The Theory and Principles of Tort Law

The Theory and Principles of Tort Law

By

Thomas Atkins Street, A.M., LL.B.

BeardBooks
Washington, DC

Reprinted 1999 Beard Books, Washington, D.C.

Printed in the United States of America

ISBN 1-893122-17-4

"The law is always approaching, and never reaching, consistency. It is forever adopting new principles from life at one end, and it always retains old ones from history at the other, which have not yet been absorbed or sloughed off. It will become entirely consistent only when it ceases to grow."

JUDGE O. W. HOLMES,
The Common Law, page 36.

To the

HONORABLE THOMAS H. MALONE:

It is fit that FOUNDATIONS OF LEGAL LIABILITY should be associated with your name; for when you, as Dean of the Law School of Vanderbilt University, caused me to be made a member of its faculty and encouraged me to undertake researches into the history of the English common law, you proximately set going the intellectual processes which have produced this work. To you it is accordingly, in grateful remembrance, dedicated.

THOMAS ATKINS STREET.

PREFACE

The present volume contains a new synthesis of the fundamental principles of tort along scientific and historical lines. The aim has been to discover and indicate the true path of legal evolution in this complicated field. As might be expected from the adoption of new methods of inquiry, and from the opening of new lines of thought, we have turned up many new ideas and have been able to present the old truths in new and more enlightening aspects. The discovery and establishment of what we have called the 'secondary trespass formation' represent, we make bold to believe, a considerable advance in legal knowledge. It gives insight into the nature of a class of torts which have hitherto proved somewhat intractable, and enables us to assign the conception of negligence to its proper place in legal theory.

The reader will find that this subject of negligence has been much stirred. We have pointed out its complexity and have shown the reason for the difficulties which are here encountered. Above all, we have illustrated this branch of the law with a copiousness of concrete cases not attempted in connection with any other subject. For the convenience of those who may desire to discriminate we have had the illustrative matter printed in a smaller type than that which is used for the ordinary text.

While admitting the efficacy, within certain limits, of that theory of negligence in which the negligent act is viewed exclusively as the breach of a positive implied legal duty, we have nevertheless pointed out the inadequacy of this theory. In chapters XIV and XV stress has been laid upon what we call the primary risk incident to maintenance of agents of harm, and upon the idea of counter-assumption of risk by the person injured. This latter idea is similar to that of contributory negligence, but is broader. In these two notions is largely to be found the explanation of the cases in which there is most talk about the legal duty to take care.

While the treatment of conversion will appear to be rather novel, it is believed that the subject is treated upon right lines. Here we have, somewhat happily it seems, hit upon the term 'disseisin of chattels' as expressive of the fundamental idea in this tort. The reader will no doubt be agreeably surprised to find how readily the law of conversion assumes consistency when viewed from the standpoint indicated in this expression.

The subject of defamation proved a fascinating one to the writer notwithstanding its idiosyncrasies. Whether or not he has been able to impart a fair measure of interest to the subject as it leaves his hand, others must say. The topic is of great importance because of the beautiful exposure of the conception of malice which occurs in this legal formation. We trust that the treatment of malice in connection with this and kindred wrongs will not be found wanting in suggestiveness.

The subject of interference with trade and calling has been treated with some fulness, for the reason that in this field we see the law in the very process of making. Even while this chapter was being written, the courts were busy laying down new and important principles. *Allen v. Flood* is already in a way out of date. The law has simply appropriated its intellectual riches and marched on.

No pains have been spared in writing the chapters on the law of deceit. Here, as in the field of negligence, is found a distinction between two conceptions of liability. There is the deceit which is actionable in the aspect of a fraud, and the deceit which is actionable in the aspect of a breach of an imposed legal obligation (warranty). But we note that in deceit the two conceptions of liability have been more constantly and more fully differentiated from each other than in the field of negligence. Apart from this clearer differentiation of the two aspects of liability, the law of deceit is not so far advanced as is the law of negligence. We have done what we could to clear the subject up. In this we have had the benefit of an important case from the House of Lords. But *Derry v. Peek* is not nearly so illuminative as the case from which so much assistance was derived in treating of interference with trade and calling.

The law concerning the negligent transmission of telegrams has come in for fuller discussion than the critical reader may think necessary. But apart from the fact that this subject has become of great practical importance in this country, and apart from the fact that here, as in the tort of interference with trade and calling, we see the law in the very process of making, the law of telegrams deserves more than passing notice because of the important questions which are here raised concerning the matter of damages. For this reason we have handled the law of telegrams with the utmost care.

The reader will note the absence of a discussion of the infringement of patents and copyrights. The reason for this omission is that the space which would have been required for a treatment of these subjects was needed for other purposes. Patent and copyright law is technical and so largely a creature of statute that a discussion of these subjects would manifestly be of little value in respect of the light which it would shed upon the general principles of tort.

In the chapters entitled Elements of Recoverable Damages and Measure of Damages we have tried to do justice in a very brief way to subjects which have the profoundest bearing on legal liability in every department of civil wrong. Many theoretical difficulties come to a focus in this narrow and yet extensive subject of damages. Naturally we have done little more than point to a few of the most important truths.

The order in which the several species of torts have been treated differs from that followed by other writers. We have adopted that sequence which best brings out the affinities of the various torts and best comports with the order of historical revelation. The violent trespass was found to furnish the starting point in the common-law theory of civil wrong, and hence trespass was put at the head of the procession. The proper initial tort having been chosen, the order in which the other wrongs should be treated was easily determined.

The reader will observe that in the citation of cases the date of the decision has been given when this was deemed material. In regard to the citation of old authorities we may observe that it is not always easy to say just when a particular decision was made. The date in such cases can often be determined only after a calculation based upon the term and regnal year of the decision and the date of the ascension of the sovereign. Nor even then is the result always absolutely certain. Where the decision is of importance we have taken much pains in fixing the date. As to others, we take it that a mistake of a year either way is not very material.

To the discerning reader the fact that the material for this work has been largely drawn from the decisions of English courts will require no word of explanation or comment. The history of the earlier stages of legal development is, of course, to be made out exclusively from English authorities. As to the later stages of legal growth, it is reasonable to suppose that the utterances of the English courts are on the whole in closer and more direct succession to the original common-law doctrine than are the decisions of the American courts. This conjecture is found, upon examination, to be fully borne out. But apart from so obvious a truth as this, the utterances of the English judges commend themselves to the intelligent reader no less by reason of their form than their learning. The better English opinions are pervaded by a terseness and sprightliness which are seldom found in the opinions of the American courts. Doubtless we work our judges too hard. The English judges have well maintained the ancient tradition of their school for the originality and piquancy, as well as for the learning, of their discourse.

In conclusion we wish to express a special sense of obligation to the writers whose contributions to the theory of tort have been of material assistance to us in this work. Our greatest indebtedness is to those who have published books of selected cases. The present treatise is truly a product of the inductive study of decided cases, and we have naturally turned often to those repositories where the most important decisions are to be found gathered together and properly edited. English Ruling Cases (in twenty-six volumes, London and Boston, 1894–1902) has proved to be of quite unique value. The two volumes of Cases on Torts (1893), edited respectively by Professor James B. Ames and Professor Jeremiah Smith, have also been very serviceable to us in the prosecution of these labors. We should be ungrateful not to acknowledge further indebtedness to the unpretentious but excellent book of Cases on the Law of Tort, by Mr. Courtney S. Kenny (1904). The notes to Professor Bigelow's Leading Cases on Torts (1875) have been found helpful in the treatment of a few subjects.

Among authors whose writings on the theory of tort have served to enlighten us, we should first mention Sir Frederick Pollock. Not infrequently a seeming casual remark from the pen of this gifted scholar has opened up most fruitful lines of inquiry. Judge Holmes's book on the Common Law proved to be very stimulating on the subjects of trespass and negligence. It was also helpful in other connections. We have gotten a number of good suggestions from articles by different writers in the Harvard Law Review and the Law Quarterly Review. We have in all cases referred to such articles in notes at the proper places.

CONTENTS

CHAPTER VI

NEGLIGENCE.

CHAPTER VII

NEGLIGENCE.—*Continued.*

CHAPTER VIII

NEGLIGENCE.—*Continued.*

CHAPTER IX

NEGLIGENCE.—*Continued.*

CHAPTER X

NEGLIGENCE.—*Continued.*

CHAPTER XI

NEGLIGENCE.—*Continued.*

CHAPTER XII

NEGLIGENCE.—*Continued.*

CHAPTER XIII

NEGLIGENCE.—*Continued.*

CHAPTER XIV

COGNATE NUISANCE.

CHAPTER XV

NUISANCE.

CHAPTER XVI

DISSEISIN OF CHATTELS.

CHAPTER XVII

DISSEISIN OF CHATTELS.—*Continued.*

CHAPTER XVIII

INTERFERENCE WITH DOMESTIC RELATIONS.

CHAPTER XIX

DEFAMATION.

CHAPTER XX

DEFAMATION.—*Continued.*

CHAPTER XXI

DEFAMATION.—*Continued.*

CHAPTER XXII

SLANDER OF TITLE AND DEFAMATION OF GOODS.

CHAPTER XXIII

MALICIOUS PROSECUTION.

CHAPTER XXIV

MAINTENANCE.

CHAPTER XXV

INTERFERENCE WITH CONTRACT RELATIONS.

CHAPTER XXVI

INTERFERENCE WITH TRADE OR CALLING.

CHAPTER XXVII

DECEIT.

CHAPTER XXVIII

DECEIT.—*Continued.*

CHAPTER XXIX

UNFAIR COMPETITION.

CHAPTER XXX

NEGLIGENT TRANSMISSION OF TELEGRAMS.

CHAPTER XXXI

ELEMENTS OF RECOVERABLE DAMAGE.

CHAPTER XXXII

MEASURE OF DAMAGES.

CHAPTER XXXIII

DAMAGE AND INJURY.

CHAPTER XXXIV

CONCLUSION.

INTRODUCTION

In the present state of knowledge, no writer can undertake to expound the theory of tort without the gravest misgivings. Considered as a distinct and self-consistent body of law, the subject of torts is comparatively new, and only within the memory of living men have fruitful efforts been made to show that there is really such a thing as a law of torts at all. During the whole of the past history of the English common law there has, of course, been an abundance of legal rules concerning those wrongs which are now treated under the head of torts, but the law pertaining to each of the several different kinds of wrong has been conceived and treated as forming a body of principle quite distinct from that pertaining to other torts. As a result we find that prior to the later years of the nineteenth century little effort was made to ascertain the relations of the different torts and define their common elements.

Past history in this field can be briefly summed up by saying that the law of torts has gone through the successive processes of integration and disintegration and is now going through a process of reintegration along new lines.

The common-law actions of trespass and case furnished the nuclei around which integration first took place. But as time went on and as the field of delictual liability was extended it was seen that the line of demarcation between the wrongs of trespass and of trespass on the case was largely a remedial accident and did not correspond with any natural substantive seam.

Scholars were accordingly forced to steer altogether away from what we may call the historical division of torts. In consequence the various sorts of delicts fell apart. Legal thinkers thereupon seem to have assumed that this branch of the law is made up of many separate masses of rules applicable to particular situations, and, until about a half century ago, it occurred to no one that the whole subject is underlaid by general principles worth the trouble of discovery. Of course, for practical purposes, the old distinction between trespass and trespass on the case could not be forgotten as long as the forms of action were retained in the actual administration of the law, and those terms were naturally used as a sort of mnemonic, long after their worthlessness in point of substantive theory was fully demonstrated. The fact that it was impossible for the legal mind to free itself entirely from the trammels of the old classification undoubtedly retarded the process of disintegration which we have noted, and hence postponed that reintegration which the whole subject was destined to undergo.

About the time, however, that the ancient procedure began to weaken under the attack of modern legislation, legal investigators in the field of delict began to take new soundings and presently struck out on different lines. Under this impulse the modern treatment of this branch of the law had its beginning. The term 'tort,' which is an equivalent of the Latin *delictum*, was chosen to designate the wrongs to be dealt with. The first treatise on the subject appeared in 1859;[1] and such advances have since been made in the exposition of this branch of the law that no contribution to the general theory of tort which has not been published or revised within a very few years, is of much value.

It is instructive to note that the course of development in the field of contract has been somewhat different. There also we see an early integration around the common-law contractual remedies, chiefly debt and assumpsit. But this division happened to correspond with a line of substantive principle. Accordingly, when in modern times contract law is freed from the trammels of the actions and the subject has to be recast, the old distinction between the contractual duty

[1] This was the American work of Francis Hilliard. It was followed in 1860 by the English work, Addison on Torts. In 1889 Dr. Joel Prentiss Bishop published a treatise on Non-Contract Law, but the expression chosen by him was not a happy one, and has not succeeded in displacing the neater and older term.

imposed by law and the obligation incurred by promise stands out as boldly as ever.

The modern theory of tort, on the contrary, proceeds on the assumption that the old distinction between the trespass and the trespass on the case is so far worthless as to be unavailable even for purposes of secondary division. We are here bound to assert entire independence of the forms of action, and must exercise the freedom of handling the mass of rules applicable to torts solely with a view to ascertain their proper substantive relations to each other and to the body of the law in general.

This does not mean that we are to ignore past distinctions. The past must constantly be taken into account as a factor in shaping the development of legal principle and not infrequently it affords the only clue to a proper understanding of existing law. In the common law we have an organism which is almost purely of natural growth. The present vitality of this organism is undoubtedly due to the fact that it is adapted to living needs, but the sources of its life are found in the past and we can interpret its existing principles aright only when we become acquainted with the history of it.

Even the most casual survey of our system of law shows that it is of very complex texture as well as of enormous mass. But its wonderful complexity is not a result of ignorance, nor does it flow from any spirit of lawlessness. Its complexity reflects, and truly reflects, the complexity of human life and human intercourse. The common law is really the very embodiment of the spirit of law. The dominance of this spirit is conspicuously shown in its wonderful tenderness for facts and in its singular patience in working out details. A genius for searching out external truth is the peculiar mark and the peculiar strength of the English common law. The common law often appears obscure merely because in particular instances it bravely grapples with problems which in other systems would be lightly glossed over or altogether evaded.

But however great may be the merit of the common law so far as its substance is concerned. it is nevertheless true that the body of our law is exceedingly ill adapted to the manipulation of the legal theorist. This undoubtedly increases the labor of mastery and in a sensible degree retards the progress of higher learning. The mass of the common law is so formidable, and its complexity so pronounced, that even the stoutest investigator may well quail upon undertaking the task of philosophic inquiry. Too often he proceeds with insufficient knowledge of details, and with little or no insight into the processes which have made the law what it now is. One who makes this fatal blunder is naturally appalled at the outset by the vast pile of matter presented for his consideration, and he is naturally tempted to lay his foundation upon *a priori* speculations instead of searching it out from the body of the law. The scholar who yields to this temptation turns his eyes from the true source of light and is irresistibly carried into barren fields of research.

It is undoubtedly true that no advance in higher knowledge can be made without indulging in some abstract speculations. Many guesses must sometimes be made before the true solution of a great problem is discovered. Nor is it any discredit to the human mind that instead of advancing in knowledge by direct insight it is often compelled to proceed upon a purely tentative hypothesis. Such indeed is the means by which alone new portions of the infinite realm of knowledge are gradually brought within the domain of the finite human mind. But in order to be fruitful, scientific speculation must be adequately guarded. To this end it is necessary that the mind of the investigator should be open and thoroughly teachable. He must learn to appreciate the significance of facts and must have the courage to bow to the least as well as to the greatest truth; for the theory that does not adequately account for small things can be of little value in explaining the great. If the investigator is imbued with this spirit his working hypothesis will usually be found to be based upon accurate observation and the likelihood of its soundness is much enhanced. At any rate, he is not likely to go far wide of the mark.

In the conviction that further progress towards higher

legal knowledge can be made only in obedience to the principle just indicated, the following pages have been written. In the prosecution of these researches we have tried to profit as well by the mistakes as by the wisdom of earlier investigators. We have sought for that broader view which is essential to adequate knowledge, but, higher than this aim, we have placed the determination not to be betrayed into that attitude of constant strain for higher generalizations and for the so-called principle of change, which is so often the mark of an incomplete mastery of details and of a narrow view of truth.

The common law is, above all, a body of practical rules, and to a far greater extent than appears on the surface, and to a far greater extent than this law itself admits, the development of these rules has been determined by considerations of convenience or policy, working towards the ultimate end of justice. The law itself has rightly put its ideals of justice higher than considerations of scientific consistency, and these ideals, it is well to be reminded, are ideals which are the product of our own civilization and life. There are unquestionably points at which its standards fall short of the highest ideals, for in the nature of things the development of the law follows in the wake of advancing morality and cannot precede it. Its ideals, while not so good as the highest, are yet not so bad as the worst, and they must be taken on the average fairly to reflect our legal instinct and the racial conception of justice.

No definition of tort at once logical and precise can be given. The reason for this is found in the fact that the conception belongs to the highest category in legal thought. Any logical definition of tort must specify the conditions under which delictual liability arises. But there is no typical tort, and in the nature of things it is impossible that a specification of the circumstances under which delictual liability is imposed should have finality. Particular torts, as trespasses of violence, defamation, nuisance, and the like, can be defined well enough, but the term 'tort' is also used to denote wrong in general. It includes the unclassified residuum as well as the specific definable wrongs. No explicit distinction has so far been drawn by any common-law judge or by any legal writer between delict and quasi-delict.[2] The term 'tort' is used alike for all sorts of wrongs, nominate and innominate, other than breaches of contract. Hence the writer who attempts to define tort is in the same quandary as he who should try to give a definition of contract broad enough to include quasi-contract.

The term 'tort' being indefinable because of its generality, it follows that such definitions of tort as commend themselves at first glance will upon examination turn out to be spurious. The following proposition, for instance, is a terse and accurate statement of a certain legal truth, and at first blush it may appear to be a logical definition. *A tort,* we may say, *is that legal wrong, or breach of duty, which is capable of being redressed in a civil action for damages.*[3] But this proposition states no criterion for distinguishing between a breach of contract and a tort, and in fact merely amounts to this, that a tort is a legal wrong for which damages may be

[2] Lord Halsbury stated in Palmer *v.* Wick, etc., Steam Shipping Co., (1894) A. C. 333, that torts are divisible into two classes, delict and quasi-delict, but he doubted whether in dealing with an English case a judge would feel at liberty to adopt the distinction.

Yet a recognition of the distinction between delict and quasi-delict would undoubtedly be conducive to clearness of thinking at certain points. If the distinction is to be made, the place to draw the line is between positive and omissive wrong. In delict, or tort proper, we should say, liability is founded upon the doing of a positive injurious act. In quasi-delict liability results from omissive breach of duty. The unjustified refusal of an innkeeper to entertain a wayfarer or the refusal of a common carrier to convey a passenger or his goods upon demand are illustrations of the latter species of tort. A considerable part of the law of negligence appears to fall under this head of quasi-delict. Quasi-delict, it will be found, exhibits an affinity for contract similar to that affinity which quasi-contract exhibits for tort. Quasi-contract and quasi-delict together cover the ambiguous zone which separates the respective hemispheres of contract and tort.

[3] The definitions of Professor Bigelow and of Professor Pollock are as follows: "A tort," says the former, "may be said to be a breach of duty fixed by municipal law for which a suit for damages can be maintained." Bigelow on Torts, p. 3. Professor Pollock says: "A tort is a breach of some duty, between citizens, defined by the general law which creates a civil cause of action." 12 Encyc. Laws Eng., tit. *Torts,* p. 189.

recovered. The statement is true enough, but it is no definition.

The trouble encountered in the preceding attempt at the definition of tort might, one would think, be cured by describing with greater precision the nature of that duty the breach of which constitutes a tort. Thus again we may say: *A tort is a breach of a general duty (imposed by law as distinguished from the obligation which is incurred by contract) for which damages may be recovered.* This proposition really looks like the definition we are hunting for. But it is not. On examination our predicate and subject are found to be convertible terms. Breach of duty imposed by law and tort are only different names for the same thing. There is no way of knowing what general duties are imposed by law except by canvassing the situations where delictual liability is held to exist. Tort, we repeat, cannot be logically defined, because of the generality of the term.

The most successful attempt so far made to define the conditions under which delictual liability arises is, in our opinion, found in the definition of tort given by Judge Holmes. He tells us, in substance, that a tort is a wrong which consists in the infliction of temporal damage by a responsible person under circumstances of such nature that the person inflicting the damage knows, or in common experience ought to know, that his conduct is likely to result in harm.[4]

This definition has the advantage of having been framed with an eye to the phenomena found in that particular branch of the law of negligence wherein undoubtedly one of the very broadest of legal principles has been exposed. Its defect is as obvious as its merits. Having been framed with an eye to a particular class of wrongs, it cannot prove helpful in dealing with other types of wrong.

[4] The exact language of this learned writer is as follows: "I think that the law regards the infliction of temporal damage by a responsible person as actionable, if under the circumstances known to him the danger of his act is manifest according to common experience, or according to his own experience if it is more than common, except in cases where upon special grounds of policy the law refuses to protect the plaintiff or grants a privilege to the defendant." 10 Harv. L. Rev. 471.

Though tort cannot be exhaustively and accurately defined within any such reasonable compass as would make the definition really helpful, our field of inquiry can nevertheless to some extent be delimited by a process of exclusion. First, it is to be observed that no wrong whatever constitutes a tort unless the common-law courts, in the exercise of their ordinary powers, have jurisdiction to entertain a civil suit for damages based thereon. Neither spiritual offenses, nor crimes, nor violations of those equitable rights which are the subject of exclusive equity jurisdiction, constitute torts in the sense of the common law. The same is to be said of wrongs arising from the violation of such marital rights as were formerly peculiar to the jurisdiction of the ecclesiastical courts.

Again, the legal wrong which results from the breach of a contract is not a tort. Upon examination we find that here, as in many other places where distinction has to be drawn between different conceptions of liability, the line of actual demarcation is hard to draw. While the two branches of wrong are plainly enough distinguished in their general features, at their nearer points of contact the resemblances are close. In truth, the field of legal liability is a seamless whole and we cannot separate any part of it from the remainder without tearing through at least some fibres which have been knit by nature. Yet some division is necessary for purposes of investigation, and the differences between the respective departments of legal truth are not rendered less convenient or less vital by reason of the fact that the respective fields shade off into each other by imperceptible degrees.

Having, then, an eye only to larger differences, and looking rather to polar phenomena than to those which are found in the equatorial belts which separate the hemispheres of tort and contract, we find the great and obvious difference between the field of tort and that of contract to be this: In the hemisphere of tort the law deals with the consequences of positive damnific acts. In the hemisphere of contract it is concerned with the consequences of omissions to do acts which one has bound himself by contract to do, or with the consequences of failures to do such acts in the mode agreed upon. It is within the province of contract law to discover the particular conditions under which an omission or failure will constitute an actionable breach of contract. Likewise it is within the province of the law of torts to discover the conditions which must be present before liability attaches for the consequences of a damnific act. Upon this difficult enterprise we are now soon to be launched.

It will be noted that in the fields of contract and tort the respective centres of legal interest are different. In the field of contract, the uppermost idea is that of the obligation of the contract which is alleged to be broken. In the field of tort the centre of legal interest is the act wrongfully done. It will not escape the reader that this difference in the point of view is reflected in the very terms 'contract' and 'tort.' The word 'contract' indicates the source from which the obligation to act is derived, while the word 'tort' is used to indicate the wrongful act upon which liability is predicated. The true correlative of 'tort' is 'breach of contract,' and there is no word in the language to indicate that right the breach whereof constitutes a tort. Yet we constantly yoke tort and contract together as if they were true correlatives and supplements of each other.

FOUNDATIONS OF LEGAL LIABILITY

CHAPTER I

TRESPASS UPON THE PERSON.

Violence.

Chapter I

THE initial point in the law of tort is found in the idea of hurt or damage done by force. Forceful hurt to the body, forceful damage to property — these are the forms of harm which appeal most directly and most strongly to the quickening legal conscience.

Earliest in the point of historical revelation, this idea is also one of the most enduring. Nor can it be surprising that the factor upon which the law lays hold in the travail incident to the birth of civil liability should prove to be one of the most important, as it is the simplest, most conspicuous, and most definite, of all the factors which enter into the conception of legal wrong.

That the law of tort should begin with wrongs of violence would seem to be natural enough in the infancy of any human society. In the state of English society which existed when the common law began to take shape it was inevitable. To tame the might of the strong arm was among the first tasks of English royal justice.

The violent trespass.

The early history of the law of tort is largely identified with the early history of the action of trespass, and as this subject is treated elsewhere in this work[1] we shall not dwell upon it here. The highly obnoxious character of the forceful trespass is manifest in the fact that this tort was originally dealt with in the double aspect of both criminal and civil wrong. In the same proceeding the wrongdoer was both mulcted in damages for the tort and fined for his criminal

[1] See vol. 3, *Trespass.*

Volume I

misdemeanor. In modern times the criminal and civil jurisdictions are severed, but the common-law action of trespass has always retained marks of its original criminal character.

Blackstone makes violence basis of primary classification of wrongs.

No wrong stands out with greater distinctness from other torts than does that in which damage is directly done by force. Blackstone's primary division of civil wrongs was that of violent and non-violent injuries. At the beginning of his treatment of wrongs, including under this term, be it noted, breaches of contract, he says: "But I must first beg leave to premise that all civil injuries are of two kinds, the one without force or violence, as slander or breach of contract; the other coupled with force and violence, as batteries or false imprisonment. Which latter species savor something of the criminal kind, being always attended with some violation of the peace; for which in strictness of law a fine ought to be paid to the king as well as a private satisfaction to the party injured. And this distinction of private wrongs into injuries with and without force we shall find to run through all the variety of which we are now to treat."[2]

Importance of the distinction between violent and non-violent injury.

Such a primary division as this is not to be thought of at the present day. But the distinction to which Blackstone's classification points is too important to be hastily put aside. Consideration of the difference between violent and non-violent injuries will in fact give a clearer perception of certain fundamental notions underlying the evolution of civil liability than can be gotten from any other point of view. The difference can perhaps be truly indicated as follows:

Moral ingredient negligible in wrongs of violence.

In the field of trespass liability is based solely upon the fact that damage is directly done by force. No consideration is here taken of the moral qualities of the act which results in damage. The actor may or may not be culpable or morally blameworthy. He may or may not have intended to do the harm complained of. All discussion on this point is, as a matter of primary principle, entirely irrelevant. In the field of wrongs not characterized by a display of force, it is different. Here the law does not impose liability unless the injurious act or omission complained of exhibits in some

[2] 3 Bl. Com. 118.

form the element of blameworthiness. Fraud, malice, negligence, will occur to the reader as forms of blame which, in one connection or another, are accepted as a basis of liability.

Chapter I

Blameworthiness a necessary factor in non-violent injury.

The moral ingredient thus appears to be negligible in wrongs of direct violence, while in other torts it is of prime importance. The internal development of the law of tort is largely a result of the interplay of these two ideas of absolute liability and of liability conditioned upon some form of fault or actual moral delinquency. The first idea is harsh. Hence as the law becomes humanized and as the legal mind becomes educated to realize the truth that the fault of the actor is a factor which has a rightful place in determining liability, the theory of trespass is ameliorated.[3]

Interplay of the two principles.

Amelioration of the principle of trespass.

The idea of absolute liability is as characteristic of the primary strata of legal thought as the idea of liability conditioned upon the fault is characteristic of later development. The early law considers plight of the injured party, but pays little or no attention to the motive or intention of the actor.

It may be observed that liability for non-violent injuries has commonly been enforced by the action on the case. Consequently the amelioration of the law of trespass just indicated may be looked upon as a victory of the principle of case over that of trespass.

The proposition that the moral ingredient is, as a matter of primary principle, negligible in wrongs of direct violence, must be taken as meaning not that this factor is necessarily absent in such wrongs, but merely that law takes no account of it. In truth, all law starts more or less from moral roots. If no morally blameworthy act had ever been done we may be sure there would never have been any law of torts. If there had been no culpable acts of deliberate violence the law would never have concerned itself to make one man pay for damage befalling another as a result of blameless injury. But however important the moral ingredient may have been in causing the courts to take the trespass in hand, when they had once done so, a hard and fast rule was laid down that

Element of blame a remote root in all legal wrongs.

[3] An account of the steps by which this amelioration of the theory of trespass was effected will be found *post*, p. 80 *et seq.*

Volume I

left no room for consideration of the moral character of the act as reflected in the motive or intention of the actor. In trespass "the intent cannot be construed," said Rede, J., at the beginning of the sixteenth century.[4] But this harsh doctrine is merely a principle of first impression and by no means represents the final judgment of the common law.

Battery.

At the head of the catalogue of forceful trespasses stands the battery, which consists, says Blackstone, of the unlawful beating of another.[5] There are two well-defined types of this wrong. The first comprises those batteries in which actual bodily injury is done; the other comprises those in which no physical hurt is inflicted and where, in consequence, legal redress is given chiefly in respect of the insult. In the first type of batteries, actual wrongful intent on the part of the wrongdoer is not essential to liability; in the other, such intent is of the essence of the wrong.

Types of battery.

The following situations illustrate batteries of the first type:

Illustrations.

A and B are fighting and one of them accidentally gives a bystander a black eye. The latter can recover of the man who struck him, although the injury was not intentionally inflicted. But the absence of intent is material in considering the amount of the damages.[6]

Intention irrelevant where actual bodily injury results from battery.

A school boy recklessly discharges an arrow from his bow at a basket behind which another boy has taken refuge. The latter unluckily raises his head above the basket just in time to have his eye hit and put out. The boy shooting the arrow is liable, although he did not intend to shoot the plaintiff.[7]

A wantonly throws a piece of mortar at B and instead of hitting him hits C, a third person who is standing near by,

[4] Y. B. 21 Hen. VII. 28, pl. 5.

[5] 3 Bl. Com. 120.

[6] James *v.* Campbell (1832), 5 C. & P. 372, 24 E. C. L. 367.

[7] Bullock *v.* Babcock, (1829) 3 Wend. (N. Y.) 391.

and injures him. A is liable to C, although he had no intention to hit him.[8]

From the foregoing illustrations it appears that where actual physical hurt is directly inflicted, the tortfeasor cannot escape liability by showing that he did not intend that the harm in question should follow.[9] This is in harmony with the fundamental notion of absolute liability in trespass which was adverted to above. So far as the element of intention can be supposed to be material in batteries of this kind it is a matter of legal inference. A man, it is said, must be conclusively presumed to intend the natural consequences of his acts. This principle is a rule of law because it is a rule of common sense. It supplies the only possible working hypothesis for a practical administration of the law. Even in our own day, the best way to find out a man's intention is to look at what he actually did and to consider what must have appeared to him at the time as the natural consequence of his conduct.[1] Formerly when parties were generally incompetent as witnesses, this method supplied practically the sole means of discovering intention.

Presumption that one intends the natural consequences of his acts.

A rule of necessity and common sense.

The type of battery above considered runs, as the reader will perceive, into the field of negligence and it includes all injuries, done by the direct application of force, whether intentional or merely inadvertent. But it does not include injuries involving physical hurts indirectly done through independent agents. Thus, trespass for assault and battery will not lie against the master of a vicious dog who negligently places the animal so that another is bitten. Such a person may well be held in an action on the case for negligence, but he is not guilty of a battery.[2]

Battery includes all bodily injuries done by the immediate application of force.

But does not include injuries done by independent agents.

The second type of batteries represents an extension of liability which is highly characteristic of common-law modes

[8] Peterson *v.* Haffner, 59 Ind. 130.

[9] To the same effect, Welch *v.* Durand, 36 Conn. 182; Mercer *v.* Corbin, 117 Ind. 450; Fitzgerald *v.* Cavin, 110 Mass. 153; Talmage *v.* Smith, 101 Mich. 370; Percival *v.* Hickey, 18 Johns. (N. Y.) 257; Vosburg *v.* Putney, 80 Wis. 523.

[1] Stephen, Hist. Crim. Law II., p. 111.

[2] The Lord Derby, 17 Fed. Rep. 265.

Volume I

of growth. Actual physical hurt supplies the genetic idea in the tort of battery. But here that idea is transcended. The factor which the law accepts as sufficient to justify this extension is found in the wrongful or hostile intent of the wrongdoer; in his malice, as the element is termed in other departments of tort. "The least touching of another in anger is a battery," said Holt, C. J., in *Cole v. Turner* (1704).[3] But a mere touching in earnest discourse,[4] or to attract attention for a lawful purpose,[5] and without any intent to do violence, is not. A friendly touch may well be excused on the ground of implied consent or on grounds of public policy. But the hostile, rude, or insolent hand has no such claim to immunity.

Hostile touching actionable though no hurt is done.

Basis of this principle.

The hostile hitting or touching, though it falls short of an actual hurt, is treated as a battery because it tends to provoke a quarrel and is in fact itself a breach of the peace. Here "the insult is more to be considered than the actual damage." [6]

Illustrations.

Ordinary contact with another in a crowd or in a narrow passage is not a battery. It is different if one forces his way in a rude or inordinate manner, and thereby jostles one person against another.[7] It is of course a battery to spit in a man's face,[8] and it is held to be a battery on the part of parish officers to cut off the hair of a pauper without his consent.[9] To lay hands angrily or insolently upon one's clothes in order to detain him,[1] or to strike the cane which he carries is a battery, for anything attached to the person shares its inviolability.[2] Caressing a woman is a battery if she objects, provided the offender does not occupy such relation as makes the act excusable.[2*]

A special exception to liability for battery is found in the

[3] 6 Mod. 149.

[4] Turbervell *v.* Savadge, 2 Keb. 545.

[5] Coward *v.* Baddeley, 4 H. & N. 478.

[6] McKean, C. J., in Respublica *v.* De Longchamps, 1 Dall. (Pa.) 114.

[7] Bull. N. P. 16; Cole *v.* Turner, 6 Mod. 149.

[8] Reg. *v.* Cotesworth, 6 Mod. 172.

[9] Forde *v.* Skinner, 4 C. & P. 239, 19 E. C. L. 364.

[1] U. S. *v.* Ortega, 4 Wash. (U. S.) 531.

[2] Respublica *v.* De Longchamps, 1 Dall. (Pa.) 114.

[2*] Goodrum *v.* State, (1878) 60 Ga. 509.

rule that one may use such force as is necessary to repel threatened injury to himself or to those persons or things which are under his protection.[3] Before the use of force can be thus justified, however, it must appear not only that the injury inflicted was indispensable for warding off the prospective harm, but that the injury threatened was grave enough to justify the use of the particular force which was used to ward it off. The battery which is sought to be justified must be no more than is commensurate with the threatened injury.[4]

Justification of defense of self and of one's own

If one who is wrongfully assaulted repels his assailant with more force than is reasonably necessary for purposes of self-protection he himself becomes a trespasser as to the excess.[5] In such an altercation both parties are in the wrong and both, it has been held, can maintain an action against the other, the party originally assailed because of the unlawfulness of the first assault, and the original assailant because of the excess of force used by the other in defending against the original assault.[6]

Use of excessive force by way of defense.

[3] Morris *v.* Platt, 32 Conn. 75; Paxton *v.* Boyer, 67 Ill. 133.

Notwithstanding the defense of self and of one's own has long been recognized as a good justification for a battery, it appears that originally it was not so. Certainly in case of homicide the ancient doctrine was that self-defense was not a good plea. The man who was so unfortunate as to have to slay another to save himself was required to surrender and was remitted to jail, where he might hope to receive royal clemency. 3 Note Book, pl. 1216 (A. D. 1236); Y. B. 21 Edw. III. 17, pl. 22; Fleta, Lib. I. c. 23, §§ 14, 15.

In Y. B. 21 & 22 Edw. I. (Rolls ed.), p. 586, and Y. B. 12 Edw. II. 381, it was held that self-defense was not a good justification for a battery. Later year-book authorities very cautiously and guardedly admit the defense. Thus, in Y. B. 33 Hen. VI. 18, pl. 10, Prisot, C. J., in recognizing the right of self-defense lays great emphasis on the duty to retreat. See also Y. B. 2 Hen. IV. 8, pl. 40, and Y. B. 21 Hen. VIII. 39, pl. 50, where, with qualifications, the doctrine of self-defense is admitted. The year-book cases above referred to are to be found in 1 Ames & Smith, Cases on Torts, pp. 93 *et seq.*

[4] Cockroft *v.* Smith, 2 Salk. 642; Rowe *v.* Hawkins, 1 F. & F. 91; Reece *v.* Taylor, 4 N. & M. 469, 30 E. C. L. 388; People *v.* Doe, 1 Mich. 451; Cotton *v.* State, 31 Miss. 504; Ogden *v.* Claycomb, 52 Ill. 365.

[5] Thomason *v.* Gray, 82 Ala. 291; Hazel *v.* Clark, 3 Harr. (Del.) 22; Philbrick *v.* Foster, 4 Ind. 442; Rogers *v.* Waite, 44 Me. 275; Ayres *v.* Birtch, 35 Mich. 501; Gallagher *v.* State, 3 Minn. 270.

[6] Dole *v.* Erskine, 35 N. H. 503; Grotton *v.* Glidden, 84 Me. 589; Slone *v.* Slone, 2 Met. (Ky.) 339.

A different rule was declared in Elliott *v.* Brown, 2 Wend. (N. Y.)

Volume I

When taking of life justifiable.

A man can lawfully repel attempts at serious bodily injury even by taking or attempting to take the life of his assailant, but he cannot of course go that far in repelling less grave injuries.[7] A man, for instance, cannot justify a serious wounding in mere defense of the possession of property,[8] unless indeed the threatened wrong is such as would amount to a felony.[9]

Defense of relatives.

The husband can justify a battery in defense of his wife, or servant; and the servant can justify a battery in defense of his master.[1] The principle naturally extends to family relations in general, for in all these there is a sort of interdependence and a natural duty of mutual protection.[2]

Defense of the possession of chattels.

A man can justify a battery in defense of the possession of his chattels, as where another makes a show of picking his pocket or of carrying off his horse or his hay.[3] The same principle has been held to justify a battery, not attended with serious injury, inflicted in the recaption of chattels already in the hands of the wrongdoer but not yet carried away.[4] The idea is that in such situation the lawful possession of

When battery justified in recaption.

497, where it was held that by using excessive violence the party assailed forfeits his right to maintain an action against the original assailant.

[7] State *v.* Bartlett, 170 Mo. 658; People *v.* Pearl, 76 Mich. 207.

In criminal law the rule in cases of homicide is that to excuse the killing of another on the ground of self-defense, the danger of life, or great bodily injury, must be real or honestly believed to be so at the time, and upon sufficient grounds. It must be both apparent and imminent. Rippy *v.* State, 2 Head (Tenn.) 217; Darling *v.* Williams, 35 Ohio St. 58.

[8] 2 Rolle Abr. 548, pl. 5.

[9] In Gray *v.* Combs (1832), 7 J. J. Marsh. (Ky.) 478, it was held that the owner of a warehouse who has set a spring gun there for its protection at night was not civilly liable in damages to the owner of a slave when the latter was killed in the act of burglarizing the warehouse.

[1] Y. B. 19 Hen. VI. 31, pl. 59; Y. B. 11 Hen. VI. 16, pl. 8; Y. B. 9 Ed. IV. 48, pl. 4; Seaman *v.* Cuppledick, Owen 150.

[2] Leward *v.* Basely, 1 Ld. Raym. 62 (wife may justify in defense of husband); Hill *v.* Rogers, 2 Iowa 67 (parent may justify in defense of child); Drinkhorn *v.* Bubel, 85 Mich. 532 (child may justify in defense of parent).

[3] Y. B. 19 Hen. VI. 31, pl. 59; Y. B. 9 Edw. IV. 28, pl. 42; Y. B. 19 Hen. VI. 66, pl. 5; Taylor *v.* Markham, Cro. Jac. 224; Bliss *v.* Johnson, 73 N. Y. 529.

[4] Blades *v.* Higgs (1861), 10 C. B. N. S. 713, 100 E. C. L. 713; Com. *v.* Donahue, 148 Mass. 529; Hodgeden *v.* Hubbard, 18 Vt. 504; Gyre *v.* Culver, 47 Barb. (N. Y.) 592; Overdeer *v.* Lewis, 1 W. & S. (Pa.) 90.

Chapter I

the chattels is still with the owner and that the wrongful detention by the trespasser after request to surrender is the same violation of property as the taking of the chattels out of the actual possession of the owner would be.

Right to eject one trespassing on land.

Likewise the occupant or person having lawful possession of land may eject a trespasser.[5] But if he uses excessive violence or applies force in a way not calculated to answer the purpose of ejection he is liable.[6]

When restraint of madman justified.

It has been held that the forcible restraint of a madman is excusable.[7] But of course the lunatic must be dangerous before he can lawfully be confined;[8] and it is held that one who restrains a person as a lunatic must be able to show that he was in fact insane. A mere belief that a man is mad, though entertained upon reasonable grounds, is no justification.[9]

Handling drunk man.

One who out of charity takes a drunken man in hand to do him a kindly turn is not chargeable with a battery[1] provided he does not directly or negligently get him hurt while doing the friendly act.[2]

[5] Browne *v.* Dawson (1840), 12 Ad. & El. 624, 40 E. C. L. 137; Harvey *v.* Brydges, 14 M. & W. 442; Tullay *v.* Reed, 1 C. & P. 6, 11 E. C. L. 297; Com. *v.* Clark, 2 Met. (Mass.) 23.

[6] Collins *v.* Renison (1754), Say. 138. The trespasser in this case put a ladder up against the defendant's house and was proceeding to nail a board there when the defendant forbade him to do so. Upon the plaintiff's refusing to desist the defendant shook the ladder and brought him down to the ground with some violence. It was held that the force used was not justified, since the only effect of it was to bring down the plaintiff to the ground without removing him from the premises.

[7] (1348) Y. B. 22 Ass. 98, pl. 56. See also case from 10 Eliz., cited by Glanvill, J., in Beale *v.* Carter, Owen 98.

In the ancient year-book case cited above it appeared that the madman had been beaten with a rod, as well as chained in the room where he was confined. In these more humane days, when insanity is better understood and its unhappy victims generally cared for by the state, the infliction of corporal punishment by private individuals having the lunatic in charge would doubtless be less tolerantly viewed.

[8] Look *v.* Dean, 108 Mass. 116; Keleher *v.* Putnam, 60 N. H. 30; Colby *v.* Jackson, 12 N. H. 526.

[9] Y. B. 22 Ed. IV. 45, pl. 10; Fletcher *v.* Fletcher (1859), 28 L. J. Q. B. 134.

[1] Short *v.* Lovejoy (1752), cited in Bull. N. P. 16.

[2] Johnson *v.* McConnel, 15 Hun (N. Y.) 293; Hoffman *v.* Eppers, 41 Wis. 251.

Volume I

Prevention of crime.

On grounds of public policy a battery can be justified if done in order to prevent the commission of a crime.[3]

Assault.

Closely akin to the wrong of battery is the simple assault. In this tort there is no actual contact as in the battery, and hence no actual physical hurt at all is inflicted. It is enough that there is a display of hostile force under such circumstances as exhibit an intention to commit a battery and a present apparent ability, as viewed from the standpoint of the person threatened, to do the harm. So easily is the principle underlying the assault deducible from the general doctrine of battery that the assault is generally conceived as only one particular form of a generic wrong (assault and battery), of which the true battery is the other species. It will further be observed that little or no hesitancy was shown by the common-law judges in allowing the action of trespass to be maintained for assault, though apparently case would have been the normal remedy.[4]

Display of hostile force coupled with apparent ability to do hurt.

Assault derived from the battery.

The principle of assault is clearly derived from the principle of battery along a line similar to that which was followed in holding the hostile touching not accompanied by actual hurt to be actionable. The evil motive, the hostility, the unlawful purpose, is there held to destroy the *prima facie* lawfulness of the touching. So, in assault, the menacing attitude and hostile purpose are accepted as sufficient to make the assault unlawful. The seditious character of the assault was of course not overlooked in stamping it as tortious.

Principle of derivation.

Antiquity of the assault.

The recognition of the simple assault as an actionable

[3] Handcock *v.* Baker, 2 B. & P. 260.

[4] Belknap urged in Y. B. 40 Edw. III. 40, pl. 19, that for an assault without more, one cannot have a writ of trespass. But he was overruled. The reporter there adds that the action on the case is the proper remedy for menaces and assault unaccompanied by a battery, citing the observation of Danby and Choke, JJ., in Y. B. 7 Edw. IV. 24, pl. 31. The authority cited does not fully corroborate the reporter on this point. The principle on which Danby and Choke agreed was that mere threats (*minas*) are not actionable unless special damage be alleged, as that the plaintiff was thereby deterred from going about his business.

wrong took place at a very early day. Near the middle of the fourteenth century, Thorpe, C. J., ruled that the throwing of a hatchet by a nocturnal disturber at a female who had put her head out of a window was a wrong for which damage could be recovered although the plaintiff had not been hit.[5] From that day the simple assault has been prominent enough among torts of violence.[6]

Illustrations.

It has been held that the chasing of one whereby he is compelled to flee in order to escape punishment is an assault.[7] So one is guilty of an assault who advances in a threatening attitude to strike another, but is prevented by a bystander from accomplishing his purpose.[8]

Display of force essential.

Though actual contact is not necessary to make an assault, a display of force is necessary. Hence there can be no assault without some motion. One who, in order to obstruct a way, stands passive like a wall cannot be held liable as for an assault.[9]

To whom force directed.

Likewise it is always necessary in an assault that the force actually expended should be directed towards the party aggrieved. One who invades a house and demolishes its windows is not guilty of an assault upon the inmate thereof, though personal harm comes to such inmate from the consequent exposure to inclement winds.[1]

Manifestation of intention.

It is generally assumed that there must be an actual intention on the part of the assailant to do the harm which he threatens to do. All that is really required is that he should show such an intention by his external acts. In cases where he is clearly only hindered from his purpose by an intervening force, the hostile intention is sufficiently manifest. So if one raises a club over the head of another, saying that if the latter speaks he will strike, and the person menaced thereupon keeps quiet in order to avoid harm, the assailant is guilty of an

[5] Y. B. 22 Ass. 99, pl. 60. In Y. B. 45 Edw. III. 24, pl. 35, Belknap, J., says: "For an assault one shall recover damages, since he is disturbed in his business and thereby he is understood to be harmed."

[6] See 2 Rolle Abr. 545.

[7] Morton *v.* Shoppee, 3 C. & P. 373, 14 E. C. L. 355.

[8] Stephen *v.* Myers, 4 C. & P. 349, 19 E. C. L. 414.

[9] Innes *v.* Wylie, 1 C. & K. 257, 47 E. C. L. 257.

[1] Stearns *v.* Sampson, 59 Me. 568.

Volume I

assault.[2] He cannot escape liability in such case by saying that he did not intend to strike if the condition of his command had been violated. Similarly it is an assault to point a loaded gun at a man, threatening at the same time to shoot, and thereby compelling the person menaced to desist from a lawful act.[3]

Pointing of unloaded gun.

Whether it is an assault to point with hostile demonstration an unloaded gun at another is not clearly settled by the authorities. Such act has several times been held to be an assault in the eye of the criminal law,[4] but there are decisions to the contrary.[5] On strictly technical grounds the rule would doubtless be that if the person threatening to shoot thinks the gun is loaded and tries to carry his purpose into effect, he is guilty of an assault although in fact he has not the power to do so because the gun proves, contrary to his expectation, to be unloaded. On the other hand, if he knows that the gun is unloaded he cannot be said to have the intention to shoot and he certainly has not the power to do so. This rule, however, would hardly prove adequate. The party assailed is subjected to an apparent danger and the act is just as harmful in itself as the pointing of a loaded weapon. Hence there is good authority for the doctrine that if the party assailed has reason to believe that the gun may be loaded, the other is guilty of an assault in the eye of both the criminal and civil law.[6] That this conclusion is reached largely upon considerations of public policy is manifest.[7]

Imprisonment.

Antiquity of the wrong of imprisonment.

Forcefully to deprive a man of the freedom to go whithersoever he may is clearly a trespass. False imprisonment was, indeed, one of the first trespasses recognized by the common

[2] U. S. *v.* Richardson, 5 Cranch (C. C.) 348.

[3] Osborne *v.* Veitch, 1 F. & F. 317.

[4] Com. *v.* White, 110 Mass. 407; Morrison's Case, 1 Broun (Scotch) 394. See also Bishop's New Crim. Law, § 32.

[5] Chapman *v.* State, 78 Ala. 463; State *v.* Sears, 86 Mo. 169.

[6] State *v.* Shepard, 10 Iowa 126; Beach *v.* Hancock, 27 N. H. 223; Richels *v.* State, 1 Sneed (Tenn.) 606. *Contra*, Blake *v.* Barnard, 9 C. & P. 626, 38 E. C. L. 259.

[7] See reasoning of Gilchrist, C. J., in Beach *v.* Hancock, 27 N. H. 223.

law.[8] A laying of violent hands upon the person and an actual forceful deprivation of liberty is the element undoubtedly at the root of liability in this wrong. In other words, the typical original imprisonment involved a battery. But the wrong was not destined to be restricted to such narrow bounds. Just as the assault represents an extension of the conception of harm involved in the battery in one direction, so the wrong of imprisonment represents the extension of that conception in another direction. Accordingly it has long been settled that actual physical constraint, or physical contact, is not necessary to make an imprisonment.[9] Coercion of any kind, as where the person imprisoned yields without resistance to superior force or to authority, is enough. But some form of coercion is essential. One who is prevailed upon by false representations to go and remain at a particular place is not imprisoned,[1] unless, perchance, force or intimidation be used to prevent departure.

Deduced from the battery.

Physical contact and forceful constraint unnecessary.

Actual coercion essential in false imprisonment.

The tort of imprisonment is so far predicated upon restraint of personal freedom that one cannot be held liable therefor unless it affirmatively appears that detention was contrary to the will of the person alleged to be imprisoned. Thus, it has been decided that where the principal of a school wrongfully refuses to surrender to its mother a child committed to his care, an action for imprisonment cannot be maintained against him on behalf of such child in the absence of proof that the child was, against its will, restrained from going with its mother, or at least that the refusal to surrender was made in its presence.[2]

Detention must be contrary to will of person imprisoned.

The law recognizes the fact that one does not have to be actually incarcerated in order to be imprisoned. That other things besides stone walls and iron bars can make a prison was decided at an early day.[3]

Incarceration not necessary.

[8] Bracton's Note Book, II., pl. 314 (1229), pl. 465.

[9] Chinn *v.* Morris, 2 C. & P. 361, 12 E. C. L. 171; Warner *v.* Riddiford, 4 C. B. N. S. 180, 93 E. C. L. 180; Wood *v.* Lane, 6 C. & P. 774, 25 E. C. L. 645.

[1] Payson *v.* Macomber, 3 Allen (Mass.) 69.

[2] Herring *v.* Boyle, 1 C. M. & R. 377.

[3] Thorpe, C. J., in Y. B. (1348) 22 Ass. 104, pl. 85.

One is imprisoned who is con-

Volume I

But though it is conceded that one's person does not have to be touched to make an imprisonment, and that one who is compelled to stay in a particular place or to go in a particular direction is, in the legal sense, imprisoned just as much as if he were locked up in a room, it has been decided that a mere obstruction of passage in a particular direction whether by threat of personal violence or otherwise is not an imprisonment; provided the person so obstructed is left at liberty to remain where he is or to go in any other direction he pleases.[4] For a partial obstruction, case might be maintained if the obstruction is followed by actual damage, but not trespass for imprisonment. To sustain the latter action the liberty of going must be totally abridged. But a momentary abridgment of such liberty is enough.

Obstruction of locomotion in particular direction not an imprisonment.

stantly for two weeks guarded by detectives so that though he has a qualified freedom, his movements are at all times subject to the control and direction of those who have him in charge. Fotheringham *v.* Adams Express Co., 36 Fed. Rep. 252.

[4] Bird *v.* Jones, 7 Q. B. 742, 53 E. C. L. 742.

CHAPTER II

FORCEFUL DAMAGE TO PROPERTY.

Damage to Chattels.

Chapter II

THE trespass upon chattels which first attracted attention was naturally that which involved total destruction or asportation, and for these wrongs the early law had its writs of trespass *vi et armis* and trespass *de bonis asportatis.*[1] At first the royal courts appear to have taken no notice of mere injury to chattels unconnected with a destruction or asportation, such offenses being deemed too trivial to justify the suing out of an original writ.[2] But as the inferior courts, which had exclusive jurisdiction over very small trespasses, gradually perished of inanition, and as legal machinery became less cumbersome, the common-law courts proceeded without question to entertain actions for damage forcefully done to chattels, although the damage inflicted fell short of actual destruction or asportation. No doubt has ever been entertained on this point in modern times.

1 See vol. 3, title *Trespass.*

2 The Register has its writ of trespass *vi et armis* for the wrongful chasing and biting of cattle by dogs, whereby the cattle dropped their young and were otherwise injured; also for the maiming of villeins, whereby they were rendered ineffective for their master's service. Reg. Brev. Orig. 94*b* (*De jumento interfecto et ovibus fugatis, De minis factis hominibus*). Compare the vicontiel writ, 92*a* (*De ovibus fugatis,* etc.).

The writ for the chasing and biting of the cattle recites that some of the beasts were killed, and it is doubtless true that where none of a man's chattels were actually destroyed or taken away the injury was ordinarily deemed too insignificant for the king's court to take cognizance of. In such situation the plaintiff naturally preferred to apply for redress to the inferior courts. In Y. B. 12 Hen. IV. 8, pl. 15, Hankford, J., speaking in an action of trespass for private nuisance, stated that by a custom then prevailing throughout all England small trespasses were to be presented in the seignorial courts, and that for offenses there cognizable, one was not to sue out a common-law writ. It is largely for this reason, no doubt, that early instances are wanting of the use of trespass *vi et armis* for a mere injury to personalty unconnected with a destruction or asportation.

The remedy for such injury is, of course, by trespass *vi et armis* or case,[3] though trespass for assault and battery has sometimes been entertained for the unlawful beating of live things.[4]

No cause of action in absence of actual damage.

It must be noted as important in connection with trespasses upon personal property that no cause of action arises unless the trespass is followed by actual damage. The application of force by one man to the chattels of another is not *per se* unlawful. The act is merely done at the actor's risk, and if damage follows he is liable for it. The same principle here prevails as in wrongs of negligence. Actual damage is essential to the cause of action. This rule is different from that which obtains in regard to personal injuries and in trespass upon realty. Every touching of the person in anger is a battery; every intrusion upon realty is a trespass. But no application of force to chattels is actionable unless it be followed by damage. It seems fair to assume that the rule obtaining in regard to chattels is the normal doctrine, and that in the field of personal injury and trespass upon realty we are confronted with deviations from that doctrine founded upon reasons of policy and convenience.[5]

[3] Morley *v.* Gaisford, 2 H. Bl. 442; Dand *v.* Sexton (1789), 3 T. R. 37; Day *v.* Edwards, 5 T. R. 648; Rogers *v.* Imbleton, 2 B. & P. N. R. 117; Ogle *v.* Barnes, 8 T. R. 188; Leame *v.* Bray, 3 East 593; Williams *v.* Holland, 10 Bing 112, 25 E. C. L. 50.

[4] In Marlow *v.* Weeks, (1744) Barnes Notes 452, the question was raised whether trespass for assault and battery would lie for an injury forcefully done to a chattel. It was held that such an action would lie where the chattel was a live thing, like a beast, but not otherwise. Trespass for assault and battery will not lie, for instance, where the thing injured is a ship. In such case the proper remedy, of course, is by a general writ of trespass *vi et armis*, though, as stated above, for historical reasons, no such writ happens to appear upon the Register. It might very well have been held, contrary to the ruling in Marlow *v.* Weeks, that trespass *vi et armis*, or case, and not trespass for assault and battery, is the proper remedy where injury is forcefully done to a live thing; but trespass for assault and battery is only a particular form of the general writ *vi et armis* and the point was not one worth arguing. Compare Bull *v.* Colton, 22 Barb. (N. Y.) 94, where it was held that trespass for the beating of a horse was not an action of assault and battery as it purported to be, but was really an action *vi et armis* for injuring the horse.

[5] Professor Pollock is inclined to think that in strict theory it must be a trespass to lay hands on another's chattel whether damage follow or not. Poll. on Torts (6th ed.) 334. But we are of the opinion that this position is untenable.

Actual damage may be small.

Very little actual damage is sufficient to sustain an action for injury done to chattels. For instance, the scratching of the panel of a carriage is enough.[6] But actual damage of some kind there must be.[7] Not even so much as a dictum can be cited to the effect that the mere touching of a chattel is ever actionable as regards merely the application of the force. True, as we shall presently see, an assumption of the control of chattels is actionable, though no damage follow, if such assumption be coupled with an intent to convert. But here the right of action is given in respect of the interference with property right, and not in respect of the force used.

Justification on grounds of self-defense.

The doing of damage to personal property or the destruction of it can be justified on grounds of self-defense to the same extent as can a personal battery. Thus, if my premises are invaded by the dangerous mastiff of a neighbor, I may kill him if this be necessary to protect myself, my family, or my cattle.[8] So where one is attacked by a dog and is in a way to be bitten, it is lawful to shoot the creature on the spot.[9] But where the animal, after a first plunge, turns to

Right to kill dangerous trespassing beasts.

[6] Alderson, B., in Fouldes *v.* Willoughby (1841), 8 M. & W. 549.

[7] Slater *v.* Swann, 2 Stra. 872; Gaylard *v.* Morris, 3 Exch. 695.

Where the defendant was charged with striking the plaintiff's horse, it was said by Pennington, J., in Marentille *v.* Oliver, 2 N. J. L. 358: "I think it was incumbent on the plaintiff below to state an injury done to the horse, whereby the plaintiff suffered damage; that he was, in consequence of the blow, bruised or wounded and unable to perform service; or that the plaintiff had been put to expense in curing him, or the like. All the precedents of declarations for injuries done to domestic animals, as far as my recollection goes, are in that way."

The striking of a horse when another is riding or driving him may be enough to constitute an assault upon the person; in which case, of course, an action would lie for the assault as such, and without regard to the question whether damage was done to the horse. *Ib.;* also Clark *v.* Downing, 55 Vt. 259. Compare Bull *v.* Colton, 22 Barb. (N. Y.) 94; Dodwell *v.* Burford, 1 Mod. 24.

[8] Keck *v.* Halstead (1699), 3 Lutw. 481; King *v.* Kline, 6 Pa. St. 318. Compare Russell *v.* Barrow, 7 Port. (Ala.) 106 (killing of furious bull justified).

[9] Credit *v.* Brown (1813), 10 Johns. (N. Y.) 365; Reynolds *v.* Phillips, 13 Ill. App. 557. Where a vicious dog is allowed to go at large so as to become a menace to the community, it may be treated as a common nuisance and can be killed by any person with impunity. Brown *v.* Carpenter, 26 Vt. 638; Nehr *v.* State, 35 Neb. 638.

Any man may kill a mad dog or one that is justly suspected of being mad, or that is known to have been bitten by such; for it is

Volume I

run away, the shooting is not to be justified, the danger then being past.[1]

A dog or cat which uses to destroy conies in a warren can be killed while trespassing therein.[2] Likewise a dog can be killed in the act of destroying one's poultry.[3] In cases of this kind the defendant must affirmatively show that the killing or other injury was reasonably necessary to the protection of his property, otherwise justification is not made out.[4] Nor can a man justify the destruction of trespassing animais or fowls where the loss caused to the owner by such killing is disproportionately great as compared with the harm they are doing.[5]

Killing must be reasonably necessary and not disproportioned to the threatened harm.

Damage to crops by foraging beasts seems never to have been admitted as a sufficient excuse for killing them. In such case the party whose premises are invaded must content himself with the remedy of distress or his common-law action for damages. It has been held that one cannot kill his neighbor's hens or his geese merely because they run in his lot or get into his garden.[6]

Foraging animals and fowls not to be killed.

In *Mouse's Case* (1608)[7] it was held that in a case of emergency upon boat or ship arising from tempest it is law-

a nuisance and menace to the public. Woolf *v.* Chalker, 31 Conn. 121; Putnam *v.* Payne, 13 Johns. (N. Y.) 312.

[1] Morris *v.* Nugent (1836), 7 C. & P. 572, 32 E. C. L. 635.

Compare Wells *v.* Head, 4 C. & P. 568, 19 E. C. L. 531, where it appeared that the offending dog, after worrying plaintiff's sheep, crossed into an adjoining close, when the defendant pursued and shot it. It was held that the killing was not justified.

[2] Wadhurst *v.* Damme (1604), Cro. Jac. 45. Compare Barrington *v.* Turner, 3 Lev. 28.

In Aldrich *v.* Wright (1873), 53 N. H. 398, the well-known mink case, it was held that one may kill minks in the act of attacking his geese, although a statute for the preservation of fur-bearing animals in general terms prohibits the killing of minks.

[3] Leonard *v.* Wilkins, 9 Johns. (N. Y.) 233; Morse *v.* Nixon, 6 Jones L. (51 N. Car.) 293.

[4] Wright *v.* Ramscot (1667) 1 Saund. 84; Janson *v.* Brown, 1 Campb. 41; Livermore *v.* Batchelder, 141 Mass. 179; Champion *v.* Vincent, 20 Tex. 811; McIntire *v.* Plaisted, 57 N. H. 606.

[5] Ford *v.* Taggart, 4 Tex. 492; Bowers *v.* Horen, 93 Mich. 420; Ulery *v.* Jones, 81 Ill. 403; Richardson *v.* Dukes, 4 McCord L. (S. Car.) 156; Hobson *v.* Perry, 1 Hill. L. (S. Car.) 277; Priester *v.* Augley, 5 Rich. L. (S. Car.) 44.

[6] Clark *v.* Keliher, 107 Mass. 406; Johnson *v.* Patterson, 14 Conn. 1; Matthews *v.* Fiestel, 2 E. D. Smith (N. Y.) 90.

[7] 12 Coke 63.

Chapter II

ful to throw goods overboard for the purpose of lighting the vessel, if this be necessary to prevent foundering. To remedy the hardship which would follow from the strict observance of this principle, the maritime law imposes a duty on the owners of so much of the cargo as is saved by the jettison, to contribute by way of general average to make the loss good.[8]

Jettison.

Contribution in general average.

Trespass upon Realty.

Strictness of law concerning trespass upon realty.

The law pertaining to trespass upon realty is both exceptionally simple and exceptionally rigorous. "No man can set his foot upon my ground without my license but he is liable to an action."[9] Every unauthorized entry on another's soil is a trespass; for, says Blackstone, "Every man's land is, in the eye of the law, enclosed and set apart from his neighbors'; and that either by a visible and material fence, as one field is divided from another by a hedge, or by an ideal, invisible boundary existing only in the contemplation of law."[1]

Inadvertent intrusion.

Firing into field of another.

If, in mowing his own land, one inadvertently allows his blade to cut through into his neighbor's field, he is guilty of a trespass;[2] so, if from the cutting of a hedge, thorns fall over the line, and the owner follows after in order to clear the ground of them.[3] It was once ruled that the firing of a gun into a field is of itself an actionable trespass,[4] and the question has even been mooted whether an action of trespass might not be maintained for passing over one's land in a balloon.[5] But undoubtedly this must be answered in the negative.

To allow a tree to obtrude upon the premises of one's

[8] Hicks *v.* Palington, (1599) Moo. K. B. 297; Burton *v.* English, 12 Q. B. D. 218; McAndrews *v.* Thatcher, 3 Wall. (U. S.) 347; Columbian Ins. Co. *v.* Ashby, 13 Pet. (U. S.) 331; Greely *v.* Tremont Ins. Co., 9 Cush. (Mass.) 415; Price *v.* Hartshorn, 44 N. Y. 94.

[9] Entick *v.* Carington, 19 How. St. Tr. 1029.

[1] 3 Bl. Com. 209. See also Dougherty *v.* Stepp, 1 Dev. & B. L. (18 N. Car.) 371.

[2] Basely *v.* Clarkson, 3 Lev. 37.

[3] Y. B. (1466) 6 Edw. IV. 7, pl. 18.

[4] See statement of Lord Ellenborough in Pickering *v.* Rudd, 1 Stark. 56, 2 E. C. L. 32, 4 Campb. 219.

[5] *Ib.* See also observation of Blackburn, J., in Kenyon *v.* Hart, 6 B. & S. 252, 118 E. C. L. 252.

Volume I

Over-hanging boughs.

Special damage.

neighbor is so far analogous to a trespass that he may lop off the boughs,[6] or cut the roots up to his line. Such injury, however, is not so far a trespass that an independent action for damages will lie therefor[7] unless special damage be shown; as where it appears that the neighbor's cattle have eaten poisonous overhanging leaves and died.[8]

Cujus est solum ejus est usque ad coelum.

The owner of the soil is the owner of everything above and below, and one is not allowed to interfere either with superincumbent air or subjacent soil by means of any instrumentality whatever. It has been held to be a trespass if one's horse sticks his head through the fence and bites a neighbor's mare.[9]

Unauthorized entry upon friendly mission not justified.

The old *Case of the Tithes* (1507)[1] well illustrates the aversion exhibited by the common law in the admission of exceptions to the general principle of strict liability which prevails in trespass upon realty. It was there held to be actionable to enter a man's field even for the purpose of doing him a friendly turn. It appeared from the plea that the wheat to which the action related had been marked off for the parson's tithes in a field. The defendant, having taken and removed the tithes to one of the parson's barns, alleged by way of justification in an action of trespass that he did this in order to prevent the grain from being eaten by stray beasts which were foraging in the field. But this was held insufficient.

When unauthorized entry to do a friendly turn justified.

The judges proceeded on the idea that inasmuch as the beasts were trespassing in the field, the parson would have had recourse against their owner in case his tithes were eaten. Hence there was supposed to be no necessity for making an exception to the general doctrine. But it was said that if things are in danger of being destroyed by water, fire, or the like, one will be excused for entering to rescue them; "for

[6] See opinion of Coke, C. J., in Morrice *v.* Baker, 3 Bulst. 196, 1 Rolle 394.

[7] Countryman *v.* Lighthill, 24 Hun (N. Y.) 405; Grandona *v.* Lovdal, 70 Cal. 161.

[8] Crowhurst *v.* Burial Board, 4 Ex. D. 5.

[9] Ellis *v.* Loftus Iron Co., L. R. 10 C. P. 10.

[1] Y. B. 21 Hen. VII. 27, pl. 5.

there the destruction would take place without there being any right of action against any one."

Entry for purpose of recaption.

The *Case of the Thorns* (1466)[2] is often cited in discussing liability for trespasses. It was there held that an entry upon the premises of another cannot be justified by showing that the intruder entered in order to recover chattels which he himself had been instrumental in causing to be upon such premises. But it was admitted that if one's chattels are carried against his will, as by a tempest, into another's field, he may justify a proper entry to recover the same.

When justified.

Hunting upon premises of another.

As a general rule no man can hunt or sport upon another's land without the consent of the owner.[3] It is, for instance, a trespass to dig for a badger on the premises of another.[4] By way of exception to this rule it has been decided that if a person finds a noxious animal, such as a fox, on his land, and in order to kill it is compelled to follow it from his land into the premises of another, he may justify the entry provided he do as little damage as possible.[5] The exception here noted appears to be founded, at least in modern times, on the implied consent of the owner rather than on the policy of encouraging the destruction of noxious animals, for it is determined that a hunter cannot pursue such animals on to the land of another against the express objection of the latter.[6] Always, of course, if actual damage be done, as where hedges are broken,[7] or where stock is injured by the dogs of chase,[8] the hunter is liable.

When justified.

Hunter liable for actual damage.

Improper use of highway.

The unreasonable and improper use of a highway may constitute a trespass as against the owner of the soil which is subject to such easement. This is well illustrated in two

[2] Y. B. 6 Edw. IV. 7, pl. 18.

[3] Sterling *v.* Jackson, 69 Mich. 488; Paul *v.* Summerhayes (1878), 4 Q. B. D. 9; Glenn *v.* Kays, 1 Ill. App. 479.

[4] Gedge *v.* Minne, 2 Bulst. 60, 2 Rolle Abr. 558.

[5] Gundry *v.* Feltham, 1 T. R. 334. "If I come upon your land and slay a fox, a gray, or an otter, for this entry I shall not be punished because these creatures are injurious to the public (*sont encontre le common profit*)." Brooke, J., Y. B. 12 Hen. VIII. 10, pl. 2.

[6] Paul *v.* Summerhayes, 4 Q. B. D. 9; Glenn *v.* Kays, 1 Ill. App. 479.

[7] Fenner, J., in Nichol's Case, cited in Geush *v.* Mynne, 1 Brownl. & Goldes. 224.

[8] Glenn *v.* Kays, 1 Ill. App. 479.

Volume I

late English cases. In *Harrison v. Rutland,*[9] one who was entitled to use for the legitimate purpose of travel a road running through the moors of another, placed himself in the road for the avowed purpose of preventing grouse from approaching within gunshot of certain butts that had been erected by the owner not far from the road. This conduct was repeated from time to time when the owner drove his moors for grouse. It was held by the Court of Appeal that this made the person so using the highway a trespasser thereon. Said Lopes, L.J., "If a person uses the soil of the highway for any purpose other than that in respect of which the dedication was made and the easement acquired, he is a trespasser. The easement acquired by the public is a right to pass and repass at their pleasure for the purpose of legitimate travel, and the use of the soil for any other purpose, whether lawful or unlawful, is an infringement of the rights of the owner of the soil."

Interference with lawful pursuit of owner by person stationed on highway.

In the case just considered the trespasser had stationed himself on the highway. In *Hickman v. Maisey,*[1] on the other hand, the use of the highway was declared improper though the defendant kept constantly on the go, passing and repassing. It appeared that while race horses were being tried on the grounds of the plaintiff, the defendant, in order to secure information as to the respective merits of the horses, walked backwards and forwards on a portion of the highway on plaintiff's land from which a view of the trial could be had. This was held to be an unlawful use of the highway, and the defendant was consequently declared to be a trespasser.

Interference by person constantly on the move on highway.

A trespass upon realty will in many cases be deemed justifiable or excusable where it appears that the act complained of was done in obedience to the dictates of necessity or was sanctioned by public policy. Upon the latter ground it is lawful in case of invasion by a public enemy for men to go upon the land of another for the purpose of resisting the

Trespass justified on grounds of necessity and policy.

[9] (1893) 1 Q. B. 142. See also Dovaston *v.* Payne, 2 H. Bl. 527; Reg. *v.* Pratt, 4 El. & Bl. 860, 82 E. C. L. 860.

[1] (1900) 1 Q. B. 752.

enemy, and to make such use of it by digging trenches, erecting bulwarks, or otherwise as may appear to be advisable for the common defense of the realm.[2]

Destruction of house in path of flames.

Upon the ground of necessity it is settled that the blowing up and destruction of houses is justifiable when done to prevent the spread of a conflagration.[3] Where a building is a nuisance it may be destroyed by the proper authorities of the city without any liability being incurred.[4]

Abatement of nuisance.

Detour from impassable highway.

If a public highway becomes impassable as by a sudden flood, drift of snow, or by the falling of a tree, the traveler is justified in making a detour over adjacent private lands.[5]

In *Whalley v. Lancashire, etc., R. Co.* (1884) [6] the Court of Appeal had occasion to consider the circumstances under which a man will be justified in diverting a threatened danger away from his own property at the expense of his neighbor. Some nice distinctions were stated, and it was held that while a man may lawfully defend himself and his property from a common danger, even though the result of warding it off is that some other person is injured, yet if the dangerous thing is not a common danger, but has merely gotten on the premises of one man and threatens damage to him alone, he will not be justified in transferring the misfortune to another.

Diversion of threatened injury.

It appeared in this case that by reason of an unprecedented flood, a large body of water had gathered on premises of the defendant railway and threatened to eat away its embankment. Thereupon the company cut trenches and caused the flood water to flow in great volume over the plain

[2] (1469) Y. B. 9 Edw. IV. 23, pl. 41. The destruction of personal property can be justified under the war power to prevent its falling into the hands of the enemy. Ford *v.* Surget, 97 U. S. 594; Respublica *v.* Sparhawk, 1 Dall. (Pa.) 357; Ford *v.* Surget, 46 Miss. 130.

[3] Mouse's Case, 12 Coke 63; Dunbar *v.* Alcalde, etc., 1 Cal. 355; Surocco *v.* Geary, 3 Cal. 69; American Print Works *v.* Lawrence, 21 N. J. L. 249; Hale *v.* Lawrence, 21 N. J. L. 714.

[4] Fields *v.* Stokley, 99 Pa. St. 306.

[5] Absor *v.* French, 2 Show. 28; Henn's Case, W. Jones 296; Campbell *v.* Race, 7 Cush. (Mass.) 408. But such privilege does not exist where the right of way is private and conferred by a special license. Taylor *v.* Whitehead, 2 Dougl. 745; Bullard *v.* Harrison, 4 M. & S. 387.

[6] 13 Q. B. D. 131.

tiff's land, doing damage to his property. If the water had not thus been turned it would in the end by percolation have reached the plaintiff's land and flowed over it, but no damage would have been done. Brett, M. R., delivering the judgment, said: "An extraordinary misfortune happened, it fell upon the defendants, and if they had allowed things to remain as they were, they would have been the sufferers; but in order to get rid of the misfortune which had happened to them, and which, *rebus sic stantibus,* would not have injured the plaintiff, they did something which brought an injury upon the plaintiff. Under those circumstances it seems to me the defendants are liable."

Upon comparing the rule in trespass upon realty (trespass *quare clausum*) with the rule in trespass for assault and battery, we note this distinction: In the field of battery, a touching which does no physical hurt is not actionable unless it be hostile. The person touched in a friendly way is perhaps supposed to consent to the touching. At any rate there is a legal presumption in favor of the friendly hand. In the field of trespass *quare clausum* it is different. There the legal presumption is against the intruder, and to escape liability he must nearly always show actual leave to enter.[7] In both fields the state of the law seems to be such as to give the necessary protection respectively to person and property and no more. A man may well be expected to protect himself within certain limits from physical hurt. But there is often no other eye than that of the law to guard his lands.

Law of trespass upon realty stricter than law concerning trespass upon the person.

Reason for the distinction.

The reason for the stricter rule in trespass upon realty is apparently found in the fact that upon the action of trespass *quare clausum* has been largely put the burden of vindicating property right — one of the greatest ends, says Lord Camden, for which men entered into human society.[8] The

[7] This striking diversity makes a remark once made by Cockburn, C. J., look more like a sally of humor than the serious observation it was intended for. "The personal injury," said he, "is a more serious matter than damage to property." Reg *v.* Heppinstale, 7 W. R. 178. Doubtless so to the person hurt, but in the eye of the law it would seem to be otherwise.

[8] See Entick *v.* Carrington (1765), 19 How. St. Tr. 1029.

law unquestionably does not prize property more than it does personal security, but at some points it has had to put forth more energetic efforts to protect property than it has to protect personal security. When it was once determined that a man could resort to a form of trespass to settle a matter of disputed title, the character of the trespass upon realty was fixed. Thenceforth the common law, in considering liability for intrusions upon realty, could not undertake to discriminate between the much and the little. In the language of Littleton, J., "the law is all one, for great things and for small." [9]

[9] Y. B. 6 Edw. IV. 7, pl. 18.

CHAPTER III

FORCEFUL DAMAGE TO PROPERTY (CONTINUED).

Waste.

Volume I

WASTE is described by Blackstone as "a spoil and destruction of the estate, either in houses, woods, or lands, by demolishing not the temporary profits only, but the very substance of the thing,"[1] "to the disherison of him that hath the remainder or reversion in fee simple or fee tail."[2] Whatever does a lasting damage to the freehold is waste. The following acts have been held to constitute waste: The unauthorized cutting of timber, such as oak, ash, and elm, for other purposes than for the ordinary use and enjoyment of the premises;[3] the cutting of fruit trees in garden or orchard;[4] the opening of new mines;[5] and the breaking of glass windows or removal of wainscot, floors, or other things once affixed to the freehold.[6] But reasonable estovers may always be taken by the tenant, and undergrowth may be cut.[7] It is waste in the tenant of a piscary, park, or warren, unreasonably to deplete the stock of fish, deer, or other game.[8] Under the early authorities and statutes, exile of men, that is, the manumission or driving away of villeins,

Illustrations of waste.

[1] 3 Bl. Com. 223.

[2] 2 Bl. Com. 281.

See generally on the subject of waste, Bowles's Case, 11 Coke 79*b*, Tudor's Leading Cas. (4th ed.) 86.

[3] Herlakenden's Case, 4 Coke 62.

For a clear statement of the law pertaining to waste by cutting of timber, see opinion of Jessel, M. R., in Honywood *v.* Honywood (1874), L. R. 18 Eq. 306.

[4] 1 Co. Inst. 53*a*.

[5] Gaines *v.* Green Pond Iron Min. Co., 32 N. J. Eq. 86. But old mines may be worked in the customary and reasonable way. Ward *v.* Carp River Iron Co., 47 Mich. 65; Darcy *v.* Askwith, Hob. 234.

[6] Herlakenden's Case, 4 Coke 64.

[7] 2 Bl. Com. 281.

[8] Co. Litt. 53*a*.

was waste.[9] But when serfdom passed away this species of waste became unknown.

Waste as affected by varying social conditions.

There is no inflexible rule by which to tell what acts constitute waste, and the question must be determined on the particular circumstances surrounding each case. What is waste in one age and country is not in another. Thus, in England and the older States, where the protection of timber has become highly important, a strict rule is laid down respecting this species of waste.[1] But in undeveloped communities where timber is of little value, it has been declared that clearing timber, not for sale, but for purposes of cultivation, is not waste.[2] It was formerly law that to change the course of husbandry by converting arable, meadow, or pasture land into woodland, or *vice versa,* was waste.[3] But this cannot be accepted as a rule of existing law. Ill-husbandry does not ordinarily constitute waste.[4]

Criteria of waste: 1. Injury to inheritance. 2. Changing character of inheritance.

The most important criteria for determining whether waste has been committed are indicated in these two questions: Did the act complained of injure the inheritance in a material way, by diminishing its value? Did the act injure the inheritance by changing its character? Advertence to the point indicated in the latter inquiry has caused many acts to be stamped as waste which clearly do not involve actual damage. It explains why meadow could not be turned into arable land, nor wood into pasture, and why a pool or piscary could not be dried up.[5] The same idea was at the root of the erroneous opinion expressed by Coke, that the building of a new house on leased premises is waste.[6] It changed the description of the estate. To convert a corn mill into a fulling

[9] "*Exilium dici poterit cum servi manumittunter et a tenementis injuriose ejiciantur.*" Fleta, Lib. I., c. 12, § 20; Stat. Marl., c. 24.

[1] Webster *v.* Webster, 53 N. H. 18.

[2] Ward *v.* Sheppard, 2 Hayw. (3 N. Car.) 283; Owen *v.* Hyde, 6 Yerg. (Tenn.) 334.

[3] 1 Co. Inst. 53.

[4] Richards *v.* Torbert, 3 Houst. (Del.) 172; Pynchon *v.* Stearns, 11 Met. (Mass.) 304.

[5] Darcy *v.* Askwith, Hob. 234.

[6] 1 Co. Inst. 53*a*. *Contra,* as to the building of the new house. Darcy *v.* Askwith, Hob. 234; Jones *v.* Chappell, L. R. 20 Eq. 539. But it is permissive waste to allow the new house when built to fall into bad repair. Darcy *v.* Askwith, Hob. 234, 2 Rolle Abr. 814, line 20.

mill,[7] or a hand mill into a horse mill,[8] is waste, regardless of any diminution or increase of value.

Diminution of value chief criterion of waste in modern times.

In modern times little stress is laid on the second consideration mentioned, and an act which does not lessen value will not be declared to be waste unless it entirely changes the character or destroys the identity of the thing dealt with.[9] The present attitude of the equity courts on such questions is well illustrated in *Meux v. Cobley.*[1] It appeared that arable and pasture land near London had been leased, the lessee covenanting in all respects to cultivate and manage the farm in a good, proper, and husbandlike manner, according to the best rules of husbandry practiced in the neighborhood. The lessee proceeded to convert part of the demised premises into a market garden, erecting glass houses thereon for the cultivating of hot-house produce for the London market. The lessor thereupon sought to prevent the use of the premises as a market garden, but it was shown that this was a more profitable mode of cultivation, and as no injury was thereby done to the inheritance the injunction was denied. The court expressed the opinion that the act of converting the premises into a market garden was not a waste at all, but said that if this were admitted to be a technical waste at common law it was ameliorating waste which equity would not restrain, thus leaving the lessor to his common-law right of recovering nominal damages after the act should be accomplished. The doctrine that equity may refuse to restrain meliorating waste had already been established in earlier cases.[2]

Alteration of premises.

In a late case it was held to be waste to shoot rubbish onto premises leased for a different purpose, thereby raising its height about ten feet. The decision was placed on the ground that this was an unwarranted alteration of the premises, regardless of the inoffensive nature of the material and

[7] 2 Rolle Abr. 814, pl. 5.

[8] Graves's Case (1606), cited in Co. Litt. 53*a*.

[9] See language of Jessel, M. R., in Jones *v.* Chappell, L. R. 20 Eq. 541, 542.

[1] (1892) 2 Ch. 253.

[2] See Doherty *v.* Allman, 3 App. Cas. 709, and cases there cited.

regardless of a probable increase in the value of the soil as incident thereto.[3]

Permissive Waste.

Permissive waste not actionable at common law.

The acts of waste so far considered are of a positive nature. But waste can be permissive, as where a tenant allows the demised premises to go to ruin for lack of repair. Upon principle it is clear that the common law cannot of its own force impose a positive duty on a tenant to keep the premises in repair. In other words, waste which results from pure omission is not actionable. But under the interpretation formerly placed on the provisions which treat of waste in the Statutes of Marlborough [4] and Gloucester,[5] permissive waste on the part of tenants for life or for years, or on the part of tenants in dower or curtesy, was, or at least was supposed to be, actionable to the same extent as voluntary destructive waste. Coke, following Littleton, says: "The tenant at his peril must keep the houses from wasting." [6] Commenting on the *non faciant vastum* of the Statute of Marlborough he observes: "To do or make waste in legal understanding in this place includes as well permissive waste, which is waste by reason of omission or not doing, as for want of reparation, as waste by reason of commission." [7] But it cannot be pretended that these statutes operated to broaden the meaning of the term *vastum* (waste), since they merely made ordinary life tenants and tenants for years liable for waste as tenants in dower and by curtesy already clearly were,[8] and there is good reason to believe that at common law 'waste' denoted a

Statutes of Marlborough and Gloucester.

[3] West Ham Cent. Charity Board *v.* East London Waterworks Co. (1900), 1 Ch. 624.

[4] 52 Hen. VI., c. 24. "Fermors, during their terms, shall not make waste, sale, nor exile of house, woods, and men, nor of anything belonging to the tenements that they have to ferm, without special license had by writing of covenant, making mention, that they may do it; which thing if they do, and thereof be convict, they shall yield full damage, and shall be punished by amerciament." 2 Co. Inst. 144.

[5] 6 Edw. I., c. 5.

[6] Co. Litt. 53*a*.

[7] 2 Co. Inst. 145.

This view is supported by opinions expressed by judges during the year-book period. See, e. g., opinion of Hull, J., in Y. B. 12 Hen. IV. 5, pl. 11.

[8] See 2 Co. Inst. 145 (note).

Volume I

positive act of destruction.[9] The opinion of Coke has, however, often been accepted without question and appears in many dicta from his day down to the middle of the last century.[1]

Tenant at will not answerable for permissive waste.

But the tenant at will is admitted by all not to be answerable for permissive waste;[2] for he is not mentioned in the statute, and besides, his tenancy can be terminated at the will of the owner. The same rule applies to the tenant from year to year.

Effect of covenant to keep in repair.

It is obvious that where a tenant is bound by the covenants of his lease[3] or by the terms of the deed or will under which he holds,[4] to make repairs, he is liable to an action upon failure to do so. In the one case he is bound by the terms of his own contract, in the other the obligation is inferred from the acceptance of the benefit of the deed or will.

Modern view.

In modern times the courts, especially in England, have shown a disposition to hold, in conformity with the original common-law doctrine, that liability for permissive waste can never arise except where it is so imposed by the contract, deed, or devise, thus repudiating the interpretation placed upon the Statutes of Marlborough and Gloucester by the old commentators. A noteworthy step in this direction was taken when the court of equity refused to have anything whatever to do with holding an equitable tenant liable for permissive waste. This court never interposes in a case of

Court of equity repudiates idea that permissive waste is actionable.

[9] The ancient writ of waste called upon the defendant to answer "*quare vastum destructionem et exilium fecit.*" Note Book, pl. 443. Fleta says that *vastum* and *destructionem* as here used are practically synonymous: "*Vastum et destructionem fere æquipollent et convertibiliter se habent in domibus, boscis, et gardinis.*" Fleta, Lib. I., c. 12, § 20. Nor did this writer imagine that the law had been changed by the statutes in question.

To the same effect, Bracton 316*b*, § 13: "*Vastum idem est quod destructio et e converso.*"

[1] See notes to Greene *v.* Cole, 2 Saund. 252.

The rule that rent goes on though the house is destroyed is possibly a corollary from the doctrine that the tenant is bound by law to keep the premises in repair.

[2] Shrewsbury's Case, 5 Coke 13*b;* Harnett *v.* Maitland, 16 M. & W. 257; Gibson *v.* Wells, 1 B. & P. N. R. 290.

"He is not bound to sustain or repair the house, as a tenant for term of years is tied." Litt. Ten., § 71.

[3] Woodhouse *v.* Walker, 5 Q. B. D. 404.

[4] Gregg *v.* Coates, 23 Beav. 33.

permissive waste, either to grant a prohibitory injunction or to give satisfaction in damages.[5]

In the early part of the last century serious doubts for the first time arose on the question of legal liability for merely permissive waste. Sir James Mansfield and his associates in 1805 denied that such waste is actionable at all.[6] A few years later it was held in conformity with this view that an action on the case cannot be maintained for permissive waste, the sole remedy being on the express or implied contractual obligation if there be such.[7] But the question was not put at rest in England by these decisions, and doubts on the subject still remained.[8] Finally, in 1889, it was expressly held in the Chancery Division of the High Court that the estate of a deceased life tenant is not liable for permissive waste incurred during the life of such tenant.[9] The decision was placed on the broad ground that purely permissive waste gives no cause of action,[1] and not on the narrower ground that the cause of action dies with the person.

Law courts reach same conclusion.

In America, as in England, the decisions are not in harmony. Here the older doctrine seems to have more vitality than it has exhibited in England. The consequence is that, in some jurisdictions, if nothing is said about it in the lease, the tenant is bound to keep the premises in repair.[2] But

Permissive waste still actionable in some American jurisdictions.

[5] Castlemain *v.* Craven, 22 Vin. Abr. 523, pl. 11; Wood *v.* Gaynon, Ambl. 395; Powys *v.* Blagrave, 4 De G. M. & G. 448; Cannon *v.* Barry, 59 Miss. 289.

In Caldwall *v.* Baylis, 2 Meriv. 408, an injunction was granted to restrain the defendant from permitting waste in the sense of authorizing or suffering waste to be done by others; and this case is sometimes erroneously cited as authority for the proposition that equity will restrain permissive waste.

[6] Gibson *v.* Wells, 1 B. & P. N. R. 290. This was a case of permissive waste by a tenant at will, and the decision was dictum on the question of the liability of tenants for life and for years for permissive waste.

[7] Herne *v.* Bembow, 4 Taunt. 764; Jones *v.* Hill, 7 Taunt. 392, 2 E. C. L. 392.

[8] Yellowly *v.* Gower, 11 Exch. 274.

[9] *In re* Cartwright, 41 Ch. D. 532. See Turner *v.* Buck, 22 Vin. Abr. 523, pl. 9; Bacon *v.* Smith, 1 Q. B. 345, 41 E. C. L. 571.

[1] Compare Manchester Bonded Warehouse Co. *v.* Carr, 5 C. P. D. 507, discussed *post.*

[2] Stevens *v.* Rose, 69 Mich. 259; Moore *v.* Townshend, 33 N. J. L. 284; Powell *v.* Dayton, etc., R. Co., 16 Oregon 33; Long *v.* Fitzimmons, 1 W. & S. (Pa.) 530; Parrott *v.* Barney, Deady (U. S.) 405.

Volume I

there are jurisdictions in which this doctrine has not been accepted or is in a way to be uprooted.[3]

Act of God or of public enemy.

A special exception to liability for waste is recognized in cases where destruction results from an act of God, as tempest or lightning, or from the act of the public enemy.[4] But if a positive duty is imposed on the lessee by contract to keep the premises in repair; or if such a duty is imposed by a general rule of law, as under the ancient interpretation of the statutes, the tenant is bound to repair the waste wrought by such casualties in a reasonable time.[5]

Manchester Bonded Warehouse Co. *v.* Carr.

A late English case (1880)[6] sheds light on the present state of the law of England in regard to the liability of a tenant to make repairs. Certain floors in a building had been leased for warehouse purposes. There were express covenants binding the lessor on his part to keep the walls, roof, and main timbers of the premises in good repair and condition. The lessee was bound to repair and keep the inside of the premises in good condition and deliver them up at the end of the term, damage by fire, storm, or tempest, or other inevitable accident and reasonable wear and tear only, excepted. But a contingency not contemplated by any of these covenants occurred. The lessee, or rather his sublessees, loaded the floor with flour, in consequence of which the whole building fell. Loading the floor with flour was under the circumstances held to be a reasonable use of the premises. The landlord rebuilt and sued for rent and damages. The lessee was clearly liable by his express covenant for the expense incurred in putting the interior into tenantable condition. He was also liable for rent during the time the structure was be-

[3] Smith *v.* Mattingly, 96 Ky. 228; Dozier *v.* Gregory, 1 Jones L. (46 N. Car.) 100; Smith *v.* Follansbee, 13 Me. 273.

[4] Y. B. 44 Edw. III. 44, pl. 52; Y. B. 29 Edw. III. 33*a* (Waste).

Fortuna autem ignis vel hujusmodi eventus inopinati omnes tenentes excusat. Fleta, Lib. I., c. 12, § 20.

[5] In Y. B. 12 Hen. IV. 5, pl. 11, Hull, J., speaking of the destruction of tenements by the wind, said: "It shall not be adjudged waste by him (the tenant), but by act of God: still if he suffers the house to remain uncovered whereby the timbers are rotted, he shall answer for this waste because it is his default, and by the law he is required to cover the house."

[6] Manchester Bonded Warehouse Co. *v.* Carr, 5 C. P. D. 507.

ing rebuilt; for, though the lease contained a clause providing for the suspension of rent in case of a destructive fire, storm, or tempest, the accident was not of that kind. As regards the lessee's liability for the cost of rebuilding the walls, roof, and main timbers, it will be perceived that he was not excused by the wear and tear clause; for destruction by reasonable use is not 'reasonable wear and tear.' These words include destruction to some extent, as of the surface by ordinary friction, but they do not include total destruction by a catastrophe not contemplated by either party.[7]

Destruction or deterioration resulting from reasonable use is not waste.

The question of the liability of the defendant for the reconstruction of the main building therefore resolved itself into the question whether he had committed waste. It was insisted that whenever a tenant actually destroys the property demised he must restore it or compensate the landlord for his loss, except of course in cases where destruction is contemplated, as in mines and quarries. But the court declared that a lessee cannot be held liable for waste where destruction happens by using the property demised in a reasonable and proper manner, having regard to its character and the purpose for which it is intended to be used.[8] In other words, in order to constitute waste the damage complained of must be attributable to the lessee as his wilful or negligent act. This is consistent with the conclusion independently reached a few years later in the Chancery Division,[9] and brings the law of waste into harmony with other branches of the law of tort. The anomalous doctrine that purely omissive or permissive waste is actionable may therefore now be considered as extinct in England.

Extinction of idea that permissive waste is actionable.

Distinction between waste and trespass upon realty.

A word may be added concerning the relation between waste and the ordinary trespass upon realty. In point of substance they are very similar torts, for in both damage is done to real property by the direct application of force. The sole difference is that in waste the damage is done by one who

[7] Coleridge, C. J., at p. 513.

[8] See Saner *v.* Bilton, 7 Ch. D. 815, where this doctrine was first announced in a case very similar to that here under consideration.

[9] *In re* Cartwright, 41 Ch. D. 532.

3

Waste violates property only. Trespass violates possession.

has a temporary legal estate, or by one for whose act such person is answerable; while in trespass the damage is done by a stranger. The trespass violates possession. Waste violates property and is committed by one having legal possession. Inasmuch as waste is a wrong of direct violence it would seem not unreasonable to have held in the beginning that the action of trespass could be maintained for waste. But this was never done, trespass being consistently restricted to cases where there is a violation of possession. As a consequence, waste and the trespass upon realty, though they have much in common, have never been associated together, a circumstance which is due solely to one of those caprices in our legal history which give to the common law its wonderful complexity and variety.

CHAPTER IV

QUALIFICATIONS AND EXCEPTIONS.

Privilege of Sovereign.

Chapter IV

NOW that we have briefly examined the primary formation in the law of tort and have familiarized ourselves with the conception of liability which underlies the phenomena there found, namely, the idea of forceful hurt to the person or forceful material damage to property, it becomes convenient, rather than necessary, to consider at this point the subject of qualifications of liability, or, as it is otherwise put, the subject of exceptions. By this means we mark out certain territory within which liability does not exist, and thus by exclusion define the field of tort with greater precision. The qualifications which we are to note apply, it is needless to say, so far as differing situations make them applicable, to other branches of tort than that of trespass which we have just considered.

Immunity of sovereign

First is to be noted the common-law principle that a civil action cannot under any circumstances be maintained against the king. As the maxim runs, "the king can do no wrong,"[1] a doctrine which has its roots in the structure of our judicial system[2] and is grounded upon considerations of policy and convenience. The same exemption from liability is enjoyed at common law by all sovereign states, among which are to be counted the component States of the American Union.[3]

and of sovereign states.

The principle of the sovereign's immunity from suit extends to servants of the crown and officers of state so far as

[1] 1 Bl. Com. 246.

[2] All judicial authority in legal theory proceeds from the king; no court can have jurisdiction over him. 1 Bl. Com. 242.

[3] Cunningham *v.* Macon, etc., R. Co., 109 U. S. 451; Beers *v.* Arkansas, 20 How. (U. S.) 527; Williamsport, etc., R. Co. *v.* Com., 33 Pa. St. 288; Moore *v.* Tate, 87 Tenn. 725.

Volume I

Officers of state acting within limits of judicial power.

they act in a political capacity and within the limits of their lawful power.[4] But it does not protect them from liability for purely tortious acts. Such wrongs are, by necessary presumption, outside the scope of their authority, and an action lies against the wrongdoer in his individual capacity.[5]

Liability of executive officers for purely tortious acts.

The doctrine that public functionaries are personally liable for acts not within the compass of their lawful authority, even though such acts be done in the course of official employment, and perchance even in obedience to a mandate from a higher source (if it be illegal), applies to all controversies which arise out of the doing of harm by persons acting in a public or official capacity to fellow subjects of the common sovereign.[6] But where the sufferer is a foreigner a different principle applies; for it is settled that no action can be brought by an alien for damage done to him by the authority of the crown. For instance, in *Buron v. Denman* (1848)[7] it appeared that a British naval commander was stationed on the coast of Africa with instructions to suppress the slave trade. Under circumstances not necessary to be recounted, he there obtained from the ruler of a certain country a treaty for the suppression of the traffic. He thereupon destroyed barracoons belonging to the plaintiff, a Spanish slave trader, and liberated his slaves. His proceedings were subsequently adopted and ratified by the British Lords of the Admiralty and by the Secretaries of State. The plaintiff having sued the defendant in an English court for the trespass, it was held that, by ratification, the defendant's act became an 'act

Distinction where injured party is an alien.

Doctrine of act of state.

[4] Lane *v.* Cotton, 1 Ld. Raym. 646; Whitfield *v.* Le Despencer, 2 Cowp. 754; Reg. *v.* Treasury Com'rs, L. R. 7 Q. B. 387; Marbury *v.* Madison, 1 Cranch (U. S.) 166; Cunningham *v.* Macon, etc., R. Co., 109 U. S. 446. *In re* Ayres, 123 U. S. 503; Mills Pub. Co. *v.* Larrabee, 78 Iowa 97.

[5] Money *v.* Leach, 3 Burr. 1742 (the case of general warrants); Madrazo *v.* Willes, 3 B. & Ald. 353, 5 E. C. L. 313; Walker *v.* Baird, (1892) A. C. 491; Hutson *v.* New York, 9 N. Y. 163.

A failure to keep a public highway in repair makes the officer who is charged with the duty of keeping it in repair liable in damages to one who suffered special damage by reason of the failure to make the repairs. Robinson *v.* Chamberlain, 34 N. Y. 389.

[6] Walker *v.* Baird, (1892) A. C. 491.

[7] 2 Exch. 167.

of state' and that the action would not lie.[8] If the plaintiff had been a British subject the only question would have been whether the act was lawful. The peculiar doctrine which is indicated by the term 'act of state' has frequently been applied in cases arising in India between British subjects acting under authority of the Indian government, and citizens of the independent states.[9]

Immunity of sovereign recognized by comity.

Upon principles of comity the courts of common law, recognizing the general immunity of sovereigns from suit, will not entertain an action against the sovereign of a foreign state;[1] nor can property belonging to him be seized under process issuing from such courts or be in any way adversely affected by their proceedings.[2]

Privilege of Persons Acting in Judicial Capacity.

Immunity of judges.

On the highest grounds of necessity and public policy, judges cannot be held liable for acts done by them in their judicial capacity. Hence, one who is imprisoned by a judge acting within his jurisdiction has no redress even though the judge overstrains his powers and acts oppressively and maliciously.[3] Defamatory words uttered by judges in the exercise of their judicial functions are absolutely privileged.[4] The question of the good faith, malice, or even corruption of the judge is wholly irrelevant.[5] But if entire jurisdiction

Extent of privilege.

[8] See Feather *v.* Reg., 6 B. & S. 296, 118 E. C. L. 296.

[9] See "Act of State as Applied to the Government of India," by C. P. Ilbert, 1 Eng. Rul. Cas. 821 *et seq.*, citing, *inter alia,* Nabob of Carnatic *v.* East India Co., 1 Ves. Jr. 371, 2 Ves. Jr. 56; Secretary of State *v.* Kamachee Boye Sahaba, 13 Moo. P. C. 22; Forester *v.* Secretary of State, L. R. Indian App. (Supp. vol.) 10; Doss *v.* Secretary of State, L. R. 19 Eq. 509.

[1] Brunswick *v.* Rex, 2 H. L. Cas. 1; Mighell *v.* Johore (1894), 1 Q. B. 149.

[2] Wadsworth *v.* Reg., 1 Q. B. 171, 79 E. C. L. 171; Smith *v.* Weguelin, L. R. 8 Eq. 198; The Parlement Belge, 5 P. D. 197; The Constitution, 4 P. D. 39.

[3] Anderson *v.* Gorrie (1895), 1 Q. B. 668.

[4] Scott *v.* Stansfield (1868), L. R. 3 Exch. 220; Thomas *v.* Churton, 2 B. & S. 475, 110 E. C. L. 475.

[5] Fray *v.* Blackburn, 3 B. & S. 576, 113 E. C. L. 576; Pratt *v.* Gardner, 2 Cush. (Mass.) 63; Taylor *v.* Doremus, 16 N. J. L. 473.

Volume I

of the subject-matter be wanting, the judge will be liable for wrongful acts which are done under his order.[6]

Persons acting in quasi-judicial capacity.

The immunity which exists in favor of judges extends to other persons who act in a judicial capacity and within the limits of their jurisdiction, like arbitrators,[7] election officers (under some conditions),[8] church wardens when supervising vestry elections,[9] revising barristers,[1] boards of health,[2] and the like. A similar but apparently not so extensive an immunity is enjoyed by private bodies or associations which exercise quasi-judicial powers. Religious congregations and social clubs are such.

Persons executing legal process.

Executive officers, such as sheriffs and constables, who act in obedience to the lawful mandate of a court of justice or in obedience to lawful process of any sort, are protected or 'privileged' in respect of acts done under such lawful authority.[3] But the privilege is not absolute, as is that of persons who exercise judicial functions. Hence if officers who execute process abuse the authority which the law confers they become liable for the damage consequent upon such abuse.[4]

Privilege of Parents and Persons in Loco Parentis.

Qualified privilege.

Parents and persons *in loco parentis* have a general authority under the law to do sundry acts which but for the 'privilege' they enjoy would clearly be actionable. Thus a parent, guardian, or schoolmaster is not guilty of a criminal assault and battery, for the correction, within reasonable

[6] Piper *v.* Pearson, 2 Gray (Mass.) 120; Mitchell *v.* Foster, 12 Ad. & El. 472, 40 E. C. L. 98; Houlden *v.* Smith, 14 Q. B. 841, 68 E. C. L. 841.

[7] Poppa *v.* Rose, L. R. 7 C. P. 32; Jones *v.* Brown, 54 Iowa 74.

[8] Barnardiston *v.* Soame, 6 How. St. Tr. 1096; Lincoln *v.* Hapgood, 11 Mass. 350.

[9] Tozer *v.* Child, 7 El. & Bl. 377, 90 E. C. L. 377.

[1] See Willis *v.* Maclachlan, 1 Ex. D. 376.

[2] Raymond *v.* Fish, 51 Conn. 80; Underwood *v.* Green, 42 N. Y. 140.

[3] Hill *v.* Bateman, 1 Stra. 710; Dews *v.* Riley, 11 C. B. 434, 73 E. C. L. 434; Tarlton *v.* Fisher, 2 Dougl. 671; Rutland's Case, 6 Coke 52*b*.

[4] See *post, Trespass ab Initio,* p. 45.

Chapter IV

limits, of those who are under his care;[5] and of course he is not civilly liable.[6] But here, as in most other connections, abuse of the power or authority which the law confers destroys the privilege and makes the person abusing the authority liable as a trespasser. If the punishment be immoderate and excessive in fact, absence of malice in the hand that inflicts it is not a good defense.[7] That the defendant was in fact actuated by personal malice could, of course, always be shown, as this would tend to show abuse of the privilege.

Malice evidence of abuse.

By reason of a necessity arising from his exceptional responsibility, the master of a vessel is privileged in respect of acts done in the enforcement of proper discipline on ship. His authority, so far as it goes, is of a summary character,[8] resembling that of a schoolmaster over his scholars, but more radical.[9] He may inflict corporal punishment when this is necessary,[1] and in case of mutiny or of necessity arising from sudden emergency may use deadly weapons.[2] In a proper case he may imprison a seaman,[3] even putting him in irons. The general rule is that the punishment imposed by the master must be reasonable in itself, moderate in degree, and administered in a proper manner.[4] In all cases where immediate action is not necessary, due inquiry should precede pun-

Privilege of the master of a ship.

[5] Com. *v.* Randall, 4 Gray (Mass.) 36; State *v.* Pendergrass, 2 Dev. & B. L. (19 N. Car.) 365.

[6] Cooper *v.* McJunkin, 4 Ind. 290; Stevens *v.* Fassett, 27 Me. 280; Cleary *v.* Booth (1893), 1 Q. B. 465.

[7] Lander *v.* Seaver, 32 Vt. 114.

[8] U. S. *v.* Hunt, 2 Story (U. S.) 120.

[9] In one respect the shipmaster's liability is less extensive than that of the parent, guardian, or schoolmaster; for the shipmaster's authority extends only to the correction of such misconduct on the part of the crew as tends to the subversion of ship discipline. Bangs *v.* Little, 1 Ware (U. S.) 506.

[1] Lamb *v.* Burnett, 1 Cromp. & J. 291; Fuller *v.* Colby, 3 Woodb. & M. (U. S.) 1; Sampson *v.* Smith, 15 Mass. 368.

The time-honored custom of flogging has been abolished in the United States. See Riley *v.* Allen, 23 Fed. Rep. 46; U. S. *v.* Collins, 2 Curt. (U. S.) 194.

[2] U. S. *v.* Colby, 1 Sprague (U. S.) 119; Roberts *v.* Eldridge, 1 Sprague (U. S.) 54; Padmore *v.* Piltz, 44 Fed. Rep. 104.

[3] Leith *v.* Trott, 16 Nova Scotia 120; Wilson *v.* The Brig Mary, Gilp. (U. S.) 31.

[4] Murray *v.* Moutrie, 6 C. & P. 471, 25 E. C. L. 493; Elwell *v.* Martin, 1 Ware (U. S.) 53; Brown *v.* Howard, 14 Johns. (N. Y.) 119.

Volume I

ishment and the accused should be given a proper hearing.[5] The result of the inquiry should be entered on the vessel's log.[6]

Master liable for abuse of his power.

If the master abuses his authority by rash and immoderate punishment beyond that which, under the circumstances, is proper, he thereby becomes a trespasser and is civilly liable to the person injured.[7] That the master was actuated by personal malice is material as tending to show an abuse of authority, and such circumstance will support exemplary damages. "Passion is not to be indulged in the infliction of punishment, and he who has to command others is not fully prepared for the duties of that station unless he, in some degree, command himself." [8]

Doctrine of privilege founded to some extent on idea of status.

The reader will observe that the exceptional immunity enjoyed by sovereigns, judges, executive officers, parents, shipmasters and the like, in respect of acts done in the discharge of their respective functions, is similar to, and to some extent identical with, the general doctrine of status; the idea here being that the law confers upon these persons, as a class, a privilege which is withheld from others. The privilege seems to be conferred mainly in consideration of the fact that the law imposes a legal duty upon such persons to discharge the functions incident to them as a class.

Privilege incident to performance of duty imposed by custom.

Clearly, the protection exists in case of a duty imposed by ancient custom, as well as in case of a duty imposed by a general rule of law, or by positive statutory provision. This is aptly shown by a decision from the Court of Appeal for India. In that country, by custom recognized in Hindu and Mohammedan law and in the regulations of the East India Company, tanks for the collection of water have been immemorially maintained and form part of a national system of irrigation. The duty of maintaining and repairing these tanks has in many instances devolved upon the local zemindars, a class of feuda-

[5] The Agincourt, 1 Hag. Adm. 274; Sheridan v. Furbur, Blatchf. & H. Adm. 423.

[6] Murray v. Moutrie, 6 C. & P. 471, 25 E. C. L. 493.

[7] Brown v. Howard, 14 Johns. (N. Y.) 123; Flemming v. Ball, 1 Bay (S. Car.) 6.

[8] The Agincourt, 1 Hag. Adm. 289.

tory proprietors who, among other conditions of their tenure, hold subject to this duty. In the case to be referred to, it appeared that certain of these ancient tanks were maintained by the defendant, a zemindar. They were properly constructed, were adequate to resist all ordinary rainfall, and were kept in proper repair. A flood, unusual in extent, but not so extraordinary as to amount to an act of God, proved more than the sluices could carry off. The tanks accordingly burst and damaged the plaintiff's railway. It was insisted for the plaintiff that under the strict English rule of liability for damage done by accumulations of water,[9] the defendant must answer for this damage. It was, however, held that as the defendant was under a legal duty to maintain the tanks he was not within the ordinary rule of liability applicable to such cases.[1] But it was admitted that if the tanks or sluiceways had been negligently built the defendant would have been liable.

Legal Authorization.

Privilege incident to performance of authorized act.

From the decisions so far considered in connection with the subject of qualifications of liability, it appears that wherever a positive duty is imposed by law upon one as a member of a particular class, or wherever general permissive authority to do a particular act is recognized as belonging to a person as a member of a particular class, such person will be protected either absolutely or conditionally in the doing of that act. But the doctrine of legal privilege is far broader than any idea of class status, and it extends to all acts which are done under the special authority of law.

In England, under the compensation acts, and in America under constitutional provisions governing the exercise of the power of eminent domain, land cannot be taken under special authority of the law for private enterprise except upon certain terms which must, of course, be complied with. But beyond the mere question of compensation for property

[9] Rylands *v.* Fletcher, L. R. 3 H. L. 330.

[1] Madras R. Co. *v.* Zemindar of Carvatenagarum, L. R. 1 Indian App. 364, Kenny's Cases on Torts 131.

Volume I

Privilege incident to prosecution of lawful enterprise.

taken, another question often arises, namely, how far one is liable for damage done in the prosecution of a specially authorized enterprise after he has it going. This question comes up most frequently in connection with the operation of railways.

When railroad company not liable for vibration caused by operation of trains.

In *Hammersmith, etc., R. Co. v. Brand* (1869)[2] it appeared that by reason of the operation of a railway after it had been constructed, the houses of the plaintiff were subjected to vibration from passing trains and were thereby depreciated in value. There was no structural damage or taking of property such as would make a case for compensation under the statutes; and such harm as was done was a necessary incident of the careful and proper operation of the railway. It was held by the House of Lords, reversing the Court of Exchequer Chamber, that no action would lie. "If the legislature authorizes the doing of an act, which if unauthorized would be a wrong and a cause of action, no action can be maintained for that act, on the plain ground that no court can treat that as a wrong which the legislature has authorized; and consequently the person who has sustained a loss by the doing of that act is without remedy unless in so far as the legislature has thought it proper to provide for compensation to him."[3] If damages could be recovered for the doing, in a proper way, of an act which the legislature has authorized, then the person injured could also maintain an injunction, and it is a *reductio ad absurdam* to suppose that the legislative purpose which intends the doing of the act is thus to be defeated.[4]

Reasonable precaution must be used.

As applied to the operation of railways the doctrine now under consideration was first declared in *Vaughan v. Taff Vale R. Co.* (1860),[5] where it was held that a company which

[2] L. R. 4 H. L. 171.

[3] Blackburn, J., L. R. 4 H. L. 196.

[4] Lord Cairns in Pryce *v.* Monmouthshire Canal, etc., Cos., 4 App. Cas. 215.

[5] 5 H. & N. 679. But it had already been held in a criminal proceeding that an indictment for nuisance will not lie for the operation, near a highway, of a railway under legislative charter whereby unsophisticated horses are frightened. Rex *v.* Pease (1832), 4 B. & Ad. 30, 24 E. C. L. 17.

operates its trains under the authority of law, using every reasonable precaution for preventing damage, is not liable for a fire caused by a spark from a passing engine. In *Atty.-Gen. v. Metropolitan R. Co.*[6] it appeared that the defendant company operating trains through a tunnel, for purposes of better ventilation enlarged an aperture over the tunnel, with the result that the plaintiff's house was depreciated in value by the increased outpour of smoke, steam, and foul air. It was held that the plaintiff had no right of action, the damage being merely incidental to the lawful operation of the railway. In *London, etc., R. Co. v. Truman* (1885)[7] it was held that an action would not lie for the harm incidentally resulting from the maintenance of a cattle yard which the defendant was specially authorized to operate, though without such authority the maintenance of the yard would have been a nuisance.

Legal authority as a defense to action for nuisance.

As may be readily imagined, the courts in interpreting the special authority under which immunity from liability is claimed, are not over-liberal. The presumption is that the legislature intended the power to be exercised in conformity with the principle by which private rights are ordinarily determined and that it did not intend to confer license to maintain a nuisance.[8] An authority to a waterworks company to use and collect water in a particular way has been held not to protect the company from liability for befouling it.[9]

Presumption against legislative intent to authorize maintenance of nuisance.

In America the doctrine that special legal authorization confers immunity in respect of damage consequentially resulting from the doing of an act authorized by the legislature seems in effect to be accepted in most quarters,[1] but judicial utterances on this subject are not so clear here. For one thing, constitutional provisions safeguarding property rights, even apart from their immediate effect, have given rise to a particular judicial attitude favorable to individual right. The

Doctrine of legal authorization not applied with liberality in America.

[6] (1894) 1 Q. B. 384.

[7] 11 App. Cas. 45.

[8] Metropolitan Asylum Dist. *v.* Hill (1881), 6 App. Cas. 193.

[9] Clowes *v.* Staffordshire Potteries Waterworks Co., L. R. 8 Ch. 125.

[1] Uline *v.* New York Cent., etc., R. Co., 101 N. Y. 98; Struthers *v.* Dunkirk, etc., R. Co., 87 Pa. St. 282. But see Chicago, etc., R. Co. *v.* Hall, 90 Ill. 42.

Volume I

legislative authority must in all cases be very explicit,[2] and doubts are sometimes expressed as to the power of the legislature to authorize one person indirectly to deprive another of the ordinary enjoyment of his property by imposing a nuisance upon it, even as a necessary incident to the operation of an authorized enterprise.[3] Some courts declare emphatically that one cannot justify the maintenance of a nuisance under legislative authority at all, but the effect of this sweeping proposition is parried by the qualification that, within limits, enterprises carried on under legislative authority are not nuisances at all.[4] This merely shifts the burden of inquiry from 'how far are specially legalized enterprises protected by privilege,' to the question 'what is a nuisance.' But the American decisions are not in entire harmony.[5]

American doctrine.

[2] Cogswell *v.* New York, etc., R. Co., 103 N. Y. 10.

[3] Pennsylvania R. Co. *v.* Angel, 41 N. J. Eq. 316. See also case cited in preceding note.

[4] Randall *v.* Jacksonville St. R. Co., 19 Fla. 409; State *v.* Louisville, etc., R. Co., 86 Ind. 114; Chope *v.* Detroit, etc., Plank Road Co., 37 Mich. 195; Beseman *v.* Pennsylvania R. Co., 50 N. J. L. 235, 52 N. J. L. 221; Grey *v.* Paterson, 60 N. J. Eq. 385.

[5] In Pennsylvania it is said that no principle of law is better settled than that a common-law action will not lie against a corporation for consequential injuries occasioned by the construction and operation of its works. Hence in that jurisdiction, as in England, damages cannot be recovered for annoyance and inconvenience occasioned by cinders, smoke, and hindrance to passage occasioned by passing trains. Struthers *v.* Dunkirk, etc., R. Co., 87 Pa. St. 282.

But in Illinois, under a constitutional provision declaring that "private property shall not be taken *or damaged* for public use without just compensation," the contrary has been held. Rigney *v.* Chicago, 102 Ill. 64; Chicago, etc., R. Co. *v.* Hall, 90 Ill. 42.

In Baltimore, etc., R. Co. *v.* Washington Fifth Baptist Church, 108 U. S. 332, it was said by Field, J.: "The acts that a legislature may authorize, which without such authorization would constitute nuisances, are those which affect public highways or public streams, or matters in which the public have an interest and over which the public have control"—a proposition that is no doubt true. But the further statement by the same learned judge, that the "legislative authorization exempts only from liability to suits civil or criminal, at the instance of the state; it does not affect any claim of a private citizen for damages for any special inconvenience and discomfort not experienced by the public at large" reflects a narrower view of the effect of legal authorization than is generally held.

See generally, Daniels *v.* Keokuk Water Works, 61 Iowa 549; Rumsey *v.* New York, etc., R. Co., 133 N. Y. 79; Valparaiso *v.* Hagen, 153 Ind. 337; Danville, etc., R. Co. *v.* Com., 73 Pa. St. 29; Hatch *v.* Vermont Cent. R. Co., 25 Vt. 49.

Where the facts are sufficient to make out a case of injury so direct as to constitute something like a trespass, as where sewage is deposited, or naturally collects, on the soil of a riparian owner, the damage may be recovered,[6] for here the damage is not consequential but direct, and the doctrine of legal authorization applies only where the question is one of liability for consequential damage.

Cannot be invoked where the damage is direct.

It will be observed that even in jurisdictions where the doctrine that damages cannot be recovered for consequential injury resulting from the operation of an authorized enterprise is fully accepted, it is nevertheless determined that negligence on the part of the party conducting the enterprise will give a right of action.[7] Negligence thus appears to be a factor that is destructive of legal privilege. It is like abuse of authority in the field of trespass *ab initio.*

Trespass ab Initio.

The doctrine of trespass *ab initio* is peculiar and important in itself, and mastery of the idea involved in it furnishes an important clue to the solution of grave difficulties in other branches of tort.

As we have already learned, one is generally liable for hurt or damage done by the direct or intentional application of force. As an exception to this principle appears the doctrine stated above, to the effect that one who acts under the authority of law is not so liable. He is protected by the privilege with which the law clothes him. Now, as an exception to this exception appears the doctrine of trespass *ab initio,* which is to the effect that one who abuses legal authority loses his privilege and is to be treated as a trespasser from the beginning. In other words, abuse of legal authority is an

Abuse of legal authority makes one trespasser *ab initio.*

[6] Platt *v.* Waterbury, 72 Conn. 531; Franklin Wharf Co. *v.* Portland, 67 Me. 46.

Damage resulting from mere concussion due to blasting, there being no direct injury from flying material, is held to be of a consequential character, and cannot be recovered where the blasting is necessary to accomplish a work authorized by statute and is done with due care. Booth *v.* Rome, etc., Terminal R. Co., 140 N. Y. 267.

[7] Peck *v.* Michigan City, 149 Ind. 670.

element which destroys privilege in the field of trespass just as malice does in the law of libel. The doctrine is very often invoked against officers who are charged with the execution of legal process,[8] but the principle is of universal application throughout the field of trespass.

Illustrations of trespass *ab initio.*

The following illustrations show somewhat of the scope of the doctrine: If a lessor who enters to view for waste, damages the house, or even stays all night;[9] if a purveyor, who takes cattle for the royal household, converts them to his own use by selling;[1] if a commoner, who lawfully enters the common, cuts down trees;[2] if a man who enters an inn continues all night against the will of the taverner;[3] if the lord of a fair or market works a horse distrained for toll;[4] or if an officer who has attached goods keeps possession of the house wherein they are taken, for an unreasonable time, without removing the goods to a place of safety;[5] in all these cases the wrongdoer is a trespasser *ab initio.* The placing of a drunken and incompetent deputy to keep guard over attached goods on the premises where they are seized, and until they can be removed, has been held to make the officer a trespasser *ab initio.*[6]

Positive misfeasance essential.

In regard to the nature of the act which is necessary in order to make one a trespasser *ab initio* it may be observed that the act must be a positive act of misfeasance, such as would in itself constitute a trespass apart from all question of privilege. A sale of distrained goods is such an act, for it amounts to a conversion.[7] But if a guest enters an inn and is supplied with wine, his subsequent failure to pay therefor, being a mere nonfeasance, is not sufficient to make him trespasser *ab initio.*[8] It is otherwise where a person, having

[8] Smyth *v.* Tankersley, 20 Ala. 212; Gay *v.* Burgess, 59 Ala. 575; Brock *v.* Berry, 132 Ala. 95; Jefferson *v.* Hartley, 81 Ga. 716; Taylor *v.* Jones, 42 N. H. 25.

[9] 2 Rolle Abr. 561 (G), pl. 2.

[1] 2 Rolle Abr. 561 (G), pl. 3.

[2] Six Carpenters Case, 8 Coke 146*b*.

[3] Rolle Abr. 561 (G), pl. 5.

[4] 2 Rolle Abr. 562, pl. 12.

[5] Reed *v.* Harrison, 2 W. Bl. 1218.

[6] Malcom *v.* Spoor, 12 Met. (Mass.) 279.

[7] Pledall *v.* Knap, Anderson 65, pl. 139.

[8] Six Carpenters Case, 8 Coke 146.

gained an entry into the inn by reason of its public character, subsequently does an act of vandalism.

An officer who, having made money upon an execution, fails to pay an unconsumed residue to the judgment debtor, does not thereby become a trespasser *ab initio*, for his failure to pay is a mere nonfeasance.[9] Nor does a sheriff become a trespasser *ab initio* by reason of a mere omission to sell, after he has lawfully seized property upon execution.[1]

Nonfeasance cannot make trespass *ab initio*.

It is worth observing that no subject has been more misunderstood from Coke's day to our own than that of trespass *ab initio*. The original difficulty was to push the action of trespass far enough to enable the person injured to use it as a remedy here. One well-known limitation of the action of trespass was that it lay only where there was a violation of possession. This was a wholly accidental and artificial limitation,[2] but it was generally supposed to be grounded in the very nature of the remedy. Now, as a person who acts under legal authority does not violate possession by his original entry upon land or seizure of chattels, it appeared that the action of trespass could not be used in case of an abuse of the authority subsequent to the entry or seizure. This barrier appeared very real to the early judges. Hence they were compelled to overcome it by an artificial presumption to the effect that the subsequent abuse was evidence of a wrongful intent from the beginning, which supposititious wrongful intent was given the effect of making the original entry or seizure a trespassory violation of possession. "The law adjudges," says Coke, "by the subsequent act, *quo animo*, or to what intent, he entered, for *acta exteriora indicant interiora secreta*."[3] An artificial difficulty was thus overcome by artificial means, with the result that true legal theory was obscured. The intent, about which there is so much talk in discussion of the doctrine of trespass *ab initio*,[4] has nothing to do with legal

Difficulty in giving recognition to the trespass *ab initio*.

Obstacle to use of the action of trespass.

Presumption of wrongful intent.

[9] Abbott *v.* Kimball, 19 Vt. 551.

[1] Bell *v.* North, 4 Litt. (Ky.) 133.

[2] See vol. 3, *Trespass*,

[3] Six Carpenters Case, 8 Coke 146.

[4] See, e. g., in Com. *v.* Rubin, 165 Mass. 453.

liability in this connection. It is, or was formerly supposed to be, material in order to permit trespass to be brought, and for this purpose a fictitious intent was as good as any.

Function of this fictitious intent.

Essentials of trespass *ab initio.*

The elements that must in fact concur in order to make one liable as a trespasser *ab initio* are these: (1) there must be an act which upon general principle is a trespass; (2) the act must be privileged in law; and (3) there must be an abuse of that privilege such that the law will withdraw its protection. What makes an abuse of the authority such as will destroy the privilege is a question of law and fact in each particular case. The element of the intent of the wrongdoer is wholly foreign to the question of liability save only so far as it tends to establish the fact of abuse. For instance malice, which is the most reprobated form of intent, might be relevant to show that a particular act constitutes an abuse. But it is needless to say that intent in this sense is a different thing from that original fictitious trespassory intent of the authorities.

CHAPTER V

SECONDARY TRESPASS FORMATION.

Responsibility for Agents of Harm.

Chapter V

Distinction between liability and responsibility.

AT the outset of this discussion the reader will note the distinction between the terms 'liability' and 'responsibility.' A man is legally liable in all cases where he is subject to an action for damages. He is said to be responsible only in those situations where he is held accountable for damage done by independent agents. Liability is a general term; responsibility, only one of its particular phases.

When we consider the matter in its bald outlines and altogether apart from its relations to actual human affairs, it seems strange that a man should ever be held liable for unintended harm which befalls another from the operation of an agent not immediately under his direction. No principle of vicarious suffering, one would say, should be admitted in any system of human law. The necessity for a recognition of some such principle becomes manifest, however, when we consider more minutely the nature and complexities of human relations. But a doctrine under which a man may be held liable for harm not directly done by himself, but by some creature of his for which he is answerable, is so far peculiar as to be worthy of serious consideration.

Agents of harm.

The agents of harm for which a man may be held responsible in law are chiefly three: (1) Human Agents, (2) Animals, (3) Inanimate Dangerous Agents, such as fire, explosives, and artificial accumulations of water. The doctrine of responsibility for the acts of human agents belongs to the law of contracts as well as to the law of tort, and this profoundly interesting topic is dealt with elsewhere in this work.[1]

[1] See vol. 2, *Representation.*

In the present connection we are to consider responsibility for harm done by (2) animals and (3) inanimate agents.

Noxal surrender.

The early history of tortious responsibility for harm done by animals and inanimate things is connected with noxal surrender (*noxæ deditio*), a subject which in recent years has been pretty fully considered by Judge Holmes[2] and Professor Wigmore.[3] A few words concerning this antiquarian matter will here suffice:

Non-liability for acts of independent agents.

The idea that a man is not liable for harm done by his slaves, his animals, or by inanimate things belonging to him provided he will surrender the harmful agent itself, is found to be characteristic of certain stages of development in all legal systems of which we have knowledge.

The most primitive view of liability can perhaps be truly indicated in the proposition that a man is liable — absolutely liable — for the direct and immediate consequences of his acts. Conversely, he is not liable at all for the consequences of acts which are not immediately attributable to him. In this view the agent of harm which acts independently of direct human control must bear the consequence of its own evil. "If an ox gore a man or a woman that they die, then the ox shall be surely stoned; . . . but the owner of the ox shall be quit." [4]

The deodand.

The doctrine of deodands has its root in this stratum of primitive thought. That which compasses or is even concerned in the death of a man is an accursed thing, whether it be animate or inanimate. The tree that falls on one, the wagon wheel that crushes him, the railway engine that runs over him, are treated in like case with the living animal. In one age they are given to the kinsman by way of compensation or *wer*. In another they are, or may be, devoted to pious uses for the benefit of the dead. In a still later and less superstitious age they are seized upon as a source of revenue

[2] The Common Law, pp. 7 *et seq.*
[3] Responsibility for Tortious Acts, 7 Harv. L. Rev. 325 *et seq.*
[4] Exodus xxi. 28.

to the crown.[5] Horses, oxen, carts, boats, mill-wheels and cauldrons are noted as the commonest of deodands.

Chapter V

This primitive notion that a man is not liable for the harm done by his creature or his chattel, but that the thing itself shall be condemned, necessarily has to give way. A beginning is made when the law imposes a positive duty on the person having control of the worker of harm to surrender it for condemnation. The alternative is that upon refusing so to surrender the chattel, the person having control of it shall himself become personally liable. In this way does the law educate itself to the idea of making the individual responsible for harms which he does not himself go about to do. Such is Judge Holmes's theory of the origin of the conception of legal responsibility, and it seems to be plausible enough.[6]

Origin of conception of responsibility.

Domestic Animals.

Passing the more modern aspects of the subject, we proceed to consider the principle of responsibility as applied to damage done by animals. Here we have to note the somewhat curious fact that in the common law a man is so far identified with his beasts of the field, like horses, sheep, and kine, that an action of trespass lies against him when such

The trespassing animal.

[5] 2 Poll. & Mait. Hist. Eng. Law (2d ed.) 473. See 1 Bl. Com. 300. As late as 1842, a railway engine that had run over a man was declared forfeited as a deodand. Reg. *v.* Eastern Counties R. Co., 10 M. & W. 58. Deodands were abolished in England by statute of 9 & 10 Vict., c. 62.

[6] On the other hand it should be added that Messrs. Pollock and Maitland agree with Professor Wigmore that the early English and German authorities tend to show that the doctrine of noxal surrender appears in mitigation of an already existing principle of absolute liability for all harm with which a man can in any way be connected. This much at least must, it seems, be conceded to the researches of these scholars, namely, that at the beginning of authentic history, English law had already reached the point where it could be explicitly affirmed that a man is in fact *prima facie* responsible for harms done by his animate or inanimate agent, and in order to escape liability must surrender the thing and free himself by oath. See Responsibility for Tortious Acts, 7 Harv. L. Rev. 325, 328; 2 Poll. & Mait. Hist. Eng. Law (2d ed.) 472 *et seq.* The particular process by which this result was reached does not appear to be clear.

Volume I

animals intrude upon the premises of his neighbor and do damage by treading down his herbage, spoiling his trees, or eating his grain.[7] Under modern rationalizing processes liability here is generally referred to the negligent keeping of the animals.[8] And this is doubtless in a way true; for, though a man is absolutely responsible for damage done to or upon his neighbor's property if he lets his cattle escape, regardless of the care he may have used in keeping them,[9] he cannot be held responsible if he is in no way at fault, as where a meddlesome third person interferes to turn his cattle out.

Responsibility of the owner based on negligence,

The law here evidently proceeds on the idea that the mischievous propensity of cattle — a term, by the way, which includes horses [1] and pigs [2] — to do damage to realty in straying abroad, must be known of all men. Knowledge of this mischievous quality is taken as a sufficient ground for making the owner responsible and therefore liable. The rule in question also reflects the characteristic strictness of the common law in regard to injuries done to real property.

or on the idea of reasonable foresight of harm.

In *Ellis v. Loftus Iron Co.* (1874),[3] a stallion belonging to the defendant poked his head through the fence and bit the mare of his neighbor. It was held that the owner of the stallion was liable for the damage thus done. The known propensity of stallions to bite must be taken as the main ground of this decision, though it may also be rested upon the idea of trespass in transgressing the bounds of the owner's premises and upon the idea of negligence in the maintenance of an insufficient fence.[4]

It is admitted that one is not responsible where his beasts

[7] Reg. Brev. Orig. 94 (*de herba et bladis depastis*).

[8] 3 Bl. Com. 211.

[9] Tonawanda R. Co. *v.* Munger, 5 Den. (N. Y.) 267; Wells *v.* Howell, 19 Johns. (N. Y.) 385; Noyes *v.* Colby, 30 N. H. 143. Compare Wagner *v.* Bissell, 3 Iowa 396; Union Pac. R. Co. *v.* Rollins, 5 Kan. 174.

[1] Wright *v.* Pearson, L. R. 4 Q. B. 582.

[2] Child *v.* Hearn, L. R. 9 Exch. 176.

[3] L. R. 10 C. P. 10. Compare Decker *v.* Gammon, 44 Me. 322

[4] In Barnes *v* Chapin, 4 Allen (Mass.) 444, it was held that the one who turns his horse on the highway is responsible for damage done by its kicking a colt which is there running beside its dam.

are driven upon his neighbor's land by a stranger;[5] and other exceptions grounded on considerations of convenience are made. Thus if, in ploughing land which adjoins the soil of another, my beast in turning takes a mouthful of the neighbor's grass, the latter has no action.[6] So where a beast, driven along a path over which one has a right of way, casually crops grain against the will of the driver.[7] Likewise it is said if one drives cattle through a town and, out of perversity, one bolts into a dwelling, the owner of the beast is not liable.[8]

Owner not responsible for act of stranger,

or for casual and unpreventable damage.

This principle is illustrated in the modern case of *Tillett v. Ward* (1882),[9] where an ox while being driven along a street betook himself to the pavement and before he could be turned again to the street passed through an open doorway into the plaintiff's shop and did damage. It was held that the owner of the ox was not liable unless chargeable with negligence.

In respect to unusual harms done by domestic animals which get abroad, the strict rule noted above does not apply. Here actual knowledge of the vicious propensity must be shown.[1] In *Mason v. Keeling* (1700),[2] Lord Holt observed that if a horse or ox breaks the hedge and runs into the highway and there kicks or gores a passer-by, an action will not lie against the owner in the absence of notice that the creature had done such thing before. This principle is illustrated in *Cox v. Burbridge* (1863),[3] where it appeared that the defendant's horse got into the highway and there kicked the plaintiff, a child of about five years. There was no evidence to show how the horse got to the spot or that it was known to its owner as being given to the habit of kicking. It was held that the defendant was not liable.[4]

Knowledge of vicious propensity essential where the harm done is of unusual type.

The kicking horse.

5 See Chapman *v.* Thumblethorp, Cro. Eliz. 329.

6 Y. B. 22 Edw. IV. 8, pl. 24.

7 2 Rolle Abr. 566 (K), pl. 1; Catesby, J., in Y. B. 22 Edw. IV. 8, pl. 24.

8 Doderidge, J., in Millen *v.* Fandrye, Popham 162.

9 10 Q. B. D. 17.

1 Buxendin *v.* Sharp, 2 Salk. 662, Reynolds *v.* Hussey, 64 N. H. 64.

2 1 Ld. Raym. 608.

3 13 C. B. N. S. 430, 106 E. C. L. 430.

4 Compare Fallon *v.* O'Brien, 12 R. I. 518; Dickson *v.* McCoy, 39 N. Y. 400; Goodman *v.* Gay, 15 Pa. St. 188.

Volume I

Injury done by dogs.

Dogs are taken to be *prima facie* harmless creatures, since they are accustomed to go hither and thither with freedom and their excursions are usually innocent. Hence before an owner or harborer [5] of a dog can be held liable for damage done by it against his will, it must appear, as in case of unusual harms done by domestic animals, that he had actual knowledge of its vicious nature.[6]

In *Millen v. Fandrye* (1624),[7] it appeared that the plaintiff's sheep were trespassing upon the defendant's premises and the latter turned his dog upon them to chase them out. The dog followed them beyond the bounds of his master's ground in spite of the latter's chiding. It was held that the owner of the dog was not liable for the chasing of the sheep beyond the limits of his land. Evidently, "a man cannot have such power upon his dog as to recall him when he pleaseth, and a dog is ignorant of the bounds of land." If the dog had been of an unusually fierce temper, the result would have been different, for in such case the owner would have been bound properly to restrain him at his peril. The trespass, if there was any, in this case was said not to be actionable, because involuntary.

In *Beckwith v. Shordike* (1767),[8] one who was out with gun and dogs entered into the plaintiff's close where there was no footpath. One of the dogs ran into an adjoining paddock and killed a deer. The hunter was held liable in trespass. The circumstance which distinguishes this case from *Millen v. Fandrye* is that here the defendant was apparently himself a trespasser by being in the plaintiff's close, while in the other case he was engaged in a lawful act. But very probably the defendant would have been held liable for the killing of the deer by the incursion of his dog into the plaintiff's paddock even though he had himself been on a highway

[5] M'Kone *v.* Wood, 5 C. & P. 1, 24 E. C. L. 187.

[6] Anonymous, 1 Dyer 25*b*, pl. 163; Mason *v.* Keeling, 12 Mod. 332; Card *v.* Case, 5 C. B. 622, 57 E. C. L. 622; Hartley *v.* Harriman, 1 B. & Ald. 620; Judge *v.* Cox, 1 Stark. 285, 2 E. C. L. 114; Brown *v.* Giles, 1 C. & P. 118, 11 E. C. L. 337.

But see Doyle *v.* Vance, 6 Vict. L. Rep. 87.

[7] Popham 161.

[8] 4 Burr. 2092.

and had made due effort to recall the dog. We apprehend that the doctrine of *Millen v. Fandrye* would not be applied to a case where a dog kills or seriously injures stock on the premises of their owner.[9]

Remedy where the action is founded on the *scienter.*

In conclusion it will be noted that in those situations where the right of action is grounded upon an actual knowledge, or *scienter,* as it is called, of the vicious trait in a dog or domestic animal, the remedy is not by writ of trespass, but by an action on the case.[1] The reason assigned for this is that in such cases the right of action is grounded upon the negligence of the owner. This however is a somewhat artificial explanation, since the keeper of an animal of known vicious habits is absolutely liable for harm which it does, regardless of the care he may use in keeping it.[2]

Wild Animals.

Injuries done by animals *feræ naturæ.*

As regards damage done by animals *feræ naturæ,* like bears and lions, which are naturally fierce and incapable of being brought to the same degree of tameness as dogs and domestic animals, liability is so strict as to amount to virtual insurance against harm. Every one is chargeable with knowledge that such creatures are dangerous, and they are kept at peril.[3] The strictness of the rule of liability here may be gathered from an observation once made by Bramwell, B.: "If a man kept a tiger and lightning broke his chain, and he got loose and did mischief, I am by no means sure that the man who kept him would not be liable." [4] But for reasons that will hereafter appear the question thus mooted must be answered in the negative.[5]

Strictness of the rule of liability.

[9] Compare Doyle *v.* Vance, 6 Vict. L. Rep. 87.

[1] Hartley *v.* Harriman, 1 B. & Ald. 620.

[2] Card *v.* Case, 5 C. B. 622, 57 E. C. L. 622.

[3] May *v.* Burdett, 9 Q. B. 101, 58 E. C. L. 101; Besozzi *v.* Harris, 1 F. & F. 92; Filburn *v.* People's Palace, etc., Co., 25 Q. B. D. 258; Jackson *v.* Smithson, 15 M. & W. 563; Congress, etc., Spring Co. *v.* Edgar, 99 U. S. 651; Decker *v.* Gammon, 44 Me. 322; Vredenburg *v.* Behan, 33 La. Ann. 627; Manger *v.* Shipman, 30 Neb. 352; Moss *v.* Pardridge, 9 Ill. App. 492.

[4] Nichols *v.* Marsland, L. R. 10 Exch. 260.

[5] See *post,* pp. 84, 85.

Volume I

Fire.

Of dangerous inanimate agents for which a man is held responsible fire was first to come under the notice of the courts, and the action on the case upon the custom of the realm for damage done by this agent is very ancient. So strict was the common-law rule of liability here that the fact that the fire was purely accidental was no defense. A man was liable where the fire was due to the act of a servant or even of a guest; but it was admitted that for the act of a stranger he could not be held.[6]

Responsibility for damage done by accidental fires.

The custom of the realm requiring a man absolutely to keep his fire safe originally applied more particularly to cases where the fire occurred in a dwelling. But at an early day a right of action founded on negligence was declared to exist where the fire originated anywhere on the defendant's premises.[7]

Under the strict common-law rule, negligence on the part of the defendant in the keeping of his fire was not necessary to be shown when the fire originated in his dwelling; but it was generally alleged, and when there was negligence in fact this furnished an *a fortiori* argument for holding him liable. By statute of 6 Anne, c. 31,[8] the common-law principle was so far altered as to abolish liability for damage resulting from accidental fires originating in dwellings. The term 'accidental' as used in this statute is construed as having reference to fires which cannot be traced to any cause. Hence the statute does not take away the right of action for fires which originate in one's house by the negligence of himself or of his servant.[9]

Statute of Anne abolishes responsibility for accidental fires.

Forces naturally tending to mitigate the harshness of the common-law rule have co-operated with the statute just men-

[6] Beaulieu *v.* Finglam, Y. B. 2 Hen. IV. 18, pl. 5.

[7] Anonymous, Cro. Eliz. 10; Turberville *v.* Stamp, 1 Comyns 32.

[8] This statute has either been reenacted in the several American States or is declared to be effective as a part of our common law. Taylor, Landlord and Tenant, § 196; Lansing *v.* Stone, 37 Barb. (N. Y.) 15.

[9] Filliter *v.* Phippard, 11 Q. B. 347, 63 E. C. L. 347.

Chapter V

tioned, and as a result, we find that in modern times the law concerning liability for fire has in America, at least, substantially reached the basis of negligence. That is to say, one is liable for damage done by fire which he is lawfully using, only where he is in some way at fault. The mere fact that a dangerous agent is used imposes, of course, a duty to use a greater degree of care than would be necessary in the use of less dangerous agents. But some negligence must generally be shown. This is illustrated in cases where the damage results from the emission of sparks from locomotive engines. The company is held not to be liable unless negligence either as regards the equipment of the engine or in its operation is proved.[1] No presumption of negligence arises from the mere fact that a fire is communicated by sparks from a locomotive.[2]

Mitigation of the common-law doctrine.

Negligence essential to cause of action.

The English courts place the immunity in the railway cases as the ground of privilege incident to special legal authorization. Accordingly where the statutory power to operate a tramway does not include power to operate locomotives by steam, the company is liable for fires communicated by a spark from such an engine, although it is properly built and operated.[3]

Modern English rule.

Firearms.

As firearms are instruments whose destructive power is obvious to every one, the law is very strict in imposing liability for damage done by them. When the damage results from the discharge of firearms actually in hand or under immediate control, one is almost absolutely responsible; but here the tort belongs to the primary trespass formation, and the authorities bearing upon the question of liability in such cases are considered hereafter.

[1] Vaughan *v.* Taff Vale R. Co., 5 H. & N. 679; Field *v.* New York Cent. R. Co., 32 N. Y. 349.

[2] Lyman *v.* Boston, etc., R. Corp., 4 Cush. (Mass.) 288; Burroughs *v.* Housatonic R. Co., 15 Conn. 124; Sawyer *v.* Davis, 136 Mass. 239.

[3] Jones *v.* Testiniog R. Co., L. R. 3 Q. B. 733. In Powell *v.* Fall, 5 Q. B. D. 597, it was held that where a traction engine is used on a highway the owner is liable for the burning of a hayrick near by, although the engine is properly con-

Dixon v. Bell (1816)[4] is commonly referred to on the question of responsibility for harm done by firearms not directly under a man's control. It looks like a hard case, but its authority has not been disputed and it well illustrates the strictness with which liability is enforced in such cases. The plaintiff and defendant both lodged at the house of one Leman, where the defendant kept a gun loaded, in consequence of several robberies having been committed in the neighborhood. The defendant left the house, and sent a mulatto girl, his servant, of the age of about fourteen, for the gun, desiring Leman to give it to her and to take the priming out. Leman accordingly took out the priming, told the girl so, and delivered the gun to her. She put it down in the kitchen, but soon afterwards took it up again, and presented it, in play, at the plaintiff's son (a child between eight and nine), saying she would shoot him, and drew the trigger. The gun went off and inflicted serious injury. Some of the priming had either been left or some grains of powder escaped through the touch-hole. The defendant was held liable on the theory that he was chargeable with the negligence of Leman. He was also to blame for sending an indiscreet person to fetch the gun.

Strictness of the law regarding injury by firearms.

In a late Irish case it appeared that the possessor of a gun placed it near a private path in a field. A casual passer-by took it up and carelessly wounded the plaintiff with it. It was held that the person who left the gun in the place where it was found by the intermeddler, was responsible and liable for the damage which was done by it.[1]

The difficult case of *Langridge v. Levy* (1837)[2] is partially explained by reference to the doctrine of strict liability in connection with damage done by firearms.[3] It appeared

structed and is operated with reasonable care. This decision exhibits a tendency to revert to the strict common-law theory.

[4] 5 M. & S. 198.

[1] Sullivan *v.* Creed (1904), 2 Ir. R. 317. We are indebted to Mr. Kenny, Cases on Torts, 588, note, for reference to this case. Unless the intermeddler in this case was quite young the decision is erroneous.

[2] 2 M. & W. 519.

[3] See the comments on this case in Winterbottom *v.* Wright, 10 M. & W. 109, and George *v.* Skivington (1869), L. R. 5 Exch. 1.

that the plaintiff's father had purchased a gun of the defendant, who was a gunmaker, for the use, as he told the defendant, of himself and his two sons. The defendant represented the arm to be of a certain well-known and excellent make. This representation was knowingly false, however, and the gun by reason of inherent defects exploded in the plaintiff's hands and did the injury complained of. The seller was held liable.

Explosives.

Dangerous explosives.

Explosives such as dynamite, powder, gas, and steam are considered in like case with firearms, though the rule of liability is hardly so strict. Of course where such agents are kept in a way that makes the keeping of them a nuisance the person so keeping them is absolutely liable for all damage that they do.[4] In *Prussak v. Hutton* (1898),[5] for instance, it was held that in such case the fact that an explosion results from a stroke of lightning is no defense. But even apart from connection with nuisance or other illegal act such as trespass, the law is very strict, approaching to an absolute duty of insurance against harm.

Selling explosive to child.

It has been held that a man who sells a dangerous explosive like powder to a child is responsible for damage which happens to it and its associates from the improper use of such explosive.[6]

Leaving dangerous things accessible to children.

In *Williams v. Eady,*[7] the defendant, a schoolmaster, kept a bottle of phosphorus (which he used for making hockey balls luminous when played with at night) in the room where the pupils' cricketing things were kept. One of the boys carried off the bottle of phosphorus to the playground, where it was ignited, and another one of the boys was hurt by the explosion. The master was held to be responsible and liable.

A person who knowingly sells an explosive to a retail

[4] Hazard Powder Co. *v.* Volger (C. C. A.), 58 Fed. Rep. 152; Wilson *v.* Phœnix Powder Mfg. Co., 40 W. Va. 413.

[5] 30 N. Y. App. Div. 66.

[6] Binford *v.* Johnston, 82 Ind. 426; Carter *v.* Towne, 98 Mass. 567.

[7] 9 Times L. Rep. 637, 10 Times L. Rep. 41.

Volume I

Duty to give notice of dangerous character of thing sold.

dealer to be resold, without giving notice of its dangerous character, is liable to a consumer who in ignorance of its true character is injured by an explosion of it.[8] In *Farrant v. Barnes* (1862),[9] an action was brought by the plaintiff to recover damages for an injury sustained by him from the explosion of a carboy of nitric acid which he was employed to carry for the defendant. It appeared that no notice had been given to the plaintiff of the highly dangerous character of the thing which he was employed to carry; and on this ground the court held that there was a breach of duty for which the defendant was liable.

Poisonous Drugs.

Poisons are *per se* dangerous agents, and one who dispenses such drugs as and for some other thing is held responsible for the harm that is done. Liability is here generally rested upon the conception of negligence, though it is perhaps also referable to the idea of breach of implied warranty.

Responsibility of druggists.

The leading case on this subject is *Thomas v. Winchester* (1852).[1] The defendant, a compounding chemist, put extract of belladonna, a poison, into a jar labeled 'extract of dandelion,' which is a harmless drug, and sold it as extract of dandelion to a retail druggist. The latter, believing the substance to be what it purported to be, sold it upon a prescription of a physician to the plaintiff. The result was serious injury. The defendant was held liable. "Nothing but mischief like that which actually happened," say the court, "could have been expected from sending the poison falsely labeled into the market, and the defendant is justly responsible for the probable consequences of the act." As observed by the same court in a later case, "it was in its nature an act imminently dangerous to the lives of others."[2] The negli-

[8] Wellington *v.* Downer Kerosene Oil Co., 104 Mass. 64; Elkins *v.* McKean, 79 Pa. St. 493.

[9] 11 C. B. N. S. 553, 103 E. C. L. 553.

[1] 6 N. Y. 409.

[2] Loop *v.* Litchfield, 42 N. Y. 359. As to liability of a druggist who sells for immediate consumption, see Smith *v.* Hays, 23 Ill. App. 244; Walton *v.* Booth, 34 La. Ann. 914; Brunswig *v.* White, 70

gence of the defendant in sending the harmful agent abroad under a false label was said to be the ground of the action.

Where a druggist grinds his harmless drugs in a mill previously used to grind poisonous drugs, without cleansing, he is liable for injuries that are done by such drugs.[3] So where a druggist delivers one medicine when a different drug is called for.[4]

Negligence on part of druggist essential to cause of action.

Though the liability of the druggist in cases of this kind is so strict as to border on absolute insurance against harm, some degree of negligence must be proved; and if it appears that an error has occurred without fault on his part, he is not liable.[5] But just what it would take to make out a case of accident so far inevitable as to excuse the dispenser of the drug is hard to say. In *Brown v. Marshall* (1882),[6] Judge Cooley suggested that proof of intermeddling by a stranger would be a good defense; and this is certainly true. It is supposed that a retail druggist might exculpate himself by proof that his mistake was due to an error of a reputable wholesale druggist from whom he purchased. If this exception exists it does not apply, so it has been held, where the retailer breaks the package and deals the stuff out in small quantities, the idea being that in such case he has opportunity to determine the character of the drug.[7]

The most important English case on the subject of responsibility for harm wrought by deleterious drugs seems to be *George v. Skivington* (1869).[8] The defendant was a chemist and as such professed to sell a compound which was made of ingredients known only to himself, which he represented to be a harmless and beneficial hair wash. The plaintiff bought a bottle for the use of his wife and injury resulted. An action was sustained on the ground of negligence in the preparation of the hair wash.

Tex. 507; Norton *v.* Sewall, 106 Mass. 143; Davis *v.* Guarnieri, 45 Ohio St. 492; Fisher *v.* Golloday, 38 Mo. App. 540.

[3] Fleet *v.* Hollenkemp, 13 B. Mon. (Ky.) 227.

[4] Brown *v.* Marshall, 47 Mich. 577.

[5] Beckwith *v.* Oatman, 43 Hun (N. Y.) 265.

[6] 47 Mich. 577.

[7] Howes *v.* Rose, 13 Ind. App. 674.

[8] L. R. 5 Exch. 1.

Volume I

Dangerous Accumulations of Water.

The question of responsibility for harm done by dangerous accumulations of water was considered in the leading English case of *Rylands v. Fletcher* (1868).[9] The defendant, it appeared, had collected by means of a reservoir on his premises a considerable body of water. Under the reservoir there had long before been mine workings which were unknown to the defendant. From these workings a shaft communicated with the ground selected for the reservoir. Competent engineers and contractors were employed to build the reservoir, and in accomplishing the work the existence of the old mine shaft became known to them. It was filled in, but, as afterwards turned out, the filling was not made sufficiently strong to bear the pressure of the superincumbent water. As a result, when the reservoir was half filled the water escaped through the shaft and flooded the plaintiff's mine. It was held that the plaintiff could recover. The analogy of the rule of liability for damage done by dangerous animate creatures was followed, and the doctrine was broadly laid down that one who for his own purposes brings on his land and collects and keeps there anything likely to do mischief must keep it at his peril and is answerable for all damage which is the natural consequence of its escape, subject of course to such defenses as act of God, *vis major,* and plaintiff's own fault.

Damage resulting from artificial accumulation of water.

The decision is sometimes criticised, but to the mind of the writer a correct result was reached. The reservoir was defective and the defect was due to negligence of the contractors. It is true that the defendant would not have been liable for damage due to the negligence of independent contractors in a matter connected solely with their execution of the job, as in depositing materials, handling tools, or constructing temporary safeguards. But where the very thing contracted for is improperly done and the owner of the premises, as in

True basis of Rylands *v.* Fletcher.

[9] L. R. 3 H. L. 330 (in House of Lords); reported in Exchequer Chamber as Fletcher *v.* Rylands, L. R. 1 Exch. 265; in Exchequer as Fletcher *v.* Rylands, 3 H. & C. 774.

Chapter V

this case, accepts the finished work as a structure upon his land, he thereby becomes responsible for damage due to its defects.[1] The correct result was reached, we say, not because there was a duty of absolute insurance against harm, but because there was negligence which was imputable to the defendant. There can be no doubt that the general principle laid down was too broad.

Explosion of steam boiler.

The cases in which *Rylands v. Fletcher* (1868)[2] has been criticised are mostly cases which present a different state of facts. Thus in *Losee v. Buchanan* (1873),[3] the question was one of liability for damage resulting from the explosion of a steam boiler. It was held that where one places a steam boiler on his premises and operates the same with care and skill he is not liable in case of an explosion due to latent defect of manufacture which was unknown to him and which he could not discover upon careful examination or by known tests. Here no fault whatever could be justly imputed to the defendant. There seems to be good reason why a different rule of responsibility should be applied where the agent of harm is a chattle of common utility which has to be bought in a manufactured state, and where it is a structure on one's own land for which the building contract is specifically let.[4]

Artificial lake flooded by extraordinary downpour.

In *Nichols v. Marsland* (1876)[5] the English Court of Appeal had occasion to consider the exceptions of act of God and *vis major* as applied to escape of water from artificial reservoirs. The defendant was owner of a series of artificial ornamental lakes, which had existed for a great number of years, and had never previous to the 18th day of June,

[1] See Gorham *v.* Gross, 125 Mass. 240; Wilson *v.* New Bedford, 108 Mass. 261.

[2] L. R. 3 H. L. 330.

[3] 51 N. Y. 476. To the same effect, see Marshall *v.* Welwood, 38 N. J. L. 339.

[4] For an instructive American decision on the principle which was applied in Rylands *v.* Fletcher, L. R. 3 H. L. 330, but upon a different state of facts, see Cahill *v.* Eastman, 18 Minn. 324.

In Pennsylvania Coal Co. *v.* Sanderson, 113 Pa. St. 126, some strictures were made upon Rylands *v.* Fletcher, L. R. 3 H. L. 330, but the case was entirely different. The question was one of pollution of a stream, and the defendant had brought nothing upon his land nor accumulated anything there.

[5] 2 Ex. D. 1 (in Court of Appeal); (1875) L. R. 10 Ex. 255 (in Exchequer).

1872, caused any damage. On that day, however, after a most unusual fall of rain, the lakes overflowed, the dams at their end gave way, and the water out of the lakes carried away the county bridges lower down the stream. The jury found that there was no negligence either in the construction or the maintenance of the reservoirs, but that if the flood could have been anticipated, the effect might have been prevented. It was held that the defendant was not liable.

Act of God.

After declaring that escape by act of God or public enemy is a good defense in cases of this kind, Mellish, L. J., adverting to the question whether the flood in this case was in fact an act of God, observed: "The jury have distinctly found, not only that there was no negligence in the construction or the maintenance of the reservoirs, but that the flood was so great that it could not reasonably have been anticipated, although, if it had been anticipated, the effect might have been prevented; and this seems to us in substance a finding that the escape of the water was owing to the act of God. However great the flood had been, if it had not been greater than floods that had happened before and might be expected to occur again, the defendant might not have made out that she was free from fault; but we think she ought not to be held liable because she did not prevent the effect of an extraordinary act of nature which she could not anticipate. In the late case of *Nugent v. Smith* (1876),[6] we held that a carrier might be protected from liability for a loss occasioned by the act of God if the loss by no reasonable precaution could be prevented, although it was not absolutely impossible to prevent it."[7]

[6] 1 C. P. D. 423.

[7] The defense of "act of God" was ineffectually interposed in Nitro-Phosphate, etc., Chemical Manure Co. *v.* London, etc., Docks Co. (1877), 9 Ch. D. 503, where the damage was caused by an extraordinary tide four feet and five inches high overflowing a wall which it was the duty of the defendant to maintain. The court found that the defendant breached a statutory duty in failing to maintain a retaining wall at the height of at least four feet. He was therefore guilty of negligence and was held liable for entire damages. Under the circumstances it was impossible to apportion the damage done by the water which flowed

Chapter V

Inanimate Agents Not Dangerous per Se.

Responsibility for agents not dangerous *per se,*

The applicability of the conception of responsibility to cases where damage is done by the three sorts of agents which we have considered is at once manifest. But apart from harms done by human agents, animals, and inanimate agents which are dangerous *per se,* the question naturally arises, how far the conception of responsibility is explanatory of liability in still a fourth class of cases, namely, that wherein harm is wrought by inanimate agents not dangerous *per se,* like wild beasts and explosives, but which, as the event turns out, are dangerous in the particular case.

but dangerous under the particular conditions.

Any extended discussion of this type of cases must necessarily be postponed until we have learned something about negligence. Nevertheless reference to a few cases will show how the conception of responsibility for agents of harm, which underlies the secondary trespass formation, can be pushed along. *Clark v. Chambers* (1878)[8] supplies a wonderfully apt illustration of the transition from the idea of responsibility for agents dangerous *per se* to that of responsibility for agents which are merely dangerous in the concrete case. It appeared that the defendant, who was in the occupation of certain premises on a private road consisting of a carriage and footway, which premises he used for the purposes of athletic sports, had erected a barrier armed with spikes (called *chevaux de frise*) across the road to prevent persons driving vehicles up to the fence surrounding his premises and overlooking the sports. In the middle of this barrier was a gap which was usually open for the passage of vehicles, but which, when the sports were going on, was closed by means of a pole let down across it. It was admitted that the defendant had no legal right to erect this barrier. Some person, without the defendant's authority, removed a part of the *chevaux de frise,* from the carriageway where the defendant had placed it, and put it in an upright position across the path-

Barrier across road.

over after the tide reached the top of the wall but before it reached the statutory four feet, and that which poured over after the tide had reached the full four feet.

[8] 3 Q. B. D. 327.

way. The plaintiff, on a dark night, was lawfully passing along the road on the way from one of the houses to which it led. He felt his way through the opening in the middle of the barrier, and getting onto the footpath was proceeding along it when his eye came in contact with one of the spikes and was injured. The jury found that the use of the *chevaux de frise* in the road was dangerous to the safety of persons using it. It was held that the defendant, having unlawfully placed that instrument in the road, was responsible for injury occasioned by it, although a more immediate cause of the mischief was the intervening act of a third person in removing it from the carriageway to the footpath.

Leaving carriage unattended in crowded thoroughfare.

In the following cases the transition is seen to be complete: In *Illidge v. Goodwin* (1831),[9] the defendant's cart and horse were left standing in the street without any one to attend them. A passer-by tapped the horse with a whip, whereupon it backed the cart against the plaintiff's window and did damage. The owner of the cart and horse was held to be responsible. "If," ruled Tindal, C. J., "a man chooses to leave a cart standing in the street, he must take the risk of any mischief that may be done."

Lynch v. Nurdin (1841)[1] is a similar but still more striking example. There, as in the other case, the defendant's cart had been left standing unguarded in the street. The plaintiff, a child of seven, playing in the street with other boys, attempted to get in. At the same time another boy made the horse move on. The plaintiff was thrown down and the wheel fractured his leg. The defendant was held. Said Denman, C. J., in effect: If I am guilty of negligence in leaving anything dangerous where I know it to be extremely probable that some other person will unjustifiably set it in motion to the injury of a third, and if that injury should be so brought about, the sufferer may unquestionably have redress against me.[2]

[9] 5 C. & P. 190, 24 E. C. L. 272.
[1] 1 Q. B. 29, 41 E. C. L. 422.
[2] 1 Q. B. 35, 41 E. C. L. 425.

Chapter V

Principle Underlying Secondary Trespass.

Conception of responsibility.

The brief survey which has just been taken of torts involving harms done by independent agents prepares us for the important conclusion that we are here confronted with a reduplication of the phenomena which are found in the field of trespass. The conception of responsibility is founded upon an axiomatic principle by which, so far as legal consequences are concerned, the act of an agent or instrument of harm is ascribed or attributed to a man, or is identified as his act. This idea will be fully expounded in considering responsibility for the acts of human agents. We here merely observe, in passing, that as in the field of agency the law accepts the act of the servant or agent as being to all intents and purposes the act of the master or principal, so in regard to responsibility for animate or inanimate agents of harm, the law so far identifies the creator, maintainer, or user of the harmful agent with the thing itself that he becomes legally responsible for the damage it does. The conception is so far fundamental that no rational explanation of it can be given in any simpler terms. Reason, common sense, law, all have to pass in one way or another on the question whether responsibility can be held to exist in a particular case; and whenever these determine that responsibility exists, the situation is governed, as regards liability, by the same principles that apply in cases of trespass proper.

Identification of the act of the agent as the act of the person who is responsible.

Fundamental nature of the conception.

In regard to the degree of strictness with which liability is enforced this is to be observed, viz., that as the obviousness of danger increases, responsibility increases; and as the danger decreases, responsibility decreases. When the danger is great and obvious, responsibility is so nearly absolute that the law virtually reaches the plane of insurance against all harm. As the danger becomes less obvious we observe that the factor of negligence begins to make its presence felt, even if not always in some degree present; and when we reach the field where harm is done by agents which, as ordinarily used, are not dangerous *per se,* negligence is admittedly the ground of responsibility.

Responsibility increases with obviousness of danger.

Place of negligence in theory of responsibility.

Volume I

So far as any general rule can be laid down by which to determine the question whether a defendant is responsible for harm done in any given case by an independent agent of harm, the following statement seems to supply the true criterion, that is to say: One who creates, maintains, uses, or sends abroad a harmful agent is responsible for unintended harms which it does, provided a prudent person, having knowledge of the facts which that person knows or ought to know, could foresee harm to others as a natural result of the creation, maintenance, or use of the agent in question. This is perhaps the broadest generalization known to the law of tort, yet the principle stated belongs exclusively to the field of secondary trespass.

Reasonable foresight of harm the test of responsibility.

Responsibility for Intended Harms Done by Dangerous Things.

For the purpose of bringing the conception of responsibility for unintended harms into clear relief, we have thus far avoided reference to injuries done by independent agents under such circumstances that a positive intention to compass the injury can be attributed to the person who is held responsible. We shall now refer to a few cases where the injury was of this kind. The trap and spring-gun cases are in point. Here the creator of the dangerous agent not only contemplates, but intends, that harm shall be done to any person or thing that perchance comes into contact with it. In *Bird v. Holbrook* (1828),[3] it appeared that the defendant, for the protection of a valuable flower garden, had placed therein a spring gun. The plaintiff, not knowing of the presence of the gun, climbed over the garden wall for the innocent purpose of getting back a stray pea-fowl and thus got shot. No general notice, by posting or otherwise, of the setting of the gun had been given. The defendant was held liable.[4] The same result has been reached in favor of one hurt by a spring

Intended harms.

Spring-gun cases.

[3] 4 Bing. 628.

[4] To the same effect, see Jay *v.* Whitfield (1817), cited in 3 B. & Ald. 308, 5 E. C. L. 297, 4 Bing. 644. Compare Wootton *v.* Dawkins (1857), 2 C. B. N. S. 412, 89 E. C. L. 412.

gun when bent upon a less legitimate enterprise than that of recovering his own fowl.[5]

Trespasser who has notice takes the risk.

Ilott v. Wilkes (1820)[6] established the doctrine in England that where notice of the presence of spring guns has been given, a trespasser goes upon the dangerous premises at his peril, and cannot hold the owner liable for consequent harm. Though the judges were somewhat hard pressed to find good reason for the judgment, the decision in question is supported by hard common sense and is correct.[7] It is essentially just that the risk should be placed on one who deliberately goes into a place of danger on forbidden premises.[8] Yet in strict theory you have no right to shoot a man because he persists, against your threats, in trespassing on your fields.[9]

This decision, it may be added, caused much excitement in England and presently led to a statutory abridgment of the 'right' to set spring guns.[1] The broad doctrine laid down in *Ilott v. Wilkes* (1820)[2] has not met with favor in some American jurisdictions, but no case holding the contrary on the particular facts has come under our observation.[3]

Upon consideration of these and analogous cases involving intended harms done by independent agents, the question

[5] Hooker *v.* Miller, 37 Iowa 613 (trespasser hurt while taking fruit from vineyard).

[6] 3 B. & Ald. 304, 5 E. C. L. 295.

[7] See *post, Assumption of Risk.*

[8] Abbott, C. J., afterwards Lord Tenterden, was careful not to commit himself to any of the several theories advanced by his fellow judges, and placed the decision on the sole ground that the plaintiff having actual notice of the placing of the spring guns took the risk upon himself in thereafter intruding on the premises. This is substantially what the other judges meant by appealing to the maxim *volenti non fit injuria.* One who deliberately puts himself in the way of harm shall not lay the blame on another.

[9] See Simpson *v.* State, 59 Ala. 1. The right to protect the habitation or person by use of spring guns rests upon a much sounder basis than the right so to protect premises at large. State *v.* Moore, 31 Conn. 479.

[1] 24 & 25 Vict., c. 100, § 31 (reenacting 7 & 8 Geo. IV. (1827), c. 18). The enactment is subject to an exception for the protection of dwelling houses at night, and it is further declared that traps usually set to destroy vermin are not illegal.

[2] 3 B. & Ald. 304, 5 E. C. L. 295; Johnson *v.* Patterson, 14 Conn. 1; Woolf *v.* Chalker, 31 Conn. 121, 131; Clark *v.* Keliher, 107 Mass. 406.

[3] See Hooker *v.* Miller, 37 Iowa 613.

Distinction between trespass and secondary trespass.

arises whether there is any need to appeal to the conception of responsibility here. In such situations the damnific act is really as much the act of the original mover as if the injury had been directly inflicted by an instrument actually in his hands. Only the train of causation is a little longer and the psychology of the act a little more complex. The truth is that cases of this kind are somewhat ambiguous, and with very little strain upon legal theory, liability here could probably be brought within the strict limits of the conception of trespass. Yet it seems best to assign such torts to the head of secondary trespass, inasmuch as the injury is not directly accomplished.

CHAPTER VI

NEGLIGENCE.

Place of the Conception of Negligence.

Chapter VI

Negligence and trespass.

WE are now prepared to consider the relation between the conception of negligence and liability in the two trespass formations. This is a sort of necessary introduction to the fuller treatment of the subject of negligence which is to follow. The first observation to be made in a discussion of negligence is that it figures almost exclusively in wrongs wherein the harm element manifests itself in physical hurt to the body or in forceful damage to property.[1] To say that negligence is confined to torts involving forceful injury to person or property is another way of saying that the factor figures exclusively in the field of trespass and secondary trespass; for, as the matter is presented in this work, trespass and secondary trespass together cover the entire field of wrong characterized by forceful injury to person or property.

As thus viewed torts of negligence fall within the category of trespass or secondary trespass, as the facts may in each case indicate. If injury is directly done in the immediate performance of a negligent act, as where a carriage driver so negligently guides his vehicle that it runs over a pedestrian or collides with another carriage, the tort comes within the conception of trespass. If the damage complained of is not thus directly done, but follows consequentially, as is said, from negligence in the creation or maintenance of an agent of harm, as where a carriage is negligently left unguarded

[1] The most notable exception to this statement is found in actions against telegraph companies for the negligent transmission of messages, a subject to be hereafter considered. The statement made in the text also leaves out of account those cases where pecuniary damage results from negligence in the breach of contract, like bailment.

and some one is injured thereby, the tort falls under the head of secondary trespass.

Negligence thus appears to be a factor which has a certain bearing upon liability in the two respective fields of primary and secondary trespass, but it has no title to be considered a distinctive tort. This idea has often suggested itself to legal scholars,[2] but heretofore it could not be vindicated for the reason that there has been no accepted category of wrong to which torts of negligence, not falling under the head of trespass proper, could be referred. The discovery of the secondary trespass formation and the consequent establishment of this new and distinctive category of tort obviates this trouble and enables us to put the conception of negligence where it properly belongs. Negligence is not a specific injury, but, like fraud and malice, it is a factor which plays an important part in large groups of wrong.

Negligence not a distinct tort.

Nature of the Conception of Negligence.

Now what are these factors — negligence, malice, fraud? They certainly serve a very similar function in three distinctive bodies of wrong: negligence, in the field of primary and secondary trespass; malice, in the field of malicious injury; and fraud, in the field of deceit. If we say that they represent states of the mind, we would not miss the truth far; yet, as regards negligence at least, the proposition would be received in some quarters with derision. We do assert that all these conceptions have reference, if not to an actual state of the actor's mind, yet to a relation which exists between the act or course of conduct which is under consideration and the faculties from which that conduct emanates. In their respective fields, negligence, malice, and fraud are competent to raise acts productive of damage into the category of legal wrong, which would not be wrongful if those factors

Negligence, malice, fraud.

Represent states of mind.

[2] Note, for example, the observation of Professor J. H. Wigmore: "It has been customary to treat the subject of Negligence as if it were a specific injury by itself, instead of merely a question of Responsibility liable to arise in connection with various kinds of harm; but this obscures the true situation." 8 Harv. L. Rev. 206.

were absent. Of these three factors, malice, it may be observed, is the least efficacious, for the law does not admit that malice is of itself adequate to convert an act which is *prima facie* lawful into a legal wrong, although such an act be followed by damage. The utmost that malice can do is in certain situations to take away exceptional immunity or, as we say, to destroy legal privilege. But fraud and negligence are, in their respective fields, entirely adequate to convert a damnific act which would otherwise be clearly lawful into an actionable wrong.

Definition of negligence.

For present purposes we may define negligence as an improper disregard on the part of one for the safety of the person or property of another. The term "covers all those shades of inadvertence . . . which range between deliberate intention on the one hand and total absence of responsible consciousness on the other."[3] This latitude in the meaning of the term is due to the fact that in one situation the law denounces as improper and unlawful a degree of disregard and inadvertence which in another situation would not give rise to liability. A similar latitude of meaning, attributable to the same cause, is observed in the term 'malice,' which is used to cover all degrees of positive advertence to the harm which is done, from that spite and ill-will towards the party injured, which constitutes malice in fact, to that responsible consciousness in doing the reprobated act which constitutes malice in law or implied malice. It is worth observing that negligence lies about as far on the negative side, or side of omission, as malice does on the opposite side. Negligence implies a blameworthy antecedent inadvertence to possible harm; malice implies antecedent advertence to intended harm.

Latitude in meaning of the term.

Analogy between negligence and malice.

Negligence in the Field of Trespass.

We now proceed to consider the relation between the conception of negligence and liability in the field of trespass.

[3] Holland, Jurisprudence (4th ed.), 94.

Volume I

Absolute liability for intentional trespass.

The proposition on which attention is here to be focused is this: For intentional injury done by the direct application of force a man is absolutely liable. For injury done by the direct application of force under such circumstances that the law can ascribe to the actor an intention to do the harm, he is also absolutely liable. But where actual intention is absent and the circumstances are such that the law will not raise a presumption of intention against the actor, there liability cannot exist, unless negligence, in the sense of some degree of blameworthy remissness or lack of care, on the part of the actor is shown. In other words, negligence is essential to liability for unintentional injury, and it is good defense in an action of trespass for unintended harm for the defendant to show that he was in no way negligent or to blame in doing the act which proximately caused the damage.

Negligence essential to liability for unintentional trespass.

Consistent as this principle is with common sense as well as with legal theory, the common law was very slow in giving full recognition to it. This was due to erroneous notions, prevailing from an early day, as to the nature and extent of liability in the action of trespass. The theory of trespass for many hundred years may be shortly summed up by saying that the conception of negligence is unknown to the law of trespass. Here liability is so strict that a man is held regardless of the state of his mind. If he is negligent he is liable, and if he is not negligent he is liable just the same. If a defendant is shown to have done damage by the direct or immediate application of force, he is liable in trespass without regard to the mode in which his faculties were correlated with the act which did the damage. Let us inquire why it is that the law of trespass should thus at its point of origin overshoot and exclude all consideration of the fault or negligence of the person who is held liable.

Original theory of trespass excludes conception of negligence.

First trespass a wrong of intentional violence.

It is an undoubted fact of legal history that the trespass which was first punished by the royal courts was a wrong of intentional violence. This is manifest from the criminal or quasi-criminal nature of the early action of trespass as well as from the nature of the trespasses which are described in the early writs.[4] To this extent, then, our law of trespass can be said to proceed from a moral source, and one might imagine that from such a beginning a rational system of law would not be long in reaching a point where negligence or some form of moral culpability would be recognized as being always essential to liability.

But from the earliest period a notion has been at work here which tends to prevent the law of trespass from reaching the indicated goal. This is the idea that a man must be taken to intend the immediate natural consequences of his acts. Such a principle was perhaps not openly formulated in the early period, but it certainly operated with effect. When the damage is immediate and no chain of causation, with its incidental metaphysics, intervenes between the wrongful act and the harm which is done, the law, if it is to be of practical moment as a factor in governing human conduct, must somewhere shut off inquiry into the state of the agent's mind, and must hold him liable regardless of the mode in which his faculties are correlated with his act. The early common-law judges appreciated this, and the attempt to state it resulted in a generalization to the effect that in the field of trespass liability is absolute.

A man is presumed to intend the natural consequences of his acts.

At the time when this notion was shaping, the civil and criminal aspects of the wrong of trespass were coming to be distinguished; and it seems to have occurred to the judges that presence or absence of trespassory intent supplied the proper criterion for discriminating between the two forms of liability. The plausible view thus became current that so far as the immediate consequences of a man's acts are concerned, he is civilly liable regardless of the state of his mind, and consequently the absence of an intent to do the harm or the absence of negligence is no defense. This proposition, taken with the qualification that civil liability is strictly limited to such consequences as are immediate, constitutes the original common-law theory of trespass.

Trespassory intent essential to criminal liability but not essential to civil liability.

The doctrine that civil liability in trespass is unqualified

[4] See vol. 3, *Trespass*.

Volume I

Illustrations:

(1) The falling timber.

was well set forth in the argument of Brian (afterwards a famous judge) in *The Case of Thorns* (1466):[5] "In my opinion," says he, "when any man does a thing, he is bound to do it in such a way that his act shall cause no hurt or harm to others. Thus if, when I am building a house and the timbers are being reared, a piece of timber falls on the house of my neighbor and breaks into it, he will have a good action against me; and yet the building of my house was lawful, and the timber fell against my will. And so if a man makes an assault upon me and I cannot avoid him, and he wants to beat me, and I in defense of myself raise my stick and strike him, and in raising it I hurt some man who is behind my back, this man will have an action against me. And yet it was lawful for me to raise my stick to defend myself, and it was against my will that I hurt him." So Fairfax, J., in the same case, illustrating the difference between criminal and civil liability, said: "If some one cuts trees and the boughs fall on a man and hurt him, in such a case that man would have an action for trespass. And so, sir, if an archer shoots at a mark and his bow swerves in his hand and against his will he kills a man, this, as has been said, is no felony. But if he hurts a man with his archery, this man will have a good action of trespass against him, although archery is lawful and the wrong which the archer did was against his will."

(2) Accidental striking.

(3) The glancing arrow.

Felling thorns on neighbor's land.

In the case in which these argumentative illustrations were used, it was held that a man who cut thorns on his own premises so that they fell upon the ground of his neighbor was liable in trespass for entering to take them away. Choke, J., observed that to say the thorns fell in the neighbor's close against the defendant's will was not sufficient; and that the plea should have alleged that he could not cut the thorns in any other way or that he had no power to keep them out.[6]

Intention irrelevant in trespass.

At a later day Rede, C. J., remarked, in a case of trespass upon realty: "So far as regards the defendant's intention, it was a good one. Yet here the intention cannot be con-

[5] Y. B. 6 Edw. IV. 7, pl. 18; Kenny's Cases on Torts, 379 *et seq.*

[6] Y. B. 6 Edw. IV. 7, pl. 18; Brooke Abr., *Trespass*, pl. 310.

sidered; but in felony it would be. As, where a man is shooting at the butts, and kills some one; there is no felony, for he had no intention to kill. And so of a tiler on a housetop, who with a tile kills a man unknowingly, there is no felony. But where some one is shooting at the butts and wounds a man, though it is against his will, yet he shall be reckoned a trespasser, against his intention."[7] As Brian once said, in another connection, after he had become Chief Justice: "It is trite learning that the thought of man is not triable, for the devil himself knows not the thought of man."[8]

Idea characteristic of early stages of the law.

The idea that civil liability for the immediate consequences of the direct application of force is an absolute liability seems to be fundamentally inherent in the primary stages of legal thought; and the common-law judges in adjusting the law of trespass to that conception were only reverting unconsciously to a conception which was vastly older than that royal justice of which they were the mouthpiece. *Qui inscienter peccat scienter emendet,* say the so-called laws of Henry I, of the case where hurt is accidentally done by the javelin or arrow which goes astray.[9]

Early law knows no 'accident.'

It is the same in Anglo-Saxon and early Germanic law.[1] "The early law," says Brunner, "knows no such thing as an accident, but seeks always for something to make answerable, and determines it by a scarcely appreciable causation-nexus, from the conditions of the harmful result."[2]

[7] Y. B. 21 Hen. VII. 27, pl. 5; Brooke Abr., *Trespass,* pl. 213.

[8] Y. B. 17 Edw. IV. 2, pl. 2.

[9] Leges Henrici Primi, c. 88, § 6; c. 99, § 11.

[1] Responsibility for Tortious Acts, J. H. Wigmore, 7 Harv. L. Rev. 319 *et seq.*

[2] Brunner, Deutsche Rechtsgeschichte, vol. II., p. 549, 7 Harv. L. Rev. 319.

As illustrations of the perdurance of the notion that civil liability in trespass is absolute, Professor Pollock refers to a passage in Bacon's Maxims of the Law (Reg. 7) and to a statement by Erskine in a celebrated argument. Bacon, in conformity with the doctrine propounded by Rede, C. J., says that if a man is accidentally hurt or maimed by an arrow at butts, an action of trespass lies though it be done against the party's mind and will.

Erskine used the following language: "If a man rising in his sleep walks into a china shop and breaks everything about him, his being asleep is a complete answer to an indictment for trespass, but he must answer in an action for everything he has broken." Rex *v.* S. Asaph, 21 How. St. Tr. 1022.

Volume I

Basis of the doctrine.

This conception of the inevitableness of liability in trespass is, we repeat, due to the proximity between the act which the early law denounces and the harm which is occasioned by it. In this stage of legal thought an arbitrary presumption of intention seems to suppress the idea of negligence entirely. But it is manifest that as more complicated acts are brought within the judicial ken and as the courts are compelled to take account of consequences more remote — in other words, as the scope of trespass is extended — attention must more and more be paid to the relation which exists between the act which causes the damage and the faculties from which it proceeds. This brings us to consider the steps by which the theory of trespass has been so mitigated. Cases involving violent accidental harm are in point.

Violent Accidental Injury.

The old view finds expression in a few decisions to which attention must be directed.

Accidental injuries done with firearms.

1. In *Weaver v. Ward* (1617),[3] trespass was brought against one who had injured the plaintiff by accidentally shooting him with a musket. The defendant pleaded that he and the plaintiff were trained soldiers in the city of London and that as such they were skirmishing for exercise in the military art under the command of their captain, against another squad. While so engaged the defendant, as the plea alleged, casually and by chance, against his own will, in discharging his piece, did the hurt which was the subject of complaint. Judgment was given for the plaintiff on the ground that "no man shall be excused of a trespass (for this is in the nature of an excuse and not of a justification) except it may be judged utterly without his fault."[4]

The fact that such a doctrine should be propounded by learned men even in loose speech or non-judicial writing is highly suggestive of the naturalness of the conception with which we are dealing.

[3] Hob. 134.

[4] To illustrate the meaning of this expression "utterly without his fault," it was added: "As if a man by force take my hand and strike you, or if here the defendant had said, that the plaintiff ran across his piece when it was discharging, or had set forth the case with the circumstances, so as it had appeared to the court that it had been inevitable, and that the defendant had committed no negligence to give occasion to the hurt."

Menaces from others are not sufficient to justify a trespass against a third person. In Gilbert *v.* Stone, (1625) Aleyn 35, Style 72, the plaintiff sued in trespass for the taking of his gelding. The defend-

2. In *Dickenson v. Watson* (1682),[5] another case of injury by discharging a gun, the defendant pleaded that while he was lawfully shooting his pistol the plaintiff casually passed that way and was hit. The plea was held to be bad on the ground that nothing short of unavoidable necessity would be a sufficient excuse in such case.

Unavoidable necessity sole defense.

3. In *Underwood v. Hewson* (1723),[6] the defendant was uncocking a gun and it went off, hurting the plaintiff, who was an onlooker. It was held that trespass would lie for such an accidental injury.

4. In 1803, Grose, J., said, "Looking into all the cases from [that of the Tithes][7] down to the latest decision, I find the principle to be that if the injury be done by the act of the party himself at the time, or be he the immediate cause of it, though it happened accidentally or by misfortune, yet he is answerable in trespass."[8] The case which called forth this observation was one in which the question was merely whether trespass or case was the proper remedy for damage done by collision with a carriage which was being driven by the defendant on the wrong side of the road on a dark night. It was held that trespass could be maintained.

In most of the foregoing cases the classical year-book illustration of accidental injury in shooting at butts is referred to without question, and it has been accepted as good law in the dicta of other decisions.[9]

Milder doctrine now established.

Notwithstanding these authorities the proposition that a man is liable in trespass for all direct harm accidentally done by him in the immediate performance of a lawful act is un-

ant pleaded that for fear of his death at the hands of twelve armed men who threatened to kill him, he was constrained to enter the plaintiff's premises and take the horse in question. It was held that the plea was bad.

[5] T. Jones 205.

[6] 1 Stra. 596.

[7] Y. B. 21 Hen. VII. 27, pl. 5.

[8] Leame *v.* Bray, 3 East 593. In the light of a subsequent development this summary of Grose, J., must now be interpreted as if the final clause were this: "He is answerable in trespass, *if he is legally liable at all.*" See Shaw, C. J., in Brown *v.* Kendall, 6 Cush. (Mass.) 295. In Holmes *v.* Mather, L. R. 10 Exch. 268, 269, Bramwell, B., said: "The result of the decisions is this, and it is intelligible enough: If the act that does an injury is an act of direct force *vi et armis*, trespass is the proper remedy (if there is any remedy) where the act is wrongful, either as being wilful or as being the result of negligence. Where the act is not wrongful for either of these reasons, no action is maintainable, though trespass would be the proper form of action if it were wrongful."

[9] E. g., by T. Raymond, J., in Bessey *v.* Olliot, T. Raym. 467, sub nom. Lambert *v.* Bessey, T. Raym. 421; also by Blackstone, J. (dissenting), in Scott *v.* Shepherd, 2 W. Bl. 892.

Volume I

tenable; and the milder doctrine is now accepted that a defendant in trespass can always excuse himself by showing that the injury complained of was purely accidental, and that it happened without any fault of his. Some degree of negligence or blame must be imputable to the defendant or he cannot be held.

Element of blame must be present.

Castle v. Duryee (1865)[1] furnishes a good illustration of the view taken of the firearm cases in a period when judicial instinct has finally come round to the proposition that liability for harm directly done is not absolute even in trespass and that there must always be some degree of fault or negligence on the part of the actor. It there appeared that at a regimental review of state militia the defendant, as colonel of the regiment, after exercising his men at target practice, had caused them to be drawn up for a few volleys with blank cartridges. What appears to have been judicious and reasonable precautions were taken to see that none but blank cartridges were used, and the guns were sounded for unejected balls. Nevertheless it so happened that some officer or man failed in his duty or some ear failed in catching the true sound of the rammer, and an accident was the result; for when the first volley was fired in front of a crowd, upon the defendant's order, the plaintiff, a spectator, was badly hurt. The trial court submitted to the jury the question whether the defendant in giving the order to fire as he did was guilty of negligence. They found for the plaintiff and the judgment was affirmed. The negligence consisted, said the court, in firing at all in the direction of the crowd of people without positive knowledge that no musket contained more than a blank cartridge.

Injury done in military practice.

But we anticipate. The following cases illustrate the gradual strengthening of the modern doctrine:

1. In *Davis v. Saunders* (1771)[2] the owners of different sloops were severally endeavoring to secure an abandoned raft. While they were working to this end the sloop of the defendant, which had come up after the plaintiff's sloop had made fast, was veered around

[1] 2 Keyes (N. Y.) 169.

[2] 2 Chit. 639, 18 E. C. L. 437.

Chapter VI

Purely accidental damage happening without fault of person causing the same is not actionable.

by the wind and struck the plaintiff's sloop, causing damage to it. It was held, in the King's Bench, that trespass would not lie, the court being of the opinion that the original act of the defendant in coming up and fastening to the raft as he did was a lawful act. This decision supports the proposition that purely accidental damage done in the prosecution of a lawful act gives rise to no ground of action.

2. *Wakeman v. Robinson* (1823)[3] furnishes authority to the same effect. The plaintiff's wagon and an ordinary coach were passing each other on the highway. The defendant's gig attempted at the same time to pass between them, there being plenty of room. The horse in the gig was frightened by the approach of a butcher cart and made a plunge, with the result that his shaft broke and killed the horse of the plaintiff. The defense was unavoidable accident. The trial judge charged in conformity with the old theory that, the action being in trespass, if the injury was occasioned by the immediate act of the defendant it was immaterial whether the act was wilful or accidental. This was held to be erroneous, and it was said that if the accident happened without default on the part of the defendant, or blame imputable to him, the action would not lie. However, the court came to the conclusion on the evidence that the defendant was guilty of negligence, inasmuch as he pulled the wrong rein and failed to go straight ahead. Hence the error in the charge was error without injury, and the judgment was affirmed. In this case we find for the first time the doctrine clearly enunciated that there must at least be negligence even in cases where damage is directly done.[4]

3. In *Hall v. Fearnley* (1842)[5] the defendant drove a cart so near the pavement at the edge of which the plaintiff was walking, that the latter was knocked down and his leg crushed. The defense was that the real cause of the hurt was that the plaintiff slipped on the curbing at the moment the defendant was passing and so got his leg under the wheel. It was admitted that this, if true, was sufficient to negative liability.[6]

4. In *Holmes v. Mather* (1875)[7] it appeared that the defendant's horses, which were being driven by his servant, ran away, and

[3] 1 Bing. 213, 8 E. C. L. 478.

[4] M'Laughlin *v.* Pryor (1842), 4 M. & G. 48, 43 E. C. L. 34, is another case where negligence plainly appeared.

[5] 3 Q. B. 919, 43 E. C. L. 1037.

[6] But it was held, very artificially, it must be admitted, that such a defense had to be specially pleaded. The idea was that the cart being under the guidance and control of the defendant, at the time of the injury, the crushing of plaintiff's limb was clearly a trespass and required special matter of defense to negative liability. It was admitted that this would not have been necessary if the injury had been done by superior agency, as in Gibbon *v.* Pepper, 2 Salk. 637, 1 Ld. Raym. 38, where the defendant's horse ran away and became uncontrollable.

[7] L. R. 10 Exch. 261.

Volume I

Unavoidable accident caused by runaway horse.

became so unmanageable that the servant could not stop them, but could, to some extent, guide them. The defendant, who sat beside his servant, was requested by him not to interfere with the driving, and complied. While unsuccessfully trying to turn a corner safely, the servant guided them so that, without his intending it, they knocked down and injured the plaintiff, who was in the highway. The jury found that there was no negligence in any one. It was held that the defendant was not liable.

The glancing shot.

In *Stanley v. Powell*[8] we find the ancient illustration of the glancing arrow put to test under modern conditions. The defendant, who was out with a shooting party, fired at a pheasant. One of the shot glanced off the bough of a tree and injured the plaintiff's eye. The jury found that the defendant was not negligent in firing as he did. It was held that an action could not be maintained.

Accidental blow to person standing behind.

The American case of *Brown v. Kendall* (1850)[9] is instructive. This case put to the test Brian's illustration of the accidental striking of one standing behind. It appeared that the defendant had interfered, as he properly might, in a dog fight, and raised his stick to part the combatants. In so doing he accidentally struck the plaintiff, who was standing behind him. The court held that if he was guilty of no negligence in fact and was using proper means to stop the dog fight, he could not be held liable in an action of trespass.

It is to be observed that the relaxation of principle which has just been indicated does not in practice operate as radically as one would naturally expect; for in many injuries which at first appear to be purely accidental, it is not difficult, upon close inspection of the facts, to fix some element of blame or negligence on the party who is sought to be held liable. And any degree of negligence is sufficient, in case of direct injuries done by dangerous instruments to make the actor responsible and liable. The case of *Castle v. Duryee*, above referred to, shows how the courts make out blame and negligence upon states of fact where under the older theory it would have been merely said that the defendant was liable

[8] (1891) 1 Q. B. 86.

[9] 6 Cush. (Mass.) 292.

because he was guilty of a trespass and liability in trespass is absolute.

Chapter VI

The following illustrations taken from modern firearm cases illustrate the same point:

Illustrations.

A is at a village store with a loaded gun. As he starts away, the gun, on being raised to his shoulder, is, in some unexplainable way, discharged. B's horse, which is hitched near by, is killed. The discharge of the gun was accidental in the sense that it was wholly unintentional on A's part. A is liable for the damage.[1] "The very fact that the gun went off under the circumstances implies of necessity some inadvertent act or want of proper caution on the part of the defendant. The lock must either have been defective or some agency must have been exerted, unintentionally and perhaps unconsciously, by the defendant; otherwise the discharge of the gun could not have happened."

C, being out with his gun, is requested by M to assist in driving an unruly cow across a stream. In so doing C gives the cow a punch with his gun and as he replaces the weapon across his horse the hammer strikes the saddle and the gun is discharged, killing M's slave. C is liable for the damage so caused.[2]

A and B are lying in the bottom of an express wagon. A discharges a revolver for amusement, and as he fixes the hammer preparatory to putting the weapon in his pocket it is discharged and B is thereby injured. A is liable.[3] "The shooting," say the court, "was an accident, but in no sense an unavoidable accident. It would not have occurred but for the defendant's carelessness. The test of liability is not whether the injury was accidentally inflicted, but whether the defendant was free from blame."[4]

[1] Tally *v.* Ayres, 3 Sneed (Tenn.) 681.

[2] Morgan *v.* Cox, 22 Mo. 373.

[3] Judd *v.* Ballard, 66 Vt. 668.

[4] To the same effect see Atchison *v.* Dullam, 16 Ill. App. 42; Bahel *v.* Manning, 112 Mich. 24. But see Sutton *v.* Bonnett, 114 Ind. 243, where the court refused to disturb a verdict in favor of the defendant, a boy, who, while handling a loaded pistol, had accidentally shot his companion.

Volume I

Negligence in Secondary Trespass.

Blame element also necessary in secondary trespass.

The idea naturally occurs that the principle thus laboriously worked out in the field of trespass also applies throughout the secondary trespass formation. That some degree of fault or blameworthy negligence is essential to liability for unintended harm wrought by things not dangerous *per se* goes without saying. In regard to damage done by things inherently dangerous, we cannot speak with such certainty; for the grounds of liability in this field have not been fully canvassed and the subject has not been generally understood. Unquestionably the law must in the end reach the same basis as in the field of trespass.

In the celebrated *Nitro-glycerine Case* (1872),[5] the Supreme Court of the United States held that an express company could not be held responsible for damage done by a dangerous explosive which was being transported by it in innocent ignorance of the true nature of the compound. The idea here applied was that the absence of blame or negligence negatives liability.

Consideration of the cases already cited in connection with such dangerous agents as fire, explosives, poisons, and dangerous accumulations of water, will show that the law in

[5] 15 Wall. (U. S.) 524. It appeared that the defendants, who were expressmen engaged in carrying packages between New York and California, by way of the Isthmus of Panama, received at New York a box containing nitro-glycerine to be carried to California. There was nothing in the appearance of the box tending to excite any suspicion of the character of its contents. It was received and carried in the usual course of business, no information being asked or given as to its contents. On arriving at San Francisco its contents were leaking and resembled sweet oil. The box was then taken for examination, as was the custom with the defendants when any box carried by them appeared to be damaged, to the premises occupied by them, which were leased from the plaintiff. Whilst a servant of the defendants, by their direction, was attempting to open the box the nitro-glycerine exploded, injuring the premises occupied by them, and other premises leased by the plaintiff to, and occupied by, other parties. The defendants had no knowledge of, and no reason to suspect, the dangerous character of the contents. They repaired the injuries to the premises occupied by them. It was held that they were not liable for the damage caused by the accident to the premises occupied by the other parties.

these several departments is gradually reaching the basis indicated. We can see no reason why the same principle should not also finally gain recognition in connection with damage done by wild beasts, and thus negative the suggestion of Bramwell, B., in *Nichols v. Marsland* (1875),[6] that the act of God is not a good defense.

[6] L. R. 10 Exch. 260.

CHAPTER VII

NEGLIGENCE (CONTINUED).

Twofold Aspect of the Conception of Negligence.

Volume I

Bi-facial aspect of conception of negligence.

IN what has preceded, negligence has been treated as standing for a certain relation between the faculties of the actor and the act or conduct which is brought in question. It now becomes necessary to turn the conception around, as it were, and view it from an entirely different point; for liability in the field of negligence is, as we shall presently see, inherently two-faced. The double aspect of the conception is indicated in the words 'commission' (positive wrong) and 'omission' (breach of duty). There is no tort of negligence which cannot indifferently be viewed either in the light of positive or omissive wrong; though it appears that the conception of positive wrong more naturally belongs to that stratum of negligence which is associated with the primary formation of trespass, while the idea of omissive wrong is more naturally associated with the secondary trespass formation. Thus, where damage is immediately done by the negligent driving of a carriage we naturally conceive of liability as being founded upon a positive wrongful act, though we may also say that liability results from the failure or omission of the driver to use due care; while if damage results from the leaving of the carriage unguarded, we naturally think of liability as being based upon omission; though we may also conceive of it as arising from a positive tortious act, in this, that the owner of the carriage, in leaving it unguarded, wrongfully created and maintained an agent of harm for which he was legally responsible.

Negligence viewed as positive wrong.

Negligence viewed as omissive wrong.

To say that liability in the field of negligence can be viewed either in the light of positive or of omissive wrong may seem to be a rather unimportant proposition. It is really fraught with the deepest significance, as the following observations will show:

Artificial nature of distinction between contract and tort.

All who are in any degree conversant with our law are aware that the ordinary division of the field of legal liability into Contract and Tort is exceedingly artificial. If we were to suggest a new, but similar and perhaps more satisfactory, division it would be something like this, namely, Delict (or Positive Wrong) and Breach of Duty (Omissive Wrong). In other words, the division would be along the lines of affirmative commission and negative omission. Under the head of Delict would fall all positive torts; while under the head of Breach of Duty would fall contract law, including debts, quasi-debts (the so-called quasi-contracts), and assumptual obligations.

New classification suggested.

In placing torts of negligence in the suggested classification, one would be confronted with a difficulty, for it would be found that in so far as liability should be conceived as arising from positive acts these wrongs should be placed under the head of Delict, but in so far as liability should be conceived as arising from omission, they should be placed under the head of Breach of Duty. Negligence thus lies along the equatorial belt which divides one hemisphere of legal liability from the other. In one aspect the law of negligence finds its affinity in pure tort, and in another aspect it finds its affinity in the law of contract. The subject of negligence is bisected, we affirm, by the most fundamental seam known to legal theory. In one part and from one point of view the law of negligence is controlled by and subject to principles which have been worked out in the field of pure tort; while in another aspect and from another point of view it is controlled by principles which have been worked out in the field of contract. The law of negligence is thus the product of an antinomy between principles belonging to different spheres.

Difficulty in placing conception of negligence.

Affinity to tort law.

Affinity for contract.

Fusion of tort and contract conceptions of liability.

In order that the reader may be able to appreciate the significance of the fact that the law of negligence in one aspect belongs to the same hemisphere as contract and in another aspect to the hemisphere of pure tort, it will be well to refer to an important point where there is a diversity of doctrine

Volume I

in the two departments. We refer to the rule as regards the extent of liability in the respective fields of contract and tort.

Extent of liability in field of contract.

If there is any proposition that can be safely laid down in the law it is that in the field of contract a man is liable only for those results of the breach of his contract which a reasonable man, looking ahead at the time the contract was made, would foresee as the likely consequences of his failure to fulfil his contract under the then known circumstances.[1] As was held in the leading case of *Hadley v. Baxendale* (1854),[2] the recovery in case of the breach of a contract is limited to such damages as may reasonably be supposed to have been in the contemplation of both parties at the time they made their contract, as the probable result of the breach of it. What can a reasonable man really foresee? that is the extent of liability in contract.

Liability in field of tort

In the field of delict liability is much more far-reaching. Here the rule is that the wrongdoer is liable for all the consequences which naturally follow from his wrongful act, provided only they be not too remote.[3]

This principle is illustrated in some New York cases, in two of which the defendant was guilty of a technical trespass and in the other of an assault. In each case he was held liable for damage which can hardly be said to have been reasonably foreseeable, but which yet was a natural consequence of the wrongful act in question.

extends to all consequences not remote.

1. In *Guille v. Swan* (1822),[4] the defendant, an aëronaut, went up in a balloon and came down, contrary to his wishes and in spite of his efforts to prevent, in the plaintiff's garden, thereby committing a trespass. A crowd of people rushed in, partly to extricate him and partly from curiosity. The result was that the plaintiff's vegetables and flowers were trodden down. It was held that the aërial navigator was chargeable with the damage done by the crowd.

[1] See article by Morris Wolf, 42 Am. L. Reg. N. S. 734.

[2] 9 Exch. 341.

[3] "In tort the defendant is liable for all the consequences of his illegal act where they are not so remote as to have no direct connection with the act." Quain, J., in Sneesby *v.* Lancashire, etc., R. Co. (1874), L. R. 9 Q. B. 268. See also 42 Am. L. Reg. N. S. 745.

[4] 19 Johns. (N. Y.) 381.

Chapter VII

2. *Eten v. Luyster* (1875):[5] A landlord wrongfully dispossessed a tenant and demolished a stable built by the latter. In an action for damages the tenant claimed that he kept a wad of money in the feed box of the stable and that this was lost as a result of the demolition of the stable. It was held that the defendant, as trespasser, was liable for the loss of the money if plaintiff's story was believed.[6]

3. *Vandenburgh v. Truax* (1847):[7] A difficulty occurred between the defendant and a negro boy. The latter fled and was pursued by the defendant with a pickax. The boy ran into the plaintiff's store, and to save himself, as he supposed, from being struck with the ax, took refuge under the counter. In fleeing he knocked out the faucet from a cask of wine and a portion of plaintiff's liquor was thereby spilled. The defendant was held liable for the wine thus wasted.

Confluence of Contract and Tort Conceptions of Liability.

From the foregoing it appears that, broadly speaking, foresight and hindsight respectively furnish the key to the question of the extent of liability in the respective fields of contract and tort. Now on the question of the conditions and extent of liability in negligence we find judicial opinion to be apparently in a state of conflict. It is frequently said that liability for negligence extends to all natural consequences. As said by the Supreme Court of Vermont, in *Stevens v. Dudley* (1883):[8] "The general rule is that the person who is guilty of a negligent act is responsible for all the injurious results which flow therefrom by ordinary natural sequence, without the interposition of any other negligent act or overpowering force. . . . It is the unexpected rather than the expected that happens in the great majority of the cases of negligence."[9]

Liability for negligence.

Does it extend to all natural consequences

On the other hand it has been supposed that one who is guilty of negligence can in law and reason be held liable only for foreseeable consequences. More than fifty years ago,

or only to foreseeable consequences?

[5] 60 N. Y. 252.

[6] Compare the very different rule which is applied in contract, where the shipper of goods is denied the right to recover for valuables lost in transit when he has concealed their nature and value from the carrier. Gibbon *v.* Paynton, 4 Burr. 2298; Relf *v.* Rapp, 3 W. & S. (Pa.) 21; Chicago, etc., R. Co. *v.* Thompson, 19 Ill. 578.

[7] 4 Den. (N. Y.) 464.

[8] 56 Vt. 158.

[9] 56 Vt. 166.

Volume I

Pollock, C. B., in discussing liability for negligence had the insight to say: "A person is expected to anticipate and guard against all reasonable consequences, but he is not, by the law of England, expected to anticipate and guard against that which no reasonable man would expect to occur." [1] This milder doctrine which assimilates liability in negligence to the contract rule finds favor with modern thinkers.[2]

True view.

The true view is this, viz., that in so far as we conceive negligence as an omissive breach of duty, the contract conception of liability is the proper one; while in so far as we assimilate liability to pure delict by treating negligence as a tort factor (positive legal wrong), the rule of liability worked out in the field of tort is applicable.

Fusion of the two ideas.

But here we are truly confronted with a great marvel, for we find that the law of negligence is not made up of these two conceptions of liability considered as separate and distinct from each other, but is a product of their fusion. The law of negligence is not double though it has two aspects. It is one single, homogeneous body of legal principle, and we cannot dissever negligence considered as pure delict from negligence considered as a breach of positive imposed duty.

Mr. Beven's statement of the doctrine.

To formulate a proposition that will correctly state the mutual relations of these two conceptions of liability, as they subsist in our law of negligence considered as a unitary whole, requires no mean effort of legal and philosophic acumen. To Mr. Beven, author of an English treatise on the law of negligence, belongs the credit of the most successful attempt hitherto made in this direction. This writer advances the theory that reasonable foresight of harm (which as we have seen is the contract test) supplies the criterion for determining the preliminary question as to whether negligence in fact exists in a particular case, but that nevertheless, negligence being established, the extent of liability is determined by the rule of liability which applies in tort; that is to say, liability for established negligence extends to all consequences of

[1] Greenland *v.* Chaplin (1850), 5 Exch. 248.

[2] See Poll. on Torts, 6th ed., 40.

which that negligence can be considered the legal, natural, and proximate cause.[3]

Chapter VII

Two important principles are involved in this theory, namely, (1) that foresight of harm is an essential antecedent condition of liability, and (2) that when negligence is shown the defendant's conduct thereby becomes tortious, or, as it were, unlawful *per se,* and he is then chargeable with all injurious consequences which proximately follow and which are not too remote. Authorities tending to establish the correctness of these propositions will presently be produced.

Negligence as a Breach of Implied Legal Duty.

Duty to take care.

From what has been said the reader will perceive that at the very outset of any intelligent inquiry into the subject of negligence account must be taken of the duty to take care, in its aspect of a positive obligation in the nature of an assumpsit. This we shall now consider, albeit even at the cost of a little digression.

Obligation in nature of assumpsit.

In the second volume of this work we shall have occasion to discuss the subject of quasi-contract in some detail. The reader will there discover that for most part the ordinary quasi-contracts consist of duties in the nature of the common-law debt. There are, however, certain obligations known to the law which are in the nature of true assumptual obligations. Now in one aspect the law of negligence is clearly referable to this head of implied assumptual obligation. We do not say that this is the most satisfactory view to take of negligence. In fact, for reasons presently to be stated, we think this idea of implied duty fails to furnish an adequate theory of negligence. Nevertheless it contains an element of truth which must not be overlooked.

[3] See 1 Beven, Negligence in Law, 106. Unfortunately we have not Mr. Beven's treatise before us, and we can merely express the hope that in the statement above made we have not unduly misrepresented his views. We wish to add further that we have not, in working out this subject of negligence, taken Mr. Beven's theory for granted, but have accepted it only because our own investigations have led up to it. On this point our researches have been entirely independent of those of the English writer, and may thus be said to corroborate his conclusions from another and different standpoint.

The general doctrine may be laid down thus: In every situation where a man undertakes to act or to pursue a particular course he is under an implied legal obligation or duty to act with reasonable care, to the end that the person or property of others may not be injured by any force which he sets in operation or by any agent for which he is responsible. If he fails to exercise the degree of caution which the law requires in a particular situation, he is held liable for any damage that results to another just as if he had bound himself by an obligatory promise to exercise the required degree of care. In this view, statements so frequently seen in negligence cases, to the effect that men are bound to act with due and reasonable care, are really vital and significant expressions. If there had been any remedial necessity for so declaring, it could obviously have been said without violence to principle that men who undertake to act are subject to a fictitious or implied promise to act with due care.

Negligence viewed as breach of implied duty.

One of the most luminous decisions on the subject of negligence in its aspect of breach of implied duty to take care is found in *Heaven v. Pender* (1883);[4] it appeared that a dock owner had provided staging for a ship which had stopped at his dock. This staging was used by a painter who was employed by the ship owner to paint the sides of the vessel. Being defective, the staging gave way and the painter was hurt. It was held that the dock owner was liable.[5]

[4] 11 Q. B. D. 503.

[5] It will be noted that the duty to take care was here imposed upon the person who supplied the staging, although he was not the owner or occupant of the premises. Lords Cotton and Bowen, JJ., proceeded upon the idea that when a ship is received into dock for repair, those who come upon the vessel for the purpose of making repairs are there by the invitation and with the consent of the dock owner. The latter has an interest in the doing of the work there because the patronage of his dock is dependent upon it. Consequently the dock owner owes to the workman the duty of taking reasonable care that the appliances are in a fit state to be used.

Brett, M. R., placed the decision upon a much broader ground. The conclusion reached by him is stated in his own words as follows: "Whenever one person is by circumstances placed in such a position with regard to another that every one of ordinary sense who did think would at once recognize that if he did not use ordinary care and skill in his own conduct with regard to those circumstances he would cause danger of injury to the

In this case Brett, M. R. (afterwards Lord Esher), in the most powerful judicial effort which has ever been put forth to generalize the theory of negligence, laid great stress upon that view of negligence which looks upon it as the breach of positive legal duty to take care. The same learned judge has emphasized this in other connections, and the view held by him may be said to be prevalent of late years.[1] Undoubtedly his lordship did, in that case, state a true test of negligence when he said that it is to be determined by reference to reasonable foresight of harm. But whether or not he was correct in assuming that negligence must always be viewed as a breach of positive imposed legal duty to take care is quite another thing. The idea underlying this view is that in order to discover whether a man has been guilty of negligence in a given situation you have merely to determine whether he was under a legal duty to take care and whether that duty was violated. The notion of positive duty to take care is thus supposed to furnish a universal criterion by which to determine the existence of negligence.

Lord Esher's generalization.

But obviously in many cases the proposed test is more illusory than real. If there were any known means by which the existence of a duty to observe due care and skill could be discovered without reference to the problem of negligence, then it could certainly be said that the breach of that duty would constitute actionable negligence. Here the existence of negligence would be determined by reference to a higher, independent legal category. But this cannot be done. Actionable negligence and breach of duty to take care are convertible terms (when the latter is used generally), and both stand for the same general problem. Hence to use one as a test for the other or as explanatory of it, merely begs the question and advances us no whit in knowledge.

Inadequacy of the theory.

The truth of the matter is that when the conception of

person or property of the other, a duty arises to use ordinary care and skill to avoid such danger."

[1] "A person cannot be held liable for negligence unless he owed some duty to the plaintiff and that duty was neglected." Lord Esher in Lane *v.* Cox (1897), 1 Q. B. 415. "A man is not liable for negligence unless he is subject to a duty." English judge, quoted by O. W. Holmes in 10 Harv. L. Rev. 471.

Volume I

Reason for its defect.

negligence is so far broadened as to apply to human relations and human affairs in general, discussions of the duty to take care, largely lose their significance. The expression 'duty' properly imports a determinate person to whom the obligation is owing as well as the one who owes that obligation. There must be two determinate parties before the relationship of obligor and obligee of a duty can exist.

There can be no actual duty without relation of privity.

Now so long as the law of negligence is limited to a conception of duty to take care as between determinate persons occupying a definite legal relation to each other, as of contract, bailment, or lease, discussions of the duty to take care are really helpful. The duty arises out of the privity of relationship between the parties. But just so soon as one goes outside of cases where some such relation exists, the duty, having become a general duty extending to and including all mankind, no longer has the same significance. A perception of the necessity for privity of relationship before a true duty can exist was undoubtedly the factor which caused Lords Cotton and Bowen to look askance at Lord Esher's broad generalization in *Heaven v. Pender,* and which caused them to rest the decision in that case on the narrower ground stated in their opinions. There is something essentially strained and artificial in the conception of a duty to use care to avoid harm as regards all the world; [2] or at least this much must be

[2] What is said here involves a more or less effective criticism on the method of exhibiting the principles of tort adopted by some learned writers. Thus Professor Bigelow in his excellent little book reduces all tort law to terms of breach of legal duty: Deceit is a breach of duty to forbear misleading a man to his damage by false and fraudulent representations; false imprisonment is a breach of duty to forbear from totally restraining a man's freedom of locomotion; trespass (on realty) is a breach of duty to forbear entering one's close, etc., etc. We cannot see that this mode of statement has any advantage over that in which the respective torts are defined by simply stating the constituent elements of the legal wrong, as that deceit consists in misleading a man to his damage by false or fraudulent representations, etc. The law of negligence is more easily reducible to terms of breach of duty not only because in certain branches of the subject there is clearly an actual positive duty owing by and to determinate persons, but also because the law of negligence belongs to the department of omissive wrong and has, as we have shown, a real and natural affinity with contract law. But even here the idea of breach of legal duty is not helpful beyond a certain point.

conceded: that in cases where there is no particular relation of privity the legal problem is as easily and perhaps more simply handled without regard to the conception of duty. The question to be discussed in such situations is simply this: Was the defendant guilty of negligence considered as a sort of legal delinquency? And such, in fact, do we find to be the course which judicial discussion commonly takes in cases where no sort of privity exists. The idea of breach of legal duty is not helpful beyond a certain point.

Dispute as to the Nature of Negligence.

Is negligence a state of mind,

or mere breach of positive duty?

The inherent ambiguity of the conception of negligence which results from its double aspect is reflected in the long-standing dispute between writers on legal theory as to the nature of negligence and the meaning of the term. The analytical jurists view negligence as a mental state and they think of it, along with fraud and malice, as a sort of *mens rea.*[3] On the other hand, the authors of the practical modern treatises repudiate the idea that negligence has anything to do with the mental state. "Negligence," says Prof. Pollock, "is the contrary of diligence, and no one describes diligence as a state of mind." [4] These writers perforce accept the 'duty' theory of negligence as universally applicable.

Each view has its element of truth, and, looking only casually at the controversy, one is reminded of the story of the knights who disputed with arms the question whether a shield which they approached from opposite directions was embossed with gold or silver, when the truth was that it was embossed with those different metals on its opposite faces. It is apparently not very material whether we say when a man starts about a lawful enterprise, that the law makes him liable for damage done to the person or property of another if he is guilty of negligence (considered as a sort of moral

[3] 1 Austin, Jurisprudence, 3d ed., Lect. XX., 438 *et seq.;* Holland, Jurisprudence, 4th ed., 94. In Professor Salmond's view, negligence is a form of "*mens rea.*" Jurisprudence, 433.

[4] Poll. on Torts, 6th ed., 421. See also Clerk & Lindsell on Torts, 3d ed., 431; Psychology of Negligence, by Chas. Morse, 41 Can. L. J. 233.

Volume I

delinquency), or whether we say that the law imposes on him in all his undertakings the positive duty of taking due and reasonable care that no harm shall come to another.

Standard of Care.

Test of existence of negligence.

The legal test of negligence, whether negligence be conceived as a sort of legal or moral delinquency or whether it be conceived as a breach of implied duty, is this: Did the defendant in doing the alleged negligent act use that reasonable care and caution which an ordinarily prudent person would have used in the same situation? If not, then he is guilty of negligence. Stated in another way, conduct is said to be negligent when a prudent man in the position of the tortfeasor would have foreseen that a harmful effect was sufficiently probable to warrant his foregoing the conduct or guarding against its consequences.

Conduct of the prudent man.

The 'external standard.'

The standard to which a man is held is thus found in the conduct of the prudent man. The law here adopts what Judge Holmes has aptly called the external standard.[5] The existence of negligence in a given case is not determined by reference to the judgment of the actor. To say that liability in negligence should only be coextensive with the judgment of the individual would make liability for negligence as variable as the foot of each individual.[6] To descend into a minute analysis of the faculties of a particular individual in order to ascertain what would have been prudent in him would pass the possibility of rational inquiry. The law considers what would be reckless, blameworthy, or negligent in the man of ordinary intelligence and prudence, and determines liability by that. Personal idiosyncracies are deliberately left out of sight.[7] The idea was once expressed by Alderson, B., in words that have often been quoted: "Negligence is the omission to do something which a reasonable man, guided

Personal equation disregarded.

[5] Holmes, Common Law, 107.

[6] Said by Tindal, C. J., in Vaughan *v.* Menlove, 3 Bing. N. Cas. 475, 32 E. C. L. 212.

[7] Holmes, Common Law, 108; Com. *v.* Pierce, 138 Mass. 176, *per* Holmes, J.

upon those considerations which ordinarily regulate the conduct of human affairs, would do; or doing something which a prudent and reasonable man would not do." [8]

On the question as to what would constitute the conduct of a prudent man in a given situation, abstract speculations cannot be of value, but this much can profitably be said: Reasonable men govern their conduct by the circumstances which are before them or are known to them. They are not, and are not supposed to be, omniscient of the future. Hence they can be expected to take care only when there is something before them to warn of danger. Could a reasonable man foresee harm? that is the question which is finally determinative. Thus again are we led to the conclusion that reasonable foresight of harm is always essential before negligence can be held to exist. This is the truth which, as we have seen, is embodied in the first branch of Mr. Beven's theory of negligence, and it is identical in substance with the generalization by which Lord Esher would determine the existence of the duty to take care.

Foresight of harm ultimate criterion.

The rule that a man is held to the exercise of the degree of care which an ordinarily prudent man would exercise in the same situation, is subject to one or two exceptions which are apparent rather than real. Thus, it is said that if a person is highly skilled about a particular business, and knows that to be dangerous which another, not so skilled as he, does not know to be dangerous, the law will hold him guilty of negligence in failing to use such expert skill.[9] Another apparent, but only apparent, exception to the general principle is indicated in the expression 'assumption of skill.' Here the rule is that if a man holds himself out as being specially competent to do things requiring professional skill, he will be held liable for negligence if he fails to exhibit the care and skill of one ordinarily an expert in that business. In *Dean v. Keate* (1811),[1] the defendant, who was not a veterinarian, officiously undertook to doctor a horse when he should have pro-

Highly skilled person.

Assumption of professional skill.

[8] Blyth *v.* Birmingham Waterworks Co. (1856), 11 Exch. 784.
[9] Rolfe, B., in Wilson *v.* Brett (1843), 11 M. & W. 113.
[1] 3 Campb. 4.

cured the service of one who knew the business. The result was that the animal died of his unskiled treatment. He was held liable. The same is true of persons who act or assume to act as medical practitioners. They are held liable if they fall short of the skill shown by those who are ordinarily versed in that art.[2]

Degrees of Negligence.

Degree of care.

The subject of the degrees of negligence may be dismissed with a very few words. It is a matter about which much unprofitable discussion has been indulged. From what has already been said it appears that the amount of care and diligence which a man is required to use in a particular situation in order to avoid the imputation of negligence varies with the obviousness of the risk. If the danger of doing injury to the person or property of another by the pursuance of a certain line of conduct is great, the individual who proposes to pursue that particular course is bound to use great care in order to avoid the foreseeable harm. On the other hand, if the danger is slight, only a slight amount of care is required. It is thus seen that there are infinite shades of care or diligence, from the slightest momentary thought or transient glance of attention to the most vigilant anxiety and solicitude. The proposition that there are *degrees of care* therefore embodies a certain amount of truth.

Gross, ordinary, and slight negligence.

Now in dealing with the law of bailment it was thought convenient by the older writers to distinguish just three degrees of care, namely, slight care, ordinary care, and great care. Ordinary care, in the sense intended by these writers, is that care which "every person of common prudence and capable of governing a family takes of his own concerns."[3] But writers on bailments have gone further, and recognized three degrees of negligence corresponding inversely with the three degrees of care above specified. Thus if, in a particular situation, a man is bound to use only a slight degree of care

[2] Jones *v.* Fay, 4 F. & F. 525.
[3] Jones on Bailments, Am. ed. (1806), 6.

to avoid harm, and fails to do so, he is said to be guilty of gross negligence. If he is bound to use ordinary care and fails to do so, he is guilty of ordinary negligence; while if he is bound to use great care and fails to do so, he is said to be guilty of slight negligence.[4]

Fallacy of recognizing degrees in negligence.

This division of negligence into the degrees indicated is clearly fallacious. It overlooks the important fact that the term 'negligence' refers only to that legal delinquency which results wherever a man fails to exhibit the care which he ought to exhibit, whether it be slight, ordinary, or great. If a man is bound to use slight diligence and fails to do so he is legally delinquent and is guilty of actionable negligence. It is the same where he is bound to use ordinary, or great, care and fails to do so.

Source of the error.

In all cases the failure to use the degree of care which the law then and there requires is negligence. And simple negligence is all that can be made of it. In the very nature of things there can be no degree of negligence. But the earlier writers on the law of bailment did not perceive this. The error was due to a misunderstanding of Roman law by Lord Holt and Sir William Jones. Judge Story perpetuated their mistake.[5] Modern investigators have shown that the Roman law recognized only two degrees of negligence, and very little stress is to be laid even upon this distinction.[6]

Perhaps the first English judge to call direct attention to

[4] The application of these so-called 'standards' to the law of bailment is stated by Judge Story in these words: "When the bailment is for the sole benefit of the bailor, the law requires only slight diligence on the part of the bailee, and of course makes him answerable only for gross neglect. When the bailment is for the sole benefit of the bailee, the law requires great diligence on the part of the bailee, and makes him responsible for slight neglect. When the bailment is reciprocally beneficial to both parties, the law requires ordinary diligence on the part of the bailee, and makes him responsible for ordinary neglect." Story on Bailments, § 23.

This statement of the law is substantially an abridgment of what Sir William Jones had previously said on the same subject. Jones on Bailments, Am. ed. (1806), 11, 12.

[5] See Story on Bailments, § 18.

[6] The work of Hasse, Die Culpa des Römischen Rechts, first published in 1815, is the foundation of the modern literature of the subject. Wharton, in his Treatise on Negligence, gives a résumé of Hasse's Theories. See also Holland, Jurisprudence, 9th ed., 107; Bigelow on Torts, 292, 293.

Volume I

Repudiation of degrees in negligence.

the impropriety of distinguishing degrees in negligence was Rolfe, B., who in *Wilson v. Brett* (1843),[7] insisted that negligence of any degree is merely negligence, and that gross negligence is only negligence with a vituperative epithet. His language on this point has been referred to with approval numberless times. Justice Curtis, on one occasion,[8] argued against the use of the term 'gross negligence,' and the opinion expressed by him has found favor in many quarters.[9]

The notion that there are degrees in negligence can be said to be exploded, but the idea is so thoroughly rooted in our law of bailment that it is not likely soon to be altogether eradicated.[1]

[7] 11 M. & W. 113.

[8] The Steamboat New World *v.* King, 16 How. (U. S.) 474.

[9] See Beal *v.* South Devon R. Co., 3 H. & C. 337; Grill *v.* General Iron Screw Collier Co., L. R. 1 C. P. 600; New York Cent. R. Co. *v.* Lockwood, 17 Wall. (U. S.) 357; Gill *v.* Middleton, 105 Mass. 479; Reed *v.* Western Union Tel. Co., 135 Mo. 661; Lyons First Nat. Bank *v.* Ocean Nat. Bank, 60 N. Y. 278; Perkins *v.* New York Cent. R. Co., 24 N. Y. 196.

[1] See opinion of Lord Chelmsford, in Giblin *v.* McMullen (1868), L. R. 2 P. C. 318, 3 Eng. Rul. Cas. 613.

CHAPTER VIII

NEGLIGENCE (CONTINUED).

Chapter VIII

Limited value of abstract discussion.

IN the presentation which is now to be made of the fundamental rules in the law of negligence, we shall make free use of concrete illustrations. The subject is of such nature that abstract discussion can at best be of only limited use. Here, more than anywhere else in the law, is it necessary to study the principles in the decided cases. At the same time it should be borne in mind that the law of negligence is so rich and complicated that no presentation of concrete illustrations can, within reasonable limits, exhaust the subject. It may be added that the cases from which these illustrations are drawn have been chosen with the greatest possible care.

Foresight of Harm.

Criterion of negligence.

That reasonable foresight of harm is the criterion by which to determine the existence of negligence in a given case is very patent after attention has once been directed to the matter; nevertheless this truth is largely obscured in the actual decisions by a confusion with the rule which is applied in regard to the extent of liability. The following cases furnish apt illustrations of the doctrine in question:

Spontaneous combustion of hayrick.

1. *Vaughan v. Menlove* (1837):[1] The defendant was possessed of a close of land, with certain buildings and a hayrick thereon near the plaintiff's cottage. Owing to the spontaneous ignition of this hayrick, fire was communicated to the defendant's buildings. The fire spread to the plaintiff's cottages and they were thereby consumed. It appeared that the hay in the rick was in such a state when put together as to give rise to discussion on the probability of fire and though there were conflicting opinions on the subject and the defendant was repeatedly warned of the danger, he said he "would

[1] 3 Bing. N. Cas. 468, 32 E. C. L. 208.

Volume I

chance it." It was held that the defendant was guilty of negligence and was liable.

Mooring boat in swift current.

2. *McGrew v. Stone* (1866):[2] A bargeman moored his boat to a pier of a bridge in the centre of a rapid current. From some cause impossible to state the barge broke loose, sank, and drifted underneath the plaintiff's boat (moored below in a crowded basin) and damaged it. There was no proof of lack of care in the mooring, and the only alleged negligent act was the mooring of the boat in an exposed place. It was held that if the defendant could, as a reasonable person, foresee danger to the boats below as a probable consequence of his mooring of the boat in that place, his conduct in so mooring it there was negligent.

Sparks from locomotive.

3. *Smith v. London, etc., R. Co.* (1870):[3] Workmen employed by a railroad company cut grass and trimmed hedges along the right of way. The material thus cut in the course of two weeks became very dry and combustible. It was then raked up into heaps which presently were ignited by a spark from a passing engine. The fire spread over the stubble until it reached and consumed a cottage two hundred yards away belonging to the plaintiff. It was held that a jury might upon these facts find that the company was guilty of negligence in leaving the dry heaps near the track. The particular harm which befell perhaps could not be easily foreseen, but the communication of fire to the heaps could be foreseen as a possible natural consequence of their being allowed to remain there.[4]

Defective steering apparatus on ship.

4. *The European* (1885):[5] A steamship fitted with a steam-steering gear ran into a vessel at anchor in the Thames, owing to the steering gear suddenly not acting; every effort was unavailingly made to avoid the collision. A few days before, on the previous voyage of the same steamship, the same apparatus had similarly refused to act, but no cause for it so doing could be seen on examination. Large numbers of the gears were in use on other steamers. In an action for damage it was held that inasmuch as the steering gear had similarly refused to act a few days before, it was negligent to trust the control of the ship to the self-same apparatus in the crowded and intricate navigation of the Thames. The conclusion

[2] 53 Pa. St. 436.

[3] L. R. 6 C. P. 14.

[4] Said Kelly, C. B.: "It may be that they did not anticipate, and were not bound to anticipate, that the plaintiff's cottage would be burnt as a result of their negligence; but I think the law is, that if they were aware that these heaps were lying by the side of the rails, and that it was a hot season, and that therefore by being left there the heaps were likely to catch fire, the defendants were bound to provide against all circumstances which might result from this, and were responsible for all the natural consequences of it." L. R. 6 C. P. 20.

[5] 10 P. D. 99.

was the more readily reached as the ship's hand-steering gear was available but was not used.

Damage done by crowd listening to public harangue.

5. *Fairbanks v. Kerr* (1871):[6] The defendant, for the purpose of making a political harangue, mounted a pile of flagstones which had been put near the curbing of a street for paving purposes by the plaintiff, a contractor. A crowd collected to hear defendant's speech and some of his auditors mounted another pile of the flagstones to listen. Their combined weight caused a number of the stones to break. It was held that the defendant's liability depended upon the question whether, when he stopped to make his speech, he could have foreseen as a natural and probable consequence of his act that persons collecting to hear him would mount the pile of stones. This question was held to be a proper one for the jury. It will be noted that the making of a speech in a public street is not a nuisance or otherwise unlawful, and the sole ground on which the defendant in this case could be held liable was that he had negligently chosen an inopportune place for his oratorical effort.

Loosening support of scaffold.

6. *Phillips v. Wilpers* (1870):[7] The plaintiff suspended a scaffold in front of a house which he was employed to paint, by fastening one of the ropes to the chimney of the defendant's adjoining house. The evidence tended to show that the defendant, being informed that his chimney was endangered, went upon his roof and handled the rope, making it less secure than before. The next day the plaintiff returned to work and the scaffold fell, causing serious injury. It was held that while the defendant might have removed the rope altogether, since to fix it there constituted a trespass on the part of the plaintiff, he was nevertheless responsible for the accident if he negligently loosened the rope without proper regard to the safety of the painter, for he thereby created an agent of harm in the nature of a trap.[8]

From the foregoing cases as well as from others which will be referred to in different connections, it appears that

[6] 70 Pa. St. 86.

[7] 2 Lans. (N. Y.) 389.

[8] White *v.* Twitchell (1853), 25 Vt. 620. The plaintiff erected a temporary staging as a preliminary to shingling his barn. For one of the supports he used a wooden bar belonging to the defendant without the latter's consent. The defendant came along and without the knowledge of the plaintiff removed this bar, thereby rendering the staging less secure. As a consequence the plaintiff, on subsequently mounting the scaffold, got a fall and was hurt. It was held that as the bar belonged to the plaintiff he had a right to retake it without notice and that he was not liable for the injury. The cases on the question of responsibility for foreseeable harm done by dangerous traps were not considered, and the value of the opinion is thereby lessened.

Volume I

Foresight of the concrete harm not essential.

in determining the question of the existence of negligence it is not necessary that one should be able to foresee the particular harm which actually befalls.[9] It is enough if an ordinarily prudent person should be able to see danger or harm of some sort ahead. Harm in the abstract, not harm in the concrete, is the idea.

In the following cases negligence was held not to exist, because a person of ordinary prudence could not be expected to foresee harm as a consequence of the course of conduct which was pursued by the defendant.

Unruly horse.

1. *Hammack v. White* (1862):[1] The defendant bought a horse at Tattersall's and upon taking the animal out to try it, it became unmanageable and swerved from the roadway to the pavement. A pedestrian was there struck and fatally injured. It did not appear that the defendant had omitted to do anything he could have done to prevent the accident. The plaintiff insisted that the mere fact that the defendant had brought into a public place a horse with whose temper he was not acquainted was evidence of negligence. But the court was of the opinion that a man is not to be charged with want of due caution merely because he rides a horse whose qualities he does not happen to know.

Extraordinary and unforeseeable event.

2. *Blyth v. Birmingham Waterworks Co.* (1856):[2] A water company laid its mains and pipes according to law, inserting properly constructed fireplugs as safety valves in pursuance of statute. For twenty-five years the apparatus worked all right, but finally an unprecedented frost occurred, such as ordinarily would not be expected anywhere south of the polar regions. For this reason the valves became incrusted with ice and failed to work, with the result that the water escaped and made its way to the plaintiff's premises near by, doing considerable damage. It was held that the defendants having taken sufficient precautions against such cold as a prudent man might reasonably expect, were guilty of no negligence and hence were not liable.

3. *Sharp v. Powell* (1872):[3] The defendant had washed a van in the street. The water which he used flowed down a gutter towards a sewer at some little distance. The weather being frosty, a grating, through which water flowing down the gutter passed into the sewer, had become frozen over, in consequence of which the water sent down by the defendant, instead of passing into the sewer, spread

[9] Hill *v.* Winsor, 118 Mass. 251.

[1] 11 C. B. N. S. 588, 103 E. C. L. 588.

[2] 11 Exch. 781.

[3] L. R. 7 C. P. 253.

Chapter VIII

over the street and became frozen, rendering the street slippery. As the plaintiff's horse passed along it slipped and was injured. There was no evidence that the defendant knew of the grating being obstructed. It was held that he was not liable. The injury was not of such character as the defendant could have contemplated as the ordinary or likely consequence to result from his permitting his van to be washed in the public street.[4]

Unforeseeable consequence.

4. *Manzoni v. Douglas* (1880):[5] A horse which was drawing a brougham ran away without any assignable cause and injured the plaintiff, who was on the pavement. It was held that there was no evidence of negligence upon the part of the defendant which could go to the jury.[6]

Runaway horse.

5. *East Indian R. Co. v. Mukerjee:*[7] The plaintiff's intestate, a passenger on the defendant's railway, was killed by an accidental explosion of fireworks which a fellow passenger had brought into the compartment in which the deceased was traveling. Suit was brought against the company on the theory that it was guilty of negligence in allowing the combustibles to be brought into the train. There was nothing to show that any servant of the company knew of the fact that the explosives were being brought aboard or knowingly suffered them to remain. Nor was there any proof to show that the package containing them was calculated to excite inquiry as to its contents. It was held that the company was not responsible.

Explosive on passenger train.

6. *Daniel v. Metropolitan R. Co.* (1871):[8] The authorities of the city of London were authorized by law to execute certain works over the line of the Metropolitan Railway Company. In carrying out their plans a girder was allowed to fall upon a passing train and the plaintiff, a passenger on the train, was hurt. The work was being carried on by an independent contractor employed by the city of London. It was held that the mischief in question was not one which the railway company could be expected to foresee and guard against. Hence they were not negligent and could not be held responsible.

Injury of passenger by falling girder.

[4] Bovill, C. J., L. R. 7 C. P. 259.

[5] 6 Q. B. D. 145.

[6] Compare Gibbons *v.* Pepper (1694), 1 Ld. Raym. 38, where it appeared that the defendant was riding a horse upon the highway and without any fault on his part the creature ran away. The plaintiff, a bystander, was run over and hurt. It was held that on this state of facts the plaintiff had no cause of action. But for defective pleading judgment was given for the plaintiff.

In Brown *v.* Collins, 53 N. H. 442, horses were frightened at a locomotive, without fault on the part of the driver, and becoming uncontrollable ran upon the plaintiff's premises and broke down his lamppost. It was held that an action would not lie.

[7] (1901) A. C. 396.

[8] L. R. 5 H. L. 45.

Volume I

Unmanageable ship.

7. *Doward v. Lindsay* (1873):[9] The ship charged with the damage had been moored to a buoy with the sanction of the authorities of the port. A storm being expected, the anchor had been got ready to drop. The shackle band of the buoy gave way under the stress of weather, and, on the anchor being let go, the windlass jammed. The ship was then driven against, and damaged, another ship lying at moorings. It was held that there was no negligence the damage being due to an inevitable accident which a reasonable man could not be expected to foresee and guard against.

Thumb crushed by door of railway carriage.

8. *Metropolitan R. Co. v. Jackson* (1877):[1] J was a passenger by a railway; the carriage in which he rode was full. At station C three persons forced themselves in and were obliged to stand. There was no evidence that a complaint on this matter had been made to the railway officials, or that they knew of the fact. At station E some other persons opened the door of the carriage, shut it again and went away. There was afterwards a rush on the platform and other persons opened the door of the carriage. J stood up to prevent their entering; the train moved; J, to save himself from falling put his hand upon the edge of the door of the carriage; at that moment a railway porter came up, pushed the persons trying to get in, and slammed the door to, in doing which J's thumb was caught and crushed. It was held that the evidence did not establish such negligence on the part of the company as could be said to have occasioned the hurt. It was observed by Lord Chancellor Cairns "These persons [who were improperly attempting to get in the train] had opened the door, and thereupon it was not only proper but necessary that the door should be shut by the porter; and as the train was on the point of passing into a tunnel, he could not shut it otherwise than quickly or in this sense violently."[2] In other words the act which caused the hurt was, under the particular conditions done in the proper way and there was nothing to warn the porter that fingers might be hurt by his slamming of the door at that juncture.

Crossing street at unaccustomed place.

9. *Cotton v. Wood* (1860):[3] This was an action for the negligent driving of an omnibus whereby the plaintiff's wife was run down and killed. The deceased attempted to cross a street on a dark wintry night at a point other than the accustomed crossing place. Defendant's omnibus was on the proper side of the street and was going at a moderate pace. The woman had passed in front of the omnibus, but became alarmed by the approach of another vehicle coming up on the other side of the street from the opposite direction. She thereupon turned back and was struck by the omnibus. It was held that there was no affirmative proof of negligence

[9] L. R. 5 P. C. 338.
[1] 3 App. Cas. 193.
[2] 3 App. Cas. 198.
[3] 8 C. B. N. S. 568, 98 E. C. L 568.

on the part of the defendant. The party who founds his claim upon an imputation of negligence must establish negligence, and where there is an even balance upon the evidence whether the injury complained of has resulted from the want of proper care on the one side or the other, the plaintiff must fail.

Res Loquitur Ipsa.

Presumption of negligence.

In the following cases the maxim *res loquitur ipsa* was applied. By this maxim the fact is indicated that upon the particular circumstances of the case the law raises a presumption of negligence or considers negligence as *prima facie* established.

Bags falling from warehouse.

1. *Scott v. London, etc., Docks Co.* (1865):[4] The plaintiff, who was passing in front of a warehouse in the dock, was struck and hurt by several falling bags of sugar. It was held that the mere happening of such an accident gave rise to an inference of negligence. Erle, C. J., observed: "Where the thing is shown to be under the management of the defendant or his servants, and the accident is such as in the ordinary course of things does not happen if those who have the management use proper care, it affords reasonable evidence, in the absence of explanation by the defendants, that the accident arose from want of care."[5]

Collapse of wall.

2. *Mullen v. St. John* (1874):[6] The plaintiff, while properly on the sidewalk of Van Brunt street, in Brooklyn, was injured by the fall of a wall of a building owned by the defendant. There was no storm or violence to cause its fall, and no affirmative evidence of a defect or want of repair in the building sufficient to cause its fall. It was held that the mere fall of the wall raised a presumption of negligence on the part of the person in charge of the building, because "buildings properly constructed do not fall without adequate cause."

Objects falling from insecure structures

3. *Jager v. Adams* (1877):[7] The plaintiff, while passing along a sidewalk in front of a building in course of erection, was struck by a falling brick. It was held that the defendant, who had the contract for doing the masonry, was liable. It was his duty, say the court, to put safeguards and barriers there to prevent even the 'accidental' fall of a brick. Here the duty to take care reaches the virtual plane of insurance against all harm not attributable to *vis major* or external intervention by a stranger.

[4] 3 H. & C. 596.

[5] To the same effect, see Byrne *v.* Boadle (1863), 2 H. & C. 722; Briggs *v.* Oliver, 4 H. & C. 403.

[6] 57 N. Y. 567.

[7] 123 Mass. 26.

Volume I

4. *Kearney v. London, etc., R. Co.* (1870):[8] The plaintiff being upon a public highway was hurt by the fall of a brick from the supports of a girder bridge maintained overhead by the defendant railway company. The happening of the accident was held to be evidence against the company of a negligent failure to keep the bridge in proper repair.

5. *Volkmar v. Manhattan R. Co.* (1892):[9] The plaintiff was driving in a street under an elevated railway when he was struck by a broken portion of a bolt which fell from the defendant's structure overhead. It was held that the fact that the bolt was broken and that part of it fell was sufficient to raise a presumption that in that particular, defendant's railway was out of repair.

Landslide in railway cut.

6. *Gleeson v. Virginia Midland R. Co.* (1891):[1] The plaintiff was traveling on defendant's road. In a cut a landslide occurred which partly derailed the train and threw the car in which the plaintiff was riding violently forward. As a result the plaintiff was seriously injured. It was held that the defendant was liable. The mere fact that a wreck is so caused raises, it was held, a *prima facie* presumption of negligence. It is the duty of the company so to construct the banks of its cuts that they will not slide by reason of the action of ordinary natural causes such as wet weather and vibration due to the operation of trains.[2]

When maxim inapplicable.

In the foregoing cases the defendant was proved to have had the exclusive control and management of those objects or agencies from some defect in which the accident must have taken place. Where such exclusive control is not shown the maxim is not applied.

1. *Kendall v. Boston* (1875):[3] The plaintiff, while attending a concert given by the defendant city, was injured by the fall of a bust or statue, which had been placed outside an interior balcony of the hall, directly over the plaintiff's seat. During the concert the audience were requested to rise, and as they did so, the bust fell and hit the plaintiff. There was no evidence as to the manner in which the bust had been attached to or placed upon the balcony, or as to whether it had been properly secured. It was held that the evidence did not warrant a verdict for the plaintiff. The reason assigned for this was that the fall of the bust may have been due,

[8] L. R. 5 Q. B. 411 (1871), 6 Q. B. 759.

[9] 134 N. Y. 418.

[1] 140 U. S. 435.

[2] A collision between two trains of the same company is evidence of negligence on its part. Skinner *v.* London, etc., R. Co. (1850), 5 Exch. 787.

[3] 118 Mass. 234.

not to an inherent defect in the mode of its attachment, but to the wrongful or negligent act of some one of the audience in the balcony. It was observed: "It is not sufficient for the plaintiff to show that the injury may have been occasioned by the negligence of those whom he seeks to charge with it. If there were other causes which also might have produced it, he is in some way to show that these did not operate."

2. *Welfare v. London, etc., R. Co.* (1869):[4] The plaintiff, intending travel, went to a railway station to get information concerning the departure of trains. While looking at a time-table which was suspended on a wall under the portico of the station he was struck by a roll of zinc and by a plank which fell through a hole in the roof. At the same time a man was seen on the roof of the portico. It was held that the circumstances were not sufficient to raise a presumption of negligence against the company. One fact which discriminates this from other negligence cases in which the maxim *res loquitur ipsa* is applied is that the person who was busy at the repair of the roof, and to whose carelessness the injury was perhaps due, was not shown to be the servant of the company.[5]

That cases applying the maxim *res loquitur ipsa* conform to the general doctrine requiring that a reasonable person should be able to foresee harm in the abstract is manifest. One who drops a bag of sugar from a warehouse window to the sidewalk, or who maintains a bridge with loose bricks in it over a highway, or who keeps loose bolts on an elevated railway, must, in the ordinary use of his faculties, foresee injury to pedestrians below as a natural consequence of such negligent act. Hence he is guilty of negligence in that course of conduct. But of course if he could show that a stranger came along and dropped the bag or loosened the brick the presumption would be rebutted.

Conformity to test of foresight.

Proximate Cause.

We now turn to the cases on proximate or legal cause. The law on this subject proceeds from a general principle running through the entire law of tort, to the effect that al-

[4] L. R. 4 Q. B. 693.

[5] This circumstance was noted by Cockburn, C. J. But the decision was not put upon that ground. As the case was actually dealt with, the decision seems not to be in harmony with other decisions involving the same question.

Volume I

Principle underlying doctrine of proximate cause.

ways before liability can arise it is necessary that a causal relation, such as the law recognizes as being sufficient, should exist between the damage which is complained of and the act which occasions the damage.[6] If such a relation does not exist, the damage is said to be remote and cannot be recovered in any form of action. If such a relation does exist, then the damage is said to be a proximate result of the wrongful act to which it is attributed, and conversely the wrongful act is said to be the proximate cause of the damage.

Question of proximity determined on facts of each case.

The terms 'proximate' and 'remote' are thus respectively applied to recoverable and non-recoverable damage. The question whether damage in a given case is proximate or remote is one of great importance. It is a question of substantive law, and the determination of it determines legal right. It is unfortunate that no definite principle can be laid down by which to determine this question. It is always to be determined on the facts of each case upon mixed considerations of logic, common sense, justice, policy, and precedent. About all that can here be safely ventured is found in an observation of Appleton, C. J., to the effect that: "Ordinarily that condition is usually termed the cause whose share in the matter is the most conspicuous and is the most immediately preceding and proximate to the event."[7] The best use that can be made of the authorities on proximate cause is merely to furnish illustrations of situations which judicious men upon careful consideration have adjudged to be on one side of the line or the other.

[6] We have said that the distinction between proximate and remote damage runs all through the law of tort. Remote damage can no more be recovered in slander, false imprisonment, trespass, or in any other department of positive wrong, than in the field of negligence. But negligence cases are much richer than cases from any other field, in discussions of proximate and remote cause, proximate and remote damage. For this reason we have found it well to treat this topic exclusively in connection with our survey of negligence.

[7] Moulton *v.* Sanford, 51 Me. 134, 135. These words of the learned judge are preceded by a remark on 'cause' which may be of some value. "The cause of an event," says he, "is the sum total of the contingencies of every description, which, being realized, the event invariably follows. It is rare, if ever, that the invariable sequence of events subsists between one antecedent and one consequent."

Chapter VIII

Not only is the line of demarcation between proximate and remote damage undefined and undefinable — it is really a flexible line; for we find this to be true, that as the wrongful act which is alleged to have caused the damage increases in moral obliquity or in illegality, the legal eye reaches further and will declare damage to be proximate which in other connections would be considered to be remote. That in wanton trespass or in assault and battery, for instance, legal causation reaches further than in a wrong of mere inadvertence or negligence cannot be questioned. The indefiniteness and flexibility of the conception of proximate cause which we have just noted is perceptible not only when we pass from such a field as that of trespass proper to the field of negligence, but it is also noticeable when we confine our attention to a particular field like negligence. One is baffled in the attempt to define and delimit the conception of proximate cause as worked out in particular torts, no less than in the entire field of tort.

Proximity and remoteness incapable of being reduced to hard and fast rules.

The following decisions support the view that when a case of negligence has been made out, liability extends to all consequences which naturally follow from that negligence. In other words, proximate cause means natural cause; proximate damage means damage that naturally follows and which in reason can be attributed to the negligent act in question. We observe that the term 'effective legal cause,' which is now coming into use in England, is much to be preferred to 'proximate cause,' for the reason that the latter term literally means 'the nearest cause' or 'a very close cause.' As a matter of fact, a cause may be sufficiently near in law to the damage to be considered its effective legal cause without by any means being the nearest or most proximate of the causes which contribute to the injury.

Effective legal cause.

1. *Hill v. New River Co.* (1868):[8] The defendant negligently allowed water to spout up open and unfenced in the highway. The plaintiff's horses, passing along the road with his carriage, took fright at the water thus spouting up, and swerved to the other side of the road. It so happened that there was in the road an open

[8] 9 B. & S. 303.

Liability extends to all natural consequences, though not capable of being foreseen.

ditch or cutting, which had been made by contractors who were constructing a sewer and which had by them been negligently left unfenced and unguarded. Into this ditch or cutting, owing to its being unfenced, the horses fell, and injured themselves and the carriage. It was held that the owner of the outfit could recover entire damages of the company which had permitted the water to spout up and frighten his horses. By the defendant's negligence the horses had been started on their career, and the fact that the particular harm which resulted came from their falling into a ditch which a third person had wrongfully left unguarded, did not lessen the defendant's responsibility.

2. *Romney Marsh v. Trinity House* (1870):[9] The defendants' vessel, by the negligence of the captain and crew, grounded upon a shoal or sand bank within three-quarters of a mile of the wall of the plaintiffs, the immediate effect of which was that the vessel became unmanageable and beyond the control of the crew. At the time a high wind was blowing and the tide flowing towards the shore. The vessel was consequently driven and carried with great violence against the wall, and so effected the injury in question. It was held that the negligence of the ship's captain and crew in allowing the vessel to ground and so to become unmanageable was the proximate cause (*causa causans*) of the damage to the wall. Said Kelly, C. B.: "The immediate effect of the negligence was to put the vessel into such a condition that it must necessarily and inevitably be impelled in whatever direction the wind and tide were giving at the moment to the sea, and this was directly upon and towards the plaintiffs' wall."

Drifting of unmanageable vessel.

Communicated fires.

3. *Fent v. Toledo, etc., R. Co.* (1871):[1] By the negligence of X, a fire originates on his premises and spreads to the premises of Y. It is thence communicated to the property of the plaintiff, Z. It is held that the negligence of X is the proximate cause of the loss which thereby happens to the plaintiff.[2]

4. *Sneesby v. Lancashire, etc., R. Co.* (1874):[3] A herd of the plaintiff's beasts were being driven, at 11 o'clock p. m., along an occupation road to some fields. The road crossed a siding of the defendants' railway on a level, and while the cattle were crossing the siding the defendants' servants negligently sent some trucks down an incline into the siding, which divided the cattle into two lots, and frightened them, and they rushed away with the drovers after them. The drovers succeeded in recovering most of the cattle, but they were unable to recover six of them, which were ultimately found at

Harm befalling lost cattle.

[9] L. R. 5 Exch. 204.

[1] 59 Ill. 357.

[2] See to the same effect, **Hoyt *v.*** Jeffers (1874), 30 Mich. 181; Milwaukee, etc., R. Co. *v.* Kellogg (1876), 94 U. S. 469.

[3] L. R. 9 Q. B. 263, (1875) 1 Q. B. D. 42.

between 3 and 4 a. m. lying dead or dying on another part of the railway. There was no evidence as to when the train had passed which ran over the cattle. It was held that, it being admitted that the defendants had been guilty of negligence which caused the drovers to lose control over the cattle, and it being also admitted that the plaintiff's men had done all they could to recover control over the beasts and had not been able to do so before they were killed, their death was the consequence of the defendants' negligence; and the damage was not too remote.

Machinery left near highway.

5. *Harris v. Mobbs* (1878):[4] A house van attached to a steam plough was left for the night on the grassy side of a highway by the defendant. The van and plough were four or five feet from the metalled part of the way. During the evening the plaintiff's testator drove his mare in a cart along the metalled road. The mare was a kicker, but he was unaware of her vice. Passing the van she shied at it, kicked and galloped, kicking, for 140 yards. She then got her leg over the shaft, fell, and kicked her driver as he rolled out of the cart. He afterwards died from the kick so received. In an action brought by the personal representative against the defendant for damages resulting from the obstruction of the highway, it was found by the jury that the leaving of the van over night beside the highway caused an appreciable danger to vehicles passing that way and that the defendant was guilty of negligence in so leaving the van. It was also found that the injury complained of was caused by the presence of the van combined with the inherent vice of the mare; and that the deceased was guilty of no contributory negligence. Upon these findings judgment was given for the plaintiff.

Damage from burning oil.

6. *Kuhn v. Jewett* (1880):[5] A train of cars loaded with petroleum was negligently permitted to get from under control of the crew. Moving down grade of its own momentum it came into collision with a locomotive, with the result that some of the oil tanks were thrown to the earth and burst. The oil thus released spread over the roadbed and coming into contact with coals of fire from the locomotive was ignited. The flaming oil trickled down the embankment to a brook below and was carried by the water to the plaintiff's barn which stood below on the bank of the stream. It was held that the loss occasioned by the fire thus communicated was attributable to the negligent management of the train of oil cars as its proximate cause, and that the company was liable.

7. *Stevens v. Dudley* (1883):[6] The defendant was marshal of a county fair and as such undertook to clear the track preparatory to a race. In so doing he caused the team of one S to turn off the track at such an inopportune place and in such a way that S fell out and the team ran away. The plaintiff was attending the fair and

[4] 3 Ex. D. 268. [5] 32 N. J. Eq. 647. [6] 56 Vt. 158.

Turning team off fair-ground.

got run down. The trial judge charged the jury that conceding the defendant, as marshal of the fair, was negligent in turning S off the track as he did, the plaintiff could not recover unless the defendant might reasonably have expected the injury in question to result from his negligent act. This charge was held to be erroneous, the Supreme Court declaring that, conceding the defendant's conduct to have been negligent, he was liable for natural consequences, although not capable of being foreseen. Satisfactory as this decision is in point of the presentation of the principle governing liability for established negligence, its value is lessened by the fact that no recognition was there given to the equally important principle that conduct is never negligent in the sense of the law unless a prudent person would have seen danger ahead as a result of the defendant's conduct.

Injury to escaped animal.

8. *Halestrap v. Gregory:*[7] Owing to the negligence of defendant's servant in leaving open a gate, plaintiff's mare, which was being agisted by the defendant, escaped into an adjoining cricket field, and, in being driven back by the cricketers in a careful and proper manner, was injured by running against defendant's iron fence. The defendant was held liable.

Leaving team in hands of inexperienced person.

9. *Engelhart v. Farrant:*[8] The defendant employed a man to drive a cart, with instructions not to leave it, and a boy, who had nothing to do with the driving, to go along and deliver parcels. The driver left the cart in charge of the boy and went into a house to get oil for his lamp. The lad, thinking to expedite matters in the driver's absence, attempted to turn the cart around. While driving on with this object in view he ran into the plaintiff's carriage and damaged it. It was held that the negligence of the driver in leaving the cart in the hands of an inexperienced person was the effective cause of the mischief and that the defendant was liable.

Blocking stream with boat.

10. *Scott v. Hunter* (1863):[9] The defendant blocked with his boats a passage through a lock, while the river was rapidly rising. The plaintiff's boat was in consequence of the delay thus occasioned exposed to the increasing current and was swept over the dam. It was held to be a question to be submitted to the jury whether the negligent blocking of the passage was the proximate cause of the damage.

Collision of sleigh.

11. *McDonald v. Snelling* (1867):[1] The driver of a sleigh by his negligent driving collided with the sleigh of another, thereby causing the horse which was drawing the latter to run away. In its course the frightened animal ran over the plaintiff and broke his collar bone. It was held that the owner of the sleigh by the negligent driving of which the accident was primarily caused, was responsible and liable for the injury sustained by the plaintiff.

[7] (1895) 1 Q. B. 561.
[8] (1897) 1 Q. B. 240.
[9] 46 Pa. St. 192.
[1] 14 Allen (Mass.) 290.

Unsafe street.

12. *Lacon v. Page* (1868):[2] A city negligently permitted a hole to appear in a drain under a street. The plaintiff's horses ran away and his wagon was thus brought at high speed to this hole. As the wagon struck and rebounded, the plaintiff was thrown to the ground and hurt. But for the uncontrollable running away of his horses the plaintiff's wagon would not have been brought to this spot. It was held that the negligence of the city was the proximate cause of the injury. The plaintiff was not at fault, the city was.

Failure to signal approach of train.

13. *Norton v. Eastern R. Co.* (1873):[3] As the plaintiff neared a grade crossing with a wagon, a train approached without giving a warning as was required by statute, and the road was so placed that a train could not be seen until very near the spot. When the plaintiff got within thirty-six feet, the train passed and his horse, being frightened, kicked the plaintiff, thereby breaking his leg. The plaintiff would have stopped farther away if he had been warned that a train was coming. It was held that this state of facts tended to show that the failure of the company to give the warning was the cause of the injury.

Communication of fire to neighboring structure.

14. The opinion in *Milwaukee, etc., R. Co. v. Kellogg* (1876)[4] lends some countenance to the narrower view of liability for established negligence, which will presently be referred to, but the point actually decided is entirely consistent with the principle that liability for established negligence extends to all the natural consequences of the negligent act. The defendant company on the occasion of the mishap in question landed its steamer near its grain elevator, which was tall and built of combustible timber. A wind was at the time blowing a gale in the direction of the elevator and the jury found that to land the steamer there under such conditions was a negligent act. The elevator caught fire and was consumed. The wind blew the fire towards certain lumber piles of the plaintiff which were several hundred feet away. These piles were in turn consumed, together with the plaintiff's sawmill, which lay further on in the march of the flames. The jury having found that the burning of the plaintiff's property was a result naturally and reasonably to be expected from the burning of the elevator under the conditions then existing, and that such loss followed as a natural and unpreventable consequence, it was held that the plaintiff was entitled to a verdict.[5]

[2] 48 Ill. 499.

[3] 113 Mass. 366.

[4] 94 U. S. 469.

[5] Mr. Justice Strong, in discussing the subject of proximate cause, said: "What is the proximate cause of an injury is ordinarily a question for the jury. It is not a question of science or of legal knowledge. It is to be determined as a fact, in view of the circumstances of fact attending it. The primary cause may be the proximate cause of a disaster, though it may operate through successive instruments, as an article at the end of a chain may be moved by a force applied to the other end, that force being the proximate cause of the movement, or as in the oft-cited

Volume I

View that liability for established negligence is limited to foreseeable consequences.

There are decisions which are inconsistent with the principle underlying the foregoing cases. These take a narrower view of liability for established negligence, and if correct, tend to show that liability for negligence extends only to such specific damage as could reasonably be foreseen upon the particular facts confronting the tortfeasor at the time of his negligent act. In this view a negligent act is said to be the proximate cause only of foreseeable damage. Here the foresight test is applied throughout: on the question of recoverable damage as well as on the question of the existence of negligence. We are of the opinion that this view is erroneous. It seems to have resulted from a very natural confusion as regards the application of the test which is applied in determining the primary question of negligence.

Escaped sheep destroyed by bears.

1. *Gilman v. Noyes* (1876):[6] The defendant carelessly left the bars of a pasture down. In consequence the plaintiff's sheep escaped and, having strayed off, were subsequently eaten by bears. It was held that the defendant's liability depended on the question whether, in view of surrounding conditions, the eating of the sheep by bears could be foreseen as a natural and reasonable consequence of their being allowed to escape.

Burning of non-contiguous premises.

2. *Ryan v. New York Cent. R. Co.* (1866):[7] The defendant by the carelessness of its servants or through the defective condition of one of its locomotive engines set fire to its own woodshed. The plaintiff's house, situated some 130 feet away, took fire from the heat of the burning shed and was consumed. It was held that defendant's

case of the squib thrown in the market-place. The question always is, was there an unbroken connection between the wrongful act and the injury, a continuous operation? Did the facts constitute a continuous succession of events, so linked together as to make a natural whole, or was there some new and independent cause intervening between the wrong and the injury? It is admitted that the rule is difficult of application. But it is generally held, that, in order to warrant a finding that negligence, or an act not amounting to wanton wrong, is the proximate cause of an injury, it must appear that the injury was the natural and probable consequence of the negligence or wrongful act, and that it ought to have been foreseen in the light of the attending circumstances. These circumstances, in a case like the present, are the strength and direction of the wind, the combustible character of the elevator, its great height, and the proximity and combustible nature of the sawmill and the piles of lumber."

[6] 57 N. H. 627.

[7] 35 N. Y. 210.

negligence was not the proximate cause of the burning of plaintiff's house. The reason assigned for this holding was that while the burning of the shed could be foreseen as a natural result of the dropping of sparks upon it from the engine, the burning of other adjacent buildings was a result not to be anticipated as a natural consequence of that negligent act.[8]

Fire communicated by burning oil.

3. *Hoag v. Lake Shore, etc., R. Co.* (1877):[9] A train bearing crude petroleum was derailed. Oil tanks burst and the stuff becoming ignited flowed down a creek which ran by until it reached the plaintiff's premises more than a hundred yards away. The flames were communicated to the plaintiff's buildings and destroyed them. It was held that conceding the derailment of the train to have been due to the negligence of the engineer in not seeing an obstruction, the damage suffered by the plaintiff must be considered remote. The decision was placed on the ground that the injury complained of was not such as might have been foreseen as likely to flow from the negligence in question.[1]

That the doctrine of *Hoag v. Lake Shore, etc., R. Co.* is unsound not only seems clear upon theoretical grounds, but appears from the fact that the Pennsylvania court has been compelled in a measure to recede from it.

Thus, in *Bunting v. Hogsett* (1891),[2] the defendants owned a private railroad which was intersected at two points on a curve by another railroad, over which the plaintiff was traveling as a passenger. At the first point a collision took place which was due to the negligence of the defendant's engineer in running at a high rate of speed without giving warning. Upon seeing that a collision was imminent, the defendant's engineer reversed his engine and shut off steam. He then jumped off. The jar of the collision derailed one car of the plaintiff's train and at the same time opened the throttle of the defendant's engine, causing it to back around the curve to the second point of intersection with the railroad track. It there again struck the train, which had run under its original momentum to that spot and stopped. In this second collision the plaintiff was hurt. It was insisted for the defendants that no action would lie, for the reason that, inasmuch as the engineer of the engine which did the damage had shut off the steam before jumping, the second collision could not be foreseen by him as a natural and probable consequence of his conduct. The defendant was, however, held to be liable, Clark, J., saying that the engineer should be held to have foreseen whatever consequences might ensue from his negligence without the

[8] To the same effect see Pennsylvania R. Co. *v.* Kerr (1869), 62 Pa. St. 353. It should be noted that view of the New York and Pennsylvania courts on this question is not accepted in other jurisdictions. See Fent *v.* Toledo, etc., R. Co., 59 Ill. 357, *ante*.

[9] 85 Pa. St. 293.

[1] Compare Kuhn *v.* Jewett, 32 N. J. Eq. 647, *ante*.

[2] 139 Pa. St. 363.

intervention of some other independent agency, and that the defendant was liable for what might in the nature of things occur in consequence of that negligence, although in advance the actual result might have seemed improbable.[3] This is inconsistent with *Hoag v. Lake Shore, etc., R. Co.*, and is in harmony with the doctrine generally obtaining in other jurisdictions.

Damage not attributable to negligence declared on.

In the following cases the admitted or established negligence of the defendant was held not to be the effective legal cause or proximate cause of the damage or injury for which recovery was sought. It is obvious that in these cases the damage could not be said to be the natural result of the negligence declared on. It was simply due to some other factor. And the conclusion reached in these cases must be the same whether liability is supposed to extend to all natural consequences or only to such as may be foreseen:

Delay in transportation followed by loss from other cause.

1. *Morrison v. Davis* (1852):[4] A canal company which, as common carrier, had undertaken to convey plaintiff's goods, negligently started the boat on its voyage with a lame horse, by reason of which the transportation of the goods was considerably delayed. It so happened that when the boat thus delayed was at a particular point on its way, an extraordinary flood occurred by which the boat was wrecked and plaintiff's goods lost. But for the delay which was caused by the lameness of the horse as aforesaid, the boat would have escaped the disaster. It was held that the damage in this could not be attributed to the starting of the boat with the lame horse as its proximate or legal cause.

2. *Denny v. New York Cent. R. Co.* (1859):[5] The defendant company received wool of the plaintiff for transportation from N to B. By reason of a failure on the part of the company to exercise reasonable diligence the wool in question was detained at station S for several days. It was then dispatched to station A and there properly stored in a freight depot, to be turned over in due course to a connecting carrier to be conveyed to B. While so stored the wool was damaged by an extraordinary rise in a river. It was held that the negligent delay in forwarding the wool could not be considered the proximate, or legal, cause of the damage.

3. *Scheffer v. Washington City, etc., R. Co.* (1881):[6] The plaintiff's intestate sustained such injuries in a railroad accident, caused by the defendants' negligence, that within a few months he became

[3] 139 Pa. St. 374, 375.
[4] 20 Pa. St. 171.
[5] 13 Gray (Mass.) 481.
[6] 105 U. S. 249.

mentally disordered and while in this condition took his own life. It was held that the death could not be attributed to the negligence of the defendant company as its legal cause, and was too remote to give rise to a cause of action.

Chapter VIII

Suicide of injured person.

4. *Burton v. West Jersey Ferry Co.* (1885):[7] A ferryboat on which the plaintiff, an elderly woman, took passage was crowded and she was thereby unable to get a seat. The boat was driven against a bridge (under circumstances which could not perhaps be attributed to the fault of the company) and the plaintiff was thrown violently to the floor. It was held that the failure of the company to provide seats for all its passengers could not be treated as a proximate cause of the injury which the plaintiff got by the fall upon the floor.

Failure of carrier to provide seats.

In the following cases the delinquency charged against the defendant was not negligence strictly speaking, but was, in the one case, breach of contract, and in the other, trespass in the nature of a battery. But on the question of proximate cause both cases were decided upon considerations that would have been equally conclusive if the actions had been based on negligence:

1. *Glover v. London, etc., R. Co.* (1867):[8] The defendant company wrongfully ejected the plaintiff, a passenger, from its train. Owing, perhaps, to the excitement occasioned by the fact that he was being so ejected, the plaintiff forgot his race-glasses and left them behind on the train so that they were lost. He could have taken the property with him if he had thought of it. It was held that the loss of the glasses could not be attributed to the wrongful ejection as its proximate cause, and that the company was not liable for their value.

Ejection of passenger.

2. *Laidlaw v. Sage* (1899):[9] The defendant, to shield himself from an expected explosion of dynamite in the hands of one who sought to extort money, gently moved the plaintiff about fifteen inches, thereby interposing him in a measure between the defendant and the dynamiter. In the explosion which followed, the plaintiff was hurt. The explosion was so terrific as to demolish the office fixtures and to kill or injure all who were present. It was held that the act of the defendant in gently moving the plaintiff a few inches could not be considered the proximate cause of the hurt which the plaintiff received.

[7] 114 U. S. 474. [8] L. R. 3 Q. B. 25. [9] 158 N. Y. 73.

Volume I

Intervening Cause.

Inter-vening independ-ent cause.

Damage cannot be attributed to a given negligent act as its proximate cause when it appears that subsequent to that negligence, a new, independent, and unexpected factor intervenes which itself appears to be the natural and real occasion of the mischief. The intervening cause breaks the chain of legal causation and relieves the original negligent actor of responsibility.

Starting of loco-motive by meddle-some third person.

1. *Mars v. Delaware, etc., Canal Co.* (1889):[1] The defendant company negligently left an engine on a switch unguarded for a few moments. A meddlesome trespasser came along and started the engine off. In its uncontrolled career it ran into a passenger train a half mile away and hurt the plaintiff. The negligence of the company in leaving the engine unguarded was held not to be the proximate cause of the mischief, as the act of the third person in starting the engine constituted an intervening cause sufficient to break the chain of causation.

2. *McDowall v. Great Western R. Co.:*[2] The defendants' servants shunted some trucks and a brake-van, all coupled together, onto a siding which was on an incline running down to a level crossing over a highway. The siding had a catch-point to prevent vehicles, if set loose, from running down the incline; but, for the convenience of their shunting operations, the defendants' servants did not place the trucks and van beyond the catch-point, but screwed down their brakes, and left them in a position in which they would not have caused any damage if not interfered with. Some boys, trespassing on the siding, uncoupled the van from the trucks and released its brake, so that it ran down the incline and injured the plaintiff, who was lawfully passing along the highway over the level crossing. The defendants were aware that the boys were in the habit of trespassing on the siding and meddling with vehicles placed upon it. At the trial of an action by the plaintiff, the jury found that the van was in a safe position as and where left by the defendants, unless interfered with afterwards; that the accident would not have happened if the van had not been interfered with; that the interference was the act of trespassers, who acted negligently; that the danger of interference causing injury was known to and could have been guarded against by the exercise of reasonable care on the part of the defendants; and that the negligence of the defendants in not placing the van beyond the catch-point was the effective cause

[1] 54 Hun (N. Y.) 625.

[2] (1903) 2 K. B. 331, reversing (1902) 1 K. B. 618.

of the accident. Judgment having been given in favor of the plaintiff, it was held in the Court of Appeal that the evidence did not support the finding that the effective cause of the injury was negligence on the part of the defendants in failing to place the van beyond the catch-point.

3. *Marvin v. Chicago, etc., R. Co.* (1891):[3] A fire attributable to the negligence of the defendant spread, in the course of several days, over a broad expanse of country and reached Beaver Bottom, where it would ordinarily have stopped. A sudden gust of whirlwind, however, carried a brand of fire over the marsh and caused the plaintiff's cranberry field to be burned. It was held that the whirlwind constituted an intervening cause such as would break the chain of causation between the negligence of the defendant and the damage done to the plaintiff by the fire.

Conveyance of flame by whirlwind.

4. *Poeppers v. Missouri, etc., R. Co.* (1878):[4] By the negligence of the defendant company a prairie adjoining the right of way and covered by a rank growth of dry grass caught fire. The wind blew hard and the fire extended three miles before nightfall. During the night the fire kept alive, but spread slowly, owing to the abatement of the wind. At morning the wind rose and blew with great violence, carrying the fire several miles in a few hours, where it destroyed the plaintiff's property. Such violent winds being not infrequent in that country, it was held that this particular gale did not constitute an intervening cause, and consequently that the loss complained of was the proximate result of the defendant's negligence.

Conveyance of flame by ordinary wind.

5. *Alexander v. New Castle* (1888):[5] The defendant, a town, negligently suffered a pit to remain open near a sidewalk. The plaintiff, a constable, undertook to commit a prisoner to jail, and while passing the pit was pushed into it by the prisoner in order to effect an escape. It was held that the town could not be held.

6. *Daniels v. Potter* (1830)[6] is authority to the effect that the act of a child in playing with a dangerous thing which has negligently been left unguarded and insecure, is not an intervening cause sufficient to relieve the person, who is responsible for the trap, from liability. The facts were as follows: The defendants had a cellar opening into the street. The flap of the cellar had been set back while the defendants' men were lowering casks into it, as the plaintiff contended, without proper care having been taken to secure it. The flap fell and injured the plaintiff. The defendant maintained that the flap had been properly fastened, but also set up as a defense that its fall had been caused by some children playing with it. But it was ruled by Tindal, C. J., that if the defendants' men

Act of young child not an independent cause.

[3] 79 Wis. 140.
[4] 67 Mo. 715.
[5] 115 Ind. 51.
[6] 4 C. & P. 262, 19 E. C. L. 375.

had not used reasonable care to secure the flap, the fact that the injury was immediately caused by the children who played with it was no defense.

Concurring Negligence of Third Person.

Concurring negligence.

In order that a negligent act or negligent conduct should be considered the legal or proximate cause of the damage complained of, it is not essential that such act or conduct should be the sole and exclusive cause of the damage in question. Hence the negligence of A may be treated as a proximate cause of damage to B although the negligence of a third person may also concur in bringing about the mischief. These cases, like some others already noted, show that proximate cause as a term to indicate the relation of legal cause and effect is really a misnomer:

Timber insecurely piled.

1. *Pastene v. Adams* (1874):[7] By the negligence of A, timber was insecurely stacked near a street. As the plaintiff was going along a third person negligently drove his vehicle against a protruding piece and caused it to fall upon the plaintiff. It was held that A's negligence could be treated as the legal cause of the hurt, though the negligence of the stranger also contributed to the accident, and was indeed the immediate occasion of it.

Collision of vehicle.

2. *Mathews v. London St. Tramways Co.* (1888):[8] The plaintiff was a passenger on an omnibus. In descending a hill the omnibus overtook a handcart near the curb and, in order to pass it, the driver of the omnibus pulled over on a tramway line. A tramcar was at the time coming up the hill and the omnibus collided with it, causing injury to the plaintiff. An action was brought against the tramway company. It was held that if there was negligence on the part of the tramcar driver in continuing his course after seeing the omnibus on his track, and this negligence contributed to the injury, the company was liable, although the driver of the omnibus had also been guilty of negligence in getting upon the track at that time; and that consequently it was erroneous to charge that the injury must be chargeable exclusively to the negligence of the tramway company before it could be held liable.

Defective sidewalk.

3. *Carterville v. Cook* (1889):[9] A village negligently maintained a sidewalk at the edge of an embankment without a railing. As the plaintiff, a boy of fifteen, passed along he was, by the careless or inadvertent shoving of a companion, pushed off the sidewalk

[7] 49 Cal. 87. [8] 60 L. T. N. S. 47. [9] 129 Ill. 152.

into the excavation and was hurt. It was held that the village was liable.[1]

Defective gas-fittings

4. *Burrows v. March Gas, etc., Co.* (1872)[2] was a case of breach of contract, but on the question of proximate cause and concurring negligence the case was decided on principles which apply equally to cases of negligence. The facts were these: Through a breach of contract by the defendants in not serving the plaintiff with a proper pipe to convey gas from their main into his premises, an escape of gas had taken place. Whereupon the servant of a gas-fitter at work on the premises went into the part of the premises where the escape had occurred, with a lighted candle. As he was examining the pipe with the candle in his hand, an explosion took place, by which the premises were damaged. The defendants were held liable, though the explosion had been immediately caused by the imprudence of the gas-fitter's man in examining the pipe with a lighted candle in his hand.

[1] But see Rowell *v.* Lowell, 7 Gray (Mass.) 100; Kidder *v.* Dunstable, 7 Gray (Mass.) 104.
Compare Carterville *v.* Cook, 129 Ill. 152, with Alexander *v.* New Castle, 115 Ind. 51.

[2] L. R. 7 Exch. 96.

CHAPTER IX

NEGLIGENCE (CONTINUED).

Duty to Care for Self.

Volume I

Injury attributable to negligence of injured party.

IT goes without saying that where injury or damage is attributable to the negligence of the sufferer himself, he has no right of action against another who may have been concerned in the mishap. A man is required to use reasonable precautions in looking out for himself and for his own.

1. *Wilds v. Hudson River R. Co.* (1862):[1] It appeared that the plaintiff, on approaching a grade crossing, negligently failed to heed the whistle and flag which gave warning of a coming train. In consequence he was struck and killed. It was held that deceased's own negligence was the cause of the accident and that the company was not liable.[2]

[1] 24 N. Y. 430.

[2] On the question of the duty of the deceased to exercise care on approaching the crossing Gould, J., said: "If a locomotive be eminently dangerous, everybody knows it to be so. And it is as dangerous to run against, or under it, as to have it run over you. A railroad crossing is known to be a dangerous place, and the man who, knowing it to be a railroad crossing, approaches it, is careless unless he approaches it as if it were dangerous. To him, the danger is vastly greater than it is to the locomotive; he may lose his life. And if the company be bound to use very great care not to endanger him, why is not he bound to use equally great care not to be endangered? His care should be as much graduated by the danger as the company's. When every one, who knows that the railroad is there, is bound to know and to remember that a train may be approaching, not to take the very simple precaution of looking and listening, to find out whether one is coming, cannot but be want of care. To be sure, the statute requires a railroad company to give specified warnings; but it neither takes away a man's senses, nor excuses him from using them. The danger may be there: the precaution is simple. To stop, to pause, is certainly safe. His time to do so is before he puts himself in the very road of casualty. And if he fails to do so, it is of no consequence, in the eye of law, whether he merely misjudges or is obstinately reckless. His act is not careful; and he is to abide the consequences, not the company under or into whose train he saw fit to run, whether he did so in excusable ignorance or in the

2. *Gaffney v. Brown* (1890):[3] At the trial of an action for personal injuries, there was evidence that the plaintiff, a customer at a public dining room kept by the defendant, was wont to enter it by a certain door and sit at a certain table; that on the day of the accident, having dined at another table, she arose, and for the purpose of leaving the room opened another door, and without observing whither she was going, or paying any heed to her steps, passed through it, fell down a flight of stairs, and was injured. It was held that the plaintiff was not in the exercise of due care, and could not recover for her injuries.

3. *Sewell v. New York, etc., R. Co.* (1898):[4] The plaintiff, a boy of nearly thirteen years, while riding a bicycle across a railway track, was struck by a passing train and hurt. The plaintiff knew that the railroad crossed the street at that place, but paid no attention and did not look out for the cars, but out to sea, watching for a steamer. There was no evidence of negligence on the part of the persons operating the train. It was held that the plaintiff could not recover.

Contributory Negligence.

Basis of doctrine.

From the truism that a man is bound to exercise reasonable care to prevent harm to himself and his own, springs the doctrine of contributory negligence. As a matter of legal history, the case of *Butterfield v. Forrester* was the first in which the doctrine of contributory negligence was clearly enunciated. That case was after this kind:

Butterfield v. Forrester (1809):[5] The defendant, for the purpose of making some repairs to his house, which was close by the roadside at one end of a town, had put up a pole across this part of the road, a free passage being left by another street in the same direction. The plaintiff left a public house not far distant from the place in question at eight o'clock in the evening. Candles were then being lighted, but there was still sufficient daylight left to discern the obstruction 100 yards away. The plaintiff was riding violently and did not see it. He consequently rode against the obstruction and both horse and rider got a fall. Bayley, J., ruled at *nisi prius*

belief that he could run the gauntlet unharmed. Nor is the court to look about to find how he, after putting himself there, conducted; whether he then took the best means of escape, or in his confusion ran more hopelessly into the jaws of death. No degree of presence of mind, and no want of presence of mind, at that time, has anything to do with the case. He should not be there, by want of care."

[3] 150 Mass. 479.

[4] 171 Mass. 302.

[5] 11 East 60.

Volume I

that if the plaintiff was riding along the street extremely hard and without ordinary care, he could not recover. The instruction was approved in the King's Bench. Lord Ellenborough observed: "One person being in fault will not dispense with another's using ordinary care for himself."

Lindley's division of negligence cases.

The subject of contributory negligence can perhaps best be approached along the lines of classification indicated by Lindley, L. J., in the case of *The Bernina* (1887):[6] Said this learned judge: "The cases which give rise to actions for negligence are primarily reducible to three classes as follows: 1. A, without fault of his own, is injured by the negligence of B; then B is liable to A. 2. A by his own fault is injured by B without fault on his part; then B is not liable to A. 3. A is injured by B by the fault more or less of both combined; then the following further distinctions have to be made: (a) if, notwithstanding B's negligence, A with reasonable care could have avoided the injury, he cannot sue B; (b) if, notwithstanding A's negligence, B with reasonable care could have avoided injuring A, A can sue B; (c) if there has been as much want of reasonable care on A's part as on B's, or, in other words, if the proximate cause of the injury is the want of reasonable care on both sides, A cannot sue B. In such a case A cannot with truth say that he has been injured by B's negligence. He can only with truth say that he has been injured by his own carelessness and B's negligence; and the two combined give no cause of action at common law."[7]

Both parties at fault.

Cases of contributory negligence all fall within class 3. Here there is negligence on the part of both the plaintiff and defendant; and inasmuch as negligence on the part of the defendant is followed by the legal consequence of liability as stated in 1, while negligence on the part of the plaintiff is followed by the legal consequence of non-liability as stated in 2, we are here confronted with a legal antinomy. The problem is to harmonize the conflicting principles in order to ascertain the application of each, where distinction can be drawn, and to determine which principle is to prevail where

[6] 12 P. D. 58.

[7] The Bernina, 12 P. D. 89.

the two are in actual conflict. To this end account must be taken of the subdivisions made by his lordship.

Chapter IX

Successive Negligent Acts.

1. Injury Caused by Plaintiff's Negligence.

In subdivisions (a) and (b), it will be noted, the respective negligent acts of the plaintiff and defendant are not actually concurrent, but one negligent act succeeds the other by an appreciable interval or is more closely connected with the harm that is done.

The following decisions illustrate the principle of nonliability stated in subdivision (a), where the defendant, though negligent, is relieved because of the failure of the plaintiff to use reasonable precautions to protect himself or his property. From these cases it will appear that here the negligence of the plaintiff is really the proximate cause of the damage, and that the negligence of the defendant is only a remote cause. The plaintiff's negligence is thus in the nature of an intervening cause which relieves the defendant of responsibility.

1. *Trow v. Vermont Cent. R. Co.* (1852):[8] A railroad corporation was guilty of negligence in not maintaining cattle-guards and fences. The plaintiff, who lived near the railroad, negligently permitted his horse to run in the highway. The animal strayed upon the track and was killed. It appeared that the defendants were guilty of no negligence in the management of the train at the time when the horse was killed. Recovery was denied.

Stray cattle killed by train.

2. *Pennsylvania R. Co. v. Aspell* (1854):[9] The defendant company negligently carried the plaintiff, a passenger, beyond his destination. The speed of the train was slackened somewhat at the switches, but after passing these the speed became greater. The conductor warned the plaintiff not to attempt to get off while the cars were moving, and told him that he would back the train to the station. The plaintiff, however, leaped from the car and was hurt. It was held that he was guilty of contributory negligence, which was the immediate and proximate cause of the injury, and could not recover.

Negligence of alighting passenger.

[8] 24 Vt. 487.

[9] 23 Pa. St. 147.

Volume I

3. *Pennsylvania R. Co. v. Righter* (1880):[1] The plaintiff's servant was driving a carriage, containing plaintiff's wife and two daughters along a street which was crossed by a railroad. While yet at a point over thirty feet distant from the railroad a view of the track towards the south for a distance of a mile could be had. The servant, however, failed to look down the track, and as he drove across, a train coming from that direction struck the rear of the carriage, demolishing it and injuring the occupants. It was held that, notwithstanding the train may have failed to give a statutory signal, the negligence of the servant in failing to look out for trains contributed to the injury, and that an action could not be maintained.

Injury at railroad crossing.

4. *Central R., etc., Co. v. Letcher* (1881):[2] The plaintiff having boarded the defendant's passenger train for a lawful purpose on its arrival at one of the regular stations on the line of railroad, was detained by his business until after the train had started on its journey; and while the train was moving from the depot, its speed increasing each moment, he, of his own accord, to prevent being carried off, and without notifying any of defendant's employees of his presence, and without requesting any of them to slow or stop the train, and without any effort to arrest its progress, walked from the platform of one car to that of another, and with papers in his right hand, descended the steps of the car and jumped from the moving train at right angles thereto and fell, and in the fall his left arm was caught under the wheel of the car and crushed. It was held that the injury sustained by the plaintiff was attributable directly and immediately to his own thoughtless and reckless act, and he could not therefore recover, though the defendant was negligent in not giving the signals required by the statute, before and at the time the train left the station.

Jumping from moving train.

5. *Davey v. London, etc., R. Co.* (1883):[3] The plaintiff, while crossing the defendant's road from the side of the down line, was injured by a train on the up line coming round a curve. It appeared that a train coming up could not be seen from the place where he began to cross, but might have been seen in time if he had looked to the left when he was on the down line or the six-foot way. The engine driver had not used the whistle. The plaintiff was well acquainted with the crossing. It was held by a majority of the court, that although there was some evidence of negligence on the part of the company, yet the plaintiff, by his omission to look to the left before he got on the rails of the up line, had caused the mischief by his own negligence.

Injury at railroad crossing.

6. *Green v. Ashland Water Co.* (1898):[4] A waterworks company negligently furnished polluted water to the inhabitants of a town, with the consequence that plaintiff's intestate, a consumer of

Drinking of polluted water.

[1] 42 N. J. L. 181.
[2] 69 Ala. 106.
[3] 12 Q. B. D. 70.
[4] 101 Wis. 258.

the water, took typhoid fever and died. It was held that, conceding a cause of action might arise upon such a state of facts, nevertheless the decedent was guilty of contributory fault in this case because he had continued to use the water, knowing it to be contaminated.

Chapter IX

As the reader has doubtless already gathered, it is fundamental in the law of negligence that, apart from a positive duty such as arises from contract, a man cannot be held liable for negligence in failing to act altogether.[5] The law never imposes on one the duty of taking the initiative, but only holds him liable for the consequences of negligence connected with his actual undertakings. At this point we find a distinction between the conception of liability for negli-

Party threatened with injury must take steps to prevent the hurt.

[5] This principle is well illustrated in the following cases: Giles *v.* Walker (1890), 24 Q. B. D. 656. Plaintiff and defendant were owners of adjacent farms. The defendant failed to mow the thistles growing on his land so as to prevent them from seeding, and in the years of 1887 and 1888 there were thousands of thistles on his land in full seed. The consequence was that the thistle seeds were blown by the wind in large quantities onto the land of the plaintiff, where they took root and did damage. It was held that no action lay.

Here the only act charged against the defendant was an omission to act altogether, a failure to take the initiative. The case shows that an action for such a neglect or omission will not lie unless the plaintiff can point to a specific recognized legal duty, such as would arise from contract. This he could not here do. If the conduct of the defendant in this case had been such as the law recognizes as a nuisance, an action would have been maintainable in respect of the damage so caused. But the action would then have been for the nuisance and would not have been grounded upon negligence.

Compare Smith *v.* Tripp (1880), 13 R. I. 153. The city of Providence failed to keep Traverse street in repair, so that the street highways were clogged and water which might have flowed off was diverted upon plaintiff's land. It was held that the plaintiff had no cause of action in the absence of a showing of positive duty to keep the way open for the flow of water.

Cobb *v.* Great Western R. Co. (1893), 1 Q. B. 459. The plaintiff while a passenger in one of the defendant's trains, which was then stopping at a railway station, was robbed by a gang of men who entered the carriage in which he was seated. The plaintiff complained to the station master of the robbery and requested that the train be detained till the culprits could be given into custody, there being at the time a police force in the station. The station master, however, gave the signal to start the train and the plaintiff was thereby prevented, as he alleged, from recovering his property. It was held that the defendant company was not liable, there being no ground on which a positive duty could be imposed on the company to aid the plaintiff in recovering his property in the manner stated. It was also held that if the cause of action was predicated upon the negligence of the company in allowing their train to be overcrowded, the damage complained of was too remote.

gence in caring for others and for negligence in caring for one's own; for the latter idea is, as the following cases clearly show, sometimes extended so far as to impose a positive duty on a man to begin to stir. This occurs when one finds himself or his property jeopardized by the negligent conduct of another. Here the law requires that the party who is threatened with injury shall take such steps as a prudent man would take to avoid that injury.

Failure to put out fire.

1. *Hogle v. New York Cent., etc., R. Co.* (1882):[6] Owing to defects in the construction, or negligence in the management, of the defendant's engine, fire was communicated to the plaintiff's property. The plaintiff, on first discovering the fire, took no steps to put it out, though he might have done so by using practicable and reasonable efforts to that end. It was held that he was guilty of contributory negligence and could not recover.

Failure to restore fence.

2. *Loker v. Damon* (1835)[7] is an analogous case going to show that a negligent failure to take reasonable steps to avoid impending damage constitutes contributory negligence, although the original wrongful element in this case was not negligence, but a trespass. It there appeared that the defendant wrongfully demolished several rods of fencing around the plaintiff's hayfield. The defendant negligently suffered the opening to remain for many months, though it was practicable to replace it sooner. Through the opening thus made cattle came in and kept the field grazed down so that plaintiff lost the next year's crop of hay. It was held that the loss of this crop of hay could not be attributed to the original tortious act of the defendant as its proximate cause, and that the defendant was consequently liable in damage only to the extent of the cost of repairing the fence.

3. The case of *Wiley v. West Jersey R. Co.* (1882)[8] directs attention to the distinction that the negligence of a third person in failing to take steps to prevent threatened injury cannot be attributed to the plaintiff so as to make him chargeable with contributory negligence. The facts were like those in *Hogle v. New York Cent., etc., R. Co.* (1882),[9] with the difference that the person who failed to take adequate steps to put out the fire was a third person, the fire then being on the latter's premises. It was held that the railroad company was liable to the plaintiff, whose premises were afterwards reached by the fire and consumed without any immediate negligence on his part.

[6] 28 Hun (N. Y.) 363.
[7] 17 Pick. (Mass.) 284.
[8] 44 N. J. L. 247.
[9] 28 Hun (N. Y.) 363.

In the following cases it was held that under the particular facts the conduct of the plaintiff did not amount to such contributory negligence as would necessarily relieve the defendant of liability.

Chapter IX

1. *Clayards v. Dethick* (1848):[1] The defendants, acting under authority from the sewer commissioners, had made a trench along the only outlet from the plaintiff's stables. It was left unprotected by railing. The piling of the earth and rubbish along the narrow passage which was left increased the difficulty of exit. The plaintiff, a cabman, attempted to lead his horses out, when one of them fell in the trench and was killed. Before the day on which the accident happened the commissioners had given notice to the occupiers of the stables that the trench would continue open for a day or two longer, and advised them to get other stables. It was ruled that it could not be the plaintiff's duty to refrain altogether from coming out of the mews, merely because the defendants had made the passage in some degree dangerous; that the defendants were not entitled to keep the occupiers of the mews in a state of siege till the passage was declared safe, first creating a nuisance and then excusing themselves by giving notice that there was some danger; though, if the plaintiff had persisted in running upon a great and obvious danger his action could not be maintained.

Use of dangerous exit into street.

2. *Flagg v. Hudson* (1886):[2] The plaintiff, driving along a highway on a dark night, pulled his horse to the left to avoid going down an embankment on the right of the road, which had negligently been left without a railing. By so going down he was brought into collision with another vehicle which came from the opposite direction. It was held that the failure of the town authorities properly to safeguard the road was the proximate cause of the damage, and that the plaintiff was not chargeable with contributory negligence in being on the wrong side of the road.

Driving on wrong side of highway.

3. *Gee v. Metropolitan R. Co.* (1873):[3] The plaintiff was a passenger on the defendant's train. As it was passing from one station to another, he rose from his seat with a view of looking out of the window and took hold of the bar of the window and pressed against it. The pressure, such as it was, of some part of his body, upon his taking hold of the bar, caused the door to open, and the motion of the train threw him out of the carriage, whereby he sustained injury. It was held that the accident was attributable to the negligence of the company in having the door insecurely fastened, and not to any contributory negligence of the plaintiff in pressing lightly against the bar.

Insecure door to passenger car.

[1] 12 Q. B. 439, 64 E. C. L. 439. [2] 142 Mass. 289. [3] L. R. 8 Q. B. 161.

Volume I

Defective sidewalk.

4. *Mosheuvel v. District of Columbia* (1903):[4] The defendant negligently permitted a water-box which was located in a sidewalk to remain uncovered, thus making a hole into which a pedestrian might step and be hurt. The hole was immediately in front of the steps leading up to the entrance to the plaintiff's residence, and the existence of the hole was known to the plaintiff. It was so situated that in order to go from the lowest step to the sidewalk it was necessary to go either to the right or left, which one could safely do, or to step over the hole. On the occasion of the accident the plaintiff came out, noticed the opening, and, instead of going to one side, attempted to step over it. She did not step quite far enough and her foot, going into the hole, caused a fall which resulted in serious injury. It was held that it was not as a matter of law contributory negligence on the part of the plaintiff to attempt to overstep the hole, for the reason that the opening was not so far obviously dangerous that no prudent person would have attempted to overstep it. The test was held simply to be this: Did the plaintiff on this occasion use the care which a prudent person would have used in attempting to overstep the opening? If so she was not guilty of contributory negligence and was entitled to recover.

Dangerous alternative.

The following special qualification of the doctrine of non-liability stated in subdivision (a) is recognized: Where the creation of a dangerous situation is ascribable to the negligent act of a defendant, he is not to be excused from liability for consequent harm by reason of the fact that the person endangered loses self-possession and in the confusion incident to the danger takes a course which turns out not to be the safest one. In such circumstances contributory negligence on the part of the person injured is not made out unless he is shown to have acted with less caution than any person of ordinary prudence would have shown under the same trying conditions.[5]

Jones v. Boyce (1816):[6] The defendant, a coach proprietor, negligently suffered a coach to go out with defective coupling. Going down a hill, the coupling broke and the horses became frightened. The driver was thereby compelled to drive to the side of the road, where the coach struck a post and was at the point of being upset. The plaintiff, who was riding on the back part of the coach, believed himself to be in jeopardy, and in order to avoid immediate

[4] 191 U. S. 247.

[5] North Eastern R. Co. *v.* Wanless, L. R. 7 H. L. 12; Chaplin *v.* Hawes, 3 C. & P. 554, 14 E. C. L. 445.

[6] 1 Stark. 493, 2 E. C. L. 189.

danger jumped down from the coach and was hurt. As it turned out, he might have avoided harm by remaining on the coach. Lord Ellenborough charged the jury, that if they were of the opinion that the negligent omission of the defendant to provide a safe means of conveyance caused that dangerous situation to arise, then the defendant's liability depended on the further question whether the plaintiff, at the time he jumped, reasonably believed himself to be in danger and took the leap as a prudent precaution towards self-preservation. "To enable the plaintiff to sustain the action it is not necessary," said he, "that he should have been thrown off the coach; it is sufficient if he was placed by the misconduct of the defendant in such a situation as obliged him to adopt the alternative of a dangerous leap or to remain at certain peril."

Chapter IX

Jumping from position of danger.

Similarly, it is established that where by the negligence of A a situation has been created by which B is placed in danger, C is not guilty of contributory negligence in making an effort, such as a reasonable and prudent man would make in such an emergency, to rescue B, although by pursuing that course C places himself in great and obvious danger.

Danger incurred in rescue of third person.

1. *Ridley v. Mobile, etc., R. Co.* (1905):[7] The plaintiff's intestate saw a boy standing on a track in imminent danger from an approaching train, which had failed to give the statutory signals. To rescue the boy the deceased rushed upon the track immediately in front of the moving train, and in that act was killed. It was held that the jury might well find that the deceased was not guilty of contributory negligence, since a dangerous situation had been created by the negligent operation of the train, and the deceased was justified in making effort to save the boy, provided he acted with such care as a prudent person would have shown in such an emergency. The law has so high a regard for human life that it will not impute negligence to an effort to preserve it, unless the exposure is clearly rash and reckless.[8]

Rushing in front of train.

2. *Pennsylvania R. Co. v. Roney* (1883):[9] A passenger train, running at a high rate of speed, entered a switch which had carelessly been left open by the engineer and crew of another train, such persons being incompetent to the knowledge of the company. On the switch the running train collided with another train and the

Standing at post of danger.

[7] 86 S. W. Rep. 606.

[8] To the same effect see Donahoe *v.* Wabash, etc., R. Co., 83 Mo. 560; Eckert *v.* Long Island R. Co., 43 N. Y. 503; Spooner *v.* Delaware, etc., R. Co., 115 N. Y. 34; Gibney *v.* State, 137 N. Y. 6; Pennsylvania, etc., R. Co. *v.* Langendorf, 48 Ohio St. 316; Woods *v.* Caledonian Ry. Co. (Scotch), 13 Rettie 1118.

[9] 89 Ind. 453.

Volume I

engineer of the passenger train was killed. If the engineer had jumped from his engine after it entered the switch he would probably not have been hurt. Instead, he stood at his post and endeavored to stop his train in order to save the passengers on it. It was held that the failure of the engineer to desert his post could not be attributed to him as contributory negligence.[1]

2. Injury Caused by Defendant's Negligence.

The principle stated in subdivision (b) of Lord Lindley's third class of cases is illustrated in decisions like the following. It will be noted that here the negligence of the defendant is really the proximate cause of the damage and that the negligence of the plaintiff is more remote.

Pedestrian run down by cart.

1. *Boss v. Litton* (1832):[2] The plaintiff, while walking at night in the carriageway, instead of being in the footpath, was knocked down by the defendant's cart. It was ruled that if the driver of the cart was negligent the verdict should be for the plaintiff, notwithstanding the latter might better have been in the path.

Tethered donkey hurt on highway.

2. *Davies v. Mann* (1842):[3] The plaintiff, having tethered the fore feet of his ass, turned it on a public highway, eight yards wide. Here the ass remained, and was grazing on the side of the road, when the defendant's wagon and horses, coming down a slight descent at a smart pace, ran against it and hurt it. The driver of the wagon was careless in being some distance behind his horses whilst they were going so fast. The judge told the jury that the plaintiff's negligence in leaving the tethered ass on the public highway was no answer to the action, unless the creature's being there was the immediate cause of the injury. The Court of Exchequer held that as the defendant might, by proper care, have avoided injuring the animal, he was liable for the consequence of his negligence, though the animal was there through the faulty act of the plaintiff;[4] for this fault was connected with the injury remotely, and not as its proximate cause. This is the well-known "Donkey Case." It is a leading authority on this branch of law.

[1] See also Cottrill *v.* Chicago, etc., R. Co. (1879), 47 Wis. 634.

[2] 5 C. & P. 407, 24 E. C. L. 384.

[3] 10 M. & W. 546.

[4] Parke, B., observed: "Although the ass may have been wrongfully there, still the defendant was bound to go along the road at such a pace as would be likely to prevent mischief. Were this not so, a man might justify the driving over goods left on a public highway, or even over a man lying asleep there, or the purposely running against a carriage going on the wrong side of the road." Davies *v.* Mann, 10 M. & W. 548, 549.

3. *Tuff v. Warman* (1857):[5] The defendant was the pilot of the steamer Celt on the river Thames. The plaintiff was the owner of a barge which was damaged in a collision with the Celt. The proof showed that as the Celt was coming up the river below Gravesend, the plaintiff's barge was sailing down the river with a fair wind. The steamer was on the right side according to the Admiralty regulations. The defendant stated that he was standing on the poop of the steamer and saw the barge about 300 yards distant, and immediately ported his helm; that if the barge had done the same the collision would have been avoided; that he thought the barge put her helm a-starboard; and that finding a collision inevitable he put his helm hard a-port, and backed his engines, but too late. On the barge there were two men, one of whom was at the helm. It did not appear where the other was, but they kept no lookout. The man at the helm stated that the sail was in his way and that he could not see forward without stooping. He also admitted that, though he saw the steamer when a considerable distance off, he did not look out again until she was within two or three yards of him, and then it was too late to avoid a collision. Verdict and judgment against the defendant were upheld on the theory that though the plaintiff may, in the first place, have been negligent, the defendant nevertheless, in the exercise of reasonable care, would have avoided the effects of that negligence and prevented the collision.

Steamer running afoul of sailing vessel.

4. *Radley v. London, etc., R. Co.* (1876):[6] A railway was in the habit of taking full trucks from the siding of a colliery owner, and returning the empty trucks there. Over this siding was a bridge eight feet high from the ground. On a Saturday afternoon, when all the colliery men had left work, the servants of the railway ran some trucks on the siding. All but one were empty, and that one contained another truck, and their joint height amounted to eleven feet. On the Sunday evening the railway servants brought on the siding many other empty trucks, and pushed forward all those previously left on the siding. Some resistance was felt, the power of the engine pushing the trucks was increased, and the two trucks, the joint height of which amounted to eleven feet, struck the bridge and broke it down. In an action to recover damages for the injury, the defense of contributory negligence was set up, it being insisted that the plaintiff's servants ought to have moved the first set of trucks to a safe place or, at all events, should not have left the truck with the disabled truck in it so as to be likely to occasion mischief. It was held that though the plaintiff may have been guilty of negligence, and though this negligence may in fact have contributed to the accident, yet if the defendant could, by the exercise of ordinary

Negligent management of ill-laden car.

[5] 2 C. B. N. S. 740, 89 E. C. L. 740, 5 C. B. N. S. 573, 94 E. C. L. 573.

[6] 1 App. Cas. 754.

Volume I

care, have avoided the mischief, the plaintiff's negligence would not excuse him.

Jamming of wharf.

5. *Inland, etc., Coasting Co. v. Tolson* (1891):[7] The plaintiff, a wharfman, got his foot mashed between the wharf and one of the fender piles by the jamming of the defendant's boat as it was making a stern landing. It was held that notwithstanding the plaintiff was negligent in standing with his foot in that place, he might nevertheless recover if the defendant might, by the exercise of reasonable care and prudence, have avoided the consequences of plaintiff's negligence.

Statement of principle underlying (a) and (b).

From the foregoing cases illustrative of the principles stated in subdivisions (a) and (b) it is seen that wherever the court or jury can see that the harm complained of was proximately caused by the negligence of one of the parties, while the negligence of the other was only remotely connected with that harm, the person whose negligence is the proximate cause must be held responsible. If that person is the defendant then the plaintiff may recover; if that person is the plaintiff himself, then the action must fall. This principle is neatly and accurately summed up in the doctrine of 'the last chance,' which is to the effect that whenever the respective acts of negligence on the part of the plaintiff and defendant are not actually concurrent, but one succeeds the other by an appreciable interval, the person who has the last chance to avoid the impending harm and negligently fails to do so is chargeable with the whole.

Doctrine of 'last chance.'

Concurring Contributory Negligence.

Pollock's statement of doctrine of contributory negligence.

From what has so far been said it would superficially appear that all discussions of contributory negligence really turn upon the question as to whose negligence was the proximate or decisive cause of the injury. "The true ground of contributory negligence being a bar to recovery," says Professor Pollock, "is that it is the proximate cause of the mischief; and negligence on the plaintiff's part which is only part of the inducing causes will not disable him." [8] This is undoubtedly true in all cases where one can say with certainty

[7] 139 U. S. 551.

[8] Poll. on Torts, 6th ed., 446.

that the negligence of one party or the other is really the decisive factor; that is, where the negligence of one is closer in time, or causality, or perhaps grosser in the point of moral obliquity, than that of the other.

Inadequacy of this theory in cases of actual concurring negligence.

But there are undoubtedly cases where no man can say with any confidence that the negligence of one rather than the other is the decisive or proximate cause. In other words, cases arise where the negligence of either party considered by itself would be adjudged to be a proximate cause of the damage. Here two elements of negligence, each sufficient of itself to found legal responsibility upon, concur. Where this happens the legal problem cannot be determined by the simple question, Whose negligence was the proximate cause of the damage?

To meet this situation the law announces a hard and fast rule applicable to the cases included in subdivision (c) of Lord Lindley's classification, to the effect that one whose negligence directly or proximately contributes in any degree whatever to the injury which befalls him is thereby disabled from recovering damages of another whose negligence concurs with his own in producing the injury. Where there is actual conflict in applying the principles (a) and (b), the principle of non-liability indicated in (a) must prevail. This is the reason why the jury were charged in *Tuff v. Warman* (1857), *ante,* that if both parties were equally to blame and the accident was the result of their joint negligence, the plaintiff could not recover; and that if the negligence or default of the plaintiff was in any degree the proximate cause of the damage, he could not recover, however great may have been the negligence of the defendant.

Plaintiff disabled where his negligence contributed to injury in any degree.

The principle under consideration was clearly brought out in the following cases:

1. *Hawkins v. Cooper* (1838):[9] The defendant's servant was driving a cart rapidly along the highway and in so doing ran over the plaintiff, a woman, who was at the time attempting to cross the road. Tindal, C. J., charged the jury that if they thought the injury was occasioned by the negligence of the driver in driving in an im-

Pedestrian run down by carriage.

[9] 8 C. & P. 473, 34 E. C. L. 485.

Volume I

proper way under the circumstances, they should find for the plaintiff; but that if it was not so occasioned, but was attributable in any degree to the incautious conduct of the plaintiff herself in running across the road at a time when in the exercise of ordinary discretion she ought not to have done so, they should find for the defendant.

Going into place of danger.

2. *Murphy v. Deane* (1869)[1] is also instructive: A pair of skids were laid over and across a sidewalk, from a wagon in the carriageway, into the door of a warehouse. A woman, passing along the sidewalk with a basket on one arm, attempted to cross over the skids, although she saw that the wagoner with two other men was preparing to roll a heavy cask of oil from the wagon down the skids, into the warehouse. She had lifted one of her feet over or upon the skids, when one of the three men slipped from his footing, and the cask escaped from their control and rolled down upon and maimed her. In an action against the employer, grounded upon the negligence of the wagoner, it was held that there could be no recovery unless it appeared that plaintiff was in the exercise of reasonable care or that the injury was in no degree attributable to any want of care on her part.[2]

Riding on bumper of engine.

3. In *Baltimore, etc., R. Co. v. Jones* (1877)[3] it appeared that the plaintiff was one of a party of men employed by a railroad company in repairing its roadway. They were usually conveyed by the company to and from the place where their service was required in a box-car. The plaintiff, on one occasion, was riding on the bumper or pilot of the locomotive instead of being in the box-car, where he ought to have been. In passing through a tunnel the train collided with cars which had, through the negligence of the company's employees, been left standing on the track, and plaintiff was hurt. Those in the box-car escaped without injury. The plaintiff had been

[1] 101 Mass. 455.

[2] Note further from this case that, in Massachusetts, the rule is adopted that the burden of proving that plaintiff was in the exercise of due care at the time of the injury is upon the plaintiff. To the same effect see Allyn *v.* Boston, etc., R. Co. (1870), 105 Mass. 77. This doctrine prevails in a very few American jurisdictions, and is repudiated in England as well as in the greater number of the American States. See 7 Am. and Eng. Encyc. of Law (2d ed.) 453. The doctrine generally held is that contributory negligence on the part of the defendant is affirmative matter of defense and the burden of proving it is upon the defendant. This is true whether it arises on a plea of not guilty or is made the subject of counter-issue. And it must appear that such negligence caused or materially contributed to the injury. Wakelin *v.* London, etc., R. Co. (1886), 12 App. Cas. 41.

By just what steps the other doctrine gained acceptance in Massachusetts we may not stop to inquire. It may be noted, however, that the majority rule gives precedence to the conception of duty to care for others; while the Massachusetts doctrine lays the stress upon the duty to take care of self.

[3] 95 U. S. 439.

warned not to ride on the bumper. It was held that plaintiff could not recover.

Chapter IX

It is to be observed that the question whether a case is really one of concurring negligence, as in subdivision (c), or whether it is a case of successive negligence in which the negligence of one may be considered the proximate cause while the negligence of the other may be considered remote, as in subdivisions (a) and (b), is often difficult to determine; and inasmuch as the legal consequences are different in (b) and (c), the decisions naturally exhibit some lack of harmony. For instance, it is clear that the case last referred to was decided on the theory of concurring contributory negligence. But why should it not have been treated as a case of successive negligence? In this view it would have been said that, though the plaintiff was primarily guilty of negligence in being on the bumper, nevertheless, he being there and being unable to get off while the train was running, it was the duty of the company to use due care not to hurt him. The obstinacy of the plaintiff in persisting to ride on the bumper after warning, made it just that the risk should be put upon him, and the court accordingly did so.

Reconciliation of principles.

Precisely the opposite conclusion was reached in *Inland, etc., Coasting Co. v. Tolson* (1891),[4] referred to above. That case was decided on the theory of non-concurring or successive negligence, inasmuch as it was held that though the plaintiff was negligent in standing where he did, that negligence was remote, while that of the defendant company in jamming the pier with its boat was the proximate cause of the injury. Evidently here is a field where considerations of policy and of justice ultimately determine the result.

The following test was propounded by the Court of Exchequer Chamber in *Tuff v. Warman* (1858),[5] as a means of determining whether the plaintiff's negligence in a given case will debar him from recovery, viz.: Did the plaintiff so far contribute to the misfortune by his own negligence or want of

Test of effectiveness of contributory negligence.

[4] 139 U. S. 551.

[5] 5 C. B. N. S. 585, 94 E. C. L. 585.

Volume I

ordinary care and caution, that, but for such negligence or want of ordinary care and caution on his part, the misfortune would not have happened? If so he cannot recover.[6]

It seems to be sometimes taken for granted that this is a universal test of the legal effectiveness of contributory negligence. But it really applies only in cases falling within (a) and (c). It has no application in the (b) cases, where, though the plaintiff first negligently puts himself in the way of harm, the defendant is nevertheless held liable, because his negligence is nearer and more proximate in point of causation.[7]

Representation in Contributory Negligence.

Plaintiff chargeable with contributory negligence of servant or agent.

Contributory negligence on the part of a servant is of course imputed to the master to the same extent as any other form of legal delinquency. Reference to *Pennsylvania R. Co. v. Righter* (1880)[8] will furnish the reader with illustration of this. The same principle applies where there is any actual relation of agency, as the following decision shows:

Otis v. Janesville (1879):[9] The plaintiff and several other persons were riding along the highway in a private conveyance drawn by a horse which was driven by one of the party, when the conveyance was overturned, owing, as was alleged, to a defect in the highway. But it appeared that the vehicle was at the time negligently being driven at a high rate of speed and that this contributed to the accident. It was held that the negligence of the driver was a bar to the plaintiff's right of action for injuries received.

[6] Wightman, J., in Tuff *v.* Warman, 5 C. B. N. S. 585, 94 E. C. L. 585.

In Massachusetts, where the burden of proving freedom from contributory negligence is on the plaintiff, the principle above stated is cast in a different form, but the substance is the same. See Murphy *v.* Deane, 101 Mass. 462, 463.

[7] This very point was noted in Tuff *v.* Warman, for Wightman, J., after stating the test indicated above, added that a plaintiff who is guilty of negligence without which the mischief would not have happened, is not thereby disentitled to recover, "if the defendant might by the exercise of care on his part have avoided the consequences of the neglect or carelessness of the plaintiff." 5 C. B. N. S. 585, 94 E. C. L. 585.

[8] 42 N. J. L. 181.

[9] 47 Wis. 422.

Chapter IX

Identification in Negligence.

A misconception of the proper limits of the doctrine stated in the preceding paragraph resulted in a judicial blunder in the Court of Common Pleas, in the following case:

Identification of passenger and driver.

Thorogood v. Bryan (1849):[1] Thorogood, a passenger in an omnibus, was killed as a result, so it appeared, partly of the negligence of the driver of the omnibus in which he was being conveyed and partly of the negligence of the driver of the defendant's omnibus. It was held that a passenger is so far identified with the owner of the omnibus in which he is conveyed that the negligence of such owner or his servant is to be considered as the negligence of the passenger himself. The plaintiff, as Thorogood's personal representative, was therefore declared to have no cause of action.[2]

Such was the doctrine of 'identification.' It extended the principle of representation entirely beyond its legitimate bounds and was untenable. A man, it may be conceded, is properly chargeable with the consequences of the acts of one who is his own agent or servant, but he is not responsible for the acts of another man's agent or servant over whom he exerts no control. It is therefore not surprising that the doctrine of *Thorogood v. Bryan* was generally repudiated by the American courts as they had occasion to pass upon the question.[3] The English Court of Admiralty also refused to fol-

[1] 8 C. B. 115, 65 E. C. L. 115.

[2] Coltman, J., said: "The negligence that is relied on as an excuse is, not the personal negligence of the party injured, but the negligence of the driver of the omnibus in which he was a passenger. But it appears to me, that, having trusted the party by selecting the particular conveyance, the plaintiff has so far identified himself with the owner and her servants that, if any injury results from their negligence, he must be considered a party to it." Cattlin *v.* Hills, 8 C. B. 130, 65 E. C. L. 130.

[3] Little *v.* Hackett (1886), 116 U. S. 366; Wabash, etc., R. Co. *v.* Shacklet, 105 Ill. 364; Danville, etc., Turnpike Road Co. *v.* Stewart, 2 Met. (Ky.) 119; Bennett *v.* New Jersey R., etc., Co. (1873), 36 N. J. L. 225; New York, etc., R. Co. *v.* Steinbrenner (1885), 47 N. J. L. 161; Chapman *v.* New Haven R. Co. (1859), 19 N. Y. 341; Covington Transfer Co. *v.* Kelly (1880), 36 Ohio St. 86.

The doctrine of 'identification' in negligence is, however, established in a few American jurisdictions on the authority of Thorogood *v.* Bryan. Lockhart *v.* Lichtenthaler, 46 Pa. St. 151; Artz *v.* Chicago, etc., R. Co., 34 Iowa 153; Prideaux *v.* Mineral Point, 43 Wis. 513. In Pennsylvania it is limited to carriers by public conveyance.

Volume I

low it,[4] and the English common-law judges looked upon the decision with disfavor.

Doctrine repudiated.

Finally the question reached the House of Lords in *Mills v. Armstrong* (1888),[5] and the doctrine was expressly overruled. It appeared in this case that a collision had occurred between the steamships Bushire and Bernina, through the fault of the masters and crews of both, and that in consequence two persons on board the Bushire, one of the crew and a passenger, neither of whom had anything to do with the negligent navigation of the ships, were drowned. In actions for damage brought by their personal representatives, it was held that the deceased persons were not identified in respect of negligence with those navigating the Bushire, and that in consequence the plaintiffs could recover full damage against the Bernina.

Imputed Negligence.

Negligence of custodian imputed to infant.

The doctrine by which the negligence of a person to whose care a child is properly committed is imputed to it as its own negligence made its appearance in *Waite v. North Eastern R. Co.* (1858).[6] The plaintiff, an infant of five, was in charge of its grandmother. By the negligence of the defendant railway company, coupled with the negligence of its grandmother, the child was hurt. It was held that it could not recover. Campbell, C. J., put the case on the ground that when a child of tender age is brought to a railway station or to any conveyance, for the purpose of being conveyed, and is wholly unable to take care of itself, the contract of conveyance is on the implied condition that the child is to be conveyed subject to due and proper care on the part of the person having it in charge.

True basis of the doctrine.

The true explanation of the principle is that infants, by reason of their natural incapacity and helplessness, must have some one to take care of them. The person having

[4] The Milan (1861), Lush. 388.

[5] 13 App. Cas. 1, reported in The Bernina, 12 P. D. 58.

[6] El. Bl. & El. 719, 96 E. C. L. 719. To the same effect, see Hartfield *v.* Roper, 21 Wend. (N. Y.) 615.

them in charge is therefore to be considered in law as occupying the relation of agent or servant; and for the negligence of such person the child is held responsible on general principles of representation. The custodian of an infant is in law its servant, although it exercises no choice and is incapable of that control which is usually incident to the relation of master and servant. The relation arises from necessity.[7]

Limitations of doctrine of imputed negligence.

Clearly imputed negligence will not defeat the action of an infant when the act of negligence imputed to him is not sufficient to make out such a case of contributory negligence as would defeat the action of an adult. Hence it is established that negligence on the part of a parent in allowing a child to be on the street cannot be imputed to a child as contributory negligence where it appears that the child while upon the street did nothing that it might not have done if its movements had been directed by an adult person of reasonable prudence.[8]

The following case embodies an application here of a principle made familiar in dealing with cases in subdivision (b) of Lord Lindley's classification:

Newman v. Phillipsburg Horse Car R. Co. (1890):[9] The plaintiff, a child of two years, was in the custody of a sister of twenty-two. By the negligence of the latter, the child got on the track of the defendant company and was run over by a horse car, the driver at the time being occupied with the collection of fares. It was held that the negligence of the sister could not be imputed to the infant so as to defeat the right of action arising from the negligence of the company.

The artificial reasoning by which the doctrine of imputed negligence has generally been supported, as witness the hypothesis of implied contract stated by Campbell, C. J., in the leading case, is no doubt partly to blame for the disfavor into which the doctrine has fallen in America. In fact we find

[7] We are unable to agree with the explanation of Professor Pollock, which, by the way, is adequate only where the negligence of the custodian of the infant is the sole proximate cause of the injury. Poll. on Torts, 6th ed., 455, 456.

[8] Wiswell *v.* Doyle (1893), 160 Mass. 42; O'Brien *v.* McGlinchy (1878), 68 Me. 552.

[9] 52 N. J. L. 446.

Volume I

that fully half, if not more, of the American courts have rejected the idea altogether and hold that the negligence of the custodian of an infant cannot be imputed to it to defeat its right of action.[1] If the infant is considered in the light of a victim of two independent wrongdoers, the defendant and its own custodian, this conclusion seems reasonable enough, for it only conforms to a general doctrine already stated.[2]

The whole difficulty is in the question whether the infant is in a relation of legal privity with its custodian. The English rule is technically strong, but the other appeals to human sympathy and it is not without support in point of reason. Where considerations are so equally balanced it is not strange that the view which sanctions the right of action on the part of the injured child should appear to be making headway.[3]

Rusticum Judicium.

In contrast with the common-law rule which denies the right of action for negligence in all cases where the plaintiff's negligence contributes to the injury is the rule applied by the admiralty courts in cases of collision. These courts here enforce a rule known as the *rusticum* (or *rusticorum*) *judicium*, by which vessels which are mutually at fault are required to bear the loss equally. Apart from the fact that the rule harmonizes with the idea of averaging losses at sea with which men engaged in maritime affairs are familiar, it has little to commend it. The rule was probably first introduced in consequence of the difficulty of determining the cause of collision, and was afterwards extended to cases where, fault in the one or both ships being proved, it was impossible to fix with precision the amount of damage done to each ship in conse-

Division of loss between colliding vessels.

Origin of rule.

[1] Berry *v.* Lake Erie, etc., R. Co., 70 Fed. Rep. 679; Government St. R. Co. *v.* Hanlon, 53 Ala. 70; Chicago City R. Co. *v.* Wilcox (Ill. 1890), 24 N. E. Rep. 419; Westerfield *v.* Levis, 43 La. Ann. 63; Norfolk, etc., R. Co. *v.* Ormsby, 27 Gratt. (Va.) 455.

[2] See *ante, Concurring Negligence.*

[3] See e. g. Mattson *v.* Minnesota, etc., R. Co. (Minn. 1905), 104 N. W. Rep. 443, where the doctrine of imputed negligence is repudiated by the Minnesota court and a previous decision recognizing that doctrine is overruled.

quence of the negligence of the other.[4] Finally by one of those perversions of doctrine which are likely to occur in the history of rules which are of uncertain origin and which rest upon insecure grounds, the rule was limited to cases where both ships are shown to be in fault. Such, at any rate, is its present extent.

Lord Stowell's statement of the doctrine.

In *The Woodrop-Sims* (1815),[5] a case where a ship and cargo had been lost by two vessels running foul of each other, Sir William Scott (Lord Stowell) stated the rules applicable in cases of collision as follows: "There are four possibilities under which an accident of this sort may occur. In the first place, it may happen without blame being imputable to either party; as where the loss is occasioned by a storm, or any other *vis major*. In that case the misfortune must be borne by the party on whom it happens to light; the other not being responsible to him in any degree.[6] Secondly, a misfortune of this kind may arise where both parties are to blame; where there has been a want of due diligence or of skill on both sides. In such a case, the rule of law is that the loss must be apportioned between them, as having been occasioned by the fault of both of them.[7] Thirdly, it may happen by the misconduct of the suffering party only; and then the rule is that the sufferer must bear his own burthen. Lastly, it may have been the fault of the ship which ran the other down; and in this case the injured party would be entitled to an entire compensation from the other." [8] From this it appears that the only situation in which there is a divergence from common-law doctrine is the second.

There are cases in which it may be manifest from the

[4] See article by R. G. Marsden, 2 L. Quar. Rev. 357, 363.

[5] 2 Dods. 83.

[6] The Itinerant (1844), 2 W. Rob. 236; Stainback *v.* Rae (1852), 14 How. (U. S.) 532; The Grace Girdler (1868), 7 Wall. (U. S.) 196.

[7] Vaux *v.* Sheffer (1850), 8 Moo. P. C. 75; Maddox *v.* Fisher (1861), 14 Moo. P. C. 103; Hay *v.* Le Neve, 2 Shaw Sc. App. 395; The Arthur Gordon (1861), Lush. 270; China, Merchants' Steam Nav. Co. *v.* Bignold (1882), 7 App. Cas. 512; The Schooner Catharine *v.* Dickinson (1854), 17 How. (U. S.) 170; The Gray Eagle (1869), 9 Wall. (U. S.) 505.

[8] Cayzer *v.* Carron Co. (1884), 9 App. Cas. 873; The Atlas (1876), 93 U. S. 302.

Volume I

Inscrutable fault.

nature of the collision, that one ship or the other was guilty of negligence, yet it may be impossible to say upon the evidence that such negligence is chargeable to one ship rather than the other. Here the fault is said to be inscrutable. This certainly seems to be a situation where the rule of *justicium rusticum* should be applied, if anywhere; but by the weight of authority, the loss lies where it falls.[9] The idea is that the damaged ship should not recover from the other at all without affirmatively proving such ship to have been in some way at fault.

It will be noted that under the admiralty rule the damages in cases of mutual fault are imposed equally upon both vessels.[1] To undertake to apportion the damages in exact accordance with the degree of blame attaching to the conduct of the crews of the respective vessels, would no doubt be impracticable.

Mutual fault necessary.

As regards what constitutes such mutual fault as will entitle either vessel to contribution from the other, it has been laid down that they must both be at fault at the time and in the acts which cause the mischief.[2] But where the negligence of both parties does thus concur, the right to insist upon contribution exists although one party may have been much more at fault than the other. Where, however, the negligence of one vessel is obvious and palpable while that of the other is so slight as not really to constitute a contributing cause, the former party must bear the whole.[3]

[9] The Worthington (1883), 19 Fed. Rep. 836; The Bark Kallisto (1877), 2 Hughes (U. S.) 128; The Schooner Summit (1854), 2 Curt. (U. S.) 150. But see The Scioto, 2 Ware (U. S.) 360, 21 Fed. Cas, No. 12,508; The David Dows, 16 Fed. Rep. 154; The Nautilus, 1 Ware (U. S.) 529.

[1] Cayzer *v.* Carron Co. (1884), 9 App. Cas. 881; Hay *v.* Le Neve, 2 Shaw Sc. App. 395; Jacobsen *v.* Dalles, etc., Nav. Co. (1901), 106 Fed. Rep. 428.

[2] Ralston *v.* The Steamboat State Rights (1836), Crabbe (U. S.) 33, 20 Fed. Cas. No. 11,540.

[3] Cayzer *v.* Carron Co., 9 App. Cas. 873; The Great Republic, 23 Wall. (U. S.) 20; Jacobsen *v.* Dalles, etc., Nav. Co., 106 Fed. Rep. 428.

Comparative Negligence.

Origin of doctrine of comparative negligence.

Comparative negligence may be dismissed in a few words. This modification of the common-law doctrine of contributory negligence originated in Illinois.[4] The doctrine of comparative negligence is to the effect that in cases where both parties are at fault, the jury shall compare their respective delinquencies, and if it be found that the plaintiff was guilty of 'slight' negligence only, while the defendant was guilty of 'gross' negligence, the plaintiff may recover. The idea in the adoption of this rule was to escape the supposed hardship of the common-law rule which prohibits recovery by a plaintiff whose negligence has contributed in any degree to the injury. The rule of comparative negligence is never applied so as to allow recovery by a plaintiff who has been guilty of 'ordinary' negligence, and *a fortiori*, it does not apply where the plaintiff is guilty of 'gross' negligence.

Unsoundness of the doctrine.

One weakness of this doctrine is that it imports into the law of negligence generally the distinction as to degrees of negligence — slight, ordinary, and gross — which had been adopted to rather poor advantage in the field of bailments, and which, as regards the law of negligence generally, is utterly specious. Slight negligence, as the term is here used, consists of a failure to exercise extraordinary care; ordinary negligence is a failure to use ordinary care, and gross negligence consists of a failure to use slight care.

Abandonment by Illinois court.

Another objection to the doctrine of comparative negligence is that, upon analysis, it has turned out to be no more than a weak, confused, and therefore misleading, effort to state the distinction which exists in common-law theory between the cases in (b) and (c) as above treated in this work. We shall not here attempt to give proof of this, more than to say that after thoroughly testing the doctrine in a great number of cases arising in that commonwealth in the course of

[4] The doctrine seems to have been first announced in Galena, etc., R. Co. *v.* Jacobs (1858), 20 Ill. 478.

Volume I

thirty years or so, the Illinois court abandoned it as unsound.[5]

[5] See Calumet Iron, etc., Co. *v.* Martin (1885), 115 Ill. 358; Lake Shore, etc., R. Co. *v.* Hessions, 150 Ill. 556; Lanark *v.* Dougherty, 153 Ill. 163; Wenona Coal Co. *v.* Holmquist, 152 Ill. 581.

In Tennessee, the doctrine of comparative negligence is repudiated, but a peculiar modification of the doctrine of contributory negligence prevails, to the effect that in cases of concurring negligence, the contributory negligence of the plaintiff does not bar the action altogether, but is to be considered by the jury in mitigation of the damages. Saunders *v.* City, etc., R. Co., 99 Tenn. 130.

In cases where the act of negligence with which the defendant is charged consists of the violation of a statute requiring certain precautions to be taken by steam railways, the plaintiff's contributory negligence will not destroy the right of action altogether, even though he be guilty of such gross negligence as is the sole proximate cause of the injury. But this is due to the wording of the statute. In ordinary cases contributory negligence which is the sole proximate cause of the injury is a good and complete defense; and the rule which allows contributory negligence to go in mitigation of damages applies only in cases of some concurring negligence on the part of both. But it is said if the parties are equally blamable, the plaintiff cannot recover. See, generally, Whirley *v.* Whiteman, 1 Head (Tenn.) 610; East Tennessee, etc., R. Co. *v.* Aiken, 89 Tenn. 245; Southern R. Co. *v.* Pugh, 97 Tenn. 624; Chesapeake, etc., R. Co. *v.* Foster, 88 Tenn. 671.

CHAPTER X

NEGLIGENCE (CONTINUED).

Dangerous Premises.

Chapter X

CASES involving harms from insecure and dangerous premises comprise a very distinct and rather difficult branch of the subject of negligence. The legal wrong in these cases is referable to the secondary trespass formation, wherein the idea of responsibility comes fully into play. It seems to be generally taken for granted that the idea of positive legal duty to take care affords a sort of key to the difficulties in this field. But that this is not true will become manifest to the careful student. We are convinced that the idea of positive duty is much overworked here and that it is by no means able to accomplish all that seems to be expected of it. These cases evidently bring us into contact with one of the very broadest conceptions of liability known to the law, and a question-begging subterfuge will not suffice to explain the problem. We shall presently give a résumé of some of the most important decisions in this field, but by way of preface we shall attempt a rational explanation of the principle upon which this branch of the law proceeds.

General principle of secondary trespass.

We first start out with the principle which was found to underlie torts of the secondary trespass formation at large, to the effect that any man who creates or maintains an agent which foreseeably and as a natural consequence may do hurt to the person or property of another, is responsible for such damage as is done by that agent. This is, in substance, the generalization of Lord Esher in *Heaven v. Pender* (1883).[1]

Now as against this, the primary risk of the author or maintainer of the thing that works the harm, we find a counter-principle which comes in to modify that risk. This is found

[1] 11 Q. B. D. 503.

Assumption of risk by person injured.

in the proposition that if the person who gets hurt or whose property is damaged himself assumes the risk, the other is relieved of responsibility. This principle is in the nature of a general qualification of the principle laid down by Lord Esher, and taken subject to that qualification there can be no doubt of the absolute accuracy of that principle and of its universal application throughout the entire secondary trespass formation.

Similarity to doctrine of contributory negligence.

It will be found that this idea of assumption of risk by the party injured occupies much the same position in torts of the secondary trespass formation that contributory negligence occupies in other negligent wrongs. The respective ideas of assumption of risk and contributory negligence are habitually confused, and indeed they have much in common; but assumption of risk is essentially the broader notion.

Principle underlying assumption of risk.

Just what is necessary to constitute an assumption of risk by the person injured so as to relieve the other party of responsibility can be truly said to constitute the great unsolved problem of the law of negligence. In general terms the principle seems to be this, viz., that before an injured person can be said to have assumed the risk it must appear that he had or ought to have had knowledge of the risk and voluntarily incurred it. But the application of this broad principle in its many relations has not been fully worked out. The law as we actually find it exemplified in the decisions seems for the most part to be the result of a very proper attempt at balancing considerations of justice as between man and man.

We now turn to the concrete illustrations, admonishing the reader that in many of these cases there is much unnecessary discussion of the duty to take care. In large part such discussions are fruitless and merely show that the courts have not always reduced the problem which they are striving to solve, to its lowest terms. A little advertence on the part of the reader to the facts stated in these illustrations will show how simply the problem can be dealt with from the point of view indicated in the two respective ideas, primary risk and counter-assumption of risk.

Chapter X

In the following cases the author or maintainer of the agent of harm was upon general principle held responsible and liable, there being no sufficient evidence to support the implication of a counter-assumption of risk by the person injured.

Primary risk incident to maintenance of agent of harm.

1. *Chapman v. Rothwell* (1858):[2] The defendant, a brewer, had a trap in the passageway which led from the street to his office along which customers were expected to go when they wished to do business with him. A person who had been there on business fell through the trapdoor on departing, and was killed. It was held that the facts stated showed a duty on the part of the defendant to take care that the customers should not fall into that trap. The simpler explanation is that the primary risk was on the defendant and there was nothing to show an assumption of risk by the person injured such as would relieve the defendant of responsibility.

Trap in passageway.

2. *Indermaur v. Dames* (1866):[3] Upon the premises of the defendant, a sugar refiner, was a hole or shoot used for raising and lowering sugar. The shoot was usual, necessary, and proper in the business. When not in use it was sometimes necessary for the purpose of ventilation that it should be open. With a view to certain improvements in the lighting of his premises, the defendant had allowed one B to instal a patent gas regulator, agreeing to pay for it if the apparatus should prove a success. The plaintiff was a journeyman gas fitter in the employment of B, and as such went upon the defendant's premises for the purpose of examining the burners as preparatory to a test of the new apparatus. Whilst thus engaged upon an upper floor of the building the plaintiff accidentally and without fault or negligence on his part fell through the hole and was injured. It was held that the defendant was liable.

Open shoot in manufacturing establishment.

3. *Francis v. Cockrell* (1870):[4] The defendant was sued for personal injury which happened to the plaintiff by the fall of a temporary stand at a steeple chase. The stand had been built by competent independent contractors, but was defective. It was held that the defendant as proprietor of the course owed to the persons who paid admission to him, a duty to see that the stand was reasonably safe.

Fall of stand at steeple chase.

4. *White v. France* (1877):[5] The plaintiff went upon the premises of the defendant with a view to getting employment. While walking there a bale of goods which had been negligently left by the defendant's servants nicely balanced at the edge of a warehouse

Bales insecurely piled.

[2] El. Bl. & El. 169, 96 E. C. L. 169.

[3] L. R. 1 C. P. 274.

[4] L. R. 5 Q. B. 184, 501.

[5] 2 C. P. D. 308.

Volume I

trapdoor, from which such bales were lowered, suddenly fell upon the plaintiff and injured him. It was held that an action would lie. The risk was not put upon the plaintiff, because he was ignorant of the risk and was there upon a commendable and lawful errand.

Slippery stairs.

5. *Miller v. Hancock:*[6] The defendant was the owner of a building which he let out in flats to tenants. The flats were reached by a common staircase, which remained in control and occupation of the defendant. The plaintiff, in the course of his business, had to call upon the tenant of one of those flats. In coming away, he slipped on the stairs, in consequence of their worn and defective condition, and broke his leg. It was held that the duty of the landlord to keep the premises reasonably safe extended to persons who should, like the plaintiff, come upon the premises to do business with the tenants.

Insecure gangway.

6. *Smith v. London, etc., Docks Co.* (1868):[7] The defendants, a dock company, provided gangways from the shore to the ships lying in their dock, the gangways being made of materials belonging to the defendants and managed by their servants. The plaintiff went on board a ship in the dock at the invitation of one of the ship's officers, and while he was on board, the defendant's servants, for the purposes of the business of the dock, moved the gangway, so that it was, and to their knowledge, insecure. The plaintiff, in the ignorance of its insecurity, returned along it to the shore; the gangway gave way and he was injured. It was held that there was a duty on the defendants towards the plaintiff to keep the gangway reasonably safe, and that he was entitled to recover damages from them for the injuries he received.

Swing bridge.

7. *Manley v. St. Helens Canal, etc., Co.* (1858):[8] A canal company was empowered to erect a swing bridge over a canal to connect the parts of an ancient highway severed by the canal. A boatman having opened the swivel bridge in the night to allow his boat to pass through, a person who was coming along the road at that time walked into the water and was drowned. It appeared that when the bridge was open the end of the highway abutting on the canal was unfenced. No lights were there to warn the pedestrian of his peril. It was held that the canal company was bound to take reasonable precautions to prevent such accidents and was therefore liable for the negligent failure to fulfil this duty.

Displaced plate over coal cellar.

8. *Braithwaite v. Watson* (1889):[9] An iron plate over a coal cellar was slightly displaced by a little boy who got into the cellar and poked about with his stick. The plaintiff walking on the pavement above set his foot on the dislocated plate and it tilted, with the result that the plaintiff was hurt. It was held that the occupant

[6] (1893) 2 Q. B. 177.
[7] L. R. 3 C. P. 326.
[8] 2 H. & N. 840.
[9] 5 Times Rep. 331.

of the premises was responsible for the accident. It was his duty, said the court, to keep the premises in a reasonably safe condition, and to this end the plate should have been made so secure that it could not be displaced by little boys who poke about with sticks.

Chapter X

9. *Coupland v. Hardingham* (1813):[1] An action was instituted against the defendant for negligence in not railing in or guarding an area before his house in Wood street, Westminster, whereby the plaintiff fell down into the area, and was severely hurt. It appeared that before the defendant's house there was an area which was descended to by three steps from the street, and from which there was a door leading into the basement story of the house; there was no railing or fence to guard the area from the street; the plaintiff, passing by on a dark night, fell in, and had his arm broken. The defense set up was, that the premises had been exactly in the same situation as far back as could be remembered, and many years before the defendant was in possession of them. But Lord Ellenborough held that "however long the premises might have been in this situation, as soon as the defendant took possession of them, he was bound to guard against the danger to which the public had been before exposed, and that he was liable for the consequences of having neglected to do so, in the same manner as if he himself had originated the nuisance. The area belongs to the house, and it is a duty which the law casts upon the occupier of the house to render it secure."[2]

Unguarded area.

The following cases are worthy of note as indicating, first, that the risk of damage resulting from the keeping of unsafe premises is primarily upon the occupant, but secondly, that, under proper conditions, others may be liable also.

Who responsible for unsafe premises.

1. *Pickard v. Smith* (1861):[3] Refreshment rooms and a coal cellar at a railway station were let by the company to the defendant. The opening for the putting in of coal was on the arrival platform. On one occasion while the plaintiff, a passenger, was passing in the usual way out of the station, he stepped into the opening which the servants of a coal dealer had insufficiently guarded. It was held that the defendant, as lessee and occupant of the cellar, was responsible and liable for the damage so done.

Occupant.

2. *Whiteley v. Pepper* (1877):[4] The defendant was a coal merchant. A carter employed by him in delivering coal at a house having a cellar below the foot pavement of the street, removed the iron plate of the coal shoot and left the place open without giving

Person guilty of actual short-coming.

[1] 3 Campb. 398.

[2] To the same effect see Irwin *v.* Sprigg (1847), 6 Gill (Md.) 200.

[3] 10 C. B. N. S. 470, 100 E. C. L. 470.

[4] 2 Q. B. D. 276.

any warning to the plaintiff, who was passing along the pavement and who, without negligence on his part, stepped into the hole and was hurt. The defendant was held liable. The fact that the occupant of the house and cellar might also have been held liable did not exonerate the merchant from liability for damages caused by the negligence of his servant.

Delegation of repairs does not lessen responsibility.

The following authorities show that where the risk incident to the keeping of unsafe premises is imposed on the owner or occupant, such risk cannot be evaded by a delegation of the care or work of repairing to a third person, not even to an independent contractor.

Insecure lamp over street.

1. *Tarry v. Ashton* (1876):[5] The defendant became the lessee and occupier of a house, from the front of which a heavy lamp projected several feet over the public foot pavement. As the plaintiff was walking along, in November, the lamp fell on, and injured, her. It appeared in evidence that in the previous August defendant employed an experienced gas fitter, C, to put this lamp in repair. At the time of the accident a person employed by defendant was blowing the water out of the gas pipes of the lamp, and in doing this a ladder was raised against the lamp-iron or bracket from which the lamp hung, and on the man mounting the ladder, owing to the wind and wet, the ladder slipped, and he, to save himself, clung to the lamp-iron, and the shaking caused the lamp to fall. On examination it turned out that the fastening by which the lamp was attached to the lamp-iron was in a decayed state. The jury found that there had been negligence on the part of C, but no negligence on the part of defendant personally; that the lamp was out of repair through general decay, but not to the knowledge of defendant; that the immediate cause of the fall of the lamp was the slipping of the ladder; but that, if the lamp had been in good repair, the slipping of the ladder would not have caused it to fall. It was held that the plaintiff was entitled to a verdict.

Gas main broken by independent contractor.

2. *Hardaker v. Idle Dist. Council:*[6] A district council, being about to construct a sewer under their statutory powers, employed a contractor to construct it for them. In consequence of his negligence in carrying out the work a gas main was broken, and the gas escaped from it into the house in which the plaintiffs (a husband and wife) resided, and an explosion took place, by which the wife was injured, and the husband's furniture was damaged. In an action by the plaintiffs against the district council and the contractor, it was held that the district council owed a duty to the public (including the plaintiffs) so to construct the sewer as not to injure the gas

[5] 1 Q. B. D. 314.

[6] (1896) 1 Q. B. 335.

main; that they had been guilty of a breach of this duty; that, notwithstanding they had delegated the performance of the duty to the contractor, they were responsible to the plaintiffs for the breach; and that the damages were not too remote to be recovered.

3. *Penny v. Wimbledon Urban Dist. Council:*[7] A district council employed a contractor to repair a way which was used by the public but which had not become repairable by the public at large. In carrying on the work the contractor negligently left in the road a heap of soil and grass unlighted and unprotected. A person walking on the road after dark fell over the heap and was injured. It was held that inasmuch as from the nature of the work danger was likely to arise to the public using the road unless precautions were taken, the negligence of the contractor was not casual or collateral to his employment, and the district council were therefore liable.

Repair of way.

Assumption of the Risk by Trespasser.

Where mischief happens to a trespasser by reason of the defective or dangerous condition of the premises upon which he trespasses, he is very properly held to assume the risk, and no recovery can be had against the keeper of those premises. As it is commonly and somewhat more artificially put, the implied duty to prevent harm from unsafe premises does not exist in favor of a trespasser.[8]

Risk of injury assumed by trespasser.

1. *Sullivan v. Boston, etc., R. Co.* (1892):[9] The plaintiff's intestate climbed upon the defendant's building to recover a ball with which he had been playing and which had lodged there. While so

Injury from electric wire.

[7] (1899) 2 Q. B. 72, affirming (1898) 2 Q. B. 212.

[8] One reason why the law does not impose a positive duty on the owner of premises to use due care to prevent injury to persons or things trespassing on his premises is this, viz.: Injury to trespassers is not reasonably foreseeable as a natural consequence of the owner's lack of care. The law justly assumes in favor of the owner that the trespasser will not ordinarily be there. That this is the true rationale of the owner's exemption sufficiently appears from decisions which hold that where the presence of a trespasser can be in fact foreseen, then the duty to use due care not to hurt such trespasser is imposed. Thus in South, etc., Alabama R. Co. *v.* Donovan (1887), 84 Ala. 141, the Alabama court held that where a railroad passes through a town where people from necessity or custom walk across the track at other points than the regular crossing, the law requires the employees operating the train to keep a vigilant lookout even for trespassers.

[9] 156 Mass. 378.

Volume I

upon the building he came into contact with a live wire used to conduct electricity from the defendant's work to an adjoining building and was killed. It was held that no action lay.

Falling into pit.

2. *Reardon v. Thompson* (1889):[1] The defendant dug a hole partly on his own premises and partly on the premises of a third person who consented to the digging. The plaintiff came along at night and fell in. The hole was not near enough to the regular path to constitute a nuisance or menace to those who were entitled to use the path. It was held that an action could not be maintained.

Collapse of old structure.

3. *Lary v. Cleveland, etc., R. Co.* (1881):[2] The plaintiff, without invitation and as a mere intruder, entered upon the uninclosed premises of the defendant, upon which was a building of the defendant in a state of visible decay. While there a sudden storm blew a fragment of the dilapidated building against the plaintiff, injuring him severely. The building had once been used as a freight house, but had been long since abandoned as a place of public business, and was not so situated with reference to any public way, as to endanger travelers thereon. It was held, in an action for damages for injuries received, that the plaintiff could not recover.

Trespassing Animals.

The doctrine that a man who keeps harmful agents on his premises is not responsible for mischief which thereby happens to a trespasser, finds exemplification in cases where trespassing animals are the subject of injury.

Stray horse.

1. *Blyth v. Topham* (1607):[3] Topham digged a pit in the common, and the plaintiff's mare having strayed, fell therein. It was held that as plaintiff's mare had no right to be in the common, the digging of the pit was lawful as against the plaintiff and hence no action lay.

Eating of yew leaves.

2. *Ponting v. Noakes:*[4] The plaintiff's colt reached over the boundaries of his master's land and ate yew leaves from a bush growing on the defendant's premises. It was held that the defendant was not responsible for the death of the colt.[5]

[1] 149 Mass. 267.

[2] 78 Ind. 323.

[3] Cro. Jac. 158.

[4] (1894) 2 Q. B. 281.

[5] Crowhurst *v.* Burial Board, 4 Ex. D. 5. A horse died of eating yew leaves from a tree which grew on the defendant's land but which overhung the plaintiff's field. The leaves eaten grew on that part of the tree which overhung the plaintiff's field. Judgment was given in favor of the plaintiff. Here the defendant's tree was the trespasser, or at least the maintenance of it was a sort of nuisance.

3. *Tennessee Chemical Co. v. Henry:*[6] The owner of a shed stored nitrate of soda sacks therein. The plaintiff's cow strayed in and ate some of the sacks, from the effects of which she died. It was held that the owner of the shed was not guilty of maintaining an attractive nuisance such as would make him liable for the value of the cow.[7]

4. But where the escape of cattle into the defendant's premises is due to a breach of positive duty on his part to keep up the fence, he is of course liable. Thus, in *Lawrence v. Jenkins* (1873),[8] it appeared that the plaintiff and defendant were the occupiers of two adjoining closes. The duty of maintaining the fence was shown, by evidence of forty years' usage, to be upon the defendant. The defendant's close was woodland, and the person to whom he had sold the fallage, felled a tree so that it fell over the fence and made a gap in it. The plaintiff's cows got through the gap and were poisoned by feeding upon the foliage of a yew tree which had been recently felled and lay near the gap. It was held that the defendant was liable for the value of the plaintiff's cows.

Breach of duty to maintain inclosure.

Assumption of Risk by Licensees, Servants, and Guests.

A doctrine very similar to that which is applied in the case of trespassers, but not quite so strict, is applied in the case of licensees, servants, and guests. These, it is held, assume all ordinary risk of getting hurt upon the premises of the licensor, master, or host. But they do not assume extraordinary risk such as is incident to a defect in the nature of a concealed trap.[9] Practically the law here seems to be a result of a balancing of considerations of justice and convenience. It is not unreasonable to hold that the licensee and servant should look out for themselves and that the visitor, by accepting hospitality, assumes the same risk that his host is exposed to. But materials for a subtler exegesis are not wanting. Thus, we may say that the law raises an implied assumpsit of risk on the part of the licensee, servant, and guest, in view of the benefit which accrues to these persons by reason of the license, employment, or entertainment. This benefit, with the corre-

Only usual risks assumed.

The implied assumpsit.

[6] (Tenn. 1905) 85 S. W. Rep. 401.

[7] To the same effect see Bush *v.* Brainard (1823), 1 Cow. (N. Y.) 78.

[8] L. R. 8 Q. B. 274.

[9] Corby *v.* Hill, 4 C. B. N. S. 556, 93 E. C. L. 556; Southcote *v.* Stanley, 1 H. & N. 247; Indermaur *v.* Dames, L. R. 1 C. P. 274.

Concerning the servant's assumption of risk in general, see *post.*

Volume I

sponding detriment to the other party, supplies a sort of legal consideration for the implied assumpsit to bear the risk. The affinity to contract theory is manifest.

Licensee injured by falling from roof.

1. *Ivay v. Hedges* (1882):[1] A house was let in apartments to tenants who were allowed to dry their linen upon the roof. The latter was covered with lead and had a rail at its outer edge. The plaintiff, a tenant, went upon the roof to remove some linen, when his foot slipped and he fell against the railing. The railing was defective and was known by the landlord to be so. In consequence the plaintiff fell through to the courtyard below and was hurt. It was held that the privilege of using the roof as a drying ground was a mere license and imposed no duty on the landlord to keep it in repair.

Going into dark warehouse.

2. *Wilkinson v. Fairrie* (1862):[2] The plaintiff, a carman, calling late for some goods at the defendant's warehouse, after waiting for some time, was directed by a servant of the defendants as to the way to go to find the warehouseman. Going along in the dark, he fell down a staircase. It was held that inasmuch as a stairway is not dangerous like a trapdoor, the defendants owed the plaintiff no duty to have the staircase or passages lighted.

Licensee falling into quarry.

3. *Hounsell v. Smyth* (1860):[3] The plaintiff opened a quarry in waste lands between two highways, but not so near as to constitute a nuisance or menace to persons who might use either. The plaintiff on a dark night accidentally strayed from one of the roads and attempted to reach the other. Having sustained injury by falling into the open quarry, it was held that he had no ground for action. Nor was the case mended by alleging in the declaration that, with the permission of the owner, the public were accustomed to use the waste land in going from one highway to the other, for this merely showed that the plaintiff was a licensee instead of a trespasser.

Bridge on private way.

4. *Gautret v. Egerton* (1867):[4] The defendant had a bridge over a canal where the same was crossed by his private road. With his permission the public was accustomed to use the way, and plaintiff's intestate upon a certain occasion fell through or from the bridge into the canal by reason of the bridge being in bad repair and was drowned. It was held that an action could not be maintained.[5]

[1] 9 Q. B. D. 80.

[2] 1 H. & C. 633.

[3] 7 C. B. N. S. 731, 97 E. C. L. 731.

[4] L. R. 2 C. P. 371.

[5] But see Campbell *v.* Boyd (1883), 88 N. Car. 129, where it appeared that the defect in the road was known to the person who maintained it for his own use and for the use of the public.

5. *Batchelor v. Fortescue* (1883):[6] The deceased was employed by a builder to watch and protect certain unfinished buildings. Workmen were employed by the defendant, a contractor, on the land near to where the deceased was on duty, to excavate the earth for the foundations of other buildings. In the performance of this operation they employed a steam crane and winch, to which were attached a chain and iron bucket by means of which the earth was raised from the excavation and thence to the carts which were to carry it away. The deceased had nothing to do with the excavations, but was standing where he need not have been, watching the defendant's men at work, and allowing the bucket to pass some three feet over his head, when the chain broke and the bucket and its contents falling upon him so injured him that he subsequently died. There was no evidence of negligence on the part of the defendant's workmen. It was held that the deceased was at most a bare licensee and that he stood where he did at his own risk.

Spectator killed by collapse of steam crane.

6. *Moffatt v. Bateman* (1869)[7] involved the question of liability for damage resulting from a defective vehicle, but it was decided upon a principle analogous with that which is applied in regard to premises; that is to say, the invited guest assumes the same risk as the person who extends accommodations. The plaintiff, a decorator, was in the service of the defendant, and the latter, wishing to have the plaintiff's assistance in papering some rooms a few miles away, offered to take the plaintiff there in a buggy. On the road the trap was smashed and the plaintiff was hurt. The accident was a result of a defective kingbolt. It was held that the plaintiff could not recover. The service of the defendant in conveying the plaintiff was gratuitous and the risk was therefore on the plaintiff.

Defective carriage.

Turntable Cases.

The turntable cases afford some highly instructive illustrations of the application of the doctrine of risk incident to the maintenance of dangerous and attractive agents. The tale told in these cases is about boys who go to ride upon railroad turntables and are brought away with broken members and, perhaps, maimed for life.

Children injured while playing on turntables.

1. *Keffe v. Milwaukee, etc., R. Co.* (1875):[8] The defendant company had a turntable on its grounds which could be easily operated, and was naturally attractive to small children. The thing was left unfastened and the plaintiff, a boy of tender years, got hurt

[6] 11 Q. B. D. 474. [7] L. R. 3 P. C. 115. [8] 21 Minn. 207.

Volume I

by the turning of the table at the hands of his playmates. It was held that the defendant was responsible.[9]

2. *Edgington v. Burlington, etc., R. Co.* (1902):[1] The defendant company fastened its turntable with a pin, bolt, or latch of some kind which could be, and on the occasion of the accident was, removed by children who went to ride upon the turntable. It was held that the question whether the company was negligent in having the table insecurely fastened was one of fact for the jury.[2]

Immature children not competent to assume risk.

In cases where the railroad company is thus held responsible and liable, it will be found that the boy who gets hurt is commonly a mere trespasser. The question arises, Why should not the risk be put upon him as upon trespassers in general? The reason simply is, that the small boy does not have legal capacity to assume a risk. The assumption of risk on the part of the injured party involves the idea of implied undertaking, or agreement to take the risk. It would clearly be contrary to principle for the law to impose such an assumpsit upon very immature children, and accordingly, by the weight of authority, it does not do so. But (from another point of view) we may say that very small children are not capable of contributory negligence.

Clearly, if a boy is sufficiently mature and discreet to have the legal capacity to assume a risk (and for this purpose the law of tort takes no notice of the period of infancy recognized in contract law, but looks only to his capacity to perceive and appreciate the danger), he ought to go upon the turntable at his peril. And so it is held.[3]

The implied invitation.

Liability in the turntable cases is frequently put upon the ground of implied invitation to children to come upon the

[9] See to same effect Sioux City, etc., R. Co. *v.* Stout (1873), 17 Wall. (U. S.) 657; Alabama G. S. R. Co. *v.* Crocker, 131 Ala. 584; Chicago, etc., R. Co. *v.* Krayenbuhl, 65 Neb. 889; East Tennessee, etc., R. Co. *v.* Cargille, 105 Tenn. 628; Ilwaco R., etc., Co. *v.* Hedrick, 1 Wash. 446. *Contra,* Frost *v.* Eastern R. Co., 64 N. H. 220; Daniels *v.* New York, etc., R. Co., 154 Mass. 349; Delaware, etc., R. Co. *v.* Reich, 61 N. J. L. 635; Walsh *v.* Fitchburg R. Co., 145 N. Y. 301.

[1] 116 Iowa 410.

[2] In Bates *v.* Nashville, etc., R. Co., 90 Tenn. 36, it was held that the company is excused if it merely fastens the turntable sufficiently to keep it securely in place.

[3] Carson *v.* Chicago, etc., R. Co. (1896), 96 Iowa 583.

premises in order to play there, the invitation being supposed to arise from the attractive nature of these dangerous engines. This hypothesis is hatched up to evade the obstacle which arises from the fact that the plaintiff is a trespasser. But it is as unnecessary as it is inadequate and artificial. Liability is to be ascribed to the simple fact that the defendant, in maintaining a dangerous agent from which harm may, under particular conditions, be expected to come, has the primary risk, and must answer in damages unless a counter-assumption of risk can be imposed on those who go there to play.

True basis of the turntable cases.

CHAPTER XI

NEGLIGENCE (CONTINUED).

Assumption of Risk by Person Injured.

Volume I

THE idea of assumption of risk by the person injured, which, as we have now seen, is so easily legible in the cases involving harms resulting from unsafe premises, is very conspicuous in a great many relations. The vehicle which is commonly used for conveying the idea underlying this defense is the legal maxim, *volenti non fit injuria.*

Volenti non fit injuria.

This maxim means that a man who consents to the doing of an act cannot maintain an action in respect of the damage which results from that act. The consent of the sufferer takes away the injurious character of the act. The idea is very rudimentary in legal science [1] and the conception was familiar in Roman law.[2]

Illustrations of the primary meaning of the maxim.

Primarily the maxim applies where there is actual consent by the sufferer to the doing of the particular act which causes the harm. A merchant, for instance, who consents to the stowage of his goods on the deck of a ship has no remedy against the ship owner for damage sustained by the cargo in consequence of such stowage.[3] And one who has agreed to take part in an operation necessitating the production of fumes injurious to health, has no cause of action in respect of bodily suffering or inconvenience resulting therefrom, though another person residing near to the seat of these operations might well maintain an action if he sustained such injuries

[1] The germ of the maxim can be traced in Aristotle. N. G. L. Child in Jurid. Rev. 43, citing Ethics, IX. 6.

[2] "*Nulla injuria est quæ in volentem fiat,*" Dig. XLVII. 10, 1, 5. An early instance of the use of the maxim in its present form, *volenti non fit injuria*, in an English court is found in Y. B. 33-35 Edw. I. (Rolls ed.), 8.

[3] Tridal, C. J., in Gould *v.* Oliver (1837), 4 Bing. N. Cas. 142, 33 E. C. L. 305.

from the same cause.[4] A husband who is consenting to adulterous conduct on the part of his wife can maintain no action for damages against her paramour.[5] Upon the same ground a woman is disabled from recovering damages of her seducer.[6] In this primary sense the maxim represents a universal qualification of legal liability and finds illustration in every department of tort.

Maxim applicable in all cases of assumption of risk by person injured.

During the last seventy-five years or so the applicability of the maxim in cases of negligence has been from time to time considered, and of late discussions of its import in this connection have become frequent, especially in England. The result has been that the scope of the maxim has been so broadened as to include all situations where the party injured can be said by implication to have assumed the risk, although in many cases there can be no pretense that he actually consented to the particular conduct which causes the harm. It is enough if he appreciates the danger and consents to take the risk. The idea embodied in the maxim is evidently a part of the same scheme of legal ideas as contributory negligence, and it occupies an analogous place.

'Spring gun' case.

Ilott v. Wilkes (1820)[7] was the first case in which the maxim was applied in the extended sense just indicated. The action was brought by a trespasser who, notwithstanding notice that a woodland was set with spring guns, went to gather nuts there and got shot. Bayley, J., said: "The maxim of law, *volenti non fit injuria*, applies; for he voluntarily exposed himself to the mischief which has happened. He is told that if he goes into the wood he will run a particular risk, for that in those grounds there are spring guns. Notwithstanding that caution, he says, 'I will go into the wood, and I will run the risk of all consequences.' Has he then any right, after he has been distinctly apprised of his danger, to bring an

[4] Lord Herschell, in Smith *v.* Baker, (1891) A. C. 360.

[5] Duberley *v.* Gunning (1792), 4 T. R. 656; Winter *v.* Henn (1831), 4 C. & P. 494; 19 E. C. L. 491; Prettyman *v.* Williamson, 1 Penn. (Del.) 224.

[6] Roll, C. J., in Norton *v.* Jason (1653), Style 398. See also Gibson, C. J., in Weaver *v.* Bachert, 2 Pa. St. 80.

[7] 3 B. & Ald. 304, 5 E. C. L. 295.

Volume I

action against the owner of the soil for the consequences of his own imprudent and unlawful act? I think not, for he had no right to enter the wood." [8]

Assumption of Risk by Servant.

Most of the cases in which the maxim, in its broadest scope, has latterly been invoked, arise out of injuries happening to servants while about their master's business, and the question is, whether the servant has assumed the risk of such injury. But of course the maxim is by no means exclusively associated with the relation of master and servant.

Servant assumes risk naturally incident to his employment.

In *Skipp v. Eastern Counties R. Co.* (1853)[9] it appeared that the plaintiff was employed by the defendant company to attach cars in making up its trains. The evidence tended to show that the work was too much for one, but the plaintiff undertook to perform the task, and did so for several months without complaint. In the end it happened that, while attaching the cars, he got knocked down and his arm was badly injured. His action for damages was dismissed on the ground that he had voluntarily assumed the risk; and it was said that if he felt endangered by reason of not having sufficient assistance he should not have accepted the work.

Assumption of risk sometimes identical with defense of contributory negligence.

In *Senior v. Ward* (1859),[1] the plaintiff's intestate, a miner, was killed by the breaking of the rope which was used to lower men into the defendant's colliery. The rope had been injured overnight by a fire, and there was a rule requiring the banksman to test the rope each morning before any person should be allowed to descend. But this rule was habitually violated to the knowledge of the plaintiff's intestate, and on the occasion of the calamity in question, the latter was told by the banksman that he should himself examine the rope before going down. The suggestion was not heeded, with the result that intestate lost his life. The maxim, *volenti non fit injuria,* was held to apply. It was also said that the contributory negligence of the deceased was fatal to the action.

[8] 3 B. & Ald. 311, 5 E. C. L. 298.

[9] 9 Exch. 223.

[1] 1 El. & El. 385, 102 E. C. L. 385.

Chapter XI

This is clearly one of the cases where the ideas of assumption of risk and of contributory negligence are equally applicable. In fact, in one aspect, contributory negligence is merely a species of the genus assumption of risk.

In *Thomas v. Quartermaine* (1887),[2] the facts were as follows: The plaintiff was employed in a cooling room in the defendant's brewery. In the room were a boiling vat and a cooling vat, and between them ran a passage which was in part only three feet wide. The cooling vat had a rim raised sixteen inches above the level of the passage, but it was not fenced or railed in. The plaintiff went along this passage to pull a board from under the boiling vat. This board stuck fast and then came away suddenly, so that he fell back into the vat and was scalded. It was held that the maxim applied and that consequently the plaintiff could not recover.

Assumption of risk distinguished from contributory negligence.

In this case it was necessary to distinguish with precision between the defense of contributory negligence and assumption of risk; for the trial court, in its finding, had specifically negatived contributory negligence on the part of the plaintiff, but had found that he knew of the danger encountered in working near the vat. Bowen, L. J., observed: "The doctrine of *volenti non fit injuria* stands outside the defense of contributory negligence and is in no way limited by it. In individual instances the two ideas sometimes seem to cover the same ground, but carelessness is not the same thing as intelligent choice, and the Latin maxim often applies when there has been no carelessness at all."[3]

Danger must be appreciated as well as perceived.

On the question whether knowledge, on the part of the plaintiff, of the danger he was in by reason of his proximity to the vat, was sufficient under the circumstances of this case to make out an assumption of risk, the same judge said: "Knowledge . . . . is not conclusive where it is consistent with the facts that, from its imperfect character or otherwise, the entire risk, though in one sense known, was not voluntarily encountered; but here, on the plain facts of the case, knowledge on the plaintiff's part can mean only one

[2] 18 Q. B. D. 685.

[3] Thomas *v.* Quartermaine, 18 Q. B. D. 697, 698.

Volume I

thing. For many months the plaintiff, a man of full intelligence, had seen this vat — known all about it — appreciated its danger — elected to continue working near it. It seems to me that legal language has no meaning unless it were held that knowledge such as this amounts to a voluntary encountering of the risk." [4]

In *Membery v. Great Western R. Co.* (1889),[5] it appeared that the defendant company had let the contract for shunting its trucks upon a particular line to a contractor, it being agreed that the company should furnish boys to assist about the business when they had boys; but if no boys were available, the shunting was to be done nevertheless. The contractor employed the plaintiff as his servant to do the shunting in question, and the latter did the work for several years, sometimes with and sometimes without assistance. It was dangerous to do the work without the help of a boy, inasmuch as the person attempting it had to guide the horse and at the same time unhook the chain from the truck while in motion. On one occasion the plaintiff asked the company's foreman for a boy; but, none being available, he proceeded to do the work alone, with the consequence that he was run over and his foot crushed. It was held in the House of Lords that, inasmuch as the plaintiff had voluntarily done the work with full knowledge of the risk he ran, the maxim applied, and he could not recover.

Essentials to assumption of risk.

Before the maxim can be invoked it must appear (1) that the plaintiff knew and appreciated the full extent of the danger to which he was subjected, and (2) that he voluntarily put himself in the way of that danger, or impliedly consented to subject himself to it.

That the first of these conditions is essential is shown by *Osborne v. London, etc., R. Co.* (1888).[6] The plaintiff in

[4] Thomas *v.* Quartermaine has been criticised on the ground that the question whether the plaintiff assumed the risk is one of fact purely and should not be held to be a matter of law. Lord Herschell in Smith *v.* Baker, (1891) A. C. 366. And this idea of Lord Herschell's seems to have been judicially accepted in Williams *v.* Birmingham Battery, etc., Co. (1899), 2 Q. B. 338.

[5] 14 App. Cas. 179.

[6] 21 Q. B. D. 220.

Chapter XI

Slippery approach to station.

this case was injured by falling on steps leading to the defendant's railway station, which the defendant had allowed to become very slippery and dangerous. The plaintiff saw that the steps were slippery and went down carefully, holding the handrail. It was held that he might recover, on the ground that it did not appear that he appreciated the full extent of the danger.[7] There was a special finding that the defendant was guilty of negligence and that the plaintiff was not guilty of contributory negligence. Wills, J., observed that, under these circumstances, before the defendants could escape on the ground of the maxim *volenti non fit injuria,* they must obtain a finding of fact "that the plaintiff, freely and voluntarily, with full knowledge of the nature and extent of the risk he ran, impliedly agreed to incur it." [8]

Open hatchway on ship.

Necessity for full appreciation of the danger also appears from a late American decision. Here plaintiff's intestate, a quarantine physician, visited a steamship at night. The vessel was coaling and her hatches were open, a thing which was unusual. After the physician had made his inspection he proceeded aft in the dark. It was necessary to pass the open hatch by way of a passage, two or three feet wide, between the hatch and the starboard rail. In so doing he was accompanied by one B, who was then superintending the coaling of the vessel. The physician was told that the hatch was open, and he doubtless saw it, but he could hardly have seen its exact extent. As the two neared the hatch, B, who was a little in the rear, told the doctor to be careful, and again, "Doctor, mind the hatch"; to which warnings the answers were, "That's all right." Proceeding a little further, the physician stepped into the hatch and, falling thirty-five feet sheer to the bottom of the vessel, was killed. The owner of the ship was held liable.[9] The idea on which the decision is to be rested is, that plaintiff's intestate did not have such

[7] In cases like this the question of assumption of risk is for the jury. Fitzgerald *v.* Connecticut River Paper Co., 155 Mass. 155; Mahoney *v.* Dore, 155 Mass. 513.

[8] Osborne *v.* London, etc., R. Co., 21 Q. B. D. 223, quoting language of Lord Esher in Yarmouth *v.* France, 19 Q. B. D. 657.

[9] Ward *v.* Dampskibselskabet Kjoebenhaven (1905), 136 Fed. Rep. 502.

Volume I

knowledge and appreciation of his danger as would justify the court in saying that he had assumed the risk.

Involuntary submission to risk.

In the following cases, knowledge of the particular conditions and appreciation of the danger were fully shown, but the maxim was held not to apply because it did not affirmatively appear that the plaintiff voluntarily incurred the risk to which he was subjected.[1]

Driving dangerous horse under protest.

Yarmouth v. France (1887)[2] presented this state of facts: The plaintiff was employed by the defendant, a wharfinger, to drive a cart and to load and unload the goods which were carried therein. Among the horses was one of a vicious nature and unfit to be driven, even by a careful driver. The plaintiff objected to driving this horse, and told the foreman of the stable that it was unfit to be driven, to which the foreman replied that the plaintiff must go on driving it, and that if any accident happened his employer would be responsible. The plaintiff continued to drive the horse, and while sitting on his proper place in the cart, was kicked by the animal and his leg broken. It was held that there was evidence to support a finding by the jury that the plaintiff did not voluntarily incur the risk.

In *Williams v. Birmingham Battery, etc., Co.*[3] it appeared that while a workman, in the course of his employment, was descending from an elevated tramway belonging to his employers, his foot slipped, with the result that he fell, receiving injuries of which he died. The employers had provided no ladder or other safe means of ascending to or descending from the tramway. It appeared that the deceased had the same means of knowing that to descend from the tramway without a ladder was dangerous, as his employers had. In an action brought by the widow of the deceased, the jury found specially that the defendants had not exercised due care to

[1] It should be observed that these decisions have been rendered since the passage of the English Employers' Liability Act, and while that act does not directly affect the principle now under consideration, it is nevertheless apparent that these cases show a visible deviation from ideas formerly held. This tendency is no doubt indirectly attributable to changes brought about by that act.

[2] 19 Q. B. D. 647.

[3] (1899) 2 Q. B. 338.

Chapter XI

Exposure of servant to unnecessary risk.

have the tramway in a proper condition for protecting their servants from unnecessary risk, and that the deceased was guilty of no contributory negligence. It also found a general verdict for the plaintiff. In the Court of Appeal the verdict was upheld. Upon the point whether the deceased had voluntarily incurred the risk, it was held that it was not enough for the defendants to show that the deceased knew the danger. A consent to incur the risk must, so it was said, affirmatively appear. As was once observed by Bowen, L. H., the maxim is *volenti non fit injuria,* not *scienti.*[4]

That mere knowledge of risk does not necessarily involve consent to assume the risk has been conclusively settled in England by the decision of the House of Lords in *Smith v. Baker.*[5] The opinions in the case are well worth a careful perusal, but the facts are not such as to admit of profitable discussion here. Reduced to its simplest terms the decision is to the effect that, in the absence of an explicit finding by the jury, an employee will not be presumed, as a matter of law, to have consented to incur an unnecessary risk incident to his employment, merely because he realizes the danger, and works on instead of refusing to do so.[6]

Doctrine of assumption of risk in America.

In America the maxim *volenti non fit injuria* has not been so extensively considered as in England, but the doctrine embodied in it is well established in the law. Sometimes the courts go upon the idea that the conduct of the plaintiff in submitting himself to an appreciated danger conclusively shows that he is not in the exercise of due care and is guilty of contributory negligence. Sometimes it is said that the defendant no longer owes him any duty; sometimes that the duty becomes one of imperfect obligation and is no longer recognized in law. In one form or other the doctrine is given effect, as showing, in a case to which it applies, that there was either no negligence on the part of the defendant, or that there was a want of due care on the part of the plaintiff. The

[4] Thomas *v.* Quartermaine, 18 Q. B. D. 696.

[5] (1891) A. C. 325.

[6] See Mahoney *v.* Dore (1892), 155 Mass. 519, 520.

late Massachusetts decisions, cited below, will be found suggestive.[7]

Fellow-servant Doctrine.

Assumption of risk by servant.

The fellow-servant rule, by which one employee is precluded from recovering damages of his master for an injury resulting from the negligence of his fellow servant, is a manifestation of the doctrine of assumed risk. A servant, it is said, upon entering employment assumes all ordinary risks incident to that employment, among which is the risk of being injured by the negligence of a fellow workman. Any satisfactory discussion of the grounds and application of the fellow-servant rule could not be brought within limits here available, and we forbear to enter upon it.

Employers' Liability Act.

One important fact, however, should be noted, namely, that it has been held that the Employers' Liability Act, which within certain limits abolishes the fellow-servant doctrine and puts employees in a measure on the same footing as strangers in respect of their right to recover damages for injury resulting from the negligence of other employees, does not take away or in any manner affect the general defense of *volenti non fit injuria.*[8] It is plain, however, that the fellow-servant rule is an offshoot from the broad doctrine of assumed risk which is embodied in the maxim. The statute thus appears to have merely pruned off an excrescence, leaving the body of the principle intact.

In *Thomas v. Quartermaine* (1887), *supra*, Lord Bowen discussed the effect of this statute in the following luminous

[7] Fitzgerald *v.* Connecticut River Paper Co. (1891), 155 Mass. 155; Anderson *v.* Clark, 155 Mass. 368; Downey *v.* Sawyer, 157 Mass. 418; Goldthwait *v.* Haverhill, etc., St. R. Co., 160 Mass. 554; Connolly *v.* Eldredge, 160 Mass. 566; Rooney *v.* Sewall, etc., Cordage Co., 161 Mass. 153; Thain *v.* Old Colony R. Co., 161 Mass. 353; Austin *v.* Boston, etc., R. Co., 164 Mass. 282; La Fortune *v.* Jolly, 167 Mass. 170; McKee *v.* Tourtellotte, 167 Mass. 69; Kennedy *v.* Merrimack Paving Co., 185 Mass. 442; Bowden *v.* Marlborough Electric Mach., etc., Co., 185 Mass. 549.

[8] Thomas *v.* Quartermaine, 18 Q. B. D. 685; Birmingham R., etc., Co. *v.* Allen, 99 Ala. 359; Bridges *v.* Tennessee Coal, etc., Co., 109 Ala. 287; O'Maley *v.* South Boston Gas Light Co., 158 Mass. 135; Mellor *v.* Merchants' Mfg. Co., 150 Mass. 362.

Chapter XI

words: "For his own personal negligence a master was always liable and still is liable at common law, both to his own workmen and to the general public who come upon his premises at his invitation on business in which he is concerned. But in the case of injuries arising out of another servant's negligence, the workmen stood, before recent legislation, at a disadvantage as compared with the world outside. For damage done by the negligence of his servants, acting within the scope of their employment, the master, on the principle of *respondeat superior,* was responsible to strangers. But a workman injured by the negligence of a fellow workman had no such redress. By entering into a contract of service the common law inferred that he had taken on himself the ordinary risks incident to such business as was lawfully carried on upon his master's premises; and the much-canvassed case of *Priestley v. Fowler* (1837),[9] and a series of decisions following in its train, had engrafted on this doctrine the grave corollary that the negligence of a fellow servant in the common employ of the master was one of such ordinary risks. The corollary gave rise to much apparent hardship and to much debate." Then, after referring to the act in question as having been passed to remedy this trouble, his lordship noted that in the situations provided for in the act, the injured workman was given (to quote the language of the statute), "the same right of compensation and remedies against the employer as if the workman had not been a workman of, nor in the service of the employer, nor engaged in his work." He then proceeded: "An enactment which distinctly declares that the workman is to have the same rights as if he were not a workman, cannot, except by violent distention of its terms, be strained into an enactment that the workman is to have the same rights as if he were not a workman, and other rights in addition. It cannot, in the case of a defect in the employer's works, be distorted into the meaning that a new standard of duty is to be imposed on the employer as regards a workman, which would not exist as regards anybody else."

Effect of the statute.

[9] 3 M. & W. 1.

CHAPTER XII

NEGLIGENCE (CONTINUED).

Breach of Statutory Duties.

I. VIOLATION OF LAW BY DEFENDANT.

Volume I

THE violation of an imposed statutory duty is a sort of negligence *per se*. Thus, where a railroad company operates its train at a higher rate of speed than the law allows, the question whether it is guilty of negligence is not debatable. This preliminary matter the law conclusively determines against the company, and the sole question to be settled in cases of this kind is whether that delinquency can be considered a proximate cause of the damage of which complaint is made.

The following cases, involving violations of statutes of one kind or another, are worthy of note:

Sale of intoxicant.

1. *Wall v. State* (1894):[1] It appeared that the defendant, in violation of a statute, sold intoxicating liquors to the plaintiff's husband, who was already drunk. In consequence he became so intoxicated as to be irresponsible, and in driving his team wildly was killed. It was held that the defendant was liable.[2]

Train run at unlawful speed.

2. *Clark v. Boston, etc., R. Co.* (1887):[3] The plaintiff's horse, having escaped into the highway without any negligence on his part, was killed at a crossing by a passing train. The train at the time was running at an unlawful speed. It was held that the jury might well find that the unlawful speed at which the train was running was the effective or proximate legal cause of the killing of the horse.

3. *Binford v. Johnston* (1882):[4] The defendant in violation of statute sold pistol cartridges loaded with powder and ball to a boy,

[1] 10 Ind. App. 530.

[2] See to the same effect Smith *v.* People (1892), 141 Ill. 447.

In King *v.* Haley (1877), 86 Ill. 106, a rumseller who violated the civil damage act was held liable for an injury which plaintiff sustained by reason of being shot by a drunken man to whom whiskey had been illegally sold.

[3] 64 N. H. 323.

[4] 82 Ind. 426.

knowing they were to be used in a toy pistol. The boy left the pistol loaded with such cartridges on the floor, where a younger brother of six got hold of it. While in his hands the pistol was discharged and the older brother who had bought the cartridges was killed. It was held that this fatality was chargeable to the unlawful sale of the cartridges as its proximate cause, and that the defendant was responsible for the harm thus done.[5]

Sale of explosive to child.

4. *Salisbury v. Herchenroder* (1871):[6] The defendant maintained a sign over the street of a city in violation of an ordinance which imposed a penalty therefor. The sign was carefully fastened. It was, however, blown down by an extraordinary gale, and in falling broke a window in a neighboring building. It was held that the owner of the sign was liable for the damage thus done; and he was not permitted to avail himself of the defense of unforeseeable accident due to *vis major.*

Maintaining sign over street.

5. *Harrison v. Berkley* (1847):[7] The defendant, a liquor dealer, sold whiskey to a slave in violation of a statute. The slave became so intoxicated that he died of drunkenness and exposure. It was held that the defendant was liable if the jury should conclude that the fatal intoxication which ensued was the natural and probable consequence of the selling of the whiskey.

Sale of liquor to slave.

The reader will observe that in the foregoing cases the illegal conduct of the defendant appears in the light of an affirmative or positive act, not an omission merely; and these authorities show that such an illegal act is done strictly at the actor's peril. He is an insurer against all harm that naturally results from the illegal act. This harmonizes fully with the general principle of liability which, as we have already seen, prevails throughout the field of positive wrong.

Liability for positive illegal act.

On the other hand, we find that where a violation of statute consists of omission merely, a different rule of liability is enforced and the defendant is held only for such damages proximately resulting from his omission, as the statute, declaring the act illegal, contemplated. Here damage cannot be recovered, it is held, unless it was foreseen by the legislative eye. The statute must show an intention to prevent just such harms. We here see the law conforming to the prin-

Liability for illegal omission.

[5] The result would have been the same, on general principles of responsibility for harm done by dangerous agents, even had the sale of the cartridges to the boy not been in violation of statute.

[6] 106 Mass. 458.

[7] 1 Strobh. L. (S. Car.) 525.

Volume I

ciple of liability worked out in contract. Omissive violations of statute are thus viewed in the same light as breaches of promissory obligations. In other words, we here discover another branch of law which is referable to the head of true quasi-assumpsit.

It must be admitted that the decisions in which the principle above stated is imbedded are not altogether satisfactory in their reasoning, but that we have stated the true doctrine of these cases seems not to be open to serious doubt.

Failure to medicine ship.

1. *Couch v. Steel* (1854)[8] is the first important case on the subject of omissive violation of statute. The plaintiff, a seaman, in an action against shipowners with whom he had sailed, alleged that they had failed to supply and keep on board a proper supply of medicine as required by statute, whereby the plaintiff's health had suffered. It was held that damages could be recovered for the suffering so caused.

This decision is now generally admitted to be erroneous,[9] and it must be so considered in any aspect. In the first place, the statute imposing the duty in that case gave a penalty for failure to comply with the requirement in question. Nowadays this provision would be accepted as showing that the legislature did not intend to give an action for damages, and the action for the penalty would be held to be the exclusive remedy. In the second place, the court erred in applying the rule of liability, which really applies only in case of affirmative illegal acts, thus extending liability to all natural as distinguished from contemplated, consequences. In the third place, even granting that liability should so extend, the damage in this case ought doubtless to be considered remote.

Improper arrangements for shipping livestock.

2. *Gorris v. Scott* (1874)[1] is a modern case illustrating the principle that damage resulting from the omissive breach of a statutory duty cannot be recovered unless the damage in question is of a kind which the legislative body had a mind to prevent in enacting the statute. The facts were these: The defendant, a shipowner, undertook to carry the plaintiff's sheep from a foreign port to England. On the voyage some of them were washed overboard and lost. No other negligence was alleged than an omission on the part of the defendant to observe certain precautions (as regards the arrangements on board the vessel for shipping of livestock) which had been prescribed by the sanitary authorities. It was held that on this state

[8] 3 El. & Bl. 402, 77 E. C. L. 402.

[9] See opinions in Atkinson *v.* Newcastle, etc., Waterworks Co. (1877), 2 Ex. D. 441, also Lord Herschell in Cowley *v.* Newmarket Local Board, (1892) A. C. 345; also disapproved in The Noddleburn, 28 Fed. Rep. 857.

[1] L. R. 9 Exch. 125.

of facts the defendant was not liable for the loss of the sheep. The statutory precautions which had been violated had no other object in view than to prevent the spread of contagious diseases among animals. And no action, founded on the breach of the statutory duty, could be maintained for other damage than that which the statute was intended to guard against. But it was admitted that if the plaintiff had generally alleged and proved negligence in the transportation of the sheep, the result would have been different.[2]

Failure to keep sufficient water pressure.

3. In *Atkinson v. Newcastle, etc., Waterworks Co.* (1877),[3] it appeared that a water company was by statute required to maintain water pipes with fire plugs charged at a certain pressure to be used in case of fire. The company failed to keep the required pressure, and as a result, so it was alleged, the plaintiff's dwelling, upon catching fire on one occasion, could not be promptly extinguished and was destroyed. It was held that the plaintiff had no cause of action. The decision was placed on the ground that the only remedy contemplated by the statute was the recovery of the penalty provided for in the statute. And it was said generally that the question whether or not the breach of a statutory duty gives a private right of action in any case must always depend upon the object and language of the particular statute.

2. Violation of Law by Person Injured.

Illegal conduct on part of person injured.

As the breach of a statutory duty is a sort of negligence *per se* on the part of a defendant, so illegal conduct on the part of the plaintiff will often bar his action in the same way that contributory negligence would be a bar. The question whether the illegal conduct of the plaintiff is a bar to his action in a given case is to be determined upon considerations not different from those which govern in connection with contributory negligence generally. As in the field of contributory negligence, the cases are here divisible into three groups.

In (a) we find the defendant has been guilty of negligence in creating a dangerous antecedent condition which might under some circumstances afford a ground of action, but is nevertheless held not to be liable because the illegal act of the

[2] See Gorris *v.* Scott, L. R. 9 Exch. 131.

The decision must be considered erroneous if it be taken as negativing liability on the facts proved in that case. But the case really decides only a point of pleading, namely, that one who declares upon a breach of statutory duty must show damage which was contemplated by the legislative power in enacting the statute.

[3] 2 Ex. D. 441.

Volume I

plaintiff supplies a closer, more direct, and therefore a proximate cause of the injury.

Imposing unlawful weight on bridge.

Welch v. Geneva (1901):[4] The plaintiff, in violation of statute, drove a traction engine of excessive weight over a highway bridge and sustained injuries from its breaking through. It was held that he could not recover though the bridge timbers might have been so defective that the bridge would have collapsed under an engine of lawful weight. There was a direct causal relation here between the plaintiff's illegal act and the injury which befell him.

In (b) we find that the plaintiff has been guilty of some delinquency which makes his conduct illegal, but he is nevertheless permitted to recover because the negligent act of the defendant supervenes extraneously upon the situation created by the plaintiff's illegal conduct, and directly produces the mischief in question. In short, wherever the illegal conduct attributed to the plaintiff is clearly seen to have no causal relation to the injury, he is upon principle entitled to recover.

Blocking street.

1. *Steele v. Burkhardt* (1870):[5] The plaintiff, in order to load his wagon, placed it transversely across a street instead of lengthwise the sidewalk, as was required by the city ordinance. While so placed, the wagon was damaged by the negligent driving of another wagon in charge of defendant's servant. It was held that plaintiff's violation of the ordinance did not *ipso facto* preclude recovery. But he could not recover if the violation of law contributed to the accident.[6]

Illegal use of firm name.

2. *Wood v. Erie R. Co.* (1878):[7] The plaintiff in violation of law conducted business under a firm name which he was not entitled to use. This circumstance was held to be no defense for a carrier when sued for goods lost in transit consigned to the plaintiff under the illegal name.

Riding on platform.

3. *Connolly v. Knickerbocker Ice Co.* (1889):[8] The plaintiff, while riding, contrary to local ordinance, upon the platform of a street car, was injured by defendant's ice wagon which was negligently permitted by its driver to collide with the car. It was held that the plaintiff could recover.

[4] 110 Wis. 388.

[5] 104 Mass. 59.

[6] To the same effect see, on this point, the case of Newcomb *v.* Boston Protective Dept., 146 Mass. 596.

[7] 72 N. Y. 196.

[8] 114 N. Y. 104.

Driving at unlawful speed.

4. *Broschart v. Tuttle* (1890):[9] The plaintiff, while driving in a city at an unlawful rate of speed, was injured by collision with the team of the defendant under circumstances attributable to the negligence of the latter. It was held that the plaintiff's unlawful speed was not fatal to his right of action.

5. In *Baker v. Portland* (1870)[1] it appeared that the plaintiffs suffered serious injury from the upsetting of their carriage in consequence of running over certain piles of stone which had been dumped in the roadway of a street by persons in the employ of the street commissioner, and left overnight without guards or lights to warn the traveler. The plaintiffs at the time of the accident were driving faster than six miles an hour, which was the maximum speed allowed by ordinance. The jury were instructed that if the plaintiff's illegal speed in no way contributed to produce the injuries complained of, it would be no bar to a recovery. This instruction was held to be correct.

Plaintiff's conduct contrary to public policy.

Where the enterprise upon which the plaintiff appears to have been bent is in itself unlawful and contrary to public policy, a stricter rule is applied, and he cannot recover damages for an injury sustained *while* engaged in that enterprise by reason of the negligence of another, although the negligent act complained of may be the immediate and proximate cause of the damage in question. This sufficiently appears from the following case:

Wallace v. Cannon (1868):[2] The plaintiff's intestate, an engineer on the Western and Atlantic Railroad, was killed in a collision which happened while he was in charge of a train conveying confederate soldiers to wage war against the federal government. It was held that as the decedent was assisting in an unlawful enterprise his representative could not recover, although there was otherwise a good cause of action arising out of the negligence of those in control of the train.

Again, there is a third class of cases (c) in which the mischief is caused by such a combination of illegal conduct on the part of the plaintiff and of negligence on the part of the

[9] 59 Conn. 1.

[1] 58 Me. 199.

This is sounder doctrine than that embodied in Heland *v.* Lowell (1862), 3 Allen (Mass.) 407, where it is held that, as a matter of law, one is precluded from recovering damages occasioned by his horse's foot going through a hole in a bridge when, contrary to ordinance, he is going "faster than a walk."

[2] 38 Ga. 199.

Illegal conduct concurring with negligence of other party.

defendant, that either factor may be considered a proximate or contributing cause. Here the defendant cannot recover. This class of cases presupposes a sort of equilibrium between the factors of illegal conduct and negligence which in practice is seldom found to exist. Usually it is possible to say with some confidence that one or the other factor supplies a proximate cause, and hence the cases generally fall under class (a) or class (b).

Springing of bridge from trotting.

Abbott v. Wolcott (1866)[3] supplies as good an illustration of cases in (c) as we are apt to find: The plaintiff received an injury from the springing of a bridge occasioned by driving at a trot when by statute he should have driven no faster than at a walk. It was held that he could not recover, although the supports of the bridge were not such as were prescribed and required by law.

Violation of Sunday Ordinance.

The cases involving injuries received by persons who at the time are engaged in the violation of Sunday statutes exhibit a great deal of conflict. The doctrine held by the majority of the courts is indicated in the following cases:

Collapse of bridge.

1. *Sutton v. Wauwatosa* (1871):[4] The plaintiff was driving his cattle to market on Sunday in violation of statute when they were injured by the breaking down of a defective bridge which the defendant was bound to maintain. It was held that the plaintiff could recover.

Defective highway.

2. *Platz v. Cohoes* (1882):[5] The plaintiff violated a statute relative to the observance of the Sabbath by driving on that day on an errand other than that of "necessity or charity." While so doing he was, without any fault on his part, upset by a pile of earth which the defendant town had negligently suffered to remain on one of its streets. The action was upheld.[6]

Doctrine of majority of courts.

The point of view of the majority is indicated in the following language of a western court in a late case where a widow sued for damages for the death of her husband, resulting from a defect in a street. At the time of the injury, the husband was engaged, contrary to statute, in work other than of necessity or charity. Said

[3] 38 Vt. 666.

[4] 29 Wis. 21.

[5] 89 N. Y. 219.

[6] To the same effect see Black *v.* Lewiston, 2 Idaho 276; Kansas City *v.* Orr, 62 Kan. 61; Sewell *v.* Webster, 59 N. H. 586; Gross *v.* Miller, 93 Iowa 72; Norris *v.* Litchfield, 35 N. H. 271; Wentworth *v.* Jefferson, 60 N. H. 158.

the Supreme Court of Kansas: "The violation of the Sunday law . . . was not the efficient or proximate cause of the injury to the plaintiff, nor an essential element of her cause of action. The general rule is that a plaintiff will not be permitted to recover when it is necessary for him to prove his own illegal act or contract as a part of his cause of action; but the time when the injury occurred does not constitute the foundation of the action, and plaintiff could prove her cause of action without proving that her husband was violating the law when the injury occurred. The time when the injury was inflicted is only an incident to the efficient cause of the injury. The injury occurred by reason of the defect in the street, and was as liable to have occurred under similar circumstances on Saturday or Monday as it did on Sunday. There was not even a remote relation between the violation of the Sunday law and the injury which resulted from the negligence of the city in maintaining its streets in a proper condition."[7]

New England rule.

In Massachusetts and a few other New England States whose courts have followed the lead of the Massachusetts court, a stricter rule prevails.

Thus, in *Bosworth v. Swansey* (1845)[8] it was held that one who travels on Sunday on business "other than that of necessity or charity," cannot recover for injury occasioned by a defect in a highway.[9]

In *McGrath v. Merwin* (1873)[1] it appeared that the plaintiff had sustained injuries by the negligence of the defendant in setting machinery in motion while the plaintiff was assisting him to clear a wheel pit on Sunday. It was held that the plaintiff could not recover.

[7] Kansas City *v.* Orr (1900), 62 Kan. 67.

The observation of the Pennsylvania court to the effect that laws relating to the observance of the Sabbath define a duty of the citizen to the state and to the state only, is sensible and pertinent. Mohney *v.* Cook (1855), 26 Pa. St. 342. See also Piollet *v.* Simmers, 106 Pa. St. 96; Philadelphia, etc., R. Co. *v.* Philadelphia, etc., Steam Towboat Co., 23 How. (U. S.) 209.

[8] 10 Met. (Mass.) 363.

[9] To the same effect see Jones *v.* Andover, 10 Allen (Mass.) 18; Connolly *v.* Boston, 117 Mass. 64; Stanton *v.* Metropolitan R. Co., 14 Allen (Mass.) 485; McClary *v.* Lowell, 44 Vt. 116; Holcomb *v.* Danby, 51 Vt. 428; Hinckley *v.* Penobscot, 42 Me. 89; Cratty *v.* Bangor, 57 Me. 423. It may be added that in at least two of these States, namely, Massachusetts and Maine, the doctrine of these cases has been abolished by recent statutes to the effect that the Sunday laws shall in no way affect the right of action for a tort or injury suffered on that day.

[1] 112 Mass. 467.

Volume I

In these cases the defendants' illegal conduct is treated as being so far the immediate or proximate cause of the damage as to bring the case within the principle of (a), or as being so far a contributory cause as to bring the case within the principle of (c). It can certainly be said, in cases like *Bosworth v. Swansey,* that if the plaintiff had not gone abroad on Sunday he would not have been hurt. In this view his illegal conduct does seem to be in a sense a proximate cause or contributory cause to the injury, since he would not otherwise be in the place to be hurt. But, though the question is one worthy to engage the faculties of the schoolmen, this does not seem to be the true test. Where the illegality of an act consists merely of disqualification as to time of performance and the illegality does not infect the act so as to make it illegal under all times and conditions, the injury can never be ascribed with any plausibility to such illegality. The injury, it can be argued, would have happened just the same if the day had been some other day.

Unsoundness of this doctrine.

But the vice of a legal rule is best seen in its fruits.

In *Lyons v. Desotelle* (1877) [2] the plaintiff went on Sunday with horse and carriage to a camp-meeting. Upon reaching the ground he hitched his horse at the side of the road, where it was presently injured by defendant's buggy being backed into it. It was held that the plaintiff could not recover, although the collision may have been due to defendant's negligence. This decision clearly violates the principle of (b) above, which was correctly applied by the Massachusetts court itself in *Steele v. Burkhardt* (1870).[3]

McGrath v. Merwin (1873)[4] and *Banks v. Highland St. R. Co.* (1884)[5] are subject to the same criticism.[6]

[2] 124 Mass. 387.
[3] 104 Mass. 59.
[4] 112 Mass. 467.
[5] 136 Mass. 485.
[6] In Banks *v.* Highland St. R. Co. (1884), 136 Mass. 485, it appeared that the plaintiff as employee of a telegraph company was set to stringing its wires across a street. While engaged in climbing a telegraph pole with his back to the street and carrying a telegraph wire attached to his person, a street railway car came along and negligently, as was alleged, ran against the wire, dragging the plaintiff down and thereby causing injury. The telegraph company had not secured permission to put its wires over the street, and hence the plaintiff in stringing the wires was engaged in an illegal act. It was held that he could not recover.

Inconsistently with its own decisions, but correctly in point of principle, the Massachusetts court has

Chapter XII

Defense unavailable in cases of wilful or wanton injury.

The subject of contributory negligence and illegal conduct contributing to injury can be dismissed with the final observation that these defenses are available only where the plaintiff's action is founded upon negligence. Hence neither defense is effective where the damage complained of is wilfully or intentionally inflicted, or is inflicted under such circumstances as to evince a wanton disregard for the safety of the person or property of the plaintiff.[7]

held that a person traveling in violation of law on Sunday can recover damages for an injury received from a dog bite while on the way. White *v.* Lang (1880), 128 Mass. 598.

[7] Jones *v.* Alabama Mineral R. Co., 107 Ala. 400; Georgia Pac. R. Co. *v.* Lee, 92 Ala. 262; Terre Haute, etc., R. Co. *v.* Graham, 95 Ind. 287; Denman *v.* Johnston, 85 Mich. 387.

Contributory negligence is no defense to an action for assault and battery, Steinmetz *v.* Kelly, 72 Ind. 442; Ruter *v.* Foy, 46 Iowa 132; or for implied wilful homicide, Matthews *v.* Warner, 29 Gratt. (Va.) 570.

In Welch *v.* Wesson (1856), 6 Gray (Mass.) 505, two persons were trotting their horses in a sleigh race on a public highway, a thing which was contrary to law, when one of them wilfully ran down the sleigh of the other and broke it. It was held that the fact that the plaintiff was busy about an unlawful enterprise when his sleigh was damaged did not preclude a recovery by him.

Volume I

CHAPTER XIII

NEGLIGENCE (CONTINUED).

History of the Development of the Conception of Negligence.

IN the presentation of the theory of negligence which is found in the preceding pages, we have purposely refrained from touching, except incidentally, upon matters of pure legal history. The subject of negligence is so complicated and has to be approached from such different avenues, that an attempt at the same time to give an adequate idea of the historical steps in the solution of the conception of negligence would only add to difficulties which are great enough already. Another consideration which has been given weight is that the law of negligence is mainly of very modern growth. Its early history, so far as it has any, is exceedingly obscure. What we have to say on this matter can therefore be said better here than at the beginning of the topic.

Law of negligence entirely modern.

The early law of negligence must be collected from different quarters. No such title is found in the year books, nor in any of the digests prior to Comyns (1762–67).[1] For the most part the subject must be dug out of the law concerning the writs of trespass and trespass on the case.[2]

Historical genesis of the conception.

The law of negligence historically starts from the idea of failure in the performance of a determinate provable legal duty. The following cases will show how this idea was from

[1] Com. Dig., *Action on the Case for Negligence.*

[2] There was one situation where the law gave a more specific but now absolute writ, viz., *de reparatione facienda.* This writ lay primarily to enforce contribution among tenants in common or joint tenants for the repair of premises, like a mill, house, or bridge, which all were equally bound to maintain. Reg. Orig. Brev. 153*b*. Subsequently it was used in situations like that where one was entitled to use a bridge, and another, who was bound to maintain the bridge, neglected to do so. Fitz. Nat. Brev. 127, C – E.

time to time dealt with, in some of the few early cases which arose in the course of nearly four centuries. Here the reader will note the presence of a positive duty to act, in the nature of an assumptual obligation arising out of prescription.

The positive legal duty.

1. *Stapleton's Case* (1354):[3] The plaintiff sued out a writ of trespass against the defendant for damage done to plaintiff's premises by water breaking over, or through, a restraining wall or bank which the defendant was bound by custom to maintain. Objection was taken that no trespass was shown, but this was overruled, the idea being that the flooding of the land was a trespassory act although not directly done. The defendant then pleaded that the overflow was caused by a tempest which greatly increased the height of the river and caused it to break over. Upon this plea and upon a general denial of the alleged duty to maintain the wall, issue was joined.

Breach of duty to keep up restraining wall.

2. *Anonymous* (1388):[4] "If one who is bound to fence against my land fails to do so, whereby the beasts of his tenants enter my fields and do damage to me, I may have an action on the case."

Failure to keep up fence.

3. *Anonymous v. Abbot of Stratford* (1406):[5] A writ in case alleged a failure on the part of the defendant properly to maintain, as he was bound to do, a restraining wall on the bank of the Thames, whereby the lands of the plaintiff were flooded. The writ was held good. That liability was here conceived as being founded upon the negligent keeping of the wall, rather than upon the trespassory act of flooding the land (as in Stapleton's Case), is shown not only by the use of the action on the case instead of trespass, but by the further fact, which appeared in the writ, that the wall in question was in the county of Essex, while the flooded premises were in Middlesex. It was held that the writ was properly sued in Essex.

Negligent maintenance of wall.

4. *Popham v. Prior of Bremour* (1410):[6] The plaintiff alleged in a writ of trespass on the case that the defendant as owner of a mill was bound by prescription to keep in repair a certain bridge on the way leading to the mill, over which bridge the plaintiff and his tenants had a right to pass at will. The defendant, it was averred, allowed the bridge to become so dilapidated that it fell. No special damage was set forth other than the loss of the use of the bridge. It was held that the action would lie. One of the judges gave this illustration: "If a man is bound to keep open a ditch through which the water has a right to flow, and he fails to do so, whereby my meadow is surrounded, I shall have a writ of trespass [on the case]."

Failure to repair bridge.

[3] Y. B. 29 Edw. III., 32*b*.

[4] 1 Rolle Abr. 105, pl. 12

[5] Y. B. 7 Hen. IV. 8, pl. 10.

[6] Y. B. 11 Hen. IV. 82, pl. 28.

Volume I

Failure to maintain divine service.

5. *Broke v. Abbot of Wobirne* (1444):[7] The plaintiff sued out a writ of trespass on the case against the defendant, alleging a failure on the part of the latter to procure and maintain a chaplain to conduct divine service for the plaintiff and his servants in a certain chapel. The duty to furnish the chaplain was alleged to be founded on prescription and immemorial custom. The writ was abated for defect in pleading the prescription, but the action on the case was recognized as an appropriate remedy for such a neglect.

Negligent keeping of fence.

6. *Anonymous* (1674):[8] It appeared that the defendants as occupiers of certain land adjoining the plaintiff's were bound to maintain the fence, but having neglected to do so, the plaintiff's mare strayed through a gap, and falling into a ditch was drowned. Judgment for plaintiff.

7. *Star v. Rookesby* (1710):[9] The plaintiff declared that he was possessed of a close adjoining the defendant's, and that the tenants and occupiers of that close had time out of mind made and repaired the fence between the plaintiff's and defendant's close, and that for want of repair defendant's cattle came into the plaintiff's close and did damage. It was held in the King's Bench that either trespass or case lay: trespass, because the beasts came upon plaintiff's land; and case, because the first wrong was a non-feasance and neglect to repair, and that omission was the gist of the action.

Neglect in office.

Another line of authority illustrating the idea of breach of actual positive duty is found in cases wherein public officers have been held liable for a failure to perform acts within the line of their official duty; as, where a sheriff failed to return a writ,[1] or to execute a summons, whereby a party was put in default.[2] Here the reader will note the presence of a legal duty to act, in the nature of an assumptual obligation derived from the statute which creates and defines the office.

Implied duty arising from public calling.

Smith.

Proceeding from the provable legal duty, like that which arises by prescription or from statute, the law next gives recognition to what may be termed an implied duty arising out of public calling. Thus, the smith was formerly bound to shoe the horse of any who applied to him,[3] subject, no doubt, to the reasonable qualification universally applied in this class of cases, to the effect that the person requiring the

[7] Y. B. 22 Hen. VI. 46, pl. 36.

[8] 1 Vent. 264.

[9] 1 Salk. 335.

[1] Marsh *v.* Astrie, 1 Rolle Abr. 93, pl. 16.

[2] 1 Rolle. Abr. 105, pl. 11.

[3] Keilw. 50, pl. 4.

service shall offer to pay what is reasonably and legally due for the service. Likewise, the innkeeper was, and is yet, bound to supply food and lodging to any wayfarer who comes his way;[4] and the common victualer to sell food and drink to any who offer to buy.[5] So a carrier is bound to convey any goods which are offered to him for transportation provided he has convenience to carry the same.[6] And a common carrier of passengers for hire is bound to convey all persons who desire to be carried, provided their character and conduct are not such as to give good ground for objecting to them.[7]

Innkeeper.

Victualer.

Carrier.

As was once said by Lord Holt, "When a man takes upon himself a public employment he is bound to serve the public as far as his employment goes, or an action lies against him for refusing."[8] The duty seems to have been originally imposed in respect not only of the exclusive privileges which may have been enjoyed by these persons in the early period of the common law, but in respect as well of the hardship which would be caused to individual members of the community by reason of a failure to serve them.

Foundation of the duty.

In 1526 the following distinction was drawn: "When a smith declines to shoe my horse, or an innkeeper refuses to give me entertainment at his inn, I shall have an action on the case. . . . But where a carpenter makes a bargain to build me a house and does nothing, no action on the case [lies], because that sounds in covenant."[9] Why the smith and the innkeeper were subject to a legal duty to act, while the carpenter was only bound when he had made a binding contract, is a phenomenon which must be explained by reference to necessity and convenience; in other words, to the public policy of that period.[1]

Public policy.

[4] Brooke Abr., *Accion sur Case*, pl. 76. See White's Case, 2 Dyer 158*b*.

[5] Y. B. 39 Hen. VI. 18, pl. 24 (Moile, J.).

[6] Jackson *v.* Rogers, 2 Show. 327.

[7] Jencks *v.* Coleman, 2 Sumn. (U. S.) 221.

[8] Lane *v.* Cotton, 1 Salk. 18.

[9] Keilw. 50, pl. 4. The point in the reference to the carpenter is that the supposed "bargain" is not binding, being merely oral and not in proper form to make a valid covenant. The idea belongs to the the binding force of mutual promises.
period antedating the conception of

[1] See article Public Callings as a Solution of the Trust Problem, by

Volume I

For obvious reasons the situations in which the law imposes a positive duty to undertake and act are few in number. As a general rule, it is better to leave the initiatory of action to a man's own impulses. Hence the duty to undertake and act is limited to persons plying public callings, and the duty can only be imposed in respect of acts falling within the line of their business.[2]

Limits of the duty.

The next step in the development of the conception of negligence is found in the recognition of an implied duty on the part of a man who has undertaken to do a thing, to be careful how he does it. The advent of this implied duty to take care marks the beginning of the conception of negligence in its ordinary sense. And while we say its recognition follows after the stages already noted have occurred, this sequence is to be understood as referring to the matter of theory

The implied duty to take care.

Bruce Wyman, 17 Harv. L. Rev. 156 *et seq.* It has been held that the callings of dyers, pressers, and bleachers are not so far impressed with a public character but that persons engaged therein may impose conditions upon receiving goods, such, for instance, as that all goods shall be subject to a lien for general balance. Kirkman *v.* Shawcross, 6 T. R. 14.

[2] The following cases embody modern applications of the idea of positive duty as incident to the pursuit of a public calling or monopolistic business. In Shepard *v.* Milwaukee Gas Light Co. (1858), 6 Wis. 539, it appeared that the defendant gas company was a chartered corporation having an exclusive right to manufacture and sell gas for the purpose of lighting the city of Milwaukee. The plaintiff was a merchant doing business on a street along which the company's pipes were laid. He had fitted up his store with the necessary pipes, tubes, and burners, and other apparatus for lighting it with gas. It was held that the company was bound to supply him with gas at usual rates and without imposing unreasonable terms.

Weymouth *v.* Penobscot Log Driving Co. (1880), 71 Me. 29, was an action by a lumberman who had hauled his logs to various landings on a river down which the defendant company had legal authority to drive all logs. Notice was given of the presence of the logs, but the company, without sufficient reason, failed to move them, whereby the logs were kept from market that year and the plaintiff was damaged. It was held that inasmuch as the company had accepted the charter right of driving all logs down the stream, its privilege in that respect thereby became exclusive and it was legally bound to drive for all who required its service.

In Griffin *v.* Goldsboro Water Co. (1898), 122 N. Car. 206, it was held that a water company enjoying the franchise of supplying the inhabitants of a town with water is legally bound to supply all persons along the line of its mains at reasonable and uniform rates.

Chapter XIII

rather than to the actual sequence in time. This phase of legal development is illustrated in cases to the effect that a ferryman is liable who negligently overloads his boat and thereby causes the horse to be drowned which he undertakes to put over the river (1347);[3] that a surgeon is liable who unskilfully hurts the wounded arm which he is employed to heal (1371);[4] that a smith is liable who negligently lames the horse which he undertakes to shoe;[5] that a bailee is liable who negligently loses the horse which he has agreed to keep safely (1472);[6] that a servant is liable if he negligently suffers cattle to perish which are intrusted to his care;[7] and that a barber is liable who negligently uses a bad razor and injures the face which he has undertaken to shave.[8]

Illustrations.

The idea in these cases is that, by assuming to do something with or about another's property, or to do something with or to him, one comes under a legal obligation to do that act properly. This conception of liability for damage to person or property resulting from a negligent misfeasance in the performance of a contract, trust, or enterprise voluntarily assumed and prosecuted at the instance of another, has an unbroken succession in the common law from the earliest to the latest period.[9]

The negligent misfeasance.

[3] Y. B. 22 Ass. 94, pl. 41.

[4] Y. B. 48 Edw. III. 6, pl. 11.

[5] Y. B. 46 Edw. III. 19, pl. 19.

[6] Y. B. 12 Edw. IV. 13, pl. 10. This case was decided for the defendant on a plea of former judgment in detinue on the same cause of action, but no doubt was expressed as the sufficiency of the writ. Big. Cas. Torts 588.

[7] 1 Rolle Abr. 105.

[8] Ras. Ent. 2*b*. 1.

[9] Elsee *v.* Gatward, 5 T. R. 143; Gladwell *v.* Steggall, 5 Bing. N. Cas. 733, 35 E. C. L. 292; Pippin *v.* Sheppard, 11 Price 400; Coggs *v.* Bernard, 2 Ld. Raym. 909. See also Thorne *v.* Deas, 4 Johns. (N. Y.) 84.

In the early cases where the courts denied the right to recover for the nonfeasance of a simple parol promise, there are abundant dicta to the effect that negligent performance gives a right of action.

Brynchesley, J.: "And so it is; and, peradventure, if, in the writ, mention had been made that the thing [a mill] had been commenced and then by negligence nothing done, it had been otherwise." Watton *v.* Brinth, Y. B. 2 Hen. IV. 3, pl. 9. But this dictum is of course too broad. The true doctrine, as stated in 1410, was this: "*Norton:* Sir, if he had made my house badly and had spoilt my timber I should have had an action on the case well enough without deed." Tirwitt, J.: "I grant in that case; for then he should answer for the tort he had done, *quia negligenter fecit.* But when a man makes a simple prom-

Volume I

Limitations of the implied duty to use care.

Two limitations of this conception of implied duty to take care should be carefully noted. In the first place, it appears as a sort of parasitic obligation in connection with an actual contract or undertaking. It is evidently easier to import a fictitious term into an actual contract or undertaking than it is to create a positive obligation in the absence of any contract relation whatever. These cases give no recognition to the idea that a man is bound to use care in his own affairs and transactions in order that he may keep from doing hurt to other persons.[1]

The common calling.

In the second place, this implied duty to use care was apparently at first limited to persons plying a common calling, like that of ferryman, surgeon, farrier, or barber. Upon other persons the law hesitated to impose such an implied duty, and would do so only where an express promise on the part of such person to perform the undertaking in connection with which negligence was charged, was alleged in the writ. In a case from 1440, against one, not a common veterinarian, who doctored a horse so negligently and carelessly that the animal died, it was held that the defendant was not liable in the absence of an express promise on his part to effect a cure.[2]

ise (*conventio*) and will not perform it, how shall you have an action without specialty?" Y. B. 11 Hen. IV. 33, pl. 60. See also the language of Martin, J., in Y. B. 3 Hen. VI. 36, pl. 33, and argument of Newton in Y. B. 14 Hen. VI. 18, pl. 58: "If a carpenter agrees to build a good strong house in a certain form and makes me a defective and frail house of a different form from that agreed, I shall have an action on the case." Again, in Y. B. 11 Hen. VI. 55, pl. 26, it is said: "If one takes upon himself to build a good serviceable house and the house is lost through his default, the plaintiff shall have his action."

In 1441 Ascoghe, J., said: "If a carpenter promises to build a house and does not, I shall not have a writ of trespass, but only covenant if I have a specialty; but if he builds the house negligently, then I shall have an action of trespass on the case, for the misfeasance is the ground of my action." Y. B. 20 Hen. VI. 34, pl. 4.

[1] The circumstance that the theory of negligence, as embodied in the action on the case for negligence, was not sufficiently developed, in the period to which we refer, to fit the case of a man who was careless in his own affairs, is not to be taken as equivalent to the statement that a person so injured could not have relief. There was the action of trespass, in which liability for injuries so inflicted was very strict.

[2] Y. B. 19 Hen. VI. 49, pl. 5.

Common bailees, like carriers and innkeepers, were chargeable with negligence in the management of

Chapter XIII

Extension of the conception of liability for negligence.

At what particular epoch in legal history the conception of common-law liability for negligence was so extended as to make one liable, in an action on the case, for damage flowing from the negligent performance of his own projects and undertakings unconnected with duty arising from statute, public calling, bailment, or prescription, we cannot say with certainty; but it probably occurred in the latter part of the seventeenth century. The extension of doctrine was apparently so natural as not to attract attention.

Taking untrained horse into public park.

In *Mitchil v. Alestree* (1686)[3] full recognition was given to the broader notion. In that case it was alleged that the defendant brought a horse into Lincoln Inn's Field, a place where people were constantly going to and fro, for the purpose of breaking him. The horse became unruly and ran over the plaintiff. For the defendant it was urged that the mischief happened against his will, and no negligence in the actual management of the horse after he became unruly was shown. But he was held liable on the ground of being at fault (i. e., negligent) in bringing a wild horse to such a place.

Neglect of vault resulting in nuisance.

Tenant v. Goldwin (1704)[4] is worthy of notice. In an action on the case the plaintiff declared that his cellar had been damaged by filth percolating from a privy of the defendant through a wall on the defendant's premises which the latter had neglected to keep in proper repair. The action was sustained. Holt, C. J., observed that "every man ought to keep and use his own so as not to damnify his neighbor." Again, "it was the defendant's wall and the defendant's filth, and he was bound of common right to keep his wall so as his filth might not damnify his neighbor; and that it was a trespass on his neighbor, as if his beasts should escape or one should make a great heap on the border of his ground, and it should tumble and roll down upon his neighbor's. . . . He whose dirt it is must keep it that it may not trespass."

It will be noted that *Mitchil v. Alestree* and *Tenant v. Goldwin* involved wrongs belonging to the secondary trespass formation. Why do we not find a case in this period laying down the same broad doctrine in the field of trespass? For

the goods in their hands without any allegation of a promise. See 1 Rolle Abr. 2 (C), Action sur Case vers Carriers, pls. 1-4. Cross *v.* Andrews, Cro. Eliz. 622; Gelley *v.* Clerk, Cro. Jac. 189; Beedle *v.* Morris, Cro. Jac. 224. Other bailees were chargeable only by the words *super se assumpsit.* Keilw. 77, pl. 25.

[3] 1 Vent. 295, sub nom. Michael *v.* Alestree, 2 Lev. 172.

[4] 1 Salk. 360.

Volume I

Late appearance of conception of negligence in field of trespass.

instance, where a man was run over by the negligence of a rider in riding carelessly, why was it not said that he was liable because the law required riders to be reasonably careful? The simple explanation is that in such situations the injury was conceived as a pure trespass, and liability was not supposed to be founded upon negligence. This is shown by the fact that until about a hundred years ago the action of trespass was the exclusive remedy in all cases where damage was directly done in the immediate performance of any act, albeit the injury was due to negligence and was not intentionally done.[5]

Action on the case for negligent injury directly done.

A change occurred soon after the beginning of the nineteenth century, when it was held that an action on the case founded on negligence would lie in such a situation, though trespass could also still be used if the plaintiff preferred.[6] This first gave recognition to negligence as a basis of liability in the field of trespass.

We have elsewhere seen how, under the old trespass régime, the law so overshot the conception of negligence as to make a man liable for injuries directly and immediately done, even though he was not in any way to blame; and by reference to what has been said in that connection, the reader will perceive that the supersession of that old idea was begun in the very period when the courts began to recognize negligence as a basis of liability in the field of trespass. The coincidence is suggestive.

By the successive steps which have been noted above, the conception of negligence was brought into its proper relations as an element of legal wrong in both trespass formations. The subsequent development of the subject has been indicated with sufficient fulness in the preceding chapters on negligence, and we accordingly here bring these remarks on the historical aspects of the matter to a close.

[5] Day *v.* Edwards (1794), 5 T. R. 648; Leame *v.* Bray (1803), 3 East 593; Taylor *v.* Rainbow (1808), 2 Hen. & M. (Va.) 423.

[6] Moreton *v.* Hardern (1825), 4 B. & C. 223, 10 E. C. L. 316; Williams *v.* Holland (1833), 10 Bing. 112, 25 E. C. L. 50. See also Claflin *v.* Wilcox, 18 Vt. 605.

CHAPTER XIV

COGNATE NUISANCE.

Chapter XIV

Place of nuisance in legal theory.

NUISANCE and its cognates, which form the subject-matter of this and the succeeding chapter, comprise a sort of tertiary trespass formation, being neither more nor less than an extension of the idea of trespass into the field of easements, servitudes, and rights appurtenant to realty. In the cognate nuisances which are treated in the present chapter the affinity to trespass upon realty is seen to be close. As we pursue our investigations the kinship is seen to fade. The cognate nuisances occupy a place in legal theory just midway between the violent trespass upon realty and nuisance proper.

The cognate nuisance.

Interference with Subjacent Support.

Any interference with subjacent soil is as much a trespass against the proprietor of the fee as if the act were done at or above the surface, since the title to realty includes the underlying soil indefinitely towards the centre of the earth.[1] But it not infrequently happens that one man has the right to dig under the soil of another, as where he has a license or a prescriptive right to take minerals, owns the subjacent strata in fee,[2] or has a leasehold interest in the same.[3] Where this happens the question of the liability of such person for damage done to the tenements above often arises. The principle here applied is that, in the absence of a binding contract, the land above has a natural right to be supported by the soil below.[4]

Right of support.

[1] See Rowbotham *v.* Wilson, 8 H. L. Cas. 348.

[2] For a statement of the distinction between ownership of subjacent strata and the prescriptive right to mine, see Wilkinson *v.* Proud, 11 M. & W. 33.

[3] Humphries *v.* Brogden, 12 Q. B. 739, 64 E. C. L. 739.

[4] Humphries *v.* Brogden, 12 Q.

Volume I

Such a situation as that here contemplated presupposes a past point of time when the entire and unqualified fee was vested in one and the same person; and when such estate was severed by a grant conveying the right to mine and reserving the surface, or granting the surface and reserving the right to mine, it must be supposed that the parties contemplated that, in the absence of express agreement, the land above should continue to be supported in its natural state by the underlying soil.[5] This right is not a mere easement held by a distinct title, it is an incident to the land itself, *sine quo res ipsa haberi non potest.*[6] Unless the right to subjacent support is qualified or taken away by contract, the person operating below is bound to answer for all damage that happens above by reason of a collapse of the soil. He is substantially an insurer against harm, and it is not necessary that he should be guilty of negligence.[7]

Theory of the right.

Extent of the right.

The right of support is not limited to what might appear to be reasonable support. "We cannot," said Lord Campbell, in *Humphries v. Brogden* (1850),[8] "measure out degrees to which the right may extend, and the only reasonable support is that which will protect the surface from subsidence and keep it securely at its ancient and natural level." The right of subjacent support, accordingly, extends not only to the land itself, but to the structures which the owner had placed on it prior to the time when the title of the subjacent proprietor began and possession was taken;[9] and also doubt-

Support of artificial structures.

B. 739, 64 E. C. L. 739; Harris *v.* Ryding, 5 M. & W. 60; Erickson *v.* Michigan Land, etc., Co., 50 Mich. 604; Coleman *v.* Chadwick, 80 Pa. St. 81; Horner *v.* Watson, 79 Pa. St. 251; Lord *v.* Carbon Iron Mfg. Co., 42 N. J. Eq. 157.

[5] Rowbotham *v.* Wilson, 8 H. L. Cas. 348; Scranton *v.* Phillips, 94 Pa. St. 15.

[6] Lord Selborne, in Dalton *v.* Angus, 6 App. Cas. 791.

[7] Pringle *v.* Vesta Coal Co., 172 Pa. St. 438; Haines *v.* Roberts, 7 El. & Bl. 625, 9 E. C. L., 625; Stroyan *v.* Knowles, 6 H. & N. 454.

But there are cases in which interference with subjacent support is discussed as if liability were predicated on negligence. Livingston *v.* Moingona Coal Co., 49 Iowa 369. Of course, if the miner be negligent, *cadit quæstio,* he is liable; but this is unnecessary.

[8] 12 Q. B. 739, 64 E. C. L. 739.

[9] Richards *v.* Jenkins, 18 L. T. N. S. 437.

Chapter XIV

less to such buildings as he may, in the proper use of the property, see fit to place upon it thereafter.[1]

Superior tenement.

The right to subjacent support in the case of tenements above ground is identical in principle with the right to have support from subjacent soil. The occupant of a flat below has no right to do any act which would impair the support of his neighbor overhead. This doctrine seems to be familiar enough to Scottish law,[2] and it would undoubtedly be applied in a proper case by common-law courts also. The right in question is absolutely necessary for any enjoyment whatever of the superior tenement.

Interference with Lateral Support.

Right to lateral support.

The right to lateral support from adjacent soil is not so absolute and unconditional as the right to support from underlying soil just considered, but it is an analogous right, and both have their origin in similar considerations of necessity and propriety.[3] In both situations the duty to refrain from interfering with support which is imposed on one proprietor for the benefit of the other illustrates the application of the maxim, *sic utere tuo ut alienum non lædas.*[4]

This difference in the point of view from which these torts are considered is to be noted. The man who is found digging under another's surface is *prima facie* a trespasser, and can

[1] See Rogers *v.* Taylor, 2 H. & N. 828; Humphries *v.* Brogden, 12 Q. B. 739, 64 E. C. L. 739; Harris *v.* Ryding, 5 M. & W. 60. The dicta in Brown *v.* Robins, 4 H. & N. 186, and Stroyan *v.* Knowles, 6 H. & N. 454, to the effect that if the weight of the house contributes to its subsidence the subjacent proprietor is not liable for damage done to the house, refer to lateral and not to subjacent support.

[2] Caledonian R. Co. *v.* Sprot, 2 Macq. H. L. 449. See Humphries *v.* Brogden, 12 Q. B. 756, 64 E. C. L. 756.

[3] Dalton *v.* Angus, 6 App. Cas. 740, 791.

[4] But this maxim it must be remembered, like many others of its kind, is merely a sort of mnemonic. As a statement of principle it is a question-begging phrase like *ubi jus ibi remedium;* for the injunction against the doing of harm (*non lædas*) must be taken to refer to that which is harmful or injurious in the eye of the law. Consequently one can never tell what situations such a maxim applies to until the category of legal harms has been first exhausted. Such a maxim can be of no assistance in determining the primary question of liability.

Volume I

only justify himself by virtue of some grant, conveyance, or prescription.[5] The man who digs in his own soil is *prima facie* privileged and can be held liable for damage thereby done to another only under conditions which are defined by law. Reference to this distinction admonishes the reader that he is now approaching a field where the strict theory of absolute liability for damage done by force is no longer applied.

The right to lateral support from adjacent soil extends only to land in its natural state, and not to the houses or other artificial structures that may be built upon it.[6] The theoretical result of this principle is that if my neighbor digs on his soil, and my *land* in consequence gives way, he is liable for the damage; but if he digs and my *house* tumbles in, he is not liable for the damage done to it unless I had by some means acquired a distinct easement of support for such house, or unless he digs negligently. But in practice, as we shall presently see, diversity of opinion exists in regard to liability for the damage done under such circumstances to the house.

Distinction between land and artificial structures.

The right to lateral support for land is not dependent upon the accident of contiguous ownership, and consequently it could in a proper case certainly be enforced against a neighboring proprietor, although the land that is burdened with the support may be separated from the land entitled to support by an intervening strip belonging to a third person. But it has been held that where the intervening proprietor has already done some act, such as the taking out of a seam of coal, which, though doing no immediate damage, yet leaves the property in jeopardy, an injunction against the operations of the remoter owner will not be granted, although if he were to proceed damage would be caused to the complainant's land by virtue of the previous operations of the intervening owner.[7] This is an illustration of the doctrine that the right of lateral support is a right to have support in the very state in which the land has been placed by nature. In the case cited the

Lateral support not limited to contiguous premises.

[5] See Rowbotham *v.* Wilson, 8 H. L. Cas. 348.

[6] Moody *v.* McClelland, 39 Ala. 45; Thurston *v.* Hancock (1815), 12 Mass. 220.

[7] Birmingham *v.* Allen, 6 Ch. D. 284.

threatened damage would be attributable to the operations of the owner of the intervening strip and not to the act of the remoter proprietor.

Right to support a property right.

The right to lateral support of land in its natural state, like the right to subjacent support, is, properly speaking, a property right and not a mere right of easement.[8] So far as the lateral support of soil is concerned, such support has obviously been afforded since the foundation of the world. Still the right of support is not infrequently spoken of as a right of easement, and the distinction is more a distinction of words than of substance.[9]

Right of support for houses,

The right to the lateral support of buildings or other artificial structures is clearly in the nature of an easement, and must be acquired by grant or prescription.[1] *Dalton v. Angus* (1881)[2] contains the fullest discussion of the English law in regard to the acquisition of the right to lateral support for houses by lapse of time. It was there held that after twenty years' uninterrupted enjoyment such right is acquired for a building proved to have been newly built or altered so as to increase the lateral pressure at the beginning of that time, provided the enjoyment of the right of support is sufficiently open that it must be known that some support is being enjoyed by the building.

acquired by lapse of time.

Not a true prescriptive right.

The doctrine that an easement for lateral support of buildings can be acquired by lapse of twenty years is undoubtedly highly artificial. It is usually spoken of as a prescriptive right, but as such it is anomalous.[3] The most that can be

[8] McGuire *v.* Grant, 25 N. J. L. 356; Stevenson *v.* Wallace, 27 Gratt. (Va.) 77.

[9] Lord Blackburn, in Dalton *v.* Angus, 6 App. Cas. 808.

[1] Lord Selborne, in Dalton *v.* Angus, 6 App. Cas. 703.

[2] 6 App. Cas. 740. See also Hide *v.* Thornborough, 2 C. & K. 250, 61 E. C. L. 250; Partridge *v.* Scott, 3 M. & W. 220; Wyatt *v.* Harrison, 3 B. & Ad. 871; 23 E. C. L. 205.

[3] To acquire an easement by prescription it is essential that the user be open and adverse and with the acquiescence of the owner of the servient tenement. In the case of lateral support, there is nothing from which the acquiescence of the adjoining owner can properly be inferred. The builder of the house does not encroach upon his soil and there is nothing of which he could complain. He might, it is true, prevent the acquisition of the right by excavating in his own soil before the twenty years elapses, but to require this is unreasonable. See Tunstall *v.* Christian, 80 Va. 1;

Volume I

said is that the rule is a positive rule of law established in England by the decisions of her courts. The right is analogous to that there recognized in favor of ancient light.

American doctrine.

In America the doctrine that an easement of support can be acquired for buildings by prescription is not accepted,[4] though there are many dicta to the contrary. The exclusive means by which a permanent right of lateral support for buildings may be acquired in this country is by grant or covenant running with the land.

Liability for negligent interference with support.

The rule that buildings are not entitled to lateral support unless such right has been acquired in some way is to be taken with the qualification that if a person tears down his own buildings or excavates his own soil in a negligent manner, and the fall of a house on premises near by is the result of such negligence, he is liable,[5] without regard to the question whether an easement of support for such building has already been acquired or not. The same is true where the person excavating or removing a structure has no right to be doing that thing. The trespasser on the premises of A is liable to an adjacent proprietor for all the damage which his acts entail upon the latter, both as regards lands and buildings; and this without regard to any easement of support which the latter may have acquired.[6]

Trespassory interference.

The rule that land is naturally entitled to lateral support, but that superincumbent buildings are not, is simple enough

also title *Support,* 12 Encyc. Laws Eng. 42.

[4] Sullivan *v.* Zeiner, 98 Cal. 346; Mitchell *v.* Rome, 49 Ga. 19; Handlan *v.* McManus, 42 Mo. App. 551, 100 Mo. 124; Tunstall *v.* Christian, 80 Va. 1.

[5] Dodd *v.* Holme, 1 Ad. & El. 493, 28 E. C. L. 128; Myer *v.* Hobbs, 57 Ala. 175; Gilmore *v.* Driscoll, 122 Mass. 199.

[6] Jeffries *v.* Williams, 5 Exch. 792; Bibby *v.* Carter, 4 H. & N. 153.

It should be further noted, for its analogy to other situations hereafter to be considered, rather than for its importance here, that there is authority to the effect that a malicious intent to damage the building of an adjacent proprietor is sufficient, when coupled with actual damage, to give a cause of action against one who excavates in his own soil under circumstances privileged but for the existence of such malice. Quincy *v.* Jones, 76 Ill. 231; McGuire *v.* Grant, 25 N. J. L. 356.

These dicta go on the assumption, doubtless justified, that a malicious intent to damage coupled with subsequent actual damage is sufficient proof of negligence in fact.

in its statement, but the practical application of it in situations where an interference with foundations causes a house to fall is not easy. The difficulty arises in connection with the question of the damages to be recovered. In some jurisdictions the very simple rule is adopted that the owner may recover for the diminution in the value of the land considered by itself, but not for the destruction or diminution in the value of the house.[7]

Rule as to recoverable damages adopted in Massachusetts.

But this is too mathematical and arbitrary, and is clearly inconsistent with the principle elsewhere universally applied in the law of torts, that a man who does a wrongful act is liable for all its natural and probable consequences. If the owner of adjacent premises who has no right to interfere with the lateral support of my land, nevertheless does this unlawful thing, why should he not be held liable for the damage? Other wrongdoers are held for consequential damages. Why should it not be so in the present case? Consideration of this circumstance has led the English and some of the American courts to the conclusion different from that reached in Massachusetts, and in this view if the act of interference with lateral support is the cause of the giving way of the foundation and the structure is thereby injured, full damages may be recovered. This goes on the very sound theory that if the wrongful act of interference had not been done, no part of the damage would have happened.[8]

English rule.

In applying this rule it must be shown that the damage to the building did not result either from its own inherent defects or from its own weight. In other words, the interference with the lateral support must be such as to cause the subsidence of the foundation soil without regard to the superincumbent weight. If this rule were not adopted the fundamental distinction between lands and houses as to the right of lateral support would be subverted. The necessity of adopting this particular qualification greatly impairs the prac-

Difficulty of applying English doctrine.

[7] Thurston *v.* Hancock, 12 Mass. 220; Gilmore *v.* Driscoll, 122 Mass. 199.

[8] Stroyan *v.* Knowles, 6 H. & N. 454; Brown *v.* Robins, 4 H. & N. 186; Busby *v.* Holthaus, 46 Mo. 161.

Volume I

tical value of the English rule, though it is otherwise unquestionably sound. To determine whether in a particular instance the foundation would have sunk in the absence of the superincumbent weight often involves guesswork. But the determination of this question, like many others too subtle for learned judges, has been conveniently put upon the broad shoulders of the jury.[9]

Obstruction and Diversion of Waters.

General principle.

The general doctrine of the law concerning the obstruction and diversion of water may be stated as follows: The proprietor of land through or by which water flows in a defined and natural channel has a right to insist that such water shall continue to flow naturally and without substantial diminution in quantity. This right can be asserted against a proprietor above who diverts the water from its natural course or obstructs it by a dam or other contrivance so as to make the flow intermittent and irregular; and likewise against the proprietor below who prevents the water from flowing off in the ordinary manner.[1]

Limits of the doctrine.

The right just defined cannot exist, except of course by contract, in waters which flow in an artificial channel.[2] Similarly surface water, which is found casually upon land and which flows in no definite course, is not a subject of riparian right. The owner of land has an unqualified right to handle such water by drainage or otherwise as he sees fit, and a neighboring proprietor cannot complain that he is thereby deprived of water which would have come upon his land.[3]

Percolating waters.

The same is true of percolating underground waters, a subject concerning which the law was fully considered by the House of Lords in *Chasemore v. Richards* (1859).[4] It was

[9] See Watson, B., in Brown *v.* Robins, 4 H. & N. 186.

[1] Mason *v.* Hill, 5 B. & Ad. 1; 27 E. C. L. 11; Roberts *v.* Gwyrfai Dist. Council (1899), 2 Ch. 608; Miner *v.* Gilmour, 12 Moo. P. C. 131; Elliot *v.* Fitchburg R. Co., 10 Cush. Mass. 191.

[2] Wood *v.* Waud, 3 Exch. 748.

[3] Rawstron *v.* Taylor, 11 Exch. 369.

[4] 7 H. L. Cas. 349, 5 H. & N. 982. See also Acton *v.* Blundell, 12 M. & W. 324; Bradford *v.* Pickles, (1895) A. C. 587.

there held that no action lies against one who sinks a well on his own premises and thereby diminishes the supply of neighboring proprietors, although he draws up more than is needed for his own use. But where the underground percolating waters flow in a defined channel the general principle applies, and one cannot abstract or divert such waters to the injury of another who is entitled to the use of the underground stream. In order to vindicate the right to underground waters which flow in a defined channel it is not necessary that the channel should be known in the sense of having been exactly ascertained by discovery prior to the abstraction. But there must be indications from which existence of a defined channel can be inferred by the jury.[5]

Nature of the riparian right.

The riparian right, like the right of support for land, is a natural incident of the possession of the riparian property. In the absence of a reservation it passes with the land without express grant, and is itself in the nature of a substantive property right.[6] It is not a mere easement.[7] It is not necessary in order to assert the right, that one should own the fee of the watercourse. It is enough if his land is washed by the stream. Lateral contact is as good as vertical.[8]

Owner of spring.

So far as the common-law riparian water right of the lower proprietor is concerned, no distinction appears to be made in favor of a higher proprietor on whose land the water originates. In other words, the owner of a spring can no more use or divert the water to the unreasonable exclusion of the owner below, than can any other riparian proprietor.[9]

The water right above defined is secured by law to every owner of land through or along which a natural watercourse flows, not for æsthetic reasons, but for practical purposes and in order that each may get such good from the water as this

[5] Black *v.* Ballymena Com'rs (1886), 17 L. R. Ir. 459.

[6] Yates *v.* Milwaukee, 10 Wall. (U. S.) 497. Compare Watuppa Reservoir Co. *v.* Fall River, 147 Mass. 548.

[7] Pine *v.* New York, 103 Fed. Rep. 337; 112 Fed. Rep. 98, 50 C. C. A. 145.

[8] Lyon *v.* Fishmongers' Co., 1 App. Cas. 682.

[9] Wadsworth *v.* Tillotson, 15 Conn. 366; Gillett *v.* Johnson, 30 Conn. 180.

Volume I

Basis of the riparian right.

beneficial gift of Providence is intended to subserve. The water of a running stream is said to be *publici juris,* and when a controversy arises between two riparian proprietors the law seems to regard the water as if it belonged in equity to both of them,[1] each being entitled to use it properly, but not ordinarily to the exclusion of the other. "The right to the reasonable and beneficial use of a running stream is common to all the riparian proprietors, and so each is bound so to use his common right as not essentially to prevent or interfere with an equally beneficial enjoyment of the common right by all the proprietors."[2] From this it follows that no man can complain of the reasonable use and consumption of flowing water by one higher up on the stream than himself.[3] But he may if the use is unreasonable.[4]

Common property in running water.

All entitled to reasonable use.

What constitutes a reasonable use of water is a question to be determined upon the facts of each particular case. "To take a quantity of water from a large running stream for agricultural or manufacturing purposes would cause no sensible or practicable diminution of the benefit to the prejudice of a lower proprietor; whereas, taking the same quantity from a small running brook passing through many farms would be of great and manifest injury to those below, who need it for domestic supply or watering cattle; and therefore it would be an unreasonable use of the water, and an action would lie in the latter case and not in the former. It is therefore, to a considerable extent, a question of degree; still, the rule is the same, that each proprietor has a right to a reasonable use of it, for his own benefit, for domestic use, and for manufacturing and agricultural purposes."[5]

What is reasonable use?

To be determined on facts of each case.

The relative situation of the respective parties and the damage done to the lower must always be considered in determining whether the use to which the higher proprietor has put

[1] Pennsylvania R. Co. *v.* Miller, 112 Pa. St. 34.

[2] Elliot *v.* Fitchburg R. Co., 10 Cush. (Mass.) 191.

[3] Springfield *v.* Harris, 4 Allen (Mass.) 494; Messinger's Appeal, 109 Pa. St. 285; Kensit *v.* Great Eastern R. Co., 27 Ch. D. 122; Davis *v.* Getchell, 50 Me. 602.

[4] Swindon Waterworks Co. *v.* Wilts, etc., Canal Nav. Co., L. R. 7 H. L. 697.

[5] Shaw, C. J., in Elliot *v.* Fitchburg R. Co., 10 Cush. (Mass.) 191.

Chapter XIV

the water is a reasonable use. A particular use may often appear to be reasonable when viewed from the standpoint of the business followed by the person using the water, which, if viewed from the standpoint of the lower proprietor, will appear to be entirely unreasonable. "The necessities of one man's business cannot be the standard of another's rights in a thing which belongs to both."[6]

Domestic and barn-yard use.

The consumption of water for domestic purposes and for watering such stock as is kept on the premises is unquestionably a reasonable use, and a lower proprietor cannot complain though the amount of the water should thereby be reduced below his own similar needs. On the other hand, one who needs water for such a purpose below could enforce the right against a superior proprietor who might wish to use the water for purely business purposes.[7] It is correct to say that one riparian proprietor has an absolute right to take running water for domestic purposes and a qualified right to consume for manufacturing and agricultural purposes. It has sometimes been made a question whether a riparian proprietor can divert water for purposes of irrigation. But it is settled that within reasonable limits he may.[8]

Manufacturing uses.

Irrigation.

Right of appropriation.

In many of the Western States, by customs which have their origin in peculiar local conditions and which have been sanctioned by statute, a person who first acquires water rights may appropriate for mining and irrigating purposes to the exclusion of other riparian owners either above or below.[9]

Contract rights in water.

The common-law right to flowing water may, as between particular proprietors, be increased or diminished by grant or reservation in a deed,[1] or by special contract or covenant. A parol agreement operates as a mere license, since no easement

[6] Wheatley *v.* Chrisman, 24 Pa. St. 298.

[7] Miner *v.* Gilmour, 12 Moo. P. C. 131; Gillett *v.* Johnson, 30 Conn. 180; Pennsylvania R. Co. *v.* Miller, 112 Pa. St. 34.

[8] Embrey *v.* Owen, 6 Exch. 353; Elliot *v.* Fitchburg R. Co., 10 Cush. (Mass.) 191.

[9] Atchison *v.* Peterson, 20 Wall. (U. S.) 507; Irwin *v.* Phillips, 5 Cal. 146; Hill *v.* King, 8 Cal. 337; Schilling *v.* Rominger, 4 Colo. 100.

[1] Goodrich *v.* Burbank, 12 Allen (Mass.) 459; Burr *v.* Mills, 21 Wend. (N. Y.) 290.

Volume I

or permanent right in land can be acquired otherwise than by deed.[2]

Prescription.

Likewise, a more extensive right than that given by law may be acquired by prescription. Hence if one proprietor, in making a particular use of water, causes it to flow back upon land above, or withholds it from flowing in its accustomed volume, or diverts it from its usual channel without resistance or opposition from the proprietor below, a grant for such use will be presumed at the end of the period of prescription.[3]

Pollution of Waters.

The common-law doctrine as to riparian water rights necessarily involves the principle that one proprietor cannot pollute the stream so as to make it unfit for the use of another below. The latter is entitled to have the flow continue substantially unaffected in quality as well as undiminished in quantity.[4]

Pollution from reasonable use.

The doctrine of reasonable use applies here as well as in cases of obstruction and diversion. Not every impurity imparted to water will give a right of action to the lower owner.[5]

[2] Stevens *v.* Stevens, 11 Met. (Mass.) 251.

[3] Bealey *v.* Shaw, 6 East 208.

The period of prescription differs in different jurisdictions. In England, and in New York, Massachusetts, and other states, the period is twenty years. Campbell *v.* Talbot, 132 Mass. 174; Belknap *v.* Trimble, 3 Paige (N. Y.) 577. In Pennsylvania and Ohio, twenty-one years. Strickler *v.* Todd, 10 S. & R. (Pa.) 63; Messinger's Appeal, 109 Pa. St. 285; Tootle *v.* Clifton, 22 Ohio St. 247. In some states the period has been made shorter by statute. Alta Land, etc., Co. *v.* Hancock, 85 Cal. 219 (five years).

[4] Aldred's Case, 9 Coke 59*a;* Clowes *v.* Staffordshire Potteries Waterworks Co., L. R. 8 Ch. 125; Goldsmid *v.* Tunbridge Wells Imp. Com'rs, L. R. 1 Ch. 349; Wood *v.* Waud, 3 Exch. 748; Norton *v.* Scholefield, 9 M. & W. 665; Holsman *v.* Boiling Spring Bleaching Co., 14 N. J. Eq. 335.

[5] Atty.-Gen. *v.* Gee, L. R. 10 Eq. 131; Hayes *v.* Waldron, 44 N. H. 580; Baltimore *v.* Warren Mfg. Co., 59 Md. 96.

This qualification of the right to have a flowing stream uncontaminated in quality is most freely applied in cases where the stream in question is available for mining and manufacturing purposes. Here the private right is sometimes made to yield in a measurable degree to considerations of public welfare, provided it be shown that the contamination complained of is a necessary incident to the proper conduct of a lawful enterprise. See Pennsylvania Coal Co. *v.* Sanderson, 113 Pa. St. 126. In this

Chapter XIV

The deposit of dyestuffs in a stream, whereby it is discolored;[6] the emptying of offensive matter from a tanyard;[7] and the discharge of poisonous and corrosive substances,[8] will not be tolerated unless it be shown that the stream was already polluted, in which event the pollution would perhaps be an instance of *damnum absque injuria*.[9] A man may have a right to use water on his own land, but he must so dispose of the corrupted water as not to injure his neighbor.[1] If filth is created on a man's premises, then, in the quaint language of Holt, C. J., "he whose dirt it is must keep it that it may not trespass."[2] A right to contaminate water in the prosecution of industry, like the right to divert it, can be acquired by grant or prescription unless the pollution is such as to constitute a public nuisance.[3]

Dyestuffs.

Tanyard.

Poisonous substances.

Grant and prescription.

Ballard v. Tomlinson (1885)[4] raised the question of liability for the pollution of underground waters. The defendant had sunk a well on his premises, but he afterwards quit the use of it as such, and turned his sewage through drainage pipes into the abandoned well. The sewage thus collected percolated through the underground strata and spoiled the plaintiff's well, which was near by. It was held in the Court of Appeal that an action would lie, for the reason that the use to which the well was being put was not its natural and proper use. "Though a man may suck dry the stratum which is a common sponge for himself and his neighbors, he is not entitled to poison the sponge."[5]

Pollution of underground waters.

state the law at this point is exceptionally favorable to the prosecution of industrial enterprises. Compare Tennessee Coal, etc., Co. *v.* Hamilton, 100 Ala. 252, which lays down a stricter, and doubtless the generally prevailing, doctrine.

[6] Crossley *v.* Lightowler, L. R. 2 Ch. 478; Holsman *v.* Boiling Spring Bleaching Co., 14 N. J. Eq. 335.

[7] Moore *v.* Webb, 1 C. B. N. S. 673, 87 E. C. L. 673.

[8] Pennington *v.* Brinsop Hall Coal Co., 5 Ch. D. 769.

[9] See opinion of Fry, J., in the case just cited.

[1] Blackburn, J., in Hodgkinson *v.* Ennor, 4 B. & S. 241, 116 E. C. L. 241.

[2] Tenant *v.* Goldwin, as reported in 1 Salk. 360, 2 Ld. Raym. 1089.

[3] Brookline *v.* Mackintosh, 133 Mass. 215; Kelley *v.* New York (Supm. Ct. Spec. T.), 6 Misc. (N. Y.) 516.

[4] 29 Ch. D. 115.

[5] See 1 Eng. Rul. Cas. 271 (note by Robert Campbell on the case of Ballard *v.* Tomlinson, 29 Ch. D. 115). Compare Hodgkinson *v.* Ennor, 4 B. & S. 241, 116 E. C. L. 241.

Volume I

Gist of interference with water rights.

In conclusion it may be observed that the element on which liability is based in infringement of water rights is the abstraction or diversion of the water in sufficient amount sensibly to affect its volume, or such contamination as appreciably affects its quality. Where this exists a cause of action arises without regard to the presence of special pecuniary or material damage.[6] The absence of appreciable damage to a lower proprietor is always strongly persuasive that there has been no improper use of the water by the owner above.[7] Thus, it has been held that there is no violation of a complainant's right where a non-riparian proprietor, with the consent of a riparian owner, takes water from a river, which, after being used, is returned to the stream unimpaired.[8] On the other hand, the fact that much loss is entailed upon the lower proprietor will be strongly persuasive that the use by the person above is improper. But the true criterion of liability in each case is to be found in the nature of the act itself under all the circumstances, and not in the material damage which it may or may not occasion.[9]

Special damage not essential.

Damage relevant on question of reasonable use.

Interference with Air.

Pursuing our inquiries in the field of tort which belongs to the fringes of property rather than property itself, we are led next to consider the obstruction and pollution of air and interference with light. Air and light, by loose English usage, have often been coupled together in pleadings upon causes of action arising out of interference with ancient light, but the law pertaining to air is quite different from that pertaining to light.[1]

Right to ventilation.

In regard to air it is established that though this substance in its free state cannot be the subject of exclusive ownership, it is nevertheless possible for the owner of a building to ac-

[6] Crooker *v.* Bragg, 10 Wend. (N. Y.) 260 (case of diversion); Wheatley *v.* Chrisman, 24 Pa. St. 298 (a case of pollution).

[7] Seeley *v.* Brush, 35 Conn. 419; Chatfield *v.* Wilson, 31 Vt. 358.

[8] Kensit *v.* Great Eastern R. Co. (1884), 27 Ch. D. 122.

[9] Gerrish *v.* New Market Mfg. Co., 30 N. H. 478.

[1] See observation of Lord Selborne in London Brewery Co. *v.* Tennant, L. R. 9 Ch. 220, 221.

Chapter XIV

quire by grant or prescription a right to have such building ventilated by the passage of air to or from it in a certain defined channel. In *Bass v. Gregory* (1890)[2] it appeared that for more than forty years a certain cellar had been ventilated through an artificial channel which terminated in the shaft of a well upon adjoining premises. The circumstances were such that the owner of the well and his predecessors must have known of the arrangement. It was held that the presumption of a grant would arise from lapse of time and that after such presumption had arisen the well could not be closed up. This was clearly a proper case for raising a presumption of grant, for the user was such that the owner of the well might, at any time before the presumption arose, have put an end to the user by stopping the vent.

Grant presumed from lapse of time.

Properly speaking, this is a case of the acquisition of an easement for the maintenance of a ventilating flue rather than the vindication of a right to air. That such is the true basis of the holding appears from decisions to the effect that a right to the access of air cannot thus arise if there is no building to which the right is appurtenant and no defined channel through which the air is derived. A windmill cannot acquire an exclusive right to the breezes of heaven.[3] Nor can one complain of the erection of a structure which causes his chimney to smoke.[4] And it is not a legal wrong to cut off the air from an open timber yard by the erection of a building on one's own land.[5]

Free air.

[2] 25 Q. B. D. 481.

[3] Webb *v.* Bird, 13 C. B. N. S. 841, 106 E. C. L. 841.

[4] Bryant *v.* Lefever, 4 C. P. D. 172.

[5] Harris *v.* De Pinna, 33 Ch. D. 238.

Bowen, L. J., gave this reason: "The passage of undefined air gives rise to no rights for the best of all reasons, the reason of common sense, because you cannot acquire any rights against others by a user which they cannot interrupt." Harris *v.* De Pinna, 33 Ch. D. 262. The meaning of this is that before one can acquire a prescriptive right by adverse user the user must itself be an infringement of a legal right of the person against whom the prescription is to be asserted. In other words, the adverse user must give rise to a right of action in favor of the person against whom the user is to become operative. This reasoning, it will be observed, is equally fatal to the acquisition of a right to light by prescription, and, in fact, it demonstrates the anomalous character of the English doctrine of light.

Volume I

Pollution of air.

In regard to pollution of air it is established that wherever the pollution is such as to amount to a nuisance, an action lies. In the early leading case on this subject it was held that the maintenance of a pigsty so near the dwelling of another as to befoul the air entering therein is an actionable wrong.[6] The same is true where a limekiln is built so near a house that the smoke enters and renders the place uninhabitable;[7] so where the smoke, stench, and unwholesome vapors of a brewery have the same effect.[8]

Interference with Light.

English law of light peculiar.

The law of air as laid down in the English cases which have been cited above is not in any way peculiar, and the principles stated are, we apprehend, accepted in all common-law jurisdictions. The English law concerning light, or air considered as a vehicle of light, is however highly eccentric.

Loss of prospect not actionable.

On general principle the act of building on one's own premises is a lawful act, and no cause of action can accrue to a neighbor whose prospect is taken away or whose windows are thereby darkened. In one of the first attempts ever made in a court of common law to maintain an action for the disturbance of light by the erection of a high building on adjoining premises, the plaintiff signally failed. The defendant's counsel asserted with a confidence which was justified by the result, that "of common right it is permitted that every man should build his own house on his own land as high as he pleases."[9]

Stoppage of light.

There can be no doubt that this principle was entirely sound. More than a hundred years later, however, a dictum appeared to the effect that the stopping of another's light by building on one's own premises is actionable. This idea happened to gain currency[1] and was accepted in 1586 by

[6] Aldred's Case (1610), 9 Coke 57*b;* State *v.* Holcomb, 68 Iowa 107.

[7] 9 Coke 59*a*.

[8] Jones *v.* Powell, Hutton 135.

[9] Y. B. 7 Edw. III. 50, pl. 25.

[1] Brooke Abr., *Accion sur Case,* pl. 57; *Nusance,* pl. 12; Sury *v.* Pigot, Popham 170 (by Whitlock, C. J.).

Chapter XIV

Conflict of authority.

the Queen's Bench in *Bland v. Moseley.*[2] But in a short time it was unanimously repudiated by the same court. "If two men be owners of two parcels of land adjoining, and one of them doth build a house upon his land and makes windows and lights looking into the other's lands, and this house and the lights have continued by the space of thirty or forty years, yet the other may upon his own land and soil lawfully erect a house or other thing against the said lights and windows, and the other can have no action; for it was his folly to build his house so near to the other's land. . . . *Cujus est solum ejus est summitas usque ad cœlum.*"[3] Curiously enough, the doctrine of *Bland v. Moseley* finally prevailed,[4] at first being limited, apparently, to cases where the light was totally cut off.

Final doctrine.

For many years the law on this subject was not clear. But it was finally settled that the stoppage of ancient lights is an actionable nuisance,[5] and that the stoppage of lights not ancient is actionable if the possessor of the premises has a right to the light by grant, express or implied. Thus, where a man built a new house on part of his land and sold the house to one and the land to another, it was held that the grantee of the house acquired a right to access of light good as against his grantor and those claiming under him.[6]

In declaring interference with ancient light to be action-

[2] Cited in Aldred's Case (1610), 9 Coke 58*a;* Bland's Case, 1 Rolle Abr. 107, pl. 17, Hutton 136.

[3] Bury *v.* Pope (1587), Cro. Eliz. 118.

[4] Aldred's Case (1610), 9 Coke 57*b;* Hughes *v.* Keymish (1610), 1 Bulst. 115; Rosewell *v.* Pryor, 6 Mod. 116.

By local customs in London and York one owner was allowed to build a new house on an old foundation as high as he pleased. Hughes *v.* Keme (1611), Yelv. 215; Hughes *v.* Keene (1611), Godb. 183. But he could not build on a vacant lot so as to obscure the light of an ancient building. Hughes *v.* Keene, Calth. 1.

[5] Anonymous, 1 Vent. 248; Palmer *v.* Fleshees (1664), 1 Sid. 167.

[6] Palmer *v.* Fletcher (1664), 1 Lev. 122; Cox *v.* Matthews, 1 Vent. 239; Swansborough *v.* Coventry, 9 Bing. 305, 23 E. C. L. 286.

An attempt to gain recognition for this particular branch of the English law of light was unsuccessfully made in Morrison *v.* Marquardt, 24 Iowa 35, the opinion in which case will be found instructive.

In England the rule is the same where the severance is effected by will. Phillips *v.* Low (1892), 1 Ch. 47.

Volume I

Exceptional nature of the law concerning light.

able the courts were governed by the analogy of the principles applied respectively to the diversion of water,[7] and to the interference with the lateral support of walls and buildings.[8] But the analogy is not close enough to support the weight imposed upon it, and the whole English doctrine concerning ancient light must be considered exceptional. It is certainly so viewed by American judges, and the idea that a right to the uninterrupted flow of light into a building can be acquired by prescription or implied grant is repudiated by the courts of this country with practical unanimity.[9]

Ancient user.

In order that a light might be considered ancient it was originally necessary in theory that the user should be shown to be coextensive with the period of legal memory. But a user for forty years was at common law held to be sufficient to raise a presumption that the light was ancient.[1] Forty years thus became the prescriptive period in case of light.

Period of prescription.

[7] Cox *v.* Matthews, 1 Vent. 237.

[8] See Palmer *v.* Fleshees, 1 Sid. 167.

[9] See Ward *v.* Neal, 37 Ala. 500; Guest *v.* Reynolds, 68 Ill. 478; Morrison *v.* Marquardt, 24 Iowa 35; Ray *v.* Sweeney, 14 Bush (Ky.) 1; Randall *v.* Sanderson, 111 Mass. 114; Parker *v.* Foote, 19 Wend. (N. Y.) 309; Rennyson's Appeal, 94 Pa. St. 147.

The American courts sometimes proceed upon the idea that even if the English rule is sound it is not applicable to the social and industrial economy of a new country. This looks like a good pretext rather than a good reason for denying the existence of the doctrine in America. It would not be hard, we think, to maintain the proposition that the English doctrine, if really suited to any sort of industrial condition, is better suited to a sparsely inhabited country where people can easily get abundance of room for building, than it is to modern urban conditions. See Law of Ancient Lights and Its Reform, 30 Law Mag. & Rev. 183, 184 (Feb. 1905).

In Parker *v.* Foote, 19 Wend. (N. Y.) 316, Bronson, J., expressed the opinion that the English law concerning ancient light was not established until about the time of the American revolution, and hence did not become law in the colonies. But this is a mistake.

The anomalous nature of the right to ancient light is well shown in the following language: "If he [the adjoining proprietor] knows that the right is accruing against him, he has no right of action against the person who enjoys his light or air, to prevent it, because he has not, and cannot have, any exclusive property in the light or air which occupies his space. He has nothing therefore to do except to stand by and lose his rights, or to erect his obstruction within a given time, simply for the purpose of protecting what was already his own." Stein *v.* Hauck, 56 Ind. 65.

[1] Lewis *v.* Price (1761), cited in 2 Saund. 175*a*, note 2; Dongal *v.* Wilson (1762), cited in 2 Saund. 175*b*.

Chapter XIV

This period was subsequently reduced to twenty years by the Prescription Act (1832).[2]

Modes of acquiring right to light in England.

As the statute just mentioned only prescribes a new mode of acquiring and claiming the right, without abolishing the right of prescription at common law, it follows that in England a right to light may be derived from grant, express or implied, or may be acquired by prescription at common law or by prescription under the act.[3] In practice the right is generally asserted under the statute.

Gist of interference with light.

Substantial diminution.

It is important to observe in regard to interference with ancient light, that the element on which liability is predicated in this tort is found in the detriment which accrues to the plaintiff by reason of the substantial diminution in the amount of light which has been accustomed to flow into his messuage; and in order to be substantial the diminution must be such as to render the occupation of the house uncomfortable according to the ordinary notions of mankind and, in case of business premises, to prevent the plaintiff from carrying on his business as beneficially as before.[4] Such is the principle recently laid down in the House of Lords,[5] in an opinion which re-

[2] Statute of 2 & 3 Wm. IV., c. 71, § 3. This enactment constitutes substantially the basis of the modern English law on the subject of light. Tapling *v.* Jones, 11 H. L. Cas. 290.

[3] As to the nature of the statutory right to light, see Kelk *v.* Pearson (1871), L. R. 6 Ch. 809; Poll. on Torts, 6th ed., 400. Also Aynsley *v.* Glover (1875), L. R. 10 Ch. 283.

[4] Colls *v.* Home, etc., Stores, (1904) A. C. 179.

[5] In this case it was said by Lord Davey: "I am of the opinion that the owner or occupier of the dominant tenement is entitled to the uninterrupted access through his ancient windows of a quantity of light, the measure of which is what is required for the ordinary purposes of inhabitancy or business of the tenement according to the ordinary notions of mankind; and that the question for what purpose he has thought fit to use that light, or the mode in which he finds it convenient to arrange the internal structure of his tenement, does not affect the question. The actual user will neither increase nor diminish the right. The single question in these cases is still what it was in the days of Lord Hardwicke and Lord Eldon — whether the obstruction complained of is a nuisance."

There was at one time supposed to be a legal presumption that a building does not interfere with ancient lights if it subtends no more than an angle of forty-five degrees when viewed from the base of the window whose light is alleged to have been interfered with. But it was held in City of London Brewery Co. *v.* Tennant, L. R. 9 Ch. 212, that there is no such presumption of law. But if the new

Volume I

pudiates the notion, lately becoming current, that the prescriptive owner is entitled to substantially all of the light which has been accustomed to come into his building, without regard to his comfort or convenience. By this very sensible judgment the law of light is put substantially on the basis of nuisance. The idea that an interference with light is not actionable unless it does enough hurt to amount to a nuisance (to the person whose rights are interfered with) was clearly announced by Lord Hardwicke as early as 1752,[6] and the notion was of course more or less implied in the fact that the writ of nuisance was originally a proper remedy for interference with light.[7] But owing to what appears to have been a too literal interpretation by the Prescription Act, this idea was apparently on the point of being lost when the House of Lords revived it in the case just referred to. The opinions of the various lords in restoring the ancient doctrine will be found instructive.

Law of light reaches basis of nuisance.

structure is no higher than forty-five degrees this is *prima facie* evidence that there is no illegal interference with light.

[6] Fishmonger's Co. *v.* East India Co., 1 Dick. 163. See also Back *v.* Stacey (1826), 2 C. & P. 465, 12 E. C. L. 218; Parker *v.* Smith, 5 C. & P. 438, 24 E. C. L. 401.

[7] Baten's Case, 9 Coke 54*b*.

CHAPTER XV

NUISANCE.

Nuisance an Interference with Incorporeal Real Rights.

Chapter XV

CONSIDERATION of the law pertaining to the diversion and pollution of natural waters and interference with air and light, brought us into contact with the conception of nuisance and acquainted us with some of its more familiar forms. We must now take a survey of the wrongs which are commonly brought together under the term 'nuisance.'

Gist of nuisance.

At the start it is well to emphasize the fact that the element common to all civil nuisances is found in the circumstance that the wrong is done in respect of some right incident to realty. Blackstone says that the nuisance is a species of real injury to a man's lands and tenements. The private nuisance he defines as "anything done to the hurt or annoyance of the lands, tenements, or hereditaments of another." [1] But taken literally this is not accurate. Nuisance does not convey the idea of injury to the realty itself. It means rather an interference with some right incident to the ownership or possession of realty. The law of nuisance is an extension of the idea of trespass into the field that fringes property. It is associated with those rights of enjoyment which are, or may become, attached to realty. Ownership or rightful possession necessarily involves the right to the full and free enjoyment of the property occupied. It may be observed that the law of nuisance proceeds on a principle which is indicated, but not defined, in the maxim *sic utere tuo ut alienum non lædas.*[2]

An extension of the conception of trespass upon realty.

[1] 3 Bl. Com. 216.

[2] "The maxim *sic utere tuo ut alienum non lædas* is mere verbiage. A party may damage the property of another where the law permits, and he may not where the law prohibits; so that the maxim can never be applied till the law is ascertained, and when it is the maxim is superfluous." Erle, J., in Bonomi *v.*

Volume I

It sometimes appears that the nuisance is an injury of a merely personal nature and that it does not involve an interference with any real right whatever. Thus, in *Brill v. Flagler* (1840),[3] it was held that if a neighbor's dog constantly comes upon one's premises, making night hideous with his howls, the nuisance may be abated with a gun. Undoubtedly even a legal mind will ordinarily conceive this situation as furnishing an instance of a wrong purely personal to the householder and his family. But in such a case as this the wrong is ultimately resolvable into an interference with that right to the undisturbed enjoyment of one's premises which is inseparable from the ownership or possession of realty. And such beyond all question is the diagnosis of every true nuisance.

Nuisance not a personal wrong.

It has been rightly surmised that the owner or master of a ship could complain of a nuisance created by an occupant on the wharf or shore which should make the ship uninhabitable.[4] But it is plain that such right of action would accrue to the master by virtue of his occupancy of ship space in the dock. The unfailing analogy between nuisance and trespass upon realty holds good even here. Trespass *quare clausum* can be maintained by any one having a lawful possession in fact,[5] and so can the action of trespass on the case for a nuisance.[6]

Interference with occupant right.

History of Nuisance.

Antiquity of the conception.

The wrong of nuisance is one of the most ancient injuries known to the common law. It was in fact a familiar subject of jurisdiction in the king's court long before the trespass acquired any standing there. This was due to the circumstance that the early remedy for nuisance, the assize of nuisance (*assisa de nocumento*), was derived directly from the familiar

Backhouse, El. Bl. & El. 643, 96 E. C. L. 643. Carpenter, J., in Ladd *v.* Granite State Brick Co., 68 N. H. 185.

[3] 23 Wend. (N. Y.) 354.

[4] Poll. on Torts, 6th ed., 385.

[5] Bac. Abr., *Trespass* (C) 3.

[6] Blackstone observes that the action on the case for nuisance is maintainable by one that hath possession only. The old assize of nuisance could be maintained only where the freehold of the dominant and servient estates was in the plaintiff and defendant respectively. 3 Bl. Com. 222.

assize of novel disseisin, being in fact only a particular form of that assize.[7] To get its writ of trespass the common law had to go into another field and the process of derivation was slower.

Criminal character of early nuisance.

As might be expected, the early nuisance, like the early trespass, was criminal. The courts were evidently on the alert to prevent encroachments on the rights of the crown, and as incident to this they very naturally fell into the habit of punishing all nuisances affecting the public at large.[8] But even the private nuisance was a misdemeanor. The idea of giving civil damages in an action for private nuisance apparently originated very much as in trespass, the damages being assessed as a sort of incidental fine along with the punitory fine which went to the king. Blackstone notes that the assize of novel disseisin was the only possessory action in which civil damages could be recovered at common law.[9] The assize of nuisance naturally inherited this feature.

Genesis of conception of civil liability.

Ancient nuisances.

From the fact that nuisance was originally redressed by a form of novel disseisin it followed that no act could be treated as a nuisance unless it involved a 'disseisin' of some right incident or appurtenant to realty. Familiar nuisances in Bracton's day were the raising of a dike or pond, exclusion of a commoner, diversion of a stream, interference with the private right of pasturage, fishery, and the like.[1]

[7] See the forms in Glanvill, Bk. XIII., c. 34–36; Reg. Brev. Orig. 198*b* *et seq.;* also Bracton 231*b* *et seq.*

[8] "A porpresture is when anything is unjustly encroached upon, against the King; as in the royal desmesnes, or in obstructing public ways, or in turning public waters from their right course; or when any one has built an edifice in a city upon the King's street. And, generally speaking, whenever a nuisance is committed affecting the King's lands, or the King's highway, or a city, the suit concerning it belongs to the King's crown." Glanv., Bk. IX., c. 11.

[9] 3 Bl. Com. 187.

[1] See Bracton, c. 43–45, 231*b* *et seq.* See also Britton 109*b*, § 14 (Bald. ed., 227). Bracton's Note Book contains a number of pleas arising upon writs of assize of novel disseisin for nuisance. The acts complained of are, for the more part, the raising of ponds and building of dams. See pleas 1081, 1196, 1253, 1785; also references in volume 1, p 182, under "Assize of Nuisance."

An interesting record of an early action of nuisance for the diversion of running water is found in Y. B. 11 & 12 Edw. III. (1338), Rolls ed., 464.

One limitation upon the ancient assize of nuisance is worthy of notice, for it gave occasion for the

Volume I

Remedy for Nuisance.

In modern times the remedies for nuisance are three: an action on the case for damages, a bill in equity for an injunction, and abatement by act of the person injured.

The action on the case.

The action on the case for nuisance does not strike directly at the abatement of the wrong, since in this action damages only can be recovered. But inasmuch as any continuation of a nuisance is treated as a new one,[2] the party aggrieved may bring a second action, recovering exemplary damages, if the other should have the hardihood to continue his wrong.[3]

Bill in equity.

The equitable remedy of injunction is much used nowadays in cases of nuisance. By this means a threatened nuisance can, in the discretion of the Court of Chancery, be prevented[4] and an existing one abated, damages being also recovered as an incident to the equitable proceedings.

A consideration of the circumstances under which this power will be exercised does not fall within the scope of the present work. One observation, however, needs to be made.

Ground of equitable interference.

When the court of equity does interfere to prevent or abate a nuisance, it does so because a legal wrong has been committed, the reason for the exercise of the equitable jurisdic-

memorable enactment authorizing the issuance of writs in case. The assize could not be maintained where the person who created a nuisance upon a neighboring freehold subsequently alienated the land. Here the person aggrieved was driven to sue out a writ of *quod permittat prosternere* — 2 Co. Inst. 405 (note), F. N. B. 124 (H) — which was in the nature of a writ of right and lay at common law for an interference with rights of common, market franchises, and other nuisances. See Reg. Brev. Orig. 155, 156, F. N. B. 123 (F) *et seq.*

To obviate the necessity of appealing to this tedious and cumbersome remedy the Statute of Westminster II. authorized the bringing of an action on the case in the nature of a writ of nuisance. This was known as the action *in casu proviso,* but incidentally the clause of general authority for the issuance of writs *in consimili casu* was inserted in the same enactment. Stat. West. II., c. 24.

[2] Weshbourn *v.* Mordant, 2 Leon. 103; Beswick *v.* Cunden, Cro. Eliz. 402.

[3] 3 Bl. Com. 220.

[4] Cooke *v.* Forbes (1867), L. R. 5 Eq. 166; Atty.-Gen. *v.* Cambridge Consumers Gas Co., L. R. 4 Ch. 71; Atty.-Gen. *v.* Sheffield Gas Consumers Co., 3 De G. M. & G. 304, 22 L. J. Ch. 811, 19 Eng. Rul. Cas. 273.

tion being the inadequacy of the legal remedy. This is not a case where there is an equitable as distinguished from a legal wrong. It follows that when a court of equity pronounces a particular act to be a nuisance, this is good authority that a legal right has been infringed. But the mere refusal of an injunction is not conclusive that the act in question may not be a nuisance, for the refusal may be based on equitable considerations governing the control of the injunctive power.

Abatement by act of person injured.

The right to abate a nuisance by personal act comes down from very ancient times. Bracton recognizes it, limiting the right to cases where the nuisance, such as the obstruction of a way, has been freshly done.[5] It has the appearance of belonging to the same archaic stratum of self help as the right to distrain, but we find no reference to it prior to Bracton. From that time on there is abundance of proof that the proper abatement of a nuisance is a lawful act.[6] The question has most frequently arisen in connection with justification in trespass.

Antiquity of this remedy.

Illustrations from early period.

The following are instances where abatement by the party concerned has been justified: If one drives stakes to make a pond which would flood my premises I may enter peacefully upon his premises and pull up the stakes though a building of his may fall in consequence.[7] So if he ditches and thereby unlawfully diverts water from my mill, I may enter and refill the ditch.[8] Likewise if a gate be placed across a highway to the nuisance of the king's subjects, any one may demolish it;[9] and if a house is built so near mine that it stops my ancient light, I may enter and tear it down.[1] It is on the ground of abating a nuisance that one is allowed to lop the limbs of a tree which overhangs his premises and to cut the roots which run into his soil.[2]

[5] Bracton 231*b*, c. 43, § 1. To the same effect see Y. B. 20 & 21 Edw. I. (1293), 462, where it is added that the nuisance cannot be abated at night.

[6] See, generally, Penruddock's Case, 5 Coke 101; Baten's Case, 9 Coke 53*b*; Lodie *v.* Arnold, 2 Salk. 458.

[7] Y. B. 9 Edw. IV. 34, pl. 10.

[8] *Ib.*

[9] James *v.* Hayward, Cro. Car. 184.

[1] Jenkins Centuries, 6th cent., pl. 57; Rex *v.* Rosewell, 2 Salk. 459; Tenant *v.* Goldwin, 6 Mod. 314.

[2] See Y. B. 8 Hen. VII. 5, pl.

Volume I

The following, among other limitations on the right to abate a nuisance, are recognized: The abatement must not be a breach of the peace, nor be done under such circumstances as to involve imminent risk of such a breach. For this reason a dwelling house in which there are inmates at the time cannot be pulled down, however unlawful its erection and maintenance may have been,[3] unless reasonable notice has been given to the occupant to depart.[4] Again, a nuisance can only be abated by one to whom it is in fact injurious.[5] Furthermore, it is determined that where a nuisance is created by one and merely continued by his successor in title, one who would abate it must first call upon the successor to remove the nuisance himself, such notice being required as a condition precedent to allowing the party aggrieved to take the law into his own hand.[6]

Qualifications of the right to abate nuisance.

Nuisance in Conduct of Business.

Having now given an account of the origin and nature of the wrong of nuisance and of the remedies available for its redress, we proceed briefly to consider the subject of nuisance as connected with the doing of an act or prosecution of a business legitimate in itself, but attended with incidental annoyance and damage to others. This subject is rendered of great importance by modern industrial development, and the law applicable to it will furnish such further illustrations of the general doctrine of nuisance as are needed for the purposes of the present work.

Nuisance incident to industry.

An action of nuisance can be maintained at common law

2; Brooke Abr., *Nuisance*, pl. 28; Lemmon *v.* Webb (1894), 3 Ch. 1; on appeal (1895), A. C. 1; Lonsdale *v.* Nelson, 2 B. & C. 311, 93 E. C. L. 98; Pickering *v.* Rudd, 4 Campb. 219.

[3] Perry *v.* Fitzhowe, 8 Q. B. 757, 55 E. C. L. 757; Jones *v.* Jones, 1 H. & C. 1.

[4] Davies *v.* Williams, 16 Q. B. 546, 71 E. C. L. 546.

[5] Brown *v.* Perkins, 12 Gray (Mass.) 89.

[6] Jones *v.* Williams, 11 M. & W. 176.

"A builds a house so that it hangs over the house of B and is a nuisance to him. A makes a feoffment to C, and B a feoffment of his house to D. Now D cannot abate the said nuisance or have a *quod permittat* for it before he makes a request to C to abate it, for C is a stranger to the wrong." Jenkins Centuries, 6th cent., pl. 57.

Chapter XV

Interference with exclusive franchise.

for the disturbance of an exclusive franchise of fair, or market, by the erection of a competing market within seven miles;[7] or for the disturbance of an ancient ferry by the erection of a rival ferry near by;[8] or for the disturbance of a mill franchise by erecting a competing mill.[9]

Business competition not actionable.

But in such situations it is necessary that the plaintiff should be able to show an exclusive franchise based upon grant or prescription. Apart from such exclusive right, mere business competition is not actionable.[1] "If my neighbor sets up a mill, and thereupon people who used to grind at my mill go to the new one instead, and so I lose my tolls, I shall not have any right of action on that account."[2]

Smokes, gases, noises, and filthy residues.

Though a legitimate business is so far lawful that it cannot be treated as a nuisance in respect of the damage done in competition, it is not absolutely privileged in respect of harm that may be otherwise done, as by the creation of noxious gases, unpleasant odors, unusual noises, and by the pollution of waters. Here the harm done touches incorporeal rights appurtenant to such realty as is situated within the radius of harm, and will be treated as a nuisance if it impinges unreasonably against those rights. It accordingly becomes important to ascertain how far a man may go in the creation of smokes, gases, smells, noises, and filthy residues without being guilty of a nuisance. In deciding this question the right

[7] 2 Rolle Abr., *Nusans* (G) 140, pls. 2, 3; F. N. B. 184 (A); 3 Bl. Com. 218. Y. B. 41 Edw. III. 24, pl. 17, where it is also observed that an action lies against one who by display of violence deters people from coming to my market.

[8] 2 Rolle Abr. 140, pl. 4.

[9] Y. B. 22 Hen. VI. 14, pl. 23; Y. B. 18 Edw. IV. 1, pl. 5.

[1] The Gloucester Grammar School Case (1410) is in point. The duly appointed masters of an ancient grammar school brought an action against the defendant, who had set up a rival school in their neighborhood whereby the plaintiffs, who had been used to obtain at least two shillings for the quarter's schooling of a pupil, were compelled by the competition to accept only one shilling. It was held that the action could not be maintained. Y. B. 11 Hen. IV. 47, pl. 21; Kenny's Cases on Torts, 174.

[2] Hankford, J., *Ib.*, 47*b*.

Compare Bracton, 221: *"Si quis in fundo proprio construat aliquod molendinum et sectam suam et aliorum vicinorum substrahat vicino, facit vicino damnum et non injuriam."* But, added this writer, this could not be done if the person making the mill was prohibited by law from constructing the mill, as he would be where the other had an exclusive franchise.

Volume I

General principle.

of the defendant is to be considered no less than that of the plaintiff.[3] The law here applies in a qualified way the moral injunction, "do unto others as you would they should do unto you;" or, as nearly the same idea is put in the form of a legal maxim, "so use your own as not to injure another" (*sic utere tuo ut alienum non lædas*). But the law applies the maxim with an eye to practical justice and only as the application of the maxim is required for the preservation of good order and a just equilibrium between the rights of man and man. The problem is to discover the exact point where such equilibrium can be maintained. This must always be done on the particular facts of each case;[4] since, generally speaking, there is no inflexible criterion for determining just when an act constitutes a nuisance.[5] Neither the fact that the business is legitimate in itself,[6] nor that it is conducted with reasonable care,[7] is a defense to an action for a nuisance, if its character as such otherwise sufficiently appears.

Applied with an eye to particular facts.

A most important factor in determining whether a particular business or manufacturing establishment is or is not a nuisance to those who may be disturbed and annoyed thereby is the place of its location. On this point it is settled that what is a nuisance in one locality may not be in another. Thus, where a business is conducted in a part of a city mainly given up through a course of years to commercial and manufacturing purposes, a court is much slower to pronounce it a nuisance than if it were recently established in a residential

Location of business.

[3] Lord Selborne in Ball *v.* Ray (1873), L. R., 8 Ch. 469.

[4] Ross *v.* Butler, 19 N. J. Eq. 294.

[5] "I do not think that the nuisance for which an action will lie is capable of any legal definition which will be applicable to all cases and useful in deciding them. The question so entirely depends on the surrounding circumstances — the place where; the time when; the alleged nuisance, what; the mode of committing it, how; and the duration of it, whether temporary or permanent." Pollock, C. B., in Bamford *v.* Turnley, 3 B. & S. 79, 113 E. C. L. 79.

[6] Aldred's Case, 9 Coke 57*b;* Jones *v.* Powell, Palmer 539; Hurlbut *v.* McKone, 55 Conn. 31.

[7] Stockport Waterworks Co. *v.* Potter, 7 H. & N. 167; Rapier *v.* London Tramways Co. (1893), 2 Ch. 588; Chicago G. W. R. Co. *v.* First M. E. Church (C. C. A.), 102 Fed. Rep. 85. But want of due care will make that a nuisance which otherwise would not be. Kinney *v.* Koopman, 116 Ala. 310.

Annoyance naturally incident to urban life.

section.[8] The taking up of a residence in a city naturally entails some inconvenience, and a man is not allowed to complain of the little annoyances which are inseparable from the turmoil of towns and the business which is normally pursued in their different sections.[9]

It was at one time accepted as law in England that a legitimate manufacturing business pursued in a proper way and in a place convenient for such business could not be declared a nuisance, however much it might annoy those dwelling near by.[1] But this view was repudiated in *Bamford v. Turnley* (1862),[2] where it was held that the mere fact that a place is

[8] Gilbert *v.* Showerman, 23 Mich. 448; Cleveland *v.* Citizens' Gas Light Co., 20 N. J. Eq. 201; Ross *v.* Butler, 19 N. J. Eq. 306. See also Hurlbut *v.* McKone, 55 Conn. 31.

[9] In St. Helen's Smelting Co. *v.* Tipping (1865), 11 H. L. Cas. 642, it was said by the Lord Chancellor: "In matters of this description it appears to me that it is a very desirable thing to mark the difference between an action brought for a nuisance upon the ground that the alleged nuisance produces material injury to the property, and an action brought for a nuisance on the ground that the thing alleged to be a nuisance is productive of sensible personal discomfort. With regard to the latter, namely, the personal inconvenience and interference with one's enjoyment, one's quiet, one's personal freedom, anything that discomposes or injuriously affects the senses or the nerves, whether that may or may not be denominated a nuisance, must undoubtedly depend greatly on the circumstances of the place where the thing complained of actually occurs. If a man lives in a town, it is necessary that he should subject himself to the consequences of those operations of trade which may be carried on in his immediate locality, which are actually necessary for trade and commerce, and also for the enjoyment of property, and for the benefit of the inhabitants of the town and of the public at large. If a man lives in a street where there are numerous shops, and a shop is opened next door to him, which is carried on in a fair and reasonable way, he has no ground for complaint because to himself individually there may arise much discomfort from the trade carried on in that shop. But when an occupation is carried on by one person in the neighborhood of another, and the result of that trade, or occupation, or business, is a material injury to property, then there unquestionably arises a very different consideration. I think, my lords, that in a case of that description, the submission which is required from persons living in society to that amount of discomfort which may be necessary for the legitimate and free exercise of the trade of their neighbors, would not apply to circumstances the immediate result of which is sensible injury to the value of the property."

[1] Hole *v.* Barlow (1858), 4 C. B. N. S. 334, 93 E. C. L. 334.

[2] 3 B. & S. 62, 66, 113 E. C. L. 62, 66.

well suited to the carrying on of a particular business does not give an unqualified right to conduct it there, even though it be properly conducted. Every man, it must be conceded, has a right to make a reasonable use of his own, but what is reasonable must be determined under all the surroundings; and the propriety of a particular location for an offensive trade is to be considered from the point of view of others as well as from the point of view of the person who plies that trade. "Nor can any use of one's own land be said to be reasonable which deprives an adjoining owner of the lawful use and enjoyment of his property."[3]

Moving into neighborhood of nuisance.

The fact that the person complaining moved into the neighborhood of the offensive establishment with a knowledge of the existence of the nuisance is not sufficient to preclude relief.[4] A legitimate business properly conducted and originally established in a section remote from active centres may thus become a nuisance by subsequent growth in the neighborhood. A contrary rule would unreasonably hamper development and sensibly impair the right of others to do what they lawfully may with their own. But a prescriptive right to carry on an offensive trade in a particular place may be acquired by twenty years' adverse user.[5] It is no defense to an action for damage resulting from the maintenance of an admitted nuisance that there are other establishments of the same kind in the same neighborhood.[6]

Prescriptive right to carry on offensive business.

Approaching the subject on its positive side, it may be laid down as a general rule concerning nuisance by annoyance that any use of property or any continuous act is a nuisance which materially interferes with the comfort of human existence.[7]

Interference with comfort of existence.

[3] Euler *v.* Sullivan, 75 Md. 620.

[4] St. Helen's Smelting Co. *v.* Tipping, 11 H. L. Cas. 642; Bliss *v.* Hall, 4 Bing. N. Cas. 183, 33 E. C. L. 315; People *v.* Detroit White Lead Works, 82 Mich. 471. Compare Perrine *v.* Taylor, 43 N. J. Eq. 128.

[5] Susquehanna Fertilizer Co. *v.* Malone, 73 Md. 268.

[6] Laflin, etc., Powder Co. *v.* Tearney, 131 Ill. 322; Ducktown Sulphur, etc., Co. *v.* Barnes (Tenn. 1900), 60 S. W. Rep. 593.

[7] Lord Romilly in Crump *v.* Lambert, L. R. 3 Eq. 409; Cleveland *v.* Citizens Gaslight Co., 20 N. J. Eq. 201; Ross *v.* Butler, 19 N. J. Eq. 294.

Smoke unaccompanied with noise or noxious vapor, noise alone, and offensive odors alone, may severally constitute a nuisance.[8]

Noxious vapors.

In a case involving nuisance from noxious vapors incident to the operation of a brickkiln, it was said that the plaintiff, whose premises were near to the kiln, had a right to have an unpolluted and untainted atmosphere; not, indeed, air as fresh, free, and pure as in its native state, but air not rendered materially less compatible with the physical comfort of human existence, judged according to the standards of the country.[9] It is not necessary that the pollution or other disturbance complained of should be actually injurious to human health.[1] It is sufficient if the comfortable enjoyment of one's home is substantially unimpaired; and this question is to be determined by the effect upon persons of ordinary sensibility.[2] It sometimes happens that the harm attributed to a nuisance consists mainly of damage to property. Where such is the case it is required that the damage be such as materially to diminish the value of the property.[3] Parties are not allowed to stand upon extreme rights and maintain an action for trifling damage.[4] It has been said that in order to be substantial the damage must be such as to be manifest to any fairly instructed eye,[5] and that it must be such as can be shown by a plain witness to a plain juryman.[6]

Injury to health not essential to nuisance.

Damage to property.

The rule of liability in cases where damage to property affords the basis of action is substantially the same as in cases where personal discomfort and inconvenience are complained of. In the first there must be substantial diminution in the

[8] Crump *v.* Lambert, L. R. 3 Eq. 409.

[9] Walter *v.* Selfe (1851), 4 De G. & Sm. 315. See also Campbell *v.* Seaman, 63 N. Y. 568.

[1] Walter *v.* Selfe, 4 De G. & Sm. 323; Rex *v.* Neil, 2 C. & P. 483, 12 E. C. L. 226; Bishop Auckland Local Board *v.* Bishop Auckland Iron, etc., Co., 10 Q. B. D. 138.

[2] Rogers *v.* Elliott, 146 Mass. 349; Price *v.* Grantz, 118 Pa. St. 402. Compare Soltau *v.* De Held, 2 Sim. N. S. 133.

[3] Euler *v.* Sullivan, 75 Md. 616; Imperial Gas-Light, etc., Co. *v.* Broadbent, 7 H. L. Cas. 600.

[4] St. Helen's Smelting Co. *v.* Tipping, 11 H. L. Cas. 642; Price *v.* Grantz, 118 Pa. St. 402.

[5] Mellish, L. J., in Salvin *v.* North Brancepeth Coal Co., L. R. 9 Ch. 713.

[6] James, L. J., L. R. 9 Ch. 709.

Volume I

Diminution of value and impairment of comfort.

value of the property, and in the second there must be substantial impairment of the plaintiff's comfort and convenience in the enjoyment of it. The suggestion made in the leading English case,[7] to the effect that the law is more tolerant of interference with personal comfort than it is of the doing of damage to property, has not been borne out by subsequent decisions. The contrary would be nearer the truth so far as equitable intervention to prevent a nuisance is concerned; for diminution in the value of property may be adequately redressed in an action for damages,[8] while personal discomfort cannot. However, the two forms of harm, depreciation of value of property and interference with personal comfort in the enjoyment of it, are nearly always found together.

Making of evidence against a right.

The only situation where an action can be maintained for a private nuisance without proof of actual damage, in one of the two forms above indicated, is where the act complained of would if persisted in make evidence of a prescriptive right.[9] The making of evidence against a right is as much of a detriment in law as actual depreciation in value.

Continuance of wrong essential in nuisance.

It should not escape notice that the conception of nuisance implies some duration of the wrong in point of time. This results almost of necessity from the fact that the nuisance is an injury to incorporeal rights appurtenant to realty and not either an injury to the realty itself or to the person of its owner. An incorporeal right, being intangible, cannot be suppressed by a blow. The only way to harm it is by continuing an act which is inconsistent with the existence of the incorporeal right and which might in course of time make evidence against it. A distinction, however, exists between the wrong which constitutes the nuisance and the harm or damage incident to its maintenance. It is not necessary that the latter should be continuous.[1]

Who is liable?

It remains to be observed that where a nuisance is maintained upon the premises which are in the hands of a tenant,

[7] St. Helen's Smelting Co. *v.* Tipping, 11 H. L. Cas. 642.

[8] Atty.-Gen. *v.* Steward, 20 N. J. Eq. 415.

[9] Harrop *v.* Hirst, L. R. 4 Exch. 43.

[1] Campbell *v.* Seaman, 63 N. Y. 568.

Chapter XV

Occupant primarily liable for nuisance.

When landlord liable.

the tenant himself is usually the proper person against whom the action should be brought, because he is the one most immediately connected with the wrong.[2] But if it appears that the nuisance existed to the landlord's knowledge when the premises were let, the landlord is also liable.[3] The same is doubtless also true where the tenant has erected a permanent nuisance which gives his landlord a right to determine the lease, which he refuses to do, for here the maintenance of it can be reasonably attributed to him.

Definition of nuisance.

The brief statement of the general doctrine of nuisance which has been made in the preceding pages may fitly be concluded by quoting the admirable definition of a private nuisance inserted by Sir Frederick Pollock in his draft of the Indian Civil Wrongs Bill: "Private nuisance is the using or authorizing the use of one's property, or of anything under one's control, so as to injuriously affect an owner or occupier of property—(a) by diminishing the value of that property; (b) by continuously interfering with his power of control or enjoyment of that property; (c) by causing material disturbance or annoyance to him in his use or occupation of that property.

"What amounts to material disturbance or annoyance is a question of fact to be decided with regard to the character of the neighborhood, the ordinary habits of life and reasonable expectations of persons there dwelling, and other relevant circumstances."[4]

Public Nuisance.

In what has been said concerning the law of nuisance, we have taken no account of the public nuisance. As a criminal and indictable offense, consideration of the public nuisance does not come within the scope of this work, but it is proper here to examine the subject for a moment in its civil aspect,

[2] Cheetham *v.* Hampson, 4 T. R. 318; Russell *v.* Shenton, 3 Q. B. 449, 43 E. C. L. 814, 2 Gale & D. 573; Rich *v.* Basterfield, 4 C. B. 783, 56 E. C. L. 783; Ahern *v.* Steele, 115 N. Y. 203.

[3] Todd *v.* Flight, 9 C. B. N. S. 377, 99 E. C. L. 377.

[4] Ind. Civ. Wrongs Bill, c. VII., § 55, in Poll. on Torts, Appendix A.

Volume I

Public nuisance may also be private nuisance.

because, as will be presently seen, the fact that a nuisance is a public one does not of necessity prevent it from being a private nuisance also, and when this is the case damages may be recovered for the harm occasioned by it to particular individuals. A nuisance may thus have a double aspect, and it is important to distinguish between the criminal and civil wrong.

Obstruction of public ways and waters.

The obstruction of public ways and waters presents a typical situation where criminal and civil liability may concur. Such obstruction is a nuisance to the public at large because it infringes the freedom of the public in regard to the use of the way. It is therefore an indictable offense. But if particular damage be thereby occasioned to an individual the act becomes as to him a private nuisance, and is actionable as such because the wrongdoer has encroached upon an individual right.

Distinction between public and private nuisance.

The common-law authorities have always insisted upon keeping the distinction between the public wrong and the private damage very clear. The public wrong swallows up, as it were, the element of damage which is common alike to all the public, and it would be neither just nor politic to allow, say, a hundred men to bring several actions against one offender, recovering merely nominal damages, in vindication of common right. "The king has the punishment of [a public nuisance] and it shall be presented in the leet and there it shall be redressed, being a nuisance common to all the lieges of the king."[5]

Particular damage.

Consequently, in order that a particular person may maintain a civil action for damage resulting from a public nuisance he must show that he suffered 'particular' or 'special' damage, as distinct from the common public harm. The first noteworthy attempt to state the distinction was made by the learned judge Anthony Fitzherbert. Speaking of the right to recover the damage resulting to an individual from an obstruction of the highway, he said: "I certainly agree that every nuisance made in the king's highway is punishable in the leet and not by [civil] action, except where a man has

Fitzherbert's statement of the principle.

[5] Baldwin, C. J., in Y. B. 27 Hen. VIII. 27, pl. 10.

greater hurt or inconvenience than others in general. . . . If one makes a ditch in the public road and I come riding along at night and myself and horse tumble in, whereby I am much damaged and inconvenienced, I shall have an action against him who made the ditch in the road, because I am damaged more than any one else." [6]

Chapter XV

The illustration here given is decidedly more apt than the language in which the distinction is stated. It is upon the existence of special or particular damage that the civil right of action for a public nuisance is based, and not upon the fact that the plaintiff may have suffered more damage than any one else. If a dozen men should travel the same way and all be hurt by the obstruction in the highway, though in different degree, each would have his several right of action, for each would suffer what the law denominates particular damage. We thus perceive that "while the wrong must be special as contradistinguished from a grievance common to the whole public, . . . it may nevertheless be the common misfortune of a number or even a class of persons, and give to each a right of redress." [7] The element of common damage in such case, for which no civil action lies, is found in the inconvenience to which the public at large is put by reason of the existence of the obstruction. Thus, if logs are scattered in the highway and people are able to make passage only by sundry turnings and windings,[8] or if a gate is hung across the road whereby those using the highway are put to the inconvenience of opening it,[9] the offense is punishable criminally and not civilly. So there is held to be no ground of civil action where the plaintiff, by reason of an obstruction, is compelled on many successive occasions to depart from the regular highway and to go to his destination by a circuitous route.[1] Nor is the expense of removing an obstruction particular damage within the meaning of the rule.[2]

Nature of special damage in law of nuisance.

[6] (1535) Y. B. 27 Hen. VIII. 27, pl. 10.

[7] Farmers' Co-operative Mfg. Co. *v.* Albemarle, etc., R. Co., 117 N. Car. 579. Compare Innis *v.* Cedar Rapids, etc., R. Co., 76 Iowa 165.

[8] 2 Rolle Abr., 137 (B), pl. 1.

[9] James *v.* Hayward, 2 Rolle Abr. 137 (C), pl. 1; Vin. Abr., *Nuisance* (B).

[1] Houck *v.* Wachter, 34 Md. 265.

[2] Winterbottom *v.* Derby, L. R. 2 Exch. 316.

Volume I

In *Paine v. Partrich* (1692)[2*] the nature of the particular damage required to sustain a civil action for a public nuisance was illustrated and defined by Lord Holt as follows: "If a highway is so stopped that a man is delayed in his journey a little while, and by reason thereof he is damnified, or some important affair neglected, this is not such a special damage for which an action on the case will lie; but a particular damage to maintain this action ought to be direct, and not consequential; as for instance, the loss of his horse, or by some corporal hurt, in falling into a trench in the highway." But this is too narrow, for a reference to modern cases both English and American shows that consequential damages are often particular within the meaning of the rule referred to. Indeed, in most cases where an individual recovers damages for a public nuisance the damage is usually consequential.

Lord Holt's statement of doctrine.

Modern illustrations.

In the following situations damage resulting from the maintenance of a public nuisance has been held to be sufficiently particular either to support a civil action for damages or to justify the issuance of an injunction at the instance of the party injured, viz.: Where the plaintiff, a dealer in coal, was deprived of the patronage of sundry customers by reason of the defendants having maliciously stopped up the road by which alone such customers could come to the plaintiff's place of business;[3] where a navigable stream was blocked so that the plaintiff's barges were unable to pass and he was compelled to convey his goods overland;[4] where the nuisance consisted of the unauthorized operation of a street railway whereby the plaintiff's property abutting on the street was rendered less valuable;[5] where access to a tradesman's shop was impeded by

[2*] Carth. 194.

[3] Iveson *v.* Moore, 1 Ld. Raym. 486, 3 Ld. Raym. 291, Carth. 451. Here the recovery was clearly for consequential damage to business. The Court of King's Bench was divided. Holt, C. J., was stoutly against the action, denying Fitzherbert's opinion, in Y. B. 27 Hen. VIII. 27, to be good law; but all the judges of the Common Pleas and Barons of the Exchequer were for the plaintiff. 1 Ld. Raym. 495. The trouble in the King's Bench seems to have arisen largely over the question of the sufficiency of the pleadings. See 2 Sim. N. S. 145 *et seq.*

This case was treated as good law by Fry, J., in Fritz *v.* Hobson (1880), 14 Ch. D. 556.

[4] Rose *v.* Miles (1815), 4 M. & S. 101.

[5] Milhau *v.* Sharp, 27 N. Y. 611.

an unreasonable use of the street or highway, whereby he lost custom or was put to extra expense;[6] where, as the result of the erection of a building on ground over which there was a prescriptive right of access to a warehouse, its rental value was impaired.[7]

The true doctrine.

The authorities upon the subject of particular damage are not capable of being fully reconciled. We are convinced that the law here rests largely upon an artificial basis and many of the decisions evince a tendency, as yet unconscious, perhaps, to reach a more solid foundation. The true doctrine seems to be embodied in the following propositions: (1) A man has no civil cause of action for the breach of common right which is incident to the maintenance of a public nuisance. The remedy is by criminal prosecution. (2) But where an individual suffers actual damage which can be attributed to the nuisance he may recover, whether the damage be immediate or consequential, though of course, if the damage be so far consequential as to be remote, no cause of action would lie.[8] In other words, in so far as a nuisance results in actual measurable

[6] Fritz *v.* Hobson (1880), 14 Ch. D. 542; Benjamin *v.* Storr (1874), L. R. 9 C. P. 400; Atty.-Gen. *v.* Brighton, etc., Co-operative Supply Assoc. (1900), 1 Ch. 276. See also Beckett *v.* Midland R. Co., L. R. 3 C. P. 82.

[7] Stetson *v.* Faxon (1837), 19 Pick. (Mass.) 147.

[8] Remoteness of the damage seems to be a sufficient reason why, in Winterbottom *v.* Derby, L. R. 2 Exch. 316, a plaintiff was not allowed to recover the expenses to which he had been put in removing an obstruction from the highway. If a stream is obstructed whereby a logman is disabled from fulfiling his contract for the delivery of logs, the logman thereby incurs actual damage and can recover. Dudley *v.* Kennedy, 63 Me. 466. But the measure of damage could not include prospective profits on the contract for the delivery of the logs. Such damage would clearly be remote, and so far as the case just cited seems to countenance the contrary view it is unsound.

In Enos *v.* Hamilton, 27 Wis. 256, it appeared that the plaintiff operated a tannery and could get his bark only by water. In consequence of an unlawful obstruction of the stream by the defendant for several weeks, the tannery was suspended and the leather thereby deteriorated. To recover this damage the action was brought. Now the damage here alleged was certainly consequential, following indeed so far off from the illegal act that it may well seem too remote to be recoverable in any aspect. But it was held that the action would lie. In this, as in the Maine case, there is a confusion between the conception of special or particular damage in the present connection, and the conception of special consequential damage, which is generally recoverable when specially alleged in the pleading. This fact of itself is significant, for it shows that

Volume I

damage to a particular individual it thereby and to that extent becomes as to him a private nuisance and is actionable as such.

In this view 'particular' or 'special' damage, as used in this connection, is merely a discriminative epithet. If the term 'particular damage' really meant anything more than the actual damage which is requisite in all civil actions for private nuisance, the law would here be anomalous and unjust, for then a man could in a degree fortify himself against civil liability by increasing his nuisance until it becomes criminal. But this is not the case. Criminality is no privilege, and it can never operate as a shield to protect a wrongdoer from civil liability where actual damage is done.

Actual appreciable damage necessary to private right of action.

But unquestionably it is settled that before a public nuisance can be the subject of a civil action the damage must be of appreciable amount. Where the damage is inconsiderable the law inclines to the convenient, if not logical, view that the tort is swallowed up in the criminal misdemeanor, although the nominal damage may be in other respects special and particular. This is the reason why one who is compelled to turn aside with but little trouble and expense cannot recover for the obstruction of a highway. But if he is put to much expense or has to change his carrier,[9] the damage may be recovered. In both cases there is some actual damage, but in the first case it is nominal and in the other it is considerable. There is then, after all, undoubtedly some truth in the statement of Fitzherbert, that the individual right of action for a public nuisance is given in respect of the doing of much harm (*grand damage*). Those courts which hold to a contrary view and deny, as in Massachusetts,[1] a right of action for the

the idea that damage must be direct and immediate in order to be particular is fading out. Formerly consequential damage could not be recovered, now consequentiality, as we may call it, is a characteristic feature of particular damage. The idea that the particular or special damage recoverable for a public nuisance is identical with the special consequential damage which is always recoverable if specially laid in the declaration, also appears in Givens *v.* Van Studdiford, 86 Mo. 158.

[9] Rose *v.* Miles, 4 M. & S. 101.

[1] See Blackwell *v.* Old Colony R. Co., 122 Mass. 1. In Blood *v.* Nashua, etc., R. Corp., 2 Gray (Mass.) 137, it was held that the owner of a sawmill cannot recover for the obstruction of a stream whereby he is impeded and put to extra expense in getting his logs.

Chapter XV

obstruction of a way whereby one is compelled to transport his goods by another route and at a greatly increased expense, apply a rule which is at least consistent. But it appears unjust and is opposed to many good precedents.

Modern English doctrine.

In England, by virtue of what appears to be a reactionary decision of the House of Lords rendered in 1867, it seems to be law that the owner or occupant of premises near to a highway cannot recover damages for an obstruction of the same, whereby his business is interrupted and his patronage diminished.[2] But in this case the obstruction was a temporary one and was erected at some distance from the plaintiff's place of business. Subsequent decisions evince a tendency to limit this pronouncement of the lords to the exact facts which called it forth,[3] and it is well settled that where an obstruction materially impedes immediate access to the plaintiff's place of business, or amounts to a blocking up of his doorway, an action will lie for the loss of patronage and for other damage thereby occasioned.[4]

See also Brayton *v.* Fall River, 113 Mass. 218.

[2] Ricket *v.* Metropolitan R. Co., L. R. 2 H. L. 175. In this case Lord Chelmsford accepted substantially the criterion of particular damage which had been laid down by Lord Holt. He did not indeed insist that the damage must be direct, but he said that the injury complained of must be "personal to himself, either immediately or by immediate consequence," thus overruling Baker *v.* Moore, cited in 1 Ld. Raym. 491 (note by Gould, J.), and Wilkes *v.* Hungerford Market Co., 2 Bing. N. Cas. 281, 29 E. C. L. 336. In Shaw *v.* Boston, etc., R. Co., 159 Mass. 597, substantially the same doctrine is declared as in the Ricket case.

[3] See Fritz *v.* Hobson, 14 Ch. D. 555, where Fry, J., distinguishes Ricket's case. In Lyon *v.* Fishmongers' Co. (1876), 1 App. Cas. 662, the House of Lords held that a riparian proprietor who was licensed by the Conservators of the Thames to erect an embankment in front of his own land abutting on the river, was liable in damages to another riparian proprietor who was, by the erection of such embankment, injuriously affected as regards his own convenience of access to the water. How far this decision is really consistent with Ricket *v.* Metropolitan R. Co. is undetermined. See Poll. on Torts, 6th ed., 389 (note).

[4] Benjamin *v.* Storr, L. R. 9 C. P. 400; Atty.-Gen. *v.* Brighton, etc., Co-operative Supply Assoc. (1900), 1 Ch. 276. "I apprehend that the right of the owner of a private wharf or of a roadside property, to have access thereto, is a totally different right from the public right of passing and repassing along the highway." The Vice-Chancellor, in Atty.-Gen. *v.* Conservators, 1 Hem. & M. 1, cited with approval by Fry, J., in Fritz *v.* Hobson, 14 Ch. D. 554.

Volume I

Nuisance involves interference with right appurtenant to realty.

At the beginning of our treatment of the subject of the private nuisance it was stated to be of the essence of this wrong that there should be an infringement of a right appurtenant to real property. We may now add that this is also true of public nuisances which by the infliction of particular damage become civilly actionable as a private nuisance. There are, however, sundry criminal offenses classed as public nuisances which relate only to conduct, such as blasphemy, common scolding, gaming, disturbing public meetings, and the like. These offenses can never become civilly actionable as nuisances, and this for the very reason that they do not involve any encroachment upon individual rights appurtenant to realty.

Law of nuisance not founded on idea of responsibility.

In the field of nuisance the imaginative faculty constantly impels us to conceive of the nuisance as a distinct legal entity. It is the smoke or the noise or the filth which causes the immediate distress, and hence, in our first thought, the nuisance itself is the real offender against our comfort. Presently we look around for the person who is the originator or maintainer of this harmful agency, and proceed to hold him liable in damages, on the theory that he is responsible in law for the acts of this his creature. But this is not the true theory of nuisance. In law a person is held liable for nuisance, not on the ground of his responsibility for the acts of an independent agent of harm, but on the ground that he is liable to answer for the consequences of his own acts. The smoke or the noise or the filth is only a manifestation of his will and power, and there is no need for the law to adopt any metaphysical theory such as is embodied in the conception of legal responsibility in order to make him liable for the damage which he does by maintaining the nuisance.

CHAPTER XVI

DISSEISIN OF CHATTELS.

Gist of Conversion.

Chapter XVI

THE law of conversion is in a state of great confusion, and from this we may safely infer that the underlying principle in this tort has not as yet been grasped with sufficient distinctness. Let us see what can be done in this direction.[1]

Gist of conversion.

The root principle in the field of conversion is undoubtedly found in the idea of interference with that dominion which is incident to the general or special ownership of chattels. This conception is utterly different from that idea of damage to the property itself which is inseparable from tres-

[1] *Asportation, Detention, Disposal.*— At first glance it would seem that the subject of conversion might be rationally handled in its present form by merely distinguishing the different conversions according to the manner in which the rights of the owner, or possessor, are interfered with. Thus we might say that a conversion consists either of (1) a wrongful taking, (2) a wrongful detention, or (3) a wrongful disposal of chattels. But this classification will not be found to be helpful. It proceeds along lines accidentally established in the evolution of remedial law, and is not based in any way upon substantive principle. For the wrongful taking, the common-law remedy was the action of trespass *de bonis asportatis;* for the wrongful detention there was the action of detinue; and for the vaguely defined wrongful disposal, there was the still more vaguely defined action of trover. It is true that in legal classification we sometimes follow the lines marked out by the common-law actions, but this should be done only when those lines coincide with seams of substantive principle. Here we are necessarily compelled to depart from the remedial classification, for it does not follow substantive lines. The division referred to in this note is the one lately used by Mr. J. W. Salmond, 21 L. Quar. Rev. 43. It savors a little of the ironical that this writer after animadverting, somewhat unduly we believe, upon the common-law forms of action, should adopt a division of conversions which corresponds precisely with the ancient lines of trespass, detinue, and trover. Verily, these "ghosts which still haunt the precincts of the law," and which "in their life were powers of evil and even in death have not wholly ceased from troubling," have come back to confound the writer who attempts to banish them utterly to the realm of outer darkness.

Volume I

pass and which seems, but only seems, to show itself in one branch of conversion. To state it in another way, we may say that interference with or obstruction of the rightful power of controlling and disposing of chattels is unlawful and amounts to a conversion. The gist of the wrong consists in an unauthorized assumption of the power of a rightful possessor, or in the obstruction of the true owner or possessor or one having the right of possession, in the exercise of that right.

Interference with dominion and control.

In conversion that exclusive power and dominion which is inseparably connected with the general or special property in chattels is conceived as an object of harm apart from the property itself. This dominion is clearly a distinct legal entity and interference with it the law here reprobates. On the surface this all may seem a little far-fetched, especially in view of the fact that the fields of trespass and trover largely overlap; but the truth of the proposition that in the theory of our law conversion denotes an invasion of a right incident to the ownership of chattels, and does not imply damage to the chattels themselves, will become more apparent at a later stage of our present investigations. That trespass and trover overlap at some points is accounted for by the fact that the same wrongful act can sometimes be viewed either as causative of damage to the property or as an interference with that dominion which is incident to the ownership or to the right of possession.

Does not involve idea of damage to property.

The disseisin.

The idea underlying the tort is aptly conveyed by the word 'disseisin,' which we now make bold to adopt and apply.[2]

[2] The expression 'disseisin of chattels' is unknown to the common law, but, as Professor Ames has shown, the idea which the expression conveys is not wholly alien to our modes of thought. 3 Harv. L. Rev. 23 *et seq.*

We are convinced that in the present state of the law it is entirely legitimate to draft the word 'disseisin' into service in the field of conversion. In the first place, the word is here badly needed. In the second place, it has no historical associations which would impair its usefulness; and finally, we think the word and the idea belong in this very place if they belong anywhere in the common-law system of legal ideas. We are not unmindful of that 'disseisin' by trespass to which Professor Ames has directed attention and which operated to transfer to the wrongdoer the property in the chattels taken by him. See 3 Harv. L. Rev. 28 *et seq.* But this act was never referred to by the common-law judges as a

Chapter XVI

The word 'conversion,' as everybody should now know, is a verbal pitfall and a snare.[3] Though we cannot escape altogether from the usage which has fastened a misleading name on a large and important class of wrongs, we can partially rob it of its deceptive power.

Let us now note a few judicial utterances which serve to make clear the exact nature of that disseisin of chattels which is called conversion. "What," says Lord Holt, "is a conversion, but an assuming upon one's self the property and right of disposing of another's goods?"[4] The technical meaning of conversion, says Martin, B., in *Burroughes v. Bayne* (1860),[5] is the "detaining goods so as to deprive the person entitled to the possession of them of his dominion over them." Such expressions as 'interference with the dominion of the true owner,'[6] 'deprivation of the property of the plaintiff,'[7] 'exercise of dominion to the exclusion and in defiance of the plaintiff's right,'[8] and 'unauthorized assumption of the powers of a true owner,'[9] are familiar forms in which the gist of this wrong is described. Not a bad definition of conversion is that approved by Bramwell, B., in *Hiort v. Bott* (1874),[1] viz., "an unauthorized act which deprives another of his property permanently or for an indefinite time." If we should say "deprives another of the dominion of his property permanently or for an indefinite time," this definition would perhaps be all that could be desired.[2] However the language be

Assumption of property.

Unlawful detention.

Deprivation of property.

Definition.

disseisin. They called it a trespass.

[3] Note the words of Bramwell, B., in Hiort *v.* Bott, L. R. 9 Exch. 86: "This is an action for conversion, and I lament that such a word should appear in our proceedings, which does not represent the real facts, and which always gives rise to a discussion as to what is and what is not a conversion."

[4] Baldwin *v.* Cole, 6 Mod. 212. But the broad dictum of the learned judge in this case, to the effect that a refusal to surrender chattels is always a conversion *per se,* and not merely evidence of a conversion, is erroneous.

[5] 5 H. & N. 296.

[6] Pollock, B., in England *v.* Cowley, L. R. 8 Exch. 126.

[7] Bayley, J., in Keyworth *v.* Hill, 3 B. & Ald. 685, 5 E. C. L. 422.

[8] Bristol *v.* Burt, 7 Johns. (N. Y.) 254. Thesiger, L. J., in Jones *v.* Hough (1879), 5 Ex. D. 128, puts it thus: The defendant was guilty of a conversion, "he having exercised dominion over the goods."

[9] Poll. on Torts, 6th ed., 342.

[1] L. R. 9 Exch. 86. This definition is substantially adopted in the Indian Civil Wrongs Bill, c. VI., § 44 (2), Poll. on Torts, 607, though the wrong is not there given any specific name.

[2] Under the Common-Law Proc.

Volume I

framed it is obvious that the gist of conversion is found in the disseisin of the owner or in an interference with legal rights which are incident to ownership, such as the right to have possession. The idea of damage to the property itself does not enter into it at all.

Intent to Convert.

As might be conjectured, we shall find on coming to consider the nature of the various acts which are capable of working a disseisin, that some of these acts have a much more pronounced tendency in this respect than others. For instance, some acts will be found to operate as disseisins *per se,* or as conversions in law, while other acts are of an ambiguous character and only amount to disseisins when coupled with proof of an intent to deprive the true owner of his lawful dominion. Consequently the general principle on which evidence of intent is relevant in the law of conversion is this: Wherever the disseisory character of an act is so manifest that the law can stamp it at once as a disseisin, the plaintiff is not required to show that the defendant intended to disseise him of his goods; and similarly a defendant cannot escape liability by showing that he did not intend to deprive the true owner of his goods.

Relevancy of intent to convert.

The latter branch of this proposition is illustrated in *Hiort v. Bott* (1874),[3] where it appeared that one Grimmett, a broker, had caused his principal to consign goods to the defendant, though none had been ordered by him. The shipment having been made, Grimmett appeared before the defendant and represented that the shipment of the goods to him was a result of mistake, and requested that he indorse the delivery order to him. The defendant did so, thereby intending to restore the goods to the plaintiffs through their broker. Grimmett, having obtained the goods, disposed of the same and absconded. It was held that by the unauthorized indorsement of the delivery order the defendant had exercised such a do-

Conversion in law.

Act, 1852, 15 & 16 Vict., c. 76, the form of declaring in trover was that "the defendant converted to his own use or wrongfully deprived the plaintiff of the use and possession of the plaintiff's goods."

[3] L. R. 9 Exch. 86.

Chapter XVI

minion over the plaintiffs as to constitute a conversion, and that the absence of an intent to convert was immaterial.

In cases, however, where the tendency of a particular act to work a disseisin is not so pronounced, in a word, where the act is ambiguous, the presence of an intent to deprive the owner of his goods turns the scale against the intermeddler, and similarly the absence of such intent may be conclusive in his favor. Intention to convert is generally shown by assertions of ownership on the part of the wrongdoer which accompany and qualify the act of disseisin.

Absence of intent.

The general principle just stated may be illustrated thus: B embarks upon a ferryboat with his horses. A dispute having arisen between B and the boat's manager, the latter refuses to transport the horses, and in order to get them off the boat, takes them by the bridle and leads them to the landing-slip, where they are turned loose. The manager is not liable as for a conversion,[4] since the act of leading the horses ashore is consistent with the property right of the owner, and there is no intent to convert such as would turn the act into adverse dominion. Again, C, who is traveling through a slave state, attaches to himself as his servant a mulatto who represents himself to be a freedman, but who is really a slave. C thus innocently enables the negro to escape to a free state. He is not liable for a conversion, because he had no knowledge that the negro was the property of the plaintiff and had no intent to deprive him of it.[5]

Basis of the distinction.

The reason why intent may be relevant on the question of conversion is this: A disseisin of the lawful owner implies of necessity a corresponding acquisition of hostile dominion by the wrongdoer. Now, a man cannot acquire a hostile dominion over another's property without his own consent, and in cases where the alleged act of disseisin does not sufficiently declare its quality, we may look into the mind of the person charged with the conversion in order to ascertain whether

[4] Fouldes *v.* Willoughby, 8 M. & W. 540.

[5] Nelson *v.* Whitman, 1 Rich. L. (S. Car.) 318. But if the thing which B thus attached to himself had been something which he must have known was the property of somebody, the result would have been different.

Volume I

he has that intent which makes his dominion hostile, and thus exclusive of the right of the true owner. The law concerning disseisin of chattels at this point will be seen to be analogous to that principle which, in the field of real property, admits evidence of intention as a factor in determining whether possession is adverse.

When proof of intention material.

The expression, 'with intent to deprive the true owner,' or, 'with intent to convert,' is sometimes incorporated into definitions of conversion,[6] as if the element of intention were a universal qualification of the wrong. But really it is only material when the act complained of does not speak for itself.

Overt act essential to conversion.

Although, as we have just seen, an intent to deprive the owner of his dominion may stamp a doubtful act as a disseisin, it is well settled that a mere intent to convert will not alone make a conversion. There must be some positive overt act of adverse dominion.[7] A man whom I trust to convey my cotton to a factory, and who delivers it at the right place, does not become guilty of a conversion merely by taking the receipt in his own or some other person's name, though he may at the time intend subsequently to dispose of the receipt and thereby convert the property.[8]

Mere claim of ownership not a conversion.

A claim of ownership, unaccompanied by an act of dominion, by one who has neither possession nor physical control of chattels is not a conversion, for such a claim merely evidences an intention or desire to appropriate, and this of itself is not enough.[9] Mere words, uncoupled with possession or control, cannot make a conversion.[1]

Nor threats.

Nor are mere threats enough. A man may be compelled by threats, or even by physical coercion, to forego the full exercise of his own dominion as owner, yet if the wrongful act falls short of a disseisin of the property, the wrongdoer is not guilty of a conversion. This is illustrated in *England v. Cowley* (1873),[2] where the only interference on the part of

[6] Chambre & Holroyd in Shipwick *v.* Blanchard, 6 T. R. 299, approved with qualification by Alderson, B., in Fouldes *v.* Willoughby, 8 M. & W. 540.

[7] Smith *v.* Young, 1 Campb. 439.

[8] Penny *v.* State, 88 Ala. 105.

[9] Fernald *v.* Chase, 37 Me. 289.

[1] Earl, C., in Gillet *v.* Roberts, 57 N. Y. 32.

[2] L. R. 8 Exch. 126.

the defendant was to prevent the plaintiff from removing certain goods without himself taking possession or exercising any control over them. Said Bramwell, B.: "The defendant did not 'convert' the goods to his own use, either by sale or in any other way. Nor did he deprive the plaintiff of them. All he did was to prevent, or threaten to prevent, the plaintiff from using them in a particular way. 'You shall not remove them,' he said, but the plaintiff still might do as he pleased with them in the house." This decision shows the difference between a partial abridgment of the owner's liberty in disposing of goods and an actual disseisin. It is plain that if there be an entire and not merely a partial suppression of the owner's liberty of use for an appreciable interval, this would amount to a disseisin. Thus, if you become purchaser at an execution sale of chattels which are on my premises, and by my threats you are prevented from entering in a reasonable time to cart them away, I have disseised you of those goods.[3]

Partial abridgment of right of control not a conversion.

A mere nonfeasance is not a conversion. One who fails to perform an affirmative act, the duty to do which is assumed by contract or imposed by law, will be liable for the breach of such duty in assumpsit or case, but trover cannot be maintained.[4]

Nonfeasance does not work a disseisin.

A bailee or other person having the custody of goods does not convert them by negligently keeping them, whereby they become deteriorated or are wholly lost.[5] Hence the failure of a warehouseman,[6] wharfinger,[7] innkeeper,[8] or carrier,[9] to de-

Negligent keeping by bailee.

[3] Nichols *v.* Newsom, 2 Murph. (6 N. Car.) 302.

[4] Severin *v.* Keppel, 4 Esp. 156; Bolling *v.* Kirby, 90 Ala. 215; Forehand *v.* Jones, 84 Ga. 508.

If you lose goods which have been sent to you unasked, no action of any sort is maintainable against you. Howard *v.* Harris, 1 Cab. & El. 253. Trover would not lie, for the failure to keep safely is merely a nonfeasance, and the sending of goods unasked does not impose any contractual or other legal duty. A man cannot be made a bailee against his will. Lethbridge *v.* Phillips, 2 Stark. 544, 3 E. C. L. 523.

[5] Mulgrave *v.* Ogden, Cro. Eliz. 219; Heald *v.* Carey, 11 C. B. 977, 73 E. C. L. 977; Duncan *v.* Fisher, 18 Mo. 403.

[6] Davis *v.* Hurt, 114 Ala. 147.

[7] Ross *v.* Johnson, 5 Burr. 2825.

[8] Williams *v.* Gesse, 3 Bing. N. Cas. 849, 32 E. C. L. 353.

[9] Anonymous, 2 Salk. 655; Wamsley *v.* Atlas Steamship Co., 168 N. Y. 533.

Volume I

liver goods which have unaccountably disappeared, or which have been lost by negligent omission, will not support the action of trover. "If a carrier loseth goods committed to him a general action of trover doth not lie against him." [1] Nor is an attaching officer guilty of a conversion by a negligent failure to keep the goods safely.[2]

Positive Acts Which Work a Conversion.

Appropriation and consumption by wrongdoer.

Of the positive acts which are sufficient to work a disseisin, certainly the most unequivocal is a consumption or the using up of the goods. This is that 'conversion to the defendant's own use' which seems to have been the starting point in this branch of the law. Here the term 'conversion' originated, and it has clung to the action of trover with fatal pertinacity through all its mutations. If I drink up your wine,[3] or consume your substance without authority, I thereby, of necessity, disseise you, and am guilty of a conversion. If the chattels are not immediately consumable, an appropriation to one's own use and purpose is quite as effective a disseisin as is a direct consumption. It is upon this idea of conversion by appropriation that the wearing of a pearl or other jewel has been held to be a conversion.[4]

Sale and delivery operates as a conversion.

One of the most common means by which goods are wrongfully appropriated is by sale and delivery to a third person. Every sale without restriction implies an assertion of title in the seller, and amounts to a conversion if some other happens to own the goods, or to have other interest in them of which he can be disseised.[5] Nor is it any defense that the seller is ignorant of the interest of the other and has no intention to convert.[6] Sale is obviously a conversion *per se.* Even an officer of the law is not protected if he innocently

Ignorance no defense.

[1] Owen *v.* Lewyn, 1 Vent. 223.

[2] Dorman *v.* Kane, 5 Allen (Mass.) 38.

[3] Philpott *v.* Kelley, 3 Ad. & El. 106, 30 E. C. L. 40.

[4] Petre *v.* Heneage, 12 Mod. 519. Compare Y. B. 20 Hen. VII. 4, pl. 13.

[5] Cooper *v.* Willomatt, 1 C. B. 672, 50 E. C. L. 672; Edwards *v.* Hooper, 11 M. & W. 363; Featherstonhaugh *v.* Johnston, 8 Taunt. 237, 4 E. C. L. 86; Clark *v.* Whitaker, 19 Conn. 319; Gilman *v.* Hill, 36 N. H. 311.

[6] Harris *v.* Saunders, 2 Strobh. Eq. (S. Car.) 370.

sells the wrong man's goods under a writ of execution.[7] It has been held that the mere sending of a piano by the hirer of it to an auctioneer to be sold is a conversion, though the instrument be not actually sold, for the hirer thereby departs from the purpose of the bailment and asserts an adverse right.[8] But one who is authorized to sell chattels for cash does not convert by selling on time, though he may be otherwise liable for the violation of his authority.[9]

Creation of adverse lien.

The creation of a lien, as by pledge or mortgage, accompanied by delivery, is equally effective as an outright sale, provided the act is an act of adverse dominion.[1] The purchaser, or pledgee, is also guilty of a disseisin as much as the wrongful seller, or pledgor, if he assumes possession or disposes of the goods in any way, and this is true though he may have acted in entire good faith and in ignorance of the owner's rights.[2]

Liability of purchaser or pledgee.

In some jurisdictions it is held that a *bona fide* purchaser, who has not disposed of the goods or used them up himself, is not liable in trover unless demand has been made for their return,[3] but the weight of authority is to the effect that demand is not necessary.[4] The rule requiring a demand applies only where the defendant originally acquires a lawful possession. This cannot be said to be the case where a man buys from one having no title.

[7] Cooper *v.* Chitty, 1 Burr. 20; Glasspoole *v.* Young, 9 B. & C. 696, 17 E. C. L. 474; Grainger *v.* Hill, 4 Bing. N. Cas. 221, 33 E. C. L. 333.

[8] Loeschman *v.* Machin, 2 Stark. 311, 3 E. C. L. 423. In this case the auctioneer acquired a lien on the piano for the expenses incurred by him, good as against the person who put the instrument there, and in legal effect this was the same as if the goods had been pledged.

[9] Loveless *v.* Fowler, 79 Ga. 134.

[1] M'Combie *v.* Davies, 6 East 538; Halsey *v.* Bird (C. C. A.) 99 Fed. Rep. 525; Hotchkiss *v.* Hunt, 49 Me. 213; Thrall *v.* Lathrop, 30 Vt. 307.

[2] Loeschman *v.* Machin, 2 Stark. 311, 3 E. C. L. 423; M'Combie *v.* Davies, 6 East 538; Lee *v.* Bayes, 18 C. B. 599, 86 E. C. L. 599; Burroughes *v.* Bayne, 5 H. & N. 296; Carpenter *v.* Hale, 8 Gray (Mass.) 157; Carter *v.* Kingman, 103 Mass. 517; Gilmore *v.* Newton, 9 Allen (Mass.) 171; Williams *v.* Merle, 11 Wend. (N. Y.) 80.

[3] Metcalfe *v.* Dickman, 43 Ill. App. 284; Valentine *v.* Duff, 7 Ind. App. 196.

[4] Woods *v.* Rose, 135 Ala. 297; Robinson *v.* McDonald, 2 Ga. 116; Whipple *v.* Gilpatrick, 19 Me. 427; Heckle *v.* Lurvey, 101 Mass. 344; Rice *v.* Yocum, 155 Pa. St. 538; Deering *v.* Austin, 34 Vt. 330; Hilbery *v.* Hatton, 2 H. & C. 822.

Volume I

To the rule that a sale, pledge, or mortgage of chattels by one not the owner of them is a conversion when accompanied by delivery, there is a qualification which at once tends to establish the truth of the proposition that the gist of conversion is in the disseisin of the owner's interest, and illustrates how that conception enters into this tort. That qualification is this: If the person dealing with the goods has himself a substantive interest in them which is itself capable of sale, pledge, or assignment, and under cover of that interest he deals with the goods, he will not be liable for a conversion. One of two tenants in common of chattels can, of course, sell or transfer his interest at pleasure, and it has even been thought in some quarters that the ownership of part interest in a chattel protects a cotenant from liability for a conversion, though he disposes, or attempts to dispose, of the entire interest in it.[5] A pledgee, or pawnee, also has an interest which can be assigned or sub-pledged,[6] but the ordinary bailee for hire for a limited period,[7] and the bailee at will [8] have not. Nor is a mere lien such an interest as gives the holder a right to transfer the property subject to it; for a lien perishes when possession is gone from the person entitled to assert it.[9] In the cases where the interest is not assignable, the transferee, if he takes possession, is liable for conversion, as is the assignor.

Sale or pledge by person having assignable interest in goods.

Tenant in common.

Pledgee.

Lienor.

Donald v. Suckling (1866)[1] is an important case on the subject now under consideration. There A deposited debentures with B as a security for the payment of a bill indorsed by A and discounted by B. It was agreed that if the bill were not paid when due, B should have the power to dispose of the debentures. Before the maturity of the bill, B pledged

[5] Farrar *v.* Beswick, 1 M. & W. 682; Morgan *v.* Marquis, 9 Exch. 145; Tubbs *v.* Richardson, 6 Vt. 442. But in most American jurisdictions a tenant in common who sells the entire property in the chattel is guilty of a conversion of his cotenant's interest. Weld *v.* Oliver, 21 Pick. (Mass.) 559; Dyckman *v.* Valiente, 42 N. Y. 549; Wilson *v.* Reed, 3 Johns. (N. Y.) 175.

[6] Jarvis *v.* Rogers, 15 Mass. 408; Bailey *v.* Colby, 34 N. H. 35.

[7] Sargent *v.* Gile, 8 N. H. 325.

[8] Bailey *v.* Colby, 34 N. H. 29.

[9] Mulliner *v.* Florence (1878), 3 Q. B. D. 484; Everett *v.* Saltus, 15 Wend. (N. Y.) 474, 20 Wend. (N. Y.) 267.

[1] L. R. 1 Q. B. 585.

the debentures to C to secure a loan for an amount larger than the bill. The bill was dishonored, and while it still remained unpaid, A, the original pledgor, sued C in detinue for the debentures. It was held that the action could not be maintained without payment or tender of the amount of the bill. To the extent of this interest the sub-pledgee had acquired rights good as against the plaintiff, and his possession was not wrongful.

Damaging property not in itself a conversion.

An act which results in damage to a chattel[2] does not amount to a conversion unless the person entitled to the property, or to the possession of it, is at the same time disseised. The fact that trespass or case was the original remedy for impairment of a chattel, and that trover was permitted to be maintained only at a comparatively late day, sufficiently shows that such a wrong is not primarily and of itself viewed as a conversion. In *Simmons v. Lillystone* (1853)[3] it appeared that certain timbers belonging to the plaintiff became imbedded in the soil of the defendant. The latter, in digging a saw-pit, cut through the timbers. Part of them remained imbedded in the soil, but part were carried away by the tide. It was held that there was no conversion.

Destruction of chattels not in itself a conversion.

A total destruction of personal property, like the impairment of its value, if accompanied by a disseisin of the owner's interests, amounts to a conversion, otherwise not. If a poacher makes an incursion into your park and shoots your game, he may be held liable in trover for such as he takes away, but not for that which he leaves dead without having had his hands upon it. As to this he is only a trespasser.

Wrongful removal.

One who intermeddles with goods by wrongfully removing them from one place to another, does not convert, unless the removal amounts to a technical asportation, which term implies a disseisin of the owner. Thus the plaintiff's cow, running at large upon the highway, accidentally falls in with the defendant's herd and is driven away to a remote section for summer pasturage. The defendant afterwards discovers that he has the plaintiff's beast, and returns her to him upon

[2] Byrne *v.* Stout, 15 Ill. 181.

[3] 8 Exch. 431.

demand in the fall. There has been no conversion.[4] A removal of another's goods not being an act of disseisin *per se*, the plaintiff who seeks to hold one liable for conversion by such an act must show that it was done with intent to deprive the true owner of his rights.[5] If the property of A gets on the land of B, the latter may remove it to another place, and if he does so, recognizing A's right in the property, the removal is no conversion.[6] The facts in *Kirk v. Gregory* (1876)[7] exhibit a situation where a removal or intermeddling with goods falls short of a disseisin, and hence is not a conversion, but where, nevertheless, the intermeddler is liable in trespass or case. It appeared that the defendant, a near relative of a deceased person, being in the house at the death, removed certain valuable jewelry from one room to another with the *bona fide* intention of preserving them. But it was not shown that the removal was necessary, and it did not appear that sufficient precautions were taken in bestowing them in a place of safety. The jewelry having been lost, the defendant was held liable as for a trespass.[8]

Intermeddling with goods of deceased person.

Liability of Servants and Agents.

One who lends his active assistance in a conversion of goods generally becomes liable, though not acting for himself. Thus, one who receives goods from B, and for accommodation pawns them in his own name, turning the proceeds over to B, is guilty of a conversion if it turns out that B had no title.[9] A clerk who, in the course of his employment, receives and turns over goods to his employer under such circumstances as make the latter liable for a conversion, is him-

Person assisting in conversion.

[4] Wellington *v.* Wentworth, 8 Met. (Mass.) 548.

[5] Fouldes *v.* Willoughby, 8 M. & W. 540.

[6] Shea *v.* Milford, 145 Mass. 525.

[7] 1 Ex. D. 55.

[8] Liability is here really based on the conception of negligent misfeasance in the carrying out an enterprise which the defendant had voluntarily assumed. The actual basis of liability was not determined by the court in that case because forms of action had been abolished, a circumstance which is significant to show that something has been lost by the modern revolutions in the law of pleading, however much may have been gained.

[9] Parker *v.* Godin, 2 Stra. 813.

self personally liable also;[1] for an actual tortfeasor cannot escape liability by showing that he acted as the servant of another.[2]

Chapter XVI

In considering the liability of servants and agents for conversion, it is important to bear in mind that a servant or agent may sometimes escape liability when the master or principal is clearly liable. Thus, a manufacturer of yarns, who purchases and works up cotton to which the seller has no title, is guilty of a conversion, but his various employees who do sundry acts in working it up, may well be held not to be so liable.[3] A little difficulty might be presented in such a case by the fact that the employees collaborate to one end, and hence assist in an unlawful act. But where the servant or agent merely does an independent act, which does not of itself amount to a disseisin, he would certainly not be liable in trover. The servant, it may be generally stated, is liable for a conversion when the particular act which he does would be enough to fasten liability on the master if he had done that particular act himself and nothing more.

When servant or agent not personally liable.

In *Donahue v. Shippee* (1887),[4] an employer put his servant to cutting his grass, but the latter, not knowing the exact boundary, cut some grass on a neighbor's land. He did no other act, however, and other servants of the same master came independently and took it away. The servant who cut the grass was clearly guilty of a trespass, but whether he was guilty of a conversion is possibly open to question. The court held that he was so liable, a decision which is no doubt justified in the existing state of the law and as a matter of practical convenience; but it apparently loses sight of the cardinal principle that to work a conversion there must be a disseisin of the goods.

The cutting of grass.

To the general rule that one who, as servant or agent, does an act which amounts to a disseisin of the chattels of a

[1] Stephens *v.* Elwall, 4 M. & S. 259.

[2] McEntire *v.* Potter, 22 Q. B. D. 438; Perkins *v.* Smith, cited in Stephens *v.* Elwall, 4 M. & S. 259; Edgerly *v.* Whalan, 106 Mass. 307; Thorp *v.* Burling, 11 Johns. (N. Y.) 285; Donahue *v.* Shippee, 15 R. I. 453; Elmore *v.* Brooks, 6 Heisk. (Tenn.) 45.

[3] See Poll. on Torts, 6th ed., 347.

[4] 15 R. I. 453.

Volume I

Exception in favor of agent engaged in common calling.

third person, is liable for a conversion the same as if he acted for himself, there are certain exceptions. Thus, it is now pretty well settled that a man who serves the public at large in certain callings, wherein it is necessary to assume control and dispose of goods for others, is not liable for conversion when he surrenders them or their proceeds to the person who intrusted him with them, or to his order, provided he does this in the ordinary course of his business and without knowledge of the defective title of such person.[5]

Factors, carriers, auctioneers.

Factors[6] and common carriers[7] are within the protection of this exception, and so in principle are auctioneers;[8] but the weight of authority is against this latter class of

[5] The distinction between ordinary servants or agents and persons plying a calling of public agency was first drawn by Abbott, C. J. (Lord Tenterden), in Greenway *v.* Fisher, 1 C. & P. 190, 11 E. C. L. 362. The validity of the test has been questioned by no less high authority than Lord Blackburn. Hollins *v.* Fowler, L. R. 7 H. L. 768 (approving remarks of Brett, J., in Fowler *v.* Hollins, L. R. 7 Q. B. 629). But notwithstanding these strictures the test seems to be substantially sound.

[6] Roach *v.* Turk, 9 Heisk. (Tenn.) 708.

[7] Bigham, J., in Union Credit Bank *v.* Mersey Docks, etc., Board (1899), 2 Q. B. 216.

[8] Frizzell *v.* Rundle, 88 Tenn. 396; Rogers *v.* Huie, 2 Cal. 571 (but see Swim *v.* Wilson, 90 Cal. 126). *Contra,* Hoffman *v.* Carow, 22 Wend. (N. Y.) 285; Coles *v.* Clark, 3 Cush. (Mass.) 399; Consolidated Co. *v.* Curtis (1892), 1 Q. B. 495.

The following distinction was made in a late English case by Romer, J., in regard to the liability of the auctioneer: "If an auctioneer or broker does nothing more than settle the price as between a vendor and a purchaser of goods and takes his commission, he is not liable as for a conversion should it turn out that the vendor was not entitled to sell. That is the case put by Lord Bramwell in Cochrane *v.* Rymill, 27 W. R. 777, as one where the auctioneer would act merely as a conduit pipe, and not be liable for a conversion. But where, as here, the auctioneer receives the goods into his custody, and, on selling them, hands over the goods to the purchasers with a view to passing the property in them, then I think the auctioneer has converted the goods, and is liable accordingly; and for this the case of Cochrane *v.* Rymill is an authority, and I may also refer to Featherstonhaugh *v.* Johnston, 8 Taunt. 237, 4 E. C. L. 86, and Adamson *v.* Jarvis, 4 Bing. 66, 13 E. C. L. 343. The general rule is that where an agent takes part in transferring the property in a chattel and it turns out that his principal has no title, his ignorance of this fact affords him no protection. I was referred to the cases of a carrier and packing agent as supporting the case of the auctioneers. But the carrier and packing agent are generally held not to have converted, because by their acts they merely purport to change the position of the goods, and not the property in them." Barker *v.* Furlong (1891), 2 Ch. 181 *et seq.*

persons on this point. It has been held that a packer who inadvertently ships goods in the usual course for a person who has no authority to dispose of them is not liable for conversion, although he makes a *pro forma* affidavit at the custom house that he is the owner.[9]

Packer.

In cases where the agent is not held liable it will be found that he acts in a purely ministerial capacity and serves as a mere conduit, as it were, by which the property is transferred from one to another, or from place to place. While he is a mere conduit pipe in the ordinary course of trade, he is not liable.[1] To make persons who ply common callings virtually insurers of the title of all goods handled by them would involve unreasonable hardship. Of course, if the agent or intermediary is affected with notice before the goods or their proceeds are out of his control, he is liable.[2]

Broker.

One of the most instructive decisions on the liability of intermediaries is *Hollins v. Fowler* (1874).[3] There a broker, having in mind the needs of a certain customer of his, bought thirteen bales of cotton in the expectation that such customer would take it off his hands. The customer did in fact do so, the broker charging a commission on the sale. It turned out that the person from whom the cotton was bought had no title. The House of Lords held that the broker was liable for conversion. The reason is that the broker did not act merely in his capacity as such. He bought the goods in his own right and exercised an independent and adverse dominion for an appreciable interval. The subsequent acceptance of the goods by the customer whom he had in mind could not operate to make him agent *ab initio* as against the real owner, whose goods he had already converted.[4]

[9] Greenway *v.* Fisher, 1 C. & P. 190, 11 E. C. L. 362.

[1] Abbott, C. J., in Greenway *v.* Fisher, 1 C. & P. 190, 11 E. C. L. 362.

[2] Lord Blackburn, Hollins *v.* Fowler, L. R. 7 H. L. 767.

[3] L. R. 7 H. L. 757.

[4] In this case Lord Blackburn stated that in his opinion the liability of an agent or intermediary is to be determined not by the test of public employment, but by this rule: "One who deals with goods at the request of the person who has the actual custody of them, in the *bona fide* belief that the custodier is the true owner, or has the authority of the true owner, should be excused for what he does if the act is of

Volume I

Demand and Refusal.

Refusal to surrender possession.

The law pertaining to the subject of demand and refusal is easily understood by reference to the central conception of disseisin. A refusal to surrender the possession of chattels to one entitled to have them is a conversion if it is made under such circumstances as to work a disseisin of the defendant's interest; otherwise not. If the refusal amounts to an absolute denial of the true owner's right to the possession it is a conversion, for the possession of the wrongdoer thereby becomes adverse, and adverseness of possession is the heart of the idea of disseisin.[5]

Adverse possession.

If the refusal is a qualified one,[6] or goes upon some other ground than that of denying the right of the true owner, it is not a conversion. One who has acquired lawful possession of another's property is entitled to keep possession until he is reasonably assured that he is turning it over to the right person.[7] A finder does not convert goods by saying to one who claims them, "Bring some one to prove it is your property and I will give it to you." [8] It is no conversion for the immediate custodian of goods to require an order from the person in authority over him as a condition precedent to surrendering possession, provided the situation be one where a demand is necessary. The claimant in such case must make demand of the person who really has control and possession.[9]

Qualified refusal.

In *Cobbett v. Clutton* (1826)[1] the defendant had posses-

such a nature as would be excused if done by the authority of the person in possession, if he was a finder of the goods, or intrusted with their custody." Hollins *v.* Fowler, L. R. 7 H. L. 766, 767. His lordship, however, added that this rule, though it solved a great many difficulties, would not solve all.

[5] See Observations on Trover and Conversion, by J. W. Salmond, 21 L. Quar. Rev. 48.

[6] Dent *v.* Chiles, 5 Stew. & P. (Ala.) 383; McEntee *v.* New Jersey Steamboat Co., 45 N. Y. 34.

[7] Vaughan *v.* Watt, 6 M. & W. 492.

The question whether a refusal to surrender is made under such circumstances as to amount to a conversion is, in doubtful cases, submitted to the jury. Burroughes *v.* Bayne, 5 H. & N. 296; McEntee *v.* New Jersey Steamboat Co., 45 N. Y. 34.

[8] Green *v.* Dunn, 3 Campb. 215 (note).

[9] Alexander *v.* Southey, 5 B. & Ald. 247, 7 E. C. L. 85.

[1] 2 C. & P. 471, 12 E. C. L. 221.

sion of a box containing sundry deeds and other papers belonging to the estate of a decedent. He agreed to surrender the box to the personal representative provided the latter would furnish him a schedule of its contents. It was held that the defendant had no right to insist upon this condition, and that a refusal to yield possession without compliance with it, made him liable for the conversion of the papers.

Unreasonable condition.

Prima facie, of course, a refusal to surrender to one entitled to possession makes the holding adverse; but the refusal is open to explanation. This is generally expressed by saying that a refusal to surrender upon demand is only *prima facie* evidence of a conversion. This formula is entirely correct. Lord Holt's remark that "the very denial of goods to him that has a right to demand them is an actual conversion, and not only evidence of it,"[2] taken literally is not true. If there be a denial of the property in the plaintiff and adverse possession is asserted, this is a disseisin, and it works a conversion of his goods. This is the kind of refusal that his lordship evidently had in mind.[3]

Refusal a *prima facie* conversion.

Demand and refusal often figure in actions for conversion against bailees. In regard to this class of persons, it should be noted that their failure to deliver the chattels may result from the fact that (1) the property has been unaccountably or negligently lost; that (2) it has been destroyed, consumed, or otherwise disposed of by the bailee; or (3) the failure to deliver may be due to a mere omission to comply with the trust implied in the bailment or imposed by contract. In the first of these situations no action for conversion lies at all, since the bailee is merely guilty of a nonfeasance.

Refusal by bailee.

In the second situation no demand is necessary if the plaintiff can independently prove the fact of destruction, consumption, or disposal by the bailee, since destruction, consumption, or disposal puts an end to the trust relation which is implied in the bailment, and works a disseisin of the

[2] Baldwin *v.* Cole, 6 Mod. 212.

[3] Mr. Salmond's criticism of the generally accepted formula is unsound. While this writer asserts that a detention after demand is a conversion in itself and not merely evidence of it, he is at once compelled to qualify by saying the detention must be adverse. 21 L. Quar. Rev. 48.

Volume I

owner.[4] But in this situation demand should usually be made when it is intended to bring trover against the bailee, because the failure to surrender would furnish *prima facie* evidence of a conversion, and the wrongdoer would not be able to rebut it.

When demand necessary.

Where the bailee has not lost, destroyed, or consumed the goods, nor exercised any other act of independent dominion which amounts to a termination of the bailment and disseisin of the owner, but merely detains them contrary to his trust or to the terms of his contract, the action of trover cannot be maintained at all unless demand be first made, followed by a refusal to surrender. The mere failure to deliver may be a

[4] Cooper *v.* Willomatt, 1 C. B. 672, 50 E. C. L. 672; Loeschman *v.* Machin, 2 Stark. 311, 3 E. C. L. 423.

A delivery by a carrier or other bailee to a person not entitled to have the goods is a wrongful disposal and amounts to a conversion. Youl *v.* Harbottle, Peake N. P. (ed. 1795) 49; Stephenson *v.* Hart, 4 Bing. 476; Devereux *v.* Barclay, 2 B. & Ald. 702; Syeds *v.* Hay, 4 T. R. 260; Louisville, etc., R. Co. *v.* Barkhouse, 100 Ala. 543. But if the chattel is stolen or tortiously taken from the bailee by a stranger, trover will not lie. Traylor *v.* Hughes, 88 Ala. 617; Kearney *v.* Clutton, 101 Mich. 106.

"There is a class of cases in which a person having a limited interest in chattels, either as hirer or lessee of them, dealing tortiously with them, has been held to determine his special interest in the things, so that the owner may maintain trover as if that interest had never been created. But I think in all these cases the act done by the party having the limited interest was wholly inconsistent with the contract under which he had the limited interest; so that it must be taken from his doing it, that he had renounced the contract, which, as was said in Fenn *v.* Bittleston, 7 Exch. 160, operates as a disclaimer of a tenancy at common law, or, as it is put by Williams, J., in Johnson *v.* Stear, 15 C. B. N. S. 330, 341, 109 E. C. L. 330, 341, he may be said to have violated an implied condition of the bailment. Such is the case where a hirer of goods, who is not to have more than the use of them, destroys them or sells them; that being so wholly at variance with the purpose for which he holds them, that it may well be said that he has renounced the contract by which he held them, and so waived and abandoned the limited right which he had under that contract. It may be a question whether it would not have been better if it had been originally determined that, even in such cases, the owner should bring a special action on the case, and recover the damage which he actually sustained, which may in such cases be very trifling, though it may be large, instead of holding that he might bring trover, and recover the whole value of the chattel without any allowance for the special property. But I am not prepared to dissent from these cases, where the act complained of is one wholly repugnant to the holding." Blackburn, J., in Donald *v.* Suckling, L. R. 1 Q. B. 614.

breach of the bailee's contract, but it is a nonfeasance and is not a conversion, though it should last forever. But when a demand is made and the bailee refuses to deliver the goods, they being then in his control, his possession thereby becomes adverse and trover lies for the conversion.

Nature of the demand.

Demand, in order to be effective, must be for a surrender of the goods. A demand is ineffective where the demandant insists that the person having possession shall return the chattel to a designated spot, as, for instance, to the place where he got it,[5] or do any other act than merely to give up the chattel.[6] Such a defect in the demand is not, however, available where the bailee totally repudiates the demandant's right, or bases his refusal to surrender on other grounds.[7]

[5] Durgin *v.* Gage, 40 N. H. 302; Farrar *v.* Rollins, 37 Vt. 295. See also Phelps *v.* Gilchrist, 28 N. H. 277.

[6] Rushworth *v.* Taylor, 3 Q. B. 699, 43 E. C. L. 932; Wells *v.* Crew, 5 U. C. Q. B. O. S. 209. In these cases there was a demand upon a bailee to restore the chattels, which had been damaged while in his possession, in as good condition as when he received them. The demand was held to be ineffectual.

[7] Sharp *v.* Pratt, 3 C. & P. 34, 14 E. C. L. 197.

CHAPTER XVII

DISSEISIN OF CHATTELS (CONTINUED).

Conversion Violates Possession or Right of Possession.

Volume I

PARADOXICAL as the statement may at first appear, disseisin, which is the essence of conversion, is not a wrong against the owner in respect of his ownership. In its ultimate analysis disseisin is not a wrong against ownership at all. It is an infringement of the right to control or of the right to possession, which is usually an incident of ownership, but not always. Ownership is an intangible entity, and in strict theory of law one cannot be disseised of ownership by a wrongful act. No mere tortfeasor ever really becomes the owner of the goods which he takes or withholds from their true owner. So long as they can be traced or identified they may be recovered. The statement that one cannot be disseised of ownership is made with full appreciation of all the talk in the books about wrongdoers obtaining property by a tortious taking and with a full appreciation of the truth that in the early common law the right of action which accrued to the owner upon such taking was subject to so many casualties that the owner was often in as bad a fix as if he had in fact been disseised of the ownership.[1] This aspect of the subject belongs to the history of the evolution of our remedial law, and the trouble which was encountered arose from the absence in our early law of just such remedies as detinue and trover finally came respectively to be, namely, actions of property and possessory right in a full, broad, and complete sense.

Conversion not a wrong against ownership,

but is a wrong against the right of dominion and control.

No, one cannot be disseised of the ownership of a chattel, but he can be disseised of the thing itself, and this is done

[1] These casualties are graphically portrayed by Professor Ames in his articles on Disseisin of Chattels, 3 Harv. L. Rev. 23, 313, 337.

by excluding him from the possession or by disabling him from the exercise of dominion and control. There can be no wrong of conversion where there is nothing to disseise, and this in the literal sense of the word 'disseise'— a taking away of a tangible thing from the control of one who has actual possession, or the exclusion of such a thing from the dominion of the person entitled to exercise it. It follows that where possession, or the right of possession, is vested in one person and the ultimate ownership in another, the former can be disseised, but the latter cannot be. This principle finds expression in the rule that in order to maintain trover, a plaintiff must be able to show either possession in himself at the time of the conversion, or a right to immediate possession. There are many judicial utterances to the effect that the plaintiff must be able to show property right conjoined with a right to possession.[2] But these expressions are used in cases where the plaintiff, although owner, has failed because he did not happen to have a right to immediate possession; and an analysis of the cases conclusively shows that either an actual possession or the right to immediate possession is enough.[3] This distinction, however, will be noted — that where one has not actual possession, a right to immediate possession can hardly exist unless it is supported by some sort of property right. Hence, in this situation there is a conjunction of the property right with the right to possession, and it is to this truth that expressions like that of Ashurst, J., point. That right to immediate possession which, as well as actual possession, will support the action of trover is sometimes called virtual possession,[4] or possession implied by law as annexed to or incident to the general ownership.

Chapter XVII

Plaintiff must show possession or right of possession.

Property right not essential.

That a violation of possession or right of possession is alone sufficient to sustain trover is manifest from decisions to the following effect: A boy finds a jewel, thereby acquiring lawful possession. He carries it to a goldsmith to know its value. The latter, under pretense of weighing, takes out the

Finder of chattel.

[2] See Ashurst, J., in Gordon *v.* Harper, 7 T. R. 9.

[3] See Big. Cas. Torts, note on Possession and Property, 424 *et seq.* Also Bac. Abr., *Trover* (C).

[4] Bac. Abr., *Trover* (C).

Volume I

stones and returns the socket empty. He is liable for conversion at the suit of the finder.[5] A sheriff may maintain trover against one who takes away goods which he has seized in execution,[6] though the process be void. And the purchaser who acquires possession under a void execution sale may do likewise.[7] Even a gratuitous bailee may sue in trover for a wrongful dispossession of goods by a stranger.[8] So also may any one having actual possession, though he himself be a wrongdoer. Thus in *Jefferies v. Great Western R. Co.* (1856)[9] it was held that the defendants who had dispossessed the plaintiff could not show when sued for the conversion, that the plaintiffs had no title to the goods.

Gratuitous bailee.

Person having actual possession.

Outstanding title.

Generally speaking, the defendant in trover cannot set up an outstanding title in a third person with which he does not connect himself.[1] But where a plaintiff is out of possession at the time of the conversion, his right of action being here based on that right to possession which can only subsist in conjunction with some sort of property right, it is permissible even for a stranger to show in an action against him for conversion that the title to the goods is in a third person.[2] It is obvious that where ownership in the plaintiff is material to make out his right to possession, the absence of such ownership is good defensive matter, and this may be established by proof of outstanding title in a third person.

Resale by seller.

For lack of a violation of possession or right to immediate possession, trover cannot be maintained in situations like these: Where the vendee leaves goods in the possession of the seller, he cannot maintain trover against the latter for

[5] Armory *v.* Delamirie, 1 Stra. 505. Compare Bridges *v.* Hawkesworth, 7 Eng. L. & Eq. 424, 21 L. J. Q. B. 75.

[6] Wilbraham *v.* Snow, 2 Saund. 47*a;* Barker *v.* Miller, 6 Johns. (N. Y.) 195. Compare Thayer *v.* Hutchinson, 13 Vt. 504.

[7] Duncan *v.* Spear, 11 Wend. (N. Y.) 54; Schermerhorn *v.* Van Volkenburgh, 11 Johns. (N. Y.) 529.

[8] Nicolls *v.* Bastard, 2 C. M. & R. 659; Burton *v.* Hughes, 2 Bing. 173, 9 E. C. L. 368.

[9] 5 El. & Bl. 802, 85 E. C. L. 802; Northam *v.* Bowden, 11 Exch. 70; Bartlett *v.* Hoyt, 29 N. H. 317.

[1] Cook *v.* Patterson, 35 Ala. 102; Harker *v.* Dement, 9 Gill (Md.) 7. *Contra*, Stephenson *v.* Little, 10 Mich. 433; Boyce *v.* Williams, 84 N. Car. 275.

[2] Morey *v.* Hoyt, 65 Conn. 516; Krewson *v.* Purdom, 13 Oregon 563.

Chapter XVII

the disposal of them until he has paid or tendered the purchase price.[3] So where goods are purchased and left in the hands of the seller subject to his lien for unpaid purchase money, the buyer cannot maintain trover against a stranger who wrongfully takes them away.[4] Here the existence of the vendor's lien deprives the purchaser of that right to immediate possession which is usually incident to ownership. Similarly a mortgagee under a bill of sale of chattels of which the mortgagor is to remain in possession until default in payment, cannot maintain trover for them;[5] nor a landlord for chattels leased for a term to a tenant.[6]

Effect of vendor's lien.

The principle here considered, namely, that the plaintiff in trover must always be able to show a violation either of actual possession or of the right to immediate possession, fully explains the decisions heretofore considered, wherein it is held that a pledgee may sub-pledge or even sell the goods while the original debt remains unpaid, and that the sub-pledgee or purchaser may hold without being liable for a conversion so long as that debt is unpaid and no tender made. In *Halliday v. Holgate* (1868),[7] a holder of scrip certificates for shares borrowed of the defendant a sum of money, payable on demand, pledging the shares. The debtor having become bankrupt, the defendant wrongfully sold some of the shares without demand and notice. The assignee in bankruptcy then sued in trover to recover the value of the shares, without tendering the amount of the debt for which the shares had been pledged. It was held that the action could not be maintained.

Sale by sub-pledgee.

It should be observed in regard to bailments that the bailee can maintain trover for a conversion because of his lawful possession. True, the authorities frequently use the term 'special property' as descriptive of the interest which en-

Special property of the bailee.

[3] Bloxam *v.* Saunders, 4 B. & C. 941, 10 E. C. L. 477.

[4] Lord *v.* Price, L. R. 9 Exch. 54.

[5] Bradley *v.* Copley, 1 C. B. 685, 50 E. C. L. 685.

A second mortgagee of personal property cannot maintain an action for the conversion of it against a purchaser to whom the first mortgagee, being entitled to the possession, has sold the entire property. Landon *v.* Emmons, 97 Mass. 37.

[6] Gordon *v.* Harper, 7 T. R. 9.

[7] L. R. 3 Exch. 299.

Volume I

ables the bailee to maintain this action, but on analysis this appears to be merely another name for the possessory right acquired under the bailment.[8]

Owner liable to bailee for conversion.

That the bailee may even bring trover for conversion against the owner, when the latter retakes possession before the term of the bailment expires, is settled by the authorities. In the old books the bailee's right to maintain trover is sometimes said to be based, like his right to maintain trespass, on the fact that he is responsible to the owner if the goods are lost.[9] This idea may have had some weight with the courts when the bailee was permitted to bring detinue in the days before the advent of trover, but the explanation is now inadequate and, so far as it goes, superfluous.

Owner's right of action against stranger.

A concession to all bailees of the right of suing for a conversion of the chattels bailed would seem of necessity to exclude the bailor from the right to bring such an action, since in trover damages to the extent of the full value of the goods are recovered, and to allow the bailor also to sue in such case apparently exposes the tortfeasor to the danger of being forced to pay double damages. Ordinarily, it is true, as once said by Bramwell, B., that "two men cannot be entitled to maintain trover for the same goods." [1] Nevertheless it is determined that in all bailments which are determinable at the will of the bailor, the latter may sue a stranger for a conversion of the goods in the hands of the bailee, because here the bailor has the right to possession whenever he chooses to assert it.[2] It is different where the bailor has not the immediate right to possession.[3] The bailment for carriage, like

[8] See vol. 2, *Bailment.* Roberts *v.* Wyatt, 2 Taunt. 268; Chamberlain *v.* Neale, 9 Allen (Mass.) 410; Hickok *v.* Buck, 22 Vt. 149. But there is ground for believing that case is here the technically proper remedy.

[9] Wilbraham *v.* Snow, 1 Sid. 438; Bac. Abr., *Trover* (C), 645 (Bouv. ed.).

[1] Lord *v.* Price, L. R. 9 Exch. 54.

[2] Nicolls *v.* Bastard, 2 C. M. & R. 659; Cooper *v.* Willomatt, 1 C. B. 672, 50 E. C. L. 672; Hardy *v.* Reed, 6 Cush. (Mass.) 252; Morgan *v.* Ide, 8 Cush. (Mass.) 420; Robinson *v.* Bird, 158 Mass. 357; Oliver Ditson Co. *v.* Bates, 181 Mass. 455.

[3] Fairbank *v.* Phelps, 22 Pick. (Mass.) 535.

Chapter XVII

ordinary bailments at will, is held not to be inconsistent with the general right of possession in the owner, and the latter may bring trover against a converter.[4] It should be added that in all cases where there is a concurrent right of action in both bailor and bailee against the same wrongdoer, the one who sues first ousts the other of his action; the rule here being the same in trespass and trover.[5]

Measure of Damages.

Value of the goods.

Normally the measure of damages in cases of conversion is the value of the goods at the time the conversion occurs.[6] But the action of trover, being a form of case, is in the nature of an equitable action,[7] and in certain cases where the plaintiff's interest falls short of full ownership — but not in all cases where this is so — the recovery has been restricted to the actual damages suffered. The mitigation of the rule of liability here indicated seems to be permitted only in those cases where the question of liability comes up as between a general and special owner, and is not recognized in actions against a stranger. If a bailor takes the chattels from his bailee before the term expires, the latter can recover, not the value of the goods, but the value of his interest. So if a bailee converts, by using or disposing of the goods in a way different from that in which he is entitled to use or dispose of them, the bailor can recover only so much as the goods were worth, less the value of the bailee's interest. For instance, in an action by a pledgor against a pledgee, the latter may recoup to the extent of his debt and lien against the value of the goods.[8] A common carrier who becomes liable for a conversion by a misdelivery of goods can reduce the recovery by the amount of his charges for their carriage.[9] In trover by a chattel mortgage against

Exception as between general and special owner.

[4] "The carrier is no more than his servant," says Grose, J., in Gordon *v.* Harper, 7 T. R. 12. But this is an unsafe assertion.

[5] See *In re* Winkfield, (1902) P. 42.

[6] Johnson *v.* Lancashire, etc., R. Co., 3 C. P. D. 499.

[7] Ludden *v.* Buffalo Batting Co., 22 Ill. App. 415.

[8] Ludden *v.* Buffalo Batting Co., 22 Ill. App. 415.

[9] Forbes *v.* Boston, etc., R. Co., 133 Mass. 154.

Volume I

the mortgagor or those claiming under him, the plaintiff can recover only the amount of the mortgage debt, in case the value of the chattels exceeds that amount; and similarly the mortgagor as against the mortgagee can recover the value of the mortgaged property less the mortgage debt.[1]

Explanation of this exception.

We are inclined to think that the proper interpretation of those decisions in which, as between general and special owners, recovery is limited to the actual damage suffered, is that we are here confronted with what is really a perversion of the action of trover. The proper remedy as between general and special owners is by an action on the case, and not by an action of trover at all.[2] But the action of trover is now, it seems, universally held to be a proper remedy as between such parties. The result is that in these cases a rule of liability has been declared which, while entirely consistent with the theory of the case, is not fully consistent with the theory of trover.

Perversion of trover.

In *Chinery v. Viall* (1860),[3] a purchaser of sheep left them with the vendor, subject to his lien for the unpaid purchase price. The vendor having disposed of the sheep to a third person, it was held, in an action brought by the first purchaser against the vendor for a conversion, that the plaintiff could recover no more than the loss sustained by him as a result of the defendant's breach of contract. The perversion of the remedy is here very plain. There was no actual conversion, because the plaintiff had not at any time been entitled to possession. But an action of trover was allowed to be maintained instead of case, and the court, in order to prevent injustice, was compelled to modify the rule of damages which

[1] Brink *v.* Freoff, 40 Mich. 610. See also Brierly *v.* Kendall, 17 Q. B. 937, 79 E. C. L. 937.

[2] In Lee *v.* Atkinson, Yelv. 172, where it appeared that a bailor had wrongfully retaken the chattels before the term of bailment expired, it was suggested that case was the proper remedy. See also Forbes *v.* Parker, 16 Pick. (Mass.) 462. In Donald *v.* Suckling, L. R. 1 Q. B. 614, Lord Blackburn regrets that it had not always been insisted that case should be used in actions between general and special owners.

[3] 5 H. & N. 288, overruling in effect Gillard *v.* Brittan, 8 M. & W. 575.

is generally applied in trover, thus establishing an exception which, if not vexatious, at least has to be accounted for.

Chapter XVII

In England it has been held that where a bailee has a mere lien, like that of the innkeeper, for instance, which ceases to exist when possession is gone, he cannot, in an action of conversion for the wrongful disposal of the goods, set off the amount of his lien.[4]

Miscellaneous Doctrines.

Among eccentric doctrines which have become imbedded in the law of conversion is the old rule, that one who hires a horse to go to a specified place is guilty of a conversion if he goes to some other destination.[5] This is merely a judicial blunder which has been perpetuated in modern times. The proper and original remedy for an abuse of a chattel by a bailee is by the action on the case for the damage consequent upon the abuse.[6] Underlying the anomaly seems to be some such idea as this, namely, that the bailee's deviation from his contract is such a breach of the trust as makes him a trespasser *ab initio*. Yet the idea is not consistently applied. To ride a horse to Carlisle, when you hired him to go to York, can amount to a conversion only when the act appears to have been done with intent to disseise the owner. The riding to Carlisle is of itself no disseisin, since the bailee has lawful possession, and, as we have already seen, asportation alone is not a conversion *per se*, even when done by a wrongdoer. To hold the hirer generally liable in such case in an action of trover is clearly contrary to principle. But in truth the full consequence of this perversion of principle is avoided by limiting the rule to those cases where the horse is lost or actually harmed in consequence of the deviation from the contract.

Conversion of horse by departure from terms of hiring.

Principle anomalous.

It has been held that a slave is converted if the hirer uses

[4] Mulliner *v.* Florence, 3 Q. B. D. 484. But in Massachusetts it has been held that a carrier who wrongfully sells to enforce his lien can set off his charges against the value of the goods. Briggs *v.* Boston, etc., R. Co., 6 Allen (Mass.) 246.

[5] Wheelock *v.* Wheelwright, 5 Mass. 104; Woodman *v.* Hubbard, 25 N. H. 67; Fisher *v.* Kyle, 27 Mich. 454.

[6] See vol. 3, *Trover;* Y. B. 21 Edw. IV. 76, pl. 9 (by Nele, J.); also vol. 2, *Bailment.*

Volume I

Conversion of slave by use in hazardous employment.

Sublease of chattels.

him in a hazardous business, such as blasting rock;[7] or if he uses him in any way contrary to express agreement.[8] These decisions present the same kind of anomaly as is found in the cases concerning the hiring of horses. But an unauthorized subleasing of property is rightly held to be a conversion, because this is an assumption of ownership and is a virtual disseisin.[1]

Dilution of liquor.

When a conversion.

What appears, at first blush, to be a similar but less pronounced deviation from principle, is found in the ruling that the pouring of water into the wine, or rum, of another is a conversion of the liquor.[2] Such an act deteriorates the stuff and literally converts it into a thing of different quality; but, we may ask, wherein is there a disseisin of the owner? To this it may be answered that the facts incident to such adulteration will generally show an act of dominion inconsistent with the right of the true owner, as that bulk has been broken in transit, or that part has been taken out. Where such an act is shown there is no difficulty in holding the wrongdoer liable in trover. But if a mere trespasser pours water or other adulterant into wine or liquor, and does no more, he is not guilty of a conversion, because he does not disseise the owner.[3]

Seller's right of action against fraudulent vendee.

Another situation where there is a seeming, but only seeming, violation of principle is presented by decisions to the effect that trover can be maintained by a seller against a vendee who has procured the sale and delivery of goods by means of fraud. The leading American authority on this point is found in *Thurston v. Blanchard* (1839),[4] where goods were sold upon a fraudulent misrepresentation, the seller taking the purchaser's note for their price. On discovering the

[7] Mullen *v.* Ensley, 8 Humph. (Tenn.) 428.

[8] Horsely *v.* Branch, 1 Humph. (Tenn.) 199. The contract stipulated against the use of the slave about water. This agreement was violated and the slave was drowned.

[1] Crocker *v.* Gullifer, 44 Me. 491.

[2] Richardson *v.* Atkinson (1723), 1 Stra. 576; Dench *v.* Walker, 14 Mass. 500.

[3] Trespass *vi et armis* for forceful damage to the liquor was the original remedy where one wrongfully drew some wine from the jar and filled it up again with water. Reg. Brev. Orig. 95*b* (*de vino a dolio extracto et aqua maritima impleto*).

[4] 22 Pick. (Mass.) 18.

fraud the seller, without making any demand for the goods or offering to surrender the note, sued the purchaser for a conversion. It was held that the action would lie, the plaintiff, of course, being required to produce and surrender the note at the trial.[5] That replevin, which, in its modern scope, is undoubtedly as much an action of property as detinue, should be maintainable under such circumstances is plain,[6] but to sanction trover here seems, on first impression, to require a decided stretch of the principle which underlies conversion.[7] The fraudulent vendee does not, it is true, obtain a good title, but he undoubtedly gets a legal possession coupled with a defeasible title, and an innocent subsequent purchaser for value from him acquires, of course, an indefeasible title.[8] The taking of possession by the fraudulent vendee, then, certainly does not of itself work a disseisin. The actionable wrong in these cases appears to consist, not in the taking, but in the wrongful detention of the goods against the seller's right to have possession, a right which is unquestionable whenever he elects to assert it. Wrongful detention here operates as a disseisin exactly as it does in the case of bailees.

Explanation of the doctrine.

With the question as to what it takes to make a fraudulent sale within the meaning of the rule above stated, we are not here concerned. It may be observed, however, that where the fraud is of such nature that the sale is totally void, the very taking of possession by the fraudulent purchaser is a disseisin. Having no title at all, he cannot in this case transmit title of any sort, even to an innocent purchaser, and trover can be maintained by the seller against any person into whose hands the goods may come. The most common illustration of this

When taking of possession under fraudulent sale a conversion.

[5] To the same effect are Noble *v.* Adams (1816), 7 Taunt. 59, 2 E. C. L. 59; Kilby *v.* Wilson (1825), R. & M. 178, 21 E. C. L. 409; Hawse *v.* Crowe, R. & M. 414, 21 E. C. L. 477; Bristol *v.* Wilsmore (1823), 1 B. & C. 514, 8 E. C. L. 218; Farwell *v.* Hanchett, 120 Ill. 573; Moody *v.* Drown, 58 N. H. 45; Waters *v.* Van Winkle, 3 N. J. L. 154; Ladd *v.* Moore, 3 Sandf. (N. Y.) 589; Warner *v.* Vallily, 13 R. I. 483; Gage *v.* Epperson, 2 Head. (Tenn.) 669.

[6] Koch *v.* Lyon, 82 Mich. 513; Farley *v.* Lincoln, 51 N. H. 577.

[7] See observations of Professor Ames, 11 Harv. L. Rev. 386.

[8] Sheppard *v.* Shoolbred, C. & M. 61, 41 E. C. L. 39; Traywick *v.* Keeble, 93 Ala. 498.

Volume I

is where one fraudulently obtains goods by personating or using the name of another. For instance: Alfred Blenkarn, who occupies a room in a house looking onto Wood street, Cheapside, orders goods of a manufacturer, giving his address as "37 Wood street, Cheapside," and signs the order as being from "Blenkiron & Co." There is a reputable firm, W. Blenkiron & Co., carrying on business at 123 Wood street. The manufacturer, thinking he is dealing with this firm, sends the goods as ordered. Blenkarn receives the goods ordered by him and disposes of them to the defendants, who are ignorant of the fraud. The defendants are liable for conversion.[9]

Innominate tort against reversioner and remainderman.

In conclusion, it may be noted that the owner of a reversionary or remainder interest in chattels cannot maintain an action of trover for a conversion which takes place before the particular estate is determined,[1] for he has neither the possession nor the right of possession. Such owner is in the same plight as is the bailor who has made a bailment for a definite term.[2] The tort, however, is an innominate injury, and the remedy is by an action on the case or, perhaps, in some jurisdictions, by bill in equity. It cannot be called a true conversion. The damage which will give rise to such right of action must be of a permanent and not merely of a temporary character.[3]

Not a true conversion.

Now that forms of action have been abolished in most jurisdictions, it has been suggested that the meaning of the term 'conversion' should be extended so as to include these innominate wrongs against reversioners and remaindermen.[4] But this would subvert the entire theory of the law of conversion and hopelessly confound the treatment of it. The abolition of actions does not render less necessary the preserva-

[9] Cundy *v.* Lindsay, 3 App. Cas. 459; Kingsford *v.* Merry, 1 H. & N. 503; Stephenson *v.* Hart, 4 Bing. 476; Rogers *v.* Dutton, 182 Mass. 187.

[1] Nations *v.* Hawkins, 11 Ala. 859; Lewis *v.* Mobley, 4 Dev. & B. L. (20 N. Car.) 323; Philips *v.* Martiney, 10 Gratt. (Va.) 333.

[2] Fairbank *v.* Phelps, 22 Pick. (Mass.) 535.

[3] Mears *v.* London, etc., R. Co., 11 C. B. N. S. 850, 103 E. C. L. 850.

[4] Observations on Trover and Conversion, 21 L. Quar. Rev. 53, 54.

Chapter XVII

tion of distinctions between the different sorts of wrongs, and the conception of conversion must not be allowed to contradict the notion of disseisin on which the tort is founded.

Disseisin of Real Property.

Doctrine of conversion not extended to real property.

The doctrine of conversion has some analogies, but is not duplicated in the field of real property. This is due to the very simple fact that land is a thing which cannot be made off with. If one is disseised of land, his rights are adequately protected by remedies for the recovery of the property itself, or possession of it. Hence the law has not made those who acquire adverse possession of real property liable in damages to the extent of its value. The action of trespass for mesne profits, which lies at common law after judgment for the plaintiff in ejectment, to recover damages for unlawful use and occupation [5] does not, it may be observed, proceed upon the theory of a desseisin of the land. This remedy is merely a form of the ordinary action of trespass upon realty (*quare clausum fregit*).

Wrongful diversion of title.

Though plainly one cannot convert land in the sense of making way with it, he undoubtedly may sometimes become liable by wrongfully diverting title from the owner and causing him thereby to lose it, as where land fraudulently acquired is sold to an innocent purchaser. The injured party here has a right of action for the fraud, and there is no need to appeal to the doctrine of conversion.

Misappropriation by trustees.

A principle very similar to that underlying conversion is applied to trustees who misappropriate trust funds or trust property of any kind. They are compelled to account for the full value of the property, though some, or even all of it, can be recovered. In Massachusetts a case lately arose of this kind: A mortgagee of land, under a mortgage containing a power of sale upon default in the payment of the debt, wrongfully sold before default occurred. The property was purchased by a third person on behalf of the mortgagee (who

Abuse of trust by mortgagee.

[5] Donford *v.* Ellys, 12 Mod. 138; Aslin *v.* Parkin, 2 Burr. 665; Wilkinson *v.* Kirby, 15 C. B. 430, 80 E. C. L. 430; Doe *v.* Wright, 10 Ad. & El. 763, 37 E. C. L. 222.

thereby acquired at most a defeasible title). He subsequently sold to an innocent purchaser for value. It was held by a majority of the court that the mortgagor could recover damages of the mortgagee to the full extent of the value of the property, just as in case of the conversion of chattels.[6] But even this singular case does not show that disseisin of land is a basis of liability for civil damage. The ground of action here is the abuse of trust, and it merely happens that upon the particular facts the measure of damage was here held to be the same as if there had been a conversion.

[6] Rogers *v.* Barnes, 169 Mass. 179 (three judges dissenting).

CHAPTER XVIII

INTERFERENCE WITH DOMESTIC RELATIONS.

Husband and Wife.

AT a very early day the common law began to take notice of interferences with the domestic relations. In the Register there appears a writ *de uxore abducta,*[1] which was available to the husband where his wife eloped with another, or was forcibly taken away. Curiously enough, the writ mentioned the wife as being taken along with the husband's chattels, and doubtless it was because of the fact that the taking of the wife could be treated as being *in consimili casu* with the taking of the gown and petticoat which she wore,[2] that this wrong of abduction got recognition. Pleasantries are sometimes indulged over the alleged fact that at common law the married woman is no more than a chattel. That she is sometimes treated as being in like case with chattels, so far as to admit of the use of the ordinary common-law remedies for the redress of wrongs done to the husband in respect of his conjugal rights, is undoubtedly true. Otherwise some of the most grievous injuries must have gone without redress.

Chapter XVIII

Abduction.

In abduction we have a derivative trespass in which the wrong consists of an interference with the husband's right of consortium which is incident to the conjugal relation. The loss of consortium is plainly the gist of the wrong. Similar to the husband's action for abduction is the action which he has, in his own right, for a battery or assault of the wife. This right of action is distinct from that which is maintainable by the husband and wife in right of the wife for the injury done to her, and is based exclusively on his loss of consortium.[3]

A derivative trespass.

Loss of consortium gist of the wrong.

[1] Reg. Brev. Orig. 97*a*.

[2] Hyde *v.* Scyssor, Cro. Jac. 538.

[3] Guy *v.* Livesey, Cro. Jac. 501, is an illustration of the husband's ac-

Volume I

Criminal conversation.

Rape of the wife necessarily involves a violent battery, and is actionable by the husband.[4] Even criminal conversation with a married woman is held to be actionable as a trespass at the suit of the husband.[5] This ruling proceeds on the rather artificial ground that the wife's consent to the act is invalid to take away its trespassory character, at least as against the husband.[6] "The law will not allow her a consent in such case to the prejudice of her husband, because of the interest he has in her."[7]

Tort transcends theory of trespass.

If the earlier judges, instead of leaning so heavily on the theory of trespass, had boldly declared that there is an independent right to immunity from interference with conjugal relations, then the action on the case would have been recognized as the proper remedy. In fact we find that in course of time, as the existence of such an independent right became more and more apparent, the action on the case did come into use, and men began to wonder how the action of trespass ever happened to be used at all.[8] Clearly we are here confronted with a class of wrongs which historically have their roots in the law of trespass, but which, nevertheless, in maturity lie altogether beyond the field of trespass and belong to that body of legal injuries in which harm is conceived as being done, not to person or property, but to rights incident to them. "The husband has the right to the conjugal fellowship of his wife, to her society, her aid, and her fidelity in every conjugal relation. Any act of another by which he is deprived of this right constitutes a personal wrong for which the law gives him a redress in damages."[9]

Disability of wife.

The wife has no corresponding right to legal redress as

tion in his own right for loss of consortium.

Russell *v.* Corne, 2 Ld. Raym. 1032, is an illustration of the right of action by husband and wife in right of the wife for the personal injury to her.

[4] In the old books this action is usually associated with abduction. Brooke Abr., *Trespass,* pl. 43.

[5] Woodward *v.* Walton, 2 B. & P. N. R. 482; Galizard *v.* Rigault, 2 Salk. 552; Bull. N. P., *Adultery,* 26*a.*

[6] Bedan *v.* Turney, 99 Cal. 653; Wales *v.* Miner, 89 Ind. 118.

[7] Holt, C. J., in Rigaut *v.* Gallisard, 7 Mod. 78.

[8] Macfadzen *v.* Olivant, 6 East 387.

[9] Bedan *v.* Turney, 99 Cal. 653.

against a woman who has intercourse with her husband.[1] This results from her common-law disability to sue alone; but other reasons, more or less artificial, have been assigned for it.[2]

Master and Servant.

Passing from the relation of husband and wife to that of master and servant, we find a very conspicuous right recognized by law as incident to this relation, namely, the right of the superior in the relation to the service of the inferior. Interference with this right to service is obnoxious to the law and constitutes a ground of legal liability in the same way that interference with the conjugal relation is treated as a ground of liability in the relation of husband and wife. The Register has its writ of trespass for the abduction of a servant (villein) no less than for the abduction of a wife.[3] So it gives a writ for the besieging of one's premises whereby his servants are prevented from coming to their duty.[4]

Right to service.

Interference with relation of service.

The taking of any servant or apprentice out of the service of another is an actionable trespass.[5] The early law of course contemplated a forceful taking, this being necessary to make out a trespass *vi et armis*. But in course of time, by an extension of the common-law doctrine, due perhaps as much to the influence of the policy of the Statute of Laborers as to anything else, the enticement or procurement of a servant to leave his master's employment became actionable. The remedy for this injury is by an action on the case.[6] The mere employment or harboring of one who is known to have quit

Abduction, enticement, and harboring of servant.

[1] Kroessin *v.* Keller, 60 Minn. 372.

[2] E. g., 3 Bl. Com. 142, 143.

[3] Reg. Brev. Orig. 96*b* (*de nativis abductis*); also *ib.*, 96*b* (2d par.).

[4] Reg. Brev. Orig. 95*a* (*de manso obsesso*), cited in note to Martinez *v.* Gerber, 3 M. & G. 90, 42 E. C. L. 56.

[5] Bottiller *v.* Newport, Y. B. 21 Hen. VI. 31, pl. 18; Y. B. 22 Hen. VI. 30, pl. 49; Y. B. 14 Hen. IV. 32, pl. 45; 2 Rolle Abr. 551, pl. 8; F. N. B. 91, I.

[6] Hart *v.* Aldridge, 1 Cowp. 54; Reg. *v.* Daniel, 1 Salk. 380; Y. B. 11 Hen. IV. (1409) 23, pl. 46; Brooke Abr. *Laborers*, pl. 21; Fitz. Abr., *Laborers*, pl. 16. Coleridge, J., in Lumley *v.* Gye, 2 El. & Bl. 255, 75 E. C. L. 255, gives full account of the year-book authorities above cited. The interpretation placed on them by him, it may be added, is too narrow. For a modern case on the enticement of a son *per quod servitium amisit* see Caughey *v.* Smith, 47 N. Y. 244.

Volume I

the service of another whom he is legally obliged to serve is not actionable at common law,[7] but was made so by the statute.[8]

Beating of servant.

The battery of a servant constitutes a wrong against the master in so far, and only in so far, as it interferes with the relation of service.[9] Hence the beating must be sufficiently grievous to disable the servant in some degree from giving the service which is due to his master. The consequential loss of service is the ground and gist of the master's action.[1]

Double right of action.

As the servant has his own action for every battery, the wrongdoer may thus become separately liable to both master and servant, the master recovering for the loss of service and the servant for the personal injury. "And thus damages are recovered twice for the same trespass, *diversis respectibus*."[2]

Remedy of master.

As a matter of abstract theory the master's remedy should be by an action on the case, but, like the husband, he was permitted to use trespass.[3]

Unlawful imprisonment of servant.

It must not be imagined that the master's right of action for injury to his servant is limited to cases where the wrongdoer is guilty of a technical trespass upon the servant. The master has his action if there be a legal injury of any kind whereby loss of service ensues.[4] The unlawful imprisonment

[7] Adams *v.* Bafealds, 1 Leon. 240. See Blake *v.* Lanyon, 6 T. R. 221, where it was held that the retention of one in service, after notice of service due to previous employer, gives a right of action. This decision can only be supported by resting it on the Statute of Laborers. Coleridge, J., in Lumley *v.* Gye, 2 El. & Bl. 252, 75 E. C. L. 252.

[8] 25 Edw. III. For form of the writ upon the statute see F. N. B. 167, B.

For a modern case of enticing a servant and harboring after notice, see Hartley *v.* Cummings, 5 C. B. 247, 57 E. C. L. 247.

[9] Y. B. 21 Hen. VI. 8, pl. 19; Brooke Abr., *Trespass*, pl. 139; *ib.*, pl. 131.

[1] Mary's Case, 9 Coke 113*a;* Hodsoll *v.* Stallebrass, 11 Ad. & El. 301, 39 E. C. L. 94.

"If one beat my servant lightly, except the master lose his servant, no action lieth." Crogate *v.* Morris, 1 Brownl. & Goldes. 197.

[2] Y. B. 19 Hen. VI. 45, pl. 94; 2 Rolle Abr. 552, pl. 7 (top); Brooke Abr., *Trespass*, pl. 131.

[3] Ditcham *v.* Bond, 2 M. & S. 436; Osborn's Case, 10 Coke 130*b*.

[4] But where the servant could sue only in case, the master's remedy is, of course, also in case. Martinez *v.* Gerber, 3 M. & G. 88, 42 E. C. L. 55.

Chapter XVIII

of a servant,[5] or the negligent injury of him in transportation,[6] gives the master a right of action to the same extent as a direct disabling battery.[7]

Negligent injury.

Guardian and Ward.

The early common law gave to the father (or other proper ancestor), and to the guardian, a right of action for the taking away and marrying of an heir or ward.[8] The wrong here recognized had its root in that obsolete incident of feudal tenure known as the right of marriage,[9] and the loss of the marriage was the gist of the action.[1] It was not based on loss of service, for service was not recognized as a legal incident of the relation.[2]

Loss of marriage.

In *Barham v. Dennis* (1599),[3] the doctrine that loss of the marriage is the gist of the father's action and that the right of action extends only to the abduction of a son or daughter who is also heir, and not to the taking of other children, was accepted.[4]

Parent and Child.

Though the common law has never given formal recognition to the broad right of the parent to the consortium of

[5] Woodward *v.* Washburn, 3 Den. (N. Y.) 369.

[6] Ames *v.* Union R. Co., 117 Mass. 541.

[7] See Louisville, etc., R. Co. *v.* Willis, 83 Ky. 57; Larson *v.* Berquist, 34 Kan. 334.

[8] F. N. B. 90 H; Ratcliffe's Case, 3 Coke 38.

[9] See 1 Poll. & Mait. Hist. Eng. Law (2d ed.) 318 *et seq.*

[1] Y. B. 12 Hen. IV. 16, pl. 9; Y. B. 29 Ass. 164, pl. 35; Ratcliffe's Case, 3 Coke 38.

[2] Y. B. 22 Hen. VI. 31*a*, pl. 49. Newton, J.: "He [my son and heir] can serve where he pleases and I cannot constrain him to serve me against his will."

In Gray *v.* Jefferies, Cro. Eliz. 55, it was held that an action will not lie at the suit of the father for a battery of his son whereby the son is made lame and decrepit. Here there was no allegation of a loss of service nor any suggestion that such allegation would have supported the action if made.

[3] Cro. Eliz. 769.

[4] But not without dissent. Said Glanvill, J.: "The father hath an interest in every of his children to educate them and to provide for them; and he hath his comfort by them. Wherefore it is not reasonable that any should take them from him, and to do him such an injury, but that he should have his remedy to punish it." Cro. Eliz. 770. The common law, it is needless to add, has never reached this high plane. It does not recognize the pleasure

Volume I

Action for loss of service.

children as it has done in the relation of husband and wife, such right is nevertheless sanctioned by the deepest instincts of nature, and it has at times pressed very hard for recognition. The courts have so far yielded to this pressure as to give qualified recognition to such right in the action for loss of service. An important step forward was taken when the courts dispensed with proof of actual service, declaring that the law will presume some service from the mere relation of parent and child.[5] This rule embodies what may be considered an entirely normal extension of doctrine, and it is applied in all sorts of harms to minor children who are in fact old enough to be capable of some service however little.[6] But if a child is very young, an action of trespass grounded on loss of service will not lie, because of its incapacity to do service.[7] As regards the measure of damages, it will be observed that in case of ordinary violent injury, the parent's right of action is limited to the value of the service lost and the consequential damage resulting to the parent by way of expense.[8] No account can here be taken of the hurt to parental feelings.[9]

Seduction of daughter or other female dependent.

Where the wrong consists of the seduction of a female dependent and the getting of her with child, strict theory is laid aside and the parent or other person *in loco parentis* is allowed to recover not only for the loss of service and consequential damage in the way of expenditures, but damage for the parental disgrace and injured feelings. That the law ought to

and comfort which a parent derives from the society of his children as a legal right.

[5] Jones *v.* Brown, 1 Esp. 217, Peake N. P. (ed. 1795) 233 (a case of battery of a son).

[6] In an action for enticing a child away *per quod servitium amisit,* no contract of service and no relation of service other than the relation of service implied by law need be proved. Evans *v.* Walton, L. R. 2 C. P. 615.

[7] Hall *v.* Hollander, 4 B. & C. 660, 10 E. C. L. 436. But a father who is put to necessary expense in curing his infant child can maintain an action on the case for the consequential damage thus indirectly imposed on him. Durden *v.* Barnett, 7 Ala. 169; Sykes *v.* Lawlor, 49 Cal. 236; Dennis *v.* Clark, 2 Cush. (Mass.) 347; Oakland R. Co. *v.* Fielding, 48 Pa. St. 320.

It has been held that the expense of removing from the child a deformity due to the injury after the wound itself is cured is too remote. Karr *v.* Parks, 44 Cal. 46.

[8] Oakland R. Co. *v.* Fielding, 48 Pa. St. 320.

[9] Flemmington *v.* Smithers, 2 C. & P. 292, 12 E. C. L. 131.

recognize the right of the head of a family to see to it that those dependent on him, especially females, are not debauched and that he should have an action for any invasion of this right which results in the getting of them with child needs no argument. The real anomaly of the action for seduction is not found in the fact that the law here permits recovery for the parental disgrace and sorrow, but in the circumstance that the courts have continued to restrict the action within the limits of servitial relations. But the circumstance is not without its instructive feature, as it illustrates the truth that legal evolution is always along the line of least resistance. To give a new action is to recognize a new species of liability and to create a new right. To extend an established remedy, even beyond its legitimate reach, is a far easier thing. Trespass for battery resulting in loss of service supplied the easiest approach to remedying the wrong of seduction, and it was adopted.[1] Hence it is that a relation of service, implied in case of minor females living in the household, actual in case of other dependent females, must always be shown before recovery can be had for seduction.[2]

Action limited to relation of service.

[1] As in Tullidge *v.* Wade (1769), 3 Wils. C. Pl. 18. The idea in allowing trespass for assault and battery to be used in an action for seduction is that the girl's consent to the act of intercourse is irrelevant as against the father, just as the consent of the wife is irrelevant as against the husband in an action for criminal conversation.

The action of trespass *quare clausum fregit* supplies a means of approach to an action for seduction in cases where the wrongdoer comes upon the plaintiff's premises. Here the seduction of the daughter can be given in evidence in aggravation of the trespass upon the realty. Sippora *v.* Basset, 1 Sid. 225. Compare Holt, C. J., in Russell *v.* Corne, 2 Ld. Raym. 1032. The fact that in most cases the entering upon the plaintiff's premises is with his express or implied consent is often an obstacle to the maintenance of the action in the form *quare clausum fregit.* Norton *v.* Jason (1653), Style 398.

License to enter is fatal to an action of trespass *quare clausum fregit* brought to recover consequential damages for the seduction of a daughter, but it cannot be given in evidence under the general issue. Bennett *v.* Allcott, 2 T. R. 166.

[2] Postlethwaite *v.* Parkes, 3 Burr. 1878; Tullidge *v.* Wade, 3 Wils. C. Pl. 18; Satterthwaite *v.* Dewhurst, 4 Dougl. 315, 26 E. C. L. 378; Irwin *v.* Dearman, 11 East 23; Dean *v.* Peel, 5 East 45; Manly *v.* Field, 7 C. B. N. S. 96, 97 E. C. L. 96; Bennett *v.* Allcott, 2 T. R. 166; Hedges *v.* Tagg, L. R. 7 Exch. 283. The case of Ellington *v.* Ellington, 47 Miss. 329 is instructive.

Volume I

Person *in loco parentis.*

Where females not living under the care of their parents are seduced, one occupying the position of a parent or standing *in loco parentis,* as it is called, can maintain an action on like grounds and subject to the same limitations as the parent.[3]

Seduction of self-supporting girl.

For lack of relation of service a parent cannot maintain an action for the seduction of a daughter who is working out to support herself, though she be not of age at the time and though the care and maintenance of her during confinement actually falls upon the parent.[4] Nor is the rule changed by the circumstance that the seduction is accomplished at the parent's home, the girl at the time being there merely on a short visit.[5] A melancholy commentary on the effect of thus adhering to loss of service as the gist of the action for seduction is that it "affords protection to the rich man whose daughter occasionally makes his tea, but leaves without redress the poor man

[3] Manvell *v.* Thomson, 2 C. & P. 303, 12 E. C. L. 136 (uncle); Paterson *v.* Wilcox, 20 U. C. C. P. 385 (brother); Ball *v.* Bruce, 21 Ill. 161 (guardian); Davidson *v.* Goodall, 18 N. H. 423 (cousin); Certwell *v.* Hoyt, 6 Hun (N. Y.) 575 (grandfather).

But it must appear that the parent has no right of action on the particular facts. Blanchard *v.* Ilsley, 120 Mass. 487.

[4] Grinnell *v.* Wells, 7 M. & G. 1033, 49 E. C. L. 1033.

The student will note that consequential damages which fall upon a parent by reason of necessary expenditures in connection with the confinement of his seduced daughter, there being no relation of service interfered with, are not recoverable; while, as we have seen above (note, p. 268), expenditures made necessary in curing an infant (too young to be of service) are recoverable by the parent. The distinction is a sound one. The doing of violent injury to the infant is in law a wrongful act in itself, and the child has its own right of action therefor. The act being wrongful in itself, the wrongdoer is held liable for consequential damage resulting therefrom, even though such damage be incurred by a third person, to wit, the parent. But the getting of a daughter with child, as a result of seduction, is not of itself a trespass as against her, because she gives consent. This act then is not a legal wrong in and of itself. Hence in the case supposed (i. e., where there is no interference with a relation of service) there is no basis on which to support an action for purely consequential damage. Consequential damage can no more be the basis of a ground of action than the elements of fraud, malice, or negligence. There must be some recognized right infringed, from which infringement the consequential damage flows.

[5] Hedges *v.* Tagg, L. R. 7 Exch. 283.

whose child, as here, is sent unprotected to earn her bread amongst strangers." [6]

But if, by this process, the right of action for seduction is in one direction rendered less extensive than feeling suggests is proper, in another direction the cause of action is thereby made more extensive than the actual ends of justice require. Thus it is determined that an employer may maintain an action for debauching his servant *per quod servitium amisit,* though he is in no way related to her by blood or marriage.[7] And the recoverable damages are not strictly limited to actual pecuniary loss.[8] The right of action here recognized is of comparatively little moment, and it by no means compensates for the shortcomings of the action for seduction above noted.

Employer's right of action for seduction of servant.

The reader will observe that the wrong of seduction is an analogue of the wrong of criminal conversation. Historically both are derivative trespasses, but as a matter of substantive theory they lie entirely without the sphere of trespass and embody the conception of injury done in respect of a right incident to family relation. In legal evolution they belong to a much later formation than that of trespass. Appreciation of the truth that seduction does not belong to the same legal formation as trespass appears in the remark of Buller, J., to the effect that the action on the case is the common-law remedy for debauching a man's daughter whereby he loses her service (no unlawful entry on the premises being alleged).[9] On this point he was wrong, for as a matter of legal history, the action is in form an action of trespass.[1] But as a matter of fact, case has been commonly used in modern times,[2] theory thus triumphing in a degree over mere legal history.

Nature of the action for seduction.

[6] Note by Manning and Granger to Grinnell *v.* Wells, 7 M. & G. 1044, 49 E. C. L. 1044.

[7] Fores *v.* Wilson, Peake N. P. (ed. 1795) 55; McKersie *v.* McLean, 6 Ont. 428.

[8] But the injury to feelings and the element of disgrace are not to be considered as in an action by the parent. Ford *v.* Gourlay, 42 U. C. Q. B. 552.

[9] See Bennett *v.* Allcott, 2 T. R. 167.

[1] Woodward *v.* Walton, 2 B. & P. N. R. 476.

[2] Dean *v.* Peel, 5 East 45; Irwin *v.* Dearman, 11 East 23; Verry *v.* Watkins, 7 C. & P. 308, 32 E. C. L. 520. Trespass or case may be used at the pleader's option. Chamberlain *v.* Hazelwood (1839), 5 M. & W. 515.

Volume I

Seduced female has no cause of action against seducer.

It need hardly be added that the female who is seduced and got with child has no cause of action at common law for the wrong done to her.[3] Her consent, though deceitfully obtained, takes away the trespass, and the seducer's fraud is not recognized as a ground of action in case. But it is allowable in some jurisdictions to prove a seduction in aggravation of damage in a suit for breach of marriage promise.[4] The rule which disables a woman from suing for her own seduction has lately been abrogated in many American jurisdictions,[5] and it is doubtless modified in some degree by the enactments fixing the so-called age of consent.[6] Where the female is given a right to sue for her own seduction the tort thus recognized is in the nature of deceit.

[3] Woodward *v.* Anderson, 9 Bush (Ky.) 624; Paul *v.* Frazier, 3 Mass. 71; Hamilton *v.* Lomax, 26 Barb. (N. Y.) 615.

[4] Millington *v.* Loring, 6 Q. B. D. 190; Sherman *v.* Rawson, 102 Mass. 395; Conn *v.* Wilson, 2 Overt. (Tenn.) 233. *Contra,* Burks *v.* Shain, 2 Bibb (Ky.) 341; Baldy *v.* Stratton, 11 Pa. St. 316.

[5] See e. g. Hood *v.* Sudderth, 111 N. Car. 215.

[6] Thus, it has lately been held in New York that a guardian who seduces his ward can be sued by her, she being under age of consent at the time of the seduction. Graham *v.* Wallace, 50 N. Y. App. Div. 101.

CHAPTER XIX

DEFAMATION.

History and General State of the Law of Slander and Libel.

Chapter XIX

IN the history of the development of our law of defamation there was a perversion of evolutionary processes, and as a result we are here confronted with a rather heterogeneous pile which should normally have gone to form a consistent body of legal doctrine, but which, on the contrary, comprises many disconnected fragments moving in a confused way under the impulse of different principles. "Marred in the making," is the verdict which the student is bound to pass when he comes to examine the outward structure and internal relations of this branch of the law.

Heterogeneity of the law of defamation.

That our law of defamation is full of anomalies is now well recognized, and we need waste no words in showing that it is so. The cause for existence of such a state of affairs is to be discovered of course in legal history. As has been well said, "the crooked and wrenched form of the law of slander and libel can be accounted for, but it must be accounted for in the way we account for the distorted shape of a tree — by looking for the special circumstances under which it has grown and the forces to which it has been exposed." [1] Fortunately the history of the growth of this branch of the law has lately been explored by competent scholars with historical insight.[2]

Explanation found in historical causes.

[1] Slander and Libel (1872), 6 Am. L. Rev. 597 (by N. St. John Green).

[2] See English Law of Defamation, by Frank Carr, 18 L. Quar. Rev. (1902) 255, 388, *et seq.*; also History and Theory of Law of Defamation, by Van Vechten Veeder, 3 Columbia L. Rev. 546 *et seq.*, 4 Columbia L. Rev. 33 *et seq.* The unsigned article by the late Mr. N. St. John Green, entitled Slander and Libel, in 6 Am. L. Rev. (1872), 593, is brilliant and original. This writer was the first to attempt to interpret the law of defamation in the light of legal history. The ingenious explanations which he advances, however, cannot be fully accepted.

Gist of defamation.

But before attempting to deal with the idiosyncrasies of this branch of English law, let us ascertain the conception which is at the root of this tort of defamation — the general principle which has struggled for utterance in the decisions of our courts, albeit with only partial success. This fundamental notion is unquestionably found in the idea of harm as incident to interference with one's good name or reputation. The repute in which one is held among his fellow men has been proved by the experience of the human race to be a most potent factor in determining his moral, social, and even material well-being. No mere poetic fancy suggested the truth that a good name is rather to be chosen than great riches. Poor indeed is he who is robbed of it. Accordingly no system of civil law can fail to take some account of the right to have one's reputation remain untarnished by defamation. Infringement of the right to reputation being the gist of the wrong of defamation, it follows that the problem now before us is to discover what acts constitute an infringement of this right.

Means by which the wrong is accomplished.

It is manifest at the outset that the repute in which one is held in a community can only be injured by the communication of spoken or written words, or by signs, pictures, or effigies which are equally competent to convey thought. Reputation represents a consensus of the judgment of others upon one's real character, and that judgment can only be affected by such instrumentalities as are capable of reaching the seat of judgment, which is in the mind. Hence, in the law of defamation we have to deal only with the effect of ideas, which have been communicated in some way, as by spoken or written words, by the sign language of deaf-mutes, or by pictures, signs, or effigies.

Falsity essential to defamation.

Again, it is plain that no civil cause of action can ever arise out of any communication of ideas from one person to another unless the communication or idea conveyed be false. To say that a particular communication is defamatory necessarily implies falsity in some respect or in some particular. However reprehensible in morals it may sometimes be for A to tell the truth about B, and however harmful it may be to the latter to have the truth known, a civil court cannot take notice

Chapter XIX

of a truthful communication as giving rise to a cause of action. More than one reason, founded on considerations of good sense and policy, may be assigned in support of this. The common one is that "the law will not permit a man to recover damages in respect of an injury to a character which he either does not or ought not to possess."[3] This goes on the assumption that conceding an injury to be done, the plaintiff's want of equity eats up his cause. "The law bars the party of a redress which he does not deserve."[4]

But in this view a cause of action is created merely in order to be demolished, and the simpler solution is to be found in the proposition that the speaking of the truth is not a ground of legal liability at all. The law evidently starts from the proposition that only what is in fact or effect a lie can be the basis of a civil action for damages. It was hard enough to get our courts to recognize that a lie may sometimes be civilly actionable, and they have never admitted that the telling of the truth may be a ground of action though the motive be ever so bad. The view commonly entertained, namely, that the speaking of the truth, if it be *prima facie* defamatory, gives rise to a cause of action, but that the law, for equitable reasons, disables the party injured from obtaining redress, is based solely on the fact that the truth of words which are *prima facie* actionable cannot be given in evidence unless specially pleaded; but we think this rule is capable of a different interpretation.

Truthful communication gives no cause of action.

The truth of the proposition that no cause of action can arise from truthful statements is conclusively shown by decisions to the effect that even the existence of express malice on the part of the person speaking or writing will not suffice to make him liable if he can show the truth of the statement which he made.[5] If the contrary view were correct, namely, that the cause of action which accrues by reason of the speaking or writing is taken away upon proof of its truthfulness, then it would follow, by analogy to other similar situations,

Malice does not make truth actionable.

[3] M'Pherson *v.* Daniels, 10 B. & C. 272, 21 E. C. L. 74.

[4] Poll. on Torts, 6th ed., 254.

[5] Castle *v.* Houston, 19 Kan. 417; Foss *v.* Hildreth, 10 Allen (Mass.) 76. In this case it is stated by way of dictum that this rule applies only in slander; but that is a mistake.

Volume I

that existence of express malice would prevent the defendant from taking advantage of the truth of his words; for, as we shall hereafter more fully perceive, malice is destructive of 'privilege'— but it cannot give rise to legal liability where there is none to begin with.

Communication must be defamatory.

Again, it is plain that before a false communication can be a basis of legal liability it must be of a defamatory nature; that is, it must be such as in fact to touch and tarnish the reputation, or such as manifestly tends to do so.

Now when all the factors above specified concur, that is, when a false communication is made by one person to another concerning a third which brings reproach and shame upon him and substantially impairs his good name, there is a legal wrong for which damage may be recovered. The proposition just stated is undoubtedly in harmony with true legal theory and with the law of all civilized states, ancient and modern, of which we have any knowledge, except English law; and it is at this very point that the peculiarity of our law of defamation becomes apparent.

Common-law doctrine of defamation.

The English law, instead of accepting the general principle that the publication of false matter which substantially impairs one's reputation, or which manifestly tends to do so, is actionable, requires that at least one of certain other conditions shall exist. The result is that in common-law jurisdictions the law of defamation is narrower than that which prevails in other jurisdictions, and with us what defamatory utterances and communications are a ground of action is determined not by any general principle, but by the enumeration of arbitrary classes of cases. Thus, in English law matter which tends to hurt one's reputation is actionable in any of the following situations, viz.:

Words imputing offense.

I. If it imputes a criminal offense the perpetration of which would subject the offender to corporal punishment;[6] or, as is sometimes ruled, a criminal offense which involves moral tur-

[6] Elliot *v.* Ailsberry, 2 Bibb(Ky.) 473; Buck *v.* Hersey, 31 Me. 558; Birch *v.* Benton, 26 Mo. 153; Billings *v.* Wing, 7 Vt. 439.

Chapter XIX

pitude;[7] or disgrace;[8] or which would subject the offender to infamous punishment;[9] or any offense which is indictable and involves moral turpitude and corporal punishment;[1] or, still more broadly, any criminal offense whatever.[2]

Cognizable in common-law courts.

But the offense charged must of course be cognizable in the common-law courts. To call a man a heretic is not actionable, for heresy is only a spiritual offense, and the common-law judges naïvely pretended that they could not know what it took to make heresy.[3]

The inability of the courts to agree upon the exact criterion of the rule which they have here attempted to frame shows that the basis of this whole edifice is purely artificial.

Imputation of loathsome disease.

II. Matter also constitutes actionable slander if it imputes to the person slandered an affliction of the plague, leprosy, or venereal disease.[4]

Aspersion in respect of one's profession.

III. Or if it casts an injurious imputation upon one in respect of his office, profession, or business.[5]

[7] Frisbie *v.* Fowler, 2 Conn. 707; Hoag *v.* Hatch, 23 Conn. 585; Redway *v.* Gray, 31 Vt. 292; Murray *v.* McAllister, 38 Vt. 167.

[8] Miller *v.* Parish, 8 Pick. (Mass.) 384; Brown *v.* Nickerson, 5 Gray (Mass.) 1; Ranger *v.* Goodrich, 17 Wis. 78.

[9] McKee *v.* Wilson, 87 N. Car. 300; Harris *v.* Terry, 98 N. Car. 131.

[1] Griffin *v.* Moore, 43 Md. 246; Brooker *v.* Coffin, 5 Johns. (N. Y.) 188.

[2] Webb *v.* Beavan, 11 Q. B. D. 609.

[3] Y. B. 27 Hen. VIII. 14, pl. 4; 1 Ames & Smith, Cases on Torts, 394.

[4] Villers *v.* Monsley, 2 Wils. C. Pl. 403; Taylor *v.* Perkins, Cro. Jac. 144; Bloodworth *v.* Gray, 7 M. & G. 334, 49 E. C. L. 334.

[5] How *v.* Prinn, 2 Salk. 694, affirmed by House of Lords, 7 Mod. 113; Foulger *v.* Newcomb, L. R. 2 Exch. 327; Evans *v.* Gwyn, 5 Q. B. 844, 48 E. C. L. 844; Highmore *v.* Harrington, 3 C. B. N. S. 142, 91 E. C. L. 142; Collier *v.* Simpson, 5 C. & P. 73, 24 E. C. L. 219; Edsall *v.* Russell, 4 M. & G. 1090, 43 E. C. L. 560.

For distinction as regards actionability of imputations in cases of offices of honor and offices of profit, see Alexander *v.* Jenkins (1892), 1 Q. B. 797.

But the connection between the slander and the plaintiff's calling must be made clear. Dorley *v.* Roberts (1837), 3 Bing. N. Cas. 835, 32 E. C. L. 346.

In Ayre *v.* Craven, 2 Ad. & El. 2, 29 E. C. L. 11, the declaration for slander alleged that the defendant used words imputing adultery to the plaintiff, a physician; and the words were laid to have been spoken of him in his profession. No special damage was laid, and after verdict for the plaintiff, judgment was arrested, the court holding that such words, merely laid to be spoken of a physician, were not actionable without special damage; and that if they were so spoken as to convey an imputation

Volume I

Words of disherison.

IV. Or if the matter is such as tends to the disherison of one who acquires land by descent, as where he is represented as being illegitimate.[6]

Pecuniary damage.

V. If no one of these several conditions is present, then defamatory matter becomes actionable if the plaintiff can show that it was followed by actual pecuniary damage such as might have been expected naturally to follow from it.[7]

Written defamation.

VI. Finally, the publication of defamatory matter is actionable if it be propagated by means of writing, printing, pictures, or effigy. In this case the defamatory matter is addressed to the ocular sense, and the injury is termed 'libel.'

Narrowness of common-law doctrine.

It will be observed that in taking the course they did English judges repudiated the idea that words which merely "sound in disgrace"[8] can be a basis of legal liability. In effect this was a repudiation of the universal and fundamental notion which, as we have stated at the outset, is at root of the law of defamation, namely, the idea of the actionability of harm which results from interference with one's reputation. Not all harms, say the English judges, which are incident to the circulation of defamatory matter are a basis of legal wrong. There must be an imputation of crime, or of contamination by loathsome disease, or an imputation hurtful to one in his business, or which tends to disherison, or which is followed by special damage; or the defamation must be in the form of a libel. Nothing could be more illogical than this enumeration; it cannot be called a classification of actionable defamations, for it proceeds upon no principle whatever. It is clear that our law of defamation was atrophied in its first stages and has not yet succeeded in breaking the bonds which stunted its growth.

Law of slander illogical.

Law of libel a normal and logical product.

Yet out of this heterogeneous pile has come forth one shoot, and that the youngest, which exhibits every symptom of entirely normal development. We refer to the law of libel. In this branch of the law of defamation, the fundamental con-

upon his conduct in his profession, the declaration ought to have shown how the speaker connected the imputation with the professional conduct.

[6] Humphry *v.* Stanfeild, Cro. Car. 469, 1 Rolle Abr. 38, pl. 21.

[7] Vaughan *v.* Ellis, Cro. Jac. 213; Bac. Abr., *Slander* (C).

[8] Heake *v.* Moulton, Yelv. 90.

ception that the doing of appreciable harm to one's reputation by the publication of defamatory matter is a source of legal liability is fully accepted. Hence our law of libel, being in conformity with the universal principle, harmonizes with the law of defamation as it exists in other countries, and stands in creditable contrast with that acephalous mass which makes up the law of spoken defamation, or slander.

Chapter XIX

Gist of libel.

From what has been said, it appears that in the field of libel the gist of the action is interference with the right to reputation; in the field of slander there is, properly speaking, in the present state of the law, no one element which can be said to be the gist of the various actions. In the first group of cases the gist of the action appears on analysis to be the jeopardy of criminal prosecution into which one is brought by the circulation of a false report that he is guilty of a crime. But this is clearly an insufficient basis for the right of action, at least in modern times; for hearsay talk is not now admissible in a criminal trial and cannot be said to involve legal jeopardy. In the second group of cases the gist of the action appears to consist in the infringement of a right to social intercourse,[9] which right is of course impaired by falsely telling of one that he is afflicted with a loathsome disease. But this too is entirely artificial. Except as connected with the right to a clean and decent reputation,[1] and except as connected with pecuniary damage,[2] the right to social intercourse is wholly unknown to our law. In other groups of cases the risk of pecuniary loss is the gist of the action, as where one is slandered in his office, business, or profession, or where words are spoken which tend to his disherison. This element also is a spurious basis of liability. Clearly, "the risk of temporal

Gist of slander: 1. Danger of prosecution;

2. Infringement of right to social intercourse;

3. Risk of pecuniary loss;

[9] "It is avoiding him for fear of contagion, and refusing to keep him company, that is the legal notion of damage. And when he is cured those inconveniences will not attend him." Hence it is not actionable to say that one has had the pox. Taylor *v.* Hall, 2 Stra. 1189.

[1] A distinctive right to the 'consortium' of one's neighbors was foreshadowed in Medhurst *v.* Balam, 1 Rolle Abr. 35, pl. 7; but this case was subsequently overruled in Barnes *v.* Bruddel, 1 Lev. 261; Roberts *v.* Roberts, 5 B. & S. 384, 117 E. C. L. 384.

[2] Moore *v.* Meagher (1807), 1 Taunt. 39.

loss is not the same as temporal loss. The risk of suffering injury is not the same as to suffer injury."[3] Yet in these cases risk of injury is given the same legal effect as if it were actual injury.

4. Pecuniary damage.

In still another group of cases the gist of the action is found in the special pecuniary damage which is consequent upon the speaking of the defamatory words. It would be misleading to say that this basis of actionability is spurious; for the idea that a particular act may be a legal wrong when followed by pecuniary damage, but not where there is no such damage, is well grounded in our law. But here the right of action is in one respect too narrow; in another, as we shall hereafter see, too broad. It is plain that in all of these groups of cases the law rests upon a wholly artificial foundation, and space would fail us to state the artificial reasoning to which judges have been wont to resort in order to keep these various rights of action from toppling off their insecure pedestals.[4]

Law of slander should conform to theory of libel.

Nevertheless, it is perfectly plain that the general principle stated is in truth at the basis of liability in the several groups of cases referred to, just as it is at the basis of the law of libel. If the general principle had been accepted from the first that impairment of one's reputation by the dissemination of defamatory speech is a legal wrong, all trouble would have been removed. This is the very principle to which common-law courts have refused to be committed. But it is obvious that a state of stable equilibrium can never be here attained until this truth is fully recognized. It seems probable that before many generations the combined effects of enlightened judicial decision and legislative action will put this branch of law on the correct basis and harmonize it with the law of libel. Otherwise we must admit the final triumph of error.

History of law of defamation.

How our law of slander got into the predicament which we have noted may be briefly told. The law of defamation as administered in the king's courts is of comparatively late

[3] Bowen, L. J., in Chamberlain *v.* Boyd, 11 Q. B. D. 416.

[4] See generally, the papers by Frank Carr and Van Vechten Veeder, above referred to: also Chapter in History of Libel, 10 L. Quar. Rev. 158; also the paper on Slander and Libel (July, 1872), 6 Am. L. Rev. 598.

Chapter XIX

Defamation originally punished in local courts.

origin. In the earliest period of our legal history this tort was punished both civilly and criminally in the local courts; and so far as has been discovered, those courts rightly accepted the general principle that the speaking of any defamatory words is actionable.[5] As the local courts waned and as the king's courts, or courts of common law, waxed strong in power and influence, this jurisdiction over the tort of defamation should normally have fallen to them, and we may perhaps expect to find on the Register appropriate writs for the speaking of false words. But such are not there. "In 1295 a picturesque dispute between two Irish magnates had been removed to Westminster, and Edward I's court declared in solemn fashion that it would not entertain pleas of defamation." [6] The day had not yet come when injuries which did not touch person or property could be remedied in the royal courts. And so the law remained for more than two hundred years.[7] A series of statutes beginning in the reign of Edward I gave the courts power, it is true, to punish slander upon mighty personages (*scandalum magnatum*),[8] but this offense was considered to be of a political character; and so far as we can see, the law concerning it exerted little influence upon the development of common-law civil jurisdiction over defamation.

Scandalum magnatum.

The refusal to entertain civil suits for the speaking of

[5] "We find that in the local courts, not only were bad words punished upon presentment in a summary way, but regular actions for defamation were common. We may gather that in such an action the defendant might allege that his words were true; *veritas non est defamatio.* We may gather that the English for *meretrix* was actionable, though an interchange of this against the English for *latro* left one shilling due to the man. We already hear that a slander was uttered 'of malice aforethought' and sometimes a plaintiff alleges 'special damage.'" 2 Poll. & Mait. Hist. Eng. Law (2d ed.) 538.

[6] 2 Poll. & Mait. Hist. Eng. Law (2d ed.) 536, citing Rot. Parl. i. 133: "*et non sit usitatum in regno isto placitare in curia Regis placita de defamationibus.*"

[7] Very few cases of defamation are reported in the year books. Statham's Abridgment (1498) contains no reference to the action on the case for words. The same is true of Fitzherbert's Abridgment.

[8] Statutes *de Scandalis Magnatum:* 3 Edw. I., c. 34; 2 Rich. II., c. 5; 12 Rich. II., c. 11.

The law concerning *scandalum magnatum,* after having been long disregarded in the actual administration of justice, was abolished in England by statute in 1887.

Ecclesiastical jurisdiction over defamation.

defamatory words seemed the more proper to our early judges for the reason that the ecclesiastical courts exercised a spiritual jurisdiction over this offense. This jurisdiction dated back to that ordinance of the Conqueror which finally separated the spiritual from the temporal courts,[9] and was confirmed from time to time by royal or parliamentary authority.[1] The canonists treated defamation as a sin and punished it by inflicting penance.

Common-law courts assume jurisdiction over defamation.

With this sort of satisfaction ordinary Englishmen, who happened to be slandered, had to be content until the time of Elizabeth, when the common-law courts began to reconsider their position and to take a limited jurisdiction over the offense. In doing this they were of course compelled to take account of what the ecclesiastical courts were doing or could do, and they were thus considerably hampered by the claims of their spiritual rivals. Not a few clashes of jurisdiction over this matter had to be settled by writs of prohibition.[2]

Rivalry of courts.

State of the law in time of Coke.

From the cases collected by Coke,[3] and other cases from the same period, it appears that by the early years of the seventeenth century a common-law action would lie for defamatory words spoken of one in his office, as for instance, where a justice of the peace was charged with corruption,[4] or an attorney with incompetence or double dealing.[5] So an action would lie for injurious words in respect of one's business, as where one who buys and sells is called a bankrupt.[6] Likewise defamatory words imputing a crime were actionable,[7] and it was

[9] Stubbs, Select Charters, 85; Stubbs, 1 Const. Hist. 307; Gee & Hardy, Documents of Church Hist. 57; Adams & Stephens, Sel. Documents Eng. Const. Hist. 1.

[1] Circumspecte Agatis, 13 Edw. I., c. 1; Articuli Cleri, 9 Edw. II.

[2] Y. B. 12 Hen. VII. 22, pl. 2; Brooke Abr., *Prohibition*, pl. 9, 13, 21; *ib.*, *Accion sur Case*, pl. 115. See the account given in Palmer *v.* Thorpe, 4 Coke 20*b*, of the case of the Abbot of St. Albans.

[3] Actions for Slander, 4 Coke 12*b*–20.

[4] Stucley *v.* Ballard, 4 Coke 16; Beaumont's Case, Jenk. 348; Cæsar *v.* Curseny (1593), Cro. Eliz. 305; Beamond *v.* Hastings, Cro. Jac. 240; Masham *v.* Bridges, Cro. Car. 223. But it is not actionable to accuse a justice of mere stupidity. Bill *v.* Neal, 1 Lev. 52.

[5] Byrchley's Case, Jenk. 284, 4 Coke 16; Bestney's Case, Jenk. 361; Martyn *v.* Burlings (1597), Cro. Eliz. 589.

[6] Squire's Case, Jenk. 350; Terry *v.* Hooper, 1 Lev. 115; Selby *v.* Carrier, Cro. Jac. 345.

[7] Snag *v.* Gee, 4 Coke 16; Barham's Case, 4 Coke 20; Bittridge's

Chapter XIX

a cause of action to charge man or woman with a lack of virtue, if his or her prospective marriage was thereby broken off.[8] So to charge one who had land by descent with being illegitimate was held to be actionable, for this tended to his disherison and disturbance by suit.[9] It was likewise actionable falsely to say of another that he had a loathsome venereal disease, like the great pox,[1] or that he had the leprosy.[2]

Temporal damage ground of common-law jurisdiction.

As a starting point these decisions are good enough. The strange thing is that these several kinds of defamation should be accepted as final and exhaustive categories. It is easy to see that the ground of defamation was the doing of 'temporal' harm, that is, such harm or damage as was a subject of civil jurisdiction in the common-law courts, as distinguished from such harms as were of exclusive spiritual cognizance. But the courts were not consistent. Why did not the jurisdiction continue to spread until all words which tended to take away a man's reputation had become actionable? There was a time when it seemed that this indeed would come to pass. In 1610 the Court of the King's Bench unanimously declared, with a view to laying down a definite rule for future guidance, that "where the words spoken do tend to the infamy, discredit, or disgrace of the party, there the words shall be actionable."[3] Nothing could be sounder or more satisfactory in point of theory than this pronouncement.

Courts overrun by actions for defamatory words.

But a few years later the same court was compelled in self-defense to recede from this advanced position. It did indeed look as if the fountains of the deep had been broken up, such a flood of suits for defamation began to pour into the common-law courts. And such a filthy stream! No writer on the law of defamation, we may safely say, will ever undertake to bring

Case, 4 Coke 19; Buckley *v.* Wood, 4 Coke 14*b*. But no action would lie where the imputation or charge of crime was made in legal proceedings. Cutler *v.* Dixon, 4 Coke 14*b*.

[8] Davies *v.* Gardiner, 4 Coke 16*b*; Morison's Case, Jenk. 347, Cro. Jac. 163; Matthew *v.* Croze, 1 Rolle Abr. 34 (D) pl. 1, 5. By custom in London an action would lie for calling a woman a whore without special damage being alleged. Oxford *v.* Cross, 4 Coke 18.

[9] 1 Rolle Abr. 37, pl. 16.

[1] 1 Rolle Abr. 66, pl. 14, 15; Lymbe *v.* Hockly, 1 Lev. 205; Jeames *v.* Rutlech, 4 Coke 17*b*.

[2] Taylor *v.* Perkins, Cro. Jac. 144, 1 Rolle Abr. 44, pl. 4.

[3] Smale *v.* Hammon, 1 Bulst. 40.

to the light of day the material which found its way into some fifty-five pages of Rolle's Abridgment (1668) which are devoted to this topic. Hardly any incident in our legal history is more astonishing than the avidity with which this new action for words was seized upon as a means of gratifying personal spite. Professor Maine, speaking of the annexation of Indian provinces to the British Empire in our own time, has remarked upon the curious and instructive rush of suitors which follows the first establishment of the civil courts.[4] Forbidden to fight, the people go to law. The mere fact that a new remedy is to be had stimulates litigation to abnormal activity. The same spring of action must now have been touched in England, otherwise Englishmen of the seventeenth century stand convicted of being more given to scurrility and billingsgate than any other people under the sun.

Hostile attitude of King's Bench.

At any rate, the Court of the King's Bench was clearly justified in taking a hostile attitude to actions which were constantly being brought merely to revenge personal insult. Accordingly, in *Crofts v. Brown* (1616),[5] Chief Justice Coke, voicing the sentiment of his fellow judges, emphatically said: "We will not give more favor unto actions upon the case for words, than of necessity we ought to do, where the words are not apparently scandalous, these actions being now too frequent; but they were not so in former times." It can easily be imagined what could be accomplished in the way of retarding the growth of a wrong, then in its precocious youth, by a court which was presided over by a judge of the learning and ingenuity of Coke. If not, one need only look for illustration to that elaborate system of technical interpretation built up by them under which defamatory words were construed *in mitiori sensu*,[6] and were required to have a certainty comparable only with the certainty of legal pleadings.[7]

Law of defamation retarded.

Construction of defamatory words.

If the court had been less precipitate, some relief might

[4] Early History of Institutions, p. 289.

[5] 3 Bulst. 167.

[6] Gardiner *v.* Spurdance, 1 Rolle Abr. 71 (Z), pl. 1. This very artificial doctrine is now exploded and defamatory words are taken in their natural sense. Peake *v.* Oldham, 1 Cowp. 275; Hankinson *v.* Bilby, 16 M. & W. 442.

[7] Collobine *v.* Vinor, 1 Rolle Abr. 79, pl. 1.

Chapter XIX

Words of personal insult not necessarily defamatory.

have been found by drawing a distinction between the hot words which pass in angry personal altercation, spoken to insult the individual, and words which are spoken to be heard of others and which are intended, or which tend, to impair the reputation. The notion of defamation does not, even in the scope which we have assigned it, properly include the idea of personal insult. It is not a direct wrong to the individual, but is exclusively an injury incurred by impairment of repute.

But the King's Bench had no time for such fine distinction. The upshot was that English law got fastened upon it a theory of defamation which made possible such perversions of justice as result from holding that a woman cannot maintain an action against one who falsely boasts himself to have had unlawful connection with her, nor against one who charges her with being a bawd, unless she proves loss of a prospective marriage;[8] and that a man cannot maintain an action for words charging the most disgraceful of acts, if perchance such act be not a punishable crime in the particular jurisdiction.[9]

Special pecuniary damage.

The result would not have been quite so deplorable as it was, if the judges had applied the doctrine of special damage in a liberal way. It would have been rational to say that to prove an actual loss or impairment of reputation consequent upon the slander would be a sufficient damage to satisfy the theory of the law. And so, indeed, it was at one time laid down.[1] But the judges of the Restoration overruled this concession,[2] and according to accepted doctrine the special damage, if it does not consist of a loss of marriage, or, under some conditions, of a loss of consortium of a spouse,[3] must be of a

[8] Morison *v.* Cade, Cro. Jac. 162; Barnes *v.* Bruddel, 1 Lev. 261. See also Bac. Abr., *Slander* (C). But it is not necessary to show, it seems, that the lost suitor was actually engaged to marry the plaintiff or that he actually intended to marry her. It is enough that on account of the slander he desisted from paying court, or that communication concerning the marriage was broken off. Matthew *v.* Croze, 1 Rolle Abr. 34 (D) *et seq.*; Bridge *v.* Langton, Lit. C. Pl. 193.

[9] Coburn *v.* Harwood, Minor (Ala.) 93.

[1] Medhurst *v.* Balam (1623), 1 Rolle Abr. 35, pl. 7.

[2] Barnes *v.* Bruddel (1669), 1 Lev. 261, 1 Sid. 396.

[3] See Lynch *v.* Knight, 9 H. L. Cas. 577.

Volume I

pecuniary kind.[4] In *Moore v. Meagher* (1807),[5] the requirement of pecuniary damage was held to be satisfied where the plaintiff showed that prior to the publication of the slander she had been received in the houses of sundry friends who gratuitously entertained her and supplied her with meat and drink, and that by reason of the slander this hospitality had been withdrawn.

Loss of employment as result of a slander.

In conformity with the narrow view which has generally been taken of special damage in suits for defamation, it was held by Lord Ellenborough, a judge, by the way, whose ability has often been overrated, that an action will not lie for words imputing malicious mischief, though the charge be made for the express purpose of causing an employer to discharge the person about whom the words are spoken and though the lie be in fact followed by such a discharge from employment.[6] The idea underlying this decision is that the damage is in such case too remote and is to be attributed, not to the falsehood which was intended to bring about and did bring about the discharge, but to the wrongful discharge itself; the sole remedy being, in the opinion of the court, against the employer for such discharge, where there is any remedy at all. In effect this is equivalent to saying that special damage in the law of slander means necessary and direct damage. If this were true, what we know as consequential damage (i. e., that which follows along a little further off from the harmful cause, yet not so far as to break the chain of natural and logical causation) could never be special damage in this connection, although it be both a natural and intended consequence of the slander.

Special damage must be direct and immediate.

Damage is special if forseeable as a probable consequence of the slander.

This notion was partially exploded by the House of Lords in *Lynch v. Knight* (1861)[7]—a decision which in many respects is quite as unsatisfactory as the earlier one; for here it was held that if slanderous words are spoken by A and special damage follows by reason of the conduct of B,

[4] Chamberlain *v.* Boyd, 11 Q. B. D. 407.

[6] Vicars *v.* Wilcocks (1806), 8 East 1.

Chapter XIX

who hearkens to the slander, then an action will lie provided B's conduct could have been foreseen as likely, but not otherwise. In this case it appeared that the defamer had persistently represented to a husband that his wife before their marriage had been guilty of immoral conduct, by reason of which calumny the husband put her away. The court concluded that the husband ought not to have taken this radical step; that his conduct was in fact unreasonable and unjustified and was not such as might have been anticipated. Hence the court held that the wife could not recover for the loss of consortium, though it was alleged that the defendant did in fact intend to bring about the separation.[8] The innocent was thus compelled to bear the 'risk of harm,' a burden which would better be put on the defamer.

Damage as cause of action.

The English cases, if sound, establish the proposition that where spoken words are not actionable in themselves the cause of action is not the original speaking, but the damage itself.[9] The true view is that the speaking of the noxious words constitutes the wrong, and the special pecuniary damage suffered is the extent of recovery.

Repetition of slanderous words.

Another ruling which shows the sorry confusion into which able judges may come when they are content to build upon bad foundations is found in *Parkins v. Scott* (1862).[1] It there appeared that the defendant, in the absence of a husband, had accused the wife of adultery, this charge, it will be remembered, not being, in that jurisdiction, actionable *per se*. The wife, unfortunately for herself, voluntarily repeated the slander to her husband, who thereupon refused further to cohabit with her. It was held that this loss of consortium was too remote to be chargeable as special damage to the slanderer. The court rested this decision on the principle laid down in *Ward v. Weeks*,[2] to the effect that damage which follows from the repetition of words not actionable *per se* by

[8] The most able of the judges in this case, Lord Wensleydale (formerly Baron Parke), it may be noted, dissented from the judgment.

[9] Bramwell, L. J., in Bree *v.* Marescaux, 7 Q. B. D. 434; Maule, J., in Wilby *v.* Elston, 8 C. B. 142, 65 E. C. L. 142.

[1] 1 H. & C. 153.

[2] 7 Bing. 211, 20 E. C. L. 104.

Volume I

Damage remote.

a third person is too remote to be attributed to the original calumniator. It follows that, as a general rule, damage cannot be called special unless the person who is influenced and whose action causes the loss, actually hears the calumny spoken. But it is conceded that the damage may be treated as special in this connection if the slanderer expressly authorizes the repetition of the slanderous words,[3] or if, perhaps, they are repeated to the person who is influenced, by one who acts in the performance of legal, moral, or official duty.[4] This rule, even with the qualification stated, appears very favorable to the slanderer. He should, one would think, be held responsible when it can be proven that the tale which he set going did come to the ears of the one who acted upon it to the plaintiff's pecuniary damage.[5] But it must be confessed that this would certainly open the door to extensive speculation, and would be in many respects radical, as it would assimilate the legal position of the calumniator to that of the man who turns loose a wild beast, making him liable for all the harm it may do in its rounds. Calumny is known to have a wonderful faculty of increasing in power and hurtfulness as it goes, and to make the originator of it liable for the damage it may do in another's hands, by reason perchance of an additional sting which the latter is able to impart to it, is too much. The remedy for such damage is against the person who republishes. "Wrongful acts of independent third persons, not actually intended by the defendant, are not regarded by the law as natural consequences of his wrong, and he is not bound to anticipate the general probability of such acts any more than a particular act by this or that individual." [6]

Authorized republication.

The principle that a slanderer cannot be held liable for damage which results not from his speaking, but from unauthorized republication, is therefore in the main sound, but it was certainly perverted and misapplied in *Parkins v. Scott* (1862).[7] It is to be contemplated that an honest wife will

Fallacy of Parkins *v.* Scott.

[3] Ward *v.* Weeks, 7 Bing. 211, 20 E. C. L. 104.

[4] Poll. on Torts, 6th ed., 237.

[5] See observations of Leonard, C., in Bassell *v.* Elmore, 48 N. Y. 568.

[6] Burt *v* Advertiser Newspaper Co., 154 Mass. 247.

[7] 1 H. & C. 153.

inform her husband of a slander which affects her character, and when she tells it to him there is not a republication such as will give her a cause of action against an independent third person. She cannot be liable to herself. Such a communication is clearly privileged.

Chapter XIX

In connection with the question as to when pecuniary loss or damage which in fact follows from a particular slander is chargeable to its originator, this further observation is to be made: If such person sets the falsehood afoot maliciously, that is, with the intention to compass a particular sort of pecuniary loss to the person slandered, then he will be liable although the harm actually comes by reason of its republication by an unauthorized person. This principle is admitted to apply to spoken as well as written matter.[8] Here we perceive that the intent to do a particular harm, or malice in fact, makes that particular damage special, though it would otherwise be remote. This is a notion which appears in several connections in the law of tort and is often an important factor in determining questions of proximate cause and remoteness of consequential damage.

Intention to compass particular harm makes that damage special.

In *Allsop v. Allsop* (1860)[9] it was held that where in consequence of an imputation of unchastity a woman falls ill and becomes unable to attend to her household duties, and her husband, besides losing her service, is put to expense in endeavoring to restore her, this is not such special pecuniary damage as will support the action. This is in harmony with the rule applied in the field of personal injury, where it is held that nervous and mental shock alone cannot constitute a ground of action.[1]

Remote damage.

In 1891 a short and halting step towards the correction of the worst features of the law of slander was taken in England by an enactment which provided that thereafter special damage

[8] See Ratcliffe *v.* Evans (1892), 2 Q. B. 524. Said Bowen, L. J.: "That an action will lie for written or oral falsehoods, not actionable *per se* nor even defamatory, where they are maliciously published, where they are calculated in the ordinary course of things to produce, and where they do produce, actual damage, is established law."

[9] 5 H. & N. 534.

[1] Victorian R. Com'rs *v.* Coultas, 13 App. Cas. 222, criticised by Prof. Pollock, Torts, 6th ed., 50 *et seq.*

Volume I

Statutory improvement of law of slander.

need not be shown in actions for words imputing unchastity or adultery to women.[2] In America, by the combined operation of somewhat freer judicial decision and statutory enactments, the law of slander has been brought to a little better state than it has yet reached in England; for in all American jurisdictions women have long been able to maintain actions for words imputing want of chastity, without proof of special damage,[3] and in some jurisdictions men are on the same footing.[4] However jealous the law of England may be of actions for mere words,[5] the American judges are not, nowadays at least, accustomed to indulge their ingenuity to find arbitrary and technical limits to such causes.[6]

State of the law in America.

The rule requiring that there must be a showing of special pecuniary damage, apart from mere contempt and disgrace, before recovery can be had for slanderous words not actionable in themselves, is of course accepted in this country.[7] But cases like *Vicars v. Wilcocks* (1806),[8] *Lynch v. Knight* (1861),[9] and *Parkins v. Scott* (1862)[1] do not appear to have been duplicated in this country. The doctrine of *Allsop v. Allsop* (1860),[2] to the effect that mental anguish accompanied by the impairment of the physical health of the person slandered is not such special damage as will impart actionability to spoken words, has been accepted.[3] But in some American

[2] Slander of Women Act (1891), 54 & 55 Vict., c. 51.

[3] See Newell on Defamation, etc. (1890), 156 *et seq.*

[4] Beasley *v.* Meigs, 16 Ill. 139; McGee *v.* Sodusky, 5 J. J. Marsh. (Ky.) 185; Hackett *v.* Brown, 2 Heisk. (Tenn.) 264; Birch *v.* Benton, 26 Mo. 153.

[5] Observations of Martin, B., in Allsop *v.* Allsop, 5 H. & N. 534.

[6] Holmes, C. J., in Rutherford *v.* Paddock, 180 Mass. 293.

[7] Woodbury *v.* Thompson, 3 N. H. 194; Moody *v.* Baker, 5 Cow. (N. Y.) 351; Bassell *v.* Elmore, 48 N. Y. 561; Ross *v.* Fitch, 58 Tex. 148.

The rule laid down in Ward *v.* Weeks, 7 Bing. 211, 20 E. C. L. 104, that damage resulting from unauthorized republication of words not actionable *per se* is not recoverable against the person who first sets them afoot, is also accepted in America. Shurtleff *v.* Parker, 130 Mass. 293; Gough *v.* Goldsmith, 44 Wis. 262.

[8] 8 East 1.

[9] 9 H. L. Cas. 577.

[1] 1 H. & C. 153.

[2] 5 H. & N. 534.

[3] Shafer *v.* Ahalt, 48 Md. 171. Here it was held that the rule applies though there be an allegation of loss by reason of consequent hindrance in transaction of ordinary affairs and of expense in employing medical assistance.

jurisdictions it is held that loss of time from ordinary pursuits, and pecuniary expenditures made necessary by reason of the impairment of one's health as a result of a slander, make the same actionable.[4]

Libel.

We have so far considered rules peculiar to slander or spoken defamation. Let us now consider doctrines peculiar to autoptic defamation or libel, a wrong in which the injury complained of results from appeals to the ocular sense. The term 'written defamation' is generally used as coextensive with libel, but this expression is not quite broad enough, since libel may be perpetrated by painting, effigy, or signs, as well as by writing. Still, the law of libel is chiefly concerned with written matter, and principles applicable to the whole subject have been first worked out in regard to this form of libel.

Political associations of the law of libel.

The English law of libel was originally separated from the law of slander by historical causes rather than by reasons inherent in the nature of the subject. Those causes we cannot here pause to trace at large.[5] Suffice it to say that this branch of the subject has a criminal as well as a civil aspect and has always been more or less intimately associated with political life. The doctrine that in its civil aspect the law of libel is more stringent than the law of slander first made its appearance in the common-law courts about 1670, when it was held in the Exchequer by Hale and his associates that any matter which tends to bring one into discredit and disgrace is civilly actionable if put in writing.[6] "To say of anybody that he is a dishonest man is not actionable, but to publish so, or put it up upon posts, is actionable."[7] Before this

Severance of libel from slander.

[4] McQueen *v.* Fulgham, 27 Tex. 463; Underhill *v.* Welton, 32 Vt. 40.

[5] See the articles by Mr. Frank Carr and Mr. Veeder, above referred to. For the criminal side of the subject see 2 Stephen's Hist. Crim. Law 298–385.

[6] King *v.* Lake, Hardres 470. Afterwards affirmed on writ of error in Exchequer Chamber, as appears from statement in Austin *v.* Culpeper, Skin. 124.

[7] By the court in Austin *v.* Culpeper (1683), Skin. 124, 2 Show. 313.

Volume I

pronouncement of 1670 writings were on the same footing as oral words as regards civil liability.[8]

Explanation of severity of law of libel.

The notion that libel is an exceptionally aggravated form of defamation had been deeply impressed on the popular and professional mind during the preceding generation by the proceedings of the Court of Star Chamber, a tribunal whose activity in punishing political libels had brought it into disrepute and had finally caused its abolition (1640). After that event the punishment of criminal libels fell exclusively to the common-law courts, and it was not strange that a form of defamation which had criminal associations should be treated with exceptional severity when the courts came to consider it in its civil aspect. The reason assigned by Sir Matthew Hale in justification of this was that writing and publication show more malice than the mere speaking of words on a single occasion,[1] the idea being that committing of the defamatory matter to writing requires deliberation, and the multiplication of copies or transmission of the paper from hand to hand constitutes new publications and hence aggravates the wrong. Much energy has lately been expended in the effort to show that there is no rational basis for the distinction referred to. To a certain extent the criticism is true — but the real point in the situation is easily misconceived. We are far from sharing the opinion that Hale and his associates were wrong in pursuing the course they did. The real mistake which was made was in holding that spoken defamatory words are not actionable unless they fall within particular classes of cases. Hale and his associates were not primarily responsible for this error, and in the existing state of authorities, and in view of the political ferment which was going on at the time, they are not to be criticised for refusing to tighten the law of oral defamation. What they really did was to seize upon a consideration which in a normal state of the law would have merely gone in aggravation of damage and to make that consideration a ground of broader liability. By thus adopting

Writing shows malice.

Distinction between slander and libel artificial.

[8] See e. g. Boughton *v.* Bishop, Anderson 119, referred to by Mr. Frank Carr, 18 L. Quar. Rev. 394.

[1] King *v.* Lake, Hardres 470.

Chapter XIX

a division which was purely artificial they were able to rescue an important branch of our law of defamation from the utter confusion into which other parts of it had fallen. In this circumstance do we perceive the true rationale of that distinction between written and spoken words which commended itself as reasonable to great judges like Hale, Holt, and Hardwicke.[2]

Distinction between slander and libel established.

Thorley v. Kerry (1812)[3] is a leading case on this subject. The Court of Exchequer Chamber, speaking through its chief justice, Sir James Mansfield, there confirmed the principle in question, but not without animadverting upon the factitious and inadequate reasons which have been assigned in support of the distinction, such as more deliberate malignity, more general diffusion, and tendency to provoke a breach of the peace. These reasons are wholly apart from the real basis of the rule. Spoken words may, under some conditions, be more malignant, more generally diffused, and more hurtful than any libel, and certainly when spoken face to face are more likely to provoke a breach of the peace.

We must, however, add that in one aspect the distinction points to a most important truth. Spoken words as often as not are merely the vehicle of personal insult, and in so far are not defamatory, for nothing can be defamatory which does

[2] See King *v.* Lake, Hardres 470 (Hale, C. B.); Cropp *v.* Tilney, 3 Salk. 225, Holt K. B. 422 (Holt, C. J.); Bradley *v.* Methuen, 2 Ford 78, 79 (Lord Hardwicke). Also Villers *v.* Monsley, 2 Wils. C. Pl. 403 (Wilmot, L. C. J.); Bell *v.* Stone, 1 B. & P. 331; Harman *v.* Delany, Fitzg. 254.

[3] 4 Taunt. 355. Reference to the opinion in this case will show the mistaken point of view from which the schism between libel and slander is often considered. Realizing that in true theory the actionable character of words ought not to depend on the question of their form, such consideration going merely to the matter of recoverable damage, the court assumes that the mistake was originally made in putting libel on a different basis from that of slander. In this view all would be right if the common-law courts had kept the law of libel strictly within the same limits as the law of slander. If this course had in fact been followed our law of libel would have been as irrational as the law of slander. As it is, the law of libel is a fairly consistent and rational body of legal truth Mr. Jos. R. Fisher, writing in 10 L. Quar. Rev. 158, is sound enough on the proposition that the actionable character of words ought never to depend on their form, but he falls into the error in point of view just indicated.

Volume I

Greater offensiveness of the libel.

not touch the reputation. Written words, on the other hand, by reason of the very form in which the matter is cast, almost inevitably touch or tend to touch a man at this vital point of reputation. Much which, if only spoken, might be passed as idle blackguardism, doing no discredit save to him who utters it, when invested with the dignity, permanence, and circulative power of print, becomes capable of doing serious injury.[4] Hence libel is rightly deemed more pernicious than slander and does not so easily admit of justification.[5] Fugitive words may be forgotten. *Litera scripta manet.*

Libelous effigy or sign.

On the whole, it seems not inapt to say that, as the distinction which separates libel from slander rests on an artificial basis, the law of libel may be said to be derived by illicit process; but as the premises from which departure was originally made were false, our law of libel is nevertheless entirely sound. The law of libel went right in spite of logic. At any rate, in the way that has been indicated, the principle was fully established that written defamation is actionable whenever it exposes the person libeled to hatred and contempt or tends to bring him into ridicule and disgrace.[6] The same is true of a picture which exhibits one in a disgraceful situation;[7] or waxen effigy which represents one as the perpetrator of murder.[8] To put a lamp before a dwelling of another and keep it burning there all day is a libel, where such sign is understood to be the mark of a bawdy house.[9] Libels which tend to blacken the memory of the dead are indictable, but are not a subject of civil action.[1]

[4] Tillson *v.* Robbins, 68 Me. 295; Colby *v.* Reynolds, 6 Vt. 489; M'Corkle *v.* Binns, 5 Binn. (Pa.) 340; Hillhouse *v.* Dunning, 5 Conn. 391.

[5] Kent, C. J., in Dole *v.* Lyon, 10 Johns. (N. Y.) 449.

[6] Clement *v.* Chivis, 9 B. & C. 172, 17 E. C. L. 353; Stewart *v.* Swift Specific Co., 76 Ga. 280; State *v.* Brady, 44 Kan. 435; Cerveny *v.* Chicago Daily News Co., 139 Ill. 345; Smith *v.* Smith, 73 Mich. 445; Moore *v.* Francis, 121 N. Y. 199; Williams *v.* Karnes, 4 Humph. (Tenn.) 9; Solverson *v.* Peterson, 64 Wis. 198.

[7] Du Bost *v.* Beresford, 2 Campb. 511; Levi *v.* Milne, 4 Bing. 195, 13 E. C. L. 396.

[8] Monson *v.* Tussaud (1894), 1 Q. B. 671.

[9] Jefferies *v.* Duncombe, 11 East 226.

[1] Bradt *v.* New Nonpareil Co., 108 Iowa 449; Wellman *v.* Sun Printing, etc., Assoc., 66 Hun (N. Y.) 331.

Chapter XIX

Special damage not required in law of libel.

As a result of the acceptance of the broad doctrine above indicated, the courts have been able to dispense altogether, in the law of libel, with the conception of special damage as a basis of legal liability, that element which in the field of slander has made no end of trouble.

CHAPTER XX

DEFAMATION (CONTINUED).

Publication.

Volume I

WE now turn our attention to certain general doctrines which, though they pertain to defamation at large, have yet been more fully worked out in the field of libel, in consequence of which our authorities will be largely drawn from this branch of the subject. And first of publication. No statement, however untruthful, becomes defamatory until it is published so as to be seen or heard of some person other than defamer and defamed. This follows from the fundamental principle that defamation involves injury to reputation and is not based on personal insult.

Publication essential in libel and slander.

There is no publication such as to give rise to a civil action where libelous matter is sent to the person libeled,[1] unless the sender intends or has reason to suppose that the matter will reach third persons (which in fact happens) or such result naturally follows from the sending.[2] If the person libeled himself makes the contents public, he of course has no cause of action.[3] It is not necessary to show, in order to maintain the action, that the obnoxious matter was widely disseminated. Enough if one person sees or hears it or is so placed that in the ordinary use of his faculties he could do so.[4] Things that are said within hearing distance are *prima facie* presumed to

Communication to person defamed.

Extent of dissemination immaterial.

[1] Clutterbuck *v.* Chaffers, 1 Stark. 471, 2 E. C. L. 181. But for the purposes of criminal prosecution the sending of defamatory matter to the person libeled is a publication; for, it is said, this tends to a breach of the peace. State *v.* Avery, 7 Conn. 266, 18 Am. Dec. 105; Sheffill *v.* Van Deusen, 13 Gray (Mass.) 304.

[2] Delacroix *v.* Thevenot, 2 Stark. 63, 3 E. C. L. 317; Pullman *v.* Hill (1891), 1 Q. B. 524.

[3] Fonville *v.* M'Nease, Dudley L. (S. Car.) 303.

[4] Harris *v.* Zanone, 93 Cal. 59; Youmans *v.* Smith, 153 N. Y. 214; Adams *v.* Lawson, 17 Gratt. (Va.) 250. But on the question of damages the extent of the circulation of the defamatory matter is of course material.

be heard.[5] It has been held that libelous matter on an envelope or postal card is published by transmission through the mail, though no one is shown to have actually seen or read it.[6]

Chapter XX

Transmission through mail.

Publication occurs when a libelous manuscript passes through the hands of a compositor, though the author suppresses the copies before they issue;[7] or where a copy of the paper containing the libelous matter is delivered to an officer at the stamp office.[8] So where libelous matter is transmitted by telegraph,[9] or even delivered to the company for transmission.[1]

Printing.

Transmission by telegraph.

Where matter is dictated to a stenographer and by the latter committed to writing, publication of necessity occurs, for the stenographer is bound to see the libel after he writes it out.[2] But if the matter thus communicated to the stenographer is subject to qualified privilege, as between the person dictating and the person to whom the communication is addressed, the fact that it thus passes through the hands of a stenographer is not treated as publication to an outsider.[3]

Dictation to stenographer.

Because of the confidential relation between husband and wife, the author of defamatory matter is held not to publish it by merely showing or telling it to his spouse.[4] But, as a man is entitled to the protection of his reputation in the sacred circle of his family no less than in the community at large, it is held that a publication does take place when the defamer communicates the slander or libel to the wife of the person whom he attacks, or any other member of his household.[5]

Communication between husband and wife.

[5] Hall *v.* Hennesley, Cro. Eliz. 486.

[6] Robinson *v.* Jones, 4 L. R. Ir. 391; Muetze *v.* Tuteur, 77 Wis. 236.

[7] Baldwin *v.* Elphinston, 2 W. Bl. 1037.

[8] Rex *v.* Amphlitt, 4 B. & C. 35, 10 E. C. L. 275.

[9] Peterson *v.* Western Union Tel. Co., 65 Minn. 18, 72 Minn. 41, 75 Minn. 368; Union Associated Press *v.* Heath, 49 N. Y. App. Div. 247.

[1] Monson *v.* Lathrop, 96 Wis. 386.

[2] Pullman *v.* Hill (1891), 1 Q. B. 524. *Quære*, whether the reduction of the matter to shorthand notes is a publication. Apparently so, for the reduction is by the authority of the person who dictates, and the stenographer sees and understands it in such form.

[3] Boxsius *v.* Freres (1894), 1 Q. B. 842; Owen *v.* J. S. Ogilvie Pub. Co., 32 N. Y. App. Div. 465.

[4] Wennhak *v.* Morgan, 20 Q. B. D. 635; Sesler *v.* Montgomery, 78 Cal. 486.

[5] Wenman *v.* Ash, 13 C. B. 836,

Volume I

Procuring publication of defamatory matter.

On general principle, a person is liable as the publisher of a libel where he communicates defamatory matter to another, requesting or expecting him to publish it, which is accordingly done. Nor is it necessary to this end that the matter be published in the exact words of the defamatory communication. It is enough if the substance of it appear.[6]

Assisting in publication.

Likewise, one who assists in the publication of defamatory matter is liable to the same extent as the prime mover. Telegraph companies, for instance, are liable for transmitting libelous matter which another puts into their hands.[7] But only, of course, where the libelous nature of the writing is apparent on its face. The printer [8] of libelous matter, and the managing editor [9] of a newspaper in which it appears, are liable to the same extent as the actual writer, while of course the proprietor of the enterprise is also liable.[1]

The news dealer.

But the doctrine above stated is not to be pushed to unreasonable limits, and in order to make one unqualifiedly liable as participator in the wrong, he must assist in or contribute to the act of original publication. One who is merely a channel for the dissemination of a libel after it has already been published is not necessarily liable.[2] This is illustrated in *Emmens v. Pottle* (1885),[3] where news venders sold papers containing a libel on the plaintiff. The jury found that the defendants did not know that the newspapers at the time they sold them contained the obnoxious matter, and that they were guilty of no negligence in failing to ascertain the fact. It was held that no action lay. "A newspaper," said Bowen,

76 E. C. L. 836; Schenck *v.* Schenck, 20 N. J. L. 208; Miller *v.* Johnson, 79 Ill. 58.

[6] Parkes *v.* Prescott, L. R. 4 Exch. 169.

[7] Archambault *v.* Great North Western Tel. Co., 4 Montreal Q. B. 122; Nye *v.* Western Union Tel. Co., 104 Fed. Rep. 628; Peterson *v.* Western Union Tel Co., 65 Minn. 18, 72 Minn. 41, 75 Minn. 368.

[8] Rex *v.* Dover, 6 How. St. Tr. 547.

[9] Watts *v.* Fraser, 7 C. & P. 369, 32 E. C. L. 544; Bruce *v.* Reed, 104 Pa. St. 408; Smith *v.* Utley, 92 Wis. 133.

[1] Storey *v.* Wallace, 60 Ill. 51; International Fraternal Alliance *v.* Mallalieu, 87 Md. 97; Long *v.* Tribune Printing Co., 107 Mich. 207; Saunders *v.* Baxter, 6 Heisk. (Tenn.) 369.

[2] Day *v.* Bream, 2 M. & Rob. 54.

[3] 16 Q. B. D. 354. See also Chubb *v.* Flannagan, 6 C. & P. 431, 25 E. C. L. 472.

L. J., "is not like a fire; a man may carry it about without being bound to suppose that it is likely to do an injury." [4] But the burden of proving an excusable ignorance of the contents of the libelous publication is on the person who is shown to have aided in spreading it abroad.[5] We imagine that one who casually hands a paper around, directing the attention of others to defamatory matter, would not be held liable unless it were shown that he indorsed the libel. But as against men who disseminate by selling, the rule is more strict.

Every repetition of slander a new publication.

As regards slander the rule is that every repetition is a new publication and every person who passes the lie on is liable to a separate action, though he expressly credit the statement to its originator.[6] This is so far recognized that, as we have already seen, the original author cannot be held for damage which follows from the repetition.

Interpretation of Defamatory Words.

Construction of defamatory matter.

The subject of the interpretation of defamatory words can be briefly dismissed. The artificial rule recognized in early cases by which such matter was construed *in mitiori sensu* has of course been long exploded,[7] and defamatory words are now taken by the courts in the sense in which they were intended and were understood to bear.[8] The rule of judicial interpretation here is the rule of common sense. Though the language be in the form of direct affirmation, it will be construed as defamatory if it conveys the imputation alleged to have been intended.[9] Words calculated to induce suspicion are sometimes more effective to destroy reputation than if the false charge were directly made. Hypothetical,[1] interroga-

Words taken in sense intended by defamer.

[4] Emmens *v.* Pottle, 16 Q. B. D. 358.

[5] Vizetelly *v.* Mudie's Select Library (1900), 2 Q. B. 170; Staub *v.* Van Benthuysen, 36 La. Ann. 467.

[6] Nicholson *v.* Rust (Ky. 1899), 52 S. W. Rep. 933.

[7] Harrison *v.* Thornborough, 10 Mod. 196; Goodrich *v.* Davis, 11 Met. (Mass.) 473; Eckart *v.* Wilson, 10 S. & R. (Pa.) 44.

[8] Mulligan *v.* Cole, L. R. 10 Q. B. 549; Downing *v.* Wilson, 36 Ala. 717; Sillars *v.* Collier, 151 Mass. 50.

[9] Haynes *v.* Clinton Printing Co., 169 Mass. 512.

[1] Clarke *v.* Zettick, 153 Mass. 1.

Volume I

tive,[2] ironical,[3] and metaphorical[4] language is a favored vehicle for slanderous and libelous charges.

Pleading.

Where the language alleged to be defamatory does not appear to be such on its face, the plaintiff is required to state fully in his declaration the circumstances which make the words actionable. This is done by setting forth, in addition of course to the words actually used,[5] what is called the inducement, the colloquium, and the innuendo. The first term is applied to the narrative of the extrinsic circumstances under which the words were used and which are necessary to be known before the defamatory meaning can attach.[6] The office of the colloquium is to connect the spoken or written words with the circumstances disclosed in the inducement,[7] while the innuendo interprets the meaning of the language used in the light of the surrounding circumstances and discloses its sting to the court. The purpose of all this elaborate apparatus is merely to enable the court to ascertain with certainty the meaning which the language was really intended and understood to have. Consequently, it is settled that there can be no enlargement of the meaning of words by innuendo beyond that which they may properly bear under the facts disclosed in the inducement and colloquium.[8]

Inducement.

Colloquium.

Innuendo.

Justification.

Justification by proof of truth.

The topic which next claims our attention is justification. As we have already indicated, the very conception of defamation involves the idea of falsity. Hence wherever it appears that the charge complained of was true in fact and in substance at the time when it was made, the action for defamation

[2] Goodrich *v.* Davis, 11 Met. (Mass.) 473.

[3] Johnson *v.* St. Louis Dispatch Co., 65 Mo. 539.

[4] Hoare *v.* Silverlock, 12 Q. B. 624, 64 E. C. L. 624.

[5] Zenobio *v.* Axtell, 6 T. R. 162; Cook *v.* Cox, 3 M. & S. 110.

[6] Andrews *v.* Woodmansee, 15 Wend. (N. Y.) 232.

[7] Beswick *v.* Chappel, 8 B. Mon. (Ky.) 486.

[8] Goldstein *v.* Foss, 4 Bing. 489; Angle *v.* Alexander, 7 Bing. 119, 20 E. C. L. 71; Holt *v.* Scholefield, 6 T. R. 691; Barnes *v.* State, 88 Md. 347; Bloss *v.* Tobey, 2 Pick. (Mass.) 320; Posnett *v.* Marble, 62 Vt. 48.

fails, however defamatory the publication may appear to be on its face.

Chapter XX

Pleading matter of justification.

In the nature of things, proof of the truthfulness of a charge which is *prima facie* libelous or slanderous must come from the defendant, and the wise rule is adopted that such matter of justification must always be specially pleaded with particularity of detail. Thus if, as usually happens, the alleged defamatory matter consists of a general charge such as that one is a swindler,[9] or impostor,[1] the defendant's justification must set out the specific instance of misconduct which supplies the basis of the charge.[2] Under the modern system of pleading the rule is the same, and the defendant's bill of particulars must still be as explicit as the plea was formerly required to be.[3] "The particulars must be as precise as would be necessary in an indictment."[4]

Particularity required.

In harmony with the foregoing is the further rule that the justification must be fully as broad as the hurtful innuendo of the defamatory matter. The justification must go to a whole. Hence a plea of justification is bad which justifies as to part only.[5] A charge that one has been guilty of a particular sort of misconduct on more than one occasion cannot be justified by showing only one instance of such misconduct.[6] But the general charge that one is a card sharper can be justified by showing that he has cheated at cards on two occasions, and it is not necessary to show other instances.[7]

Justification must go to the whole charge.

A defamatory written statement must be true in every hurtful feature, or it cannot be justified. Whatever in fact stings, or as said by Maule, J.,[8] whatever "is injurious to the plain-

[9] I'Anson *v.* Stuart, 1 T. R. 748.

[1] Zierenberg *v.* Labouchere (1893), 2 Q. B. 183.

[2] Van Ness *v.* Hamilton, 19 Johns. (N. Y.) 349; Wachter *v.* Quenzer, 29 N. Y. 552.

[3] Wren *v.* Weild, L. R. 4 Q. B. 213, 38 L. J. Q. B. 88; Tilton *v.* Beecher, 59 N. Y. 176.

[4] See Lord Esher, M. R., in Wren *v.* Weild, *ante;* also Alderson, B., in Hickinbotham *v.* Leach, 10 M. & W. 363.

[5] Mountney *v.* Watton, 2 B. & Ad. 673, 22 E. C. L. 164; Bishop *v.* Latimer, 4 L. T. N. S. 775; Clement *v.* Lewis, 3 Brod. & B. 297, 7 E. C. L. 444, 3 B. & Ald. 702, 5 E. C. L. 427.

[6] Wakley *v.* Cooke, 4 Exch. 511; Clarkson *v.* Lawson, 6 Bing. 266, 19 E. C. L. 78.

[7] Reg. *v.* Labouchere, 14 Cox C. C. 419.

[8] Helsham *v.* Blackwood, 11 C. B. 111, 73 E. C. L. 111.

Volume I

tiff," must be shown to be true. Thus if a charge of having committed murder in a duel is published about a man, and the libel goes on to state circumstances of aggravation, the plea of justification must show the truth of such aggravating circumstances, although they would not affect the degree of the homicide in a legal prosecution.[9] The result in this case would doubtless have been different had the defamatory matter been merely spoken, since it could have been injurious in law only so far as it charged the legal crime.

Plea of justification disfavored.

A praiseworthy consideration for the innocent victims of calumny has certainly led the courts to the adoption of strict rules in this field, and pleas of justification can truly be said to be disfavored. This is illustrated in *Leyman v. Latimer* (1878),[1] where it was held that to write a man down as a 'felon editor' or 'convicted felon' cannot be justified by showing that he has once been convicted of felony, if he can show in reply that he has served his term out, his disability being thereby removed.[2]

In the nature of the thing a defendant who justifies thereby embarks in a counter-attack, and such enterprise has been found to be a very delicate and dangerous business. If he fails to establish his charge his obstinacy in persisting in it may be indicative of malice, and he loses the benefit of mitigating circumstances.[3] Truly this is an instrument with which one may in a proper case bring down his adversary with unfailing certainty; but if it be improperly chosen or unskilfully used, it acts only as a boomerang.

Fair Comment and Criticism.

Closely related to justification by truth is the defense of fair comment and fair criticism. This question comes up in

[9] Helsham *v.* Blackwood, 11 C. B. 111, 73 E. C. L. 111.

[1] 3 Ex. D. 15, 352.

[2] In the Court of Appeal, Bramwell, L. J., went on the theory that the words "felon editor" implied that the plaintiff had been guilty of felony, and the justification did not allege that he had actually committed felony; and therefore although the plaintiff might be "a convicted felon," yet the justification, being pleaded to the whole cause of action, was too wide and formed no defense. Brett and Cotton, L. JJ., went on the theory that by statute a person convicted of felony after enduring the punishment is no longer a felon.

[3] Newell on Defamation, 882.

libel cases where the alleged defamatory matter consists of strictures upon undertakings, enterprises, and works which appeal to the public and about which individuals have a right to speak their mind. The injury in these cases usually consists of special damage in respect of the plaintiff's work or business and does not involve injury to personal reputation.

Chapter XX

Strictures upon works of art and enterprises which concern the public.

The subject of fair comment is sometimes confused with the subject of privilege, which is presently to be dealt with, but the defense of fair comment is quite a different thing from the defense of privilege. Just as the truthfulness of a statement prevents it from being libelous, so the fact that comment is fair prevents such comment from being libelous; and just as it would be improper to say that a truthful statement is privileged in law, so it is incorrect to say that fair comment is privileged. Privilege implies an exceptional immunity by which matter *prima facie* defamatory is held to be protected. Fair comment is clearly not an instance of protection against the ordinary legal consequences of wrongful act. When proved it shows that there has been no wrong at all. As was said by Bowen, L. J., in *Merivale v. Carson* (1887),[4] it is only when one goes beyond the limits of fair criticism that his matter passes into the region of libel at all. The question whether this limit has been transcended is one for the jury.[5]

Defense of fair comment distinct from privilege.

A distinction is to be drawn between statement of purported facts and comment or criticism upon facts. If a statement of fact be false *cadit quæstio,* it is libelous, provided only it tends to defame, and no amount of soberness in the criticism will cure the wrong.[6] But if the statement of facts be true, then within the limits of the application of the rule, the fairness of the comment is a good defense although the strictures are such as to bring the thing criticised into disrepute.

Facts and comment on facts.

Literary and art criticism is the field in which the principle

[4] 20 Q. B. D. 283. See also Lopes, L. J., in South Hetton Coal Co. *v.* North-Eastern News Assoc. (1894), 1 Q. B. 143.

[5] Campbell *v.* Spottiswoode, 3 B. & S. 769, 113 E. C. L. 769; Wason *v.* Walter, L. R. 4 Q. B. 73; Fay *v.* Harrington, 176 Mass. 270.

[6] Merivale *v.* Carson, 20 Q. B. D. 275; Davis *v.* Shepstone (1886), 11 App. Cas. 187.

Volume I

Book criticism.

Theatrical performance.

To be fair, criticism must be honest and relevant.

just stated is most commonly invoked. When an author places his book before the public he invites criticism, and however hostile that criticism may be and however much damage it may cause in preventing the sale of the book, the critic is not liable in an action for libel provided he does not materially misrepresent the contents of the book and does not attack the character of the author.[7] So likewise it is not libelous fairly to criticise a theatrical performance,[8] a painting,[9] or other work of art,[1] however strong the terms of censure may be. The same principle applies to honest strictures upon all things which are intended to edify or serve the public or to procure its patronage; in short, to all things in which the public may be properly interested.[2]

As regards the meaning of the term 'fair,' the remarks of Collins, M. R., in a late case involving a criticism upon a musical play, are instructive: "One thing, however," said he, "is perfectly clear, and that is that the jury have no right to substitute their own opinion of the literary merits of the work for that of the critic, or to try the fairness of the criticism by any such standard." [3] Accordingly this judge defined fair criticism as being that which is honest and also relevant.[4]

It would doubtless be very hard in any case to maintain an action of libel for comment on an enterprise or work really open to public discussion which is a *bona fide* expression of the writer's opinion untinctured by malice and not associated with garbled statements of fact. *Henwood v. Harrison,* (1872)[5] shows how far a court may go in sustaining the right of free and open discussion. In this case the alleged libel was found in a communication to the Admiralty, which criticised certain plans of the plaintiff for the improvement of the

[7] Dowling *v.* Livingstone, 108 Mich. 321; Carr *v.* Hood, 1 Campb. 355 (note).

[8] Merivale *v.* Carson, 20 Q. B. D. 275.

[9] Thompson *v.* Shackell, M. & M. 187, 22 E. C. L. 286; Battersby *v.* Collier, 34 N. Y. App. Div. 347.

[1] Soane *v.* Knight, M. & M. 74, 22 E. C. L. 255.

[2] Eastwood *v.* Holmes, 1 F. & F. 347; Heriot *v.* Stuart, 1 Esp. 437; Crane *v.* Waters, 10 Fed. Rep. 619; Bearce *v.* Bass, 88 Me. 521; Fay *v.* Harrington, 176 Mass. 270.

[3] McQuire *v.* Western Morning News Co. (1903), 2 K. B. 109.

[4] (1903) 2 K. B. 110.

[5] L. R. 7 C. P. 606.

navy. The communication ended with an animadversion upon "the known antecedents of the author." Assuming this to be *prima facie* libelous, the court held that the absence of malice on the part of the defendant was a good defense. As regards the particular ground on which this decision was placed by the majority, the conclusion seems to be wrong. The true ground of the decision no doubt is that the words complained of referred to the scientific attainments of the author and not to his moral antecedents. The scientific equipment of a man who brings forward plans for a radical departure in the navy is certainly pertinent on the question of the value of those plans. But his moral character is of course irrelevant, and reference to it could not be so justified.

Chapter XX

Scientific attainments open to criticism.

Consideration of the subject of fair comment in all its aspects leads us to the conclusion that the doctrine properly applies only to criticisms upon undertakings, enterprises, and art productions and that it has no application to strictures upon the character of individuals. Of course it is legitimate, as we shall hereafter see, in many circumstances, to make fair criticisms upon character. But wherever words touch the reputation of the man as distinct from his enterprise or work, fairness of comment is a good defense only in so far as the situation giving rise to the comment is privileged in law.[6]

Limits of the defense of fair comment.

[6] *Malicious Aspersions on Character.*— That the existence of malice is fatal to the defense of fair comment in all cases where the criticism complained of makes aspersions upon the person whose work is ridiculed is too well settled to admit of cavil. Soane *v.* Knight, M. & M. 74, 22 E. C. L. 255; Campbell *v.* Spottiswoode, 3 F. & F. 426; Morrison *v.* Belcher, 3 F. & F. 614; Hedley *v.* Barlow, 4 F. & F. 224; Cherry *v.* Des Moines Leader, 114 Iowa 298; Bearce *v.* Bass, 88 Me. 539, 540; Battersby *v.* Collier, 34 N. Y. App. Div. 347.

It may be said that malice in this connection has merely the effect of showing that the comment is unfair in fact, since that which is recklessly defamatory, as malicious criticisms usually are, cannot be deemed fair. See Cockburn, C. J. (to jury), in Hedley *v.* Barlow, 4 F. & F. 230, 231. But it is not unreasonable to say that in all cases where the alleged defamatory comments involve the character of the individual as well as the nature of his work, malice is destructive of privilege and is not to be treated solely as persuasive of unfairness. The American cases at least all go upon the theory that criticisms which involve an attack upon individual character owe their immunity, where this exists, to legal privilege. And the older, as well as some of the late, English cases take this view also. See e. g.,

We close these observations on the subject of fair comment and fair criticism with the remark that the point of view above indicated will perhaps only become altogether clear to the reader when he has perused what is hereinafter said on the subject of privilege and malice.

Green *v.* Chapman, 4 Bing. N. Cas. 92, 33 E. C. L. 288; Henwood *v.* Harrison, L. R. 7 C. P. 606. Compare the observations of Bowen, L. J., in Merivale *v.* Carson, 20 Q. B. D. 282, 283; and also remarks of Collins, M. R., in McQuire *v.* Western Morning News Co. (1903), 2 K. B. 112.

CHAPTER XXI

DEFAMATION (CONTINUED).

Privilege.

Chapter XXI

Definition of privilege.

PRIVILEGE implies exceptional immunity whereby one is excused from the consequences of an act which upon general principle would furnish a ground of action. Privilege in defamation, as in other fields, may be either absolute or conditional. If absolute, the defamatory utterance gives no cause of action, though it be made falsely, knowingly, and with express malice. In cases where the privilege is conditional, the protection is taken away and the immunity lost if the privilege which the law gives is abused. As might be imagined, the occasions where matter is absolutely privileged are few in number and arise out of the highest considerations of necessity and public policy.

Illustrations of absolute privilege.

Instances of absolute privilege are: Official utterances of administrative functionaries, such as the chief executive of the nation and governors of the several states;[1] communications relating to affairs of state between officers of state in the course of official duty;[2] reports made concerning a subordinate officer by his superior officer acting in the course of his military duty;[3] utterances of members of Parliament, or other legislative body, made in the course of legislative proceedings;[4] utterances of judges,[5] attorneys,[6] witnesses,[7] jurors,[8]

[1] See Kirkpatrick *v.* Eagle Lodge No. 32, 26 Kan. 390.

[2] Chatterton *v.* Secretary of State (1895), 2 Q. B. 189.

[3] Dawkins *v.* Paulet, L. R. 5 Q. B. 94.

[4] Dillon *v.* Balfour, 20 L. R. Ir. 600; Coffin *v.* Coffin, 4 Mass. 1. Compare Rex *v.* Creevey, 1 M. & S. 273; Rex *v.* Abingdon, 1 Esp. 226.

[5] Scott *v.* Stansfield, L. R. 3 Exch. 220.

[6] Munster *v.* Lamb, 11 Q. B. D. 588.

[7] Seaman *v.* Netherclift, 2 C. P. D. 53; Cooley *v.* Galyon, 109 Tenn. 1. Nor is it material that the party scandalized is not a party to the proceeding in which the testimony is given. Henderson *v.* Broomhead, 4 H. & N. 569.

[8] (Petit juror) Dunham *v.* Powers, 42 Vt. 1. (Grand juror) Fisk *v.* Soniat, 33 La. Ann. 1400; Rector *v.* Smith, 11 Iowa 302.

Volume I

and even of parties litigant,[9] made in the course of judicial proceedings, or made before a tribunal having attributes similar to those of a court of justice, such as a military court of inquiry [1] or legislative committee.[2]

In America the courts have been more loath than the English courts to declare privilege in any particular case to be absolute; and it is here generally held that the privilege of lawyers, witnesses, and parties is conditional upon the pertinence of the matter to the question in hand, and its materiality.[3]

Qualified privilege.

Situations in which there is a qualified or conditional privilege are numerous. It may be laid down that wherever one speaks in the exercise of a common and recognized right, or in obedience to a legal or moral duty, his utterance is privileged. The officious and meddlesome volunteer, on the other hand, does not receive much consideration. He speaks, as it were, at his peril.[4] That is, if he says hurtful words which are false, he is liable, regardless of his belief in their truth. The speaker who is conditionally privileged, if he speaks honestly and says things relevant to the matter in hand, is not liable. But he cannot make the privileged occasion a mere cloak for private spleen or malice.

Illustrations.

The following communications illustrate the application of the doctrine of qualified privilege: Complaints addressed by private citizens to public functionaries having the power to redress the grievance complained of;[5] complaints in regard to the character or conduct of a public official when addressed to the proper superior officer;[6] communications

[9] Doyle *v.* O'Doherty, C. & M. 418, 41 E. C. L. 230; Bartlett *v.* Christhilf, 69 Md. 219; Crockett *v.* McLanahan, 109 Tenn. 517.

[1] Dawkins *v.* Rokeby, L. R. 8 Q. B. 255.

[2] Goffin *v.* Donnelly, 6 Q. B. D. 307.

[3] Smith *v.* Howard, 28 Iowa 51; Barnes *v.* McCrate, 32 Me. 442; Wright *v.* Lothrop, 149 Mass. 385; Gilbert *v.* People, 1 Den. (N. Y.) 41; White *v.* Carroll, 42 N. Y. 161. See also 18 Am. and Eng. Encyc. of Law (2d ed.) 1023, 1024.

[4] Norfolk, etc., Steamboat Co. *v.* Davis, 12 App. Cas. (D. C.) 328; Krebs *v.* Oliver, 12 Gray (Mass.) 239; Joannes *v.* Bennett, 5 Allen (Mass.) 169; Byam *v.* Collins, 111 N. Y. 143.

[5] Wright *v.* Lothrop, 149 Mass. 390; Woods *v.* Wiman, 122 N. Y. 445.

[6] Harrison *v.* Bush, 5 El. & Bl. 344, 85 E. C. L. 344; White *v.*

concerning the fitness of applicants for office when made to the appointing power.[7]

Communications concerning official conduct.

In regard to communications made by one private citizen to another or to the public at large concerning the official conduct of a public officer, or of one holding a position of public trust, or concerning the fitness of a candidate for public office, there is a diversity of opinion. It is everywhere held that if the facts stated are true, fair comment and criticism thereon are privileged,[8] and the courts are inclined, in this connection, to allow very free discussion. In some jurisdictions it is held that even statements of facts which are relevant to the question of official fitness are so far privileged that no action will lie when it appears that the defendant circulating the report honestly believed it to be true,[9] or where it appears that there was reasonable ground for so believing.[1] But in other jurisdictions the privilege is held to extend only to comment and criticism and not to the facts on which the criticism is based. In this view charges imputing criminal offenses, or grave moral delinquency, to officers or candidates for office, are libelous if false.[2]

Accounts of judicial proceedings.

The question of privilege is often raised in connection with the publication of accounts of judicial proceedings by the ordinary purveyors of news. The rule is that such accounts are privileged if they are fair and not garbled.[3] There must be

Nicholls, 3 How. (U. S.) 266. See Hebditch *v.* MacIlwaine (1894), 2 Q. B. 54.

[7] Coogler *v.* Rhodes, 38 Fla. 240.

[8] Parmiter *v.* Coupland, 6 M. & W. 105; Seymour *v.* Butterworth, 3 F. & F. 372; Turnbull *v.* Bird, 2 F. & F. 508; State *v.* Grinstead, 10 Kan. App. 78; Burt *v.* Advertiser Newspaper Co., 154 Mass. 242; Wilcox *v.* Moore, 69 Minn. 49; Rowand *v.* De Camp, 96 Pa. St. 493.

[9] Bays *v.* Hunt, 60 Iowa 251; State *v.* Balch, 31 Kan. 465; Marks *v.* Baker, 28 Minn. 162.

[1] Briggs *v.* Garrett, 111 Pa. St. 404.

[2] Davis *v.* Shepstone, 11 App. Cas. 187; Post Pub. Co. *v.* Hallam (C. C. A.), 59 Fed. Rep. 530; Rearick *v.* Wilcox, 81 Ill. 77; Bronson *v.* Bruce, 59 Mich. 467; Wheaton *v.* Beecher, 66 Mich. 307.

[3] Saunders *v.* Mills, 6 Bing. 213, 19 E. C. L. 60; Bathrick *v.* Detroit Post, etc., Co., 50 Mich. 629; Post Pub. Co. *v.* Moloney, 50 Ohio St. 71.

Upon considerations of public policy the privilege is held not to extend to the publication of scandalous, indecent or blasphemous matter which may be brought to light in legal proceedings. But this rule seems to be applied only in criminal proceedings. Rex *v.* Salisbury, 1 Ld. Raym. 341; Rex *v.* Carlile, 3

Volume I

no material addition to or suppression of facts, but it is not necessary that everything connected with the business be told.[4] So far as the report goes, it must be a truthful mirror of what actually occurs in the proceedings or of what is contained in the judicial record.[5] The privilege extends, of course, to reports of judgments rendered, and it is not necessary to set out the evidence on which it was based.[6]

In order that the privilege may exist, the proceedings reported must be of a judicial character,[7] and must take place before a properly constituted legal tribunal acting in its judicial capacity.[8] Accounts of preliminary and *ex parte* proceedings are protected if such proceedings are judicial.[9]

Report of legislative proceedings.

A privilege similar to that allowed to fair reports of judicial proceedings is that accorded to accounts of legislative and parliamentary proceedings. No cause of action arises from the publication of parliamentary debates, though they contain matter injurious to the reputation of individuals.[1] But as in case of judicial proceedings, the report must always, so far as it goes, be an accurate and truthful transcript of what was said. If extraneous libelous matter is included in the report, it is actionable even though such matter be incorporated in obedience to a resolution of the House and though the House declare that such insertion is a matter of parlia-

B. & Ald. 167, 5 E. C. L. 252; Com. *v.* Costello, 1 Pa. Dist. 745.

[4] Delegal *v.* Highley, 3 Bing. N. Cas. 950, 32 E. C. L. 398; Andrews *v.* Chapman, 3 C. & K. 289; Hoare *v.* Silverlock, 9 C. B. 20, 67 E. C. L. 20.

[5] Lewis *v.* Levy, El. Bl. & El. 537, 96 E. C. L. 537.

[6] Macdougall *v.* Knight, 17 Q. B. D. 636.

[7] Cowley *v.* Pulsifer, 137 Mass. 392.

[8] M'Gregor *v* Thwaites, 3 B. & C. 24, 10 E. C. L. 6; Ryalls *v.* Leader, L. R. 1 Exch. 296; Lewis *v.* Levy, El. Bl. & El. 537, 96 E. C. L. 537; McDermott *v.* Evening Journal Assoc., 43 N. J. L. 488.

[9] Kimber *v.* Press Assoc. (1893), 1 Q. B. 65; Usill *v.* Hales, 3 C. P. D. 319; McBee *v.* Fulton, 47 Md. 403.

[1] Wason *v.* Walter, L. R. 4 Q. B. 73; Rex *v.* Wright, 8 T. R. 293; Terry *v.* Fellows, 21 La. Ann. 375.

There is a conflict as to whether reports of the proceedings of inferior legislative bodies, such as municipal councils, are privileged. In theory they should be privileged wherever the speaker's words are privileged as to himself. Wallis *v.* Bazet, 34 La. Ann. 131; Buckstaff *v.* Hicks, 94 Wis. 34. In this latter case the words reported seem not to have been spoken in connection with the exercise of the council's legislative power.

mentary privilege.[2] Such question is to be determined by the court.

Communications between parties occupying confidential relations.

One of the most extensive heads of qualified privilege is found in connection with communications between individuals concerning matters that are of moment to one or both of the parties. Communications between parties occupying confidential relations, as between principal and agent,[3] master and servant,[4] physician and patient,[5] attorney and client,[6] clergyman and parishioner,[7] parent and child,[8] are privileged so far as the substance of such communications pertains to matters about which the relation of confidence exists. Here the parties have a common interest in the subject-matter of the communication.

Statements by mercantile agencies.

But it is not necessary that both maker and recipient should have such interest. The interest of the maker alone, or recipient alone, may be sufficient to impart a qualified privilege to the communication. Communications to particular subscribers made by mercantile agencies concerning the character and standing of a business man are privileged,[9] but the statements published by such agencies to their subscribers at large are not.[1]

Reflection on servant.

Words spoken by a master in regard to the character of a servant, in response to inquiry from a prospective employer, are *prima facie* privileged,[2] and one who takes a servant upon the recommendation of another, if he finds that the servant does not justify the character given him, may communicate such fact to the person who gave the recommendation.[3] One

[2] Stockdale *v.* Hansard, 9 Ad. & El. 1, 36 E. C. L. 13.

[3] Atwill *v.* Mackintosh, 120 Mass. 181; Rothholz *v.* Dunkle, 53 N. J. L. 438; Allen *v.* Cape Fear, etc., R. Co., 100 N. Car. 397.

[4] Somerville *v.* Hawkins, 10 C. B. 583, 70 E. C. L. 583.

[5] Humphreys *v.* Stilwell, 2 F. & F. 590.

[6] Levy *v.* McCan, 44 La. Ann. 528.

[7] Davies *v.* Snead, L. R. 5 Q. B. 608; Shurtleff *v.* Stevens, 51 Vt. 501.

[8] Todd *v.* Hawkins, 8 C. & P. 88, 34 E. C. L. 304; Harriott *v.* Plimpton, 166 Mass. 585.

[9] King *v.* Patterson, 49 N. J. L. 417; State *v.* Lonsdale, 48 Wis. 348; Todd *v.* Dun, 15 Ont. App. 85.

[1] Dun *v.* Weintraub, 111 Ga. 416; Sunderlin *v.* Bradstreet, 46 N. Y. 188; Pollasky *v.* Minchener, 81 Mich. 280.

[2] Weatherston *v.* Hawkins, 1 T. R. 110; Child *v.* Affleck, 9 B. & C. 403, 17 E. C. L. 405.

[3] Rogers *v.* Clifton, 3 B. & P.

Volume I

who has given his servant a good character may subsequently give him a bad one if he finds out that the better opinion was not justified.[4] The fact that a person volunteers information concerning the character of a servant does not necessarily take the communication out of the category of privilege, but such fact may be persuasive of malice.[5]

Communication made in obedience to social duty.

The obligation imposed by moral or social duty may alone be enough to impart qualified privilege to a communication,[6] but the limits of this doctrine are not easy to state. In *Stuart v. Bell*,[7] it appeared that the defendant was entertaining as his guest one B who had his valet along. The host, having received information from the authorities in a city where B had been staying, to the effect that B's valet was suspected of having committed theft in a hotel there, communicated such fact to B, who thereupon discharged his valet on the ground that suspicions were entertained against his honesty. The suspicion proved groundless and the discharged servant brought suit for slander against the defendant, alleging his discharge as special damage. It was held that the communication, being made in obedience to social duty, was privileged.

Mistake as to existence of duty.

It has been determined that one who makes an injurious communication under a sense of duty is not protected if it appears that he was mistaken in regard to the existence of the duty. Belief that there is a duty to communicate is irrelevant on the question whether the occasion is privileged.[8] But it is relevant on the question of malice.

What has been said illustrates, as far as may here be done, the scope and application of the doctrine of qualified privi-

587; Dixon *v.* Parsons, 1 F. & F. 24.

[4] Gardner *v.* Slade, 13 Q. B. 796; 66 E. C. L. 796; Fowles *v.* Bowen, 30 N. Y. 20.

[5] Fresh *v.* Cutter, 73 Md. 87.

[6] See Whiteley *v.* Adams, 15 C. B. N. S. 392, 109 E. C. L. 392.

[7] (1891) 2 Q. B. 341.

[8] Lindley, L. J., in Stuart *v.* Bell (1891), 2 Q. B. 341; Esher, M. R., in Hebditch *v.* MacIlwaine (1894), 2 Q. B. 60, 61. On this particular point the opinion of Tindal, C. J., in Coxhead *v.* Richards, 2 C. B. 594, 52 E. C. L. 594, seems to be untenable. But in other respects his presentation of the law in that case is generally accepted as sound. See Lindley, L. J., in Stuart *v.* Bell (1891), 2 Q. B. 347; Lord Blackburn in Davies *v.* Snead, L. R. 5 Q. B. 611

Chapter XXI

lege in the law of slander and libel. The reason for holding any occasion privileged is the common convenience and welfare of society, and no definite line can be drawn so as to mark off with precision those occasions which are privileged and separate them from those which are not. This is strikingly illustrated in *Coxhead v. Richards* (1846),[9] where four eminent judges were equally divided upon the question whether, on the particular facts, the showing of a letter which the defendant had received from the mate of a vessel, reflecting on the conduct of the captain, was a privileged communication.

Basis of the doctrine of privilege.

Malice.

We now come to consider that element which when present takes away qualified privilege and makes the person communicating defamatory matter liable as if the privilege did not exist. This element is 'malice,' a term used to indicate the fact that the defamer is prompted by personal ill-will or spite, and speaks not in response to duty, but merely to injure the reputation of the person defamed. The fundamental notion with which we here come in contact, namely, that the mental attitude of the actor may turn a privileged act into an actionable wrong, is one of the most profoundly instructive conceptions with which the student of the law of tort has to deal. It ramifies, in fact, through many departments of tort, appearing in different forms in different connections. In the law of defamation alone do we find a legal formation where that conception is exposed in its simplicity. The law will not tolerate that privilege which it intends as a protection to the honest, should be used as a means of gratifying personal venom.

Meaning of malice.

A very satisfactory aspect of the matter is obtained in the statement that proof of actual malice shows that the speaker did not act under the privilege at all. Thus, Bramwell, L. J., discussing the effect of malice in the publication of certain judicial proceedings, once used the following language: "It is said . . . that [this] publication was

Malice destructive of privilege.

[9] 2 C. B. 560, 52 E. C. L. 560.

Volume I

with a view of giving information to the public and therefore the communication is privileged; but it must be shown that the defendant did act under the privilege. The jury have found that the report was sent with a certain amount of malice. The defendant did not act under the privilege. His motive for the publication was not a desire to give information to the public. . . . Suppose a man be applied to for the character of a servant and he is angry with that servant, and says 'He is a bad servant, he has stolen my spoons'; that communication would be privileged if the man has acted *bona fide,* intending honestly to discharge a duty. It is a privilege created by the application of the servant." [1]

Words, then, may be spoken in anger and yet not in malice. The term 'malice' implies an intention to do ulterior and unjustifiable harm.[2] The principle that actual malice destroys the qualified privilege of spoken or written words, or shows that the person making the communication did not act under the privilege, is applied in a clear-cut way throughout the entire subject of defamation, and such illustrations as are needed may be found in the cases cited below.[3] It is needless to observe that the existence of actual malice in any given case can be proved either by extrinsic, internal, or circumstantial evidence, like any other fact necessary to make out the plaintiff's case.[4]

How malice to be proved.

The question naturally arises whether there are other things besides malice which will take away qualified privilege. It is clear that malice is held to be destructive of privilege because the existence of it shows an abuse of the privilege. Accordingly there is no reason why the same thing should not happen when the abuse takes other forms.[5] For instance,

Abuse of privilege.

[1] Stevens *v.* Sampson, 5 Ex. D. 55.

[2] "Maliciously" means and implies an intention to do an act which is wrongful, to the detriment of another. Bowen, L. J., in Mogul Steamship Co. *v.* McGregor, 23 Q. B. D. 612.

[3] Proctor *v.* Webster, 16 Q. B. D. 112; Rex *v.* Abingdon, 1 Esp. 226; Preston *v.* Frey, 91 Cal. 107; Denehy *v.* O'Connell, 66 Conn. 175; State *v.* Burnham, 9 N. H. 34; Jackson *v.* Pittsburgh Times, 152 Pa. St. 406; Tillinghast *v.* McLeod, 17 R. I. 208; Saunders *v.* Baxter, 6 Heisk. (Tenn.) 369.

[4] Oddy *v.* Paulet, 4 F. & F. 1009; Rogers *v.* Clifton, 3 B. & P. 587; Gilpin *v.* Fowler, 9 Exch. 615; Mielenz *v.* Quasdorf, 68 Iowa 726.

[5] This is in harmony with the

it has been held that when the writer of a privileged letter directs the reader to read it to all persons he sees fit, and its contents are thereby disseminated, the privilege is taken away.[6] So it has been held that where the words are not spoken in the proper place and manner they are not entitled to privilege.[7]

In some jurisdictions the same effect is given to want of probable cause for making the injurious statement.[8] Here, it is usually said, want of probable cause is evidence of malice; but this appreciably warps the meaning of malice and tends to confusion, creating a new kind of malice in law. In England it is admitted that a statement recklessly made, without caring whether it be true or false, is not privileged,[9] but want of probable cause does not there suffice to take the privilege away.[1] Nor is privilege destroyed by the mere fact that a third person happens to be present and hears the privileged communication. But if the privileged speaker were to seek an opportunity of making the injurious communication in the presence of others than the party interested, this would tend to show malice.[2] The use of heated and exaggerated language might, it seems, be treated as being such an abuse of privilege as would make a party using it liable, but the prevailing doctrine is that excessive language is destructive of privilege only so far as it establishes malice.[3] The English rule substantially is that malice and malice alone destroys the

Want of probable cause.

Reckless statements.

Heated language.

analogy of the doctrine of trespass *ab initio*, an analogy which is not so remote as may at first appear.

[6] Coles *v.* Thompson, 7 Tex. Civ. App. 666.

[7] Karger *v.* Rich, 81 Wis. 177.

[8] Locke *v.* Bradstreet Co., 22 Fed. Rep. 771; Toothaker *v.* Conant, 91 Me. 438; Briggs *v.* Garrett, 111 Pa. St. 404.

[9] Clark *v.* Molyneux, 3 Q. B. D. 237; Royal Aquarium, etc., Soc. *v.* Parkinson (1892), 1 Q. B. 431.

[1] Clark *v.* Molyneux, 3 Q. B. D. 237. See to the same effect, Bays *v.* Hunt, 60 Iowa 255, 256; Haft *v.* New Castle First Nat. Bank, 19 N. Y. App. Div. 425; Hemmens *v.* Nelson, 138 N. Y. 524.

[2] Toogood *v.* Spyring, 1 C. M. & R. 181.

[3] Gilpin *v.* Fowler, 9 Exch. 615; Wright *v.* Woodgate, 2 C. M. & R. 573; Fryer *v.* Kinnersley, 15 C. B. N. S. 422, 109 E. C. L. 422; Sullivan *v.* Strathan-Hutton-Evans Commission Co., 152 Mo. 268; Kent *v.* Bongartz, 15 R. I. 72.

Where the jury finds that a statement made upon a privileged occasion was couched in excessive language, yet finds that there was no malice, the speaker is protected. Nevill *v.* Fine Arts, etc., Co. (1895), 2 Q. B. 156.

Volume I

legal privilege — a rule to be commended for its simplicity and certainty rather than for its theoretical soundness. In strict theory any abuse of the privilege is enough.

Burden of proving malice.

It should be added that the burden of proving express malice is always upon the plaintiff,[4] a circumstance which has sometimes been overlooked because so much is said in the books about malice being implied from the mere publication of defamatory matter.

Malice in Law.

The reader will observe that in what has been said concerning defamation, nothing has fallen from us on a topic which, during the nineteenth century, exercised the judges more than almost any other connected with this species of wrong, and which even yet is a source of much confusion. This is malice in law. The sooner all the learning about it is forgotten the better it will be both for scientific and judicial precision.

Tort of defamation not founded on malice.

If the preceding investigations into the subject of defamation taught us any one thing it is that malice is not the gist of the wrong. Malice, as we have seen, enters into this branch of the law and qualifies it in the particular way we have noted, but it is not primarily at the basis of liability. It would be just as accurate to say that intention to convert is the gist of conversion as to say that malice is the gist of defamation. Even the judges of the sixteenth century, who cannot be accused of too much learning on this subject, were wise enough to know that malice is not the gist of defamation. Hence we find it laid down in the early books that in a civil action for slanderous words it need not be alleged and proved that the words were maliciously spoken.[5] A very casual dic-

[4] Jenoure *v.* Delmege, (1891) A. C. 73.

[5] Anonymous (1652), Style 392; Mercer *v.* Sparks, Owen 51, Noy 35; Anonymous, Moo. K. B. 459, pl. 637.

Rolle Abr., *Act. sur Case pur Parols,* contains no suggestion that malice is an essential ingredient in the wrong, and Comyns says it is sufficient to allege that the words were falsely spoken or were spoken with intention to harm (*machinans pejorare*). 1 Com. Dig., Action upon the Case for Defamation (G. 5), citing authorities. But the same

tum to the contrary appeared in *Smith v. Richardson* (1737),[6] where the court is reported to have agreed that malice is the gist of the action. The notion made no progress for nearly a century.

Origin of the conception of malice in law.

Finally, in *Bromage v. Prosser* (1825),[7] it was taken up with much show of learning and made into a man of straw only to be demolished. It is true, said Bayley, J., "that malice, in some sense, is the gist of the action," and he thereupon proceeded to fix upon this element of malice which he conceived to be the primary basis of liability, an artificial meaning such as would lend plausibility to this theory. It was, of course, necessary to draw a distinction between this element and that malice which is destructive of privilege. "Malice," says he, "in common acceptation means ill-will against a person; but in its legal sense it means a wrongful act, done intentionally, without just cause or excuse." Now it is undoubtedly true that there are connections in which the term 'malice' has acquired this broad meaning. But the step now taken was altogether gratuitous and misleading; gratuitous, because one legal fiction was set up only to be demolished by another fiction;[8] misleading, because it lends countenance to the notion that there was perhaps some period in the past when an action for defamation would lie only upon proof of actual malice.

Idea causes much trouble.

But the learned talk in *Bromage v. Prosser* had its effect, and soon the judges were saying that malice is the foundation of the wrong of defamation.[9] For three-quarters of a century implied malice, or malice in law, proved to be a veritable bugbear in the law of slander and libel. The work of demolishing the spectre in England seems to have been begun

writer says, without vouching any proof, that "the declaration must show a malicious intent in the defendant." This inaccurate and unsupported observation seems to mark the beginning of the error.

[6] Willes 24.

[7] 4 B. & C. 247, 10 E. C. L. 321.

[8] The legal fiction that malice is essential to the action is destroyed by the fiction that the necessary malice will be presumed. See the incisive opinion of Gaynor, J., in Prince *v.* Brooklyn Daily Eagle (Supm. Ct. Spec. T.), 16 Misc. (N. Y.) 187, 188; also Ullrich *v.* New York Press Co. (Supm. Ct. Tr. T.), 23 Misc. (N. Y.) 168.

[9] See opinion of Erle, C. J., in Whiteley *v.* Adams (1863), 15 C. B. N. S. 414, 109 E. C. L. 414.

Volume I

by Lord Blackburn, who once observed: "A publication calculated to convey an actionable imputation is *prima facie* a libel, the law, as it is technically said, implying malice, or as I should prefer to say, the law being that the person who so publishes is responsible for the natural consequences of his act."[1]

Lord Herschell's statement of function of malice in defamation.

A few years later the function of malice in the law of defamation was discussed by Lord Herschell in these enlightened words: "Some of the learned judges cite actions of libel and slander as instances in which the legal liability depends on the presence or absence of malice. I think this a mistake. The man who defames another by false allegations is liable to an action, however good his motive, and however honestly he believed in the statement he made. It is true that in a limited class of cases the law, under certain circumstances, regards the occasion as privileged, and exonerates the person who has made false defamatory statements from liability if he has made them in good faith. But if there be not that duty or interest which in law creates the privilege, then, though the person making the statements may have acted from the best of motives, and felt it his duty to make them, he is none the less liable. The gist of the action is that the statement was false and defamatory. Because in a strictly limited class of cases the law allows the defense that the statements were made in good faith, it seems to me, with all deference, illogical to affirm that malice constitutes one of the elements of the torts known to the law as libel and slander."[2]

Right of Privacy.

The question of the existence of a right of privacy which has lately been mooted in several quarters[3] and which has finally reached one or two courts of last resort for decision,

[1] Capital, etc., Bank *v.* Henty, 7 App. Cas. 787.

[2] Allen *v.* Flood, (1898) 1 A. C. 125, 126.

[3] The Right to Privacy, by S. D. Warren and L. D. Brandeis, 4 Harv. L. Rev. 193 *et seq.* The Rights of the Citizen: To His Reputation, by E. L. Godkin, Scribner's Magazine, July, 1890. See also Legal Relations of Photographs (1869), 8 Am. L. Reg. N. S. 1.

Chapter XXI

illustrates in an interesting way the process by which the validity of new principle is tested. It is supposed that if such a right is to be born it must come in some way from the law of libel.[4] Those who contend for a right of personal security broad enough to include a general right "to be let alone" would not perhaps admit this, but unquestionably the law of libel furnishes a nearer approach to the indicated goal than any other branch of tort.

Publication of photograph of another not actionable.

A typical situation is presented in *Roberson v. Rochester Folding Box Co.* (1902),[5] where it appeared that the defendant had, without the plaintiff's consent, printed and extensively circulated for advertising purposes lithographic prints, photographs, and likenesses of her. It was insisted for the plaintiff that the defendant had thereby invaded the right of privacy and committed a legal wrong. A person, it was argued, has a right to pass through life, if he wills, without having his picture published, his business enterprises discussed, or his eccentricities commented upon either in hand bills, circulars, or newspapers, whether the comment be favorable or otherwise. The court, however, held that such publication cannot be actionable unless it be defamatory, and an injunction against the continued circulation of the plaintiff's likeness was denied. The decision necessarily negatives the right to recover general damages, even nominal, for such an act as that here complained of.[6]

If the plaintiff in this case had alleged that the circulation of her pictures by the defendant in the manner stated tended to lower her in the esteem of the people who knew her, and that the defendant was in fact guilty of libeling her, another question would have arisen. Could it not be truthfully said that such circulation of the picture would be accepted by the

[4] In Monson *v.* Tussaud (1894), 1 Q. B. 671, an action was brought to enjoin the exhibition of a wax effigy which tended to connect the plaintiff, whose likeness was exhibited, with a murder. Counsel on both sides agreed that the right of action depended solely on the principles of libel, and no suggestion was made that the action could be rested on any other ground than interference with the right of reputation.

[5] 171 N. Y. 538. See also Corliss *v.* E. W. Walker Co., 57 Fed. Rep. 434, 64 Fed. Rep. 280.

[6] Now otherwise, under Laws N. Y. 1903, c. 132.

public as being done with her consent, and hence would be taken as an indication of vulgarity and immodesty? Such a concession would give recognition to the idea that a representation which leads to a false inference as to the character of the person about whom it is made may be libelous. Such notion would be new, but it would not be an anomaly. *Pavesich v. New England L. Ins. Co.* (1905)[7] is in point as countenancing the idea that a misrepresentation which is only by inference hurtful to character, may be a ground of action. Here the defendant, an insurance company, had caused to be printed as an advertisement in a newspaper a recognizable likeness of the plaintiff, accompanied by a statement that he was insured in that company. This statement was false and naturally tended, so the court declared, to raise in the minds of the plaintiff's acquaintances who knew its falsity, a suspicion that he might be improperly propagating a falsehood, either gratuitously or for a consideration. The right of action was accordingly upheld.[8]

Misrepresentation which is hurtful by inference is actionable.

In declaring that an independent right to privacy as distinct from the right to reputation does not in the present state of the law exist, the court of New York was in our opinion unquestionably correct. Whether such a right shall ever acquire recognition will depend upon the view which the highest courts take of the policy of recognizing it and of the social necessity for so doing.[9] Innovations like this are usu-

[7] 122 Ga. 190, N. Y. L. J., April 12, 1905, p. 148.

[8] The Supreme Court of Georgia (Cobb, J.) in this case argued strongly in favor of the right of privacy and rejected the doctrine of the Roberson case, 171 N. Y. 538. But the decision can apparently be more securely rested on the narrower ground indicated above. "A right of privacy," say this court, "is derived from natural law, recognized by municipal law, and its existence can be inferred from expressions used by commentators and writers on the law as well as by judges in decided cases." We merely observe that appeals to 'natural law' are long since out of fashion.

[9] Mr. Kenny, Cases on Torts, p. 367, calls attention to Gokal Prasad *v.* Radho, Indian L. R. 10 Allahabad 358, in which we are told by the court that a right of privacy exists in some of the Indian provinces by immemorial custom. Says Edge, C. J.: "Owing to differences in the conditions of domestic life this custom, perfectly reasonable in India, is unknown in England. But in these provinces of India *Parda* [seclusion of ladies] has for centuries been strictly ob-

ally taken by courts of last resort only under strong pressure, and one may surmise that, if the recognition of such a right be really needed, the legislative power will anticipate the courts in giving it legal standing.

served by all Hindus except those of the lowest castes, and by all Muhammadans except the poorest. The male relations of a *parda-nashin* woman — and the woman herself — would consider it a disgrace were her face to be exposed to the gaze of male strangers. . . . In the hot weather, great numbers of *parda-nashin* women are compelled by the climate to sleep in the open air, that is, in the courtyards or verandahs of their houses. A neighbor should not be allowed to open new doors or windows in such a way as would substantially interfere with those parts of his neighbor's premises which are used by *parda-nashin* women of the latter's family."

CHAPTER XXII

SLANDER OF TITLE AND DEFAMATION OF GOODS.

Slander of Title.

Volume I

Special damage as basis of liability.

Slander of title.

The injurious words may be spoken or written.

IN treating of slander we saw that the common law, while denying the actionability of defamatory spoken words in general, made certain exceptions, one of which was that defamatory words which result in special damage are actionable. Here the courts treated the special damage, and not the injury to reputation, as the basis of liability. It will be readily perceived that the recognition of this principle easily leads to a radical extension of the action for words. If the special damage be the basis of liability, then words which are false and which result in special damage need not be defamatory or injurious to personal reputation at all in order to be a ground of action. This conclusion was so far accepted by the courts as to cause them to recognize the right of action for slander of title, a wrong which is defined as a false and malicious statement, oral or written, made in disparagement of a person's title to real or personal property, or of some other property right of his, and causing special damage.[1] The impossibility of bringing slander of title under the principle of ordinary slander was shown in *Malachy v. Soper* (1836),[2] where it was also declared that in this wrong the law is the same as regards both written and spoken words. That the cause of action for special damage resulting from slander of title does not die with the person [3] strikingly illustrates the fact that the wrong differs widely from defamation of character.

In conformity with modes of speech prevailing in slander

[1] 25 Am. and Eng. Encyc. of Law (2d ed.) 1074. On the subject of slander of title see the cases and notes in 9 Eng. Rul. Cas. 169–185.

[2] 3 Bing. N. Cas. 371, 32 E. C. L. 161.

[3] Hatchard *v.* Mege, 18 Q. B. D. 771.

and libel it has been said that the false statement must be made with malice in order to give rise to an action.[4] But it is clearly sufficient if there be merely a knowledge of its falsity, or absence of reasonable ground for believing it to be true, or a reckless disregard of its truth or falsity.[5] Where the party making the harmful assertion knows that there is no ground for it the law infers an intention to do the harm which thereupon ensues, and there can be said to be malice in law such as was recognized in *Bromage v. Prosser* (1825).[6]

Knowledge of falsity.

But in the sense of ill-will, malice, as a distinctive element, evidently enters into slander of title in exactly the same way that it does into slander and libel, that is, malice is not the gist of the action; but where the occasion of the communication would ordinarily be treated as privileged, the existence of malice takes the privilege away. The notion, however, that actual malice is at the basis of liability in this tort is deeply rooted, at least in dicta.[7] Perceiving, unconsciously perhaps, that special damage is hardly adequate to sustain liability, the courts have tried to put this other pillar of malice under the wrong. Thus has it apparently come to pass that "bad faith as well as special damage is the gist of the action." [8]

Malice in fact not essential to liability.

But 'bad faith' of some sort is necessary.

Defamation of Goods.

Disparagement of manufactured goods.

Akin to slander of title is defamation of manufactured goods, a wrong which consists of the unjustifiable publication of a statement disparaging the quality of the goods of

[4] Hargrave *v.* Le Breton, 4 Burr. 2422; Smith *v.* Spooner, 3 Taunt. 246.

[5] Green *v.* Button, 2 C. M. & R. 707; Linville *v.* Rhoades, 73 Mo. App. 223; Andrew *v.* Deshler, 45 N. J. L. 172; Hopkins *v.* Drowne, 21 R. I. 20.

[6] 4 B. & C. 247, 10 E. C. L. 321.

[7] See Wren *v.* Weild, L. R. 4 Q. B. 730; Halsey *v.* Brotherhood, 19 Ch. D. 386; Harrison *v.* Howe, 109 Mich. 479; John W. Lovell Co. *v.* Houghton, 116 N. Y. 520; Cardon *v.* McConnell, 120 N. Car. 461.

[8] Poll. on Torts, 6th ed., 302. In 14 L. Quar. Rev. 131, Professor Pollock says in regard to malice in slander of title: "We incline to think that the word has no proper application here, and that what is meant is — as in the action for deceit — merely the defendant's knowledge that he is telling or representing a falsehood." In our view this latter observation is entirely sound.

Volume I

another.[9] A showing of special damage is of course necessary here.[1]

Application of doctrine of fair comment.

As defamation of goods is a wrong done in respect of things put before the public for their patronage or approval, the doctrine of fair comment and criticism is applicable. Hence criticism, however caustic, will be tolerated unless it exceed the limits of fair criticism, or in other words, is prompted by that privilege-destroying element malice. But reckless disregard of truth is enough.[2]

Words injurious to business.

In treating of slander we further saw that defamatory words spoken of one in respect of his office, profession, or business, are *per se* actionable at common law. This notion also has in it a potentiality of extension beyond the domain of personal reputation, just as does the notion of the actionability of words causing special damage. At any rate, by combining the two conceptions the courts arrived at such a proposition as this, namely, that words not defamatory are actionable if they cause special damage to a man in his business. In *Ratcliffe v. Evans*[3] it appeared that the plaintiff carried on a business as engineer and boiler-maker under the name of Ratcliffe & Sons, having become entitled to the goodwill of the business on the death of his father. The defendant falsely published in his paper a statement to the effect that the plaintiff had ceased to carry on his business of engineer and boiler-maker and that the firm of Ratcliffe & Sons did not then exist. By reason of this statement a general loss of business occurred. It was held that an action lay in respect of such general loss, and the plaintiff was not required to show special damage in the sense of losing particular customers. Bowen, L. J., said, *inter alia:* "That an action will lie for written or oral falsehoods, not actionable *per se* nor even defamatory, where they are maliciously published, where

Actual damage necessary to be shown.

[9] Western Counties Manure Co. *v.* Lawes Chemical Manure Co., L. R. 9 Exch. 218; Thorley's Cattle Food Co. *v.* Massam, 14 Ch. D. 763; White *v.* Mellin, (1895) A. C. 154.

[1] Dudley *v.* Briggs, 141 Mass. 582; Dooling *v.* Budget Pub. Co., 144 Mass. 258; Swan *v.* Tappan, 5 Cush. (Mass.) 104.

[2] Gott *v.* Pulsifer, 122 Mass. 235.

[3] (1892) 2 Q. B. 524.

they are calculated in the ordinary course of things to produce, and where they do produce, actual damage, is established law. Such an action is not one of libel or of slander, but an action on the case for damage wilfully and intentionally done without just occasion or excuse, analogous to an action for slander of title. To support it, actual damage must be shown, for it is an action which only lies in respect of such damage as has actually occurred." [4] It is needless to add that malice on analysis here proves to be just as fatuous an element, considered as the primary basis of liability, as in the wrongs already considered.

[4] (1892) 2 Q. B. 527.

CHAPTER XXIII

MALICIOUS PROSECUTION.

Malicious Prosecution for Crime.

Volume I

THE examination which we have made into the law of defamation, and the attendant discussion of the subsidiary topics of privilege and malice, place us in a position to understand the nature of the wrong of malicious prosecution. We have seen that at common law to charge a man falsely with the commission of a criminal offense, or to speak words which injure him in his business or which cause special damage to him, is an actionable wrong. We have also learned that while, as a general rule, one who acts under the authority or sanction of law is privileged in respect of things done under that authority, there are nevertheless certain elements, chiefly malice, which operate to take this privilege away. Now for the application of these principles to malicious prosecution. And first we shall speak of malicious criminal proceedings.

Criminal proceedings ordinarily privileged in law.

It is evident that the institution of criminal proceedings by one individual against another amounts to a publication of the charge that he is guilty of the crime for which he is prosecuted. We may even go further and say that this is a mode of publication which, above all others, is dangerous to the reputation of the person who is charged with crime. It tends to fix upon him the stigma of dishonor much more effectually than the spoken word or the printed libel. This being so, it follows that, but for the privilege which the law confers, the making of a false criminal charge in course of a legal prosecution would undoubtedly be an actionable wrong. The grounds upon which the privilege is conferred are not difficult to discover. Men are morally bound to prosecute the crim-

Ground of the privilege.

Chapter XXIII

inal whose operations come within their ken. It is a duty one owes to himself and society, and there are not wanting traces of the recognition of this duty as a legal one.[1] But whether the duty is in our day a legal one or not, it is unquestionable that one has a legal right to prosecute criminals and is amply protected in so doing. The privilege is not an absolute one, and if it be abused the prosecutor becomes liable in damages to the person aggrieved. Malicious prosecution for a criminal offense is thus seen to be a wrong which embodies merely an extension of the conception underlying our law of defamation.[2] Furthermore, it is not an independent substantive wrong, but belongs to the legal formation which we know as 'breach of privilege,' or 'abuse of authority.' Considered as an independent tort, malicious prosecution must always appear to be an anomalous injury; for then the element malice would have to be conceded to be the primary basis of liability. But this, as we have now learned, malice cannot be.

The privilege is a qualified one.

The decisions on the subject of malicious prosecution will be found upon examination to contain abundant recognition of the fact that this tort, in its main segments at least, is subordinate to the more general wrong of defamation. But writers on the theory of tort have fallen into the habit of treating it as an independent malicious wrong. One reason for this

Malicious prosecution a branch of defamation.

[1] Witness the old rule that where a forcible trespass amounts to a felony, a civil action for damages cannot be maintained until after the wrongdoer has been criminally prosecuted. Wellock *v.* Constantine, 2 H. & C. 146; *Ex p.* Ball, 10 Ch. D. 673; Wells *v.* Abrahams, L. R. 7 Q. B. 554.

[2] The utterances of Lord Herschell and Lord Davey in Allen *v.* Flood (1898), A. C. 125, 172, evince an appreciation of the affinity between defamation and malicious prosecution. Professor Pollock tentatively accepts the suggestions of these learned lords as a rational justification of the law on the subject of malicious prosecution. Poll. on Torts, 6th ed., 310.

It should be remarked that the writer in 8 Encyc. Laws of England, p. 88, misses the point altogether when, in criticising the observations of Lords Herschell and Davey, he says "there is no judicial authority which will justify the proposition that the institution of legal proceedings has ever been presumed to be an actionable wrong, however vexatious they may be." Quite true. The institution of proceedings is the very thing that is not a wrong. It is the making of the criminal charge which supplies the basis of liability in this tort. The litigation is no evil. That the law countenances, and even makes the occasion of exceptional immunity.

Volume I

error is to be found in the fact that the torts of defamation and malicious prosecution sprang up in different fields and have had different historical associations. Consequently they have generally been viewed from different standpoints and their natural affinity has been in some degree obscured.

Antiquity of the tort of malicious prosecution.

How modern in its main branches is the law of defamation, we have already seen. The law of malicious prosecution, on the contrary, is very ancient. "From the very twilight of the English law," says Professor Bigelow, "it has been unlawful for men to harass each other with vexatious suits." [4]

Statutory recognition of the tort.

"Common law and common reason agree," says Staundforde, our earliest writer on criminal law, "that when a man has sustained a prosecution by which his goods, land, life, and goodwife are in jeopardy without cause or any other foundation than the malicious accusation of a person, and is found a true and loyal man, and is duly acquitted of that of which he is appealed, he ought to have amends for this against his false accuser." [5] Yet the recognition of malicious prosecution as a distinct legal wrong was originally due to statute.[6]

Conspiracy to prosecute upon a false charge.

To the early common-law judges the most aggravated form of malicious prosecution was that in which a false prosecution was set afoot by more than one person acting in conspiracy. The idea that it is a much more grievous wrong for several to be concerned in a false prosecution than merely one person evidently originated in that stage of law and society when the hired champion was a factor to be reckoned with in the administration of justice. At any rate, so odious was the wrong of conspiring to prosecute one upon a false criminal charge, that the common law gave redress by a writ of conspiracy where the prosecution was for treason or felony.[7] This writ of conspiracy antedated the statutes of

[4] Big. Lead. Cas. Torts 193.

[5] Staundf. P. C. 167*b*.

[6] Statute West. II., c. 12 (of malicious appeals). See Co. 2 Inst. 383 and notes. Statute West. II., c. 36 (false distresses). See also authorities referred to by Professor Bigelow, Lead. Cas. Torts, 190 (note) *et seq.*

[7] Reg. Brev. Orig. 134.

At a very early day parliament defined the wrong of conspiracy and extended the law concerning it. Stat. Incerti. Temp., 1 Stat. at L.

Chapter XXIII

Writ of conspiracy.

malicious prosecution, and we find that when the latter wrong obtained recognition as a ground of civil liability, no special writ for it was framed. Instead, the old writ of conspiracy was pressed into service, the allegation of conspiracy being treated as surplusage.[8] The distinction between malicious prosecution and conspiracy (resulting in a prosecution on a false charge) was thus effectually broken down, and as a distinct tort the latter wrong is now practically unknown.

The following are the general principles underlying the modern action for a malicious criminal prosecution:

General principles.

First, it must appear that the accused was innocent and that the proceedings against him are at an end, having been terminated in his favor.[9] This rule is supported by good sense and sound considerations of public policy. If the law were otherwise, a person prosecuted for crime could institute a suit for malicious prosecution pending the criminal action, hoping to compromise with the prosecutor by mutual concession. Then, again, if permitted to sue before the original prosecution is ended, the accused might possibly recover in the civil action, though he afterwards should be proven guilty and be convicted. This, it has been considered, would be a scandal on the administration of justice.

Secondly, there must have been an absence of probable cause for the prosecution, which is alleged to have been maliciously instituted. It is not enough that the accused is in-

399. By Stat. 33 Edw. I. 1, conspirators were defined as "they that do consider or bind themselves by oath, covenant, or other alliance that every of them shall aid and support the enterprise of each other falsely and maliciously to indict or cause to be indicted, or falsely to acquit people, or falsely to move or maintain pleas; and also such as cause children within age to appeal men of felony whereby they are imprisoned and sore grieved; and such as retain men with their liveries or fees for to maintain their malicious enterprises," etc. See Big. Lead. Cas. Torts 211.

[8] F. N. B. (Writ of Conspiracy) 114 D; Savile *v.* Roberts, 1 Ld. Raym. 374; Skinner *v.* Gunton, 1 Saund. 230 (note). See Comyn's Digest, Action upon the Case for Conspiracy (A); 1 Rolle Abr., 110, *Action sur Case en Nature d'un Conspiracy.*

[9] Morgan *v.* Hughes, 2 T. R. 225; Castrique *v.* Behrens, 3 El. & El. 709, 107 E. C. L. 709; Whitworth *v.* Hall, 2 B. & Ad. 695, 22 E. C. L. 173; Fisher *v.* Bristow, 1 Dougl. 215. But this rule does not apply in case of malicious abuse of process upon *ex parte* showing. Steward *v.* Gromett, 7 C. B. N. S. 191, 97 E. C. L. 191.

Volume I

nocent and has been proven to be so. The plaintiff must go further and show that there was no probable cause for thinking that he was guilty.[1]

Want of probable cause.

Probable cause in this connection is shown when it appears that circumstances were such at the time of the institution of the proceedings as to lead a reasonable person acting in good faith to the belief that the person accused was guilty.[2]

Moreover, where the accused is in fact innocent, but the circumstances are such as to cause suspicion to fall upon him and to afford reasonable ground for believing him guilty, the prosecutor, when sued for malicious prosecution, cannot take advantage of such reasonable ground unless he knew the suspicious circumstances and credited them.[3]

Prosecution only justified when conducted in good faith.

This all means that the prosecutor must act in entire good faith in order to be able to claim the protection of legal privilege where it turns out that the accused is innocent. If the prosecutor knows, or believes, that the person accused is innocent, circumstances however damning will not justify the prosecution. In effect the authorities come to this, viz.: that if an innocent man is prosecuted on a criminal charge in bad faith and without probable cause, he can maintain an action for damages. Perhaps the tersest and most satisfactory way in which to state the underlying doctrine of malicious prosecution for crime is by saying that want of probable cause, coupled with bad faith, is sufficient in law to show abuse of the privilege of prosecution.

It has been laid down in innumerable cases that malice on the part of the prosecutor is an essential ingredient of the tort of malicious prosecution and the use of the epithet 'malicious,' in naming the tort, shows that this element has been

[1] Anonymous, 6 Mod. 25, 73. Turner *v.* Ambler, 10 Q. B. 252, 59 E. C. L. 252; Ravenga *v.* Mackintosh, 2 B. & C. 693, 9 E. C. L. 225; Sanders *v.* Palmer (C. C. A.), 55 Fed. Rep. 217; Jordan *v.* Alabama G. S. R. Co., 81 Ala. 220; Cloon *v.* Gerry, 13 Gray (Mass.) 201; Evans *v.* Thompson, 12 Heisk. (Tenn.) 534.

[2] Compare definitions of probable cause in the following cases: Nevill *v.* Loadman, 2 F. & F. 313; Wheeler *v.* Nesbitt, 24 How. (U. S.) 544; Munns *v.* Dupont, 3 Wash. (U. S.) 31; Lunsford *v.* Dietrich, 93 Ala. 565; Thompson *v.* Beacon Valley Rubber Co., 56 Conn. 493; Foshay *v.* Ferguson, 2 Den. (N. Y.) 617.

[3] Haddrick *v.* Heslop, 12 Q. B. 267, 64 E. C. L. 267.

Chapter XXIII

supposed to be essential. The common way of stating the law is that the two elements, malice and want of probable cause, must concur before an action of malicious prosecution can be maintained.[4] But this proposition is immediately qualified by the admission that malice may be inferred from want of probable cause.[5] This would seem to show that want of probable cause alone is the basis of liability, and that actual ill-will when present is only an aggravating element. But this inference is not wholly warranted, for the authorities are explicit on the point that something else besides want of probable cause is essential to liability. This element is bad faith in the prosecution — an acting under some other motive than that of the furtherance of justice. Malice in this broad sense can be said to be essential to the tort.[6] A failure to use due care in ascertaining the true state of facts tends to show bad faith or malice, but it is not a legal equivalent of these elements.[7]

In what sense malice essential to cause of action.

The burden of proving want of probable cause and malice is upon the plaintiff, notwithstanding the difficulty that may arise from requiring him in effect to prove a negative.[8]

Burden of proof.

Liability for malicious prosecution is not limited to prosecutions for criminal offenses. Thus an action will lie for the institution of bankrupt proceedings maliciously and without probable cause, or for the malicious or ungrounded filing of a petition to wind up a corporation.[9] This is in conformity

Malicious institution of civil proceedings.

[4] Jordan *v.* Alabama G. S. R. Co., 81 Ala. 220.

[5] Lunsford *v.* Dietrich, 93 Ala. 565. It would be better to say that malice may be inferred from all the facts proved.

The converse is not true, for want of probable cause cannot be inferred from malice under any circumstances. Musgrove *v.* Newell, 1 M. & W. 582; Stewart *v.* Sonneborn, 98 U. S. 187.

[6] "The term 'malice' in this form of action is not to be considered in the sense of spite or hatred against an individual, but of *malus animus* and as denoting that the party is actuated by improper and indirect motives." Parke, J., in Mitchell *v.* Jenkins, 5 B. & Ad. 588, 27 E. C. L. 131.

[7] Abrath *v.* North Eastern R. Co., 11 App. Cas. 247; Brown *v.* Hawkes (1891), 2 Q. B. 718.

[8] Ravenga *v.* Mackintosh, 2 B. & C. 693, 9 E. C. L. 225; Abrath *v.* North Eastern R. Co., 11 App. Cas. 247; Legallee *v.* Blaisdell, 134 Mass. 473; Le Clear *v.* Perkins, 103 Mich. 131; Scott *v.* Shelor, 28 Gratt. (Va.) 891.

[9] Chapman *v.* Pickersgill, 2 Wils.

Volume I

with the analogy of that principle in our law of defamation which gives a right of action for words injurious to a man in his office, profession, or business.

Inquisition of lunacy.

Likewise it has been held that the malicious institution of proceedings to have a person declared a lunatic supplies a good ground of action.[1]

Special damage in malicious prosecution.

In further conformity with the analogy of slander we naturally expect to find in the law of malicious prosecution recognition of 'special damage' as a head of legal liability. And we are not disappointed. In *Savile v. Roberts* (1698),[2] Lord Holt said that there are three sorts of damage, any one of which is sufficient to support an action for malicious prosecution: (1) The damage to a man's fame, as if the matters whereof he is accused be scandalous; (2) The second sort of damages are such as are done to the person, as where a man is put in danger to lose his life, or limb, or liberty; (3) The third sort of damages is damage to a man's property, as where he is forced to expend his money in necessary charges, to acquit himself of the crime of which he is accused. The first two of these forms of damage are merely legal harms such as result from injury to person or reputation. The third form of damage is pecuniary detriment.

Malicious prosecution of ordinary civil suit actionable.

It might seem at first glance that the institution of any ordinary civil suit whatever imposes a special and necessary pecuniary detriment on the defendant to defend such action. Consequently it might be concluded that such pecuniary detriment would be a sufficient damage to enable the defendant to maintain an action for the malicious prosecution of any ungrounded civil claim whatever. And there are modern decisions in America to this effect.[3] But there must be an end of litigation somewhere, and the right to retaliate by counter-

Contrary doctrine.

C. Pl. 145; Whitworth *v.* Hall, 2 B. & Ad. 695, 22 E. C. L. 173; Quartz Hill Consol. Gold Min. Co. *v.* Eyre, 11 Q. B. D. 674; Metropolitan Bank *v.* Pooley, 10 App. Cas. 210; Stewart *v.* Sonneborn, 98 U. S. 187.

[1] Lockenour *v.* Sides, 57 Ind. 360; Davenport *v.* Lynch, 6 Jones L. (51 N. Car.) 545.

[2] 1 Ld. Raym. 374.

[3] See *post*, note 7; also, generally, The Action for Malicious Prosecution of Civil Suit, by J. D. Lawson, 21 Am. L. Reg. N. S. 281 (May, 1882).

Chapter XXIII

suit may well be limited to narrow bounds. Accordingly, in England it is now settled that an action will not lie for the malicious prosecution of an ordinary civil suit.[4] The same rule prevails in a number of the American States.[5] But if there be special damage such as is involved in a deprivation of personal liberty or of the possession, use, or enjoyment of property, as, for instance, where it is attached upon mesne process, the action lies.[6]

In a number of American jurisdictions it is determined that an action will lie for the malicious prosecution of any ungrounded civil suit, though it is begun only by process of summons and does not lead to any deprivation of property or interference with personal liberty.[7]

Costs cover all recoverable items of special damage.

The English decisions which deny the right to maintain the action proceed largely upon the idea that the costs recovered by the successful defendant are a sufficient indemnity and cover all damage which is not remote. These costs, it seems, there include the attorney's charges and the honorarium of the barrister, as well as the fees of witnesses and court costs.[8] In some of the American States the same liberality in the matter of taxing costs prevails. But in other jurisdictions recoverable costs are limited by statute to official court expenses and witness fees. The inadequacy of such a recovery to defray the natural and necessary cost of defense has caused the minority courts to break away from the English rule. If not entirely justified on theoretical grounds in so doing, they are not without justification in point of justice and common sense.

[4] See opinion of Bowen, L. J., in Quartz Hill Consol. Gold Min. Co. *v.* Eyre, 11 Q. B. D. 690.

[5] Wetmore *v.* Mellinger, 64 Iowa 741; McNamee *v.* Minke, 49 Md. 122; Bitz *v.* Meyer, 40 N. J. L. 252; Muldoon *v.* Rickey, 103 Pa. St. 110.

[6] Mitchell *v.* Southwestern R. Co., 75 Ga. 398; Fortman *v.* Rottier, 8 Ohio St. 548; Newark Coal Co. *v.* Upson, 40 Ohio St. 17.

[7] Eastin *v.* Stockton Bank, 66 Cal. 123; Kolka *v.* Jones, 6 N. Dak. 461; Pope *v.* Pollock, 46 Ohio St. 367; Lipscomb *v.* Shofner, 96 Tenn. 112; Closson *v.* Staples, 42 Vt. 209.

[8] 21 Am. L. Reg. N. S. 370.

Volume I

Malicious Abuse of Process.

Akin to the wrong of malicious prosecution is that which is known as malicious abuse of process. The leading case on the subject of malicious abuse of process is *Grainger v. Hill* (1838),[0] where, after a man had been arrested upon legal process, he was compelled by duress to surrender as a condition of his release the register of his vessel, whereby he lost certain voyages. It was held that an action would lie, and this without proof that the original proceedings had been terminated. The ground of the action is not the malicious beginning and prosecution of the proceedings, but consists in the abuse of the process, where it is admitted to have been lawfully issued.[1] Malicious abuse of process is an analogue or complement, in the field of case, of the tort of trespass *ab initio* in the field of trespass. There, as we have seen, one who forcibly interferes with person or property under circumstances which the legal process will not justify, becomes a trespasser *ab initio.* Here we learn that where the abuse complained of is not such an act as may be treated as a forcible trespass, the tort is called malicious abuse of process, and is remediable in an action on the case.

Malicious abuse of process an analogue of trespass *ab initio.*

Function of malice in malicious abuse of process.

As might be expected, it is frequently said that, as in malicious prosecution, actual malice is a necessary element in malicious abuse of process.[2] But in fact all that is necessary is that the act should be an abuse.[3] In whatever sense malice

[0] 4 Bing. N. Cas. 212, 33 E. C. L. 328.

[1] On the subject of malicious abuse of process, see Page *v.* Cushing, 38 Me. 523; Wood *v.* Graves, 144 Mass. 365; Antcliff *v.* June, 81 Mich. 477; Rossiter *v.* Minnesota Brandner-Smith Paper Co., 37 Minn. 296; Sneeden *v.* Harris, 109 N. Car. 357; Lockhart *v.* Bear, 117 N. Car. 298; Mayer *v.* Walter, 64 Pa. St. 283.

In Nix *v.* Goodhill, 95 Iowa 285, an action was maintained against one who garnished the exempt earnings of his debtor, knowing them to be exempt, with the purpose of harassing him into paying the debt out of such exempt earnings. The wrong was treated by the court as a malicious abuse of process, but it was clearly a case of malicious prosecution of a civil suit.

[2] Phœnix Mut. L. Ins. Co. *v.* Arbuckle, 52 Ill. App. 33; Nix *v.* Goodhill, 95 Iowa 282; Hearn *v.* Shaw, 72 Me. 193; Mayer *v.* Walter, 64 Pa. St. 283.

[3] "If process is wilfully made use of for a purpose not justified by the law, this is an abuse for which an

is necessary, the element will be inferred from the advertent doing of a harm which is outside the protection of the process. Express malice is only evidence of abuse. So likewise is want of probable cause. Malice is no more essential to liability here than it is in the field of trespass *ab initio,* and no one ever imagined that actual malice is there essential to liability.

Chapter XXIII

Function of Malice.

Function of malice in general.

From what has been said in the last three or four chapters concerning malice we conclude that this element is one which, however conspicuous it may be in the early stages of the evolution of any species of wrong, is yet of continually diminishing importance as the true basis of liability comes to be discovered and defined. At first malice is treated as a reserve force of sufficient weight to fix liability where no general right of action is recognized. Having thus assisted in the generation of new principle, it subsequently recedes more and more from view. In conformity with the universal law of nature the great struggle of legal theory is in parturition. When new principle has actually appeared the work of bringing it to maturity is comparatively easy.

Recession of malice as a constitutive element in legal wrong.

The recession of the element of malice as a constitutive factor in liability in the maturity of the law is aptly illustrated in *Bond v. Chapin* (1844).[4] It there appeared that the defendant, Chapin, had instituted against the plaintiff a civil suit in the name of a third person. Chapin supposed he had authority to take this step, but the suit was, in fact, unauthorized. The plaintiff was not actuated by malice, and subsequently took a nonsuit. Thereupon the defendant sued for the damages incurred by reason of the unauthorized proceedings. It is clear that the bringing of the original suit by the defendant was an abuse of that privilege of suit which the law confers on persons who have, or suppose themselves to have, a cause of action in their own right. It is furthermore

action will lie." Antcliff *v.* June, 81 Mich. 492.

[4] 8 Met. (Mass.) 31.

clear that the right of action of the injured person fell within the principle governing the tort of malicious prosecution. On this assumption the trial court charged the jury that the plaintiff must prove that the former action was prosecuted maliciously, that is to say, with some improper motive or without due care to ascertain his rights, as well as without authority and without probable cause. This was in conformity with the well-known formula used in defining the wrong of malicious prosecution. The Supreme Court of Massachusetts, however, held that malice need not be proved. The decision shows that 'abuse of the privilege of suing' is the gist of the wrong of malicious prosecution and that malice is not a necessary ingredient. It is true that the court did not put the decision on this ground, but declared instead that the right of action in case for the unauthorized institution and prosecution of a suit in the name of a third person is a different wrong from malicious prosecution. But this seems to be merely an illustration of the natural proclivity of courts to harmonize authorities by differentiation rather than to meet difficulties by direct attack upon accepted formulas.

Gist of the wrong.

CHAPTER XXIV

MAINTENANCE.

Chapter XXIV

Analogy of maintenance to malicious prosecution.

FOLLOWING up the idea of damage incurred as a result of improperly setting in motion the machinery of the law, we come to the tort of maintenance. Here the principle is recognized that it is a legal wrong on the part of A towards B to maintain C in a suit against B on a cause of action in which A is not concerned. We reach this wrong coming by insensible gradations from the tort of malicious prosecution, for it would seem that the idea of liability incurred by maintaining the suit of another differs little in principle from the idea of liability for wrongfully setting legal machinery in motion oneself. But however fine the dividing line may be, it marks the transition into a different legal formation, for the tort of maintenance does not belong to that stratum, 'abuse of privilege,' with which we have been dealing. It is an independent tort and stands on its own foundation. The tort of malicious prosecution, as we have seen, comes under an exception to an exception to a general principle. Maintenance, on the other hand, comes directly under a general principle. There is a rule of law that one must not maintain a stranger in his suit. Such act is a legal wrong and is not *prima facie* privileged at all, as is a suit which one maintains in his own behalf. The way in which the legal point of view here shifts is characteristic, and a mental note of it may be of value hereafter. It shows how nearly alike things may outwardly be and yet differ widely in point of fundamental theory.

Definition.

The wrong of maintenance is accurately described in *Termes de la Ley* as follows: "Maintenance is where any man gives or delivers to another, that is plaintiff or defendant in any action, any sum of money or other thing to maintain his plea, or takes great pains for him when he hath nothing therewith to do; then the party grieved shall have against him a writ called a writ of maintenance."[1] It consists of unauthorized intermeddling in the litigation of others, to keep it going or to influence the result. *Culpa est rei se immiscere ad se non pertinenti.*

Formerly maintenance attracted a great deal of attention, owing to social conditions which are now happily gone,[2] and its suppression taxed to the utmost the ingenuity of legislative as well as judicial heads.[3] With the passing away of the state of affairs which gave prominence to this wrong the law on the subject of maintenance has been relaxed, but it is by no means obsolete. Even yet the action for maintenance "may be in some cases the only way of redressing very cruel wrongs."[4]

Anciently any sort of busying oneself to further the suit of another could be treated as maintenance, but the commonest form of the wrong was the act of supplying sinews, in the form of money or property, with which to determine the contest or influence its result.[5]

In the leading modern case the action was sustained under these circumstances: One Bradlaugh, it appeared, had sat and voted in Parliament without taking an oath required by statute. Newdegate, a fellow member of Parliament, procured one C to sue for a penalty supposed to have been incurred by reason of Bradlaugh's failure to take the oath. The plaintiff in the *qui tam* action was of insufficient means to bear the cost of such proceeding, and after its commencement, Newdegate gave him a bond of indemnity against such costs and expenses as he might incur. The *qui tam* proceeding eventually failed, on the ground that the statute did not authorize a suit by a common informer. Bradlaugh then

[1] Termes de la Ley, *sub voce* Maintenance. See also 4 Bl. Com. 134; Co. Litt. 368*b*, 369*a*; 2 Co. Inst. 208, 212.

[2] See Stubbs, 3 Const. Hist. (5th ed.) 550 *et seq.*; Stephen, 3 Hist. Crim. Law 236 *et seq.*

[3] For an account of the legislation making maintenance and champerty criminal offenses see Stephen, 3 Hist. Crim. Law 234–240.

[4] Lord Coleridge, C. J., in Bradlaugh *v.* Newdegate (1883), 11 Q. B. D. 6.

[5] See 2 Rolle Abr., *Maintenance*, passim.

brought an action against Newdegate for maintaining the action of C. It was held that he was liable.[6]

Chapter XXIV

It will be observed that maintenance consists of giving assistance after the suit has been brought. To advise, and thus by instigation to cause the institution of a suit, is not maintenance.[7] But there is an innominate wrong for which case will lie if one moves another to bring an action for which there is no reasonable or probable ground.[8] This innominate action falls strictly within the principle of malicious prosecution.

Instigation of groundless suit.

In cases of maintenance proper, it is not necessary for the plaintiff to show that the suit which was improperly maintained was without any reasonable or probable basis. It is the intermeddling in the suit that the law reprobates, and the merit of the suit is not in question. Still, if the party whose suit is maintained turns out to be in the right, and the maintenance does not take the form of corrupt interference with the course of justice, the losing party would have difficulty in showing, to the satisfaction of a modern court at least, that he had suffered legal damage. The plaintiff, seeking to recover for an act of maintenance, should be required to show, not that there was want of probable cause, but that the suit maintained has in fact failed.

Suit maintained must be ended.

If the party who maintains the suit and the party whose suit is maintained have a common interest in the result of the suit, no action for maintenance will lie. Thus the inhabitants of a village having prescriptive rights may maintain an action in vindication of such rights, although they are not actual parties.[9] But the interest must be "an actual valuable

Common interest.

[6] Bradlaugh *v.* Newdegate, 11 Q. B. D. 1. The modern English authorities on the subject of maintenance are fully reviewed in the opinion of Lord Coleridge in this case.

[7] Flight *v.* Leman, 4 Q. B. 883, 45 E. C. L. 883.

[8] Flight *v.* Leman, 4 Q. B. 883, 45 E. C. L. 883; Pechell *v.* Watson, 8 M. & W. 691.

[9] 2 Rolle Abr., *Maintenance* (G), pl. 1. So a reversioner may assist a lessee for years in maintaining his rights under the lease where the right of the inheritance is brought in issue. *Ib.*, pl. 2.

interest in the result of the suit itself, either present, or contingent, or future."[1]

Right to maintain suit of relative.

A well-established qualification of the general rule prohibiting the maintenance of litigation in which one is not directly interested, arises out of the relation of the parties. One can maintain "his blood,"[2] and it is no wrong to assist those who are related to you by consanguinity or affinity.[3] So both master and servant are allowed to maintain each other in litigation,[4] as in broils.

Assistance given from charity.

It is also a good defense to an action for maintenance that the assistance complained of was rendered out of motives of charity, in the cause of one thought to be oppressed and who had no means of obtaining redress without such assistance.[5] To enable one to come within this benevolent exception, it is not necessary for him to show that his charity was extended after due inquiry into the merits of the cause of action.[6] Charity is not required to be discreet or considerately regardful of the interests of the supposed oppressor, as well as of the interests of the supposed victim. It is enough if the spirit of the act be right.

Infrequency of actions for maintenance.

Actions for maintenance are not frequent nowadays, and it seems needless to go further into the subject. The citations below will put the curious on the track of such matter as may prove of interest or value.[7] In America there is no more

[1] Bradlaugh *v.* Newdegate, 11 Q. B. D. 11.

[2] Martin, J., in Y. B. 9 Hen. IV. 64, pl. 17.

[3] 2 Rolle Abr. 115 (H. I.).

[4] 2 Rolle Abr. 116 (K. L.). But the servant was formerly not allowed to assist with his money or other property. *Ib.*, pl. 4, 5. His right to maintain was limited to such offices of assistance as fell within his duty as a servant, such for instance as staying with the master at the trial and doing errands to speed the cause.

[5] "I can give gold or silver to a man who is poor to maintain his plea, if he himself cannot through his poverty." Martin, J., in Y. B. 9 Hen. VI. 64, pl. 17. See also Paston, J., in Y. B. 21 Hen. VI. 16, pl. 30; and remarks by Prisot, Serjeant, in Y. B. 22 Hen. VI. 35, pl. 54.

[6] Harris *v.* Brisco, 17 Q. B. D. 504.

[7] Burke *v.* Greene, 2 Ball & B. 517; Pechell *v.* Watson, 8 M. & W. 691; Harrington *v.* Long, 2 Myl. & K. 590; Hutley *v.* Hutley, L. R. 8 Q. B. 112; Alabaster *v.* Harness (1895), 1 Q. B. 339; Wallis *v.* Portland, 3 Ves. Jr. 494; Fisher *v.* Kamala Naicker, 8 Moo. Indian App. 170; Findon *v.* Parker, 11 M. & W. 675; Master *v.* Miller, 4 T. R. 320.

than the barest recognition of the civil right of action for maintenance. There are, to be sure, many judicial dicta in this country to the effect that maintenance may give rise to a civil action for damages, and there are one or two decisions in which the point has been expressly ruled;[8] but for the most part the question of the unlawfulness of maintenance has arisen in connection with the validity of contracts.[9] The judicial feeling seems to be that the doctrine is a relic of social conditions which have passed away.[1]

[8] Fletcher *v.* Ellis, Hempst. (U.S.) 300; Goodyear Dental Vulcanite Co. *v.* White, 2 N. J. L. J. 150.

[9] Quigley *v.* Thompson, 53 Ind. 317; Manning *v.* Sprague, 148 Mass. 18; Christie *v.* Sawyer, 44 N. H. 303; Sherley *v.* Riggs, 11 Humph. (Tenn.) 53.

[1] Duke *v.* Harper, 2 Mo. App. 10.

CHAPTER XXV

INTERFERENCE WITH CONTRACT RELATIONS.

Volume I

Interference with status.

IN considering the subject of interference with domestic relations, we learned that at common law it is actionable to entice a servant from the employment of his master. The relation of master and servant is here conceived as a distinct legal entity and as the object of the reprobated harm. Consideration of this tort opens the way for the realization of a still broader conception of liability. Thus, it being admitted that it is a legal wrong to break up a relation of personal service (whether that relation subsists by reason of family tie, or, as in ancient times, by reason of villeinage, or, as in modern times, by agreement), the question naturally arises whether it is a legal wrong for one person to break up or interfere with any contract relation subsisting between other persons. Obviously this question takes us into a field where the conception of status as the object of the legal wrong can no longer be of assistance.

Interference with contract for performance of personal service.

Lumley v. Gye (1853)[1] is the leading case in this branch of the law. It there appeared that the plaintiff, as manager of a theatre, had entered into a contract with Miss Johanna Wagner, an opera singer, whereby she bound herself for a period to sing in the plaintiff's theatre and nowhere else. The defendant, knowing of the existence of this contract, and, as the declaration alleged, "maliciously intending to injure the plaintiff," enticed and procured Miss Wagner to leave the plaintiff's employment. Clearly here was a case of interference with a relation of personal service, but the relation was totally devoid of any trace of status in the true sense. It was held by the Court of Queen's Bench, Coleridge, J., dissenting, that the plaintiff could recover. For the defendant, it was insisted that the principle of liability for interference with service

[1] 2 El. & Bl. 216, 75 E. C. L. 216.

is limited to the cases of apprentices and menial servants and others to whom the Statutes of Laborers were applicable. But the majority of the judges concurred in the opinion that the principle extended to all cases of hiring. It was also intimated — but the point was not essential to the judgment — that the principle in question extends to cases of interference with contractual relation, whether the contract stipulates for personal service or not.[2]

The dissenting opinion of Coleridge, J., in *Lumley v. Gye* (1853),[3] like the dissenting opinions of Cockburn, C. J., in *Collen v. Wright* (1857),[4] and of Grose, J., in *Pasley v. Freeman* (1789),[5] is exceedingly instructive, for it brings into clear relief the fact that the decision of the majority embodied a radical extension of legal doctrine, not to say an actual departure from former precedents. Nothing better illustrates the process by which the law grows. That situation which to one judge seems to be only a new instance falling under a principle previously recognized, will to another seem to be so entirely new as not to fall under such principle. It will not infrequently be found that the judge of greatest legal acumen, the greatest analyzer, is the very one who resists innovation and extension. This, indeed, is one of the pitfalls of much learning.

Process of legal growth.

One who considers the phenomenon of legal growth to much purpose will learn that legal theory is a flexible thing; and in every case where the question is whether a particular extension of legal doctrine should be sanctioned, considerations of justice and expediency should be given due weight. Yet the judge who sees most clearly the logical limits of the principle underlying a particular tort is precisely

Considerations of policy and justice.

[2] See observations of Crompton, J., p. 229, on the contention of the plaintiff's counsel for the broader rule; also observations of Wightman, J., p. 237. On this point Green *v.* Button, 2 C. M. & R. 707, was cited as authority. There it was held that an action was maintainable against the defendant for maliciously and wrongfully causing certain persons to refuse to deliver goods to the plaintiff, by asserting that he had a lien upon them and ordering these persons to retain the goods until further orders from him.

[3] 2 El. & Bl. 244, 75 E. C. L. 244.

[4] 8 El. & Bl. 647, 92 E. C. L. 647.

[5] 3 T. R. 51.

the one who is least likely to yield to the mentor of justice and policy when it comes to a question of transcending those limits. The pride of intellectual certainty seems to shut out from the mind considerations which should in doubtful situations be given weight. In nine cases out of ten it will be found that future development justifies the more liberal view. Rare indeed is that judicial mind in which the highest analytical powers are happily blended with that practical common sense which is indispensable to the proper administration of justice.

Interference with contract relation unconnected with service.

In *Bowen v. Hall* (1881),[6] the Court of Appeal accepted the doctrine of *Lumley v. Gye*. Some doubts as to the soundness of the decision were expressed by some of the lords in *Allen v. Flood*,[7] but these doubts have now been dissipated.[8]

In *Temperton v. Russell*[9] it was decided, in conformity with the previous suggestion in *Lumley v. Gye* (1853),[1] that the right of action for maliciously procuring a breach of contract is not confined to contracts for personal services, but extends to contracts in general. In that case the contract which the defendants had procured to be breached was a contract for the supply of building material.

Bad faith but not malice essential to right of action.

The declaration in *Lumley v. Gye* alleged that the wrong complained of was maliciously done, and malice in some form is generally supposed to be an essential ingredient in cases of interference with contract relations. But clearly it is enough if the wrongdoer, having knowledge of the existence of the contract relation, in bad faith sets about to break it up. Whether his motive be to benefit himself or gratify his spite by working mischief to the employer is immaterial.[2] Malice in

[6] 6 Q. B. D. 333.

[7] (1898) A. C. 1.

[8] Quinn *v.* Leathem, (1901) A. C. 495, 510.

[9] (1893) 1 Q. B. 715, approved in Quinn *v.* Leathem, (1901) A. C. 495.

[1] 2 El. & Bl. 216, 75 E. C. L. 216.

[2] "A study of the case of Lumley *v.* Gye, 2 El. & Bl. 216, 75 E. C. L. 216, has satisfied me that in that case the majority of the court regarded the circumstance that what the defendant procured was a breach of contract as the essence of the cause of action. It is true that the word 'maliciously' was to be found in the declaration the validity of which was then under consideration; but I do not think the learned judges regarded the allegation as involving the necessity of proving an evil motive on the part of the defendant, but merely

Chapter XXV

the sense of ill-will or spite is not essential. All that is necessary is that the interference should be shown to have been without legal justification.

Legal justification.

Upon the question as to what constitutes legal justification, a good illustration was put in the leading case. If a party enters into a contract to go for another upon a journey to a remote and unhealthful climate, and a third person, with a *bona fide* purpose of benefiting the one who is under contract to go, dissuades him from the step, no action will lie.[3] But if the advice is not disinterested and the persuasion is used for "the indirect purpose of benefiting the defendant at the expense of the plaintiff," the intermeddler is liable if his advice is taken and the contract broken.[4]

An instructive decision upon this point is found in the late case of *South Wales Miners Federation v. Glamorgan Coal Co.*[5] It there appeared that certain miners employed in the plaintiff's collieries, acting under the order of the executive council of the defendant federation, violated their contract with the plaintiff by abstaining from work on certain days. The federation and council acted without any actual malice or ill-will towards the plaintiff, and the only object of the order in question was that the price of coal might thereby be kept up, a factor which affected the miners' wage scale. It was held that no sufficient justification was shown and that the federation was liable.

'Equal or superior right' necessary to justification.

In *Read v. Friendly Soc., etc.*,[6] it was held that the justification which will be sufficient to exonerate a person from liability for his interference with the contractual rights of another must be an equal or superior right in himself; and it will not be sufficient for him to show that he acted *bona fide* or without malice, or in the best interests of himself or others, or on a wrong understanding of his own rights.

as implying that the defendant had wilfully and knowingly procured a breach of contract." Lord Herschell in Allen *v.* Flood, (1898) A. C. 121.

[3] Case put by Coleridge, J., in Lumley *v.* Gye, 2 El. & Bl. 247, 75 E. C. L. 247.

[4] See language of Brett in Bowen *v.* Hall, 6 Q. B. D. 338.

[5] (1905) A. C. 239, affirming (1903) 2 K. B. 545 (in C. A.). In the King's Bench Division the contrary conclusion had been reached. (1903) 1 K. B. 118.

[6] (1902) 2 K. B. 88.

Volume I

State of law in America.

In America the doctrine of *Lumley v. Gye* is generally accepted.[7] But in a few jurisdictions the view advocated by Coleridge, J., in his dissenting opinion has found favor.[8] The opinion is held in some quarters that the right of action for malicious interference with contract relations is limited to situations where the contract is for personal service.[9] But this is untenable.[1] The real difficulty is in accepting the doctrine that interference by a stranger with a contract existing between two other persons can be actionable under any conditions. When this point is conceded, the same reason is seen to apply to contracts in general as to contracts of employment.

Interference with contract by means unlawful *per se.*

It should be observed in conclusion, that no question can arise as to the liability of one who puts an end to a contractual relation by a means which, under existing legal canons, can be denominated an unlawful means. Thus, if performance is prevented by force,[2] intimidation, coercion, or threats,[3] or by false[4] or defamatory[5] statements, or by nuisance or riot, the person using such unlawful means is, under all the authorities, liable for the damage which ensues. And in jurisdictions where the doctrine of *Lumley v. Gye* is rejected, no liability can arise from a meddlesome and malicious interference with a contract relation unless some such unlawful means as those just indicated are used.[6]

[7] Nashville, etc., R. Co. *v.* McConnell, 82 Fed. Rep. 65; Chipley *v.* Atkinson, 23 Fla. 206; Jones *v.* Blocker, 43 Ga. 331; Salter *v.* Howard, 43 Ga. 601; Walker *v.* Cronin, 107 Mass. 555; Bixby *v.* Dunlap, 56 N. H. 456; Haskins *v.* Royster, 70 N. Car. 601; Huff *v.* Watkins, 15 S. Car. 82.

[8] Boyson *v.* Thorn, 98 Cal. 578; Chambers *v.* Baldwin, 91 Ky. 121; Bourlier *v.* Macauley, 91 Ky. 135.

[9] Glencoe Land, etc., Co. *v.* Hudson Bros. Commission Co., 138 Mo. 439. See also Boyson *v.* Thorn, 98 Cal. 578.

[1] Rice *v.* Manley, 66 N. Y. 82; Jones *v.* Stanly, 76 N. Car. 355.

[2] Tarleton *v.* M'Gawley, Peake N. P. (ed. 1795) 207 (violence).

[3] Garret *v.* Taylor, Cro. Jac. 567 (menaces); Perkins *v.* Pendleton, 90 Me. 166 (threats).

[4] Rice *v.* Manley, 66 N. Y. 82 (false statement).

[5] Moran *v.* Dunphy, 177 Mass. 485 (defamatory statement).

[6] See Boyson *v.* Thorn, 98 Cal. 578; Chambers *v.* Baldwin, 91 Ky. 121; Bourlier *v.* Macauley, 91 Ky. 135.

CHAPTER XXVI

INTERFERENCE WITH TRADE OR CALLING.

Allen v. Flood.

Chapter XXVI

WE now come to consider the conditions under which liability results from an interference by a stranger with relations which are wholly unconnected either with status or contract; and our purpose is to discover whether a generalization can be framed which will define the limits of a new tort. The expression 'interference with trade or calling' points out the field in which it has for many years been thought possible that a new and independent wrong might sooner or later gain recognition.

Leading case.

A discussion of *Allen v. Flood* [1] seems to supply the best approach to the subject before us, and perhaps about all that we need to say can be brought out in connection with this great and illuminative case. The plaintiffs in this suit were shipwrights, and, at the time of the occurrence on which the action was based, were employed by the Glengall Iron Company in repairing the woodwork of a certain ship. They were employed for the job, but were liable to be discharged at any time. Some ironworkers who were employed on the ironwork of the ship objected to the plaintiffs being employed, on the ground that the plaintiffs had previously worked at ironwork on a ship for another firm, the practice of shipwrights working on iron being resisted by the trade union of which the ironworkers were members. The defendant, who was a delegate of the union, was sent for by the ironworkers and informed that they intended to leave off working. The defendant informed the employers that unless the plaintiffs were discharged all the ironworkers would be called out, or

[1] (1898) A. C. 1.

Volume I

knock off work (it was doubtful which expression was used); that the employers had no option; that the iron-men were doing their best to put an end to the practice of shipwrights doing ironwork, and that wherever the plaintiffs were employed the iron-men would cease work. There was evidence that this was done to punish the plaintiffs for what they had done in the past. The employers, the Glengall Company, in fear of this threat being carried out, which (as they knew) would have stopped their business, discharged the plaintiffs and refused to employ them again. In the ordinary course the plaintiffs' employment would have continued. The plaintiffs having brought an action against the defendant, the jury found that he had maliciously induced the employers to discharge the plaintiffs and not to engage them, and gave the plaintiffs a verdict for damages. Judgment was entered in accordance with the verdict and the case was affirmed in the Court of Appeal.[2] From this decision an appeal was taken to the House of Lords. The case being considered of much importance, the lords called upon a number of the puisne judges to hear the final argument and to give their opinions upon a question propounded by the lords to them. Of the eight judges thus summoned, six gave their opinion in favor of affirmance, while two favored a reversal.[3] The case was then decided by the lords, six being in favor of a reversal and three in favor of affirmance.[4] A judgment of reversal was thereupon entered in accordance with the opinion of the majority of the lords, a result which, as will be observed, was in accordance with the views of only eight of the twenty-one judges who had a part in the determination of the case at one stage or another. This radical disagreement of so many learned men on a fundamental principle of liability will ad-

Maliciously procuring employer to discharge workman.

House of Lords denies plaintiffs' right of action.

[2] Allen *v.* Flood (1895), 2 Q. B. 21. Kennedy, J., was the trial judge. The judges in the Court of Appeal were Lord Esher, M. R., Lopes, L. J., and Rigby, L. J.

[3] Those favoring affirmance were Hawkins, Cave, North, Wills, Lawrence, Grantham, JJ.

[4] Of the lords, Lords Watson, Herschell, Macnaghten, Shand, and Davey, and James of Hereford, favored a reversal; while the Lord Chancellor Halsbury and Lords Ashbourne and Morris favored an affirmance.

Chapter XXVI

monish the reader that the question now to be dealt with is one of difficulty and uncertainty. Happily the great intellectual efforts which the judges put forth in the decision of this case were well expended.

No breach of contract on part of the employer.

The reader will note that the Glengall Iron Company, in discharging the plaintiffs at the instigation of the defendant, did not violate any legal obligation. There was no contract by which the company was bound to keep the plaintiffs in their service till the repairs of the vessel were completed. But on the other hand, there was no reasonable doubt that but for what was done by the defendant they would have been kept at work until the termination of the repairs. The absence of a breach of contractual obligation discriminates the case from *Lumley v. Gye* and kindred cases. Again, it will be observed that though the jury found that the defendant acted maliciously, he did not in fact have a personal spite against the plaintiffs.[5] Such malice as there was consisted merely of an intention to accomplish an end which foreseeably and of necessity would result in the damage which actually ensued. But of course this was enough to support a finding of malice in most situations where malice is legally material.

Conflicting inferences of fact.

We should also, at the beginning of this discussion, direct attention to a conflict in the inferences of fact which the different judges drew from the evidence and findings. Where the dissentient judges saw unlawful threats, coercion, and intimidation in the conduct of the defendant, the prevailing judges saw nothing more than a lawful combination, intimation, or warning. Said Hawkins, J.: "Menacing action or language, the influence of which no man of ordinary firmness or strength of mind can reasonably be expected to resist, if used or employed with the intent to destroy the freedom of will in another and to compel him through fear of such menaces to do that which it is not his will to do, and which, being done, is calculated to cause injury to him or some other person, amounts to an attempt to intimidate and coerce; and if such attempt is successful, the object attained under such

(1) Intimidation and coercion;

[5] Lord Herschell at p. 131. [6] (1898) A. C. 74, 75.

Volume I

influence is attained by coercion, and the person wrongfully injured by it, whether in his person, property, or rights, may sue the coercer for reparation in damages." So Halsbury, L. C., one of the dissentient lords, adopts the terms intimidation, obstruction, and molestation as descriptive of the conduct of the defendant,[6] and he adds: "To my mind he was guilty of intimidation, and coercion through that intimidation." [7]

But the prevailing judges did not take this view of the defendant's conduct. To their mind the defendant's roar was as gentle as any sucking dove's. All that the defendant Allen did, say these judges, was to inform the employers of the plaintiffs that most of the workmen would leave them if they (the employers) should not discharge the plaintiffs.[8]

(2) Representation; warning.

Lord Herschell observed: "Even then if it can be said without abuse of language that the employers were intimidated and coerced by the [defendant], even if this be in a certain sense true, it by no means follows that he committed a wrong or is under any legal liability for his act. Everything depends on the nature of the representation or statement by which the pressure was exercised. The law cannot regard the act differently because you choose to call it a threat or coercion instead of an intimidation or warning." [9]

In a later case, the House of Lords being called upon to discover the rationale of the decision of *Allen v. Flood,* and

[7] (1898) A. C. 80.

[8] Statement by Lord Lindley in Quinn *v.* Leathem (1901), A. C. 532, citing Allen *v.* Flood, (1898) A. C. 115 (Lord Herschell); *ib.*, 148 (Lord Macnaghten); *ib.*, 161, 165 (Lord Shand); *ib.*, 175 (Lord Davey); *ib.*, 178 (Lord Davey). Said Lord Watson: "That the boiler makers . . . did seriously resent the presence among them of the respondents very plainly appears from the evidence of the respondents themselves; and that they would certainly have left the dock had the respondents continued to be employed appears to me to be an undoubted fact in the case. . . . It was clearly for the benefit of the employers that they should know what would be the result of their retaining in their service men to whom the majority of their workmen objected; and the giving of such information did not, in my opinion, amount to coercion of the employers, who were in no proper sense coerced, but merely followed the course which they thought would be most conducive to their own interests." (1898) A. C. 99.

[9] Allen *v.* Flood, (1898) A. C. 129.

to apply its doctrine to a very similar state of facts, it was said by Lord Chancellor Halsbury: "The hypothesis of fact upon which *Allen v. Flood* was decided by a majority in this House was that the defendant there neither uttered nor carried into effect any threat at all: he simply warned the plaintiffs' employers of what the men themselves, without his persuasion or influence, had determined to do, and it was certainly proved that no resolution of the trade union had been arrived at at all, and that the trade-union official had no authority himself to call out the men." [1]

Case decided upon theory that there was no actual coercion.

The difference in the inferences of fact drawn by the several judges furnishes the true clue to the solution of the decision. To the mind of the writer the inference drawn by the dissentient judges seems to be the just one to draw; and that is evidently the view taken by the jury. The question is, however, one of fact about which one who has not read the proof is hardly entitled to express an opinion. As said by Lord Lindley in *Quinn v. Leathem:* [2] "It is all very well to talk about peaceable persuasion. It may be that in *Allen v. Flood* there was nothing more. . . . What may begin as peaceable persuasion may easily become, and in trades-union disputes generally does become, peremptory ordering, with threats open or covert of very unpleasant consequences to those who are not persuaded. Calling workmen out involves very serious consequences to such of them as do not obey. Black lists are real instruments of coercion, as every man whose name is on one soon discovers to his cost. . . . A threat to call men out, given by a trade-union official to an employer of men belonging to the union and willing to work with him, is a form of coercion, intimidation, molestation, or annoyance to them and to him, very difficult to resist, and, to say the least, requiring justification."

This view apparently untenable.

The difference between the prevailing and dissentient judges on the inference of fact in *Allen v. Flood* is implicated with a corresponding divergence of opinion upon a question of law; and perhaps, after all, it will be found that the different

Conflicting views of legal principle applicable to the facts.

[1] Quinn *v.* Leathem, (1901) A. C. 506.

[2] (1901) A. C. 538.

Volume I

(1) Means used unlawful.

(2) Means used lawful.

verbiage which they used to state their respective inferences of fact was merely a result of their divergence of opinions as to the law applicable to the facts proved. This difference of opinion as to the law may be broadly indicated by saying that to the minds of the dissentient judges the communication, threat, coercion, or whatever it was, was an unlawful means for Allen to use in order to bring about the plaintiffs' discharge. To the minds of the prevailing judges, whatever Allen said or did was done in the exercise of a lawful right. In other words, he did not use an unlawful means to compass his purpose, and hence whatever he said or did was legitimate. The ultimate conclusion in the case is thus seen to be a mixed conclusion of law and of fact. It was of course taken for granted by all, that if the defendant had used a means that could be denominated unlawful in order to bring about the plaintiffs' discharge, he would be liable.

What are unlawful means of interference?

This makes it proper for us here to consider the question, what specific means or modes of interference with a man in his trade or calling can be said to be unlawful? The most obviously unlawful of all means is, of course, that of violence. Thus, if one with force of arms and display of violence prevents people of the vicinage from attending the plaintiff's fair, whereby he loses his tolls and trade, an action of trespass *vi et armis* can be maintained for the disturbance.[3]

(1) Violence.

Tarleton v. M'Gawley (1794)[4] supplies a fairly good illustration of the rule that a violent interference with trade relations gives a cause of action. It there appeared that the plaintiffs were the owners of a boat which was engaged in trading with natives on the coast of Africa. A canoe with some natives aboard came out for the purpose of establishing trade relations. A rival trader, desiring to frighten the natives from dealing with the plaintiffs, fired a cannon at the canoe, killing one of the occupants. The natives were thereby deterred from trading with the plaintiffs' vessel, whereby loss was occasioned. The plaintiffs recovered.

In *Garret v. Taylor* (1619),[5] menaces and threats were

[3] Y. B. 29 Edw. III. 18 B (Trespass).

[4] Peake N. P. 205.

[5] Cro. Jac. 567.

(2) Menaces and threats of bodily harm.

used by the defendant to deter workmen from entering the employment of a mine owner, and to deter purchasers from buying his output. There was no actual display of violence in this case, but there were threats to do bodily harm (mayhem). It was held that an action would lie.

(3) Riot and conspiracy.

It will be observed that the right of action for violent interference is not limited to relations of trade and employment, but extends to all disturbance of a man in his lawful relations with other persons, whether he be a trader or employer or not. In *Gregory v. Brunswick* (1843)[6] it was held that the plaintiff, an actor, who was interfered with in the performance of his part by the riotous conduct of a number of spectators who had conspired to hiss him down, could maintain an action for the disturbance.

(4) Other types of illegal means.

The means of interference and disturbance which are everywhere recognized as being clearly unlawful are fraud, defamation, false representation, violence, and threats of violence. Admitting that the means just enumerated are unlawful, the rationalizing faculty of the mind almost irresistibly carries us to the recognition of the further principle that any form of intimidation or coercion, moral as well as physical, is unlawful if it actually results in the substitution of the will of the actor for that of the person imposed upon, so that the latter is forced to do an act which is really contrary to his will.[7] Such was the conclusion drawn by the dissentient judges in *Allen v. Flood,* and the prevailing judges were only able to escape from this principle by holding that, as a matter of fact, there was no substitution of will, but only a submission of facts to the employer whereby he was influenced to come to his own independent conclusion.

Is moral intimidation and coercion an unlawful means?

No doubt practical difficulties must arise in attempting to

[6] 6 M. & G. 205, 46 E. C. L. 205.

[7] "I do not doubt," says Fry, L. J., in the Mogul case, "that it is unlawful and actionable for one man to interfere with another's trade . . . by molesting his customers, or those who would be his customers, whether by physical obstruction or moral intimidation." Mogul Steamship Co. *v.* McGregor, 23 Q. B. D. 626.

So in Giblan *v.* National Amalgamated Labourers' Union (1903), 2 K. B. 623, Stirling, L. J., says that in his opinion acts "in the nature of molestation and coercion," although they do not involve recourse to physical force, may be illegal.

Substitution of will.

apply the doctrine that all coercion which results in an actual substitution of will is unlawful. What state of facts would justify the inference that in a particular case of moral coercion the will of the person imposed upon has been so far superseded that the other becomes responsible, and alone responsible, for the act which he procures to be done? Is it not manifest that nothing short of legal duress will suffice? That the coercion must be of such nature as to supersede the will of the person who is induced to act, so that the act becomes exclusively the act of the mover, is apparent from another line of reasoning: In the case supposed, the employer's act in discharging his employee is a lawful act. The employee has no grievance against him. Whatever right of action he has is against the person who instigates the employer to discharge him, and this right of action can exist only in so far as the discharge is attributable exclusively to the mover. As long as any real freedom of choice is left to the employer, the act of discharging the employee is his act.

One of the most vital criticisms of the view of the dissentient judges is that it apparently leads to this anomaly, that a man is held liable for procuring an act to be done which gives no right of action against the doer of it. The only way to meet this criticism is by saying that the act in question is the act of the mover and not the act of the agent. To this end it is essential that the will of the agent should be entirely superseded by that of the party who is guilty of coercing him. Still, however great the theoretical difficulties of applying this doctrine of moral coercion may be, it involves, after all, only an inference of fact, and practically, judges and juries may be safely trusted to reach a just conclusion on the facts of each case.

Difficulty involved in recognizing coercion as an unlawful means.

However, accepting the inference of fact drawn by the majority of the judges in *Allen v. Flood* as the true one, and provisionally accepting also their conclusion that the means (intimations, persuasions, threats) used by the defendant were not such as could be classed as unlawful *per se*, we proceed to inquire whether there is any theory under which the plaintiffs were entitled to recover in this view. Now there are two, and only two, theories under which a recovery could be allowed upon the foregoing assumptions. These we shall separately consider.

I.— The plaintiff may recover if it be granted that the doing of any malicious act is sufficient to create an independent cause of action when such malicious act is followed by damage. On this proposition all of the judges substantially agreed that the action could not be maintained. Nor was this new law. More than fifty years ago Parke, B., afterwards Lord Wensleydale, in giving the judgment of an exceptionally strong court, said: "An act which does not amount to a legal injury cannot be actionable because it is done with a bad intent."[8] In that case the question was whether a count was good which averred that the defendant had maliciously distrained for more rent than was due. It was held that the averment of malice did not help the declaration. In *Bradford v. Pickles*,[9] the House of Lords itself had recently held that acts done by the defendant on his own land were not actionable when they were admittedly within his legal rights, even though his motive were to prejudice his neighbor. The Lord Chancellor said: "If it was a lawful act, however ill the motive might be, he had a right to do it. If it was an unlawful act, however good his motive might be, he would have no right to do it." This statement was confined to cases, like that then before the court, where the act complained of is done in the exercise of rights incident to the ownership of real property; but, as was pointed out by Lord Herschell in *Allen v. Flood*,[1] the principle is equally applicable to the exercise by an individual of any recognized legal right. It is thus seen that in declaring that malice will not convert a lawful act into an unlawful act the House of Lords was abundantly justified by authority.

Malice will not convert lawful act into an unlawful act.

Some surprise may naturally be felt that this should be so. Malice as a mental qualification of an act is far more

[8] Stevenson *v.* Newnham (1853), 13 C. B. 297, 76 E. C. L. 297.

[9] (1895) A. C. 587. See to the same effect, Phelps *v.* Nowlen, 72 N. Y. 39; Mogul Steamship Co. *v.* McGregor, (1892) A. C. 25.

[1] (1898) A. C. 124.

Volume I

Reason suggested.

obnoxious in point of morals than is negligence, and it is equally as obnoxious as fraud. Yet, as we elsewhere learn, both negligence and fraud, when coupled with particular forms of damage, are sufficient to support liability. Why should not the same be true of malice? The explanation is perhaps to be found in the nature of the damage with which these three factors, negligence, fraud, and malice, are severally associated. Negligence is almost exclusively associated with damage to person or property. Here the damage is sensible, tangible, and, in theory at least, measurable by human standards. Fraud is exclusively, or almost exclusively, associated with pecuniary loss. Here also the damage, if not so tangible as in case of damage to person or property, is yet measurable with some degree of certainty by human standards. In these cases a jury may safely be trusted to arrive at something like a satisfactory basis for assessing the damage. Malice, on the other hand, is exclusively, or almost exclusively, associated with a class of wrongs in which the injury is done in respect of intangible rights appurtenant to person or property. The damage, therefore, in the case of malicious torts, is of a different kind and is, in theory at least, much more difficult to measure and assess than in torts of negligence and fraud. Some such idea as this was evidently in the mind of Lord Herschell when he said: "I can imagine no greater danger to the community than that a jury should be at liberty to impose the penalty of paying damages for acts which are otherwise lawful, because they choose, without any legal definition of the term, to say that they are malicious. No one would know what his rights were. The result would be to put all our actions at the mercy of a particular tribunal whose view of their propriety might differ from our own."[2]

Is interference with calling tortious *per se?*

II.— We now turn to the second and main ground upon which it was insisted that a judgment for the plaintiffs in *Allen v. Flood* might be rested. Interference with calling or livelihood, it was argued, is tortious *per se* and actionable where damage results from the interference. In this view interfer-

[2] Allen *v.* Flood, (1898) A. C. 118.

ence with calling is in like case with the wrong of interference with contract relations. But upon this point a number of the prevailing judges appear to have concurred in denying the existence of the general action for interference with trade or calling. The clearest opinion on this point is that of Lord Herschell. It cannot be denied that previous authorities fall somewhat short of giving recognition to this tort.

Keeble v. Hickeringill (1706)[3] was relied on by the plaintiff's counsel as authority for the broad proposition that every man has a right to pursue his trade or calling without molestation or obstruction, and that any one who by any act, though it be not otherwise unlawful, molests or obstructs him is guilty of a wrong unless he can show a lawful justification or excuse for so doing. That case was an action by the owner of a decoy pond against one who had driven away his wild fowl by firing guns with intent to damnify the plaintiff. It appears that the plaintiff possibly used the decoy as a means of obtaining a livelihood, and Lord Holt, in deciding for the plaintiff, observed that "this employment of his ground to that use is profitable to the plaintiff, as is the skill and management of that employment." But, as was pointed out by the majority lords, it is not conceivable that the right of action depended upon the circumstance that the plaintiff traded in the ducks which he obtained by his decoy. The case is sustainable on the theory that the defendant was guilty of a wilful disturbance of the plaintiff in the enjoyment of his own land, and hence he was liable on the ground of nuisance.[4]

Driving wild fowl from decoy.

Decision based on idea of nuisance.

But there are certain dicta of Lord Holt in the case referred to which certainly appear on their surface to lend countenance to the view that any malicious act done to a man in respect of his occupation, profession, or livelihood will, if damage ensues, give rise to a cause of action. He gives the following illustrations: If H should lie in the way with guns and fright boys from going to school, and their parents would not let them go thither, sure that schoolmaster would

Interference with occupation or livelihood.

[3] 11 East 574 note, Holt K. B. 14, 17, 19, 11 Mod. 74, 130, 3 Salk. 9.

[4] Lord Davey in Allen *v.* Flood, (1898) A. C. 174; Lord Herschell, *ib.*, 133.

Illustrations.

have an action for the loss of his scholars. A man hath a market to which he hath toll of horses sold; a man is bringing his horse to market to sell; a stranger hinders and obstructs him from going to the market; an action lies, because it imports damage. Again, an action on the case lies against one that by threats frightens away his tenants at will.[5] Lord Herschell correctly observes, upon these illustrations given by Lord Holt, that the acts of interference are unlawful *per se.*[6]

In the two hundred years that have elapsed since the decision in *Keeble v. Hickeringill* was made, it cannot be said that the case has gained recognition as establishing any general doctrine of law,[7] and it certainly is not adequate of itself to bear the weight of the broad proposition that it is unlawful to interfere with a man in his calling.

Now if all of the majority judges in *Allen v. Flood* had agreed upon this point, it would have followed as a matter of course that the plaintiffs could not recover in this aspect of the case, and further discussion would have been unnecessary. But some of the majority judges adopted a secondary line of reasoning which makes the point just stated unnecessary to the decision of that case, and hence it cannot be said that such point was conclusively adjudicated. In fact, in the later case of *Quinn v. Leathem* [8] we find a decision which strongly tends to show, even if it does not establish, the principle that the general cause of action referred to does in fact exist. The American authorities, it may be added, confirm this view.

Was the defendant's conduct privileged in law?

The major premise in this secondary line of reasoning does not seem to have been explicitly stated by any of the judges in *Allen v. Flood,* but the argument is this: Even

[5] Keeble *v.* Hickeringill, 11 East 574 note.

[6] Lord Herschell in Allen *v.* Flood, (1898) A. C. 135.

[7] Keeble *v.* Hickeringill was somewhat blindly followed in Carrington *v.* Taylor, 11 East 571. Everybody agrees that this case, so far as appears from the report, was wrongly decided; though it may be of value as showing that the judges of the King's Bench in 1809 did not regard the judgment in Keeble *v.* Hickeringill as being founded on interference with trade or dependent on the presence of malice. See Lord Herschell in Allen *v.* Flood, (1898) A. C. 135, 136.

[8] (1901) A. C. 495.

Chapter XXVI

conceding that there is a general right of action for malicious interference with a man in his calling or livelihood, the action in *Allen v. Flood* must fail because the defendant's conduct was privileged in law.

This makes it necessary to consider the nature of the conduct of the defendant in order to ascertain why the exceptional favor of legal privilege should be ascribed to it. On this point it is said that in what he did the defendant Allen was acting to promote his interests and that of the workmen whom he represented, as competitors of the plaintiffs in the labor market. This view was well expressed by Lord Shand in *Quinn v. Leathem*: "The ground of judgment of the majority of the House, however varied in expression by their lordships, was, as it appears to me, that Allen in what he said and did was only exercising the right of himself and his fellow workmen as competitors in the labor market, and the effect of injury thus caused to others from such competition, which was legitimate, was not a legal wrong."

Privilege incident to competition in labor market.

It is undoubtedly true that competition in trade and labor (unconnected with fraud) is a matter of very high, perhaps of absolute, legal privilege. On this the authorities, both ancient and modern, are explicit, as will appear from two important and well-known cases decided respectively in 1411 and 1892. In the *Gloucester Grammar School Case*[1] two masters of a grammar school brought an action of trespass on the case against another master who had set up a rival school in the same neighborhood and thereby deprived the plaintiffs of patronage and forced them to reduce their fees. It was held that the action would not lie. In *Mogul Steamship Co. v. McGregor*,[2] the plaintiffs and the various defendants were shipowners engaged in the tea-carrying trade between China and England. The plaintiffs alleged that the defendants had injured them by entering into a conspiracy to prevent the vessels of the plaintiffs from being employed by shippers in Chinese ports to carry their cargoes of tea to London. The conspiracy was alleged to have been put into effect by bribes,

Competition in business subject of high privilege.

Rival schoolmasters.

[1] Y. B. 11 Hen. IV. 47, pl. 21.

[2] (1892) A. C. 25, affirming 23 Q. B. D. 598, and 21 Q. B. D. 544.

Volume I

coercion, and threats. It was proved, among other instances of this, that the defendants had offered a special discount to those exporters who employed them alone; and also had organized a plan for sending steamers of their own to meet any vessels sent to Hankow by the plaintiffs and to underbid them, even by accepting rates of freight so low as to be actually unremunerative; and, further, had forbidden their agents, on pain of dismissal, to act as agents for the plaintiffs. It was held that no action could be maintained. "If there were two shopkeepers in a village and one sold an article at cost price, not for profit therefor, but to attract customers or cause his rival to leave off selling the article only, it could not be said he was liable to an action." [3] Bowen, L. J., observed in the Court of Appeal that shipowners and merchants are not bound by law to conform to any imaginary 'normal' standard of freights or prices, and that the law courts do not undertake to say to them in respect to their competitive tariffs, "Thus far shalt thou go and no further." [4]

Rivalry in shipping trade.

In this case there were allegations that the acts complained of were maliciously done, and some evidence was adduced which might be supposed to mean that the defendants were actuated by a desire to inflict malicious injury upon the plaintiffs; but upon analysis it appeared that there was no intention to injure except in the sense that as trade was appropriated by the defendants it would at the same time necessarily be withdrawn from the plaintiff.[5] Lord Hannen observed that a different case would have arisen if the evidence had shown that the object of the defendants was a malicious one namely, to injure the plaintiffs, whether they should be benefited or not.[6]

Malice.

Now in *Allen v. Flood* it was accepted by the majority of the lords as conclusively proved that the defendant was not actuated by any personal feeling of malice towards the plaintiffs, but was exclusively bent on furthering the interests of

[3] Lord Bramwell in (1892) A. C. 48, 49.

[4] Mogul Steamship Co. *v.* McGregor, 23 Q. B. D. 615.

[5] Lord Halsbury, Mogul Steamship Co. *v.* McGregor, (1892) A. C 36.

[6] Mogul Steamship Co. *v.* McGregor, (1892) A. C. 59.

himself and those whom he represented as competitors in the labor market.[7] In this view the defendant's conduct was privileged and furnished no cause of action even though it be conceded that interference with trade or calling is *prima facie* a legal wrong.

Is labor competition as highly privileged as business competition?

The assumption that privilege of competition is as extensive and universal in labor controversies as it is in matters of trade and commerce is one that should have been subjected to closer scrutiny than it appears to have received. The American courts have not acted upon this assumption, and to this circumstance apparently is to be attributed whatever conflict exists between American and English decisions on the subject of interference with employment.

Quinn v. Leathem.

The import of *Allen v. Flood* cannot be understood without reference to the later case of *Quinn v. Leathem,*[8] in which the House of Lords had occasion to weigh the previous decision and consider its effect. This case presented a situation where the injuries complained of consisted of interferences in the trade of a butcher. The several defendants and others, members of a labor union, had confederated together to break up the plaintiff's business because he insisted on employing nonunion labor. To this end they refused to allow their union workmen to remain in his employment or in the employment of others who dealt with him. They also published the plaintiff's name in a "blacklist" circulated in the community. Furthermore, they induced persons, not members of their union, to quit the plaintiff's employment. The result was that the plaintiff was greatly harassed in his business and damaged in his trade. The House unanimously held that an action for damages could be maintained. It is of great mo-

Interference with trade.

[7] Lord Shand in Allen *v.* Flood, (1898) A. C. 163.

But the same learned judge, it should be added, observed that even if actual malice towards the plaintiff had existed in the mind of the defendant this would not have created liability. *Ib.*, 167. To his mind evidently actual competition, unaccompanied by fraud or other unlawful means, is absolutely privileged.

[8] (1901) A. C. 495.

Volume I

ment to discover the exact factor which differentiates this case from that of *Allen v. Flood.*

At the outset we are met by the striking fact that for some reason or other all of the judges in this case were able to see the facts in the same light that the dissentient judges had seen the facts in *Allen v. Flood.* All now saw coercion where before the prevailing judges had been able to see no more than arguments of self-interest addressed to the reason of the person who was induced to act.

Coercion.

Combination.

Another factor that distinguishes *Quinn v. Leathem* is the presence of conspiracy and oppressive combination. On the surface it indeed seems that this is the decisive element, and the decision seems almost to be authority for the proposition that the co-operation of several persons in interfering with the trade or calling of another is sufficient to give rise to a right of action, where exactly the same harm done by a single person would not give such a right. Such a conclusion would indeed be surprising, for the opinion is widely prevalent that an act which is lawful when done by one will not become unlawful by reason of the fact that many are concerned in it.[1] The prevailing opinion on this point is indicated in the following language from an American court: "What one man may lawfully do singly, two or more may lawfully agree to do jointly. The number who unite to do the act cannot change its character from lawful to unlawful. The gist of a private action for the wrongful act of many is not the combination or conspiracy, but the damage done or threatened to the plaintiff by the acts of the defendants. If the act be unlawful, the combination of many to commit it may aggravate the injury, but cannot change the character of the act"[2]

Co-operation of many will not make lawful act unlawful.

Nor, when rightly considered, does the decision of *Quinn v. Leathem* lend countenance to a contrary view. It is apparent that in this case the element of combination and conspiracy was treated chiefly as of evidentiary value. In this aspect it did undoubtedly turn the scale and was the decisive

[1] Huttley *v.* Simmons (1898), 1 Q. B. 181; Kearney *v.* Lloyd, 26 L. R. Ir. 268.

[2] Bohn Mfg. Co. *v.* Hollis, 54 Minn. 234.

Chapter XXVI

factor which enabled the judges to see coercion where they otherwise probably would not have found it. The true function of this factor of combination and conspiracy in *Quinn v. Leathem* seems to have been correctly set forth by Lord Lindley in the following words: "It was contended at the bar that if what was done in this case had been done by one person only, his conduct would not have been actionable, and that the fact that what was done was effected by many acting in concert makes no difference. My lords, one man without others behind him who would obey his orders could not have done what these defendants did. One man exercising the same control over others as these defendants had could have acted as they did, and, if he had done so, I conceive that he would have committed a wrong towards the plaintiff for which the plaintiff could have maintained an action."[3] Said Lord Hannen in *Mogul Steamship Co. v. McGregor:* "There are some forms of injury which can only be effected by the combination of many."[4] Where such is the case conspiracy makes the injury possible, but it is not the ground of liability. The gist of the action is the legal harm that is done. Still, it cannot be denied that the language of some of the lords was plain enough to the effect that the factor of conspiracy of itself made the interference in *Quinn v. Leathem* unlawful; and in the end it may be found that in interference with trade and calling the element of combination and conspiracy serves an exceptional function.

Combination only makes greater injury possible.

A third conspicuous factor in *Quinn v. Leathem* is the fact that the lords found that the defendants were actuated by malice towards the plaintiff in the sense of spite and ill-will. Their purpose was to injure the plaintiff in his trade, as distinguished from the purpose legitimately to advance their own interests. In other words, the situation was not such as to entitle the defendants to that legal privilege which attaches to competition in trade and labor. In this connection some of the lords used language which bears out the theory that interference with one's trade or calling by coercion of his customers, employees, or employer is *prima facie* a legal wrong,

Malice present.

[3] Quinn *v.* Leathem, (1901) A. C. 537.

[4] (1892) A. C. 60.

even though no means which is in itself unlawful be used. In such case it is incumbent on the defendant to show a legal justification, as by bringing himself within the privilege which shields a competitor in trade and labor.[5] Wanting such justification he must be held liable. This is borne out by the interpretation placed on *Quinn v. Leathem* by the Court of Appeal in *Giblan v. National Amalgamated Labourers' Union.*[6]

General conclusion.

The result is that one can now say with certainty that there is in the field where we have been working a new and distinct form of wrong which may be indicated by the term 'interference with trade or calling.' This conclusion is inconsistent with the opinions of some of the prevailing lords in *Allen v. Flood,* but it is not inconsistent with the actual result in that case as it has been interpreted by the House of Lords itself. Furthermore, it is consistent with the views of some of the majority lords in that case, and is consistent with the views of all the dissentient judges. Many of the situations in which liability for interference exists are of course referable to heads of tort already familiar, but some are not referable thereto, and it is these situations which prove that a new category of legal wrong ought to be recognized.

[5] Lord Shand, (1901) A. C. 514; Lord Brampton (formerly Hawkins, J.), *ib.*, 524; Lord Lindley, *ib.*, 536, 538.

See the interpretation which Professor A. V. Dicey places upon the so-called Conspiracy Cases in 18 L. Quar. Rev. 1-6. Says this learned writer: "Interference, in short, with the liberty of one person, N, to deal at choice with another person, A, is *prima facie* an interference with the right of N, and actionable; and if such interference is intended to damage A, and does damage A, it is also an interference is intended to damage A, and does a right of action against X, who unlawfully interferes; and if this is so in the case of X acting alone, it is so, *a fortiori,* in the case of X and Y, when acting in concert, with the object of damaging A. The same point may be put in another shape. A has a right to carry on his own business, as long as he does not break the law, in the way he himself prefers. Hence it is the legal duty of X and Y not to use intimidation or coercion towards A or his customers, with a view to preventing A from carrying on his business in the way he chooses." This, says he, seems to be the central position finally established by the House of Lords in Quinn *v.* Leathem (citing especially judgment of Lord Lindley, *ante*).

[6] (1903) 2 K. B. 600. In this case the plaintiff Giblan had incurred the ill-will of the defendants by reason of his refusal to pay a certain debt due to a union of which he had been a member but from which he was expelled. The defendants, two officers of the

Chapter XXVI

American Doctrine.

The foregoing discussion of *Allen v. Flood* and subsequent English cases bearing on the question of interference with trade and calling renders unnecessary any elaborate review of decisions from other jurisdictions.[7] Reference to a few late American decisions will, however, be of value for corroborative purposes.

It is of course everywhere accepted that an interference with trade or calling is actionable if accomplished by unlawful means, as by force, fraud, defamation, or nuisance. *Sherry v. Perkins* (1888)[8] affords illustration of an interference accompanied by nuisance and made actionable by that fact. In this case it appeared that the defendants entered into a scheme to prevent persons entering the employment of the plaintiff, who was a manufacturer, and to this end displayed in front of his premises banners with inscriptions calculated to injure his business and to deter workmen. The inscriptions

Interference amounting to nuisance.

union, in order to force him to pay the debt in question began persecuting him by causing him to be discharged from one place of employment after another. This they were able to do by means of threats to the effect that if the plaintiff were not discharged other men in the service of such employer would be called out by the union. It was held that the plaintiff could recover. The elements of liability here present were: Combination, moral coercion of the employer, express malice, absence of privileged occasion, damage. Whether the court would have seen coercion in the absence of combination is a matter of dictum and speculation. But at any rate the presence of this factor brought the case clearly within the principle of Quinn *v.* Leathem. Said Romer, L. J.: "But I should be sorry to leave this case without observing that, in my opinion, it was not essential, in order for the plaintiff to succeed, that he should establish a combination of two or more persons to do the acts complained of. In my judgment, if a person who, by virtue of his position or influence, has power to carry out his design, sets himself to the task of preventing, and succeeds in preventing, a man from obtaining or holding employment in his calling, to his injury, by reason of threats to or special influence upon the man's employers, or would-be employers, and the design was to carry out some spite against the man, or had for its object the compelling him to pay a debt, or any similar object not justifying the acts against the man, then that person is liable to the man for the damage consequently suffered."

[7] For a Canadian case see, in its various stages, Perrault *v.* Gauthier, 28 Can. Sup. Ct. 241, 6 Quebec Q. B. 65, 10 Quebec Super. Ct. 224, 6 Quebec Super. Ct. 83.

[8] 147 Mass. 212.

upon the banners were not false, nor were they in disparagement of the plaintiff's business. It was held that an action would lie, and relief by injunction against the nuisance was granted.

Picketing.

'Picketing,' which consists of the detailing of men by a labor union to watch a place of business and to speak to the workmen as they come and go, in order to induce them to quit work, is unlawful if it becomes so annoying as to amount to a nuisance.[9]

Malice not an independent ground of action.

The courts of this country generally agree that a malicious motive will not make actionable an act which is otherwise lawful.[1] On this point American authority is in harmony with the main conclusion reached in *Allen v. Flood.*

Combination.

The element of combination or conspiracy is prominent in many of the American decisions on the subject of interference with trade and calling,[2] but so far as the writer can see, this factor is treated in about the same way as in the English decisions; that is to say, an act which is lawful in itself cannot be declared unlawful because it is done by more than one,[3] but inasmuch as the combination of many persons makes possible a much greater degree of harm than could be accomplished by one person acting alone, such factor when present is usually decisive. At any rate, here, as in England, inter-

[9] Vegelahn *v.* Guntner, 167 Mass. 92. See also Lyons *v.* Wilkins (1899), 1 Ch. 255.

[1] Heywood *v.* Tillson, 75 Me. 225; Hunt *v.* Simonds, 19 Mo. 583; Walker *v.* Cronin, 107 Mass. 555; Plant *v.* Woods, 176 Mass. 499; Bohn Mfg. Co. *v.* Hollis, 54 Minn. 223; Phelps *v.* Nowlen, 72 N. Y. 45; Payne *v.* Western, etc., R. Co., 13 Lea (Tenn.) 507; Raycroft *v.* Tayntor, 68 Vt. 219; West Virginia Transp. Co. *v.* Standard Oil Co., 50 W. Va. 611.

"Malicious motives make a bad act worse, but they cannot make that wrong which in its essence is lawful." Black, J., in Jenkins *v.* Fowler, 24 Pa. St. 308.

[2] See Toledo, etc., R. Co. *v.* Pennsylvania Co., 54 Fed. Rep. 730; Arthur *v.* Oakes, 63 Fed. Rep. 310, 24 U. S. App. 239; Hopkins *v.* Oxley Stave Co. (C. C. A.), 83 Fed. Rep. 912; Wabash R. Co. *v.* Hannahan, 121 Fed. Rep. 563; Standard Oil Co. *v.* Doyle (Ky. 1904), 82 S. W. Rep. 271.

[3] Baker *v.* Sun L. Ins. Co. (Ky. 1901), 64 S. W. Rep. 967; Baker *v.* Metropolitan L. Ins. Co. (Ky. 1901), 64 S. W. Rep. 913; Bohn Mfg. Co. *v.* Hollis, 54 Minn. 223; Brackett *v.* Griswold, 112 N. Y. 454; West Virginia Transp. Co. *v.* Standard Oil Co., 50 W. Va. 611. But see *contra,* Hawarden *v.* Youghiogheny, etc., Coal Co., 111 Wis. 545.

ferences brought about by conspiracy and characterized by actual coercion and intimidation are actionable.[4]

Moral coercion.

And moral coercion brought about by combination is enough, though unconnected with violence or threat of violence, or with any other means generally recognized as unlawful *per se*. This is well shown in the boycott cases. In *Casey v. Cincinnati Typographical Union No. 3* (1891),[5] the complainant, the proprietor of a newspaper, had refused to unionize his office. Thereupon the officers and members of the union instituted a boycott. To this end, by handbills and posters, they called upon the public to withdraw its patronage from complainant's newspaper. They also issued circulars addressed to advertisers requesting them to withdraw their advertisements, threatening, in case of refusal, that such advertisers would incur the ill-will of organized labor and lose its patronage. Similar methods were used to prevent newsdealers from handling the paper. An injunction was granted against the continuation of the boycott by these methods.[6]

Boycott.

In the instructive case of *Beck v. Railway Teamsters' Protective Union* (1898)[7] it was held that a boycott to be condemned by law does not have to be accompanied by violence or threats of violence. It is unlawful if the means used are threatening in their nature and are intended, and naturally tend, to overcome by fear of loss of property the will of others and compel them to do things which they would not otherwise do.

Discharge of employee at instigation of labor union.

Turning from cases of boycott in business to cases of interference with employment, we find the same principle applied. In *Perkins v. Pendleton* (1897)[8] suit was maintained by a workman against members of a labor union who by threats and persuasions had caused an employer to discharge him. There was no allegation that the threats were threats of violence.

[4] Standard Oil Co. *v.* Doyle (Ky. 1904), 82 S. W. Rep. 271; Vegelahn *v.* Guntner, 167 Mass. 92; Plant *v.* Woods, 176 Mass. 492. See State *v.* Stockford, 77 Conn. 227.

[5] 45 Fed. Rep. 135.

[6] To the same effect, see the elaborate opinion of Green, V. C., in Barr *v.* Essex Trades Council, 53 N. J. Eq. 101. See also Brace *v.* Evans, 3 Ry. & Corp. L. J. 561, 35 Pittsb. L. J. 399; and Murdock *v.* Walker, 152 Pa. St. 595.

[7] 118 Mich. 497.

[8] 90 Me. 167.

Volume I

The circumstance that the employer was coerced into discharging one whom he would otherwise have been glad to retain was taken to be the decisive factor.

A case which on its surface appears to conflict with this view, but which really does not, is found in *Raycroft v. Tayntor* (1896).[9] The defendant was in full management of a granite quarry as superintendent. As such he entered into a contract (terminable at will) with one Libersont to cut paving blocks at the quarry. In carrying out this contract Libersont employed the plaintiff as a laborer. For some reason the defendant became angry with the plaintiff, and in order to gratify his malice requested Libersont to discharge the plaintiff, threatening in event of noncompliance that he would terminate Libersont's contract for cutting stone. The latter thereupon discharged the plaintiff from his employment. It was held that no action lay against the defendant for procuring this discharge. The reason is found in the fact that the defendant, as general superintendent of the quarry, had a right to say who should or should not work upon the premises. Hence, in insisting on the plaintiff's discharge, he was clearly acting within his unqualified legal right. The fact that he was moved by a malicious motive was, as is now everywhere accepted, insufficient of itself to give a right of action. It was admitted that if the defendant had been a stranger and had not had an unquestioned legal right to interfere as he did, the action could have been maintained.

Exercise of legal right.

Payne v. Western, etc., R. Co. (1884)[1] also affords an instance of interference with business which was held not to be actionable because the act done was within the limits of undoubted legal right. The facts presented in this case were somewhat novel. It appeared that the plaintiff, a storekeeper, had, for some reason or other, incurred the ill-will of the defendant railroad company, and out of malice and spite, as the declaration averred, the company published a notice informing its numerous employees that such of them as thereafter should trade with the plaintiff would be discharged. As

Prohibiting employees from trading with plaintiff.

[9] 68 Vt. 219.

[1] 13 Lea (Tenn.) 507.

Chapter XXVI

a result the plaintiff lost the custom of the railroad employees and his business was ruined. It was held that an action could not be maintained. The terms of employment being subject to change, it was within the legitimate power of the company in adjusting its relations with its own employees to name a condition on which alone it would continue to employ them in the future. When the announcement was made that the employees must not trade with the plaintiff, this was merely in effect to add a new term to the contract, the employees of course being free to abide by it or to quit the service as they chose. The plaintiff's damage, then, in this case appears to be *damnum absque injuria,* inasmuch as it was merely consequential upon the exercise of a legal right. But the case evidently lies very near the border which separates the legitimate from that which is illegal.[2]

Discharge of non-union laborer at instance of union.

In *Lucke v. Clothing Cutters', etc., Assembly No. 7507* (1893),[3] it appeared that a certain employee, a nonunion man, was performing his duties to the entire satisfaction of his employer, who would gladly have retained him. A labor organization, however, demanded his discharge, threatening in case of refusal to notify other labor organizations in the city that the employer's business was a nonunion one, and thus subject him to loss of patronage. The employee having

[2] In Webb *v.* Drake, 52 La. Ann. 290, the Supreme Court of Louisiana thought that the balance of reason was on the other side and sustained an action under these circumstances: The plaintiff, the proprietor of a hotel, incurred the malice of a number of local merchants. They therefore determined to ruin his business and to this end gave it out that they would not purchase goods of any drummer who stopped at that hostelry. The plaintiff's business was dependent upon this element of transient trade and he had to close up. We do not see how this decision can be sustained. The defendants had a right to buy goods of any drummer whom they saw fit to patronize; or to purchase no goods at all. And they merely threatened to withdraw their own trade from men who lodged with the plaintiff. If they had threatened to visit upon those drummers a loss of trade outside of and greater than their own patronage, and the drummers had been forced to yield to such a threat the case would have been different. Evidently the line of demarcation between the exercise of legal right and that coercion of a party which gives a right of action to him is not definable with precision. The course of legal evolution, it may safely be predicted, will be towards the extension of liability.

[3] 77 Md. 396.

been thereupon discharged, it was held that an action would lie against the labor organization which caused the discharge.

An instructive case comes from the Supreme Court of Illinois. The plaintiff, Horn, was in the employ of one A as foreman of his factory. In operating a milling machine Horn was hurt under such circumstances that he had, or was supposed to have, a right of action against A. At the time A carried an indemnity policy in an accident insurance company covering such a claim, and the latter therefore had to defend the suit. The accident company undertook to adjust the claim, but the terms offered by it were refused by the plaintiff. Angered at this and hoping to enforce compliance with his terms, the agent of the insurance company, in an interview with A, demanded that the latter should forthwith discharge Horn from his employment. He accompanied the demand with a threat that in case of refusal by A to discharge Horn, he would then and there cancel the indemnity policy which A was then carrying against future risks. A thereupon complied with the demand and discharged Horn. In ordinary course the latter would have been retained indefinitely in A's employment. It appeared that by its terms the indemnity policy referred to could be canceled by the company at its election, but five days' notice of such intention was required to be given. The agent of the company was therefore not within legal right when he threatened to cancel the policy forthwith. It was accordingly held that the plaintiff could recover.[4]

Discharge procured by threat to violate contract.

Berry v. Donovan (1905),[5] lately decided by the Supreme Court of Massachusetts, presented these facts: A union of boot and shoe workers procured a contract from an employer by which he agreed in the future to employ only union workmen and by which he also agreed to discharge any employee after receiving notice that such employee was for any reason objectionable to the union. The union took advantage of this clause to force the discharge of an employee of several years' standing who was giving satisfaction and would have

Interference in conformity with terms of invalid contract.

[4] London Guarantee, etc., Co. *v.* Horn (1904), 206 Ill. 493.
[5] 188 Mass. 353.

been retained. It was held that the clause in question was unreasonable and unlawful, inasmuch as it purported to authorize the union to interfere and deprive any workman of his employment in an arbitrary exercise of power. The result was that an action for damages was sustained. "Whatever the contracting parties may do if no one but themselves is concerned, it is evident that as against the workman, a contract of this kind does not of itself justify interference."

The general conclusion to be drawn from American authority is that there is a class of cases involving interference with trade and calling in which liability cannot be said to depend upon the use of any of the means generally recognized as unlawful *per se* and in which liability cannot be properly referred to any of the recognized heads of delict like nuisance, fraud, and trespass. This proves the existence of a new and distinct species of wrong, and corroborates the conclusion which is being reached in the latest English cases.

As suggested above, the American courts have not pushed the idea of privilege as incident to competition in the labor market as far as some of the English judges have been inclined to press it. Thus, in the boycott cases and in cases like *Perkins v. Pendleton* (1897),[6] *Lucke v. Clothing Cutters, etc., Assembly No. 7507* (1893),[7] we find no countenance given to the idea that labor organizations, by reason of being engaged in a competitive warfare with the nonunion labor element, are to be treated as subject to exceptional immunity or privilege. Judge Holmes, while on the Supreme Bench of Massachusetts, vainly strove to engraft this idea upon American jurisprudence. In his view the special immunity which is incident to competition in business, as indicated in cases like *Mogul Steamship Co. v. McGregor,*[8] applies in an equal degree to the operations of labor organizations in their efforts to drive out nonunion workmen; and such immunity goes so far, in his opinion, as to protect them against liability for any sort of coercion, intimidation, and persecution that stops short of violence or threat of violence.[9] This is wholly

Labor organizations not specially privileged.

[6] 90 Me. 167.

[7] 77 Md. 396.

[8] (1892) A. C. 25.

[9] See dissenting opinions in Ve-

Volume I

at variance with American doctrine. Nor does English authority justify any such radical view.

General conclusion.

Gist of the tort.

Finally, it is to be impressed upon the reader that the gist of this right of action for interference with relations of trade or employment is the compulsion or coercion, by a stranger to that relation, of one of the parties whereby the relation is terminated or interfered with. The court must be led to see actual coercion in some form before the plaintiff has any standing in court. In what we have said no countenance has been given to the idea that mere persuasions or influence short of compulsion can give rise to liability.

Conspiracy.

Conspiracy not a substantive tort.

What was said above in regard to the element of conspiracy in interference with trade and occupation is, it may be added, true of the same factor in other departments of tort. Though conspiracy may be a crime, it is not a substantive tort.[1] Like malice, it is an element which may serve to aggravate a legal injury, but cannot alone support legal liability. The only other tort besides interference with trade and calling in which the factor of conspiracy has at any time been prominent is that of malicious prosecution. As we have already seen, the first recognition given by statute to the latter tort was in situations where it appeared that a conspiracy had been made to prosecute upon a groundless charge of felony. And the ancient writ of conspiracy was used as the remedy.[2] But the idea that conspiracy is at the basis of liability there has been outgrown for ages. It is still true in theory that the old writ of conspiracy will not lie unless more than one person is charged with the wrong complained of, but this remedy has long given way to the action on the case in the nature of conspiracy, which will lie against one or many and without proof of any actual collusion.[3] From the foregoing it results that

gelahn *v.* Guntner, 167 Mass. 104, and in Plant *v.* Woods, 176 Mass. 504.

[1] Doremus *v.* Hennessy, 62 Ill. App. 391, affirmed in 176 Ill. 609; Kimball *v.* Harman, 34 Md. 407; Hutchins *v.* Hutchins, 7 Hill (N. Y.) 107.

[2] See *ante, Malicious Prosecution.*

[3] Savile *v.* Roberts, 1 Ld. Raym. 379.

the mere entering of two or more into an agreement to inflict certain damage upon a third person gives no right of action;[4] and even when the conspiracy has accomplished its purpose, no cause of action exists unless the resulting damage appears to be actionable by reference to recognized legal standards.[5]

On the historical aspects of the subject of conspiracy regarded as an element of civil wrong, see note by Professor Bigelow, Lead. Cas. Torts 210 *et seq.* The following authorities may be consulted to advantage: Reg. Brev. Orig. 134, *De Conspiratione;* F. N. B. 114-116; 1 Rolle Abr. 110 (P), *Action sur Case en Nature d'un Conspiracie;* Com. Dig., *Action upon Case for Conspiracy;* Encyc. Laws Eng., *Conspiracy* (treating of its criminal aspects).

[4] Cotterell *v.* Jones, 11 C. B. 713, 73 E. C. L. 713.

[5] Orr *v.* Home Mut. Ins. Co., 12 La. Ann. 255; Hutchins *v.* Hutchins, 7 Hill (N. Y.) 104.

CHAPTER XXVII.

DECEIT.

In General.

Volume I

WE here take up a head of liability which is quite different from anything that has gone before; and we shall not proceed far before the reader is aware that we are in closer proximity to the hemisphere of contract than we have heretofore been at any time in the course of these investigations in the law of tort. The law of deceit is the matrix of assumpsit, and it is therefore in effect the matrix of the greater part of modern contract law. The affinity between the obligation incurred by the making of a false representation (the most important form of deceit) and the obligation which arises out of the making of a promise is so marked that some scholars refuse to take any account whatever of false representation as a species of tort.[1] In this view false representation belongs rather to the hemisphere of contract than to that of tort. In our opinion nothing much is to be gained by this procedure. Accordingly, in conformity with common usage, we treat this entire department of the law as a branch of tort.

Affinity of deceit and contract.

Deceit consists of the fraudulent imposition of damage, and this damage commonly takes the form of pecuniary loss or risk of pecuniary loss. The idea which is at the root of liability in deceit is that of a detriment imposed by fraud. It corresponds with the conception of *dolus* in the Roman law. Let us proceed to discover the process by which the common law was led to grasp this notion of liability arising from dishonesty.

Fraudulent imposition of pecuniary loss.

[1] General Analysis of Tort Relations, 8 Harv. L. Rev. 395. Says Professor Wigmore: "The writer believes, with others, that it [false representation] is, like some parts of estoppel, akin in essence to the general subject of undertakings (including contracts)."

Chapter XXVII

One of the very oldest of common-law writs is the writ of deceit (*breve de deceptione*).[2] Consideration of the scope of this early writ shows where legal evolution in the field of fraud began. The first form of deceit which was recognized by the common law as a ground of legal liability was that which embodied a deception of the court and a consequent perversion of the ordinary course of legal proceeding.[3] Of such a wrong the common law could take notice because it was an interference with the administration of royal justice. The wrong was viewed as an offense against the king as well as a wrong against the individual who happened to be damaged. Hence the wrongdoer had to pay a fine to the king as well as damages to the individual. False personation in court proceedings, whereby actions were brought without authority or judgments recovered against persons ignorant of the pendency of a suit, was the most common grievance for which the writ of deceit was used.[4]

Writ of deceit.

Deception in judicial proceedings.

False personation.

Deceit was one of the first of common-law actions to feel the stimulus of the statute specially authorizing the issuance of writs *in consimili casu* with writs already formed;[5] and under the influence of that statute, the action of deceit or case in the nature of deceit began to be used for many other purposes than that of recovering damages for deceitful practices in court proceedings. Illustrations of the extended use of the

Extended use of the writ of deceit.

[2] The writ of deceit was already known in the time of John. 2 Poll. & Mait. Hist. Eng. Law, 2d ed., 535, citing Select Civil Pleas, pl. 111 (A. D. 1201).

[3] See F. N. B. 95 E *et seq.;* Reg. Brev. Orig. 112 *et seq.*

For an early reference to the writ of deceit as a remedy against a sheriff for false return, see Y. B. 21 & 22 Edw. I. (Rolls ed.), 44.

[4] 2 Poll. & Mait. Hist. Eng. Law, 2d ed., 534, 535. These writers cite an interesting case from 9 & 10 Edw. I. (unprinted), where one Adam was attached to answer for defrauding his wife by producing a female who personated her in the levying of a fine.

Bracton gives the form of the writ of deceit for a "malicious and manifest fraud (*falsitatem*)" whereby one A recovered land by default in proceedings in which the defendant had not been given notice, there having been a false return by the summoners. Bract. 335*b*, § 2. The corresponding writ in the Register will be found among the judicial writs. Reg. Brev. Jud. 6*b*.

For the later authorities upon the subject of deceit as a remedy for fraudulent artifice in court proceedings see, fully, Com. Dig., *Action upon Case for Deceipt* (A, 3 & 4); Rolle Abr., *Action Sur Case* (Q).

[5] Stat. West. II., c. 24.

Volume I

Illustrations.

action on the case in the nature of deceit are found in situations like these: If one who had been retained as legal counsel fraudulently colluded with his client's adversary;[6] or if one who had been retained of counsel to be at court on a certain day, failed to come, whereby the cause was lost;[7] or if a man who professed skill in a common calling like that of a smith, lamed the horse that he had undertaken to shoe;[8] or if a farrier undertook to cure a graveled horse, but on the contrary killed him;[9] in all these cases, it was held, an action on the case in the nature of deceit lay at common law.

Any fraudulent act resulting in damage a ground for action of deceit.

Reference to the authorities referred to below[1] will show that the old writ of deceit was entirely merged in or superseded by the action on the case in the nature of deceit and that in the latter form it became the general common-law remedy for fraudulent acts of any kind which result in actual damage. The remedy was broad enough to cover such wrongs as malicious prosecution and abuse of legal process, and, indeed, much of the old law on these topics is tucked away under the heading 'Deceit' in the old books.[2]

Cheating.

Cheating in all its forms,[3] such as at cards,[4] or by means of forged documents,[5] gives rise to a cause of action for deceit. The same is true of any false pretense by means of which one party wrongfully acquires the money or property of another.

False pretense.

If a woman deceitfully gives a man flattering words equivalent to a promise of marriage, whereby he is beguiled into bestowing presents and rendering valuable service at her behest, an action of deceit will lie to recover for the presents and service so expended.[6] An action on the case in the nature of deceit lies against a married man who, on the pretense of being un-

[6] Y. B. 11 Hen. VI. 18, pl. 10.

[7] Y. B. 20 Hen. VI. 34, pl. 4.

[8] Y. B. 46 Edw. III. 19, pl. 19.

[9] 1 Rolle Abr., *Action sur le Case* (P), pl. 16; Y. B. 19 Hen. VI. 49, pl. 5.

[1] Fitz. Abr., *Disceit;* Brooke Abr., *Disceit;* 1 Rolle Abr., *Action sur le Case* (P); Com. Dig., *Action upon Case for Deceipt.*

[2] See Com. Dig., *ubi citat.*

[3] Harris *v.* Bowden, Cro. Eliz. 90.

[4] Baxter *v.* Woodyard, Moo. K. B. 776, pl. 1075.

[5] Tracy *v.* Veal, Cro. Jac. 223.

[6] Rex *v.* Robinson, Cro. Eliz. 79.

married, makes love to a single woman and inveigles her into marriage.[7]

Chapter XXVII

Fraud and False Warranty in Chattel Sales.

The proper approach to the subject of fraud in its modern aspects is found in the law of chattel sales; and here we have to consider the closely related subjects of fraud and false warranty as a ground of liability. From the interfused mass of principle with which we have to deal in connection with these two subjects we shall perceive to emerge in the course of legal evolution three distinct conceptions of liability, namely, (1) delictual liability for fraud, (2) delictual liability for false warranty, and (3) liability for breach of warranty conceived as a contractual obligation. Properly to exhibit these conceptions in their resemblance as well as in their differences, we find to be one of the most difficult problems with which we have had to grapple. In the course of legal evolution these three ideas gradually become disassociated from each other and stand out with some distinctness, but they are underlaid by a mass of common principle and cover a large amount of common territory.

Different conceptions of liability.

In one of the earliest cases (1367) on the subject of fraudulent sale, it appeared that one who had tortiously taken certain beeves from their owner, drove them away and sold them "as if they had been his own." The rightful owner having reclaimed them, it was held that an action in the nature of deceit could be maintained by the purchaser against the seller for this fraud (*fauxime*).[8] It does not appear in this case that the defendant at the time of the sale actually represented that the beeves were his or that he had given any express warranty of title. But it did appear that he knew he had no title, and this was enough; for the fraud was the basis of the action.

Fraudulent sale in early law.

A few years later (1383) it was held that an action on the case in the nature of an action of deceit will lie at the instance

False warranty of title or quality.

[7] Anonymous, Skin. 119.

[8] Y. B. 42 Ass. 259, pl. 8.

of the purchaser against one who falsely warrants the nature or quality of a chattel at the time of the sale.[9]

These two decisions certainly furnished a good starting point for a satisfactory doctrine concerning the liability of the vendor of chattels. But in later years the voice of the common law on this subject was strangely halting and obscure. Groundless fears of encouraging litigation by too great laxity caused the judges to disfavor actions of deceit at the instance of disappointed purchasers. "This is a dangerous case and may be the cause of a multitude of actions," observed Popham, C. J., in a case (1605) where a purchaser sought to recover damages for a false representation as to the nature of a jewel.[1] The maxim *caveat emptor* has been accepted as embodying a general common-law principle and the courts have been loath to trench upon it.

Actions by disappointed purchasers disfavored.

Caveat emptor.

In the time of James I, the courts seem to have been unusually touchy upon the subject, and the decisions of that period bear a decidedly reactionary hue.[2] It so happened that this was a formative epoch in the law of sales, and, as a result, the work of those judges in connection with the subject of warranty and fraud in sales was more or less permanent. Laxity in applying the doctrine of *caveat emptor* would, according to the notions of common-law judges, put too much risk on the seller and appreciably tend to deaden the incentive of trade. "If one sells a horse or wine without warranty it is at the other's peril, and his eyes and his taste ought to be his judges in that case." [3] This, by the way, is a very sound principle in all cases where the buyer can use his senses; in

Formative period in law of sales.

[9] Bellewe's Cases, *Disceit; ib., Accion sur le Case;* Fitz. Abr., *Monstrauns de Faits,* pl. 160. In this case the warranty was as to the quality of a horse. It was objected by the defendant that the warranty here sued on was in the nature of a covenant. In this view the action should have been by writ of covenant and the plaintiff would have been required to show a sealed instrument to prove the warranty. The objection was overruled because the plaintiff had sued in case. In other words, he had elected to sue in tort instead of suing upon the promise.

[1] See Chandelor *v.* Lopus, 8 Harv. L. Rev. 284.

[2] Note the strictures of Tanfield, J., in Roswel *v.* Vaughan, Cro. Jac. 196, upon the case referred to above from Y. B. 42 Ass. 259, pl. 8.

[3] F. N. B. 94 C.

other words, where he has the opportunity to inspect. But it is not applicable in other situations.

It will be noted that the common-law judges have never denied the doctrine of the early cases that either fraud or breach of warranty on the part of the seller gives a right of action in tort to the purchaser. On the other hand, they have never admitted that the seller will be liable for anything short of fraud or breach of warranty. No fault is to be found here. If there is any principle which in theory and in practice has given satisfaction to the English and American judicial mind, it is the principle that the seller of a chattel is liable to the purchaser only when he is guilty of a fraud or of a breach of warranty.

Seller liable only for fraud or breach of warranty.

The peculiar complexion of the common law in regard to the seller's liability does not appear, then, in the matter of determining the grounds of that liability. It appears in connection with the two questions as to what is sufficient to constitute fraud and what is sufficient to constitute a warranty. In working out these problems narrow views have not infrequently prevailed.

On the question as to what constitutes a warranty it was determined at an early day that with one or two exceptions, attributable doubtless to the effect of statutes, there can be no such thing as a warranty without an express agreement. "The common law bindeth him not unless there be a warranty, either in deed or in law." [4] The most emphatic affirmation or representation of fact was not construed as a

Warranty must be express.

[4] Co. Litt. 102*a*. In Y. B. 9 Hen. VI. 53, pl. 37, an action on the case was brought by a purchaser against a defendant who had sold a butt of corrupt wine. It was alleged that he knew the stuff to be unfit for consumption, and furthermore, that he warranted it to be good wine. It was said that the allegation of warranty was superfluous, since it was contrary to law to sell impure food or drink. This is the warranty in law to which Coke refers. See 1 Rolle Abr. 90 (P), pl. 1, 2. A merchant who sold inferior wool stuffs (*panneus laneus*), knowing the goods to be unfulled, was also liable to an action. 1 Rolle Abr. 90 (P), pl. 3. But here the scienter was of the gist of the action. Keilw. 91, pl. 16.

The implied warranty, or warranty in law, was imposed only on common victualers, and as to them it resulted not from the common law, but from ancient statute. Burnby *v.* Bollett, 16 M. & W. 644.

Volume I

warranty, although the parties might have intended it to operate as such. Much less was there any recognition of such a thing as the implied warranty. The term 'warranty' denoted and implied express agreement. Here the law of warranty was defective, and in modern times it has of course been greatly modified.

Warranty must induce the sale.

At an early day it was recognized that the warranty in order to be effective must be the inducing cause of the sale[5]—a proposition which is as sound to-day as it ever was.[6] But in the early cases the principle in question was often put in the form of the proposition that the warranty must be given at the time of the sale.[7] In this form it appears to have been sometimes enforced with a too technical strictness.[8]

Actual knowledge of falsity essential to fraud.

On the question as to what constitutes fraud it was laid down in unequivocal and explicit terms that no representation or statement on the part of the seller can be fraudulent unless he has actual knowledge of its falsity.[9] This proposition, it may be observed, was defective (1) in that it took no account of reckless statements made without sufficient regard to their truth or falsity. Nor did it (2) take any account of statements made without reasonable grounds for belief in their truth. In modern times all authorities agree that reckless statements may be fraudulent, but on the second proposition there is a diversity of opinion.

The false representation of quality.

Between the two propositions that there can be no warranty without an express agreement and no fraud without actual knowledge of the falsity of the representation, the ingenious rascal went free. *Chandelor v. Lopus* (1603)[1] is the classical instance of a miscarriage of justice brought about by this unfortunate legal dilemma. There the plaintiff purchased of the defendant, a jeweler, a stone for one hundred pounds, on the faith of the representation that it was a bezoar

[5] Goldsmith *v.* Preston, 1 Rolle Abr. 96, pl. 1.

[6] Hopkins *v.* Tanqueray, 15 C. B. 130, 80 E. C. L. 130; McGaughey *v.* Richardson, 148 Mass. 608.

[7] Mew *v.* Russel, 2 Show. 284; Moor *v.* Russell, Skin. 104; Roswel *v.* Vaughan, Cro. Jac. 196.

[8] Thus, the proper form of declaration was upon a *warrantizando vendidit,* and in Pope *v.* Lewyns, Cro. Jac. 630, it was held that a declaration in the form *warrantizavit et vendidit* was bad.

[9] Chandelor *v.* Lopus, Cro. Jac. 4.

[1] Cro. Jac. 4, cited in 2 Rolle 5.

stone. The stone turned out not to be a bezoar stone and was worthless. It was held in the Exchequer Chamber that no action lay in the absence of an allegation that the seller knew that it was not a bezoar stone or that he warranted it to be such.[2]

Wiser by reason of this failure of his suit, the purchaser tried again with a new and stronger declaration, in which he alleged that at the time of the sale the defendant knew the stone to be false and fictitious and that the plaintiff bought in ignorance of its true nature.[3] With these averments the plaintiff thought to succeed on the ground of fraud. The court was apparently divided and the final outcome of the case is not known. But all the judges agreed that actual knowledge on the part of the defendant of the falsity of his representation was essential to his liability in this aspect of the case. Without the allegation of a scienter no action would lie.[4] The necessary allegation of a scienter being made, the fact that the defendant was a jeweler and as such presumably skilled in knowledge of the quality of precious stones should have been accepted as good proof that he knew

Scienter.

[2] In 1 Harv. L. Rev. 191, R. C. McMurtrie has attempted to vindicate the doctrine of Chandelor *v.* Lopus, Cro. Jac. 4, on the ground that the decision involved only the question of the sufficiency of the declaration and that the declaration (which failed to show a warranty or a scienter) was held to be bad because of the rule that the legal effect of a contract or conduct must be pleaded, and not the evidence by which that effect can be proved. In this view, the plaintiff, if he had satisfied the rule of pleading by alleging a warranty, might have proved it by showing the affirmation of the defendant that the stone was a bezoar; or, if he had alleged a scienter, he might have proved fraud to the satisfaction of the jury on the particular facts of the case. The first of these suggestions is squarely contrary to the view then prevailing, to the effect that an affirmation cannot amount to a warranty.

As to the other alternative, viz., alleging a scienter and proving fraud to the satisfaction of a jury on the facts of the case, the history of the second action brought by the plaintiff in that case shows that even this course was not without its difficulties.

[3] Chandelor *v.* Lopus (1605), as reported by Professor Beale from MS. in Harvard Law School Library, 8 Harv. L. Rev. 283. The plaintiff should have added that he bought upon the faith of the representation that the stone was a bezoar, but no objection was raised on this point. Popham, C. J., doubtfully admitted that the declaration disclosed a good cause of action. Tanfield, J., reserved his opinion and the case was adjourned.

[4] 8 Harv. L. Rev. 284.

Volume I

the representation to be false.[5] But such a concession would have been inadequate. What the law really needed, as later events prove, was a somewhat radical extension of the conception of warranty and a somewhat less radical extension of the conception of fraud.

False representation as to title.

In regard to defects in the title of the vendor of chattels the law in the time of James I was substantially the same as in regard to defects of quality. In order to maintain an action of deceit the vendee either had to show a plain case of fraud, and to this end it was necessary for him to allege and prove that the seller knew he had no title,[6] or he had to allege and prove an express warranty.[7] In case a warranty was declared upon the scienter was held to be immaterial, for there the seller "takes upon himself the knowledge of the title." [8] But where there was no warranty the scienter was of the gist of the action.[9]

Affirmation of ownership not equivalent to a warranty.

An affirmation of ownership by the seller was not admitted to be equivalent to a warranty of title, but one small concession was here made in favor of the buyer, namely, that where the declaration showed that the seller affirmed himself to be owner at the time of the sale, judgment in favor of the buyer would not be arrested after verdict for failure to allege an express warranty.[1] And under similar circumstances the omission to allege a scienter was held not to be fatal.[2]

Implied Warranty of Title.

From what has been said it is apparent that the law of deceit as applied to the sale of chattels during the time of

[5] J. W. Smith, note to Chandelor *v.* Lopus, 1 Smith Lead. Cas. (8th ed) 295. Compare Hedin *v.* Minneapolis Med., etc., Institute, 62 Minn. 146.

[6] Dale's Case, Cro. Eliz. 44; Sprigwell *v.* Allen, Aleyn 91; Furnis *v.* Leicester, Cro. Jac. 474.

[7] 1 Rolle Abr. 90, pl. 4.

[8] Springwell *v.* Allen, 2 East 448, note. Compare Warner *v.* Tallerd, 1 Rolle Abr. 91, pl. 7.

[9] Springwell *v.* Allen, 2 East 448, note, Aleyn 91.

[1] Harding *v.* Freeman, 1 Rolle Abr. 91, pl. 8; Furnis *v.* Leicester, Cro. Jac. 474, 1 Rolle Abr. 90, pl. 6.

[2] Cross *v.* Garnet, 3 Mod. 261; Warner *v.* Tallerd, 1 Rolle Abr. 91, pl. 7. After verdict the words 'falsely and fraudulently' will be taken to import the scienter. Cross *v.* Garnet, 3 Mod. 261.

Chapter XXVII

James I was not a very creditable body of legal doctrine; yet modern law has been built upon the foundation thus laid. That the product should lack harmony and consistency is no more than might have been expected. Legal development in this field has of course constantly been towards a broader conception of liability. Some of the manifestations of this tendency will be noted.

Warranty implied from possession.

On the question of warranty the greatest need for modification of doctrine was felt in connection with title, for in common transactions of bargain and sale the purchaser is seldom so cautious as to require an express agreement to warrant the title, and it is a great hardship that he should have no redress against a seller when it turns out that the thing belongs to another. In *Medina v. Stoughton* (1700)[3] Lord Holt held that where the seller has actual possession of the goods at the time of the sale, an affirmation of ownership amounts to a warranty; " for his having possession is a color of title and perhaps no other title can be made out." This was a distinct advance, for it tended to break down the rule that express words of warranty are necessary, and was the beginning of the modern doctrine that every affirmation is a warranty where it appears to have been so intended and understood.[4]

Implied warranty of title recognized by Blackstone.

Even with this concession the trouble was not wholly cured, for in many sales there is no express affirmation of ownership, any more than there is an express warranty. Clearly the next step was to determine that every sale of itself implies an affirmation of ownership which is equivalent to a warranty. As Popham, C. J., had observed a hundred years before, an affirmation that the goods are the proper goods of the vendor is implied in the very fact of sale.[5] Thus would an implied warranty of title gain recognition. A consciousness of the propriety and justice of the step caused Blackstone to strain previous authority somewhat by saying that a purchaser of chattels may have satisfaction from the seller, if he sells them

[3] 1 Salk. 210, 1 Ld. Raym. 593.

[4] Power *v.* Barham, 4 Ad. & El. 473, 31 E. C. L. 115; Shepherd *v.* Kain, 5 B. & Ald. 240, 7 E. C. L. 82; Carter *v.* Crick, 4 H. & N. 412.

[5] Chandelor *v.* Lopus (1605), 8 Harv. L. Rev. 284.

Volume I

as his own and the title proves deficient, without any express warranty for that purpose.[6] But the doctrine of implied warranty of title did not actually obtain full recognition in the English courts until about a hundred years later. As late as 1849, in *Morley v. Attenborough* (1849),[7] upon a full review of authorities it was considered that the sale of a chattel does not imply a warranty of title.

State of the law in 1849.

A few years later, however, in *Eichholz v. Bannister* (1864),[8] it was held that in the case of goods sold in open shop or warehouse, there is an implied warranty on the part of the seller that he is owner of the goods. Erle, C. J., said: "If the vendor of a chattel by word or conduct gives the purchaser to understand that he is the owner, that tacit representation forms part of the contract."[9] As a result of this and similar decisions, what were formerly exceptions have now come to stand for a general principle, and on this point of the question of title the rule of *caveat emptor* has dwindled into an exception. Mr. Benjamin formulates the modern English doctrine as follows: "A sale of personal chattels implies an affirmation by the vendor that the chattel is his, and therefore he warrants the title, unless it be shown by the facts and circumstances of the sale that the vendor did not intend to assert ownership, but only to transfer such interest as he might have in the chattel sold."[1]

Modern English doctrine.

American doctrine.

In America the courts, generally speaking, were quicker to adopt the idea of an implied warranty of title in the sale of chattels than were the English courts; Blackstone's statement being here accepted as a correct exposition of law.[2] But the principle has generally been restricted in America to sales of personalty in the possession of the seller.[3] This was due to the unguarded acceptance of Lord Holt's language in

[6] 2 Bl. Com. 451; 3 Bl. Com. 165.

[7] 3 Exch. 500.

[8] 17 C. B. N. S. 708, 112 E. C. L. 708.

[9] 17 C. B. N. S. 721, 112 E. C. L. 721.

[1] Benj. on Sales, 6th Am. ed., § 639.

[2] Boyd *v.* Bopst (1785), 2 Dall. (Pa.) 91; Defreeze *v.* Trumper (1806), 1 Johns. (N. Y.) 274; 2 Kent Com. 478.

[3] Huntingdon *v.* Hall, 36 Me. 501; Scranton *v.* Clark, 39 N. Y. 220; Scott *v.* Hix, 2 Sneed (Tenn.) 192.

That constructive possession of goods is a sufficient basis for an implied warranty of title is admitted

Medina v. Stoughton (1689),[4] as embodying the true reason for the rule. In England no such limitation is recognized in the modern cases.[5]

Implied warranty not properly limited to cases where seller has possession.

The reason for raising the implied warranty is that one who sells of necessity thereby affirms title to be in himself, and if the representation be false he is liable for it, the other having acted upon it to his damage.[6] This reasoning applies where the goods are out of the vendor's hands as well as where he has possession. Possession by no means furnishes a proper criterion for raising an implied warranty. The idea of scienter or knowledge, on the part of the seller, of his want of title, on which the judges used to lay stress,[7] was fully as sound. Yet that idea has long since been exploded as a criterion of liability in case of a failure of title.

Warranty of Quality.

Caveat emptor.

As regards the warranty of the nature or quality of goods, the doctrine of *caveat emptor* rightly holds its place as embodying the general common-law principle.[8] But the doctrine itself has been substantially modified and its application has been restricted by the recognition of special exceptions.

When representation operates as warranty.

In the first place, it is determined that no particular form of words is necessary to create a warranty as to the nature or quality of the goods. It is the subject-matter of the statement and the understanding of the parties, not the form of

in some jurisdictions. Shattuck *v.* Green, 104 Mass. 42; Reynolds *v.* Roberts, 57 Vt. 392.

[4] 1 Salk. 210.

[5] See Pasley *v.* Freeman, 3 T. R. 58, where Buller, J., repudiates the idea that there is a distinction as to the implied warranty of title between sales where the vendor has, and sales where he has not, the possession.

In New Hampshire, as in England, there is no distinction as to warranty of title between goods in the vendor's possession and goods out of his possession. Smith *v.* Fairbanks, 27 N. H. 521,

[6] It will be observed that the idea underlying this line of reasoning is that of fraudulent misrepresentation. This illustrates the common basis of the two conceptions, fraudulent misrepresentation and breach of warranty, and shows how impossible it is to consider one without reference to the other.

[7] Dale's Case, Cro. Eliz. 44; Kenrick *v.* Burges, Moo. K. B. 126, pl. 273.

[8] Barr *v.* Gibson, 3 M. & W. 389; Ormrod *v.* Huth, 14 M. & W. 651; Parkinson *v.* Lee, 2 East 314; Gachet *v.* Warren, 72 Ala. 288; Rasin *v.* Conley, 58 Md. 59.

Volume I

Expression of opinion.

the representation, which stamps it as a warranty.[9] Difficulty is necessarily encountered in the practical application of the rule just stated, but this does not impeach its validity. Among statements which are held not to amount to warranties are mere expressions of opinion or belief,[1] predictions of future yield,[2] and words of simple commendation.[3] Every seller has the right to extol the merit of his wares, and his ofttimes extravagant language is not to be taken too seriously. It is looked upon as an invitation to purchase, rather than as a warranty. 'Dealers' talk' is not a sufficient foundation for an action of deceit.[4] Before there can be a warranty there must be a representation as to an existing and material fact.

Dealers' talk.

To the general rule that the seller is not liable for defects in the nature or quality of goods unless he warrants them to be good, there are a number of important and well-defined exceptions. One of the most noteworthy is found in the rule that a person who, as manufacturer or maker, undertakes to supply an article for a particular purpose warrants it to be reasonably fit for that purpose.[5] The reason of the warranty here implied is that the purchaser must rely upon the skill and judgment of the vendor. The rule applies whether the article or commodity which is the subject of the contract is already manufactured and in stock or is to be made on the purchaser's order.[6]

Supplying goods for particular purpose.

Brown v. Edgington (1841)[7] supplies a fit and well-known illustration of the principle under consideration. It appeared that the defendant had undertaken to supply a crane

[9] Shippen *v.* Bowen, 122 U. S. 581; Tabor *v.* Peters, 74 Ala. 96; Hastings *v.* Lovering, 2 Pick. (Mass.) 214; Fairbank Canning Co. *v.* Metzger, 118 N. Y. 260.

[1] Schroeder *v.* Trubee, 35 Fed. Rep. 652; Tewkesbury *v.* Bennett, 31 Iowa 83; Bates County Bank *v.* Anderson, 85 Mo. App. 351; Duffany *v.* Ferguson, 66 N. Y. 482.

[2] Bryant *v.* Crosby, 40 Me. 9.

[3] Chandelor *v.* Lopus, Cro. Jac. 4; Byrne *v.* Jansen, 50 Cal. 624; McGrew *v.* Forsythe, 31 Iowa 179.

[4] Kimball *v.* Bangs, 144 Mass. 321; Worth *v.* McConnell, 42 Mich. 473.

[5] Jones *v.* Bright, 5 Bing. 533, 15 E. C. L. 529; Curtis, etc., Mfg. Co. *v.* Williams, 48 Ark. 325; Blackmore *v.* Fairbanks, 79 Iowa 282.

[6] George *v.* Skivington (1869), L. R. 5 Exch. 1. Compare Kellogg Bridge Co. *v.* Hamilton (1884), 110 U. S. 108.

[7] 2 Scott N. R. 496.

rope for hoisting wine barrels of the plaintiff from his cellar. The rope turned out to be defective and broke. It was held that there was an implied warranty of fitness. It is not a good defense that the defect was unknown to the person who undertook to supply the article and that he was guilty of no negligence.[8]

Ignorance of defect no excuse.

A warranty of fitness has, under varying conditions, been held to exist in cases where the following articles have been supplied for a known purpose: copper sheathing for vessels,[9] windmills,[1] steam boilers,[2] heating furnaces,[3] packing boxes,[4] barrels,[5] and hair restorer.[6] Firewood has been held not to be a manufactured article within the meaning of the rule.[7]

Wholesomeness of food and drink.

Sir William Blackstone supposed that in contracts for provisions there is always an implied warranty that they are wholesome,[8] and this view has been accepted as regards sales of food and drink for immediate consumption provided the seller is a common taverner, victualer, vintner, brewer, or butcher, or other person whose common calling is to supply food and drink.[9]

The warranty of wholesomeness does not arise in favor of one who purchases for purposes of trade, as in sales to dealers

[8] Randall *v.* Newson, 2 Q. B. D. 102; Nashua Iron, etc., Co. *v.* Brush (C. C. A.), 91 Fed. Rep. 214. But there is some authority to the effect that the manufacturer is not liable for the results of a latent defect which could not have been discovered by careful inspection. McKinnon Mfg. Co. *v.* Alpena Fish Co., 102 Mich. 221; Hoe *v.* Sanborn, 21 N. Y. 556.

[9] Jones *v.* Bright, 5 Bing. 533, 15 E. C. L. 529.

[1] McClamrock *v.* Flint, 101 Ind. 278.

[2] Rodgers *v.* Niles, 11 Ohio St. 48.

[3] Fuller-Warren Co. *v.* Shurts, 95 Wis. 606.

[4] Gerst *v.* Jones, 32 Gratt. (Va.) 518.

[5] Poland *v.* Miller, 95 Ind. 387.

[6] George *v.* Skivington, L. R. 5 Exch. 1.

[7] Correio *v.* Lynch, 65 Cal. 273.

[8] 3 Bl. Com. 165.

[9] Wiedeman *v.* Keller, 171 Ill. 93; Craft *v.* Parker, 96 Mich. 245; Van Bracklin *v.* Fonda, 12 Johns. (N. Y.) 468.

There is authority to the effect that it is not necessary that the seller should be a regular dealer. Hoover *v.* Peters, 18 Mich. 51. But the contrary is the generally accepted view. Wiedeman *v.* Keller, 171 Ill. 93; Giroux *v.* Stedman, 145 Mass. 439.

If one farmer sells another a dead pig there is no warranty in law that it is fit for human consumption. Burnby *v.* Bollett, 16 M. & W. 644.

Volume I

and middlemen.[1] Nor does it arise where food is sold for consumption by animals.[2]

Modern English doctrine.

In England the authorities tend to the conclusion that at common law there is no implied warranty in the sale of food that does not exist with reference to other articles.[3] Such liability as exists is there held to arise either from statute or from the fraud of the seller in selling a thing which he knows to be unfit for use. In other words, a scienter of the unwholesomeness must be proved.[4]

When maxim of *caveat emptor* does not apply.

The maxim of *caveat emptor* is based on the very sensible and practical notion that in trade the buyer must rely on his own senses to protect him from imposition rather than upon the honesty and good faith of the seller. His eye and his taste must primarily be his protection. Now where there is no opportunity for the purchaser to inspect and he is compelled to rely exclusively on the judgment of the seller, the main reason for the maxim *caveat emptor* is wanting. Hence, naturally, 'lack of opportunity to inspect' is taken as a basis for making another exception to the general doctrine. Thus, under a contract with a manufacturer or merchant dealing with goods of a particular class to supply goods of that kind, which goods the buyer has no opportunity to inspect, it is held that the goods must not only in fact answer that description; they must be salable or merchantable under that description.[5] In the leading case of *Jones v. Just* (1868),[6] the Court of Queen's Bench observed that the judges were aware of no case in which the maxim *caveat emptor* has been applied where

Opportunity of inspection.

[1] Wiedeman *v.* Keller, 171 Ill. 93; Howard *v.* Emerson, 110 Mass. 320; Goldrich *v.* Ryan, 3 E. D. Smith (N. Y.) 324. But see Sinclair *v.* Hathaway (*contra,* in sales of bread), 57 Mich. 60.

[2] Lukens *v.* Freiund, 27 Kan. 664. *Contra,* where there is no opportunity to inspect. Coyle *v.* Baum, 3 Okla. 695. And see French *v.* Vining, 102 Mass. 132, where the seller was held liable for result of latent defect known to him.

[3] See Benj. on Sales, 6th Am. ed., § 672.

[4] Emmerton *v.* Mathews, 7 H. & N. 586.

[5] Mody *v.* Gregson, L. R. 4 Exch. 49; Macfarlane *v.* Taylor, L. R. 1 H. L. Sc. 245; Drummond *v.* Van Ingen, 12 App. Cas. 284; English *v.* Spokane Commission Co. (C. C. A.), 57 Fed. Rep. 451; Gachet *v.* Warren, 72 Ala. 288; Swett *v.* Shumway, 102 Mass. 365; Hood *v.* Bloch, 29 W. Va. 244; Brantley *v.* Thomas, 22 Tex. 270; Merriam *v.* Field, 24 Wis. 640, 29 Wis. 592.

[6] L. R. 3 Q. B. 197.

there had been no opportunity of inspection or where that opportunity had not been waived.[7]

Chapter XXVII

Sales by sample.

In sales by sample there is an implied warranty that the article sold corresponds in kind and quality with that of the sample.[8] To constitute a sale by sample it must appear that the parties contracted with reference to the sample as representing the quality of the bulk. The mere exhibition of a sample is not conclusive that the sale is a sale by sample.[9]

Transition from Tort to Contract Conception of Liability for Breach of Warranty.

Breach of warranty conceived as tort.

For some four hundred years from the first recorded instance (1383)[1] of an action for breach of warranty in the sale of a chattel, the exclusive remedy was by the action on the case for deceit. Liability for the breach of warranty thus appears to have been conceived as being purely in tort. Nowadays the warranty is looked upon almost exclusively as a separate contract subsidiary to the contract of sale,[2] and the liability of the vendor which arises by reason of the breach is conceived as a breach of contract. In this view assumpsit is the proper remedy for the breach of the warranty.

Breach of warranty conceived as breach of contract.

The case of *Stuart v. Wilkins* (1778),[3] ushered in the modern epoch, that being the first reported decision in which it was judicially held that the giving of a warranty at the time of a sale creates an obligation in the nature of an assumpsit for breach of which the action of assumpsit lies.[4]

[7] L. R. 3 Q. B. 204.

[8] Gardiner *v.* Gray, 4 Campb. 144; Jones *v.* Just, L. R. 3 Q. B. 197; Bradford *v.* Manly, 13 Mass. 139; Myer *v.* Wheeler, 65 Iowa 390; Dayton *v.* Hooglund, 39 Ohio St. 671.

In Pennsylvania, the only warranty that may be implied in the absence of fraud or circumstances indicating that the sample was to be taken as a standard of quality is that the article to be delivered is to correspond with the sample in kind and substance and be simply merchantable. Selser *v.* Roberts, 105 Pa. St. 242; Fraley *v.* Bispham, 10 Pa. St. 320; Boyd *v.* Wilson, 83 Pa. St. 319.

[9] Day *v.* Raguet, 14 Minn. 273; Proctor *v.* Spratley, 78 Va. 254. See Beirne *v.* Dord, 5 N. Y. 98.

[1] Bellewe's Cases, title *Disceit;* Fitz. Abr., *Monstrauns de Faits,* pl. 160.

[2] Benj. on Sales, § 610; Tiedeman on Sales, § 180.

[3] 1 Dougl. 18.

[4] It appears, however, that the practice of declaring in assumpsit instead of in case upon a false warranty was at the time of the deci-

Volume I

The two conceptions not coextensive.

Since that date the law of warranty has been transferred almost bodily to the domain of contract. It naturally carried with it into that sphere many marks of its delictual origin.[5] But it should be borne in mind that the two species of liability, contractual and delictual, which emerge from the warranty are not coextensive though they have much territory in common.

It is certainly not a little curious that this step should have been postponed so long; but the action on the case for deceit had antedated the appearance of assumpsit by more than a hundred years, and the older remedy was thus too firmly intrenched in the field of warranty to be easily dislodged by its modern rival. The advantage of assumpsit was that a count in indebitatus for money had and received might be inserted in the declaration in order to enable the plaintiff to recover the consideration paid.[6]

The modern implied warranty.

The adoption of assumpsit vastly accelerated the development of the law of warranty in sales. The notion that knowledge (scienter) of the falsity of the warranty is essential to liability at once disappeared[7] and ere long the conception of implied warranty enabled the courts to push this branch of the law far beyond the point where it must otherwise have rested.

sion of Stuart *v.* Wilkins (1778), 1 Doug. 18, fully twenty years old. See the observations of Lawrence, J., in that case, and of Lord Ellenborough, C. J., in Williamson *v.* Allison (1802), 2 East 446.

[5] In Mahurin *v.* Harding, 28 N. H. 128, the difference in the mode of declaring upon a false warranty in case and assumpsit, was stated in the following terms: "The declaration in assumpsit always states a consideration and a promise or warranty, and complains of a breach of the warranty. The contract to warrant, of the breach of which the plaintiff complains, and the entire consideration for it, is indispensable to be stated. . . . The declaration for deceit alleges that the defendant induced the plaintiff to purchase an article by a warranty, or by statements which he knew to be false, and thereby deceived and defrauded him. It is not necessary to make any allegation in relation to the consideration or the terms of the contract of sale, unless they happen to be connected with the fraud alleged in that case; though if a party incautiously recites the particulars of such a contract he may be compelled to prove them as he states them, and may fail if any material variance occurs in his proof."

[6] Williamson *v.* Allison (1802), 2 East 446.

[7] 2 East 446.

In the state of Pennsylvania we have an instructive object lesson of the sorry plight into which American and English law might have come but for the intelligent use and extension of this newer remedy. In that state, by a singular atrophy of legal development, it is held that, apart from the implied warranty of title, nothing short of an express promise will constitute a warranty on which assumpsit will lie.[8] This proposition is manifestly an anachronism, and the injustice with which the rule has operated in that state has, as might have been expected, forced the legislature to modify it.

Pennsylvania doctrine.

[8] McFarland *v.* Newman, 9 Watts (Pa.) 55; Fraley *v.* Bispham, 10 Pa. St. 320; Jackson *v.* Wetherill, 7 S. & R. (Pa.) 480; Boyd *v.* Wilson, 83 Pa. St. 319; Selser *v.* Roberts, 105 Pa. St. 242. In Borrekins *v.* Bevan, 3 Rawle (Pa.) 23, it was held that there is an implied warranty that the article is of the kind that it is sold for. But this is an essential condition of contract as well as warranty.

CHAPTER XXVIII

DECEIT (CONTINUED).

Misrepresentation.

Volume I

Misrepresentation unconnected with sale.

THE first case in which a court of common law ever held that an action may be maintained upon a false affirmation or false representation, independent of a relation of contract or of confidence between the parties, is found in *Pasley v. Freeman* (1789).[1] This decision, therefore, marks a new point of departure in the law of fraud. Prior to that time the use of the action of deceit upon a false representation, if not strictly limited to situations where the false representation was made by a seller to his vendee as an inducement to the sale, was at least restricted to situations where the party injured was brought into legal relations with the person making the false representation.[2]

In *Pasley v. Freeman* it appeared that the defendant had represented to the plaintiff that one Falch was solvent and safely to be trusted for the value of certain goods which the plaintiff, on the faith of the representation, thereupon sold to Falch upon credit, whereby loss resulted. The representation was false to the knowledge of the defendant, and was made with the expectation that it would be acted upon. The majority of the court held that the defendant was liable.[3]

[1] 3 T. R. 51.

[2] Observe the following language of Grose, J., 3 T. R. 53: "I have not met with any case of an action upon a false affirmation, except against a party to a contract, and where there is a promise, either express or implied, that the fact is true, which is misrepresented; and no other case has been cited at the bar."

Anonymous (1683), Skin. 119, where the defendant, a married man, had inveigled the plaintiff into marriage with him, is an illustration of the then rare use of the action of deceit upon a false representation unconnected with the sale of a chattel.

[3] The majority was composed of Buller and Ashurst, JJ., and Lord Kenyon, C. J. Grose, J., dissented and as late as 1801 declared that he was unable to comprehend the

The difficulty arose out of the fact that the dishonest representation was made by one who was not in legal relations with the plaintiff. Hence the case did not fall directly under the principle which had hitherto been applied in cases of fraudulent misrepresentation by sellers. But it was conceived, and properly conceived, that the case at bar was *in consimili casu* with previous cases involving fraud, and hence was to be redressed by an action on the case. Such is the beginning of the modern law concerning fraudulent misrepresentation. In the language of one of the old judges, "fraud without damage, or damage without fraud, gives no cause of action, but where these two do concur and meet together there an action lieth." [4]

Fraud coupled with damage gives cause of action.

As generally stated in modern terms, the doctrine is that one becomes civilly liable to another when he knowingly makes a false representation of a material fact with the intention that it shall be acted upon by the person to whom it is made and the same is in fact so acted upon by him to his damage.[5] The essential factors in liability are representation, falsity, scienter, deception, damage.[6] Of these several factors something will in turn be said.

Essential elements in the wrong.

The Representation.

First is to be noted the fact that the actionable representation in the modern law of fraud usually consists of a misrepresentation by means of words. It is sometimes said that an acted misrepresentation or fraudulent concealment will give a right of action for deceit as well as express words.[7]

Misrepresentation by words.

ground on which the case was decided. Haycraft *v.* Creasy, 2 East 92. His dissent, however, is merely significant of the fact that the case embodied a new departure.

[4] Croke, J., in Baily *v.* Merrell, 3 Bulst. 95.

[5] Byard *v.* Holmes, 34 N. J. L. 296; Brackett *v.* Griswold, 112 N. Y. 454. See also Brown *v.* Castles, 11 Cush. (Mass.) 348.

[6] Church, C. J., in Arthur *v.* Griswold, 55 N. Y. 410. Compare language of Parke, B., in Watson *v.* Poulson, 7 Eng. Law & Eq. 588.

[7] "The gist of the action [of deceit] is fraudulently producing a false impression upon the mind of the other party; and if this result is accomplished it is unimportant whether the means of accomplishing it are words or acts of the defendant, or his concealment or suppression of material facts not equally within the knowledge or reach of the plaintiff." Stewart *v.*

Volume I

Misrepresentation by conduct.

This is true only with qualifications. To be sure elementary frauds, like cheating with loaded dice, marked cards, or other fraudulent devices, are referable to the head of misrepresentation by conduct. But it is well settled that where positive fraudulent device is absent, a mere concealment or failure to speak out supplies no ground of action,[8] unless the law imposes a duty of disclosure arising out of peculiar relations.[9] "To constitute fraud there must be an assertion of something false within the knowledge of the party asserting it, or the suppression of that which is true and which it was his duty to communicate."[1] In *Schneider v. Heath* (1813),[2] the master of a ship which was intended to be sold, slid her off the ways and kept her in the water in order to conceal a broken keel and worm-eaten hull. Under the circumstances it was conceived that this conduct amounted to such a fraudulent device or positive concealment of defect as to enable the purchaser, who thereby lost the opportunity to inspect, to rescind and recover the purchase money. But it is not likely that an action of deceit would lie in such a case.[3]

Representation must concern existing fact.

In the second place, it is to be observed that, as in case of warranties in chattel sales, a representation to be the basis of an action of deceit in any connection whatever, must be a representation concerning a past or existing fact.[4] A matter of mere opinion or belief, or a mere prediction as to what may happen in the future, is no more a ground for an action of deceit than it is ground for an action upon an implied contract of warranty.[5]

Wyoming Cattle Ranche Co., 128 U. S. 388.

[8] Horsfall *v.* Thomas, 1 H. & C. 90.

[9] Juzan *v.* Toulmin, 9 Ala. 662.

[1] Bramwell, B., in Horsfall *v.* Thomas, 1 H. & C. 100.

[2] 3 Campb. 506.

[3] For another instance of a concealment sufficient to invalidate a contract, but not perhaps sufficient to sustain an independent action of deceit, see Evans *v.* Edmonds, 13 C. B. 777, 76 E. C. L. 777.

[4] Chadwick *v.* Manning, (1896) A. C. 231; Munroe *v.* Pritchett, 16 Ala. 785; Milliken *v.* Thorndike, 103 Mass. 382; Cochrane *v.* Halsey, 25 Minn. 52.

[5] Bellairs *v.* Tucker, 13 Q. B. D. 562; Jorden *v.* Money, 5 H. L. Cas. 185; Gordon *v.* Butler, 105 U. S. 553; Holbrook *v.* Connor, 60 Me. 578; Mooney *v.* Miller, 102 Mass. 217; Scroggin *v.* Wood, 87 Iowa 497.

But in order that the foregoing rule may apply it is essential that the expression of opinion or belief should be intended and understood as mere matter of opinion or belief. The mere circumstance that a particular statement is put into the form of an expression of opinion is not conclusive that it is merely matter of opinion.[6] Asserting opinion or belief is an assertion of the fact of belief, and where the fact of opinion or belief is the operative element a false representation as to what that opinion is is fraudulent, provided it is made with an intention to deceive. On the other hand, a statement may be put into the form of a positive statement of fact and yet amount to no more than an expression of opinion, in which case of course it cannot be the basis of an action.[7] In the end it is the character of the statement itself and not its form which determines whether it is a matter of fact or of mere opinion.[8]

Representation concerning existing opinion.

A prediction of future events is clearly only matter of opinion, yet if one states positively that a thing will happen when he knows of a fact which renders it impossible or unlikely, his statement may be fraudulent.[9] Such a statement can at least be treated as a representation that the party who makes it knows nothing to the contrary, and in this aspect it becomes a fraudulent misrepresentation of existing fact. A misrepresentation of one's existing intention as to a future line of conduct may amount to fraud.[1]

Prediction as to future.

A representation concerning general rules of law cannot ordinarily be treated as a sufficient foundation for an action of deceit, because this must be taken as a mere expression of opinion.[2] But a statement as to the effect of general rules of law on private right in particular instances is a matter of fact.[3]

Statement of law.

[6] Smith *v.* Land, etc., Property Corp., 28 Ch. D. 15; People *v.* Peckens, 153 N. Y. 576; Simar *v.* Canaday, 53 N. Y. 298.

[7] Haycraft *v.* Creasy, 2 East 92.

[8] Cummings *v.* Cass, 52 N. J. L. 77.

[9] Murray *v.* Tolman, 162 Ill. 417; French *v.* Ryan, 104 Mich. 625.

[1] Lee *v.* Lemert, 26 Kan. 111.

[2] Rashdall *v.* Ford, L. R. 2 Eq. 750; Gormely *v.* Gymnastic Assoc., 55 Wis. 350.

[3] West London Commercial Bank *v.* Kitson, 13 Q. B. D. 360; Hirschfeld *v.* London, etc., R. Co., 2 Q. B. D. 1.

Volume I

Representation must concern material fact.

A misrepresentation supplies no ground of action unless it is about what is called a material fact. Just what it takes to make a fact material within the meaning of this rule is not very clear. At first impression it would seem that wherever a fact falsely represented to be true is of sufficient importance to cause the person to whom it is made to act upon it, such fact is a material fact and supplies a ground of action where the other elements of wrong are present. But this is not the law, and it is settled that a representation may be so trivial [4] or so irrelevant to the merit of the main transaction that the law will not take notice of it as a ground of liability.[5]

Immaterial facts.

A representation by the vendor of real property that he is a man of high social and political position is of this kind.[6] So a false statement of one's reason for desiring to purchase stock at a very low price is not material.[7] In such situations the law assumes that the conduct of intelligent men is not controlled by such irrelevant statements.

Intention.

In order that one should be liable for a representation it is not necessary that he should at the time of making the representation actually intend that the party to whom it is made should be damaged by acting upon it. In other words, malice in its radical sense is not an essential ingredient in the tort or deceit. The motive of the person guilty of a deceit is immaterial. *Polhill v. Walter* (1832)[8] is generally referred to as authority on this proposition. There the defendant accepted a bill of exchange for a drawee per procuration without being authorized to do so. The plaintiff, relying on the representation of authority thus made, took the bill in course of trade and was damaged by its subsequent dishonor. It was held that the defendant was liable though he had no wicked motive to injure the plaintiff. The defendant in this case knew that he had no authority to accept

[4] Smith *v.* Chadwick, 20 Ch. D. 27.

[5] Dawe *v.* Morris, 149 Mass. 188; Hall *v.* Johnson, 41 Mich. 286; Davis *v.* Davis, 97 Mich. 419.

[6] Farnsworth *v.* Duffner, 142 U. S. 43.

[7] Byrd *v.* Rautman, 85 Md. 414.

[8] 3 B. & Ad. 114, 23 E. C. L. 38.

for the drawee, and hence knew that his representation was false in point of fact. For this reason it was held that the fact that he believed in good faith that the acceptance would be ratified was not sufficient to relieve him of liability.

Representation not made directly to person who acts upon it.

The same decision shows that it is not necessary that the representation should be made immediately or directly to the person who acts upon it.[9] It is sufficient if under the circumstances the representation is so made that the plaintiff's conduct in acting upon it was to be expected by the person making the representation as a natural consequence.

Person intended to be influenced.

From this it follows that a representation is no ground of action unless the person who acts upon it is either the particular person for whom it is intended or falls within the class of persons who were intended to be influenced. To illustrate: the prospectus of a projected corporation is primarily intended to induce men to subscribe for the original shares. When this end is accomplished the object of the prospectus is fulfilled. Hence it is held that false representations in a prospectus afford no ground of action to a person, other than an original allottee, who buys the stock in the open market.[1]

But this rule is not an arbitrary one and where it appears that a prospectus is fraudulently issued with an intention to influence a wider circle than that of the original allottees, an action will lie at the instance of one who acts upon such prospectus to his damage.[2]

[9] See Clarke *v.* Dickson, 6 C. B. N. S. 453, 95 E. C. L. 453.

[1] Peek *v.* Gurney, L. R. 6 H. L. 377, 43 L. J. Ch. 19.

[2] Andrews *v.* Mockford (1896), 1 Q. B. 372.

A curious and anomalous case, illustrating the rule that the representation need not be made directly to the person who acts upon it, is found in Langridge *v.* Levy, 2 M. & W. 519 (in the Court of Exchequer), 4 M. & W. 337 (in the Court of Exchequer Chamber).

It appeared in this case that one Langridge purchased a gun of the defendant, a gun-maker, informing him that it was for the use of himself and of his two sons. The defendant represented and warranted that the weapon was of a certain well-known make, and on this representation the purchase was made. Subsequently the plaintiff, who was one of the purchaser's sons, and for whose use the weapon was partly purchased, undertook to hunt with it. On firing off one of the barrels with an ordinary charge, it exploded, mutilating the plaintiff's

Volume I

Falsity of Representation.

Representation must be false.

It goes without saying that in order to give a right of action for deceit, the representation complained of must be false in point of fact. If a man states the facts correctly, the circumstance that he states an erroneous conclusion from those facts does not make the statement fraudulent.[3] But a statement which is partially true and partially false is just as fraudulent as if the whole were false, provided the false portion can be considered material.[4]

When ambiguous statement fraudulent.

If a statement is ambiguous and capable of being understood either in a true or false sense, it will be treated as fraudulent if the speaker knows that the other party under-

hand. It turned out that the gun was not of the make which it had been represented to be, and to the mind of the jury it was of inferior material. The court held that the defendant was liable on the ground that he had made a false representation with a view that the plaintiff should use the instrument in a dangerous way. The weak point in the decision is that it does not appear that the false representation was communicated to the plaintiff and that he acted upon the faith of it. Parke, B., said that this was not material, the gun having been delivered in order to be used by the plaintiff. On this point he was undoubtedly wrong. The law of deceit furnishes no sufficient foundation for the judgment. If Langridge *v.* Levy is sound it must be rested on the doctrine of exceptional liability which is applied in connection with negligence in sending forth dangerous things.

Another case quite as curious in its way is Denton *v.* Great Northern R. Co., 5 El. & Bl. 860, 85 E. C. L. 860. Here the defendant railway company had prepared and printed time-tables correctly showing that a train making certain connections was dispatched at a particular hour. The company discontinued the train, but nevertheless published and circulated the time-tables after the train in question had been withdrawn by it. The plaintiff, relying on the time-table, went to the station at the hour indicated, and there for the first time learned that no such train was then being run. In consequence he was delayed in his journey and sustained damage. It was held by the Court of Queen's Bench that he was entitled to recover on the ground that the circulation of the time-table amounted to a representation on the part of the defendant that there was a train to be had at that hour, which representation was false to the knowledge of the company and was calculated to cause the plaintiff to act upon it to his damage, as he did. The theory of the decision is plausible but unsound. The case has apparently proved sterile. Such a situation would now be dealt with, it seems, from the standpoint of negligence, and the theory of negligence is hardly equal to the occasion.

[3] Stevens *v.* Rainwater, 4 Mo. App. 292.

[4] Rose *v.* Hurley, 39 Ind. 77; Bonney *v.* Bonney, 9 Manitoba 280,

stands it in the misleading sense.[5] In *Smith v. Chadwick* (1884),[6] Lord Blackburn, speaking of deceptive statements by directors which were capable of two meanings, pungently said: "It may be that they lie *like* truth; but I think they lie, and it is a fraud. Indeed, as a question of casuistry, I am inclined to think the fraud is aggravated by a shabby attempt to get the benefit of a fraud without incurring the responsibility." Again, a representation literally true in itself may be made to convey a false impression by the connection or manner in which it is stated.[7]

Suppressio veri.

A suppression of truth may amount to a suggestion of falsehood.[8] But the circumstances must be such that, on the whole, what is actually told is thereby turned into a falsehood. A man who keeps silent altogether cannot be held for deceit.[9] But when he breaks silence he must be guilty of no deception.

Silence.

Knowledge of the Falsity of the Representation.

The next factor to be considered is the scienter, or knowledge, on the part of the person speaking, of the falsity of the representation. Here the general principle is that in order to establish a right of action for deceit such knowledge on the part of the defendant must be proved. Still, there are certain things which are accepted as equivalent to actual knowledge of the falsity of a representation. Thus it is universally held that if a statement is made without an honest belief in its truth, or is recklessly made by one who cares not whether it be true or false, the person making it will be liable in an action of deceit to one who is thereby misled. In America there is a strong line of authority to the further effect that if one states as of his own knowledge material facts which are susceptible of knowledge and which are untrue, he will be liable to one who acts upon such rep-

Scienter.

Absence of honest belief.

[5] Moens *v.* Heyworth, 10 M. & W. 147.

[6] 9 App. Cas. 187.

[7] Lester *v.* Mahan, 25 Ala. 445.

[8] See Stewart *v.* Wyoming Cattle Ranche Co., 128 U. S. 388.

[9] Keates *v.* Cadogan, 10 C. B. 591, 70 E. C. L. 591; Juzan *v.* Toulmin, 9 Ala. 662; Wood *v.* Amory, 105 N. Y. 278; Kintzing *v.* McElrath, 5 Pa. St. 467.

Volume I

Misrepresentation as to existence of knowledge.

resentation although he may in good faith believe that the statement made by him is true. The falsity and fraud, it is said, consist in representing that he knows the facts to be true of his own knowledge when he has not such knowledge.[1] On the other hand, a number of American decisions favor the doctrine lately formulated by the House of Lords in *Derry v. Peek*,[2] where it was laid down that there can be no liability for deceit where the person making the representation in good faith believes it to be true.

Reckless statements.

The point then at which the two lines of authority diverge is this. Both agree that if a man makes a statement of fact as of his own knowledge, when he in fact does not know whether it is true or false, and knows that he does not know it, he will be liable. Here the statement is said to be recklessly made without regard to truth or falsity. But if he makes a statement of a fact susceptible of personal knowledge when he in fact does not know it to be true, but at the same time honestly believes that he is speaking the truth, then according to the weight of authority he cannot be held liable on the ground of fraud, while according to the other view he can.

False statement honestly believed to be true.

The leading case.

The case of *Peek v. Derry* (1889)[3] is the leading modern English authority on the subject of deceit. All the previous English authorities were there canvassed and the question of the scienter exhaustively considered, first in the Chancery Division, then in the Court of Appeal, and lastly in the House of Lords itself. It may be observed that the conclusion which was finally adopted by the House of Lords had already been reached in a number of American jurisdictions. Reference to the opinions rendered by the several judges in this case will, however, give the reader an adequate idea of the principles which are applicable in this branch of the law. Consequently a short account of this case will obviate the need of any review of cases which are in harmony with it.

[1] Litchfield *v.* Hutchinson, 117 Mass. 195; Cowley *v.* Smyth, 46 N. J. L. 380.

[2] 14 App. Cas. 374; Kountze *v.* Kennedy, 147 N. Y. 124.

[3] 14 App. Cas. 337. For a report of the case in the Chancery Division and in the Court of Appeal, see Peek *v.* Derry, 37 Ch. D. 541.

It appeared in *Derry v. Peek* that by a special act incorporating a tramway company in a certain city it was provided that the carriages might be moved by animal power and, with the consent of the local Board of Trade, by steam power. The directors issued a prospectus containing the statement that by their special act the company had a right to use steam power instead of horses. The plaintiff took shares on the faith of this statement. The Board of Trade afterwards refused its consent to the use of steam power and the company had to be wound up. The plaintiff then brought an action of deceit to recover the damage incurred by reason of the representation in question. The defendants were shown to have had an honest belief in the truth of the representations upon which the action was based, but there was no sufficient foundation for that belief. Consequently the question to be decided was this, viz., whether absence of reasonable ground for believing a statement to be true is so far equivalent to actual knowledge of its falsity as to render the person making such representation liable for the damage which is occasioned by it.

Statement believed to be true, but without sufficient grounds.

Viewed in another aspect the question was whether a negligent failure to ascertain the truth of a statement on which another is expected to act is sufficient to charge the person making the representation with knowledge of its falsity. The Court of Appeal answered these questions in the affirmative, but in the House of Lords this decision was reversed. In the House, Lord Herschell tersely summed up the law in the following terms: "I think the authorities establish the following propositions: First, in order to sustain an action of deceit, there must be proof of fraud, and nothing short of that will suffice. Secondly, fraud is proved when it is shown that a false representation has been made (1) knowingly, or (2) without belief in its truth, or (3) recklessly, careless whether it be true or false. Although I have treated the second and third as distinct cases, I think the third is but an instance of the second, for one who makes a statement under such circumstances can have no real belief in the truth of what he states. To prevent a false statement being fraudulent,

Lord Herschell's summary of the law.

Volume I

there must, I think, always be an honest belief in its truth. And this probably covers the whole ground, for one who knowingly alleges that which is false, has obviously no such honest belief." [4]

The 'negligent' statement not actionable.

It follows from Lord Herschell's summary that a negligent failure on the part of the defendant to look into the truth of the facts which he puts forth in his statement is not sufficient to make him liable as for a fraudulent misrepresentation where he has an honest belief in its truth. But, of course, such a negligent failure is relevant on the question as to whether honest belief in fact existed. "In my opinion," said Lord Herschell, "making a false statement through want of care falls far short of and is a very different thing from fraud, and the same may be said of a false representation honestly believed though on insufficient grounds." [5] But, added he, "I desire to say distinctly that when a false statement has been made the questions whether there were reasonable grounds for believing it, and what were the means of knowledge in the possession of the person making it, are most weighty matters for consideration. The ground upon which an alleged belief was founded is a most important test of its reality. I can conceive many cases where the fact that an alleged belief was destitute of all reasonable foundation would suffice of itself to convince the court that it was not really entertained, and that the representation was a fraudulent one. So, too, although means of knowledge are, as was pointed

Negligence relevant on question of honest belief.

[4] Derry *v.* Peek, 14 App. Cas. 374. With this should be compared the divergent opinion of Lopes, L. J., as stated in the Court of Appeal. Said he: "I think the result of the cases amounts to this. If a person makes to another a material and definite statement of a fact which is false, intending that person to rely upon it, and he does rely upon it and is thereby damaged, then the person making the statement is liable to make compensation to the person to whom it is made — first, if it is false to the knowledge of the person making it; secondly, if it is untrue in fact and not believed to be true by the person making it; thirdly, if it is untrue in fact and is made recklessly, for instance, without any knowledge on the subject, and without taking the trouble to ascertain if it is true or false; fourthly, if it is untrue in fact but believed to be true, but without any reasonable grounds for such belief." Peek *v.* Derry, 37 Ch. D. 585.

[5] Derry *v.* Peek, 14 App. Cas. 375.

out by Lord Blackburn in *Brownlie v. Campbell* (1880),[6] a very different thing from knowledge, if I thought that a person making a false statement had shut his eyes to the facts, or purposely abstained from inquiring into them, I should hold that honest belief was absent, and that he was just as fraudulent as if he had knowingly stated that which was false."

In *Le Lievre v. Gould*,[7] Bowen, L. J., tersely stated the effect of *Derry v. Peek* by saying that one cannot succeed in an action of fraud without proving that the defendant was fraudulent. This neat expression is all right so far as it merely states the result reached in the case referred to; but the aphorism is loaded, and we must say that as an argument it is not nearly so conclusive as it appears to be. The idea is that the action for deceit must not be allowed to transcend the root conception of liability on which that tort is founded. Yet the whole secret of common-law growth is found in just perversions of legal theory. It is by no means impossible that in *Derry v. Peek* the House of Lords fell into that vice of conservatism which sometimes possesses the most learned judges. The circumstance that a strong line of authority in America supports the view that lack of reasonable ground for believing a representation to be true is equivalent to actual knowledge of its falsity is enough to raise at least a suspicion that something may be wrong. That the conclusion reached does not harmonize with the requirements of commercial honesty may be inferred from the fact that Parliament has by statute abrogated the rule laid down in that case so far as it applies to representations made by directors in prospectuses.[8]

The decision somewhat reactionary.

While we do not venture to say with Professor Pollock that the decision is wholly wrong and ought not in any case to be followed by courts which are at liberty to disregard it,[9]

[6] 5 App. Cas. 952.

[7] (1893) 1 Q. B. 499.

[8] Directors' Liability Act (53 & 54 Vict., c. 64). This act leaves the principle of Derry *v.* Peek in force save in regard to representations made in prospectuses or notices concerning companies.

[9] See his article in 5 L. Quar. Rev. 410, on Derry *v.* Peek in the

we nevertheless do agree that the reasoning is not by any means conclusive, and we think that the doctrine of the case ought to be subjected to further scrutiny. Some most important truths, it appears to us, were overlooked by the judges who decided it.

We are quite willing to concede that if the technical limits of the common-law actions are strictly observed, then the action of deceit may properly be restricted to situations where the defendant is guilty of moral fraud, such as is involved in the making of a statement known to be false or the making of a statement without belief in its truth. At the same time we may remark that where the conscience is sufficiently educated up to the proper point, the making of a statement without reasonable grounds for believing it to be true is quite as clearly immoral as the making of a statement knowing it to be false or without belief in its truth. When it comes to hurting a man's leg we have no difficulty in conceiving that negligence is a factor deserving both of legal and moral reprobation. And, one may well ask, why is the same factor not to be reprobated when it comes to the imposition of pecuniary loss?

The implied warranty supletory to the conception of fraud.

Still, conceding that the law of deceit may properly stop short of holding a man liable for statements made in honest belief, but negligently and without reasonable grounds, it by no means follows that he may not become liable for such a representation on the theory of implied promise. We have already seen how the conceptions of fraud and implied warranty are implicated with each other, running as they do along somewhat parallel lines and each assisting the other at points of contact.

The most striking instance where the conception of implied promise or implied warranty has assisted the law of fraud and carried liability beyond the legitimate reach of the conception of fraud is found in *Collen v. Wright* (1857).[1]

House of Lords, and compare the reply of Professor Anson in 6 L. Quar. Rev. 72.

[1] 8 El. & Bl. 647, 92 E. C. L. 647.

This is a leading case in an important field, and as it accomplishes a just end its doctrine has not been questioned. The facts were these: The defendant, believing himself to be the duly authorized agent of one G, undertook to make a contract of lease between the plaintiff and his supposed principal. It turned out that the defendant in fact had no authority, and the plaintiff suffered damage by reason of his inability to secure the premises covered by the lease. There can be no doubt that on this state of facts the plaintiff had a real grievance against the defendant, since on the faith of the representation of authority the plaintiff entered into a contract which would have been binding on himself if the purported principal had chosen to ratify. The question was how to get at him. The professed agent clearly could not be sued on the contract itself, for this would have been contrary to the terms of the contract, which did not purport to bind him, but the principal; and he could not be sued in an action of deceit, because he in good faith believed that he had authority to contract for the alleged principal.

Collen *v.* Wright.

The suggestion had indeed at one time been made that the purported agent in such a case could be sued on the contract as if he were himself the principal,[2] and this suggestion had been acted upon by the English courts in one instance.[3] But the anomaly of allowing one person to be held liable on a contract made solely on behalf of another was soon perceived, and it was accordingly held that one who is found to have misrepresented his authority cannot himself be held liable on a contract made by him as agent for another specified person.[4]

Unauthorized agent not liable on contract made by him as agent.

[2] Paley, Principal and Agent (3d ed.), c. 6, § 1, p. 386; Story on Agency, c. X., § 264, and note 3.

[3] Jones *v.* Downman (1843), 4 Q. B. 235, note, 45 E. C. L. 234, note. This case was reversed in the Court of Exchequer Chamber, but solely on the ground that the absence of authority was not shown. Downman *v.* Williams, 7 Q. B. 103, 53 E. C. L. 103.

There is American authority to the same effect. See Meech *v.* Smith (1831), 7 Wend. (N. Y.) 315; Layng *v.* Stewart (1841), 1 W. & S. (Pa.) 222.

[4] Jenkins *v.* Hutchinson (1849), 13 Q. B. 744, 66 E. C. L. 744; Lewis *v.* Nicholson (1852), 18 Q. B. 503, 83 E. C. L. 503; Bartlett *v.* Tucker, 104 Mass. 336. Polhill *v.* Walter, 3 B. & Ad. 114, 23 E. C. L. 38, seems to have been the first case in which the propriety of holding an unauthorized agent liable as principal was seriously doubted, but that case

Volume I

Unauthorized agent not liable for deceit where he believes himself to have authority.

On the question of the professed agent's liability in an action of deceit, the plaintiff was confronted by the same obstacle that proved fatal in *Derry v. Peek,* namely, in the rule that deceit will lie only where the representation is false to the knowledge of the person making it, or where it is recklessly made without an honest belief in its truth.[4*] It followed that a person who made a contract with another as agent was without remedy where the professed agent had acted under an honest but mistaken impression as to his authority.

The implied warranty of authority.

The law being in this unsatisfactory shape, a way was found out of the dilemma by holding that a party who contracts as agent in the name of a specified principal impliedly warrants to the other contracting party that he has authority from the alleged principal to make the contract, and if it turns out that he has not such authority he is liable in an action on such implied warranty. One of the ablest judges who participated in the decision dissented, saying that such an implied contract was a thing unknown to our law.[5] He was fully justified in saying that the idea was a novel one. But if novelty were always fatal to the adoption of a legal principle, what would our law be?[6]

Now the question whether the law will raise an implied warranty was not considered in *Derry v. Peek,* though the judges evidently thought that the determination of the question which they actually decided was fatal to the existence of

turned upon the peculiar character of the bill of exchange, it being held that a person accepting a bill drawn upon another in the name of the drawee and without authority cannot be sued upon the bill as acceptor.

[4*] There can be no question that a pretended agent may be held liable for deceit where he knows that he has no authority. Randell *v.* Trimen, 18 C. B. 786, 86 E. C. L. 786; Clark *v.* Foster (1836), 8 Vt. 98.

[5] See opinion of Cockburn, C. J. (dissenting), 8 El. & Bl. 658, 92 E. C. L. 658.

[6] Collen *v.* Wright, 8 El. & Bl. 647, 92 E. C. L. 647, was followed in Cherry *v.* Colonial Bank, L. R. 3 P. C. 24; Richardson *v.* Williamson, L. R. 6 Q. B. 276; Weeks *v.* Propert, L. R. 8 C. P. 427. See also Firbank *v.* Humphreys, 18 Q. B. D. 54; Starkey *v.* Bank of England (1903), A. C. 114; Dickson *v.* Reuter's Tel. Co., 3 C. P. D. 1. The American authorities accept its doctrine without question. Weare *v.* Gove, 44 N. H. 196; Patterson *v.* Lippincott, 47 N. J. L. 457; Dung *v.* Parker, 52 N. Y. 494; Simmons *v.* More, 100 N. Y. 140; Kroeger *v.* Pitcairn, 101 Pa. St. 311; Hamburg Bank *v.* Wray, 4 Strobh. L. (S. Car.) 87; McCurdy *v.* Rogers, 21 Wis. 197.

any sort of liability. Such a ruling *sub silentio* is not to be accepted as having much weight. The result is that the law concerning misrepresentation in general stands in England at the precise point where the law concerning misrepresentation by professed agents stood on the eve of the decision of *Collen v. Wright*. *Derry v. Peek* seems to have silenced discussion in the English courts, and it is possible that this idea of implied warranty will not there be taken up; but that it supplies a sufficient basis to support liability in such cases cannot be doubted.

The idea of implied warranty applicable to cases like Derry v. Peek.

As previously stated, there are a number of American jurisdictions in which a conclusion has been reached different from that reached by the English House of Lords in the principal case.[7] So far as appearances go, these courts have had no assistance from the conception of implied warranty. Still, it must be considered that those American cases in which it is held that a false representation made in honest belief but without reasonable grounds for believing it to be true is actionable, are really to be supported on the ground of breach of implied warranty and none other.

The impress of the conception of implied warranty is clearly seen in decisions like *Litchfield v. Hutchinson* (1875),[8] where it was held that when one states, as of his own knowledge, facts which are susceptible of personal knowledge and which are false, such statement is actionable without regard to the defendant's belief in its truth.[9] The idea here is that the assumption of knowledge imposes a positive obligation to see that the statement conforms to truth. One who represents that he knows a certain state of facts to be true is held to warrant that state of facts to be true.

The assumption of knowledge imposes positive obligation to speak the truth.

[7] Cooper *v.* Schlesinger, 111 U. S. 148; Lehigh Zinc, etc., Co. *v.* Bamford, 150 U. S. 665; Munroe *v.* Pritchett, 16 Ala. 785; Goodwin *v.* Robinson, 30 Ark. 535; Hubbard *v.* Weare, 79 Iowa 678; Holcomb *v.* Noble, 69 Mich. 396; Johnson *v.* Gulick, 46 Neb. 817; Burgess *v.* Wilkinson, 13 R. I. 646.

[8] 117 Mass. 195.

[9] See also Hazard *v.* Irwin, 18 Pick. (Mass.) 95; Page *v.* Bent, 2 Met. (Mass.) 371; Savage *v.* Stevens, 126 Mass. 207; Cole *v.* Cassidy, 138 Mass. 437; Weeks *v.* Currier, 172 Mass. 53; Teague *v.* Irwin, 127 Mass. 217; Tucker *v.* White, 125 Mass. 347.

Still, as a mere matter of pleading there must be an allegation that

Volume I

Gratuitous information.

The principle just stated must, however, be taken subject to one qualification, which is this — the voluntary giving of information for mere accommodation, without any request on the part of the person imparting it that the other shall act upon it, does not raise an implied warranty of the truth of the statement. To justify putting the risk on the speaker there must be something like a request on his part that the other shall act upon the faith of the statement, and some sort of personal interest to be subserved by the act or course of conduct which his representation induces.

The person who gives gratuitous information for the accommodation of another party is in a very different position from that of the man who approaches another and solicits him to embark his money or credit into a particular enterprise, or to do some other act on the faith of statements then and there made. In determining the question as to who shall bear the risk of acting upon the faith of a representation, it is but fair that the law should consider all the circumstances surrounding the statement. Whose interest is to be furthered by acting on the representation? is a question of greatest importance here. If the speaker has no personal interest to be subserved, but is merely talking in a social capacity, as it were, he cannot be held responsible when others are damaged by acting on his representations. But if, on the other hand, a statement is made to influence another to do an act which the speaker wishes to be done in furtherance of his own business aims, then the implied warranty may well be held to arise. This is the point which, we say, was overlooked in *Derry v. Peek.*

The self-serving representation.

Cameron v. Mount (1893)[1] affords a good illustration of the implied warranty arising by virtue of the principle just stated. It appeared in this case that the plaintiff's husband wished to buy a gentle horse for his wife (the plaintiff) to drive. The defendant called with a horse which he represented to be kind, safe, and gentle. He invited the plaintiff

the representation complained of was fraudulently made. Holst *v.* Stewart, 154 Mass. 445.

[1] 86 Wis. 477.

to get in his buggy and drive the horse herself to prove his qualities, saying that the animal was free from tricks and bad habits. The plaintiff did as requested. The horse proved to be vicious, and by his plunges threw the plaintiff out of the buggy and hurt her badly. It did not appear that the defendant knew that his representation as to the horse's gentleness was false. The court, however, held that he was liable in tort for a breach of warranty. Most of the American cases in which defendants have been declared to be liable for false statements which they honestly believed to be true, but which were made without reasonable grounds, have arisen out of sales of property. Here there is no difficulty in declaring that when a statement is made to induce a sale, the person making the statement thereby of necessity requests the other to act upon it.

Request that representation shall be acted upon.

A mere recommendation and polite expression of hope that the person to whom the recommendation is made may see fit to accommodate the person recommended is evidently not a request in such sense as will subject the person giving the recommendation to the stricter rule of liability.[2]

Social and business courtesy.

New light on the decision in *Haycraft v. Creasy* (1801)[3] can be obtained by reference to this factor of request. In that case the declaration disclosed a state of facts similar to that involved in *Pasley v. Freeman* (1789), save that the defendant who made the representation honestly believed it to be true. A Miss Robertson who, as it turned out, was an irresponsible and dishonest person, desired to buy certain goods of the plaintiff on credit. The plaintiff, in order to assure himself that Miss Robertson was solvent and fit to be trusted for the goods, applied to the defendant for information. The de-

Recommendation of solvency.

[2] Thus, in Einstein *v.* Marshall, 58 Ala. 153, a representation of solvency was put in this form: "The bearer of this, Mr. M. Heller, is doing a small but safe business in this town. He desires to buy several hundred dollars' worth of groceries from you. He is good for all he buys, and you may safely sell him a bill. We recommend him to you, and hope you will treat him satisfactorily." Upon this it was properly said that the representation of solvency must be shown to have been knowingly false, or that it was recklessly made. "Candor and good faith are what the law requires, for the law does not convert a mere recommendation into a guaranty." Stone, J., 58 Ala. 163.

[3] 2 East 92.

Volume I

fendant said, "I can positively assure you of my own knowledge, that you may credit Miss Robertson to any amount with perfect safety." Substantially the same statement was reiterated several times with emphasis and with much assumption of particular knowledge as to the state of her affairs. The plaintiff thereupon furnished the goods desired. The defendant honestly believed that his representations were true, but was himself deceived. It was decided that he could not be held liable for the damage occasioned by the plaintiff's acting upon these representations. The court went on the theory that the action was for fraud and that there can be no fraud where there is an honest belief in the truth of the representation — a conclusion which was corroborated by *Derry v. Peek.* The decision is also explained by saying that notwithstanding the form of the representation and the assumption of particular knowledge the defendant's statement was after all a mere matter of opinion. There is possibly something in this suggestion, though it appears dangerously like a mere juggle with words.

Theory of the decision.

The true explanation, we submit, is that, on the showing of the declaration, the representation was sought for by the plaintiff himself. It was given gratuitously for accommodation only, and the declaration did not allege that the defendant requested the plaintiff to part with his goods on the faith of the statement. The case therefore falls under the rule stated above as applicable to representations made for the accommodation of the person seeking gratuitous information. The defendant owed him no duty save that he should not intentionally mislead him. The plaintiff consequently acted upon the representation at his own peril.[4]

Another explanation.

[4] But Lord Kenyon, who was no mean judge, dissented in this case. The true rationale of this dissent is revealed in the facts actually proved at the trial; for there it appeared that the defendant himself actually made application to the plaintiff on behalf of Miss Robertson for the purchase of the goods. At another time he came with her and together they selected and ordered the goods. Lord Kenyon's judicial instinct evidently seized upon this as showing that the defendant induced the plaintiff to act upon the representation by requesting him to supply the goods.

Chapter XXVIII

What the final outcome of the controversy which we have been considering will be, cannot now be predicted. It is plain, however, that the ability and learning displayed in *Derry v. Peek,* and the authoritative nature of the judgment there rendered, have for the time being put an end in England to all idea that a man may be liable upon a representation which he honestly believes to be true; while in America it has undoubtedly proved a serious blow to the forces which were making for the extension of liability. The courts which have committed themselves to the more advanced view should fortify their position by reference to implied warranty and stand their ground.[5]

Positive duty arising from confidential relation.

Where under the circumstances of a particular case the courts can find an independent positive duty to ascertain and speak the truth, no appeal to the doctrine of implied warranty of the truthfulness of the representation is necessary, though the effect is substantially the same. Such a duty exists at least in equity for purposes of rescission in all cases where a confidential relation is shown. In a number of states it is held that the directors of a bank owe a positive legal duty within certain limits to know the state of its affairs, and if they put forth or suffer to be put forth in their name a statement which is false and misleading, whereby one is induced to deposit his money in consequence of which it is lost, an action on the case will lie.[6]

Changed conditions.

If a representation is true when it is made, but, by reason of changed conditions, becomes false before it is acted upon, the person making the representation cannot be said to be guilty of a fraud in any true sense.[7] Nevertheless there is

[5] In Nash *v.* Minnesota Title Ins., etc., Co., 163 Mass. 574, the Supreme Court of Massachusetts, which has long been plainly committed to the doctrine that an assumption of knowledge about a matter susceptible of personal knowledge may be a ground of action in deceit although the person making the representation honestly believes it to be true, showed a disposition to take the back track, the decision in Derry *v.* Peek being referred to by the majority of the court with approval.

[6] Tate *v.* Bates, 118 N. Car. 287; Seale *v.* Baker, 70 Tex. 283.

[7] See, *per* Cotton and James, L. JJ., in Arkwright *v.* Newbold, 17 Ch. D. 325. See also Corbett *v.* Gilbert, 24 Ga. 454.

authority to the effect that where the changed conditions come to the knowledge of the person who made the representation, and he, knowing that the other intends to act upon it, fails to reveal such changed conditions, he may be held.[8] This rule may be supported on the artificial theory that the representation is a continuing one until it is acted upon, or on the theory that changed conditions give rise to a positive duty to make a disclosure. At any rate, it apparently puts the legal risk on the right person and is to be commended for that reason if for none other. The effect of this rule is to give a qualified recognition of an implied warranty against changed conditions, or an implied positive contractual duty to make a disclosure, and in an appreciable degree it goes beyond the legitimate reach of the conception of fraud, as expounded in *Derry v. Peek.*[9]

The duty to correct erroneous statements.

On similar grounds and with even better reason one who innocently makes a false representation must, upon discovering his error, reveal the true state of facts. Otherwise if he remains silent and suffers the person to whom he made the representation to act upon it to his damage, he will be guilty of fraud.[1] The doctrine that there is a positive duty to reveal changed conditions and to disclose the truth when one finds that he has innocently stated an untruth is usually invoked for purposes of defense against a contract or in cases where rescission is sought in equity. It is evidently much easier to raise the implied positive contractual duty where the parties enter into contractual relations than where they do not. But there is no good reason why the principle should not under proper limitations be applied in actions for deceit.[2]

[8] Reynell *v.* Sprye, 1 De G. M. & G. 660; Loewer *v.* Harris (C. C. A.), 57 Fed. Rep. 368; Mooney *v.* Davis, 75 Mich. 188; Lancaster County Bank *v.* Albright, 21 Pa. St. 228.

[9] Compare Denton *v.* Great Northern R. Co., 5 El. & Bl. 860, 85 E. C. L. 860.

[1] Reynell *v.* Sprye, 1 De G. M. & G. 660; Traill *v.* Baring, 4 De G. J. & S. 318; Davies *v.* London, etc., Marine Ins. Co., 8 Ch. D. 469.

[2] Poll. on Torts, 6th ed., 285.

Chapter XXVIII

Deception.

Plaintiff must have been misled.

The next element necessary to support an action for deceit is the fact of deception, the rule here being that the plaintiff, in order to make out his case, must show that he was in fact misled by the false representation of which he complains. If a person happens to know that a statement is false he cannot be deceived by it and hence is not allowed to maintain an action upon it.[3] The same rule is applied where the party to whom a statement is made believes that it is false, although he does not know it as a fact.[4]

Where a party is actually misled about a matter not equally open to both, it is no defense to the other when sued for false representation, that the plaintiff had easy means of detecting the falsity of the statement and yet omitted to protect himself.[5] But where a man who has equal opportunity with the other to judge of a particular fact, voluntarily shuts his eyes, he must charge his misfortune to his own credulity. Public policy, it is said, requires that persons shall be held to the exercise of ordinary prudence in their business dealings instead of calling upon the courts to relieve them from the consequences of their inattention and folly.[6]

The false representation as the inducing cause.

Again, it is necessary that the false representation should be the inducing cause of the plaintiff's conduct.[7] The general burden of proof here is on the plaintiff, but if he shows that a false representation was made about a material matter and under conditions that reasonably lead to the inference that it was the inducing cause, the law will presume that the misrepresentation supplied the operative motive. The actual

[3] Cowen *v.* Simpson, 1 Esp. 290; Hughes *v.* Sloan, 8 Ark. 146; Clopton *v.* Cozart, 13 Smed. & M. (Miss.) 363.

[4] Bowman *v.* Carithers, 40 Ind. 90.

[5] Dobell *v.* Stevens, 3 B. & C. 623, 10 E. C. L. 201.

[6] Moore *v.* Turbeville, 2 Bibb (Ky.) 602.

[7] Smith *v.* Chadwick, 9 App. Cas. 187; Moses *v.* Katzenberger, 84 Ala. 95; Brackett *v.* Griswold, 112 N. Y. 454; Boyd *v.* Shiffer, 156 Pa. St. 100. See also Arkwright *v.* Newbold, 17 Ch. D. 324 (Cotton, L. J.). The same rule applies where equitable relief is sought against the enforcement of a contract. Jennings *v.* Broughton, 17 Beav. 234; Redgrave *v.* Hurd, 20 Ch. D. 1; Slaughter *v.* Gerson, 13 Wall. (U. S.) 379.

Volume I

situation before the man at the time he acts often gives a better clue to his reason for acting than his own explicit statement subsequently made, that without the representation he would or would not have acted as he did. If the plaintiff makes out his *prima facie* case by proof that a material misrepresentation was made under such circumstances as to raise the inference that he was thereby induced to act, the defendant may rebut by showing that the plaintiff in fact acted from some other cause. Thus, if he appears to have relied exclusively on a guaranty,[8] or upon the result of investigations made by himself or by his agent,[9] he cannot treat the representation as fraudulent. And where a man makes independent investigation the presumption is that his act resulted from that and not from the representation.[1] But this is only a presumption of fact, and if it appears that without fault he was unable to discover the truth and in fact relied on the representation, he can recover.[2]

Material inducement.

It is not necessary that the false representation should be the sole inducement which operates to bring about the step which results in damage. In most human transactions there are more than one inducing cause, and it is enough for the purposes of maintaining an action of deceit or for rescinding a contract that the false representation was a material inducement. If this be shown it is immaterial what other causes or motives may have operated on the plaintiff's mind.[3] Some courts have laid down the proposition that a representation shall not be considered as an inducing cause unless the party who claims to have acted upon it would have pursued a different course in the event it had not been made.[4] But what

[8] Holdom *v.* Ayer, 110 Ill. 448; Elphick *v.* Hoffman, 49 Conn. 331.

[9] Redgrave *v.* Hurd, 20 Ch. D. 1; Saltonstall *v.* Gordon, 33 Ala. 149; Crocker *v.* Manley, 164 Ill. 282; Whiting *v.* Hill, 23 Mich. 399; Arnold *v.* Norfolk, etc., Hosiery Co., 148 N. Y. 392; Lee *v.* Burnham, 82 Wis. 209; Singer *v.* Schilling, 74 Wis. 369.

[1] Fauntleroy *v.* Wilcox, 80 Ill. 477; Anderson *v.* McPike, 86 Mo. 293.

[2] Kelley *v.* Owens (Cal. 1892), 30 Pac. Rep. 596; Meek *v.* Keene, 47 Ind. 77; Foley *v.* Holtry, 43 Neb. 133.

[3] Clarke *v.* Dickson, 6 C. B. N. S. 453, 95 E. C. L. 453; Jordan *v.* Pickett, 78 Ala. 331.

[4] Smith *v.* Kay, 7 H. L. Cas. 775; Ruff *v.* Jarrett, 94 Ill. 475; Mc-

a man would have done but for a given representation is largely a matter of speculation, and the suggested test is more plausible than sound.[5]

Uncommunicated representations.

Uncommunicated representations are not actionable, because they cannot enter as an inducing factor into the conduct of the party for whom they were intended.[6] For this reason one who has entered into a contract in his own behalf and on his own responsibility cannot complain of a false representation made to his agent but not communicated by the agent until after the transaction is finished.[7] Similarly, a representation which is made after a transaction is finished cannot furnish a ground of action for damage growing out of such transaction.[8] An *ex post facto* representation is as ineffectual to raise delictual liability as an *ex post facto* promise is ineffectual to raise liability in assumpsit, and for the same reason. In the field of contract, the promise, and in the field of tort, the representation, must be the cause of the incurring of the detriment (consideration, damage) which gives rise to legal obligation.

The subsequent representation.

The Damage.

The damage element essential to liability.

The final factor to be considered in connection with the subject of liability for false representation is that of damage. It is of the very essence of an action of deceit that the fraud should be accompanied by damage. Only where these two factors concur does an action lie.[9] The damage must take the form of an actual detriment, and this usually involves pecuniary loss or subjection to some legal obligation which will

Aleer *v.* Horsey, 35 Md. 439; Hartford Live Stock Ins. Co. *v.* Mathews, 102 Mass. 221; Safford *v.* Grout, 120 Mass. 20; Lebby *v.* Ahrens, 26 S. Car. 275.

[5] Reynell *v.* Sprye, 1 De G. M. & G. 708 (Lord Cranworth); Cabot *v.* Christie, 42 Vt. 121; James *v.* Hodsden, 47 Vt. 127.

[6] Lindsey *v.* Lindsey, 34 Miss. 432; Manhattan Brass Co. *v.* Reger, 168 Pa. St. 644.

[7] Thompson *v.* Rose, 16 Conn. 71.

[8] Everling *v.* Holcomb, 74 Iowa 722; Schelling *v.* Bischoff, 59 N. Y. Super. Ct. 562.

[9] Baily *v.* Merrell, 3 Bulst. 95 (*per* Croke, J.); Pasley *v.* Freeman, 3 T. R. 51; Bennett *v.* Terrill, 20 Ga. 83; Randall *v.* Hazelton, 12 Allen (Mass.) 414; Skowhegan First Nat. Bank *v.* Maxwell, 83 Me. 576; Bunn *v.* Ahl, 29 Pa. St. 387.

Volume I

result in such loss. There must be damage either already fallen or else inevitable.

Liability must be fixed.

It has been held that the incurring of a merely contingent liability, as where a man is fraudulently induced to indorse a note, will not support an action of deceit until the plaintiff's liability as indorser has become fixed by the dishonor of the note.[1]

In the eye of the law a man is not injured by being beguiled into the doing of a thing which he is already legally bound to do.[2] Where this happens the deceitful artifice is not a ground even for the avoidance of a contract, and, *a fortiori,* it does not afford a ground for an action of deceit.

[1] Freeman *v.* Venner, 120 Mass. 424. See also Ely *v.* Stannard, 46 Conn. 124, citing Sedgwick on Damages, 229. Compare Kimmans *v.* Chandler, 13 Iowa 327.

[2] Pheteplace *v.* Eastman, 26 Iowa 446; Atkinson *v.* Sinnott, 67 Miss. 502; Randall *v.* Hazelton, 12 Allen (Mass.) 412; Marsh *v.* Cook, 32 N. J. Eq. 262.

CHAPTER XXIX

UNFAIR COMPETITION.

Chapter XXIX

Interference with trade-marks, etc.

THOUGH, as we have already seen from the discussion of the *Mogul Steamship Case*,[1] the law is exceedingly tolerant of competition in business, there are certain forms of competition which are not allowed. Interference with trade-marks and trade names, and the wrong of unfair competition, cover a field in which competition becomes illegitimate and consequently gives rise to legal liability. The common element in these torts consists of a false representation on the part of the competitor, by means of words, names, pictures or symbols, to the effect that his goods or his business are the goods or the business of his rival. In deceit we became conversant with the idea of liability as incident to the making of false representations to an individual whereby he is himself led to act to his damage. Here we are to consider liability as incident to the making of false representations to a third person (the public) whereby such third person is misled. The law in this field is entirely modern. The best-known and most highly specialized branch of the subject is that which relates to the law of trade-marks. But unfair competition is the generic tort, and interference with trade-marks is only one of its forms. Interference with trade names is another species of the same wrong.

Gist of unfair competition.

The remedy in most cases of unfair competition, whether there be an interference with a trade-mark, or some more general wrong, is usually by bill in equity to enjoin the continuance of the wrongful interference. Such equitable relief reaches the root of the trouble and abates the injury altogether. Hence it is a more satisfactory remedy than the ordinary action at law for damages in which recovery is had

Common remedy by bill in equity.

[1] Mogul Steamship Co. *v.* McGregor, (1892) A. C. 25, discussed *ante.*

Volume I

only for injury already done. For this reason unfair competition is not a very important subject when the wrong is viewed merely as a ground of liability in an action at law. It may be suggested, furthermore, that the courts of equity, in giving their peculiar relief in cases of unfair competition, administer the law with characteristic freedom and discretion. It results that a discussion of the grounds on which an injunction will be granted against unfair competition is not exactly in place in a treatise which is chiefly concerned with strictly legal wrongs. Still, in every case of unfair competition a legal right is infringed, and equity assumes jurisdiction only because it is able to give a more perfect remedy. Furthermore, it is established that where, as in cases of unfair competition, an injunction is sought in aid of a legal right, the court is bound to grant it if the legal right is established.[2] For this reason the nature of these wrongs will be briefly explained and their respective relations to each other and to other torts will be indicated.

Equity proceeds on ground of invasion of legal right.

The Earlier Decisions.

Counterfeit trade-mark.

The first case of which we have knowledge wherein an action was maintained for infringement of a trade-mark comes from the twenty-second year of Elizabeth (1579). There an action on the case in the nature of deceit was brought by a clothier, who had gained a reputation for the making of good cloth, against one who had counterfeited his trade-mark and sold inferior goods by this means. It was held that the action would lie.[3]

Law of unfair competition develops slowly.

For some reason or other the development of the law on this subject was not rapid. In 1742, Lord Hardwicke, in a decision which is entirely inconsistent with modern doctrine,

[2] Fullwood *v.* Fullwood, 9 Ch. D. 176.

[3] See Anonymous (22 Eliz.), cited by Doderidge, J., in Southern *v.* How, Popham 144. In Croke's report of this case, Cro. Jac. 471, the purchaser of the inferior goods is represented as being the plaintiff in the action of deceit. Rolle is uncertain as to whether the plaintiff was the purchaser or the clothier. 2 Rolle 28. Popham's account of Doderidge's words is so explicit on this point that it would seem unlikely that he is in error.

refused to enjoin a defendant from making use of the Great Mogul as a stamp upon his cards at the instance of a plaintiff who claimed the exclusive right to use such stamp by royal charter.[4] In 1783, Lord Mansfield remarked by way of dictum that if one man sells a particular article of his own make under the name or mark of another, that is a fraud against the latter[5] for which an action will lie. This was in conformity with the doctrine of the early case referred to above. Twenty years later Lord Eldon enjoined a defendant from publishing a magazine which was made to resemble in appearance the plaintiff's serial magazine, and which purported to be a continuation of it.[6]

Simulation of mark.

In *Sykes v. Sykes* (1824),[7] it appeared that a manufacturer had adopted a particular mark for his goods in order to denote that they were manufactured by him. The defendant, a manufacturer of goods of the same kind but of inferior quality, adopted the same mark for the purpose of palming such goods off on the public as and for the plaintiff's goods. It was shown in evidence that the dealers who bought goods directly of the defendant knew by whom they were manufactured, but the consumers to whom the goods were finally sold did not. It was held that an action would lie.

Simulation of wrapper.

Within the next decade cases on the subject of trade-marks began to multiply, and this most important branch of the law of tort thus began to assume its present shape. In *Blofeld v. Payne* (1833),[8] the declaration stated that the plaintiff, a manufacturer of metallic hones, used certain envelopes for the same, denoting them to be his. The defendant made other hones, wrapped them in similar envelopes, and sold them as and for the plaintiff's hones. It was held that an action for damages lay without proof that the hones were of inferior quality and without proof of special damage. In this decision we perceive the ripening of the conception of absolute and exclusive property right in the trade-mark.

Another stage in the development of the idea is marked

[4] Blanchard *v.* Hill, 2 Atk. 484.

[5] Singleton *v.* Bolton, 3 Dougl. 293, 26 E. C. L. 114.

[6] Hogg *v.* Kirby, 8 Ves. Jr. 215.

[7] 3 B. & C. 541, 10 E. C. L. 176.

[8] 4 B. & Ad. 410, 24 E. C. L. 87.

Volume I

Intent immaterial.

by *Millington v. Fox* (1838),[9] where it was held that one who infringes a trade-mark is liable although he has no fraudulent intent and is in fact ignorant that the trade-mark in question belongs to another.

Lord Langdale's statement of doctrine.

In *Perry v. Truefitt* (1842),[1] Lord Langdale, M. R., stated the principle on which courts of law and equity proceed in protecting trade-marks as follows: "A man is not to sell his own goods under the pretense that they are the goods of another man; he cannot be permitted to practice such a deception, nor to use the means which contribute to that end. He cannot therefore be allowed to use names, marks, letters, or other indicia, by which he may induce purchasers to believe that the goods which he is selling are the manufacture of another person."

One must not sell his goods as and for the goods of another.

The next year, in a case which involved the broader question of unfair competition as well as that of trade-mark, the same learned judge said: "No man has a right to dress himself in colors, or adopt and bear symbols, to which he has no peculiar or exclusive right, and thereby personate another person, for the purpose of inducing the public to suppose, either that he is that other person, or that he is connected with and selling the manufacture of such other person, while he is really selling his own. It is perfectly manifest, that to do these things is to commit a fraud, and a very gross fraud. . . . No man has a right to sell his own goods as the goods of another."[2] Here it appeared that a firm known as Day & Martin had long been engaged in the manufacture of a blacking which was sold in bottles of particular design. The defendant, who was named Day, having procured the authority of one Martin to use his name, set up an establishment near by, under the firm name of Day & Martin, for the purpose of selling blacking in bottles of similar design. The labels were also similar. The fraudulent design to profit by the good will of the established business was clear, and the injunction was granted.

[9] 3 Myl. & C. 338.
[1] 6 Beav. 66.
[2] Croft *v.* Day (1843), 7 Beav. 88.

Knott v. Morgan (1836)[3] furnishes a good illustration of unfair competition as distinguished from the technical infringement of trade-mark. The plaintiffs having successfully established a certain omnibus line with coaches of a particular design and color, the defendants, in order fraudulently to obtain some of their patronage, established a rival line. The carriages were painted like those of the plaintiffs. A similar combination of words was used to indicate the name of the line, and the livery of the employees was identical. The plaintiff's symbol of star and garter was likewise imitated. An injunction was granted restraining the defendants from their imitation of the various devices which the plaintiffs had adopted for distinguishing their line of omnibuses.

Illustration of unfair competition

Trade-marks.

Though the law concerning infringement of trade-marks and that concerning unfair competition have a common conception at their root, namely, the idea that one shall not misrepresent that his goods or his business is the goods or the business of another, the law concerning trade-marks occupies in a way a somewhat higher plane. The infringement of a trade-mark, for instance, is conceived as an invasion of property. One who has identified a peculiar symbol or mark with his goods thereby acquires a property right in it, and if another infringes the trade-mark he thereby violates the exclusive right of user which is incident to the possession of the trade-mark. Here knowledge, intent, or fraudulent motive on the part of the infringer is immaterial.[4] Unfair competition, on the other hand, cannot be placed on the plane of invasion of property right. This tort is strictly one of fraud, and a fraudulent intent or its equivalent is essential to liability. The law of trade-marks is a highly specialized subject and is distinct from the law of unfair competition. It furnishes

Trade-mark represents property right.

Unfair competition a wrong of fraud.

[3] 2 Keen 213.

[4] Edelsten *v.* Edelsten, 1 De G. J. & S. 185; Hall *v.* Barrows, 4 De G. J. & S. 150; Leather Cloth Co. *v.* American Leather Cloth Co., 4 De G. J. & S. 137; McLean *v.* Fleming, 96 U. S. 245; Handy *v.* Commander, 49 La. Ann. 1119.

Volume I

its own binding rules of decision in all cases where there is a technical infringement of a trade-mark.

Confusion between the two torts.

Inasmuch as the principles applicable to trade-marks were precisely defined at an earlier day than the broader principles applicable to unfair competition, it is not surprising that some confusion should be found in the earlier decisions between these two bodies of legal doctrine. In fact it is only in very recent years that the term 'trade-mark' has been restricted to its proper technical meaning and the term 'unfair competition' adopted to indicate wrongs similar to infringement of trade-marks, but not falling within its principle. In the earlier decisions simulations of labels and packages and other fraudulent devices for palming off one's goods as those of another are intermingled under the general subject 'infringement of trade-marks.'[5]

Trade-marks protected by statute.

In England the law concerning trade-mark rights is defined and fully regulated by statutes.[6] Under these it is necessary that a trade-mark should be registered before its owner is entitled to protection. But the principles applicable to cases of unfair and fraudulent competition can of course be invoked for the protection of those who have not registered or who are not entitled to register their names or symbols as technical trade-marks.[7]

In the United States also there are statutes, both federal and state, which give protection to registered trade-marks. These statutes are only in aid of the common-law rules applicable to trade-mark cases, and give rise to no new right;[8] but registration under the federal statutes is *prima facie* evidence of title to the trade-mark.[9]

In order that a trade-mark should be entitled to protection

[5] See C. F. Simmons Medicine Co. *v.* Mansfield Drug Co., 93 Tenn. 120 *et seq.*

[6] 46 & 47 Vict. (1883), c. 57; 51 & 52 Vict. (1888), c. 50.

[7] Thompson *v.* Montgomery, 41 Ch. D. 35, affirmed in House of Lords, (1891) A. C. 217.

[8] Trade Mark Cases, 100 U. S. 82; Sarrazin *v.* W. R. Irby Cigar, etc., Co. (C. C. A.), 93 Fed. Rep. 624; Oakes *v.* St. Louis Candy Co., 146 Mo. 391.

[9] Hennessy *v.* Braunschweiger, 89 Fed. Rep. 664.

as such at common law, or to registration as a valid trade-mark under the statutes, it must conform to certain requisites:

Chapter XXIX

Requisites of valid trade-mark.

(1) Legality of business.

The business to be protected must of course be a lawful one,[1] and the mark itself must not be indecent or otherwise opposed to public policy.[2]

(2) Mark must be attached to article.

The trade-mark, to be effective, must be attached to or accompany the article with which it is associated, so that to the mind of the purchaser or consumer it may come to have a definite significance as indicating the origin of such article. The mark must go with the goods into the market.[3] But it is sufficient if the trade-mark is on the box or wrapper.[4]

Symbols, words, and arbitrary devices.

The trade-mark may consist either of a symbol or of a word or combination of words. Arbitrary devices which can have no significance except as associated with particular articles are perhaps the original norm of the trade-mark. Such devices as crests, geometrical figures, the rising sun, a star, an eagle, lion, elephant, etc., are not uncommon. Numerals and initial letters arbitrarily employed to indicate origin and not quality may constitute valid trade-marks.[5] Novelty and originality are not requisite except so far as it is necessary that no person should have previously acquired a right to the same mark.[6]

Novelty.

What words cannot be adopted as trade-marks.

In regard to the use of words and combinations of words as trade-marks, it is to be observed that words cannot be exclusively appropriated by one particular person when others are of common right entitled to use the same words. De-

[1] Portsmouth Brewing Co. *v.* Portsmouth Brewing, etc., Co., 67 N. H. 433.

[2] Cohn *v.* People, 149 Ill. 486; McVey *v.* Brendel, 144 Pa. St. 235.

[3] Lorillard *v.* Pride, 28 Fed. Rep. 434; Hazelton Boiler Co. *v.* Hazelton Tripod Boiler Co., 142 Ill. 494; Schneider *v.* Williams, 44 N. J. Eq. 391.

[4] Jay *v.* Ladler, 40 Ch. D. 649.

[5] Lawrence Mfg. Co. *v.* Tennessee Mfg. Co., 138 U. S. 537; Amoskeag Mfg. Co. *v.* Trainer, 101 U. S. 51; Boardman *v.* Meriden Britannia Co., 35 Conn. 402; Lawrence Mfg. Co. *v.* Lowell Hosiery Mills, 129 Mass. 325; Gillott *v.* Esterbrook, 48 N. Y. 374.

[6] Trade Mark Cases, 100 U. S. 94; William J. Moxley Co. *v.* Braun, etc., Co., 93 Ill. App. 183.

Volume I

scriptive [7] and geographical [8] terms are therefore not the subject-matter of a valid trade-mark. A contrary rule would seriously hamper manufacturers and traders, in the use of the common tongue.

Newly coined, arbitrary, and fanciful words are consequently the surest basis for trade-mark right when the trade-mark is a verbal one. But familiar words, if arbitrarily or fancifully used, are just as good. The following words have in particular instances been held to constitute valid trade-marks: Eureka,[9] Charter Oak,[1] Hoosier,[2] Ideal,[3] Elk,[4] Hunyadi.[5] Newly coined words like Cuticura,[6] Celluloid,[7] Bromo-Caffein,[8] and Yusea,[9] are good trade-marks.

Familiar words used arbitrarily.

Newly coined words.

A foreign word or phrase may be adopted as a trade-mark if it gives the effect of a novel, arbitrary, or fanciful term.[1] But a transliteration of the foreign name for an article, there being no English equivalent, cannot be so adopted and monopolized.[2]

Foreign words.

Though descriptive terms are incapable of being exclusively appropriated as trade-marks, a descriptive combination of words may be, provided the words are arbitrary in their selection and arrangement and are not the only words which could be employed to describe the article to which they are

Descriptive terms.

[7] Cellular Clothing Co. *v.* Maxton, (1899) A. C. 326; Rumford Chemical Works *v.* Muth, 35 Fed. Rep. 524; Hygeia Distilled Water Co. *v.* Hygeia Ice Co., 70 Conn. 516; Larrabee *v.* Lewis, 67 Ga. 561; Bolander *v.* Peterson, 136 Ill. 215; Gessler *v.* Grieb, 80 Wis. 21.

[8] McAndrew *v.* Bassett, 4 De G. J. & S. 380; Elgin Nat. Watch Co. *v.* Illinois Watch Case Co., 179 U. S. 666; Glendon Iron Co. *v.* Uhler, 75 Pa. St. 467; Telephone Mfg. Co. *v.* Sumter Telephone Mfg. Co., 63 S. Car. 313.

[9] Alleghany Fertilizer Co. *v.* Woodside, 1 Hughes (U. S.) 115 (applied to fertilizer).

[1] Filley *v.* Fassett, 44 Mo. 168 (applied to stove).

[2] Julian *v.* Hoosier Drill Co., 78 Ind. 408 (applied to grain drill).

[3] Waterman *v.* Shipman, 130 N. Y. 301 (applied to fountain pen).

[4] Lichtenstein *v.* Goldsmith, 37 Fed. Rep. 359 (applied to cigars).

[5] Saxlehner *v.* Eisner, etc., Co., 179 U. S. 19 (applied to medicinal water).

[6] Potter Drug, etc., Corp. *v.* Pasfield Soap Co. (C. C. A.), 106 Fed. Rep. 914.

[7] Celluloid Mfg. Co. *v.* Read, 47 Fed. Rep. 712.

[8] Keasbey *v.* Brooklyn Chemical Works, 142 N. Y. 467.

[9] Welsbach Light Co. *v.* Adam, 107 Fed. Rep. 463.

[1] *In re* Rotherham, 14 Ch. D. 585; Gout *v.* Aleploglu, 6 Beav. 69, note; Menendez *v.* Holt, 128 U. S. 514.

[2] Dadirrian *v.* Yacubian (C. C. A.), 98 Fed. Rep. 872.

applied. The following, among other descriptive combinations of words, have been sustained as trade-marks: Black Diamond, as applied to scythestones;[3] Moxie Nerve Food, as applied to a beverage;[4] Cream Baking Powder, as applied to a baking powder;[5] and Pirie's Parchment Bank, as applied to a particular kind of paper.[6] In this class of cases it is often difficult to say with certainty whether the decision goes on the theory of the infringement of a trade-mark or upon the theory of unfair competition. Where the imitation of the combination of words is close enough to be hurtful, the inference of fraudulent intent is irresistible, and hence the plaintiff is entitled to relief in either view.

Descriptive combination.

Unfair Competition.

From consideration of the question as to what may constitute a valid trade-mark we pass to the subject of unfair competition; and it may be remarked at once that in many situations one who fails to establish the exclusive property right which is necessary to the validity of a trade-mark may yet obtain relief on the ground of his competitor's unfairness or fraud. Any conduct may be said to be unfair competition when its effect is to pass off or tend to pass off on the public the goods of one man as the goods of another. It is not necessary that any particular means should be used to this end. The most usual devices are the simulation of labels, the imitation of another's style of putting up goods, and the reproduction of the form, color, and general appearance of his packages.[7] Another common device is found in the adoption of the same or similar trade names.[7 *]

Law of trade-marks supplemented by law of unfair competition.

Definition of unfair competition.

As a preliminary to granting relief against a defendant for a misrepresentation that his goods are those of another, it is required in courts of equity (and the rule would be the same in actions at law) that the complainant himself should

[3] A. F. Pike Mfg. Co. *v.* Cleveland Stone Co., 35 Fed. Rep. 896.

[4] Moxie Nerve Food Co. *v.* Beach, 33 Fed. Rep. 248.

[5] Price Baking-Powder Co. *v.* Fyfe, 45 Fed. Rep. 799.

[6] *In re* Goodall, 42 Ch. D. 566.

[7] C. F. Simmons Medicine Co. *v.* Mansfield Drug Co., 93 Tenn. 119, 120.

[7 *] Fite *v.* Dorman (Tenn. 1900), 57 S. W. Rep. 129.

Volume I

have been guilty of no misrepresentation. The law concerning unfair competition is not based on the idea of redressing a grievance of the public, yet the fact that there is imposition on the public goes far to support the law concerning unfair competition as a matter of policy. Hence where a complainant is shown to have himself been guilty of imposing on the public, the law will not give him relief. This principle, it may be added, applies in cases of infringement of trade-marks as well as in cases of unfair competition. One who puts a false statement on his goods or upon his label cannot maintain an action against an imitator.[8]

Plaintiff must be free from charge of misrepresentation.

Manufacturers and vendors of patent medicines have often come to grief on this rock. A false statement as to the purity of an article,[9] or of the ingredients of which it is composed,[1] or of its origin or the place of manufacture,[2] disentitles a complainant to relief. The same is true of false statements as to the person by whom the article is made.[3]

False statements by personage grieved.

Coming now to the question as to what constitutes unfair competition, we are brought to consider the element of fraudulent intent. It may be observed at the outset that the element of fraud in wrongs of unfair competition occupies a position very similar to that of malice in such torts as slander

Element of fraudulent intention.

[8] Pidding *v.* How, 8 Sim. 477; Holzapfel's Compositions Co. *v.* Rahtjen's American Composition Co., 183 U. S. 1; Manhattan Medicine Co. *v.* Wood, 108 U. S. 218; Chattanooga Medicine Co. *v.* Thedford, 58 Fed. Rep. 347; Palmer *v.* Harris, 60 Pa. St. 156.

[9] Krauss *v.* Jos. R. Peeble's Sons Co., 58 Fed. Rep. 585.

[1] Clotworthy *v.* Schepp, 42 Fed. Rep. 62.

[2] Joseph *v.* Macowsky, 96 Cal. 518; Coleman, etc., Co. *v.* Dannenberg Co., 103 Ga. 784; Kenny *v.* Gillet, 70 Md. 574; Connell *v.* Reed, 128 Mass. 477.

[3] Manhattan Medicine Co. *v.* Wood, 108 U. S. 218.

The principle now under consideration is possibly applicable in cases where question is made of the right to use a trade name. Thus individuals who without entering into articles of incorporation assume to do business under a name which necessarily imports that the business is incorporated cannot, it seems, obtain an injunction against one who adopts a similar name. McNair *v.* Cleave, 10 Phila. (Pa.) 155, 31 Leg. Int. (Pa.) 212.

But it has been held that such a name as "Standard Distilling Company," without more, does not necessarily import that the business is incorporated. Block *v.* Standard Distilling, etc., Co., 95 Fed. Rep. 978.

of title and slander of goods. Fraud and malice appear indeed to be only different names for the same mental element viewed from different points. Both are merely aggravated forms of intention to compass the harm which actually comes upon the person injured.

Recession of fraud as a constitutive element of liability.

The suggestion just made prepares the reader to anticipate that while fraudulent intent is originally at the genesis of liability in all forms of unfair competition, it is nevertheless an element which decreases in importance and more and more tends to vanish as legal evolution and legal analysis proceed. We may be sure that the courts would never at first have assumed to interfere with business competition at all, if cases had not been presented where the defendant was clearly striving to filch and dishonestly to acquire for himself the trade of the plaintiff. But having admitted that fraud in competition supplies a sufficient pretext for giving redress, it was inevitable that the courts should have difficulty in setting a limit to the jurisdiction thus acquired. Fraudulent intent is always more or less a matter of inference, and by imperceptible gradations we pass from actual fraud to fraud which is a necessary inference and to fraud which is imputed by law. Finally we are driven to accept the idea that there are other elements which may be accepted as the equivalent of fraud, and hence we conclude that fraud is not an element which is really at the basis of liability at all. Such is the inevitable course of legal development in all departments of tort where the mental quality of an act (negligence, malice, fraud) is admitted as a reason for extending liability.

Analogy in the fields of negligence and malice.

Let us now note how this thought is illustrated in the law of trade-marks and unfair competition. In the field of trademark the idea that a fraudulent intent on the part of the competitor is essential to liability has, as already stated, long been banished.[4] In the field of unfair competition the element of fraudulent intent still occupies a prominent place in legal theory as the ground and basis of liability. But the English courts have already fully accepted the correct doctrine that deception or likelihood of deception is the gist of an action

Deception or likelihood of deception gist of the wrong.

[4] Millington *v.* Fox (1838), 3 Myl. & C. 338.

Volume I

Fraudulent intent immaterial,

for unfair competition. Hence when it is once established that a competitor has used distinguishing marks or has made representations which are likely to deceive customers, the question whether his motive is fraudulent or innocent is not material. On this point the rule is exactly the same in unfair competition as in an infringement of trade-marks.[5]

Still, fraudulent intent, though it cannot be accepted as the basis of liability, is often of great evidentiary value. Thus in *Saxlehner v. Apollinaris Co.*,[6] Kekewich, J., said: "If . . . the defendants' goods on the face of them, and having regard to surrounding circumstances, are calculated to deceive, it seems to me that no evidence is required to prove the intention to deceive, nor ought time and money to be expended on any such evidence. The sound rule is that a man must be taken to have intended the reasonable and natural consequences of his acts, and no more is wanted. If, on the other hand, a mere comparison of the goods, having regard to surrounding circumstances, is not sufficient, then it is allowable to prove from other sources that what is or may be apparent innocence was really intended to deceive. There can be no better evidence of intention to deceive than that of the deceiver himself, and this evidence may be given with equal force by admissions, oral or in writing, or by inference from conduct. If the intent to deceive be once established, it is but a short step, though it is a step, and not an inevitable one, to the conclusion that the intention has been fulfilled and that the goods are calculated to deceive." Actual fraudulent intent is thus seen to furnish merely an *a fortiori* argument in favor of giving relief in situations where liability for deception exists apart from the fraud.[7]

except as bearing on the matter of deception.

It is inevitable that the courts should go further in giving relief in cases where an actual fraudulent intent appears than in cases where such intent is absent. This is well illustrated in a late and important English decision, *Reddaway v. Ban-*

[5] Cellular Clothing Co. *v.* Maxton, (1899) A. C. 326.

[6] (1897) 1 Ch. 900.

[7] See statement of Kay, L. J., in Powell *v.* Birmingham Vinegar Brewery Co. (1896), 2 Ch. 79.

ham,[8] a case which also shows that a complainant who has no standing whatever in court so far as trade-mark law is concerned may yet obtain relief against unfair competition. The plaintiff had for many years made and sold a certain belting which he called Camel Hair Belting. Camel hair was one of the ingredients of the belting material, and hence the term Camel Hair could not be treated as a technical trade-mark, being a descriptive epithet. In course of time, however, the term Camel Hair Belting acquired in the trade a secondary signification and came to mean the belting made by this particular manufacturer, the plaintiff. In this state of affairs the defendant began to make a belting of the yarn of camel hair and stamped it Camel Hair Belting. The jury found that the defendant adopted this epithet as the name of his belting to deceive purchasers and cause them to buy it as and for belting made by the plaintiff. In the Court of Appeal it was held that the term Camel Hair Belting was a substantially correct description of the goods which the defendant was selling and that he had an absolute right to call it by such name. The fact that the plaintiff had for years been selling belting made of similar material under the same name might cause confusion, it was admitted, but it could not make the defendant liable for making the representation, which was in accord with truth, that his belting was camel hair belting.[9]

The Camel Hair Belting case.

In the House of Lords the decision of the Court of Appeal was reversed on the ground that the expression Camel Hair Belting had acquired a secondary signification different from its primary meaning, and that it was used and understood in this sense by persons who had occasion to deal in belting. Among other things Lord Herschell said: I demur "to the view that the defendants in this case were telling the simple truth when they sold their belting as camel hair belting. I think the fallacy lies in overlooking the fact that a word may acquire in a trade a secondary signification differing from its primary one, and that if it is used to persons in the trade who will understand it, and be known and intended

Secondary signification of words not subject to trade-mark right.

[8] (1896) A. C. 199, reversing (1895) 1 Q. B. 286.
[9] Reddaway *v.* Banham (1895), 1 Q. B. 286.

to understand it in its secondary sense, it will none the less be a falsehood that in its primary sense it may be true. A man who uses language which will convey to persons reading or hearing it a particular idea which is false, and who knows and intends this to be the case, is surely not to be absolved from a charge of falsehood because in another sense which will not be conveyed, and is not intended to be conveyed, it is true. In the present case the jury have found, and in my opinion there was ample evidence to justify it, that the words 'camel hair' had in the trade acquired a secondary signification in connection with belting; that they did not convey to persons dealing in belting the idea that it was made of camel's hair, but that it was belting manufactured by the plaintiffs. They have found that the effect of using the words in the manner in which they were used by the defendants would be to lead purchasers to believe that they were obtaining goods manufactured by the plaintiffs, and thus both to deceive them and to injure the plaintiffs. On authority as well as on principle, I think the plaintiffs are on these facts entitled to relief." [1]

Ambiguous statement intended to deceive.

From other language of the same learned lord,[2] and from the opinion of Lord Macnaghten,[3] the conclusion is to be drawn that the decision in this case would have been different if the dishonest purpose of the defendant had not been shown.

American doctrine.

In America there are many judicial utterances to the effect that in cases of unfair competition fraudulent intent on the

[1] Reddaway *v.* Banham (1896), A. C. 212, 213.

[2] (1896) A. C. 214.

[3] (1896) A. C. 219, 220. "The whole gist of the action was that the defendants were endeavoring to palm off their goods as the goods of the plaintiffs by selling them under a designation which would enable purchasers from them in this country to deceive customers abroad. That is, as it seems to me, a charge of dishonesty, and I must say that I think the charge was established. It was proved by admissions wrung from Mr. Banham on cross-examination, and by the correspondence which was put in evidence. When a manufacturer's goods are a drug on the market so long as they bear his own name or proclaim their true origin, and yet are salable at once if marked with nothing but some common English words, and when that manufacturer holds himself out as ready and willing so to mark his goods, and does so mark them at the 'instigation,' as he says, of a purchaser, a Lancashire jury may perhaps be trusted to read the riddle."

Chapter XXIX

part of the competitor is essential to liability.[4] But such statements are generally found to be dicta. The effect of such a rule is, however, easily evaded by an appeal to the convenient subterfuge of presumed, constructive, or imputed fraud.[5] It has never been actually declared by the Supreme Court of the United States in a case where such declaration was necessary to a decision, that a complainant who shows actual deception of the public by a competitor must go further and show an actual intent to deceive. In this country as in England, one may feel assured, an actual deception of the public or sufficient tendency to deceive is all that is essential to liability; and where this is proved, the state of the wrongdoer's mind is irrelevant.[6]

Deception or tendency to deceive.

From what has been said it follows that the question whether there has been unfair competition in any particular case resolves itself into the question whether the alleged competitor has done acts whch have deceived or are calculated to deceive the public into buying his goods as those of another. This is a question of fact to be determined by the court or jury under all the facts proved.[7] Hence, as was once re-

Question for jury.

[4] See, for instance, the language of Fuller, C. J., in Elgin Nat. Watch Co. *v.* Illinois Watch Case Co., 179 U. S. 674: "Such circumstances must be made out as will show wrongful intent in fact, or justify that inference from the inevitable consequences of the act complained of."

In Gorham Mfg. Co. *v.* Emery-Bird-Thayer Dry-Goods Co. (C. C. A.), 104 Fed. Rep. 243, a case of unfair competition, Sanborn, J., said: "This suit is based on fraud. Its foundation is unfair, fraudulent competition, and the intent to deceive is an indispensable element." See also Daviess County Distilling Co. *v.* Martinoni, 117 Fed. Rep. 188; Lawrence Mfg. Co. *v.* Tennessee Mfg. Co., 138 U. S. 537.

[5] Lalance, etc., Mfg. Co. *v.* National Enameling, etc., Co., 109 Fed. Rep. 317.

[6] The converse of the proposition just stated has been declared to be law in a number of cases; that is to say, that the fraudulent intent on the part of an unfair competitor to filch another's trade furnishes no cause of action unless the devices which he uses are calculated to convey a false impression to the public mind and to deceive purchasers. Centaur Co. *v.* Marshall (C. C. A.), 97 Fed. Rep. 785; N. K. Fairbank Co. *v.* R. W. Bell Mfg. Co. (C. C. A.), 77 Fed. Rep. 869; Kann *v.* Diamond Steel Co. (C. C. A.), 89 Fed. Rep. 706. Moreover, the similarity of name, label, wrapper, or package must be sufficiently close to deceive purchasers of ordinary intelligence in the exercise of ordinary care. Stuart *v.* F. G. Stewart Co. (C. C. A.), 91 Fed. Rep. 243; Brown *v.* Seidel, 153 Pa. St. 60.

[7] Payton *v.* Snelling (1901), A. C. 310; Kroppf *v.* Furst, 94 Fed. Rep. 150; Fischer *v.* Blank, 138 N. Y. 245.

Volume I

marked by Lord Macnaghten, the facts of one case are little or no guide in the determination of another.[8]

Trade Names.

Right to use one's own name.

An instructive branch of the law concerning unfair competition is that which pertains to the use of trade names. Here we may begin with the proposition that a man has a right, amounting practically to an absolute privilege, to use his own name in connection with his own business.[9] If damage come to another by this it is *damnum absque injuria.* Hence if Thomas Turton & Sons are doing business in a certain line and a rival starts up in the same town under the name of John Turton & Sons, no legal wrong is done if the new firm is really composed of John Turton and his sons.[1] The probability that the public will be occasionally misled by the similarity of names is not sufficient to justify legal interference. "If all that a man does is to carry on the same business, and to state how he is carrying it on — that statement being the simple truth — and he does nothing more with regard to the respective names, he is doing no wrong. He is doing what he has an absolute right by the law of England to do, and you cannot restrain a man from doing that which he has an absolute right by the law of England to do."[2]

Form in which name to be used.

The name as used in connection with the new business must be true, and it must be given in full if a shorter form would cause confusion.[3]

Colorable name.

Where the name of the new business is false, colorable, or fictitious, its use will not be tolerated if this would result in a deception of the public and consequent diversion of trade.[4] The general principle is that the new proprietor or manufac-

[8] Reddaway *v.* Banham, (1896) A. C. 220.

[9] Meneely *v.* Meneely, 62 N. Y. 427; Bingham School *v.* Gray, 122 N. Car. 699; Duryea *v.* National Starch-Mfg. Co. (C. C. A.), 79 Fed. Rep. 651; Wm. Rogers Mfg. Co. *v.* Rogers, 84 Fed. Rep. 639; Rogers *v.* Rogers, 53 Conn. 121.

[1] Turton *v.* Turton, 42 Ch. D. 128. Compare Burgess *v.* Burgess, 3 De G. M. & G. 896; Rogers *v.* Rogers, 53 Conn. 121.

[2] Turton *v.* Turton, 42 Ch. D. 128, *per* Lord Esher, M. R.

[3] Saunders *v.* Sun L. Assur. Co. (1894), 1 Ch. 537; James *v.* James, L. R. 13 Eq. 421.

[4] Croft *v.* Day, 7 Beav. 84.

turer must not by any false representation lead the public to understand that his goods or his business is the same as that of the older firm; or that his business is a continuation of the older business.

Misrepresentation as to continuation of business.

One of the first and most instructive cases on this subject is *Churton v. Douglas* (1859).[5] It there appeared that upon the dissolution of a partnership which had been carried on under the style of John Douglas & Co., John Douglas assigned all his shares, rights, and interest in the business, including the good will thereof, to his late partners and others, who thereupon proceeded to carry on the business under a new style consisting of their own names with the addition of the words "late John Douglas & Co." The defendant, John Douglas, having associated others with himself, opened a new and rival business near by under the firm name John Douglas & Co. The evidence showed conduct and representations on the part of the defendant which were equivalent to a claim that the new business was identical with that conducted by the old firm of John Douglas & Co. A rather sweeping injunction was granted restraining the defendant from carrying on business in that neighborhood either alone or in partnership with others under the style of John Douglas & Co., and from holding out in any manner that he was carrying on the business in continuation or in succession to the business carried on by the old firm. If the defendant had set up the new business alone he could, of course, have used the term "John Douglas" without more.[6] But he could not in such event have added the words "& Co.," for that would have been false.

In restraining the defendant and others who were *bona fide* associated with him from doing any business at all under the name John Douglas & Co., the court went farther than the authorities warrant.[7] The really obnoxious element was the endeavor by words and conduct to represent to the world that the new business was a continuation of the old. The

[5] Johns. Ch. (Eng.) 174. [6] Johns. Ch. (Eng.) 191.

[7] Burgess *v.* Burgess, 3 De G. M. & G. 896; Meneely *v.* Meneely, 62 N. Y. 427.

Volume I

injunction should have been coextensive with such wrongful conduct and no broader.[8] In a later and somewhat similar case Fry, J., said: "The defendants [E. Fullwood & Co.] are entitled to carry on their business under the firm name which they have adopted, if they are so minded, and to carry it on where and as they like, provided that they do not represent themselves to be carrying on the business which has descended to the plaintiff [R. J. Fullwood & Co.]."[9]

Conditions imposed on use of name.

Though a court will not enjoin a man from using his own name altogether, it will, in a case where the fraudulent intent is manifest, impose rigorous conditions upon such use, requiring the fullest precautions against the deception of purchasers.[1]

[8] Fite *v.* Dorman (Tenn. 1900), 57 S. W. Rep. 129 (syllabus 7). The opinion in this case contains a very full review of all the authorities on several aspects of the law of trade names.

[9] Fullwood *v.* Fullwood, 9 Ch. D. 176. See to same effect, Meneely *v.* Meneely, 62 N. Y. 427.

[1] Royal Baking Powder Co. *v.* Royal (C. C. A.), 122 Fed. Rep. 337.

CHAPTER XXX

NEGLIGENT TRANSMISSION OF TELEGRAMS.

Place of the Tort in Legal Theory.

Chapter XXX

ACTIONS against telegraph companies for damage resulting from the failure to transmit telegrams with reasonable dispatch, or from errors in the transmission of the same, exhibit peculiarities which require treatment. It will be noted that in these cases there is to begin with a definite contract relation between two parties. The relation is analogous to that which results from the bailment of a chattel for carriage. But the legal situation is not by any means the same as in bailment; for a telegraphic message is not, in this connection at least, treated as a chattel. It is of no intrinsic value and cannot be the subject of embezzlement. The identical message is not to be carried, but its contents are to be communicated at a distance, after translation into telegraphic symbols, and then again into the original form of the message. The measure of damages for a failure to transmit and deliver it has no relation to any value of the message itself, except as such value may be disclosed by the message or agreed upon between the sender and the company.[1]

The telegraphic message.

The law concerning telegraphic messages resembles the law of bailment in this, that we here find the two distinct conceptions of liability coexisting and in a measure fusing with each other, namely, that conception in which liability is conceived as arising from breach of actual contract, and that in which liability is conceived as arising from the breach of a public duty, that is, out of pure tort. As the relation between the sender and the company is primarily one of contract, and inasmuch as in most cases where damages are sought against the company, the plaintiff is either the sender himself

Different conceptions of liability.

Contract conception.

[1] See Primrose *v.* Western Union Tel. Co., 154 U. S. 14, 15.

Volume I

or is in some sort of privity with him, and thus in privity with the contract, it naturally follows that the liability of the company is most usually conceived and treated as arising from the breach of contract. But as in the science of geology a formation which is entirely wanting in one region may be revealed by an exposure in the sides of some distant mountain, so here do we find decisions which clearly reveal the tort conception of the liability and prove it to be an existing fact in this branch of legal science. The cases which supply the evidence on this point are those in which the sendee or addressee,[2] who is in no sort of privity with the contract of sending, is allowed to maintain an action against the company for damages consequent upon its negligence.

Tort conception of liability.

The tort conception of the liability of the telegraph company results from an extension of the doctrine of negligence into this field, and to superficial observation it might seem that this step is beset with no difficulties. In reality it represents a rather radical advance in legal theory and is worthy of close study. The phenomenon in fact is highly characteristic of modes of legal growth.

Difficulty of extending the theory of negligence to subject of telegrams.

The difficulty in extending to the telegraph cases the ordinary principles of the law of negligence as those principles manifest themselves in the trespass formations will be perceived when it is pointed out that the damage element here takes the form of mere pecuniary detriment (or mental anguish), and does not take the form of physical hurt to the body or of damage to property. Nor is there any delivery of property as in bailments, on which the law can predicate a legal duty apart from the contract. The problem is, out of a simple contract relation unaccompanied by a delivery of property or by an intrusting of one's self to the care of another, to evolve a right of action broad enough to extend the one

[2] The term 'sendee' is here used, in conformity with a suggestion made by Morris Wolf in Liability of Telegraph Companies, 42 Am. Law Reg. N. S. 722, note, to indicate the person to whom a message is delivered by the company, whether late or inaccurately; while the term 'addressee' is used of a person to whom a telegram is addressed, but who, owing to some default of the company, fails to receive it altogether.

Chapter XXX

not actually in privity with the contract. The thing is not so easy as might seem; but that it is an accomplished fact, at least in American legal jurisprudence, will fully appear.

Action of Sendee and Addressee.

Sender acting as agent of sendee.

As legal evolution, like other kinds of growth, is always along the line of least resistance, it is but natural that the courts should begin with the contract conception of liability, which represents a perfectly normal application of principle, and proceed by pushing it to its utmost limits. Attacking from this point of view the problem of the right of a sendee or addressee to recover for damage caused by the failure of the telegraph company to transmit a message seasonably and accurately to him, we observe that such person may well recover where it appears that the sender of the telegram was in fact acting as his agent.[3]

Here the sendee or addressee is, by reason of the relation of agency, brought into privity with the contract. The only difficulty encountered in this situation is the fact that usually the telegraph company is not apprised of the relation of agency, and it has sometimes been supposed that to allow the sendee or addressee to recover in such case would violate that principle of agency which disables a principal from suing on a contract when the fact of agency was not disclosed.[4] But this trouble has somehow been surmounted.[5]

Sendee ratifies by paying for the message.

It is equally apparent that little difficulty is presented in cases where the telegraph company accepts a message to be transmitted for a consideration to be paid by the receiver of the message. Here the company undertakes to transmit it subject to the right of the sendee to ratify, and if the latter chooses to do so by accepting the message and paying for it the company becomes liable to him on the contract. Actual agency also sufficiently appears where the sender uses the

[3] Milliken *v.* Western Union Tel. Co., 110 N. Y. 403; Western Union Tel. Co. *v.* Millsap, 135 Ala. 415; Clement *v.* Western Union Tel. Co. (1884), 137 Mass. 463.

[4] See Western Union Tel. Co. *v.* Allgood, 125 Ala. 712.

[5] Manker *v.* Western Union Tel. Co. (1902), 137 Ala. 292, overruling the earlier case.

Volume I

telegraph at the request or suggestion of the sendee.[6] But the cases in which any sort of agency between the parties to the message appears are comparatively few.

English doctrine.

Coming now to the situations where the sendee or addressee, as plaintiff, is unable to show any sort of privity with the contract, we note that in England it has been held by the Court of Appeal that such person can maintain no action at all. Under the rule there prevailing he can have no right under the contract, and a right of action in tort for negligence is not recognized.[7]

American view.

In America the courts have generally sustained the right of action of the sendee, not in privity with the contract, upon the principle, here commonly recognized, that a stranger to the consideration may sue upon a promise made for his benefit.[8]

Difficulties of this theory.

This theory is not devoid of plausibility, but it is of course not available in those jurisdictions where the right of a third person to sue upon a promise with which he is not in legal privity is denied. Besides, the application of the doctrine is beset with difficulties. In the present state of legal development the question as to when a person to whom performance is due is entitled to sue the promisor is not clearly settled even in those jurisdictions which permit it. To

[6] Coit *v.* Western Union Tel. Co. (1900), 130 Cal. 657. See also Durkee *v.* Vermont Cent. R. Co., 29 Vt. 127.

[7] Playford *v.* United Kingdom Electric Tel. Co. (1869), L. R. 4 Q. B. 707. Also it has been held in England that when a telegram is delivered to the wrong person and acted upon by him to his damage, he has no cause of action. Dickson *v.* Reuters Tel. Co. (1877), 2 C. P. D. 62.

These cases embody what may be called the first impression or first thought of the English judges. The circumstance that the telegraph business has in that country been put into government hands has prevented the question of the liability of the company to the sendee from arising with any frequency; though the matter is still important as regards foreign telegrams. It has been suggested by more than one writer that if the question should finally be brought into the House of Lords, a result might there be reached different from that indicated above and more in conformity with the conclusions of the American courts.

[8] Whitehill *v.* Western Union Tel. Co., 136 Fed. Rep. 499; Manier *v.* Western Union Tel. Co., 94 Tenn. 448.

saddle this trouble upon the right of action of the sendee is highly undesirable.[9]

The obligation to use care.

Clearly the only satisfactory solution of the problem in all its aspects is to be found in that view which puts the right of action of the sendee on the ground of negligence viewed as a breach of pure legal duty. But, it will be asked, whence does the duty arise? To this it may be replied that, even leaving out of consideration certain statutory enactments which in a few states have imposed such a duty, the common law itself imposes a duty on the telegraph company to use due care to prevent the person to whom it undertakes to deliver a message, or to whom it does in fact deliver a message, from being damaged by its negligence in transmitting the same.

Foresight of harm.

The only condition necessary to raise the common-law duty is that there should be something in the nature of the undertaking or in the particular situation to warn the company that damage may reasonably and naturally follow from

[9] It is held, for instance, that the sendee or addressee cannot maintain an action unless the telegram shows on its face that it was intended for his benefit. The late case of Frazier *v.* Western Union Tel. Co., 45 Oregon 414, affords an illustration of this. It appeared that a telegram relating to an important deal in real estate was negligently delayed for several days in the hands of the telegraph company, as a result of which the plaintiff, the real estate broker to whom the message was directed, lost a sale of the property and consequently was damaged to the extent of his prospective commission. The message in question contained the words, "See Shepard. Take his last offer." It was held that the telegraph company was not liable, for the reason that the wording of the telegram was not such as to show on its face that the addressee of the telegram was a person who was intended to be benefited. See to same effect, Western Union Tel. Co. *v.* Wood (C. C. A.), 57 Fed. Rep. 471; Butner *v.* Western Union Tel. Co., 2 Okla. 234.

It is all right for the courts to hold, in conformity with a principle hereafter to be stated, that the company must be affected with sufficient notice of the nature of the transaction to which the message relates to enable it to foresee damage as a reasonable consequence of its negligence, and in the light of this principle the actual results in the cases just cited may, or may not, be justified. But to say that the sendee's right of action must be worked out exclusively under the contract, and that the company must be affected with notice that the contract was intended for his benefit, is to adopt an unnecessary as well as capricious test of liability.

Volume I

Extension of the theory of negligence.

any negligence on its part. There must, in other words, be reasonable foresight of harm; and if this element is present, negligence resulting in damage gives a right of action. This principle was, to be sure, originally worked out, as we have seen, in the trespass formations; but it commends itself to reason in telegraph cases, and no sufficient ground can be shown why it should not be here applied.

Language of Massachusetts court.

Accordingly we note the following language of Bigelow, C. J., in a case before the Massachusetts court, where a sendee, not in privity with the contract, had sued for damages consequent upon an error of transmission: "In the ordinary employments and occupations of life men are bound to the use of due and reasonable care and are liable for the consequences of carelessness or negligence in the conduct of their business to those sustaining loss or damage thereby." [1] Here we see the trespass generalization extended into a new field. The circumstance that the step was unconsciously taken, and without mental advertence on the part of the court to the fact that it really was an extension of a trespass doctrine into an entirely different field, commends it as a rational and natural step rather than otherwise.

Telegraph company plies public calling.

A factor which should not be overlooked in considering the matter of a general duty on the part of the company to take care in transmitting messages is found in the status of telegraph companies and the nature of their business. Upon this point an American court has trenchantly said: "[The telegraph] is a system of appliances conducting the electric current or fluid, used for the purpose of transmitting intelligence, thought, or news from one place to another. Somewhat akin is it to a common carrier, in this: that they are both carriers, and must serve all alike; but the carrier transports persons or goods, while the telegraph conveys intelligence. The very object of the invention is to quickly convey information from one to another, upon which that other may act. It is a public use, and for that reason eminent domain may be exercised in its behalf, and is engaged

[1] Ellis *v.* American Tel. Co. (1866), 13 Allen (Mass.) 234.

in a business affecting public interests to such an extent that the state may regulate the charges of companies engaged in the business. It is not an insurer of the accuracy or of the delivery of messages intrusted to it, but it is so far a common carrier as to be bound to serve all people alike, and to exercise due care in the discharge of its public duties. Nor can it provide by contract for exemption from liability for the consequences of its own negligence. Enough has been stated to show that it owes a duty to all whom it attempts to serve, independent of the contractual one entered into when it receives its messages." [2]

Analogy to calling of carrier.

It must be admitted that the decisions which recognize the existence of a general duty on the part of the company towards the sendee, apart from contract or statute, are by no means as explicit or conclusive as might be wished. A number of the American courts are clear enough in giving recognition to the tort aspect of the matter.[3] But there is a general and very natural tendency to put the right of action of the sendee upon purely contractual grounds so far as may be done; and the broad legal duty is appealed to only in situations where the contract theory is clearly insufficient. In Alabama, where happily for purposes of scientific observation the common-law forms of action are still retained, the distinction between the tort and contract aspects of the company's liability to the sendee is clearly recognized.[4]

State of the authorities.

Fusion of the Tort and Contract Conception.

The undoubted existence of a delictual right of action on the part of a sendee or addressee not in privity with a contract, shows that the law pertaining to telegraphic messages has a tort aspect throughout. That is to say, even in cases where liability can be and is supported on grounds

[2] Deemer, J., in Mentzer *v.* Western Union Tel. Co. (1895), 93 Iowa 757.

[3] Webbe *v.* Western Union Tel. Co., 169 Ill. 610; Western Union Tel. Co. *v.* McKibben, 114 Ind. 511; Mentzer *v.* Western Union Tel. Co., 93 Iowa 752; Tobin *v.* Western Union Tel. Co., 146 Pa. St. 375. See also Coit *v.* Western Union Tel. Co., 130 Cal. 657.

[4] Western Union Tel. Co. *v.* Waters, 139 Ala. 652.

Volume I

of contract, the tort aspect of liability is at most only latent, not altogether absent. That the factor should often enter into and more or less qualify liability is but natural. In fact the law pertaining to telegrams, in so far as it develops along right lines, must be a product of the reconciliation if not of the fusion of the two conceptions of liability.

Two aspects of liability.

Though it has proved to be a precocious plant, this branch of the law is still young and the courts have by no means reached the root of it. We cannot but believe that, as the courts exhaust themselves in the limitations and perplexities of the contract conception, they will turn more and more to the tort theory; or rather, as they push the contract conception onward they will discover the broader truth. For it cannot be doubted that the tort conception of liability is in a sense the true goal of legal theory wherever the two aspects of liability are found to coexist.

Fusion of the two conceptions.

What has been said prepares us to find that in the practical working out of the law of telegrams, conflict has often arisen between the courts of different jurisdictions, and not infrequently there is actual confusion in the decisions of particular courts. The tort conception often plays no little part in determining the extent of liability in the contract field, and on the other hand, the contract view will often be found to prevail in cases which sound purely in tort. In other words, a right of action which is clearly of delictual origin is by attraction made to conform to contract principles, and *vice versa*.

Illustration.

A good illustration of this war between the respective conceptions of liability is found in decisions concerning the effect of the provisions of the contract upon the liability of the company to a sendee not in privity with the contract. Under the tort or negligence theory, the provisions of the contract, as entered into by the sender and the company, would appear to have no binding effect upon such person;[5] whereas, under the theory which works out the sendee's rights under the

[5] Tobin *v.* Western Union Tel. Co. (1892), 146 Pa. St. 375.

contract of sending, its terms, so far as reasonable, are fully binding on him.[6]

Effect of contract provisions as regards rights of sendee.

An attempt at the reconciliation — or possibly it is only a confusion — of these two ideas is apparent in the decisions of those courts which hold that the sendee is not bound by the terms of the contract unless he has notice or knowledge of them and assents thereto.[7] But this is illogical. If the rights of the sendee are derived exclusively from the contract, he should be held bound by its terms whatever they be; while, on the other hand, if the right of action is conceived to be in tort, the terms of the contract are not binding upon him in a contractual sense. But it may be said, even in those cases where liability is conceived in tort, that the measure of the company's legal duty is to be found partly in its own reasonable rules and regulations. Telegraphy is a new agency and the company, though it is a public servant, has the right within reasonable limits to determine the terms and conditions upon which it will undertake responsible service. In a word, the liability of the company to the sendee, though here founded on tort, is by attraction made to conform to contract principles. This seems to be the true diagnosis of the decisions which give effect to the contract provisions as against a sendee who is not really in privity with the contract.

The Damages.

Damages in contract aspect of liability.

Coming now to the matter of the extent of the company's liability, it is in the first place to be premised that where the cause of action arises out of a breach of contract, the plaintiff is *ipso facto* entitled to recover something upon merely proving a breach of the contract. The recovery upon such proof without more is of course limited to the consideration paid, viz., the price of the telegram. This amount is

[6] Russell *v.* Western Union Tel. Co., 57 Kan. 230; Stamey *v.* Western Union Tel. Co., 92 Ga. 613; Manier *v.* Western Union Tel. Co., 94 Tenn. 442.

[7] Webbe *v.* Western Union Tel. Co., 169 Ill. 610, reversing 64 Ill. App. 331. See Western Union Tel. Co. *v.* Longwill, 5 N. Mex. 308.

Volume I

Special damage.

usually small and is treated as nominal. The great controversy in actions *ex contractu* against telegraph companies is on the question of the right to recover what is known in contract law as special damages.

Damages in tort aspect.

On the other hand, where the action is conceived *ex delicto,* the plaintiff is not entitled to recover even so much as nominal damages upon merely proving negligence on the part of the company. In actions of negligence damage is of the very gist and essence of the plaintiff's cause. Inasmuch as actions are framed *ex delicto* only where suit is brought by sendees who are not in privity with the consideration, it follows that the price paid for the telegram is not an element of recoverable damage in actions of tort against telegraph companies, for such price is not paid by the plaintiff. The consequence is that in tort the plaintiff must prove substantial damages or he recovers nothing.

Consequential damage.

Furthermore, it appears that the damage which is recoverable in tort must always be of the kind which is known as consequential damage. Telegrams never do harm directly. They cannot hit a man or smash his vehicle, like the carelessly driven carriage or locomotive. If damage comes from negligence in the transmission of telegrams it must come by reason of the fact that the same party is put in a worse position. The great controversy in actions *ex delicto* against telegraph companies must therefore always be over the right to recover consequential damage.

The problem of liability in telegraph cases is thus seen to resolve itself for the most part into a question of the right to recover special or consequential damage. It will be noted that the 'special damages' of the contract aspect of the question, and the 'consequential damages' of the tort aspect of the matter, mean substantially the same thing; or rather, by a sort of attraction, consequential damage is here subjected to the same limitations in respect to recoverability as special damage.

On the question as to when and under what condition 'special' damages can be recovered for the breach of a

Chapter XXX

contract, the case of *Hadley v. Baxendale* (1854)[8] supplies the leading authority. It was decided by a very able bench after considerable deliberation, and though the case had nothing to do with a telegram, the rule there laid down is everywhere held to be applicable in telegraph cases. The plaintiffs in that case were proprietors of a mill in Gloucester, which was propelled by steam, and which was engaged in grinding and supplying meal and flour to customers. The shaft of the engine got broken, and it became necessary that the broken shaft be sent to an engineer or foundry man at Greenwich, to serve as a model for casting or manufacturing another that would fit into the machinery. The broken shaft could be delivered at Greenwich on the second day after its receipt by the carrier. It was delivered to the defendants, who were common carriers engaged in that business between these points, and who had told plaintiffs it would be delivered at Greenwich on the second day after its delivery to them, if delivered at a given hour. The carriers were informed that the mill was stopped, but were not informed of the special purpose for which the broken shaft was desired to be forwarded. They were not told the mill would remain idle until the new shaft would be returned, or that the new shaft could not be manufactured at Greenwich until the broken one arrived to serve as a model. There was delay beyond the two days in delivering the broken shaft at Greenwich, and a corresponding delay in starting the mill. No explanation of the delay was offered by the carriers. The suit was brought to recover damages for the lost profits of the mill, caused by the delay in delivering the broken shaft. It was held that the plaintiff could not recover.

The leading case.

Anticipated profits not recovered.

From the language[9] of Baron Alderson, who delivered

[8] 9 Exch. 341.

[9] Said the learned baron here: "Where two parties have made a contract which one of them has broken, the damages which the other party ought to receive in respect of such breach of contract should be such as may fairly and reasonably be considered either arising naturally, i. e., according to the usual course of things, from such breach of contract itself, or such as may reasonably be supposed to have been in the contemplation of both parties, at the time they made the contract, as the probable result of the breach of it. Now, if the special circumstances

Volume I

the judgment of the Court of Exchequer, the following conclusions may be drawn: Recoverable damages are in all events limited to such as may reasonably be foreseen in the light of facts known to the contracting parties. But within these limits there are two sorts of damage: 1, ordinary, natural, and in a sense necessary damages; and 2, special damage.

Ordinary damage.

Ordinary damage is found in all breaches of contract where there are no special circumstances to distinguish the case specially from other contracts. The consideration paid for an unperformed promise is an instance of this sort of damage. In all such cases the damages recoverable are such as naturally and generally would result from such a breach, "according to the usual course of things." In cases involving only ordinary damage no discussion is ever indulged as to whether that damage was contemplated or not. This is conclusively presumed from the immediateness and inevitableness of the damage, and the recovery of such damage follows as a necessary legal consequence of the breach. Ordinary damage is assumed as a matter of law to be within the contemplation of the parties.

Presumed to have been contemplated.

Illustration.

What may be deemed ordinary legal damage is well illustrated in *Borradaile v. Brunton* (1818).[1] An action was brought for breach of warranty of a cable chain. It appeared that while the plaintiff's ship was riding at anchor at the mouth of the Ganges river in a dangerous position between two reefs, one of the links in the cable chain was found to have separated. The pilot, being unable to get in that part of the cable in which was the broken link, deemed

under which the contract was actually made were communicated by the plaintiffs to the defendants, and thus known to both parties, the damages resulting from the breach of such a contract, which they would reasonably contemplate, would be the amount of injury which would ordinarily follow from a breach of contract under these special circumstances so known and communicated. But, on the other hand, if these special circumstances were wholly unknown to the party breaking the contract, he, at the most, could only be supposed to have had in his contemplation the amount of injury which would arise generally, and in the great multitude of cases not affected by any special circumstances, from such a breach of contract." 9 Exch. 353, 354.

[1] 8 Taunt. 535, 4 E. C. L. 202.

it necessary for the preservation of the ship and crew to slip the cable and run to sea, which he accordingly did, thereby losing the anchor as well as the cable. The value of both anchor and cable was recovered as ordinary damage.[2]

Special damage.

Special damage, on the other hand, is such as follows less directly from the breach than ordinary damage. It is only found in cases where some external condition, apart from the actual terms of the contract, exists or intervenes, as it were, to give a turn to affairs and to increase damage in a way that the promisor, without actual notice of that external condition, could not reasonably be expected to foresee. Concerning this sort of damage, *Hadley v. Baxendale* (1854)[3] lays down the definite and just rule that before such damage can be recovered the plaintiff must show that the particular condition which made the damage a possible and likely consequence of the breach was known to the defendant at the time the contract was made.

Liability dependent on notice.

The following cases furnish good illustrations of special damage being made recoverable by specific knowledge on the part of the promisor of the condition which makes such special damage a natural and foreseeable consequence of his delinquency:

Illustrations.

1. *Smeed v. Foord* (1859):[4] The defendant contracted to deliver to plaintiff, a farmer, a threshing machine within three weeks. It was plaintiff's practice, known to defendant, to thresh wheat in the field, and send it thence direct to market. At the end of the three weeks, plaintiff's wheat was ready, in the field, for threshing; and, on plaintiff's remonstrating at the delay in the delivery of the machine, defendant several times assured him it should be sent forthwith. The plaintiff, having tried unsuccessfully to hire another machine, was obliged to carry home and stack the wheat, which, while so stacked, was damaged by rain. The machine was afterwards delivered to plaintiff, who paid defendant the contract price.

[2] Compare Brown *v.* Edgington, 2 M. & G. 279, 40 E. C. L. 371, where a rope was brought for a crane used in hoisting and letting down wine casks. The defendant supplied the rope, knowing the use to which it was to be put and warranting the same to be fit for that purpose. The rope broke and a pipe of wine was thereby lost. It was held that the value of the wine as well as the price of the rope could be recovered as ordinary actual damage.

[3] 9 Exch. 341.

[4] 1 El. & El. 602, 102 E. C. L. 602.

Volume I

The wheat was then threshed; and it was found necessary, owing to the deterioration by the rain, to kiln-dry it. When dried and sent to market, it sold for a less price than it would have fetched had it been threshed at the time fixed by the contract for the delivery of the machine and then sold, the market price of wheat having meanwhile fallen. It was held that the expense of the stacking of the wheat and the loss arising from its deterioration in the rain, as well as the expense of drying it in the kiln could be recovered; for such damage could, in the light of the defendant's knowledge of existing conditions, be foreseen by him as a natural consequence of his breach.

2. *Passinger v. Thorburn* (1866):[5] The plaintiff, a gardener, purchased certain seed of the defendant. The latter warranted the seed to be Bristol cabbage seed and that they would produce Bristol cabbage. The defendant knew the purpose for which the seeds were to be used. The seed turned out to be spurious and the plaintiff lost his crop. It was held that he could recover the difference in net value of an ordinary crop of Bristol cabbage in that year and the net value of the crop actually raised.

3. *Chisholm, etc., Mfg. Co. v. U. S. Canopy Co.* (1903):[6] A contracted to supply to B certain brackets to be used by B during the mosquito season in the manufacture of mosquito canopy frames. It was known to A that such brackets could not be bought in the open market and that they could not be manufactured by any one else in time for the mosquito season, if he should fail to supply them as he had contracted to do. He also knew that B was taking orders for the sale of canopy frames upon the faith of his own proper performance of the contract. A manufactured defective brackets. As a consequence B was unable to fill the orders which he had taken and thereby lost the profits on those orders. It was held that B could recover this loss of A.

Remote damage not recoverable as special damage.

In this connection we find a distinction which accounts for certain conflict of opinion in decisions in regard to special damage. It is this: If the damage which the plaintiff seeks to recover as special damage, appears to be so far speculative and contingent as to be legally remote, no amount of notice as to the special conditions which make that damage possible will render the defendant liable therefor. To bring damage which would ordinarily be treated as remote within the category of recoverable special damage it is necessary that the condition should actually be contracted about. It must be so far in the mind and contemplation of the parties

[5] 34 N. Y. 634. [6] 111 Tenn. 202.

as virtually to be a term of the contract. Thus, in *Smeed v. Foord* it was held that the loss arising from the fall in the market for wheat could not be recovered. This was an element of damage which was so far speculative and remote as not to be recoverable without being made a term of the contract.

Distinction between special and remote damage not clear.

Naturally the line of demarcation between special damage such as becomes recoverable by reason of special notice of existing conditions, and remote damage which is not recoverable in the absence of express stipulation, is fine and affords a margin for differences of legal opinion. The Tennessee court, for instance, treats as remote and speculative such damage as the New York court, in *Passinger v. Thorburn* (1866),[7] held to be recoverable as special damage:

Illustrations of speculative damage.

1. *Hurley v. Buchi* (1882):[8] The plaintiff purchased seed potatoes from the defendant which were represented to be 'Early Rose' potatoes, when in fact they were of another and inferior variety. The plaintiff was a gardener and wanted the potatoes for early market, as the defendant knew. It was held that the plaintiff could only recover the difference in value of the potatoes which were bought and their value if they had been of the kind which they were represented to be. The difference in value of the crops was held to be no proper element of recovery, being remote and speculative.

2. *Horne v. Midland R. Co.* (1873)[9] is a case where the damage which was sought to be recovered as special damage was really remote, and some of the judges rightly placed the disallowance of the damage on the ground that to make such damage recoverable, it must so far have been within the contemplation of the parties as to form at least an implied term of the contract. But others proceeded on the idea that the notice given to the defendant was not sufficiently full and definite. The result was the same in either view. The alleged damage was clearly remote, like the loss caused by the decline of the market in *Smeed v. Foord.* The facts in the case of *Horne v. Midland R. Co.* were these: The plaintiffs, shoe manufacturers at K, were under contract to supply by a certain day shoes to a firm in London for the French government. They delivered the shoes to a carrier in sufficient time for the goods to reach London at the time stipulated in the contract and informed the railroad agent that the shoes would be thrown back upon their hands if they did not

[7] 34 N. Y. 634.

[8] 10 Lea (Tenn.) 346.

[9] L. R. 8 C. P. 131 (in Exchequer Chamber), L. R. 7 C. P. 583 (in Common Pleas).

Volume I

reach the destination in time. The defendants negligently failed to forward the goods in due season. The sale was therefore lost, and the market having fallen, the plaintiffs had to sell at a loss.

As we have already shown, all substantial damages in telegraph cases fall under the head of special or consequential damage. Hence, applying the principle above stated concerning the recovery of special damages to the telegraph cases, we find this to be true: that before the plaintiff can recover substantial damages he must in every case show that the telegraph company upon undertaking to transmit the telegram was so far apprised of the nature of the transaction about which the telegram was sent, that it might reasonably be said to foresee and contemplate the damage which is sought to be recovered, as a natural consequence of negligence on its part.[1]

Telegraph company must have notice.

The information which is necessary to charge the company is most often found in the wording of the telegram itself. But it is enough if it be communicated by other

How communicated.

[1] Postal Tel. Cable Co. *v.* Barwise, 11 Colo. App. 328; Postal Tel. Cable Co. *v.* Lathrop, 131 Ill. 575; Western Union Tel. Co. *v.* Valentine, 18 Ill. App. 57; Evans *v.* Western Union Tel. Co., 102 Iowa 210; Smith *v.* Western Union Tel. Co., 83 Ky. 104; Squire *v.* Western Union Tel. Co., 98 Mass. 232; Beaupré *v.* Pacific, etc., Tel. Co., 21 Minn. 155; Melson *v.* Western Union Tel. Co., 72 Mo. App. 111; Mackay *v.* Western Union Tel. Co., 16 Nev. 222; Leonard *v.* New York, etc., Electro Magnetic Tel. Co., 41 N. Y. 544; Baldwin *v.* U. S. Telegraph Co., 45 N. Y. 744; McColl *v.* Western Union Tel. Co., 44 N. Y. Super. Ct. 487; Barnesville First Nat. Bank *v.* Western Union Tel. Co., 30 Ohio St. 555; Western Union Tel. Co. *v.* Edsall, 74 Tex. 329; Elliott *v.* Western Union Tel. Co., 75 Tex. 18; Western Union Tel. Co. *v.* J. A. Kemp Grocer Co. (Tex. Civ. App. 1894), 28 S. W. Rep. 905; Candee *v.* Western Union Tel. Co., 34 Wis. 471.

A mere request of the sender for the operator to 'rush' the message as important, or a statement that it pertains to stock, does not charge the company with knowledge of the nature of a cipher message, so as to make it liable for damage incident to the fluctuations of the market. There must be a more specific communication of the circumstances. Houston, etc., R. Co. *v.* Davidson, 15 Tex. Civ. App. 334; Candee *v.* Western Union Tel. Co., 34 Wis. 471.

But it is generally held to be sufficient in ordinary commercial telegrams that the company should be apprised of the fact that the telegram pertains to a commercial transaction in which damage may result from its own negligence. Postal Tel. Cable Co. *v.* Lathrop, 131 Ill. 575; Fererro *v.* Western Union Tel. Co., 9 App. Cas. (D. C.) 455; Western Union Tel. Co. *v.* Blanchard, 68 Ga. 299; Pepper *v.* Western Union Tel. Co., 87 Tenn. 554.

Chapter XXX

means. Extraneous information not derived from the message itself or even from the sender is sufficient.[2]

Company liable only for foreseeable damage.

Taken in a narrow and literal sense the proposition above stated would come to this, that substantial damages cannot be recovered of a telegraph company for negligence in transmitting a telegram unless the damage complained of is such as might reasonably be foreseen in the concrete form which it actually takes. But like most propositions which purport to lay down hard and fast rules, this is clearer in statement than in application. In an effort at greater precision the rule has been stated to be that the company is liable for such damage as both parties would have contemplated if at the time they entered into the contract they had bestowed proper attention upon the subject and had been fully informed of the facts.[3] It is not necessary, it has been said, that they should have contemplated the actual damages for which a recovery may be allowed.[4]

Qualifications.

Drift towards compound theory of liability.

Such expressions as these seem to exhibit an unconscious and perhaps inevitable drift towards that compound theory of liability prevailing in the field of negligence at large, in which foresight of harm furnishes the test of liability while natural consequence measures the extent of liability.[5] To discover the extent of this drift towards the tort view as embodied in the results of the decided cases, albeit in the decisions of the courts which insist upon the contract theory of lia-

[2] McPeek *v.* Western Union Tel. Co., 107 Iowa 356; Herron *v.* Western Union Tel. Co., 90 Iowa 129; Western Union Tel. Co. *v.* Williford (Tex. Civ. App. 1894), 27 S. W. Rep. 700.

[3] Earl, C. J., in Leonard *v.* New York, etc., Electro Magnetic Tel. Co., 41 N. Y. 567; Western Union Tel. Co. *v.* Reynolds, 77 Va. 186.

[4] Western Union Tel. Co. *v.* Church (Neb. 1902), 90 N. W. Rep. 882.

[5] In McPeek *v.* Western Union Tel. Co. (1899), 107 Iowa 356, we find the tort theory already prevailing, it being there laid down as law that in actions against a telegraph company for failure to promptly deliver a message damages may be recovered for all such injurious results as naturally flow therefrom by ordinary sequence without the interposition of any intervening cause, and are not limited to such as might reasonably have been within the contemplation of the parties. This was an action by a sendee in which, of course, resort to the tort theory of liability is more natural and more necessary than where the action is brought by the sender.

Volume I

bility, would lead us too far afield; but it is clear that if all the particular items of damage which have been recovered in telegraph cases are to be justified on the sole ground that they were within the reasonable contemplation of the parties, then the foresight which the law attributes to men is a very different thing from that foresight which is actually imbedded in the human faculties.

Cipher messages.

The most familiar illustration of the rule requiring that the company shall be affected with specific notice of the transaction about which the telegraph is sent is found in cases involving cipher messages. Here the company can get no information as to the nature of the transaction which the messages touches, from the message itself. Hence by the great weight of authority only nominal damages can ordinarily be recovered for negligence in the transmission of such messages. The rule has been compared — though the analogy seems to be more fanciful than real — to that principle which exempts the carrier from liability for goods where the owner conceals their nature or value.[6]

Nominal damages.

The rule stated above is applied whether the company's delinquency consists of an error in the wording of the cipher message,[7] or of an unreasonable delay or failure to send it altogether.[8]

Substantial damage for non-delivery of cipher message.

A few of the courts have allowed the recovery of substantial damages in cases where there is a total failure to send or an unreasonable delay in sending the cipher message, the idea apparently being that there is no relation of cause and effect between the fact that the message is in cipher and such failure or delay.[9]

[6] Candee *v.* Western Union Tel. Co., 34 Wis. 471.

[7] Primrose *v.* Western Union Tel. Co., 154 U. S. 1; Hart *v.* Western Union Tel. Co., 66 Cal. 579; Fererro *v.* Western Union Tel. Co., 9 App. Cas. (D. C.) 455.

[8] Sanders *v.* Stuart, 1 C. P. D. 326; Western Union Tel. Co. *v.* Wilson, 32 Fla. 527 (overruling Western Union Tel. Co. *v.* Hyer, 22 Fla. 637); U. S. Telegraph Co. *v.* Gildersleve, 29 Md. 232; Abeles *v.* Western Union Tel. Co., 37 Mo. App. 554; Cannon *v.* Western Union Tel. Co., 100 N. Car. 300; Fergusson *v.* Anglo-American Tel. Co., 178 Pa. St. 377; Candee *v.* Western Union Tel. Co., 34 Wis. 471.

[9] Daughtery *v.* American Union Tel. Co., 75 Ala. 168; Western Union Tel. Co. *v.* Way, 83 Ala. 542; Western Union Tel. Co. *v.*

Chapter XXX

Daughtery v. American Union Tel. Co. (1883)[1] is one of these decisions. It is instructive for more than one reason. It was decided by a very able court; it contains a wonderfully luminous exposition of *Hadley v. Baxendale* (1854);[2] and above all, it is pervaded by an error which apparently vitiates the result and which should therefore be exposed. An action of assumpsit was brought by the sender of a telegram to recover damages consequent upon the non-delivery of his message. The message contained directions to the plaintiff's agent to sell three hundred bales of cotton, but it was in cipher and unintelligible to the telegraph operator. Nor was any information given to the latter by which the telegraph company would have been warned that pecuniary damage might ensue from a failure to send the message. A decline in the market soon came, and the plaintiff by reason of the nondelivery of his message was subjected to loss. The court held that this damage could be recovered.[3] *Hadley v. Baxendale* was rightly expounded and the proper distinction drawn between that ordinary, natural, and necessary damage which is always recoverable as a matter of law upon breach of a contract, and that special damage which can only be recovered when the equitable condition as to knowledge of the transaction is fulfilled. Applying these principles the court then made the mistake of treating the damage which was shown in that case as ordinary damage. It was a clear case of special damage, as the substantial recovery sought in telegraph cases always is. The effect of the decision was

Criticism of minority doctrine.

Fatman, 73 Ga. 285. Western Union Tel. Co. *v.* Hyer, 22 Fla. 637; Western Union Tel. Co. *v.* Reynolds, 77 Va. 173. See also Western Union Tel. Co. *v.* Eubanks, 100 Ky. 604.

This seems to follow the analogy of those decisions which hold that a provision in the contract that the company shall not be liable beyond the cost of the message, unless the same is repeated, has reference only to cases where there is an error in the message, not to cases where the company delays or fails to deliver the message altogether. Western Union Tel. Co. *v.* Broesche, 72 Tex. 654; Gulf, etc., R. Co. *v.* Wilson, 69 Tex. 739.

[1] 75 Ala. 168.

[2] 9 Exch. 341.

[3] In Western Union Tel. Co. *v.* Way, 83 Ala. 542, Somerville, J., dissented from the conclusion reached by the court (of which he himself had been a member) in Daughtery *v.* American Union Tel. Co., 75 Ala. 168.

Volume I

therefore to impeach the very case which was relied upon to support the judgment.

The true import of decisions allowing the recovery of substantial damages for delays in cipher messages where no notice is given of the nature of the transaction is apparently found in the fact that we here perceive that unconscious drift towards the tort conception of the company's liability which has been noted in other connections.

Remote damage.

Finally, concerning the damage which is recoverable in telegraph cases, it is to be added that if the damage claimed is so far separated from the act of negligence charged against the defendant, as to be considered remote in law, it cannot of course be recovered. What damage has been considered to be thus remote may be gathered from the cases cited below.[4] If the damage is found not to be remote in point of legal causation, in other words if it is proximate in the sense usually understood in the law of tort, then the further question, already discussed, as to whether the damage was such as could be concretely foreseen, must be considered. And it is not until this second question has been answered in the affirmative that the plaintiff's right to recover is established.

When telegraph company liable on theory of misrepresentation.

Before dismissing this subject of telegrams, a few words must be said about the liability of the company in the light of the law of misrepresentation and deceit. A telegraph company upon delivering a telegram must in reason be taken thereby to represent to the recipient that it received that message at the point whence it purports to come and that the message was directed to him. If it turns out that the company received a different message, or that the message in question was originally directed to another person, no good reason can be suggested why the receiver who is misled by

[4] Bodkin *v.* Western Union Tel. Co., 31 Fed. Rep. 134; Stansell *v.* Western Union Tel. Co., 107 Fed. Rep. 668; Postal Tel. Cable Co. *v.* Barwise, 11 Colo. App. 328; Western Union Tel. Co. *v.* Watson, 94 Ga. 202; Western Union Tel Co. *v.* Simpson, 64 Kan. 309; Chapman *v.* Western Union Tel. Co., 90 Ky. 265; McAllen *v.* Western Union Tel. Co., 70 Tex. 243; Western Union Tel. Co. *v.* Smith, 76 Tex. 253; Fisher *v.* Western Union Tel. Co., 119 Wis. 146.

Chapter XXX

it to his damage may not recover. There is nothing in this that is contrary to the doctrine of *Derry v. Peek* (1889),[5] for a telegraph company which fails to transmit correctly has actual knowledge of the falsity of its delivery or is chargeable with that knowledge.[6] *May v. Western Union Tel. Co.* (1873)[7] affords an apt illustration of the application of the law of deceit to inaccurate or false telegraphic messages.

Inadequacy of this theory.

The inadequacy of the theory of misrepresentation appears in the fact that it cannot be applied in cases where the message is never delivered, nor where it is delivered only after an unreasonable lapse of time. The theory is doubtless objectionable from another point of view, in this, that in effect it makes the company an absolute insurer of the accuracy of the message. The law of misrepresentation, when one comes to push it to its logical and legitimate consequences, turns out to be a law of warranty, and the idea of absolute warranty is not suited to the situations presented by the telegraph cases.[8] Judicial opinion is undoubtedly crystallizing on the proposition that a telegraph company ought in no case to be held unless it is chargeable with some degree of fault.

This is well illustrated in *Western Union Tel. Co. v. Uvalde Bank* (1904).[9] It appeared that a person who was skilled in the operation of telegraphic apparatus, but who was not in the employment of the telegraph company, by

[5] 14 App. Cas. 337.

[6] The situation of the telegraph company which transmits a false message is to be discriminated from the situation involved in Derry *v.* Peek, on precisely the same ground that Lord Herschell, 14 App. Cas. 365, discriminated Polhill *v.* Walter, 3 B. & Ad. 114, 23 E. C. L. 38, namely, that the defendant makes a representation which it knows to be untrue and which is calculated from the mode in which it is made to induce another to act upon it.

[7] 112 Mass. 90. It was held in this case that in declaring in tort as upon a false representation the plaintiff need not allege an intent to deceive or that the representation was false to the knowledge of the defendant company.

[8] In Dickson *v.* Reuter's Tel. Co. (1877), 2 C. P. D. 62, Herschell, Q. C., for the plaintiff, strongly pressed the theory of deceit upon the court. But it was rejected, partly, it seems, on the erroneous idea that the guaranty of accuracy, if once recognized, would extend to all mankind. See Denman, J., at p. 68. But evidently it would extend only to the person to whom the message is rightly or wrongly delivered.

[9] 97 Tex. 219.

casual inquiry of an operator who was in the employment of the company, learned the secret call for Uvalde station. He then tapped the wire and sent a fraudulent message to a confederate at that place, purporting to come from a bank in another city and authorizing the confederate to draw upon the bank by which the telegram purported to be signed. This confederate then requested the plaintiff, the Uvalde National Bank, to cash the draft. The latter refused to do so until it should have a verification of the telegram. To this end it sent a telegram of inquiry to the other bank, which telegram was intercepted by the wire-tapper and another fraudulent telegram, purporting to come from the bank of which the inquiry was made, was sent. Upon receipt of this telegram the draft drawn by the confederate was cashed. In an action against the telegraph company brought by the losing bank it was held that the defendant could not be held to vouch absolutely for the authenticity of messages which came over its wires, but that it was liable if it failed to adopt reasonable precautions to prevent the tapping of its wires. In other words, liability was held to depend on the presence or absence of negligence.[1]

Liability dependent upon fault or negligence.

[1] In closing a word may be here added concerning still another theory of the liability of the telegraph company to the sendee, namely, the theory of misfeasance in agency. In one of the early cases involving the liability of the company to a sendee, it was suggested, by the Pennsylvania court, that perhaps the company ought to be considered as the common agent of both parties, and that at any rate the company was the agent of the sender. Being the agent of the sender, it was argued, the company would be liable to the sendee for any damage which resulted to the latter from a malfeasance in the performance of his agency. New York, etc., Printing Tel. Co. *v.* Dryburg (1860), 35 Pa. St. 303.

It is certainly true that in the making of contracts, the telegraph company is usually so far considered the agent of the sender that the sender is bound by the terms of the telegram as it reaches the sendee. Haubelt *v.* Rea, etc., Mill Co., 77 Mo. App. 672; Smith *v.* Easton, 54 Md. 138; Western Union Tel. Co. *v.* Shotter, 71 Ga. 760; Squire *v.* Western Union Tel. Co., 98 Mass. 232; Saveland *v.* Green, 40 Wis. 431. But in some jurisdictions a contrary rule prevails, the company being treated as an independent contractor. Shingleur *v.* Western Union Tel. Co., 72 Miss. 1030; Pepper *v.* Western Union Tel. Co., 87 Tenn. 554; Harrison *v.* Western Union Tel. Co. (Tex. 1885), 10 Am. & Eng. Corp. Cas. 600.

CHAPTER XXXI

ELEMENTS OF RECOVERABLE DAMAGE.

Chapter XXXI

THE telegraph cases bring us into contact with the controversy over the matter of damages for distress of mind or for mental anguish, as it is commonly called. To get at the bottom of the matter something must be said concerning the nature of damages in general.

Meaning of 'damage.'

The word 'damage' does not always bear the same significance. It is often used, like injury in its technical sense, to indicate the harm element on which liability in a given case is based. More frequently it means damage to property, just as injury in its popular acceptation means physical hurt to the body. In its plural form, 'damages,' the word has a very definite meaning and refers to the recoverable damage — that money charge into which the law commutes the element or elements of legal injury which are found in a particular case.

Types of harm.

Consideration of the subject of recoverable damage therefore involves the question, What harms constitute legal injury in such sense as to be commutable into damages? A glance over the field of tort shows that for most part these harms can be resolved into three main types, (1) injury to person, (2) injury to reputation, (3) pecuniary loss. Only in very recent years has the question been raised whether other forms of harm, like nervous shock and mental distress, can be a basis of liability. This question we are now to consider. And first in regard to nervous shock.

Nervous Shock.

As a matter of first impression it would seem sound to say that in order that physical hurt should be such as to support an action there must be some forceful impact or some agent, like poison, so applied as actually to work the injury

Volume I

Nervous shock without impact.

complained of directly and immediately. In conformity with this idea, *Victorian R. Com'rs v. Coultas* (1888)[1] was decided in the Privy Council. It there appeared that the plaintiffs, husband and wife, while out driving, came to a railway crossing and by the negligence of the person in charge of the gate were put in a position where they were in imminent danger of being killed by a passing train. They escaped, however, without being struck, but the train sped by so close that the wife was badly frightened. An action having been brought to recover damages resulting from nervous shock and mental injury, it was held that the defendants were not liable.[2] The decision was placed on the ground that the injury complained of was remote; but this is untenable. If the decision is to be sustained at all it must be upon the ground that in practice it would not be possible satisfactorily to administer a different rule,[3] and upon the ground that simple nervous shock and consequent injury to the mind, considered alone, do not as a matter of law supply a ground of action.

Injury held to be remote.

In *Dulieu v. White*[4] the Court of King's Bench had occasion to consider the question that was before the Privy Council in the Coultas case, and arrived at a different conclusion. The facts were these: The defendant's servant negligently managed a van drawn by two horses, and in consequence the team went into a shop or room in a public house where the plaintiff, a woman, was behind the bar. She was not struck, but sustained nervous shock and became seriously ill. One of the features of her case was a miscarriage brought about, as was alleged, by the shock so sustained. It was held that inasmuch as physical injury resulting from the fright had been caused, an action lay though there was no forceful impact. But this limitation was recognized, viz.: that where nervous shock incident to fright is the basis of a claim for damages it must appear that the shock arose from

Physical suffering engendered by nervous shock.

[1] 13 App. Cas. 222.

[2] To the same effect, see Haile *v.* Texas, etc., R. Co. (C. C. A.), 60 Fed. Rep. 557; Mitchell *v.* Rochester R. Co. (1896), 151 N. Y. 107; Ewing *v.* Pittsburgh, etc., R. Co. (1892), 147 Pa. St. 40.

[3] See Spade *v.* Lynn, etc., R. Co. (1897), 168 Mass. 285.

[4] (1901) 2 K. B. 669.

a fear of personal injury to one's self.[5] A woman who faints because she saw another person assaulted could have no cause of action.

It will be noted that in this case there was no actual battery or assault or other trespass such as would have given a right to recover nominal damages apart from consideration of the actual consequences to the plaintiff. If there had been such a trespass, the plaintiff could have recovered for the nervous shock without question, for it is well settled that where there is actual impact accompanied by physical injury however slight, the nervous shock is a proper element of damage. This is recognized even in jurisdictions where the doctrine of the Coultas case is accepted.[6] Bodily injury necessarily involves mental suffering. Being bound together the law refuses to separate one of these elements from the other and allows compensation for both.

Nervous shock associated with physical injury.

The telegraph cases direct attention to one situation where the negligent failure of the company to deliver a telegram with reasonable promptness is in certain jurisdictions considered the proximate cause of physical suffering. To illustrate: A person is suffering and needs the immediate attention of a surgeon or physician. A limb perchance has been broken or a woman is in confinement. A telegram asking a doctor to come at once is dispatched, but, owing to the negligence of the company, is not promptly received, whereby the physician is prevented from going and the patient's suffering is prolonged. It has been held that damages for the suffering so caused may be recovered.[7] The principle involved in these cases is not very different from that which under-

Suffering attributable to non-arrival of physician.

[5] Kennedy, J., at p. 675 (citing Smith *v.* Johnson, unreported). See Renner *v.* Canfield, 36 Minn. 90.

[6] Homans *v.* Boston El. R. Co. (1902), 180 Mass. 456; Cameron *v.* New England Telephone, etc., Co. (1902), 182 Mass. 310.

[7] Western Union Tel. Co. *v.* McCall, 9 Kan. App. 886, 58 Pac. Rep. 797; Western Union Tel. Co. *v.* Church (Neb. 1902), 90 N. W. Rep. 878; Brown *v.* Western Union Tel. Co. (1889), 6 Utah 219.

We refer to these cases here because of the fact that the negligence of the company is considered as the cause of actual physical suffering. But these authorities can hardly be supported apart from consideration of the question of bare mental distress which is discussed hereafter.

Volume I

lies *Dulieu v. White,* for in the latter case the nervous shock was treated as a species of physical hurt, while in these telegraph cases there is actual physical suffering attributable to the non-arrival of the physician, and hence to the negligence of the company.

Mental Distress.

Mental distress raises a somewhat more difficult question than physical suffering and nervous shock, for the term 'mental distress' has reference to effects which are purely metaphysical. But here again legal theory has proved equal to the emergency, and within limits not yet fully determined, it is settled that wherever there is, to begin with, an undoubted right of action apart from the mental suffering, such factor may be considered in estimating the damages, although that mental suffering is not associated with actual physical injury and though it does not amount to such a nervous shock as to involve injury to the human system. Thus, where a person is falsely imprisoned, account can be taken of humiliation and of the injury to his feeling in estimating the damages.[8] The same is true in malicious prosecution.[9] In an action for assault, also, the fright and mental suffering may be considered.[1]

Mental suffering as aggravative element of damage.

It is held that where a person is wrongfully ejected from a train he can recover for the injury to his feelings and sensibilities although he suffers no physical hurt.[2] In a case where a railway company was held liable in damages for the kissing of a woman passenger by the conductor, it was decided that the insult and humiliation to which the plaintiff

Illustrations.

[8] Stewart *v.* Maddox, 63 Ind. 51; Butler *v.* Stockdale (1902), 19 Pa. Super. Ct. 98.

[9] Fisher *v.* Hamilton, 49 Ind. 341.

[1] Kline *v.* Kline (1902), 158 Ind. 602.

[2] Head *v.* Georgia Pac. R. Co., 79 Ga. 358; Mabry *v.* City Electric R. Co., 116 Ga. 624; Shepard *v.* Chicago, etc., R. Co., 77 Iowa 58; Kansas City, etc., R. Co. *v.* Little, 66 Kan. 378.

In Sloane *v.* Southern California R. Co., 111 Cal. 668, there were paroxysms of the nervous system caused by the indignity and humiliation attendant upon the ejection which made a case of actual physical injury.

Chapter XXXI

was subjected might be taken into consideration by the jury.[3] It has been held that a parent who, by reason of the violation of his possession of a burial lot, has a right of action in trespass against one who removes the remains of his child, may recover for his injured feelings.[4] So it has been determined that where a dead body is mutilated, as by dissection, the person who has the right to the possession of it may maintain an action therefor, and where such person is the widow of the deceased she may recover for the distress occasioned to her by such mutilation.[5]

Parasitic damage.

The authorities which have just been considered bring us into contact with a factor which we may, for the sake of convenience, refer to as the parasitic element of damage. The idea which is meant to be brought out by the use of this expression is that in certain situations the law permits elements of harm to be considered in assessing the recoverable damage, which cannot be taken into account in determining the primary question of liability. It is only under this head that such factors as insult, disgrace, and anguish of feeling can get legal recognition at all. The idea is no mere modern innovation, but is familiar in all stages of legal growth.

Parasitic element in actions for seduction.

In cases of interference with the domestic establishment, we find a striking instance where the parasitic element completely overshadows the legal element of injury on which the action is in theory founded. Thus, in the action for the abduction or seduction of a daughter, interference with the relation of service is the injury which the law recognizes as the basis of liability; but this factor is completely overshadowed by the parasitic element of family disgrace and shame.[6]

In cases of the abduction or seduction of one's wife and in cases of criminal conversation with her, the action is

[3] Craker *v.* Chicago, etc., R. Co., 36 Wis. 657. Compare Savannah, etc., R. Co. *v.* Quo, 130 Ga. 125, where there was a criminal assault upon a woman passenger.

[4] Meagher *v.* Driscoll, 99 Mass. 281.

[5] Larson *v.* Chase, 47 Minn. 307. Concerning the Law of Burial, see the learned report of Ruggles, referree, in *In re* Petition of the Corporation of the Brick Presbyterian Church of New York City, 4 Bradf. (N. Y.) 503.

[6] Stevenson *v.* Belknap, 6 Iowa 103.

Volume I

not, in this day at least, considered as being founded upon loss of service. The law here treats the loss of consortium as the gist of the wrong. The phenomenon with which we are here confronted — and it is worthy of note — is that an element of damage which in one stage of legal evolution was clearly of a parasitic nature has so far come into ascendency as to be recognized as the basis of liability to the entire exclusion of the conception of service which so tenaciously holds its ground elsewhere.

Parasitic element of damage in field of contract.

It is not to be imagined that the phenomenon of parasitic damage is confined to tort law. True, it is perhaps not so familiar in the field of contract, but the idea is certainly found there. The harm which is done by the breach of a contract usually takes the form of temporary damage or pecuniary loss, just as it does in case of fraud. And in assessing the damage no account is ordinarily taken of any other element than the pecuniary loss. The disappointment of the promisee, for instance, cannot be considered. Contracts derive their vitality chiefly from the conception of pecuniary detriment to the promisee, a conception which takes the form of *quid pro quo* in debt and of consideration in assumpsit. To allow the promisee to recover for his disappointment in the breach of the contract in addition to his temporal loss would transcend the proper limits of the contractual obligation, and besides would violate that principle of contract law by which damage cannot be recovered unless it is such as was reasonably within the contemplation of the contracting parties. In breaches of contract other damage than the direct pecuniary loss which the breach entails is almost inevitably remote as a matter of law.

Apart, however, from the considerations just mentioned contract law is not averse from taking notice of other forms of harm than pecuniary loss. As a matter of principle there is nothing to prevent a physical hurt from being commuted into a money charge in an action of contract any more than in an action of tort, provided that physical hurt is the direct result of the breach of contract. The circumstance that the recoverable damages in cases of contract nearly always represent pecuniary loss has sometimes been supposed to be due to the difficulty of ascertaining the monetary equivalent of the subtler forms of injury; but clearly, contract law is just as competent to deal with that as tort law. So far as other conditions of liability can be fulfilled, the elements of damage which are recoverable in contract are precisely the same as the elements that are recoverable in tort.

Action for breach of promise.

The action for breach of promise presents some eccentric features that go to illustrate what has just been said. Mutual promises to marry are binding, because "there is a mutual contract betwixt the parties about a lawful thing."[7] At one time an apparent obstacle to the recognition of the breach of this contract, as giving a cause of action in a common-law court, was the fact that the spiritual courts had jurisdiction of matters pertaining to matrimony. But at a comparatively early day it was held that this objection had no application where the action was not brought "to compel the marriage upon the contract, but to recover damages for not doing it."[8]

Marriage was held as a matter of law to be a preferment either to man or woman and the loss of it a temporal damage; that is, the matter was cognizable in the common-law, or temporal, courts as distinguished from the spiritual courts. "Here is a temporal loss and therefore a temporal action doth lie," said Rolle, C. J., in the case of *Baker v. Smith* (1651).[9] The use of the term 'temporal' here might

[7] Ellis, J., in Holcroft *v.* Dickenson, Cart. 233.

[8] Rolle, C. J., in Baker *v.* Smith (1651), Style, 295, 304.

The earliest reported case where an action was sustained for breach of promise is Stretch *v.* Parker (1638), 1 Rolle Abr. 22, pl. 20. This case arose before the "troublesome times" of the civil war and was therefore allowed to be of better authority than the cases of later date. "Late authorities in the troublesome times are of no moment." Vaughan, C. J., in Holcroft *v.* Dickenson (1673), Cart. 233.

[9] Style 293. To the same effect, Hebden *v.* Rutter (1664), 1 Sid. 180; Harrison *v.* Cage (1697), Carth. 467, 5 Mod. 411, 1 Salk. 24. In the latter case the action was by a disappointed man; and the court refused to recognize any distinction between men and women in the matter of treating marriage as an "advancement."

Volume I

be supposed to indicate that the recoverable damages were limited exclusively to the question of disappointed pecuniary expectations. But such was not its import. The point simply was that the common-law courts had jurisdiction of the action. The question as to what elements might be considered in determining the amount of recoverable damage was not involved.

Damages for breach of promise.

Now it is upon this question of recoverable damage that the peculiarity of the action appears. To go into detail would not be worth while. Clearly the principal ground of the action is disappointed hope, and the injury complained of is a violation of faith more resembling deceit and fraud than a common breach of promise.[1] In the end the law comes to something like this: In estimating the amount of damages the jury are to compensate the plaintiff for the loss of social and worldly advancement that would have come by the marriage and for the blow which her affections have suffered by the breach. This factor of disappointment and incidental suffering is elastic enough to include an impairment of health where this actually ensues. Furthermore the jury may consider the injury to the plaintiff's future prospects of marriage, her "loss of market," as the Scotch say; also the humiliation, contempt, and mortification to which, by reason of the breach, she may be subjected in the social circles in which she moves. Likewise she can recover for outlay and expenses in making preparation for the espousals. Finally, exemplary damages may, in a proper case, be awarded, and in most jurisdictions evidence of seduction under the promise is admissible in aggravation of damages.[2]

[1] Wilde, J., in Stebbins *v.* Palmer, 1 Pick. (Mass.) 79.

[2] *Damages for Breach of Promise.*—Berry *v.* Da Costa (1866), L. R. 1 C. P. 331; Smith *v.* Woodfine, 1 C. B. N. S. 660, 87 E. C. L. 660; Grant *v.* Willey, 101 Mass. 356; Bennett *v.* Beam, 42 Mich. 349; Goddard *v.* Westcott (1890), 82 Mich. 180; Hanson *v.* Elton, 38 Minn. 493; Schmidt *v.* Durnham, 46 Minn. 227; Stratton *v.* Dole, 45 Neb. 472; Coryell *v.* Colbaugh, 1 N. J. L. 90; Thorn *v.* Knapp, 42 N. Y. 474; Ortiz *v.* Navarro, 10 Tex. Civ. App. 105; Olson *v.* Solveson, 71 Wis. 663.

Seduction Provable in Aggravation.—Hatlin *v.* Chapman, 46 Conn. 607; Kurtz *v.* Frank, 76 Ind. 594; Sherman *v.* Rawson, 102 Mass. 395; Green *v.* Spencer, 3 Mo. 318; Musselman *v.* Barker, 26 Neb. 737; Williams *v.* Hollingsworth, 6 Baxt.

The rule allowing seduction to be shown in aggravation in effect permits the female to recover damages for her own seduction. This indirectly operates to subvert that principle of tort law which disables her as a consenting party from maintaining an action for the results of the injurious act. Hence in a few jurisdictions it is held that in actions for breach of promise, seduction cannot be proved.[3]

Parasitic element.

From what has been said it is plain that the element of parasitic damage has found lodgment in the action for breach of promise just as in sundry actions *ex delicto*. The circumstance is instructive as showing that the comparative absence of other forms of damage than pecuniary loss in the field of contract is not due to any idiosyncrasy of this branch of law, but is due to causes which inhere in the nature of the wrongs with which we here have to deal. Submit to the theory of contract law a situation that justly calls for the recognition of other forms of damage than pecuniary loss, and it will prove quite as elastic and will go quite as far to meet the exigency as tort law can go.

It may be said that the recognition of the parasitic damage element in breach of promise cases substantially takes the action off the basis of contract and to that extent makes it an action *ex delicto*. Indeed it is commonly said that the action is contractual in form and that so far as the measure of damages is concerned it is an action of tort.[4] But the suggestive thing is that an action which is beyond all question founded on breach of contract should be capable of being thus perverted.[5]

(Tenn.) 12; McKinsey *v.* Squires, 32 W. Va. 41.

[3] Burks *v.* Shain, 2 Bibb (Ky.) 341; Tyler *v.* Salley, 82 Me. 128; Baldy *v.* Stratton, 11 Pa. St. 316; Perkins *v.* Hersey, 1 R. I. 493.

[4] Thorn *v.* Knapp, 42 N. Y. 474.

[5] A feature of the action for breach of promise which shows its affinity with actions *ex delicto* is that ordinarily it abates on the death of either party. Chamberlain *v.* Williamson (1814), 2 M. & S. 408 (plaintiff dies); Stebbins *v.* Palmer (1822), 1 Pick. (Mass.) 71 (defendant dies); Weeks *v.* Mays (1888), 87 Tenn. 442 (defendant dies).

But the action does not abate, it is said, where special damage is alleged: but one can hardly conceive of a case where such special damage could arise as would support the action. See Finlay *v.* Chirney,

Volume I

Mental distress as an element of damage in telegraph cases.

We are now prepared to consider the factor of mental distress or mental anguish in the telegraph cases. The reader will rightly anticipate that if this element of damage is recognized at all it must first appear in the rôle of a parasite; that is to say, a cause of action being shown apart from mental distress, the court may allow such factor to be taken into consideration in fixing the amount to be recovered, but not otherwise. The reader will also be prepared to admit the theoretical possibility of the appearance of this factor whether the cause of action is conceived to be in tort or in contract.

Present state of the law in United States.

Directing our attention now to the decisions on this question we find the actual situation to be this: In Texas (1881), Tennessee (1888), Alabama (1890), North Carolina (1890), Iowa (1895), Louisiana (1903), and in Nevada (1904), damages for mental distress caused by the negligence of a telegraph company in connection with the transmission and delivery of telegrams can be recovered.[6] In more than twenty of the states the question has not been passed upon; while in the states of Kansas (1888), Mississippi (1891), Georgia (1892), Missouri (1893), Florida (1893), Wisconsin (1894), Minnesota (1894), Ohio (1895), New York (1897), Arkansas (1898), South Carolina (1900), Indiana (1901), Virginia (1902), and in the former territory of Dakota (1884) as well as in the present territory of Oklahoma (1894), the recovery of such damages for mental distress is not permitted.[7] The same doc-

20 Q. B. D. 494; Chase *v.* Fitz, 132 Mass. 359.

If A were to promise to pay C a sum of money in consideration that the latter should promise to marry A, and A should subsequently refuse to marry C, the right of action to recover this money would not abate on the death of A. But here the real ground of action would be the breach of the contract to pay money.

[6] Western Union Tel. Co. *v.* Henderson, 89 Ala. 510; Western Union Tel. Co. *v.* Crumpton, 138 Ala. 632; Chapman *v.* Western Union Tel. Co., 90 Ky. 265; Mentzer *v.* Western Union Tel. Co., 93 Iowa 752; Graham *v.* Western Union Tel. Co., 109 La. 1069; Barnes *v.* Western Union Tel. Co., 27 Nev. 438; Young *v.* Western Union Tel. Co., 107 N. Car. 370; Green *v.* Western Union Tel. Co., 136 N. Car. 489; Wadsworth *v.* Western Union Tel. Co., 86 Tenn. 695; Gray *v.* Western Union Tel. Co., 108 Tenn. 39; So Relle *v.* Western Union Tel. Co., 55 Tex. 308; Stuart *v.* Western Union Tel. Co., 66 Tex. 580.

[7] Peay *v.* Western Union Tel.

Chapter XXXI

trine is maintained in the federal courts.[8] The cases which raise the question now under consideration are very similar in their facts, being limited, for the most part, to situations where the telegram conveys information concerning sickness or death to or from a near relative. Such illustration as may be needed will presently be given.

Damages for mental distress where liability is based on breach of contract.

Of the courts that sanction the recovery of damages for mental anguish, some proceed upon the theory that the right of action against the company is founded upon breach of contract, while others proceed upon the idea that the right of action arises out of tort. We have already shown that it is entirely possible for parasitic damage to appear in a contractual action. The decisions of those courts which treat the right of action against a telegraph company as arising *ex contractu* illustrate this point. The fact that upon mere proof of a breach of contract a plaintiff is entitled to recover at least nominal damages, makes the step of recognizing mental anguish comparatively easy in this aspect of the matter; for the existence of the right of action for nominal damages supplies the necessary liability element to which the other damages can be added. It will be noted that those courts which concede the right to recover for mental anguish in actions *ex contractu,* generally deny the right to recover

Co., 64 Ark. 538; International Ocean Tel. Co. *v.* Saunders, 32 Fla. 434; Chapman *v.* Western Union Tel. Co., 88 Ga. 763; West *v.* Western Union Tel. Co., 39 Kan. 93; Francis *v.* Western Union Tel. Co., 58 Minn. 252; Western Union Tel. Co. *v.* Rogers, 68 Miss. 748; Connell *v.* Western Union Tel. Co., 108 Mo. 459; Curtin *v.* Western Union Tel. Co., 13 N. Y. App. Div. 253; Morton *v.* Western Union Tel. Co., 53 Ohio St. 431; Lewis *v.* Western Union Tel. Co., 57 S. Car. 325; Summerfield *v.* Western Union Tel. Co., 87 Wis. 1 (the doctrine of this decision has been abrogated in this state by a subsequent statute); Western Union Tel. Co. *v.* Ferguson, 157 Ind. 64; Connelly *v.* Western Union Tel. Co., 100 Va. 51; Russell *v.* Western Union Tel. Co., 3 Dak. 315; Butner *v.* Western Union Tel. Co., 2 Okla. 234.

[8] Western Union Tel. Co. *v.* Wood (C. C. A.), 57 Fed. Rep. 471; Chase *v.* Western Union Tel. Co., 44 Fed. Rep. 554; Tyler *v.* Western Union Tel. Co., 54 Fed. Rep. 634; Gahan *v.* Western Union Tel. Co., 59 Fed. Rep. 433.

To warrant the consideration of mental suffering in fixing the amount of damages, it is said, the mental suffering must be an element of physical pain, or the natural and proximate result of some physical injury. Crawson *v.* Western Union Tel. Co., 47 Fed. Rep. 544.

Volume I

such damage where the action is brought *ex delicto*, if no damage other than the mental anguish is alleged.

The doctrine that damage for mental anguish can be recovered in an action *ex contractu* but not in an action *ex delicto* appears in the Texas decisions,[9] but it is more clearly brought out in the Alabama cases.[1]

The reader will observe that these courts assume that if a case could be stated in tort where the plaintiff had suffered some actual damage which the law recognizes as a ground of action, the plaintiff might in that case recover also for mental anguish. But such a case cannot easily arise. The difficulty in recovering damages for mental anguish in an action of tort is found in the fact that a failure to send a telegram correctly and promptly is not recognized as being in itself a legal wrong in such sense as to entitle the plaintiff to at least nominal damages, as is the case in breach of contract. It is fundamental in the law of negligence that damage — legal damage, such as the law recognizes as sufficient to support liability — is of the very gist of the action; and if no such damage is alleged, then there is nothing to support the parasitic damage element.

Damages for mental distress where liability is based on tort.

But not all of the courts which permit the recovery of damages for mental anguish are committed to the contract theory as fully as are the Alabama and Texas courts; and in a few jurisdictions it is held that such damages can be recovered even though the action be conceived *ex delicto* and no other damage is alleged than the mental anguish.[2] A mistaken notion as to the effect of the abolition of actions is partly accountable for this. At any rate we find that the courts which proceed along the line now to be considered are

[9] See Gulf, etc., R. Co. *v.* Levy (1883), 59 Tex. 542, 563.

[1] Western Union Tel. Co. *v.* Waters, 139 Ala. 652; Western Union Tel. Co. *v.* Krichbaum, 132 Ala. 535; Western Union Tel. Co. *v.* Ayers, 131 Ala. 391; Western Union Tel. Co. *v.* Crocker, 135 Ala. 492; Western Union Tel. Co. *v.* Crumpton, 138 Ala. 632; Blount *v.* Western Union Tel. Co., 126 Ala. 105; Western Union Tel. Co. *v.* Cunningham, 99 Ala. 314; Western Union Tel. Co. *v.* Wilson, 93 Ala. 32.

[2] For the authorities which countenance this view, see *post*, p. 472 *et seq.*

found in jurisdictions where forms of action have been abolished, and we find these courts not infrequently relying on the principle that since the abolition of actions a plaintiff may, in an action on the facts of the case, recover all such damages as could formerly be recovered either in an action *ex contractu* or *ex delicto* — a rough and doubtless inaccurate way of stating a certain legal truth.

One unquestionable result of the abolition of actions is that these courts deal with the question here at issue with considerable laxity and without that analytical acumen which has to be displayed in jurisdictions, like Alabama, where the common-law distinctions are preserved. The result is that it is very hard to discover the precise theory underlying those decisions which sanction the recovery of damages for mental anguish in actions *ex delicto*. The following appears to be a correct diagnosis:

Theory of the action.

Before damages for mental anguish can be recovered in an action *ex delicto* one of two assumptions must be made: first, that a failure on the part of a telegraph company to transmit a telegram promptly and correctly is a tort *per se* such as to give a right to recover at least nominal damages to begin with, to which the damages for mental anguish can be added; or secondly, it must be assumed that mental anguish is an independent cause of action. These assumptions are to outward appearance quite different, yet it is manifest that the first assumption cannot be given effect without in a way involving and, in the end, leading up to the other also.

Necessary assumptions.

Apparently none of the courts to which reference is now made openly plants itself upon either of the propositions stated above. No court openly asserts that upon proof of the failure to transmit a telegram promptly and carefully the company is liable for at least nominal damages in an action of tort, and no court asserts that mental anguish is of itself sufficient to support liability. These courts do not analyze thus far. They merely say that the company owes a legal duty and upon breach of the duty becomes liable for all damage that is the proximate result of the breach.

These assumptions not openly made.

We are by no means inclined to denounce this position,

Volume I

Company's negligence viewed as breach of simple legal duty.

or at least the result actually reached, as theoretically untenable. In point of abstract principle it is sound enough, for it is merely a result of that inevitable drift towards the tort theory of the company's liability which has elsewhere been noted. There is nothing inconsistent with principle in saying that a failure of the telegraph company to fulfil its duty is a tort *per se* and gives a right of action wherein all elements of recoverable damage may enter. Nor is there any inconsistency in going further and saying, what these decisions actually import, that mental anguish is alone sufficient to support liability. It is not a question of principle, it is only a question of sound policy; of which more will presently be said.

Parasitic damage characteristic of transition period.

The treatment of any element of damage as a parasitic factor belongs essentially to a transitory stage of legal evolution. A factor which is to-day recognized as parasitic will, forsooth, to-morrow be recognized as an independent basis of liability. It is merely a question of social, economic, and industrial needs as those needs are reflected in the organic law.

In *Cole v. Atlanta, etc., R. Co.* (1897)[3] we find a good illustration of the manner in which the parasitic damage element when once fully recognized inevitably waxes stronger until it attains a self-subsisting character. There really seems to be no good stopping place after an element of damage has once been admitted in any guise until it is recognized as an independent basis of liability. Pollock, C. B., was wise in his day when he said: "We ought to be careful not to introduce a new element of damage, recollecting to what a large class of actions it would apply and what a dangerous use might be made of it."[4]

Danger of recognizing new damage element.

[3] 102 Ga. 474. To the same effect, Georgia R., etc., Co. *v.* Baker (1904), 120 Ga. 991. Cole *v.* Atlanta, etc., R. Co. was not a case involving a telegram, but was against a railroad company. The plaintiff while a passenger on the defendant's train was abused and insulted by the conductor in rough and opprobrious language. It was held that an action lay, although there was no assault and the plaintiff was not ejected from the train.

[4] Allsop *v.* Allsop (1860), 5 H. & N. 536. The language was used in a case of slander, but it con-

The following concrete illustrations will give an idea of the manner in which the telegraph cases are dealt with by courts which recognize mental distress as an element of recoverable damage.

Right of Action Arising Ex Contractu.

1. *Stuart v. Western Union Tel. Co.* (1886):[5] The plaintiff, knowing that his brother was ill in a distant town, sent a telegram of inquiry requesting to be informed of his condition. An answer was dispatched to the effect that the brother was low and telling the plaintiff to come on first train. The message was not delivered within a reasonable time, with the result that the brother died and was buried before the plaintiff arrived. In an action *ex contractu* it was held that the plaintiff could recover for mental distress.[6]

2. *Western Union Tel. Co. v. Henderson* (1889):[7] The plaintiff's wife being very ill, he sent a telegram to a physician asking him to come at once. The company neglected to deliver the message for nearly twenty-four hours, during which time the wife continued in great agony. When the message was finally delivered the doctor responded and relieved the woman's suffering, but she presently died. It was held in an action *ex contractu* that the husband could recover for the distress which he himself suffered by reason of the absence of the physician under these circumstances.

3. *Rowell v. Western Union Tel. Co.* (1889):[8] In this case it appeared that the plaintiff had been informed by the first telegram that her mother was dangerously ill. The second telegram containing news that she was out of danger was not delivered by the company. It was held that no action lay for the uneasiness which the plaintiff suffered by reason of her failure to receive the second telegram.

4. *Cashion v. Western Union Tel. Co.* (1898):[9] The plaintiff's husband, having been killed accidentally, the plaintiff telegraphed for her brother-in-law. The message was delayed and as a result the plaintiff was much distressed by the absence of her brother-in-law and inconvenienced in connection with the funeral arrangements. It was held that she could recover. It was also said that in the near relations such as husband and wife, parent and child, brother and sister, mental anguish will be presumed, but that in remote relations, such as brother-in-law or friend, mental distress must be proved.

tains an element of conservatism and good sense that gives it value in other connections.

[5] 66 Tex. 580.

[6] To the same effect, Western Union Tel. Co. *v.* Cunningham, 99 Ala. 314.

[7] 89 Ala. 510.

[8] 75 Tex. 26.

[9] 123 N. Car. 267.

Volume I

5. *Western Union Tel. Co. v. Crocker* (1902):[1] The father of a sick child sent a telegram summoning his mother-in-law, the grandmother of the child, to its bedside. The message was delayed and in consequence the sendee did not reach the child before its death. It was held that the father could recover for the distress which he suffered by reason of the absence of the child's grandmother. It was said that the relationship existing between the sender, sendee, and the person concerning whom the message was sent was of such close degree as to warrant a presumption of natural love and affection.[2]

Right of Action Conceived as Arising Ex Delicto.

1. *Mentzer v. Western Union Tel. Co.* (1895):[3] The plaintiff's mother died in a distant state. A telegram informing him of that fact and of the date of the funeral was dispatched, but, through negligence, was not delivered until the obsequies were over. The plaintiff was thereby prevented from going to the burial, as he otherwise could and would have done. In an action *ex delicto* it was held that he could recover for the mental distress which he suffered by reason of his inability to attend the funeral. The decision was placed on the grounds that the defendant company, by violating a legal duty owing by it to the plaintiff, became liable for all damage which should naturally flow therefrom, and that mental anguish is an injury which the law recognizes as an element of recoverable damage. The opinion in this contains one of the strongest arguments in favor of the tort theory of the company's liability and in favor of the allowance of damages for mental anguish that is to be found in the reports.

2. *Lyne v. Western Union Tel. Co.* (1898):[4] One R met with a fatal accident in the city of Richmond, Va. A message was thereupon dispatched to his wife in Raleigh, N. C., notifying her that her husband was hurt and could live only a short time. The message was unduly delayed and the wife was thereby deprived of the privilege of being with her husband at his death. In an action *ex delicto* it was held that she could recover for the distress occasioned to her by her absence.

3. *Western Union Tel. Co. v. Frith* (1900):[5] The plaintiff's child died in a distant place while it, together with its mother, was visiting her relations. A telegram was sent to the father notifying him of the death and telling him to come forthwith. The tele-

[1] 135 Ala. 492.

[2] But in Western Union Tel. Co. *v.* Ayers, 131 Ala. 391, where the relationship between the sendee and the infant mentioned in the message was that of uncle and niece, it was held the relationship was too remote.

[3] 93 Iowa 752.

[4] 123 N. Car. 129.

[5] 105 Tenn. 167.

gram was not delivered and the father was thus prevented from going, as he otherwise would have done, to the burial. In an action of tort it was held that he could recover for the grief and disappointment which he suffered by reason of his absence from the burial of his child and by reason of his distress in not being able to be with his wife in her grief.[6]

Mental distress as an element of damage figures almost exclusively in cases where the telegram refers to sickness or death. Here are two cases where the distress was not of that poignant kind which is usually the subject of legal consideration in this type of cases:

1. *Barnes v. Western Union Tel. Co.* (1904):[7] The plaintiff being in Grand Junction, Colo., and wishing to go to Lovelock, Nev., but not having means to buy a ticket further than to Ogden, Utah, telegraphed to a brother to wire him a ticket from Ogden to Lovelock. The telegraph company neglected to deliver the message for an unreasonable time and the plaintiff received no ticket, as he would have done if the message had been promptly delivered. Not receiving the ticket the plaintiff proceeded afoot, or beating his way on trains when opportunity afforded. Thus with much discomfort and even suffering from cold and hunger, he proceeded some hundreds of miles on his journey. It was held that the telegraph company was liable for the suffering and mental worry as well as for the labor expended.

2. *Green v. Western Union Tel. Co.* (1904):[8] The plaintiff, a girl of sixteen, started alone upon a trip from Weldon, N. C., to Spartanburg, S. C. It was necessary, in order to make railway connection, that she should stay over during the greater part of a night at Columbia, S. C. In this city was a friend to whom the father of the girl, after the latter's departure, sent a telegram asking that the young lady should be met at the train in Columbia. The telegram was not delivered and in consequence no one was there to meet her upon arrival at midnight. She was naturally much disturbed and upset, but the conductor put her in charge of the matron at the station. After some delay a carriage was procured and she was safely driven to the home of her friend. It was held that she could recover for the inconvenience and distress which she suffered by reason of the failure of the company to deliver the telegram.[9]

[6] Wadsworth *v.* Western Union Tel. Co., 86 Tenn. 695; Western Union Tel. Co. *v.* Mellon, 96 Tenn. 66; Gray *v.* Western Union Tel. Co., 108 Tenn. 39. There is a statute in this state that telegraphic messages shall be transmitted correctly and without unreasonable delay. This statute has been relied on by the Tennessee court as creating the legal duty.

[7] 27 Nev. 438.

[8] 136 N. Car. 489.

[9] It is necessary for the plaintiff to show in such a case as this that the sendee of the telegram

Volume I

Louisville, etc., R. Co. v. Hull (1902)[1] presents this question of damages for mental distress in a still different aspect. The plaintiff was conveying the body of his wife from Asheville, N. C., to his home in Kentucky for burial. At Nashville, Tenn., where a change was necessary to be made, the body was, by the negligence of the company's servants, either dispatched on the wrong road or left in the depot. As a result the body was left behind. The husband was naturally worried and distressed and the funeral arrangements had to be postponed. It was held that he could recover for his mental suffering caused by this mishap.[2]

Doctrine that mental distress is not an element of recoverable damage.

The position of the courts which refuse to allow the recovery of damages for mental anguish in the telegraph cases can be briefly stated. Such damage, it is said, is legally remote or is purely of a sentimental character and hitherto unrecognized by law. These arguments contain certain elements of truth, but at most they appear to be criticisms rather than refutations. When a person, who could and would go on a moment's notice to the bedside or to the burial of a parent, or brother or sister, or husband or wife, fails to get the telegram which should, if duly forwarded, notify him to come, common sense will attribute the grief which he feels at his inability to be present, to the negligence of the telegraph company, and there is no sufficient reason why the law should not attribute it to that also. Nor does the suggestion that the injury is purely sentimental appear to be conclusive. We may not altogether agree with the observation of Bleckley, C. J., in a case of wrongful ejectment from a railroad train, that the wounding of a man's feelings is as much actual damage as breaking his limbs, the only difference being that one is internal while the other is external;[3] yet we must admit that such a wound is of a very real kind. Nor is the novelty of this element of damage a fatal objection.

could and would have met the train if the telegram had been received, and this fact ought to be alleged in the declaration: otherwise the chain of legal causation is not shown to be complete and the distress must be considered as remote in point of law. So far as appears from the report of this case, no such allegation was made in the pleadings. But the point was not raised.

[1] 113 Ky. 561.

[2] To the same effect, Hale *v.* Bonner, 82 Tex. 33.

[3] Head *v.* Georgia Pac. R. Co., 79 Ga. 358.

Granting that legal principle expands as new conditions arise which educate the human mind to higher and subtler conceptions of injury, there appears to be no theoretical reason why this new form of damage should not be given recognition if it really answers the needs of a complex and enlightened society.

Question resolved into one of policy.

This final *if* brings us into contact with what is, after all, the really vital question. Is it practicable? Is it just? Is it a part of sound legal policy to recognize hurt to the feelings as a ground of action in these cases? On this ground of public policy the heresy of mental anguish, if such it be, must be met and extinguished. A strong presentation of this aspect of the matter is found in the following language of Lurton, J.: "Depending largely upon physical and nervous condition, the suffering of one under precisely the same circumstances would be no test of the suffering of another. Vague and shadowy, there is no possible standard by which such an injury can be justly compensated, or even approximately measured. Easily simulated and impossible to disprove, it falls within all of the objections to speculative damages, which are universally excluded because of their uncertain character. That damages so imaginary, so metaphysical, so sentimental, shall be ascertained and assessed by a jury with justness, not by way of punishment to the defendant, but as mere compensation to the plaintiff, is not to be expected."[4] To expect that the jury will separate the anguish and grief which result from the delayed information and the consequent inability to respond to the call of affection, from that grief which is a material incident of the death of the loved one, and that it will assess damages for the former to the exclusion of the latter, is to expect an unnatural and impossible thing. So far as sound public policy demands the penalizing of the telegraph company, the matter may well be left to the legislative power.

[4] Wadsworth *v.* Western Union Tel. Co. (1888), 86 Tenn. 721.

CHAPTER XXXII

MEASURE OF DAMAGES.

Volume I

Difficulties of the law concerning measure of damage.

NO term in the range of legal science is more misleading than 'measure of damages,' if by that expression one is to understand that there is some definite canon by which the amount of recoverable damages is to be alike determined and limited in every case. There is no such rule. As was once observed by Lord Halsbury, "The whole region of inquiry into damages is one of extreme difficulty. You very often cannot even lay down any principle upon which you can give damages; nevertheless, it is remitted to the jury, or those who stand in place of the jury, to consider what compensation in money shall be given for what is a wrongful act. Take the most familiar and ordinary case: how is anybody to measure pain and suffering in moneys counted? Nobody can suggest that you can by any arithmetical calculation establish what is the exact amount of money which would represent such a thing as the pain and suffering which a person has undergone by reason of an accident. . . . But nevertheless the law recognizes that as a topic upon which damages may be given." [1]

The various obstacles which make it impossible to generalize the theory of legal wrong under any one universal principle all exist in the field of damage, and likewise make it impossible here to state any single canon for assessing damages. Many theoretical difficulties are brought to a focus in this narrow subject. Something at least is gained if we realize at the outset that the principles which underlie the law of damage are even more complex and multiform than the principles which determine liability. That these difficulties have not been fully explored is due, not to their absence,

[1] The Steamship Mediana *v.* The Lightship Comet, (1900) A. C. 116.

but to our convenient habit of leaving hard things to the jury.

The ultimate aim of law is the realization of justice, and justice can only be realized by a proper balancing of all the factors which are present in each case. The faculty of wisdom is manifest not only in the process of the actual balancing of these factors, but in the judgment which is shown in determining just when one consideration rather than another shall be allowed to control. Here human experience is of course the great and best teacher. It follows that the law cannot always work with the same immediate or proximate end in view.

Realization of justice the end of law.

In considering the amount of damages which may be awarded in civil actions, the law keeps in mind two ideas, namely, punishment and compensation. In certain situations it lays stress upon one of these ideas, in other situations it permits the other to control. Both of these conceptions necessarily also involve the idea of the prevention of future wrong by deterrent example, though this object is more conspicuous in the idea of punishment. Clearly the idea of prevention is merely secondary to the two main ideas of punishment and compensation. "Damages," said Lord Mansfield, in one of the famous cases involving the validity of the general warrants, "are designed not only as a satisfaction to the injured person, but likewise as a punishment to the guilty to deter from any such proceeding for the future, and as a proof of the detestation of the jury to the action itself." [2]

Punishment; compensation.

Prevention.

The conception of punishment arises chiefly from a contemplation of the wrongful act viewed in its moral aspect. The notion of compensation arises from a contemplation of the act as it affects the sufferer. That both punishment and compensation are rational ends in the administration of law is a proposition from which few will dissent.[3]

[2] Wilkes *v.* Wood, 19 How. St. Tr. 1167, Lofft (3 Geo. III.) 19.

[3] In passing we note that Prof. J. W. Salmond has advanced the idea that punishment is the exclusive rational object in the administration of law and that the idea of compensation is *per se* an irrational aim, only to be supported as a species of punishment. Essays in Jurisprudence and Legal History, pp. 127-129.

Volume I

The idea of punishment finds its completest expression in the criminal law, and it might seem that in an ideal system of jurisprudence the ideas of punishment and compensation would respectively be limited exclusively to the fields of criminal and civil wrong. But the common law has never been guilty of the folly of putting theory entirely before practical ends, and hence we find that the idea of punishment still holds its ground in the administration of civil justice.[4]

The idea of compensation for civil injury is one which, from its very nature, must be more or less present in every stratum of legal thought. The idea of punishment is chiefly conspicuous in wrongs which are characterized by the wanton or intentional infliction of injury or by oppression. Naturally the idea of punishment is conspicuous enough in the early law of liability, for the wrongs of which the law first takes cognizance are characterized by the intentional infliction of injury. The several forms of violent trespass are in point.

Recession of the idea of punishment in the theory of civil wrong.

As the horizon of legal wrong broadens, we find that the idea of punishment becomes less prominent, and the law is compelled to work more and more with an eye to the mere compensation of the sufferer. Hence the recognition of several types of injury, such as negligence, in which actual damage is of the essence of the right of action.

In modern times it has been a great question among eminent lights whether or not in all cases damages must be assessed upon the sole principle of compensation for the injury done. The affirmative view was supported by Professor Greenleaf. The negative was maintained by Mr. Sedgwick. As is often the case in controversies of this kind, it will be

[4] It should be noted that the civil courts do not admit that the idea of pure vengeance has any place in the administration of the law. Said Lord Herschell in Allen *v.* Flood, (1898) A. C. 131: "When a court of justice awards punishment for a breach of the law the object is not vengeance. The purpose is to deter the person who has broken the law from a repetition of his act and to deter other persons also from committing similar breaches of the law." This looks very much like an effort to give an appearance of modern refinement to a crude instinct which nevertheless is one of the mainsprings of human action in all stages of society.

Chapter XXXII

found that each of these opposing views has its element of truth. But as a matter of practical fact, the weight of authority is with Mr. Sedgwick. The view which treats compensation as the exclusive object of the law of civil injury presupposes a theoretical unity in the principles underlying the law of damages which does not exist. It is generalization pushed too far. Perhaps it will be well to state the point in controversy a little more fully.

Controversy over the principle on which damages should be assessed.

"Damages," says Professor Greenleaf, "are given as a compensation, recompense, or satisfaction to the plaintiff, for an injury actually received by him from the defendant. They should be precisely commensurate with the injury, neither more nor less; and this whether it be to his person or estate."[5] As is admitted by all, this proposition correctly states the rule of law in all breaches of contract and in most torts. The difference of opinion arises when we come to consider a comparatively small class of torts.

Principle of compensation.

Says Mr. Sedgwick: "In actions of tort, when gross fraud, malice, or oppression appears, the jury are not bound to adhere to the strict line of compensation, but may, by a severer verdict, at once impose a punishment on the defendant and hold him up as an example to the community."[6] Such damages are called vindictive, exemplary, or punitory damages; or, as is sometimes said, 'smart money.' In this view damages may be given, to use the language of Lord Mansfield, "for more than the injury received."[7] Over this proposition is the dispute.

Exemplary damages.

To go fully into the matter is neither desirable nor practicable, but one or two salient points may be noted. Most important is the fact that these two opposing views, while not capable of being reconciled in point of strict theory, yet practically in many cases work out about the same results.

[5] Greenl. Evidence (14th ed.), § 253. Professor Greenleaf's argument in favor of this proposition is found in a lengthy note to the section cited.

[6] 1 Sedgw. Damages, § 347.

[7] Said this learned judge in Wilkes *v.* Wood, 19 How. St. Tr. 1167: "I have formerly delivered it as my opinion on another occasion, and I still continue of the same mind, that a jury have it in their power to give damages for more than the injury received."

Volume I

Practical application of two conflicting theories.

This comes from the different significance which the two parties to the controversy attach to the elements of injury in cases where the question in dispute arises. In a case of malice or oppression, for instance, the courts which accept Professor Greenleaf's view, say that the defendant's malice or oppression operates to increase or aggravate the actual legal injury. In assessing compensatory damages for the legal wrong under this view, the element of malice and oppression are necessarily taken into consideration. On the other hand, the courts which adhere to the opinion of Mr. Sedgwick take a less comprehensive view of the elements of legal injury. The malice and oppression are here considered as constituting a factor altogether apart from the actual legal injury, and after allowing compensatory damages for the injury, other additional damages must be awarded by way of punishment or example.

Controversy in part purely theoretical.

It follows that damages which in one jurisdiction are recoverable as exemplary damages are, in another jurisdiction, recovered under the guise of compensatory damages for mental suffering, insult, or outrage.[8] The controversy thus appears to dwindle into a dispute over the import and latitude of the word 'injury' as applied to the various sorts of wrong.

It is, however, manifest that the contrariety of opinion on this point cannot altogether be thus reconciled; for after all, it is one thing to tell a jury that they cannot transcend the extent of the injury in giving damages, and quite another to tell them that they may assess full damages for the injury

[8] In Brown *v.* Swineford, 44 Wis. 289, Ryan, C. J., observed: "The distinction between compensatory damages for wounded feeling, sense of insult, etc., and punitory damages is sometimes very vague, as may be seen by comparison of Wilson *v.* Young, 31 Wis. 574, and Craker *v.* Chicago, etc., R. Co., 36 Wis. 657. And the vagueness of this distinction, in practice as well as in theory, is illustrated by the three reports of Bass *v.* Chicago, etc., R. Co., 36 Wis. 450, 39 Wis. 636, 42 Wis. 654. The case was three times tried, in different counties; twice upon instructions allowing exemplary damages, and once upon instructions disallowing them. And yet the verdict on each trial was for the same sum. Apparently, what was allowed on two trials for exemplary damages, was allowed on the third trial for compensatory damages for wounded feelings."

and also additional damages by way of punishment and example.

Chapter XXXII

The most powerful effort that has been put forth to refute the supposed heresy of exemplary damages is found in *Fay v. Parker* (1872),[9] where the Supreme Court of New Hampshire undertook to show that, in all civil actions whatever, the recoverable damages are limited to such as will exactly compensate the plaintiff for the injury inflicted upon him.[1] The opinion in this case furnishes as strong a brief in favor of Professor Greenleaf's thesis as is likely to be written. Nevertheless its arguments do not appear to be conclusive, and the view therein advocated is accepted in only a very few of the American States.[2]

Minority view.

The great weight of authority in this country, as in England, is to the effect that exemplary damages may be awarded, as stated by Mr. Sedgwick, in cases where the wrongful act is characterized by gross fraud, malice, or oppression, or by wanton disregard of the rights of the plaintiff.[3] It is even held that exemplary damages may be given where the plaintiff's injury results from gross negligence or recklessness.[4]

Prevailing doctrine.

[9] 53 N. H. 342.

[1] The precise point decided in this case was that where the wrongful act which supplies the ground of action is also punishable criminally, exemplary damages cannot be awarded; but the opinion was directed towards the establishment of the broader principle indicated above. The notion that when an act is punishable criminally exemplary damages cannot be assessed in a civil action finds expression in a few jurisdictions. The idea is that a different rule would subject the wrongdoer to double punishment. Cherry *v.* McCall, 23 Ga. 193; Taber *v.* Hutson, 5 Ind. 322; Butler *v.* Mercer, 14 Ind. 479. But this results in the inconsistency of giving less damages in grave cases than in those where the act is not so serious. The better view, and that supported by the majority of the courts, is that the liability to criminal punishment in no way affects the question of the civil damages to be recovered. If the defendant suffers twice it is because his act creates criminal as well as civil liability.

[2] Barnard *v.* Poor, 21 Pick. (Mass.) 378; Detroit Daily Post Co. *v.* McArthur, 16 Mich. 447; Boyer *v.* Barr, 8 Neb. 68; Bixby *v.* Dunlap, 56 N. H. 456; Spokane Truck, etc., Co. *v.* Hoefer, 2 Wash. 45.

[3] Bell *v.* Midland R. Co., 10 C. B. N. S. 287, 100 E. C. L. 287; Scott *v.* Donald, 165 U. S. 58; Clark *v.* Bales, 15 Ark. 452; Dorsey *v.* Manlove, 14 Cal. 553; St. Ores *v.* McGlashen, 74 Cal. 148; Welch *v.* Durand, 36 Conn. 182; McNamara *v.* King, 7 Ill. 432; Wanamaker *v.* Bowes, 36 Md. 42; Smith *v.* Matthews, 152 N. Y. 152; Devine *v.* Rand, 38 Vt. 621.

[4] Emblen *v.* Myers, 6 H. & N. 54;

Volume I

The principle upon which exemplary damages may be awarded has been clearly stated by the Supreme Court of Pennsylvania in these words: "In actions on contract, except promises to marry, the amount recoverable is limited to the actual damages caused by the breach, the measure being the same whether the defendant fails to comply with his contract through inability, or wilfully refuses to perform it. But in torts the rule is different; the motive of the defendant becomes material. In those that are committed through mistake, ignorance, or mere negligence, the ordinary rule is mere compensation; but in such as are committed wilfully, maliciously, or so negligently as to indicate a wanton disregard of the rights of others, the jury are not restricted to compensation merely. They may, if the evidence justifies it, give vindictive or exemplary damages, such as will not only compensate the injured party, but at the same time tend to prevent a repetition of the wrong, either by the defendant or others." [5]

When exemplary damages recoverable.

In *Day v. Woodworth* (1851)[6] Justice Grier used the following language: "It is a well-established principle of the common law, that in actions of trespass and all actions on the case for torts, a jury may inflict what are called exemplary, punitive, or vindictive damages upon a defendant, having in view the enormity of his offense rather than the measure of compensation to the plaintiff. We are aware that the propriety of this doctrine has been questioned by some writers; but if repeated judicial decisions for more than a century are to be received as the best exposition of what the law is, the question will not admit of argument. By the common, as well as by statute law, men are often punished for aggravated misconduct or lawless acts, by means of a civil action, and the damages, inflicted by way of penalty or punishment, given to the party injured. In many civil actions, such as libel, slander, seduction, etc., the wrong done to the plaintiff is inca-

Defamation; seduction.

Milwaukee, etc., R. Co. *v.* Arms, 91 U. S. 489; Mobile, etc., R. Co. *v.* Ashcraft, 48 Ala. 15; Linsley *v.* Bushnell, 15 Conn. 225; Cochran *v.* Miller, 13 Iowa 128; Wiley *v.* Keokuk, 6 Kan. 94; Wilkinson *v.* Drew, 75 Me. 360; Von Fragstein *v.* Windler, 2 Mo. App. 598; Byram *v.* McGuire, 3 Head (Tenn.) 530.

[5] Pittsburgh, etc., R. Co. *v.* Lyon (1889), 123 Pa. St. 150.

[6] 13 How. (U. S.) 371.

pable of being measured by a money standard; and the damages assessed depend on the circumstances, showing the degree of moral turpitude or atrocity of the defendant's conduct, and may properly be termed exemplary or vindictive rather than compensatory. In actions of trespass, where the injury has been wanton and malicious, or gross and outrageous, courts permit juries to add to the measured compensation of the plaintiff which he would have been entitled to recover, had the injury been inflicted without design or intention, something farther by way of punishment or example, which has sometimes been called 'smart money.' This has been always left to the discretion of the jury, as the degree of punishment to be thus inflicted must depend on the peculiar circumstances of each case. It must be evident, also, that as it depends upon the degree of malice, wantonness, oppression, or outrage of the defendant's conduct, the punishment of his delinquency cannot be measured by the expenses of the plaintiff in prosecuting his suit."[7]

Wilful trespass.

The following abstracts of cases in which the assessment of exemplary damages has been approved illustrate the steps by which the doctrine has taken shape, and at the same time give an idea of its limits.

[7] The following instructive language of Lord Blackburn upon the subject of the amount of recoverable damages is worthy of a place here: "I do not think there is any difference of opinion as to its being a general rule that, where any injury is to be compensated by damages, in settling the sum of money to be given for reparation of damages you should as nearly as possible get at that sum of money which will put the party who has been injured, or who has suffered, in the same position as he would have been in if he had not sustained the wrong for which he is now getting his compensation or reparation. That must be qualified by a great many things which may arise — such, for instance, as by the consideration whether the damage has been maliciously done, or whether it has been done with full knowledge that the person doing it was doing wrong. There could be no doubt that there you would say that everything would be taken into view that would go most against the wilful wrongdoer—many things which you would properly allow in favor of an innocent mistaken trespasser would be disallowed as against a wilful and intentional trespasser on the ground that he must not qualify his own wrong, and various things of that sort." Livingstone *v.* Rawyards Coal Co., 5 App. Cas. 39.

Volume I

Illegal commitment under general warrant.

1. *Huckle v. Money* (1763):[8] The plaintiff, a journeyman printer, was taken into custody by the defendant, a king's messenger, upon suspicion of having printed number 45 of the *North Briton*. The defendant kept him in custody for about six hours, but used him very civilly by treating him with beef-steaks and beer, so that he suffered little or no actual damages. In an action for false imprisonment the defendant justified under the authority of a general warrant of the secretary of state to apprehend the printers and publishers of the paper referred to. Such warrant was held to confer no authority upon the defendant to arrest the plaintiff and the jury thereupon gave £300 damages. Upon a motion to set the verdict aside as being outrageously excessive, Pratt, L. C. J., among other things, said: "If the jury had been confined by their oath to consider the mere personal injury only, perhaps £20 damages would have been thought damages sufficient; but the small injury done to the plaintiff, or the inconsiderableness of his station and rank in life did not appear to the jury in that striking light, in which the great point of law touching the liberty of the subject appeared to them at the trial. They saw a magistrate over all the King's subjects, exercising arbitrary power, violating Magna Charta, and attempting to destroy the liberty of the kingdom by insisting upon the legality of this general warrant before them; they heard the King's counsel, and saw the Solicitor of the Treasury, endeavoring to support and maintain the legality of the warrant in a tyrannical and severe manner. These are the ideas which struck the jury on the trial, and I think they have done right in giving exemplary damages."

Exemplary damages in case of seduction.

2. *Tullidge v. Wade* (1769):[9] In an action of trespass against the defendant for the seduction of the plaintiff's daughter, Wilmot, L. C. J., said, "Actions of this sort are brought for example's sake; and although the plaintiff's loss in this case may not really amount to the value of twenty shillings, yet the jury have done right in giving liberal damages." And Bathurst, J., added, "In actions of this nature, and of assaults, the circumstances of time and place, when and where the insult is given, require different damages; as it is a greater insult to be beaten upon the Royal Exchange than in a private room."

3. *Merest v. Harvey* (1814):[1] The plaintiff, a gentleman of fortune, was shooting upon his estate in a common field contiguous to the highway, when the defendant, a banker, a magistrate, and a member of parliament, who had dined and drank freely after taking the same diversion of shooting, passed along the road in his carriage, and, quitting it, went up to the plaintiff and told him he would join his party, which the plaintiff positively declined, in-

[8] 2 Wils. C. Pl. 205.
[9] 3 Wils. C. Pl. 18.
[1] 5 Taunt. 442, 1 E. C. L. 150.

Chapter XXXII

quired his name, and gave him notice not to sport on the plaintiff's land; but the defendant declared with an oath that he would shoot, and accordingly fired several times, upon the plaintiff's land, at the birds which the plaintiff found, proposed to borrow some shot from the plaintiff, when he had exhausted his own, and used very intemperate language, threatening, in his capacity of a magistrate, to commit the plaintiff, and defying him to bring an action. The jury found a verdict for all the damages claimed, viz., £500, and the verdict was upheld. Gibbs, C. J., said the court could not grant the rule for a new trial unless they were to lay it down that the jury must give no more in such cases than the absolute pecuniary damage. Heath, J., remembered a case where £500 was given for merely knocking a man's hat off; and he observed, "It goes to prevent the practice of dueling, if juries are permitted to punish insult by exemplary damages." It goes almost without saying that under modern conditions so large a verdict in cases of this kind would not be allowed to stand.

Trespass accompanied by insult.

4. *Sears v. Lyons* (1818):[2] The defendant strewed poisoned barley on the plaintiff's premises and his own with the purpose of destroying the plaintiff's poultry, which sometimes escaped and trespassed upon the defendant's premises. Some of the fowls died, but it did not appear whether from eating the barley which was thrown on the plaintiff's premises or on the defendant's. Abbott, J., in charging the jury, observed that "it had always been held that for trespass and entry into the house or lands of the plaintiff, a jury might consider not only the mere pecuniary damage sustained by the plaintiff, but also the intention with which the fact had been done, whether for insult or injury;" and he said that they "were not confined in this case to the mere damage resulting from throwing poisoned barley on the land of the plaintiff, but might consider also the object with which it was thrown, taking care at the same time to guard their feelings against the impression likely to have been made by the defendant's conduct." The jury found for the plaintiff to the extent of £50.

Wanton poisoning of poultry.

5. *Warwick v. Foulkes* (1844):[3] In an action of false imprisonment the defendant pleaded by way of justification that the plaintiff had committed a felony. At the trial, his counsel abandoned the plea and exonerated the plaintiff from the charge. It was held that the putting of such a plea upon record was a persisting in the charge contained in it and ought to be taken into account by the jury in estimating the damages.

False imprisonment.

6. *Emblem v. Myers* (1860):[4] It appeared that the plaintiff was in possession of a small piece of ground at Houndsditch, which he claimed as his freehold, and on which he had built a stable and

[2] 2 Stark. 317, 3 E. C. L. 426.
[3] 12 M. & W. 507.
[4] 30 L. J. Exch. 72. Compare *id.*, 6 H. & N. 54.

Volume I

loft for the purposes of his trade as a carman and coal and coke dealer. The defendant had recently purchased two old houses adjoining the plaintiff's premises, and employed a laborer to pull them down. In doing this the plaintiff's stable was injured, and a piece of timber falling from the defendant's houses on the plaintiff's stable, knocked part of the roof in, which, falling upon the horse and cart of the plaintiff, injured them. Evidence was also adduced, on the part of the plaintiff, showing that there had been an actual trespass in pulling down of part of the stables, and that the defendant was anxious to obtain possession of the land claimed by the plaintiff, and that in consequence of the plaintiff refusing to give it up the defendant was annoyed, and caused the old houses to be taken down in a reckless and hasty manner. The jury were told by Wilde, B., that if they thought that the proceeding was done with a high hand, wilfully, and with a view to getting a poor man out of possession, damages might be awarded for more than the actual pecuniary loss inflicted upon the plaintiff. This instruction was held to be correct. Pollock, C. B., in the Court of Exchequer said: "I think it is felt by all persons who have occasion to consider questions of compensation, that there is a difference between that which is purely the result of accident, the party who is responsible being perfectly innocent, and the case where he has accompanied the wrong, be it wilfulness or negligence, with expressions that make the wrong an insult as well as an injury. Not that in this case what are called vindictive damages should have been given, but a different measure of damages might be fairly given, according to the nature of the injury." [5]

Wanton disregard for the rights of others.

7. *Borland v. Barrett* (1882): [6] The defendant with his wife had for a considerable period boarded at the Atlantic Hotel in the city of Norfolk, and had occupied certain seats in the dining room. Upon their going away for the summer the seats in question were assigned to the plaintiff and wife. When the defendant returned in the autumn, he insisted that the seats formerly occupied by himself and his wife should be given up to him. Upon the plaintiff's refusal to do so defendant struck plaintiff over the head with a bottle of sauce. A very ugly scene ensued, but the parties were soon separated. The sauce bottle was broken and the plaintiff's head was cut so that it bled. The jury gave a thousand dollars' damages and the verdict was sustained, the court observing that the assault was wilful and wanton and that the jury were amply

Wanton assault and battery.

[5] Channell, B., in the same case, observed: "In an action of trespass, that is, in some actions of tort, you may give evidence of damage beyond the actual injury sustained, in consequence of insulting circumstances connected with the trespass; and I can see no reason why that should be limited to one kind of action of tort, namely, trespass, and should not extend to an action which, in substance, is for negligence committed under circumstances which might have supported an action of trespass."

[6] 76 Va. 128.

justified in giving vindictive damages. It was also said that to make out a case for exemplary damages it was not necessary that the defendant should have been actuated by actual malice in making the assault or that he should have had a deliberate design to injure the plaintiff. The existence of actual malice may be shown in an aggravation of such damages, but its absence does not defeat the right to their recovery.

Insult conceived as aggravative of the injury.

Here are two cases which are worth noting as showing how the factors of aggravation which are usually treated as supplying a basis for assessing exemplary damages, supplementary to the damages for the legal injury, may be considered merely as aggravation of the injury itself, in which view they go to increase the compensatory damages:

1. *Smith v. Holcomb* (1868):[7] In trespass for assault and battery the plaintiff gave evidence that the defendant unlawfully struck him. The trial judge charged the jury that the plaintiff could recover for all the direct injurious results of the assault and could also recover for the insult and indignity inflicted upon him by reason of the blow given him by the defendant.

The Supreme Court said: "The insult and indignity inflicted upon a person by giving him a blow with anger, rudeness, or insolence, occasion mental suffering. In many cases they constitute the principal element of damage. They ought to be regarded as an aggravation of the tort, on the same ground that insult and indignity, offered by the plaintiff to the defendant, which provoked the assault, may be given in evidence in mitigation of the damage."

2. *Keyse v. Keyse* (1886):[1] In divorce proceedings the plaintiff, a husband, sought to recover damages of the co-respondent for alienation of the wife's affections and for illicit cohabitation with her. Sir James Hannen, President, in charging the jury said: "You must remember that you are not here to punish at all. Any observations directed to that end are improperly addressed to you. All that the law permits a jury to give is compensation for the loss which the husband has sustained. That is the only guide to the amount of damages to be given. But undoubtedly, if it is proved that a man had led a happy life with his wife, that she has taken care of his children, that she has assisted in his business, and then some man appears upon the scene and seduces the wife away from her husband, then the jury will take those facts into consideration."

Abstractly speaking, the view which limits damages to such as are actually compensatory has much to commend it,

[7] 99 Mass. 552.

[1] 11 P. D. 100.

Volume I

Law of damage outstrips the theory of civil wrong.

and there is reason to suspect that the notion of compensation is the true goal of the theory of civil damage. What seems really to have happened here, is that in the course of legal development the law of damage has outstripped the conception of legal wrong. This was due to the looseness with which of necessity the law of damage has been administered.

Freedom of jury in dealing with elements of harm.

If it had been practicable for the judges to analyze and define for the jury with precision all the elements of legal harm which enter into every case, there would have been no necessity for the recognition of the idea of punishment as a proper end in the administration of the law of civil wrong. But they did not essay this task and it was felt that the jury should be left to deal with the undefined factors of harm with a pretty free hand. The doctrine of exemplary damages answered this end well enough for practical purposes, and hence gained currency. As our theory of wrong catches up with the law of damage, the idea of punishment will appear more and more out of place in the civil system, and it may possibly in time altogether disappear.

Amount of exemplary damages left to discretion of jury.

The amount of damages which may be assessed in a proper case under the head of exemplary damages is in a measure arbitrary. The jury may do what they please, and their verdict is subject to revision only in case of a palpable miscarriage of justice.[2]

Assessment of compensatory damages.

The amount of damages which may be given under the head of compensation would appear at first blush not to be thus arbitrary. But practically the court and jury are often as much at sea when working out the problem of compensation as when dealing with the matter of punishment. As we have already seen, the difficulty is most apparent in wrongs which do not involve pecuniary loss; where there has been, for instance, interference with some intangible right incident to the person, or where the harm element takes the subtler form of physical or mental suffering. In such cases the jury has substantially the same freedom as in assessing exemplary

[2] Creed *v.* Fisher, 9 Exch. 472; Humphries *v.* Parker, 52 Me. 502; Dye *v.* Denham, 54 Ga. 224; Vinal *v.* Core, 18 W. Va. 1.

damages, and the verdict will be set aside only when the result is so clearly unjust as to give rise to the inference that the jurors were controlled by passion or prejudice.[3]

Proximity and remoteness of damage.

Then, again, the question whether a particular item of damage is proximate or remote has to be answered in every case. How far is the chain of legal causation to be allowed to run? Even in cases of pecuniary damage this question is often difficult. It is easy enough to say that in an action of tort the measure of damages is to be ascertained by reference to the natural and proximate consequences of the wrongful act.[4] But what difficulties are thus brought within the range of contemplation! We have elsewhere learned that there is no definite rule by which to determine proximity or remoteness. In one class of wrongs the range of causation is relatively much circumscribed, as in certain actions of slander; in another, as in trespass and negligence, causation runs on until some external and independent factor intervenes to break the chain. The subject of legal causation has already been discussed as fully as can be done within the limits of this work, and we shall not again take it up. A further observation which may be made in this place is that the mental attitude of the wrongdoer is of capital importance in determining whether a given element of damage is proximate or remote. Where the mind of the actor looks through coming complications and foresees and wills particular damage to another as a result of his conduct, that damage will not be held remote, however far off it may be in point of logical sequence. The factor of malice (in the sense of intending particular harm) is thus often important in determining whether damage can be treated as a proximate result of a given wrongful act.

Mental attitude of wrongdoer.

[3] Chambers *v.* Caulfield, 6 East 245; Williams *v.* Currie, 1 C. B. 841, 50 E. C. L. 841; Dwyer *v.* St. Louis, etc., R. Co., 52 Fed. Rep. 87; Denver *v.* Dunsmore, 7 Colo. 328; McMurray *v.* Basnett, 18 Fla. 609; Western, etc., R. Co. *v.* Lewis, 84 Ga. 211; Gilbert *v.* Woodbury, 22 Me. 246; Goodno *v.* Oshkosh, 28 Wis. 300.

[4] 2 Greenl. Evidence, § 261.

Volume I

Liability of joint tortfeasors.

As a final word upon the subject of damages, we shall briefly refer to the well-known principle, that where more than one join in the commission of an unlawful act, the whole of the damages may be recovered from each, all, or so many of them as the plaintiff sees fit to sue.[5] This rule undoubtedly represents a normal idea in law and requires no explanation. The different rule prevailing in contract [6] has its basis in the nature of the contractual obligation.

No contribution among tortfeasors.

Connected with the rule that a plaintiff can enforce reparation against one or more of the wrongdoers to the exclusion of others, is the further principle that one joint tortfeasor who pays or is compelled to pay all the damages, cannot obtain indemnity or contribution from those who are equally guilty as himself, or even more guilty than he. Such, in broad terms, was the ruling in *Merryweather v. Nixan* (1799).[7] This is a necessary consequence of the principle embodied in the maxim *ex turpi causa non oritur actio*. Modern decision has limited the doctrine to situations where the person who claims contribution must be presumed to have known that he was doing an unlawful act.[8] The obligation among wrongdoers to indemnify or contribute, so far as it exists, is of a quasi-contractual nature and hence must be enforced in an action of general assumpsit for money paid or in equity. Consideration of the particular circumstances under which such an obligation arises consequently has no place here.

[5] De Bodreugam *v.* Arcedekene (1302), Y. B. 30 Edw. I. (Rolls ed.), 106–108; Mitchell *v.* Tarbutt (1794), 5 T. R. 649; Rich *v.* Pilkington, Carth. 171. See also Child *v.* Sands, Carth. 294.

[6] Boson *v.* Sandford, 2 Salk. 440, Skin. 278, 3 Lev. 258.

[7] 8 T. R. 186. To the same effect are Peck *v.* Ellis, 2 Johns. Ch. (N. Y.) 131; Rhea *v.* White, 3 Head (Tenn.) 121; Spalding *v.* Oakes, 42 Vt. 343; Atkins *v.* Johnson, 43 Vt. 78; Davis *v.* Gelhaus, 44 Ohio St. 69.

[8] Adamson *v.* Jarvis, 4 Bing. 66, 13 E. C. L. 343; Palmer *v.* Wick, etc., Steam Shipping Co., (1894) A. C. 324; Thweatt *v.* Jones, 1 Rand. (Va.) 328. Compare Battersey's Case, Winch. 48.

CHAPTER XXXIII

DAMAGE AND INJURY.

Chapter XXXIII

Injury; damage.

THE technical term for that element which is inseparably associated with right of action is injury (*injuria*). Where injury is absent no action lies. The term 'damage' is in one way broader and in one way narrower than injury. It is broader in that it includes certain harms or detriments which do not amount to injury, and narrower in that there are harms which amount to legal injury though actual damage is not present.

Damage not a universal element of wrong.

It is true that by a strained and artificial mental process, damage is sometimes supposed to be an active element in every legal injury. From the mere fact that injury exists, the law is said to import damage.[1] But this is clearly only a legal fiction, which the law indulges in order that the action may be so far effective as to give the plaintiff a vindication of his legal right and to enable him to recover his costs. In no exact or helpful sense can the damage element (in the sense of the infliction of an actual detriment or loss) be said to be a universal element in legal wrong.[2] But of course

[1] See Holt, C. J., in Ashby *v.* White, 2 Ld. Raym. 938.

[2] We note that Professor Salmond adopts the opposite view, viz., that in every case damage to the plaintiff is in legal theory essential to the existence of a wrong. "The true distinction," says he, "is not between cases in which damage is, and cases in which it is not, requisite; but between cases in which damage must be proved and cases in which it is presumed by law to exist." Essays in Jurisprudence and Legal History, p. 134. The conclusion which we have reached on this point is not a first thought, as may be gathered from the following statement of personal experience in dealing with the matter. At the beginning of the present volume, and before we had seen Professor Salmond's essay, we became convinced in the course of our preliminary studies that the damage element is in fact after all, and notwithstanding some superficial appearances to the contrary, the one universal element in legal liability — precisely the same conclusion as that announced by Professor Salmond. To sustain this thesis we went into a somewhat extensive analysis, and the results were summed up in a few pages which were meant to be inserted in our in-

Volume I

'damages' conceived as a monetary equivalent of the various elements of harm which are present in a given case, is an inseparable incident of every action.[3] Legal theory is evidently much embarrassed here by the fact that the word 'damage' not only has a fluctuating and uncertain sense in the singular form, but has in the plural a meaning entirely different from any that attaches to it in the singular.

Damnum absque injuria.

The distinction between damage and injury is ancient. Bracton notes that from injury a right of action always follows, but that damage does not always amount to a legal injury.[4] The expression *damnum absque injuria* is used to indicate the situation where an actual detriment, loss, or harm is held not to be actionable because the element of legal injury is wanting. Under this head fall all conceivable harms which do not come under some recognized category of legal wrong; also all harms which, though coming under some recognized head of wrong, are by some special rule or exception rendered nonactionable under that head. The violation of a moral or social duty, such as is not recognized as being legally binding, involves damage without injury, in so far as such violation is productive of harm at all.

Competition in business affords one of the commonest illustrations of damage unaccompanied by legal injury. Said

troductory chapter. We found in the end, however, that the point of view indicated in the proposition which we had set out to maintain was unsatisfactory, inasmuch as it appeared that to that 'damage element' which seemed to be a true universal factor in liability, we had been forced to give a meaning substantially identical with that of the term 'injury.' The inquiry having thus turned out to be unfruitful, what had been written was consigned to the waste basket. It taught us the valuable lesson that search for a universal factor in legal liability, other than that which is indicated by the broad term 'injury,' is the veritable chase of an *ignis fatuus*.

[3] See North Vernon *v.* Voegler, 103 Ind. 314.

[4] "Non omne damnum inducit injuriam, sed econtra injuria damnum. Injuria autem dici poterit omne id quod non jure fit et ex injuria sequitur actio ad tollendum injuriam et id quod injuria fit sed ubi damnum et nulla injuria non sequitur actio ad tollendum nocumentum per quod fit damnum." Bract. 45*b*, c. 19, § 2.

An illustration of *damnum absque injuria* is given by Bracton in the case of a proprietor who in the exercise of his legal right uses or diverts water to the damage of his neighbor. The author is here discoursing on the subject of nuisance. Bract. 232*b*, c. 44.

Chapter XXXIII

Hankford, J., in the case where the masters of the grammar school of Gloucester long since sought to recover damages against one who established a rival school: "There can be damage without injury (*damnum absque injuria*); as if I have a mill and my neighbor builds another whereby the profit of my mill is diminished, I shall have no action against him, still there is a loss to me."[5] The law has never recognized ordinary competition in business as giving rise to liability in any aspect or under any head of tort.

General principle of non-actionable damage.

In general terms the principle is that wherever an act is done without negligence and in the exercise of legal right, such damage as comes to another thereby is damage without injury. And the same principle applies whether the act is lawful on general principle,[6] or is lawful merely because it is done under special legal authorization.[7]

In a rather singular case involving an instance of pecuniary loss without legal redress, Dr. Lushington observed: "It is essential to an action in tort that the act complained of should, under the circumstances, be legally wrongful as regards the party complaining. That is, it must prejudicially affect him in some legal right. Merely that it will, however directly, do him harm in his interests, is not enough. Cases are of daily occurrence in which the lawful exercise of a right operates to the detriment of another, necessarily and directly, without being actionable."[8]

Nonactionable injury.

From what has been said, it appears that injury is always a prerequisite condition of liability and without injury no right of action can exist. In theory the converse ought to be true, namely, that wherever legal injury is done a right of action accrues to the person injured as a necessary consequence.[9] But this is not exactly true. For instance, in cases

[5] (1410) Y. B. 11 Hen. IV. 47, pl. 21.

[6] Chasemore *v.* Richards, 7 H. L. Cas. 349.

[7] Dunn *v.* Birmingham Canal Nav. Co., L. R. 7 Q. B. 244; Dixon *v.* Metropolitan Board of Works, 7 Q. B. D. 418; Rigney *v.* Chicago, 102 Ill. 64; Lincoln *v.* Com., 164 Mass. 368.

[8] Rogers *v.* Rajendro Dutt, 8 Moo. Indian App. 103.

[9] In 1329, Scrope, J., in an action of conspiracy and false imprisonment, gave utterance to these significant words, "We are not

Volume I

of nuisance, where the loss or injury which results to one individual is not distinguished from that which accrues to the public at large, no action lies on behalf of such individual. To maintain his action the plaintiff must be able to show, in addition to the violation of public right, that he has suffered special damage.[1]

Civil wrong merged in felony.

The ancient and now practically obsolete rule which denied the right to maintain an action for damages where the injurious act amounted to a felony, affords an instance of injury without legal remedy. Here the civil wrong was said to be merged in the felony. The doctrine was never, it seems, successfully involved in connection with any other wrongs than such as amount to a technical felonious battery, or to a larcenous asportation of chattels. The reason and policy of the doctrine are uncertain. One very practical reason for a denial of the right of action in such case is found in the fact that the civil action would necessarily be futile, as, at common law, the goods of all felons were forfeited to the state. Nor was forfeiture abolished in England until 1870.[2] Another reason which, though it may not have operated with much force in originating the rule, has at least been used as an afterthought to explain it, is found in the fact that parties injured by the perpetration of a felony are morally bound to prosecute the wrongdoer. Now if the person aggrieved were allowed to prosecute the civil action, it would clearly be to his interest to relax diligence in securing the punishment of the offender, since conviction of the felon would result in the forfeiture of his estate and thereby make the civil action fruitless. Hence public policy discountenances private suits for the recovery of damage accruing to individuals as the result of crimes.

Reasons for the rule.

minded to abate this writ, for the law sees to it that in every case where one is endamaged he shall have a remedy without regard to the quantity of the damage." Y. B. 3 Edw. III. 19, pl. 34. The term 'endamaged' is here clearly used in the sense of 'injured.'

[1] Ricket *v.* Metropolitan R. Co., L. R. 2 H. L. Cas. 175; Iveson *v.* Moore, Holt K. B. 10; Caledonian R. Co. *v.* Ogilvy, 2 Macq. H. L. 229; Metropolitan Board of Works *v.* McCarthy, L. R. 7 H. L. 243; Caledonian R. Co. *v.* Walker, 7 App. Cas. 259.

[2] 33 & 34 Vict., c. 23.

Chapter XXXIII

Doctrine not in force in America.

In America, where forfeiture does not exist and where there are public prosecutors to conduct all criminal proceedings, the doctrine that the trespass is merged in the felony is generally denied.[3]

Doctrine obsolescent in England.

In England, too, though the existence of the rule in question has been often incidentally recognized and sometimes applied in judicial decisions, it has in recent years been much impaired and is probably in a fair way to be completely extinguished.[4] Thus, it has been there held that the right of action is not absolutely merged in the felony, but is only suspended in order that public justice may first be satisfied.[5] Hence, where one act constitutes both a tort and a felony, a civil right of action does arise; and the plaintiff, suing on the tort, ought to show that the felon has been prosecuted; or, at least, that he has not been remiss in performing his public duty.[6]

[3] Boston, etc., R. Corp. *v.* Dana, 1 Gray (Mass.) 83; Atwood *v.* Fisk, 101 Mass. 363; Quimby *v.* Blackey, 63 N. H. 77; Van Duzer *v.* Howe, 21 N. Y. 531; Ballew *v.* Alexander, 6 Humph. (Tenn.) 433; Cook *v.* Darby, 4 Munf. (Va.) 444. See, however, Morton *v.* Bradley, 27 Ala. 640.

[4] Markham *v.* Cob, Latch, 144, Noy 82; Dawkes *v.* Coveneigh, Style 346; Cooper *v.* Witham, 1 Sid. 375. In White *v.* Spettigue (1845), 13 M. & W. 603, it was held that where one's goods are stolen he can maintain trover against a third person who innocently purchases them from the thief.

[5] Crosby *v.* Leng, 12 East 409.

[6] *Ex p.* Ball, 10 Ch. D. 667, *per* Baggallay, L. J. See also Stone *v.* Marsh, 6 B. & C. 551, 13 E. C. L. 249; Wells *v.* Abrahams, L. R. 7 Q. B. 554; Wellock *v.* Constantine, 2 H. & C. 146; Roope *v.* D'Avigdor, 10 Q. B. D. 412; Ward *v.* Lloyd, 7 Scott N. R. 499.

CHAPTER XXXIV

CONCLUSION.

Volume I

NOW that we are at the end of our survey of the law of torts, a few observations by way of general conclusion are in place.

Successive legal formations.

The law of torts is to be conceived as a body of legal truth which is made up of many successive formations. To use a different figure, we may say that the several wrongs appear to be only so many waves in one large sea of delict. Each successive wave has its distinguishing feature, yet all are moved by the same impulse. In this intricate system of interrelated legal ideals, each species of wrong subsists by virtue of its own principle, yet each appears to be the fruit of some idea whose germ is found elsewhere.

Process of evolution.

The process by which a new species of wrongs attains recognition is well illustrated at many points in the preceding pages, and a general idea of that process can perhaps be here set forth in a few words: The several generic wrongs are found upon inspection to be each underlaid by some particular principle or conception of liability. Beginning with such a principle the courts proceed, as occasion requires, to extend or apply that principle to situations similar to those in which the principle has already been applied, but which nevertheless are not the same. Presently that principle is found, as a result of this process of extension, to have been transcended. This gives rise to an accrescent body of doctrine *in consimili casu* with the main principle, but which cannot, strictly speaking, be brought under that principle. Looking at this body of derivative doctrine in a narrow way one might be inclined to think it exceptional, perhaps even anomalous and unsound. But this conjecture is soon belied by subsequent development. For in the next stage we see the new idea putting forth its tentacles in various directions and drawing strength from many sources. It is found to be in harmony with the general scheme of legal ideas. Principles imported from other departments of tort are found to sustain it, and considerations of justice, convenience, or policy rally to its support.

Finally, when the new principle is securely grounded in all directions and its relations to other bodies of doctrine determined, it disattaches itself altogether from the maternal tort and is accepted as the basis of an independent species of legal wrong. The philosophic mind can now state in definite terms the corresponding right and duty to which birth has thus been given. The result is the addition of another tort to the catalogue of nominate wrongs.

Primary types of wrong.

The process of evolution above outlined presupposes the existence of certain primary types of wrong from which the derivative torts are evolved. Dogmatism is perhaps unsafe at this point, but we are inclined to think that there are just five torts which ought to be considered primary types. These are Trespass, Nuisance, Conversion, Defamation, and Deceit. These were not so much evolved as they were discovered. They seem to embody conceptions of wrong so rudimentary and necessary that their recognition follows at once when the mind is directed to the right situation. The only condition which is necessary in actual practice is that the system of remedial law should be equal to the task of giving effect to the self-evident truth.

Legal growth subject to requirements of policy and justice.

From what has been said above it appears that the secret of legal growth is to be found in the capacity of the law to recognize the validity of derivative or accrescent bodies of legal doctrine. But it should be noted that legal growth is always conditioned upon the fact that in the particular case extension is required by considerations of reason, justice, and public policy. These latter elements alone supply the atmosphere in which new legal doctrines can germinate.

In the process of the evolution of legal principle the courts are naturally and, as it were, irresistibly borne along by the current of an ever-broadening stream. The judges do not assume to make new law by their mere judicial fiat. Indeed,

Volume I

Function of the courts.

they vehemently renounce the idea that they have any such power;[7] and although new doctrines come into being, the judges insist that they are rather instruments for declaring what the law was than makers of new law. The courts only have the power, so it is claimed, to apply the old law to new situations.

Taken literally, such statements are misleading. The courts do in fact and in truth make new law in the very act of applying recognized principles to new facts. The thinly veiled fiction of the antecedent immortality of legal principle is a pleasing fancy, and it is no doubt indulged by the judges out of a sense of responsibility. It is certainly in some degree elevating to look upon the judge, not as a legislator and originator of law, but only as an oracle of its eternal truth. But for our own part we prefer to believe that legal truth comes into being and has life only as it is recognized and declared.[8]

[7] "The judges cannot make new law by new decisions; they do not assume a power of that kind; they only endeavor to declare what the common law is and has been from the time when it first existed. But inasmuch as new circumstances, and new complications of fact, and even new facts, are constantly arising, the judges are obliged to apply to them what they consider to have been the common law during the whole course of its existence, and therefore they seem to be laying down a new law, whereas they are merely applying old principles to a new state of facts." Brett, M. R., in Munster *v.* Lamb (1883), 11 Q. B. D. 599.

[8] On the question as to what is the exact nature of the function performed by the judge in deciding a case presented to him for solution, difference of opinion has arisen among jurists. The view generally entertained among lawyers is that indicated in the language of Brett just quoted. It had its origin with Blackstone. This writer observes that the judge is sworn to determine "not according to his own private judgment, but according to the known laws and customs of the land; . . . not delegated to pronounce a new law, but to maintain and expound the old." 1 Bl. Com. 69. In the same connection, speaking of overruled cases he adds: "But even in such cases the subsequent judges do not pretend to make a new law, but to vindicate the old one from misrepresentation. For if it be found that the former decision is manifestly absurd or unjust, it is declared, not that such a sentence was bad law, but that it was not law."

This theory was criticised by Bentham, and Austin denounced "the childish fiction employed by our judges that judiciary or common law is not made by them, but is a miraculous something made by nobody, existing from eternity." 3 Austin Jurisprudence, Campbell's ed., 655.

Time, which is the greatest of

Courts have no power of direct innovation.

Two salutary ideas are, however, contained in the proposition that the judges have no power to make new law. They cannot create a new species of liability or create a new defense which has no recognition in the existing scheme of legal ideas, and they must not, in applying a given principle, suffer that principle to be violated. Direct creative power the courts do not possess, and they are bound to preserve established truth unimpaired. Development there must be, but it cannot take place by leaps and bounds. There must be no ellipsis of any intermediate process. In the course of legal growth older principles are transcended, but this must take place by steps so natural and inevitable as to be in a measure unconscious. The transcension of a legal principle, it should be further observed, involves a going beyond the reach and support of that principle, but does not necessarily imply a violation of it. For it may well be, as indicated above, that the derivative doctrine finds support in other principles, or in considerations of policy, and hence is able to stand with little assistance from the principle which it transcends.

Doctrine of judicial precedent.

The double principle referred to above, namely, that a court cannot create new law and that it must preserve established truth unimpaired, finds expression, in the common-law system, in a peculiar and characteristic doctrine of judicial precedent. This doctrine is to the effect that a judicial decision of a court of competent jurisdiction has an authoritative binding force on the court that renders the decision and upon all courts inferior to that court. The decision is not merely persuasive of what the law is. All points necessary to the decision, as well as the point actually decided, become

teachers, has done much to discredit the Blackstonian theory. Unwritten laws change as social conditions alter, and the judges are the ones who effect the changes. The silent evolution of the law is much more manifest, because much more rapid, to-day than it was in Blackstone's day. The Blackstonian theory is rejected with practical unanimity by modern writers on theoretical jurisprudence. See Maine's Anc. Law, p. 31; E. C. Clark, Practical Juris., Pt. II., c. 3, 5. Professor W. G. Hammond, editor of a late edition of Blackstone's Commentaries, expresses his approbation of that writer's opinion as to the function of the judge. See his note to Blackstone, *ubi citat.*, and also Lieber's Hermeneutics, ed. 1880, p. 327.

Volume I

binding rule of law unless the decision is reversed or perchance overruled. Until thus impeached the decision must be followed in all situations where the *ratio decidendi* can be considered applicable, however different the facts may be from those which called the decision forth.[9]

English veneration for precedents.

No common-law principle has been more carefully cherished. Our veneration for precedent has without doubt often retarded progress, but it has given us a priceless treasure in the law reports — that continuous record, extending over more than six centuries, of the reasoned decisions of the English judges. It furnishes indubitable evidence of the law-abidingness of the English-speaking people, a feature which is indelibly stamped upon every aspect of their civic and political life.

9 The doctrine of judicial precedent is commonly indicated in modern times by the expression *stare decisis.* The full maxim is *stare decisis et non quieta movere.*

The idea is very ancient. Professor Pollock finds evidence of it in the records of a date soon after the Conquest. Essays in Jurisp. & Ethics, p. 215. In Y. B. 32 Edw. I. (Rolls ed.), p. 32, a reference to the binding force of precedent is found in a remark of Herle, counsel for one of the parties, who admonished the judges that the decision then to be rendered would be an authority in every similar action in England. In Y. B. Hen. VI. 41*a*, pl. 17, Prisot, C. J., remarked upon the special value of the principle in reference to the interpretation of statutes.

Roman law and modern continental systems deriving from it, wholly reject the idea that a judicial decision can have any authoritive force. Indeed, the Prussian and Austrian codes have expressly provided that judgments shall not have the force of law, and in Prussia judicial reference either to the opinions of teachers of the law or to previous judgments has been expressly forbidden. In other countries, such as Belgium and France, the recognized rule is that previous decisions are instructive as belonging to the body of existing 'jurisprudence,' but have no binding force. This notion was fixed in the Roman law by a constitution of one of the emperors, subsequently embodied in the Code VII. 45, 13: *Cum non exemplis sed legibus judicandum sit* — a provision which was construed as prohibiting the use of precedents altogether.